AF269164

FIFTY-NINE SERMONS

BY

GEORGE WHITEFIELD

© 2010 Benediction Classics..

Contents

1 The Seed of the Woman, and the Seed of the Serpent 3
2 Walking With God 17
3 Abraham's Offering Up His Son Isaac 30
4 The Great Duty of Family Religion 41
5 Christ the Best Husband: Or an Earnest Invitation to Young Women to come and See Christ 52
6 Britain's Mercies, and Britain's Duty 64
7 Thankfulness for Mercies received, a necessary Duty 75
8 The Necessity and Benefits of Religious Society 86
9 The Folly and Danger of Being Not Righteous Enough 98
10 A Preservative against unsettled Notions 112
11 The Benefits of an Early Piety 126
12 Christ the Believer's Husband 135
13 The Potter and the Clay 155
14 The Lord our Righteousness 169
15 The Righteousness of Christ, an Everlasting Righteousness 184
16 The Observation of the Birth of Christ 196
17 The Temptation of Christ 205
18 The Heinous Sin of Profane Cursing and Swearing 216
19 Christ the Support of the Tempted 225
20 Worldly Business no Plea for the Neglect of Religion 234
21 Christ the only Rest for the Weary and Heavy-Laden 242
22 The Folly and Danger 251
23 Marks of a True Conversion 265
24 What think ye of Christ? 278
25 The Wise and Foolish Virgins 293
26 "The Eternity of Hell-Torments" 307
27 Blind Bartimeus 317
28 Directions how to hear Sermons 328
29 The Extent and Reasonableness of Self-Denial 336
30 Christ's Transfiguration 345
31 The Care of the Soul urged as the one thing needful 357
32 A Penitent Heart 372
33 The Gospel Supper 386
34 The Pharisee and Publican 398
35 The Conversion of Zaccheus 408
36 The Marriage of Cana 419

37 The Duty of searching the Scriptures. 431
38 The Indwelling of the Spirit 440
39 The Resurrection of Lazarus 451
40 The Holy Spirit 469
41 Saul's Conversion 481
42 Marks of having Received the Holy Ghost 494
43 The Almost Christian 505
44 Christ, the Believer's Wisdom, Righteousness, Sanctification and Redemption 515
45 The Knowledge of Jesus Christ the best Knowledge 527
46 Of Justification by Christ 535
47 The Great Duty of Charity Recommended 544
48 Satan's Devices 554
49 On Regeneration 565
50 Christians, Temples of the Living God 575
51 Christ the only Preservative against a Reprobate Spirit 585
52 The Heinous Sin of Drunkenness 596
53 The Power of Christ's Resurrection 606
54 Intercession every Christian's Duty 615
55 Persecution every Christian's Lot 624
56 An Exhortation 635
57 Georgia Sermon 640
58 The Method of Grace 654
59 The Good Shepherd 667

Sermon 1 The Seed of the Woman, and the Seed of the Serpent

Genesis 3:15 "And I will put Enmity between thee and the Woman, and between thy Seed and her Seed, it shall bruise thy Head, and thou shalt bruise his Head."

On reading to you these words, I may address you in the language of the holy angels to the shepherds, that were watching their flocks by night: "Behold, I bring you glad tidings of great joy." For this is the first promise that was made of a Savior to the apostate race of Adam. We generally look for Christ only in the New Testament; but Christianity, in one sense, is very near as old as the creation. It is wonderful to observe how gradually God revealed his Son to mankind. He began with the promise in the text, and this the elect lived upon, till the time of Abraham. To him, God made further discoveries of his eternal council concerning man's redemption. Afterwards, at sundry times, and in divers manners, God spoke to the fathers by the prophets, till at length the Lord Jesus himself was manifested in flesh, and came and tabernacled amongst us.

This first promise must certainly be but dark to our first parents, in comparison of that great light which we enjoy: And yet, dark as it was, we may assure ourselves they built upon it their hopes of everlasting salvation, and by that faith were saved.

How they came to stand in need of this promise, and what is the extent and meaning of it, I intend, God willing, to make the subject-matter of your present meditation.

The fall of man is written in too legible characters not to be understood: Those that deny it, by their denying, prove it. The very heathens confessed, and bewailed it: They could see the streams of corruption running through the whole race of mankind, but could not trace them to the fountainhead. Before God gave a revelation of his Son, man was a riddle to himself.

And Moses unfolds more, in this one chapter (out of which the text is taken) than all mankind could have been capable of finding out of themselves, though they had studied to all eternity.

In the preceding chapter he had given us a full account, how God spoke the world into being; and especially how he formed man of the dust of the earth, and breathed into him the breath of life, so that he became a living soul. A council of the Trinity was called concerning the formation of this lovely creature. The result of that council was, "Let us make man in our image, after our likeness. So God created man in his own image, in the image of God created he him." Moses remarkably repeats these words, that we might take particular notice of our divine Original. Never was so much expressed in so few words: None but a man inspired could have done so. But it is remarkable, that though Moses mentions our being made in the image of God, yet he mentions it but twice, and that in a transient manner; as though he would have said, "man was made in honor, God make him upright, `in the image of God, male and female created he them.' But man so soon fell, and became like the beasts that perish, nay, like the devil himself, that it is scarce worth mentioning." How soon man fell after he was created, is not told us; and therefore, to fix any time, is to be wise above what is written. And, I think, they who suppose that man fell the same day in which he was made, have no sufficient ground for their opinion. The many things which are crowded together in the former chapter, such as the formation of Adam's wife, his giving names to the beasts, and his being put into the garden which God had planted, I think require a longer space of time than a day to be transacted in. However, all agree in this, "man stood not long." How long, or how short a while, I will not take upon me to determine. It more concerns us to inquire, how he came to fall from his steadfastness, and what was the rise and progress of the temptation which prevailed over him. The account given us in this chapter concerning it, is very full; and it may do us much service, under God, to make some remarks upon it.

"Now the serpent (says the sacred historian) was more subtle than any beast of the field which the Lord God had made, and he said unto the woman, Yes, hath God said, ye shall not eat of every tree of the garden?" Though this was a real serpent, yet he that spoke was no other than the devil; from hence, perhaps, called the old serpent, because he took possession of the serpent when he came to beguile our first parents. The devil envied the happiness of man, who was made, as some think, to supply the place of the fallen angels. God made man upright, and with full power to stand if he would: He was just, therefore, in suffering him to be tempted. If he fell, he had no one to blame except himself. But how must Satan effect his fall? He cannot do it by his power, he attempts it therefore by policy: he takes possession of a serpent, which was more subtle than all the beasts of the field, which the Lord God had made; so that men who are full of subtlety, but have no piety, are only machines for the devil to work upon, just as he pleases.

"And he said unto the woman." Here is an instance of his subtlety. He says unto the woman, the weaker vessel, and when she was alone from her husband, and therefore was more liable to be overcome; "Yes, hath God said, ye shall not eat of every tree of the garden?" These words are certainly spoken in answer to something which the devil either saw or heard. In all probability, the woman was now near the tree of knowledge of good and evil; (for we shall find her, by and by, plucking an apple from it) perhaps she might be looking at, and wondering what tree was in that tree more than the others, that she and her husband should be forbidden to take of it. Satan seeing this, and coveting to draw her into a parley with him, (for if the devil can persuade us not to resist, but to commune with him, he hath gained a great point) he says, "Yea, hath God said, ye shall not eat of every tree in the garden?" The first thing he does is to persuade he, if possible to entertain hard thoughts of God; this is his general way of dealing with God's children: "Yea, hath God said, ye shall not eat of every tree of the garden? What! Hath God planted a garden, and placed you in the midst of it, only to tease and perplex you? Hath he planted a garden, and yet forbid you making use of any of the fruits of it at all?" It was impossible for him to ask a more ensnaring question, in order to gain his end: For Eve was here seemingly obliged to answer, and vindicate God's goodness. And therefore, -- Verses 2 & 3. The woman said unto the serpent, "We may eat of the fruit of the trees of the garden: But of the fruit of the tree which is in the midst of the garden, God hath said, ye shall not eat of it, neither shall ye touch it, lest ye die." The former part of the answer was good, "We may eat of the fruit of the trees of the garden, God has not forbid us eating of every tree of the garden. No; we may eat of the fruit of the trees in the garden (and, it should seem, even of the tree of life, which was as a sacrament to man in the state of innocence) there is only one tree in the midst of the garden, of which God hath said, ye shall not eat of it, neither shall ye touch it, lest ye die." Here she begins to warp, and sin begins to conceive I her heart. Already she has contracted some of the serpent's poison, by talking with him, which she ought not to have done at all. For she might easily suppose, that it could be no good being that could put such a question unto her, and insinuate such dishonorable thoughts of God. She should therefore have fled from him, and not stood to have parleyed with him at all.

Immediately the ill effects of it appear, she begins to soften the divine threatening. God had said, "the day thou eatest thereof, thou shalt surely die;" or, dying thou shalt die. But Eve says, "Ye shall not eat of it, neither shall ye touch it, lest ye die." We may be assured we are fallen into, and begin to fall by temptations, when we begin to think God will not be as good as his word, in respect to the execution of his threatenings denounced against sin. Satan knew this, and therefore artfully "Said unto the woman, (ver. 4) Ye shall not surely die," in an insinuating manner, "Ye shall not surely die. Surely; God will not be so cruel as to damn you only for eating an apple, it cannot be." Alas! How many does Satan lead captive at his will, by flattering them, that they shall not surely die; that hell torments will not be eternal; that God is all mercy; that he therefore will not punish a few years sin with an eternity of misery? But Eve found God as good as his word; and so will all they who go on in sin, under a false hope that they shall not surely die.

We may also understand the words spoken positively, and this is agreeable to what follows; You shall not surely die; "It is all a delusion, a mere bugbear, to keep you in a servile subjection." For (ver. 5) "God doth know, that in the day ye eat thereof, then shall your eyes be opened, and ye shall be as gods, knowing good and evil." What child of God can expect to escape slander, when God himself was thus slandered even in paradise? Surely the understanding of Eve must have been, in some measure, blinded, or she would not have suffered the tempter to speak such perverse things. In what odious colors is God here represented! "God doth know, that in the day ye eat thereof, ye shall be as gods," (equal with God.) So that the grand temptation was, that they should be hereafter under no control, equal, if not superior, to God that made them, knowing good and evil. Eve could not tell what Satan meant by this; but, to be sure, she understood it of some great privilege which they were to enjoy. And thus Satan now points out a way which seems right to sinners, but does not tell them the end of that way is death.

To give strength and force to this temptation, in all probability, Satan, or the serpent, at this time plucked an apple from the tree, and ate it before Eve; by which Eve might be induced to think, that the sagacity and power of speech, which the serpent had above the other beasts, must be owing, in a great measure, to his eating that fruit; and, therefore, if he received so much improvement, she might also expect a like benefit from it.

All this, I think, is clear; for, otherwise, I do not see with what propriety it could be said, "When the woman saw that it was good for food." How could she know it was good for food, unless she had seen the serpent feed upon it?

Satan now begins to get ground space. Lust had conceived in Eve's heart; shortly it will bring forth sin. Sin being conceived, brings forth death. Verse 6, "And when the woman saw that the tree was good for food, and that it was pleasant to the eyes, and a tree to be desired to make one wise, she took of the fruit thereof, and did eat, and gave also unto her husband, and he did eat." Our senses are the landing ports of our spiritual enemies. How needful is that resolution of holy Job, "I have made a covenant with mine eyes!" When

Eve began to gaze on the forbidden fruit with her eyes, she soon began to long after it with her heart. When she saw that it was good for food, and pleasant to the eyes, (here was the lust of the flesh, and lust of the eye) but, above all, a tree to be desired to make one wise, wiser than God would have her be, nay, as wise as God himself; she took of the fruit thereof, and gave also unto her husband with her, and he did eat. As soon as ever she sinned herself, she turned tempter to her husband. It is dreadful, when those, who should be help-meets for each other in the great work of their salvation, are only promoters of each other's damnation: but thus it is. If we ourselves are good, we shall excite others to goodness; if we do evil, we shall entice others to do evil also. There is a close connection between doing and teaching. How needful then is it for us all to take heed that we do not sin any way ourselves, lest we should become factors for the devil, and ensnare, perhaps, our nearest and dearest relatives? "she gave also unto her husband with her, and he did eat." Alas! What a complication of crimes was there in this one single act of sin! Here is an utter disbelief of God's threatening; the utmost ingratitude to their Maker, who had so lately planted this garden, and placed them in it, with such a glorious and comprehensive charter. And, the utmost neglect of their posterity, who they knew were to stand or fall with them. Here was the utmost pride of heart: they wanted to be equal with God.

Here's the utmost contempt put upon his threatening and his law: the devil is credited and obeyed before him, and all this only to satisfy their sensual appetite. Never was a crime of such a complicated nature committed by any here below: Nothing but the devil's apostasy and rebellion could equal it.

And what are the consequences of their disobedience? Are their eyes opened? Yes, their eyes are opened; but, alas! It is only to see their own nakedness. For we are told (ver. 7) "That the eyes of them both were opened; and they knew that they were naked." Naked of God, naked of every thing that was holy and good, and destitute of the divine image, which they before enjoyed. They might rightly now be termed Ichabod; for the glory of the Lord departed from them. O how low did these sons of the morning then fall! Out of God, into themselves; from being partakers of the divine nature, into the nature of the devil and the beast. Well, therefore, might they know that they were naked, not only in body, but in soul.

And how do they behave now they are naked? Do they flee to God for pardon? Do they seek to God for a robe to cove their nakedness? No, they were now dead to God, and became earthly, sensual, devilish: therefore, instead of applying to God for mercy, "they sewed or platted fig-leaves together, and made themselves aprons, "or things to gird about them. This is a lively representation of all natural man: we see that we are naked: we, in some measure, confess it; but, instead of looking up to God for succor, we patch up a righteousness of our own (as our first parents platted fig-leaves together) hoping to cover our nakedness by that. But our righteousness will not stand the severity of God's judgment: it will do us no more service than the fig-leaves did Adam and Eve, that is, none at all.

For (ver. 8) "They heard the voice of the Lord God walking in the trees of the garden, in the cool of the day; and Adam and his wife (notwithstanding their fig-leaves) hid themselves from the presence of the Lord God, among the trees of the garden." They heard the voice of the Lord God, or the Word of the Lord God, even the Lord Jesus Christ, who is "the word that was with God, and the word that was God." They heard him walking in the trees of the garden, in the cool of the day. A season, perhaps, when Adam and Eve used to go, in a n especial manner, and offer up an evening sacrifice of praise and thanksgiving. The cool of the day. Perhaps the sin was committed early in the morning, or at noon; but God would not come upon them immediately, he staid till the cool of the day. And if we would effectually reprove others, we should not do it when they are warmed with passion, but wait till the cool of the day.

But what an alteration is here! Instead of rejoicing at the voice of their beloved, instead of meeting him with open arms and enlarged hearts, as before, they now hide themselves in the trees of the garden. Alas, what a foolish attempt was this? Surely they must be naked, otherwise how could they think of hiding themselves from God? Whither could they flee from his presence? But, by their fall, they had contracted an enmity against God: they now hated, and were afraid to converse with God their Maker. And is not this our case by nature? Assuredly it is. We labor to cover our nakedness with the fig-leaves of our own righteousness: We hide ourselves from God as long as we can, and will not come, and never should come, did not the Father prevent, draw, and sweetly constrain us by his grace, as he here prevented Adam.

Verse 9. "And the Lord God called unto Adam, and said unto him, Adam, where art thou?" "The Lord God called unto Adam." (for otherwise Adam would never have called unto the Lord God) and said, "Adam, where art thou? How is it that thou comest not to pay thy devotions as usual?" Christians, remember the Lord keeps an account when you fail coming to worship. Whenever therefore you are tempted to withhold your attendance, let each of you fancy you heard the Lord calling unto you, and saying, "O man, O woman, where art thou? It may be understood in another and better sense; "Adam, where art thou?" What a condition is thy poor soul in? This is the first thing the Lord asks and convinces a sinner of; when he prevents and calls him effectually by his grace; he also calls him by name; for unless God speaks to us in particular, and we know where we are, how poor, how miserable, how blind, how naked, we shall never value the redemption wrought out for us by the death and obedience of the dear Lord Jesus. "Adam, where art thou?" Verse 10. "And he said, I heard thy voice in the garden, and I was afraid." See what cowards sin makes us. If we knew no sin, we should know no fear. "Because I was naked, and I hid myself." Ver. 11, "And he said, who told thee that thou was naked? Hast thou eaten of the tree, whereof I (thy Maker and Law-giver) commanded thee, that thou shouldest not eat?" God knew very well that Adam was naked, and that he had eaten of the forbidden fruit, But God would know it from Adam's own mouth. Thus God knows all our necessities before we ask, but yet insists upon our asking for his grace, and confessing our sins. For, by such acts, we acknowledge our dependence upon God, take shame to ourselves, and thereby give glory to his great name.

Verse 12. "And the man said, the woman which thou gavest to be with me, she gave me of the tree, and I did eat." Never was nature more lively delineated. See what pride Adam contracted by the fall! How unwilling he is to lay the blame upon, or take shame to himself. This answer is full of insolence towards God, enmity against his wife, and disingenuity in respect to himself. For herein he tacitly reflects upon God. "The woman that thou gavest to be with me." As much as to say, if thou hadst not given me that woman, I had not eaten the forbidden fruit. Thus, when men sin, they lay the fault upon their passions; then blame and reflect upon God for giving them those passions.

Their language is, "the appetites that thou gavest us, they deceived us; and therefore we sinned against thee." But, as God, notwithstanding, punished Adam for hearkening to the voice of his wife, so he will punish those who hearken to the dictates of their corrupt inclinations. For God compels no man to sin. Adam might have withstood the solicitations of his wife, if he would. And so, if we look up to God, we should find grace to help in the time of need. The devil and our own hearts tempt, but they cannot force us to consent, without the concurrence of our own wills. So that our damnation is of ourselves, as it will evidently appear at the great day, notwithstanding all men's present impudent replies against God.

As Adam speaks insolently in respect to God, so he speaks with enmity against his wife; the woman, or this woman, she gave me. He lays all the fault upon her, and speaks of her with much contempt. He does not say, my wife, my dear wife; but, THIS WOMAN. Sin disunites the most united hearts: It is, the bane of holy fellowship. Those who have been companions in sin here, if they die without repentance, will both hate and condemn one another hereafter. All damned souls are accusers of their brethren. Thus it is, in some degree, on this side of the grave. "The woman whom thou gavest to be with me, she gave me of the tree, and I did eat." What a disingenuous speech was here! He makes use of no less than fifteen words to excuse himself, and but one or two (in the original) to confess his fault, if it may be called a confession at all. "The woman which thou gavest to be with me, she gave me of the tree;" here are fifteen words; "and I did eat." With what reluctance do these last words come out? How soon are they uttered are they uttered? "And I did eat." But thus it is with an unhumbled, unregenerate heart; It will be laying the fault upon the dearest friend in the world, nay, upon God himself, rather than take shame to itself. This pride we are all subject to by the fall; and, till our hearts are broken, and made contrite by the spirit of our Lord Jesus Christ, we shall be always charging God foolishly. "Against thee, and thee only, have I sinned, that thou mightest be justified in thy saying, and clear when thou art judged," is the language of none but those, who, like David, are willing to confess their faults, and are truly sorry for their sins. This was not the case of Adam; his heart was not broken; and therefore he lays the fault of his disobedience upon his wife and God, and not upon himself; "The woman which thou gavest to be with me, she gave me of the tree, and I did eat." Verse 13. "And the Lord God said, What is this that thou hast done?" What a wonderful concern does God express in this expostulation! "What a deluge of misery hast thou brought upon thyself, thy husband, and thy posterity? What is this that thou has done? Disobeyed thy God, obeyed the devil, and ruined thy husband, for whom I made thee to be an help-meet!

What is this that thou hast done?" God would here awaken her to a sense of her crime and danger, and therefore, as it were, thunders in her ears: for the law must be preached to self-righteous sinners. We must take care of healing before we see sinners wounded, lest we should say, Peace, peace, where there is no peace. Secure sinners must hear the thunderings of mount Sinai, before we bring them to mount Zion. They who never preach up the law, it is to be feared, are unskillful in delivering the glad tidings of the gospel. Every minister should be a Boanerges, a son of thunder, as well as a Barnabus, a son of consolation. There was an earthquake and a whirlwind, before the small still voice came to Elijah: We must first show people they are condemned, and then show them how they must be saved. But how and when to preach the law, and when to apply the promises of the gospel, wisdom is profitable to direct. "And the Lord God said unto the woman, What is this that thou has done?" "And the woman said, The serpent beguiled me, and I did eat." She does not make use of so many words to excuse herself, as her husband; but her heart is as unhumbled as his. What is this, says God, that thou hast done?

God here charges her with doing it. She dares not deny the fact, or say, I have not done it; but she takes all the blame off herself, and lays it upon the serpent; "The serpent beguiled me, and I did eat." She does not say, "Lord, I was to blame for talking with the serpent; Lord, I did wrong, in not hastening to my husband, when he put the first question to me; Lord, I plead guilty, I only am to blame, O let not my poor husband suffer for my wickedness!" This would have been the language of her heart had she now been a true penitent. But both were now alike proud; therefore neither will lay the blame upon themselves; "The serpent beguiled me, and I did eat. The woman which thou gavest to be with me, she gave me of the tree, and I did eat." I have been the more particular in remarking this part of their behavior, because it tends so much to the magnifying of Free-grace, and plainly shows us, that salvation cometh only from the Lord. Let us take a short view of the miserable circumstances our first parents were now in: They were legally and spiritually dead, children of wrath, and heirs of hell. They had eaten the fruit, of which God had commanded them, that they should not eat; and when arraigned before God, notwithstanding their crime was so complicated, they could not be brought to confess it. What reason can be given, why sentence of death should not be pronounced against the prisoners at the bar? All must own they are worthy to die. Nay, how can God, consistently with his justice, possibly forgive them? He had threatened, that they day wherein they eat of the forbidden fruit, they should "surely die;" and, if he did not execute this threatening, the devil might then slander the Almighty indeed. And yet mercy cries, spare these sinners, spare the work of thine own hands. Behold, then, wisdom contrives a scheme how God may be just, and yet be merciful; be faithful to his threatening, punish the offense, and at the same time spare the offender.

An amazing scene of divine love here opens to our view, which had been from all eternity hid in the heart of God! Notwithstanding Adam and Eve were thus unhu7mbled, and did not so much as put up on single petition for pardon, God immediately passes sentence upon the serpent, and reveals to them a Savior.

Verse 14. "And the Lord God said unto the serpent, because thou hast done this, thou art accursed above all cattle, and above every beast of the field; upon thy belly shalt thou go, and dust shalt thou eat all the days of thy life;" i.e. he should be in subjection, and his power should always be limited and restrained. "His enemies shall lick the very dust," says the Psalmist. (Verse 15.) "And I will put enmity between thee and the woman, and between thy seed and her seed: it shall bruise thy head, and thou shalt bruise his heel." Before I proceed to the explanation of this verse, I cannot but take notice of one great mistake which the author of the WHOLE DUTY OF MAN is guilty of, in making this verse contain a covenant between God and Adam, as though God now personally treated with Adam, as before the fall. For, talking of the second covenant in his preface, concerning caring for the soul, says he, "This second covenant was made with Adam, and us in him, presently after the fall, and is briefly contained in these words, Gen.

3:15 where God declares, 'The seed of the woman shall break the serpent's head; and this was made up, as the first was, of some mercies to be afforded by God, and some duties to be performed by us." This is exceeding false divinity: for those words are not spoken to Adam; they are directed only to the serpent. Adam and Eve stood by as criminals, and God could not treat with them, because they had broken his covenant. And it is so far from being a covenant wherein "some mercies are to be afforded by God, and some duties to be performed by us," that here is not a word looking that way; it is only a declaration of a free gift of salvation through Jesus Christ our Lord. God the Father and God the Son had entered into a covenant concerning the salvation of the elect from all eternity, wherein God the Father promised, That, if the Son would offer his soul a sacrifice for sin, he should see his seed. Now this is an open revelation of this secret covenant, and therefore God speaks in the most positive terms, "It shall bruise thy head, and thou shalt bruise his heal." The first Adam, God had treated with before; he proved false: God therefore, to secure the second covenant from being broken, puts it into the hands of the second Adam, the Lord from heaven. Adam, after the fall, stood no longer as our representative; he and Eve were only private persons, as we are, and were only to lay hold on the declaration of mercy contained in this promise by faith, (as they really did) and by that they were saved. I do not say but we are to believe and obey, if we are everlastingly saved. Faith and obedience are conditions, if we only mean that they in order go before our salvation, but I deny that these are proposed by God to Adam, or that God treats with him in this promise, as he did before the fall under the covenant of works. For how could that be, when Adam and Eve were now prisoners at the bar, without strength to perform any conditions at all?

The truth is this: God, as a reward of Christ's sufferings, promised to give the elect faith and repentance, in order to bring them to eternal life; and both these, and every thing else necessary for their everlasting happiness, and infallibly secured to them in this promise; as Mr. Rastan, an excellent Scots divine, clearly shows, in a book entitled, "A view of the covenant of grace." This is by no means an unnecessary distinction; it is a matter of great importance: for want of knowing this, people have been so long misled, They have been taught that they must do so and so, and though they were under a covenant of works, and then for DOING this, they should be saved. Whereas, on the contrary, people should be taught, That the Lord Jesus was the second Adam, with whom the Father entered into covenant for fallen man; That they can now do nothing of or for themselves, and should therefore come to God, beseeching him to give them faith, by which they shall be enabled to lay hold on the righteousness of Christ; and that faith they will then show forth by their works, out of love and gratitude to the ever blessed Jesus, their most glorious Redeemer, for what he has done for their souls. This is a consistent scriptural scheme; without holding this, we must run into one of those two bad extremes; I mean Antinomianism on the one hand, or Arminianism on the other: from both which may the good Lord deliver us!

But to proceed: By the seed of the woman, we are here to understand the Lord Jesus Christ, who, though very God of very God, was, for us men and our salvation, to have a body prepared for him by the Holy Ghost, and to be born of a woman who never knew man, and by his obedience and death make an atonement for man's transgression, and bring in an everlasting righteousness, work in them a new nature, and thereby bruise the serpent's head, i.e. destroy his power and dominion over them. By the serpent's seed, we are to understand the devil and all his children, who are permitted by God to tempt and sift his children. But, blessed be God, he can reach no further than our heel.

It is to be doubted but Adam and Eve understood this promise in this sense; for it is plain, in the latter part of the chapter, sacrifices were instituted. From whence should those skins come, but from beasts slain for sacrifice, of which God made them coats? We find Abel, as well as Cain, offering sacrifice in the next chapter: and the Apostle tells us, he did it by faith, no doubt in this promise. And Eve, when Cain was born, said, "I have gotten a man from the Lord," or, (as Mr. Henry observes, it may be rendered) "I have gotten a man, -- the Lord, -- the promised Messiah." Some further suppose, that Eve was the first believer; and therefore they translate it thus, "The seed, (not of the, but) of this woman:" which magnifies the grace of God so much the more, that she, who was first in the transgression, should be the first partaker of redemption. Adam believed also, and was saved: for unto Adam and his wife did the Lord God make coats of skins, and clothed them: which was a remarkable type of their being clothed with the righteousness of our Lord Jesus Christ.

This promise was literally fulfilled in the person of our Lord Jesus Christ. Satan bruised his heel, when he tempted him for forty days together in the wilderness: he bruised his heel, when he raised up strong persecution against him during the time of his public ministry: he in an especial manner bruised his heel, when our Lord complained, that his soul was exceeding sorrowful, even unto death, and he sweat great drops of blood falling upon the ground, in the garden; He bruised his heel, when he put it into the heart of Judas to betray him: ad he bruised him yet most of all, when his emissaries nailed him to an accursed tree, and our Lord cried out, "My God, my God, why hast thou forsaken me?" Yet, in all this, the blessed Jesus, the seed of the woman, bruised Satan's accursed head; for, in that he was tempted, he was able to succor those that are tempted. By his stripes we are healed. The chastisement of our peace was upon him. By dying, he destroyed him that had the power of death, that is, the devil. He thereby spoiled principalities and powers, and made a show of them openly, triumphing over them upon the cross.

This promise has been fulfilled in the elect of God, considered collectively, as well before, as since the coming of our Lord in the flesh: for they may be called, the seed of the woman. Marvel not, that all who will live godly in Christ Jesus, must suffer persecution. In this promise, there is an eternal enmity put between the seed of the woman, and the seed of the serpent; so that those that are born after the flesh, cannot but persecute those that are born after the spirit. This enmity showed itself, soon after this promise was revealed, in Cain's bruising the heel of Abel: it continued in the church through all ages before Christ came in the flesh, as the history of the Bible, and the 11th chapter of the Hebrews, plainly show. It raged exceedingly after our Lord's ascension; witness the Acts of the Apostles, and the History of the Primitive Christians. It now rages, and will continue to rage and show itself, in a greater or less degree, to the end of time. But let not this dismay us; for in all this, the seed of the woman is more than conqueror, and bruises the serpent's head. Thus the Israelites, the more they were oppressed, the more they increased. Thus it was with the Apostles; thus it was with their immediate followers. So that Tertullian compares the church in his time to a mowed field; the more frequently it is cut, the more it grows. The blood of the martyrs was always the seed of the church. And I have often sat down with wonder and delight, and admired how God has made the very schemes which his enemies contrived, in order to hinder, become the most effectual means to propagate his gospel. The devil has had so little success in persecution, that if I did not know that he and his children, according to this verse, could not but persecute, I should think he would count it his strength to sit still. What did he get by persecuting the martyrs in Queen Mary's time?

Was not the grace of God exceedingly glorified in their support? What did he get by persecuting the good old Puritans? Did it not prove the peopling of New-England? Or, to come nearer our own times, what has he got by putting us out of the synagogues? Hath not the word of God, since that, mightily prevailed? My dear hearers, you must excuse me for enlarging on this head; God fills my soul generally, when I come to this topic. I can say with Luther, "If it were not for persecution, I should not understand the scripture." If Satan should be yet suffered to bruise my heel further, and his servants should thrust me into prison, I doubt not, but even that would only tend to the more effectual bruising of his head. I remember a saying the then Lord Chancellor to the pious Bradford: "Thou hast done more hurt, said he, by thy exhortations in private in prison, than thou didst in preaching before thou was put in," or words to this effect. The promise of the text is my daily support: "I will put enmity between thy seed and her seed; it shall bruise thy head, and thou shalt bruise his heel." Further: this promise is also fulfilled, not only in the church in general, but in every individual believer in particular. In every believer there are two seeds, the seed of the woman, and the seed of the serpent; the flesh lusting against the spirit, and the spirit against the flesh. It is with the believer, when quickened with grace in his heart, as it was with Rebekah, when she had conceived Esau and Jacob in her womb; she felt a struggling, and began to be uneasy; "If it be so says she, why am I thus?" (Gen. 25:22) Thus grace and nature struggle (if I may so speak) in the womb of a believers heart: but, as it was there said, "The elder shall serve the younger;" so it is here, -- grace in the end shall get the better of nature; the seed of the woman shall bruise the serpent's head. Many of you that have believed in Christ, perhaps may find some particular corruption yet strong, so strong, that you are sometimes ready to cry out with David, "I shall fall one day by the hand of Saul." But, fear not, the promise in the text insures the perseverance and victory of believers over sin, Satan, death, and hell. What if indwelling corruption does yet remain, and the seed of the serpent bruise your heel, in vexing and disturbing your righteous souls? Fear not, though faint, yet pursue: you shall yet bruise the serpent's head. Christ hath died for you, and yet a little while, and he will send death to destroy the very being of sin in you. Which brings me To show the most extensive manner in which the promise of the text shall be fulfilled, vis. at the final judgment, when the Lord Jesus shall present the elect to his Father, without spot or wrinkle, or any such thing, glorified both in body and soul.

Then shall the seed of the woman give the last and fatal blow, in bruising the serpent's head. Satan, the accuser of the brethren, and all his accursed seed, shall then be cast out, and never suffered to disturb the seed of the woman any more. Then shall the righteous shine as the sun in the kingdom of their Father, and sit with Christ on thrones in majesty on high.

Let us, therefore, not be weary of well-doing; for we shall reap an eternal harvest of comfort, if we faint not. Dare, dare, my dear brethren in Christ, to follow the Captain of your salvation, who was made perfect through sufferings. The seed of the woman shall bruise the serpent's head.

Fear not men. Be not too much cast down at the deceitfulness of your hearts. Fear not devils; you shall get the victory even over them. The Lord Jesus has engaged to make you more than conquerors over all. Plead with you Savior, plead: plead the promise in the tent. Wrestle, wrestle with God in prayer. If it has been given you to believe, fear not if it should also be given you to suffer. Be not any wise terrified by your adversaries; the king of the church has them all in a chain: be kind to them, pray for them; but fear them not. The Lord will yet bring back his ark; though at present driven into the wilderness; and Satan like lightening shall fall from heaven.

Are there any enemies of God here? The promise of the text encourages me to bid you defiance: the seed of the woman, the ever-blessed Jesus, shall bruise the serpent's head. What signifies all your malice? You are only raging waves of the sea, foaming out your own shame. For you, without repentance, is reserved the blackness of darkness for ever. The Lord Jesus sits in heaven, ruling over all, and causing all things to work for his children's good: he laughs you to scorn: he hath you in the utmost derision, and therefore so will I. Who are you that persecute the children of the ever blessed God? Though a poor stripling, the Lord Jesus, the seed of the woman, will enable me to bruise your heads.

My brethren in Christ, I think I do not speak thus in my own strength, but in the strength of my Redeemer. I know in whom I have believed; I am persuaded he will keep that safe, which I have committed unto him. He is faithful who hath promised, that the seed of the woman shall bruise the serpent's head. May we all experience a daily completion of this promise, both in the church and in our hearts, till we come to the church of the first-born, the spirits of just men made perfect, in the presence and actual fruition of the great God our heavenly Father!

To whom, with the Son, and the Holy Ghost, be ascribed all honor, power, might, majesty, and dominion, now and for evermore. Amen.

Sermon 2 Walking With God

Genesis 5:24, "And Enoch walked with God: and he was not; for God took him."

Various are the pleas and arguments which men of corrupt minds frequently urge against yielding obedience to the just and holy commands of God. But, perhaps, one of the most common objections that they make is this, that our Lord's commands are not practicable, because contrary to flesh and blood; and consequently, that he is `an hard master, reaping where he has not sown, and gathering where he has not strewed'. These we find were the sentiments entertained by that wicked and slothful servant mentioned in the 25th of St. Matthew; and are undoubtedly the same with many which are maintained in the present wicked and adulterous generation.

The Holy Ghost foreseeing this, hath taken care to inspire holy men of old, to record the examples of many holy men and women; who, even under the Old Testament dispensation, were enabled cheerfully to take Christ's yoke upon them, and counted his service perfect freedom. The large catalogue of saints, confessors, and martyrs, drawn up in the 11th chapter to the Hebrews, abundantly evidences the truth of this observation. What a great cloud of witnesses have we there presented to our view? All eminent for their faith, but some shining with a greater degree of luster than do others. The proto-martyr Abel leads the van. And next to him we find Enoch mentioned, not only because he was next in order of time, but also on account of his exalted piety; he is spoken of in the words of the text in a very extraordinary manner. We have here a short but very full and glorious account, both of his behavior in this world, and the triumphant manner of his entry into the next. The former is contained in these words, `And Enoch walked with God'. The latter in these, `and he was not: for God took him'.

He was not; that is, he was not found, he was not taken away in the common manner, he did not see death; for God had translated him. (Heb. 11:5.) Who this Enoch was, does not appear so plainly. To me, he seems to have been a person of public character; I suppose, like Noah, a preacher of righteousness. And, if we may credit the apostle Jude, he was a flaming preacher. For he quotes one of his prophecies, wherein he saith, `Behold, the Lord cometh with ten thousands of his saints, to execute judgment upon all, and to convince all that are ungodly among them, of all their ungodly deeds which they have ungodly committed, and of all their hard speeches, which ungodly sinners have spoken against him'. But whether a public or private person, he has a noble testimony given him in the lively oracles.

The author of the epistle to the Hebrews saith, that before his translation he had this testimony, `that he pleased God'; and his being translated, was a proof of it beyond all doubt. And I would observe, that it was wonderful wisdom in God to translate Enoch and Elijah under the Old Testament dispensation, that hereafter, when it should be asserted that the Lord Jesus was carried into heaven, it might not seem a thing altogether incredible to the Jews; since they themselves confessed that two of their own prophets had been translated several hundred hears before. But it is not my design to detain you any longer, by enlarging, or making observations, on Enoch's short but comprehensive character: the thing I have in view being to give a discourse, as the Lord shall enable, upon a weighty and a very important subject; I mean, WALKING WITH GOD. `And Enoch walked with God.' If so much as this can be truly said of you and me after our decease, we shall not have any reason to complain that we have lived in vain.

In handling my intended subject, I shall, FIRST, Endeavor to show what is implied in these words, WALKED WITH GOD.

SECONDLY, I shall prescribe some means, upon the due observance of which, believers may keep up and maintain their WALK WITH GOD. And, THIRDLY, Offer some motives to stir us up, if we never walked with God before, to come and walk with God now. The whole shall be closed with a word or two of application.

FIRST, I am to show what is implied in these words, `walked with God'; or, in other words, what we are to understand by WALKING WITH GOD.

And FIRST, WALKING WITH GOD implies, that the prevailing power of the enmity of a person's heart be taken away by the blessed Spirit of God.

Perhaps it may seem a hard saying to some, but our own experience daily proves what the scriptures in many places assert, that the carnal mind, the mind of the unconverted natural man, nay, the mind of the regenerate, so far as any part of him remains unrenewed, is enmity, not only an enemy, but enmity itself, against God; so that it is not subject to the law of God, neither indeed can it be. Indeed, one may well wonder that any creature, especially that lovely creature man, made after his Maker's own image, should ever have any enmity, much less a prevailing enmity, against that very God in whom he lives, and moves, and hath his being. But alas! so it is. Our first parents contracted it when they fell from God by eating the forbidden fruit, and the bitter and malignant contagion of it hath descended to, and quite overspread, their whole posterity. This enmity discovered itself in Adam's endeavoring to hide himself in the trees of the garden. When he heard the voice of the Lord God, instead of running with an open heart, saying Here I am; alas! he now wanted no communion with God; and still more discovered his lately contracted enmity, by the excuse he made to the Most High: 'The woman (or, this woman) thou gavest to be with me, she gave me of the tree, and I did eat'. By saying thus, he in effect lays all the fault upon God; as though he had said, If thou hadst not given me this woman, I had not sinned against thee, so thou mayest thank thyself for my transgression. In the same manner this enmity works in the hearts of Adam's children. They now and again find something rising against God, and saying even unto God, What doest thou? 'It scorns any meaner competitor (says the learned Dr. Owen, in his excellent treatise on indwelling sin) than God himself.' Its command is like that of the Assyrians in respect to Ahab _ shoot only at the king. And it strikes against every thing that has the appearance of real piety, as the Assyrians shot at Jehoshaphat in his royal clothes. But the opposition ceases when it finds that it is only an appearance, as the Assyrians left off shooting at Jehoshaphat, when they perceived it was not Ahab they were shooting at. This enmity discovered itself in accursed Cain; he hated and slew his brother Abel, because Abel loved, and was peculiarly favored by, his God. And this same enmity rules and prevails in every man that is naturally engendered of the offspring of Adam. Hence that a averseness to prayer and holy duties which we find in children, and very often in grown persons, who have notwithstanding been blessed with a religious education. And all that open sin and wickedness, which like a deluge has overflowed the world, are only so many streams running from this dreadful contagious fountain; I mean a enmity of man's desperately wicked and deceitful heart. He that cannot set his seal to this, knows nothing yet, in a saving manner, of the Holy Scriptures, or of the power of God. And all that do know this, will readily acknowledge, that before a person can be said to walk with God, the prevailing power of this heart-enmity must be destroyed: for persons do not use to walk and keep company together, who entertain an irreconcilable enmity and hatred against one another. Observe me, I say, the prevailing power of this enmity must be taken away; for the in-being of it will never be totally removed, till we bow down our heads, and give up the ghost. The apostle Paul, no doubt, speaks of himself, and that, too, not when he was a Pharisee, but a real Christian; when he complains, 'that when he would do good, evil was present with him'; not having dominion over him, but opposing and resisting his good intentions and actions, so that he could not do the things which he would, in that perfection which the new man desired. This is what he calls sin dwelling in him. `And this is that Fronhma sarko", which (to use the words of the ninth article of our church,) some do expound the wisdom, some sensuality, some the affectation, some the desire, of the flesh, which doth remain, yea, in them that are regenerated.' But as for its prevailing power, it is destroyed in every soul that is truly born of God, and gradually more and more weakened as the believer grows in grace, and the Spirit of God gains a greater and greater ascendancy in the heart.

But SECONDLY, Walking with God not only implies, that the prevailing power of the enmity of a man's heart be taken away, but also that a person is actually reconciled to God the Father, in and through the all-sufficient righteousness and atonement of his dear Son. `Can two walk together, unless they are agreed?' Jesus is our peace as well as our peace-maker. When we are justified by faith in Christ, then, but not till then, we have peace with God; and consequently cannot be said till then to walk with him, walking with a person being a sign and token that we are friends to that person, or at least, though we have been at variance, yet that now we are reconciled and become friends again. This is the great errand that gospel ministers are sent out upon. To us is committed the ministry of reconciliation; as ambassadors for God, we are to beseech sinners, in Christ's stead, to be reconciled unto God, and when they comply with the gracious invitation, and are actually by faith brought into a state of reconciliation with God, then, and not till then, may they be said so much as to begin to walk with God.

Further, THIRDLY, Walking with God implies a settled abiding communion and fellowship with God, or what in scripture is called, `The Holy Ghost dwelling in us'. This is what our Lord promised when he told his disciples that `the Holy Spirit would be in and with them'; not to be like wayfaring man, to say only for a night, but to reside and make his abode in their hearts. This, I am apt to believe, is what the apostle John would have us understand, when he talks of a person `abiding in him, in Christ, and walking as he himself also walked'. And this is what is particularly meant in the words of our text. `And Enoch walked with God', that is, he kept up and maintained a holy, settled, habitual, though undoubtedly not altogether uninterrupted communion and fellowship with God, in and through Christ Jesus. So that to sum up what has been said on this part of the first general head, WALKING WITH GOD consists especially in the fixed habitual bent of the will for God, in an habitual dependence upon his power and promise, in an habitual voluntary dedication of our all to his glory, in an habitual eyeing of his precept in all we do, and in an habitual complacence in his pleasure in all we suffer.

FOURTHLY, WALKING WITH GOD implies our making progress or advances in the divine life. WALKING, in the very first idea of the word, seems to suppose a progressive motion. A person that walks, though he move slowly, yet he goes forward, and does not continue in one place. And so it is with those that walk with God. They go on, as the Psalmist says, `from strength to strength'; or, in the language of the apostle Paul, `they pass from glory to glory, even by the Spirit of the Lord'. Indeed, in one sense, the divine life admits of neither increase nor decrease. When a soul is born of God, to all intents and purposes he is a child of God; and though he should live to the age of Methuselah, yet he would then be only a child of God after all. But in another sense, the divine life admits of decays and additions. Hence it is, that we find the people of God charged with backslidings and losing their first love. And hence it is that we hear of babes, young men, and fathers in Christ. And upon this account it is that the apostle exhorts Timothy, `to let his progress be made known to all men'. And what is here required of Timothy in particular, by St. Peter is enjoined on all Christians in general. `But grow in grace, (says he), and in the knowledge of our Lord and Savior Jesus Christ'. For the new creature increases in spiritual stature; and though a person can but be a new creature, yet there are some that are more conformed to the divine image than others, and will after death be admitted to a greater degree of blessedness. For want of observing this distinction, even some gracious souls, that have better hearts than heads, (as well as men of corrupt minds, reprobates concerning the faith) have unawares run into downright Antinomian principles, denying all growth of grace in a believer, or any marks of grace to be laid down in the scriptures of truth. From such principles, and more especially from practices naturally consequent on such principles, may the Lord of all lords deliver us!

From what then has been said, we may now know what is implied in the words, `walked with God', viz. Our having the prevailing enmity of our hearts taken away by the power of the Spirit of God; our being actually reconciled and united to him by faith in Jesus Christ; our having and keeping up a settled communion and fellowship with him; and our making a daily progress in this fellowship, so as to be conformed to the divine image more and more.

How this is done, or, in other words, by what means believers keep up and maintain their walk with God, comes to be considered under our second general head.

And, FIRST, Believers keep up and maintain their walk with God by reading of his holy word. `Search the scriptures', says our blessed Lord, `for these are they that testify of me'. And the royal Psalmist tells us `that God's word was a light unto his feet, and a lantern unto his paths'; and he makes it one property of a good man, `that his delight is in the law of the Lord, and that he exercises himself therein day and night'. `Give thyself to reading', (says Paul to Timothy); `And this book of the law, (says God to

Joshua) shall not go out of thy mouth'. For whatsoever was written aforetime was written for our learning. And the word of God is profitable for reproof, for correction, and for instruction in righteousness, and every way sufficient to make every true child of God thoroughly furnished unto every good work. If we once get above our Bibles, and cease making the written word of God our sole rule both as to faith and practice, we shall soon lie open to all manner of delusion, and be in great danger of making shipwreck of faith and a good conscience. Our blessed Lord, though he had the Spirit of God without measure, yet always was governed by, and fought the devil with, 'It is written'. This the apostle calls the 'sword of the Spirit'. We may say of it, as David said of Goliath's sword, 'None like this'. The scriptures are called the lively oracles of God: not only because they are generally made use of to beget in us a new life, but also to keep up and increase it in the soul. The apostle Peter, in his second epistle, prefers it even to seeing Christ transfigured upon the mount. For after he had said, chap. 1:18. 'This voice which came from heaven we heard, when we were with him in the holy mount'; he adds, 'We have also a more sure word of prophecy; whereunto ye do well that ye take heed, as unto a light shining in a dark place, until the day dawn, and the day-star arise in your hearts': that is, till we shake off these bodies, and see Jesus face to face. Till then we must see and converse with him through the glass of his word. We must make his testimonies our counselors, and daily, with Mary, sit at Jesus' feet, by faith hearing his word. We shall then by happy experience find, that they are spirit and life, meat indeed and drink indeed, to our souls.

SECONDLY, Believers keep up and maintain their walk with God by secret prayer. The spirit of grace is always accompanied with the spirit of supplication. It is the very breath of the new creature, the fan of the divine life, whereby the spark of holy fire, kindled in the soul by God, is not only kept in, but raised into a flame. A neglect of secret prayer has been frequently an inlet to many spiritual diseases, and has been attended with fatal consequences. Origen observed, "hat the day he offered incense to an idol, he went out of his closet without making use of secret prayer" It is one of the most noble parts of the believers' spiritual armor.

'Praying always', says the apostle, 'with all manner of supplication.' 'Watch and pray', says our Lord, 'that ye enter not into temptation.' And he spake a parable, that his disciples should pray, and not faint. Not that our Lord would have us always upon our knees, or in our closets, to the neglect of our other relative duties. But he means, that our souls should be kept in a praying frame, so that we might be able to say, as a good man in Scotland once said to his friends on his death-bed, 'Could these curtains, or could these walls speak, they would tell you what sweet communion I have had with my God here'. O prayer! Prayer! It brings and keeps God and man together. It raises man up to God, and brings God down to man. If you would there, O believers, keep up your walk with God; pray, pray without ceasing. Be much in secret, set prayer. And when you are about the common business of life, be much in ejaculatory prayer, and send, from time to time, short letters post to heaven upon the wings of faith. They will reach the very heart of God, and return to you again loaded with spiritual blessings.

THIRDLY, Holy and frequent meditation is another blessed means of keeping up a believer's walk with God. `Prayer, reading, temptation, and meditation', says Luther, make a minister.' And they also make and perfect a Christian. Meditation to the soul, is the same as digestion to the body.

Holy David found it so, and therefore he was frequently employed in meditation, even in the night season. We read also of Isaac's going out into the fields to meditate in the evening; or, as it is in the margin, to pray. For meditation is a kind of silent prayer, whereby the soul is frequently as it were carried out of itself to God, and in a degree made like unto those blessed spirits, who by a kind of immediate intuition always behold the face of our heavenly Father. None but those happy souls that have been accustomed to this divine employ, can tell what a blessed promoter of the divine life, meditation is. `Whilst I was musing', says David, `the fire kindled.' And whilst the believer is musing on the works and word of God, especially that work of works, that wonder of wonders, that mystery of godliness, `God manifest in the flesh', the Lamb of God slain for the sins of the world, he frequently feels the fire of divine love kindle, so that he is obliged to speak with his tongue, and tell of the loving-kindness of the Lord to his soul. Be frequent therefore in meditation, all ye that desire to keep up and maintain a close and uniform walk with the most high God.

FOURTHLY, Believers keep up their walk with God, by watching and noting his providential dealings with them. If we believe the scriptures, we must believe what our Lord hath declared therein, `That the very hairs of his disciples' heads are all numbered; and that a sparrow does not fall to the ground, (either to pick up a grain of corn, or when shot by a fowler), without the knowledge of our heavenly Father'. Every cross has a call in it, and every particular dispensation of divine providence has some particular end to answer in those to whom it is sent. If it be of an afflictive nature, God does thereby say, `My son, keep thyself from idols': if prosperous, he does, as it were by a small still voice, say, `My son, give me thy heart'. If believers, therefore, would keep up their walk with God, they must from time to time hear what the Lord has to say concerning them in the voice of his providence. Thus we find that Abraham's servant, when he went to fetch a wife for his master Isaac, eyed and watched the providence of God, and by that means found out the person that was designed for his master's wife. `For a little hint from providence', says pious Bishop Hall, `is enough for faith to feed upon.' And as I believe it will be one part of our happiness in heaven, to take a view of, and look back upon, the various links of the golden chain which drew us there; so those that enjoy most of heaven below, I believe, will be the most minute in remarking God's various dealings with them, in respect to his providential dispensations here on earth.

FIFTHLY, In order to walk closely with God, his children must not only watch the motions of God's providence without them, but the motions also of his blessed Spirit in their hearts. `As many as are the sons of God, are led by the Spirit of God', and give up themselves to be guided by the Holy Ghost, as a little child gives its hand to be led by a nurse or parent. It is no doubt in this sense that we are to be converted, and become like little children. And though it is the quintessence of enthusiasm, to pretend to be guided by the Spirit without the written word; yet it is every Christian's bounden duty to be guided by the Spirit in conjunction with the written word of God. Watch, therefore, I pray you, O believers, the motions of God's blessed Spirit in your souls, and always try the suggestions or impressions that you may at any time feel, by the unerring rule of God's most holy word: and if they are not found to be agreeable to that, reject them as diabolical and delusive. By observing this caution, you will steer a middle course between the two dangerous extremes many of this generation are in danger of running into; I mean, ENTHUSIASM, on the one hand, and DEISM, and DOWNRIGHT INFIDELITY, on the other.

SIXTHLY, They that would maintain a holy walk with God, must walk with him in ordinances as well as providences, etc. It is therefore recorded of Zachary and Elizabeth, that `they walked in all God's ordinances, as well as commandments, blameless'. And all rightly informed Christians, will look upon ordinances, not as beggarly elements, but as so many conduit-pipes, whereby the infinitely condescending Jehovah conveys his grace to their souls. They will look upon them as children's bread, and as their highest privileges. Consequently they will be glad when they hear others say, `Come, let us go up to the house of the Lord'. They will delight to visit the place where God's honor dwelleth, and be very eager to embrace all opportunities to show forth the Lord Christ's death till he come.

SEVENTHLY and LASTLY, If you would walk with God, you will associate and keep company with those that do walk with him. `My delight', says holy David, `is in them that do excel' in virtue. They were, in his sight, the excellent ones of the earth. And the primitive Christians, no doubt, kept up their vigor and first love, by continuing in fellowship one with another. The apostle Paul knew this full well, and therefore exhorts the Christians to see to it, that they did not forsake the assembling of themselves together. For how can one be warm alone? And has not the wisest of men told us, that `As iron sharpeneth iron, so doth the countenance of a man his friend?' If we look, therefore, into church history, or make a just observation of our own times, I believe we shall find, that as the power of God prevails, Christian societies, and fellowship meetings prevail proportionably. And as one decays, the other has insensibly decayed and dwindled away at the same time. So necessary is it for those that would walk with God, and keep up the life of religion, to meet together as they have opportunity, in order to provoke one another to love and good works.

Proceed we now to the third general thing proposed: to offer some motives to excite all to come and walk with God.

And, FIRST, walking with God is a very honorable thing. This generally is a prevailing motive to persons of all ranks, to stir them up to any important undertaking. O that it may have its due weight and influence with you in respect to the matter now before us! I suppose you would all think it a very high honor to be admitted into an earthly prince's privy council, to be trusted with his secrets, and to have his ear at all times and at all seasons. It seems Haman thought it so when he boasted, Esther 5:11, that besides his being 'advanced above the princes and servants of the king; yea, moreover, Esther the queen did let no man come in with the king unto the banquet that she had prepared, but myself; and to-morrow am I invited unto her also with the king'. And when afterwards a question was put to this same Haman, Chap. 6:6. 'What shall be done unto the man whom the king delighteth to honor?' he answered, verse 8. 'Let the royal apparel be brought which the king used to wear, and the horse that the king rideth upon, and the crown royal which is set upon his head; and let this apparel and horse be delivered to the hand of one of the king's most noble princes, that they may array the man withal whom the king delighteth to honor, and bring him on horseback through the street of the city and proclaim before him, Thus shall it be done to the man whom the king delighteth to honor.' This was all, then, it seems, that an ambitious Haman could ask, and the most valuable thing that he thought Ahasuerus, the greatest monarch upon earth, could give. But, alas, what is this honor in comparison of that which the meanest of those enjoy, that walk with God! Think ye it a small thing, sirs, to have the secret of the Lord of lords with you, and to be called the friends of God? And such honor have all God's saints. The secret of the Lord is with them that fear him: and 'Henceforth(says the blessed Jesus) call I you no longer servants, but friends; for the servant knoweth not the will of his master'. Whatever you may think of it, holy David was so sensible of the honor attending a walk with God that he declares, 'he had rather be a door-keeper in his house, than to dwell even in the tents of ungodliness'. O that all were like-minded with him!

But, SECONDLY, As it is an honorable, so it is a pleasing thing, to walk with God. The wisest of men has told us, that 'wisdom's ways are ways of pleasantness, and all her paths peace'. And I remember pious Mr. Henry, when he was about to expire, said to a friend, `You have heard many men's dying words, and these are mine: A life spent in communion with God, is the pleasantest life in the world'. I am sure I can set to my seal that this is true. Indeed, I have been listed under Jesus' banner only for a few years; but I have enjoyed more solid pleasure in one moment's communion with my god, than I should or could have enjoyed in the ways of sin, though I had continued to have gone on in them for thousands of years. And may I not appeal to all you that fear and walk with God, for the truth of this? Has not one day in the Lord's courts been better to you than a thousand? In keeping God's commandments, have you not found a present, and very great reward? Has not his word been sweeter to you than the honey or the honeycomb? O what have you felt, when, Jacob-like, you have been wrestling with your God? Has not Jesus often met you when meditating in the fields, and been made known to you over and over again in breaking of bread? Has not the Holy Ghost frequently shed the divine love abroad in your hearts abundantly, and filled you with joy unspeakable, even joy that is full of glory? I know you will answer all these questions in the affirmative, and freely acknowledge the yoke of Christ to be easy, and his burden light; or (to use the words of one of our collects), `His service is perfect freedom'. And what need we then any further motive to excite us to walk with God?

But methinks I hear some among you say, `How can these things be? For, if walking with God, as you say, is such an honorable and pleasant thing, whence is it that the name of the people of this way is cast out as evil, and every where spoken against? How comes it to pass that they are frequently afflicted, tempted, destitute, and tormented? Is this the honor, this the pleasure, that you speak of?' I answer, Yes. Stop a while; be not over hasty. Judge not according to appearance, but judge righteous judgment, and all will be well. It is true, we acknowledge the `people of this way', as you, and Paul before you, when a persecutor, called them, have their names cast out as evil, and are a sect every where spoken against. But by whom? Even by the enemies of the most high God. And do you think it is disgrace to be spoken evil of by them? Blessed be God, we have not so learned Christ. Our royal Master has pronounced those `blessed, who are persecuted, and have all manner of evil spoken against them falsely'. He has commanded them `to rejoice and be exceeding glad', for it is the privilege of their discipleship, and that their reward will be great in heaven. He himself was thus treated. And can there be a greater honor put upon a creature, than to be conformed to the ever-blessed Son of God? And further, it is equally true that the people of this way are frequently afflicted, tempted, destitute, and tormented. But what of all this? Does this destroy the pleasure of walking with God? No, in no wise; for those that walk with God are enabled, through Christ strengthening them, to joy even in tribulation, and to rejoice when they fall into divers temptations. And I believe I may appeal to the experience of all true and close walkers with

God, whether or not their suffering times have not frequently been their sweetest times, and that they enjoyed most of God when most cast out and despised by men?

This we find was the case of Christ's primitive servants, when threatened by the Jewish sanhedrin, and commanded to preach no more in the name of Jesus; they rejoiced that they were accounted worthy to suffer shame for the sake of Jesus. Paul and Silas sang praises even in a dungeon; and the face of Stephen, that glorious proto-martyr of the Christian church, shone like the face of an angel. And Jesus is the same now as he was then, and takes care so to sweeten sufferings and afflictions with his love, that his disciples find, by happy experience, that as afflictions abound, consolations do much more abound. And therefore these objections, instead of destroying, do only enforce the motives before urged, to excite you to walk with God.

But supposing the objections were just, and walkers with God were as despicable and unhappy as you would represent them to be; yet I have a third motive to offer, which if weighed in the balance of the sanctuary, will over-weigh all objections, viz. That there is a heaven at the end of this walk. For, to use the words of pious bishop Beveridge, 'Though the way be narrow, yet it is not long: and though the gate be strait, yet it opens into everlasting life'. Enoch found it so. He walked with God on earth, and God took him to sit down with him for ever in the kingdom of heaven. Not that we are to expect to be taken away as he was: no, I suppose we shall all die the common death of all men. But after death, the spirits of those who have walked with God shall return to God that gave them; and at the morning of the resurrection, soul and body shall be for ever with the Lord; their bodies shall be fashioned like unto Christ's glorious body, and their souls filled with all the fullness of God. They shall sit on thrones; they shall judge angels. They shall be enabled to sustain an exceeding and eternal weight of glory, even that glory which Jesus Christ enjoyed with the Father before the world began. 'O gloriam quantam et qualem', said the learned and pious Arndt, just before he bowed down his head, and gave up the ghost. The very thought of it is enough to make us 'wish to leap our seventy years', as good Dr. Watts expresses himself, and to make us break out into the earnest language of the royal Psalmist, 'My soul is athirst for God, yea, for the living God. When shall I come to appear in the presence of my God?' I wonder not that a sense of this, when under a more than ordinary irradiation and influx of divine life and love, causes some persons to faint away, and even for a time lose the power of their senses.

A less sight than this, even the sight of Solomon's glory, made Sheba's queen astonished; and a still lesser sight than that, even a sight of Joseph's wagons, made holy Jacob faint, and for a while, as it were, die away.

Daniel, when admitted to a distant view of this excellent glory, fell down at the feet of the angel as one dead. And if a distant view of this glory be so excellent, what must the actual possession of it be? If the first fruits are so glorious, how infinitely must the harvest exceed in glory?

And now, what shall I, or, indeed, what can I well say more to excite you, even you that are yet strangers to Christ, to come and walk with God?

If you love honor, pleasure, and a crown of glory, come, seek it where alone it can be found. Come, put ye on the Lord Jesus. Come, haste ye away and walk with God, and make no longer provision for the flesh, to fulfill the lust thereof. Stop, stop, O sinner! Turn ye, turn ye, O ye unconverted men, for the end of that way you are now walking in, however right it may seem in your blinded eyes, will be death, even eternal destruction both of body and soul. Make no longer tarrying, I say: at your peril I charge you, step not one step further on in your present walk. For how knowest thou, O man, but the next step thou takest may be into hell? Death may seize thee, judgment find thee, and then the great gulf will be fixed between thee and endless glory for ever and ever. O think of these things, all ye that are unwilling to walk with God. Lay them to heart. Show yourselves men, and in the strength of Jesus say, Farewell, lust of the flesh, I will no more walk with thee! Farewell, lust of the eye, and pride of life! Farewell, carnal acquaintance and enemies of the cross, I will no more walk and be intimate with you! Welcome Jesus, welcome thy word, welcome thy ordinances, welcome thy Spirit, welcome thy people, I will henceforth walk with you. O that there may be in you such a mind! God will set his almighty fiat to it, and seal it with the broad seal of heaven, even the signet of his holy Spirit.

Yes, he will, though you have been walking with, and following after, the devices and desires of your desperately wicked hearts ever since you have been born. 'I, the high and lofty One', says the great Jehovah, 'that inhabiteth eternity, will dwell with the humble and contrite heart, even with the man that trembleth at my word.' The blood, even the precious blood of Jesus Christ, if you come to the Father in and through him, shall cleanse you from all sin.

But the text leads me to speak to you that are saints as well as to you that are open and unconverted sinners. I need not tell you, that walking with God is not honorable, but pleasant and profitable also; for ye know it by happy experience, and will find it more and more so every day.

Only give me leave to stir up your pure minds by way of remembrance, and to beseech you by the mercies of God in Christ Jesus, to take heed to yourselves, and walk closer with your God than you have in days past: for the nearer you walk with God, the more you will enjoy of him whose presence is life, and be the better prepared for being placed at his right hand, where are pleasures for evermore. O do not follow Jesus afar off! O be not so formal, so dead and stupid in your attendance on holy ordinances! Do not so shamefully forsake the assembling yourselves together, or be so niggardly or indifferent about the things of God. Remember what Jesus says of the church of Laodicea, 'Because thou art neither hot nor cold, I will spew thee out of my mouth'. Think of the love of Jesus, and let that love constrain you to keep near unto him; and though you die for him, do not deny him, do not keep at a distance from him in any wise.

One word to my brethren in the ministry that are here present, and I have done. You see, my brethren, my heart is full; I could almost say it is too big to speak, and yet too big to be silent, without dropping a word to you. For does not the text speak in a particular manner to those who have the honor of being styled the ambassadors of Christ, and stewards of the mysteries of God. I observed at the beginning of this discourse, that Enoch in all probability was a public person, and a flaming preacher. Though he be dead, does he not yet speak to us, to quicken our zeal, and make us more active in the service of our glorious and ever-blessed Master? How did Enoch preach! How did Enoch walk with God, though he lived in a wicked and adulterous generation! Let us then follow him, as he followed Jesus Christ, and ere long, where he is there shall we be also. He is not entered into his rest: yet a little while and we shall enter into ours, and that too much sooner than he did. He sojourned here be-low three hundred years; but blessed be God, the days of man are now shortened, and in a few days our walk will be over. The Judge is before the door: he that cometh will come, and will not tarry: his reward is with him. And we shall all (if we are zealous for the Lord of hosts) ere long shine as the stars in the firmament, in the kingdom of our heavenly Father, for ever and ever. To Him, the blessed Jesus, and eternal Spirit, be all honor and glory, now, and to all eternity. Amen, and Amen.

Sermon 3 Abraham's Offering Up His Son Isaac

Genesis 22:12 "And he said, Lay not thine hand upon the lad, neither do thou any thing unto him, for now I know that thou fearest God, seeing thou hast not withheld thy Son, thine only Son from me."

The great Apostle Paul, in one of his epistles, informs us, that "whatsoever was written aforetime was written for our learning, that we through patience and comfort of the holy scripture might have hope." And as without faith it is impossible to please God, or be accepted in Jesus, the Son of his love; we may be assured, that whatever instances of a more than common faith are recorded in the book of God, they were more immediately designed by the Holy Spirit for our learning and imitation, upon whom the ends of the world are come. For this reason, the author of the epistle to the Hebrews, in the 11th chapter, mentions such a noble catalogue of Old Testament saints and martyrs, "who subdued kingdoms, wrought righteousness, stopped the mouths of lions, etc. and are gone before us to inherit the promises." A sufficient confutation, I think, of their error, who lightly esteem the Old Testament saints, and would not have them mentioned to Christians, as persons whose faith and patience we are called upon more immediately to follow. If this was true, the apostle would never have produced such a cloud of witnesses out of the Old Testament, to excite the Christians of the first, and consequently purest age of the church, to continue steadfast and unmoveable in the profession of their faith. Amidst this catalogue of saints, methinks the patriarch Abraham shines the brightest, and differs from the others, as one star differeth from another star in glory; for he shone with such distinguished luster, that he was called the "friend of God," the "father of the faithful;" and those who believe on Christ, are said to be "sons and daughters of, and to be blessed with, faithful Abraham." Many trials of his faith did God send this great and good man, after he had commanded him to get out from his country, and from his kindred, unto a land which he should show him; but the last was the most sever of all, I mean, that of offering up his only son. This, by the divine assistance, I propose to make the subject of your present meditation, and, by way of conclusion, to draw some practical inferences, as God shall enable me, from this instructive story.

The sacred penman begins the narrative thus; verse 1. "And it came to pass, after these things, God did tempt Abraham." After these things, that it, after he had underwent many severe trials before, after he was old, full of days, and might flatter himself perhaps that the troubles and toils of life were now finished; "after these things, God did tempt Abraham." Christians, you know not what trials you may meet with before you die: notwithstanding you may have suffered, and been tried much already, yet, it may be, a greater measure is still behind, which you are to fill up. "Be not high-minded, but fear." Our last trials, in all probability, will be the greatest: and we can never say our warfare is accomplished, or our trials finished, till we bow down our heads, and give up the ghost. "And it came to pass, after these things, that God did tempt Abraham." "God did tempt Abraham." But can the scripture contradict itself? Does not the apostle James tell us, "that God tempts no man;" and God does tempt no man to evil, or on purpose to draw him into sin; for, when a man is thus tempted, he is drawn away of his own heart's lust, and enticed. But in another sense, God may be said to tempt, I mean, to try his servants; and in this sense we are to understand that passage of Matthew, where we are told, that, "Jesus was led up by the Spirit (the good Spirit) into the wilderness, to be tempted of the devil." And our Lord, in that excellent form of prayer which he has been pleased to give us, does not require us to pray that we may not absolutely be led into temptation, but delivered from the evil of it; whence we may plainly infer, that God sees it fit sometimes to lead us into temptation, that is, to bring us into such circumstances as will try our faith and other Christian graces. In this sense we are to understand the expression before us; "God did tempt or try Abraham." How God was pleased to reveal his will at this time to his faithful servant, whether by the Sheckinah, or divine appearance, or by a small still voice, as he spoke to Elijah, or by a whisper, like that of the Spirit to Philip, when he commanded him to join himself to the eunuch's chariot, we are not told, nor is it material to inquire. It is enough that we are informed, God said unto him, Abraham; and that Abraham knew it was the voice of God: for he said, "Behold, here I am." O what a holy familiarity (if I may so speak) is there between God and those holy souls that are united to him by faith in Christ Jesus! God says, Abraham; and Abraham said (it should seem without the least surprise) Behold, here I am.

Being reconciled to God by the death and obedience of Christ, which he rejoiced in, and saw by faith afar off; he did not, like guilty Adam, seed the trees of the garden to hide himself from, but takes pleasure in conversing with God, and talketh with him, as a man talketh with his friend. O that Christ-less sinners knew what it is to have fellowship with the Father and the Son! They would envy the happiness of saints, and count it all joy to be termed enthusiasts and fools for Christ's sake.

But what does God say to Abraham? Verse 2. "Take now thy son, thine only son Isaac, whom thou lovest, and get thee into the land of Moriah, and offer him there for a burnt-offering upon one of the mountains which I shall tell thee of." Every word deserves our particular observation. Whatever he was to do, he must do it now, immediately, without conferring with flesh and blood.

But what must he do? "Take now thy son." Had God said, take now a firstling, or choicest lamb or beast of thy flock, and offer it up for a burnt-offering, it would not have appeared so ghastly; but for God to say, "take now thy son, and offer him up for a burnt-offering," one would imagine, was enough to stagger the strongest faith. But this is not all: it must not only be a son, but "thine only son Isaac, whom thou lovest." If it must be a son, and not a beast, that must be offered, why will not Ishmael do, the son of the bond-woman? No, it must be his only son, the heir of all, his Isaac, by interpretation laughter, the son of his old age, in whom his soul delighted, "whom thou lovest," says God, in whose life his own was wrapped up: and this son, this only son, this Isaac, the son of his love, must be taken now, even now, without delay, and be offered up by his own father, for a burnt offering, upon one of the mountains of the which God would tell him.

Well might the apostle, speaking of this man of God, say, that "against hope he believed in hope, and, being strong in faith, gave glory to God." For, had he not been blesses with faith which man never before had, he must have refused to comply with this severe command. For now many arguments might nature suggest, to prove that such a command could never come from God, or to excuse himself from obeying it? "What! (might the good man have said) butcher my own child! It is contrary to the very law of nature: much more to butcher my dear son Isaac, in whose seed God himself has assured me of a numerous posterity. But supposing I could give up my own affections, and be willing to part with him, though I love him so dearly, yet, if I murder him, what will become of God's promise? Besides, I am now like a city built upon a hill; I shine as a light in the world, in the midst of a crooked and perverse generation: How then shall I cause God's name to be blasphemed, how shall I become a by-word among the heathen, if they hear that I have committed a crime which they abhor! But, above all, what will Sarah my wife say? How can I ever return to her again, after I have imbrued (to wet or stain) my hands in my dear child's blood? O that God would pardon me in this thing, or take my life in the place of my son's!" Thus, I say, Abraham might have argued, and that too seemingly with great reason, against complying with the divine command. But as before by faith he considered not the deadness of Sarah's womb, when she was past age, but believed on him, who said, "Sarah thy wife shall bear thee a son indeed;" so now, being convinced that the same God spoke to and commanded him to offer up that son, and knowing that God was able to raise him from the dead, without delay he obeys the heavenly call.

O that unbelievers would learn of faithful Abraham, and believe whatever is revealed from God, though they cannot fully comprehend it!

Abraham knew God commanded him to offer up his son, and therefore believed, notwithstanding carnal reasoning might suggest may objections. We have sufficient testimony, that God has spoken to us by his son; why should we not also believe, though many things in the New Testament are above our reason? For, where reason ends, faith begins. And, however infidels may stile themselves reasoners, of all men they are the most unreasonable: For, is it not contrary to all reason, to measure an infinite by a finite understanding, or think to find out the mysteries of godliness to perfection?

But to return to the patriarch Abraham: We observed before what plausible objections he might have made; but he answered not a single word: no, without replying against his Maker, we are told, verse 3, that "Abraham rose up early in the morning, and saddled his ass, and took two of his young men with him, and Isaac his son, and clave the wood for the burnt- offering, and rose up and went unto the place of which God had told him." From this verse we may gather, that God spoke to Abraham in a dream, or vision of the night: For it is said, he rose up early. Perhaps it was near the fourth watch of the night, just before break of day, when God said, Take now thy son; and Abraham rises up early to do so; as I doubt not but he used to ruse early to offer up his morning-sacrifice of praise and thanksgiving. It is often remarked of people in the Old Testament, that they rose early in the morning; and particularly of our Lord in the New, that he rose a great while before day to pray. The morning befriends devotion; and, if people cannot use so much self-denial as to rise early to pray, I know not how they will be able to die at a stake (if called to it) for Jesus Christ.

The humility as well as the piety of the patriarch is observable: he saddled his own ass (great men should be humble) and to show the sincerity, though he took two of his young men with him, and Isaac his son, yet he keeps his design as a secret from them all: nay, he does not so much as tell Sarah his wife; for he knew not but she might be a snare unto him in this affair; and, as Rebekah afterwards, on another occasion, advised Jacob to flee, so Sarah also might persuade Isaac to hide himself; or the young men, had they known of it, might have forced him away, as in after-ages the soldiers rescued Jonathan out of the hands of Saul. But Abraham fought no such evasion, and therefore, like an Israelite indeed, in whom there was no guile, he himself resolutely "clave the wood for the burnt-offering, rose up and went unto the place of which God had told him." In the second verse God commanded him to offer up his son upon one of the mountains which he would tell him of. He commanded him to offer his son up, but would not then directly tell him the place where: this was to keep him dependent and watching unto prayer: for there is nothing like being kept waiting upon God; and, if we do, assuredly God will reveal himself unto us yet further in his own time. Let us practice what we know, follow providence so far as we can see already; and what we know not, what we see not as yet, let us only be found in the way of duty, and the Lord will reveal even that unto us. Abraham knew not directly where he was to offer up his son; but he rises up and sets forward, and behold now God shows him: "And he went to the place of which God had told him." Let us go and do likewise.

Verse 4. "Then on the third day Abraham lifted up his eyes, and saw the place afar off." So that the place, of which God had told him, was no less than three days journey distant from the place where God first appeared to him, and commanded him to take his son. Was not this to try his faith, and to let him see that what he did, was not merely from a sudden pang of devotion, but a matter of choice of deliberation? But who can tell what the aged patriarch felt during these three days? Strong as he was in faith, I am persuaded his bowels often yearned over his dear son Isaac. Methinks I see the good old man walking with his dear child in his hand, and now and then looking upon him, loving him, and then turning aside to weep. And perhaps, sometimes he stays a little behind to pour out his heart before God, for he had no mortal to tell his case to. Then, methinks, I see him join his son and servants again, and talking to them of the things pertaining to the kingdom of God, as they walked by the way. At length, "on the third day, he lifts up his eyes, and saw the place afar off." And, to show that he was yet sincerely resolved to do whatsoever the Lord requested of him, he even how will not discover his design to his servants, but "said, verse 5. To his young men," (as we should say to our worldly thoughts, when about to tread the courts of the Lord's house) "Abide you here with the ass; and I and the lad will go up yonder and worship, and come again to you." This was a sufficient reason for their staying behind; and, it being their master's custom to go frequently to worship, they could have no suspicion of what he was going about. And by Abraham's saying, that he and the lad would come again, I am apt to think he believed God would raise him from the dead, if so be he permitted him to offer his child up for a burnt-offering. However that be, he is yet resolved to obey God to the uttermost; and therefore, Verse 6. "Abraham took the wood of the burnt-offering, and laid it upon Isaac his son; and he took the fire in his hand, and a knife, and they went both of them together." Little did Isaac think that he was to be offered on that very wood which he was carrying upon his shoulders; and therefore Isaac innocently, and with a holy freedom (for good men should not keep their children at too great a distance) "spake unto Abraham his father, and said, My father; and he (with equal affection and holy condescension) said, Here am I, my son." And to show how careful Abraham had been (as all Christian parents ought to do) to instruct his Isaac how to sacrifice to God, like a youth trained up in the way wherein he should go; Isaac said, "Behold the fire and the wood; but where is the lamb for a burnt-offering?" How beautiful is early piety! How amiable, to hear young people ask questions about sacrificing to God in an acceptable way! Isaac knew very well that a lamb was wanting, and that a lamb was necessary for a proper sacrifice: "Behold the fire and the wood; but where is the lamb for a burnt-offering?" Young men and maidens, learn of him.

Hitherto, it is plain, Isaac knew nothing of his father's design: but I believe, by what his father said in answer to his question, that now was the time Abraham revealed it unto him.

Verse 8. "And Abraham said, My son, God will provide himself a Lamb for a burnt-offering." Some think, that Abraham by faith saw the Lord Jesus afar off, and here spoke prophetically of that Lamb of God already slain in decree, and hereafter to be actually offered up for sinners. This was a lamb of God's providing indeed (we dared not have thought of it) to satisfy his own justice, and to render him just in justifying the ungodly. What is all our fire and wood, the best preparations and performances we can make or present, unless God had provided himself this Lamb for a burnt-offering?

He could not away with them. The words will well hear this interpretation.

But, whatever Abraham might intend, I cannot but think he here made an application, and acquainted his son, of God's dealing with his soul; and at length, with tears in his eyes, and the utmost affection in his heart, cried out, "Thou art to be the lamb, my Son;" God has commanded me to provide thee for a burnt-offering, and to offer thee upon the mountain which we are now ascending. And, as it appears from a subsequent verse, Isaac, convinced that it was the divine will, made no resistance at all; For it is said, "They went both of them together;" and again, when we are told, that Abraham bound Isaac, we do not hear of his complaining, or endeavoring to escape, which he might have done, being (as some think) near thirty years of age, and, it is plain, capable of carrying wood enough for a burnt-offering. But he was partaker of the like precious faith with his aged father, and therefore is as willing to be offered, as Abraham is to offer him: And "so they went both of them together." Ver. 9 At length "they came to the place of which God had told Abraham. He built an altar there, and laid the wood in order, and bound Isaac his son, and laid him on the altar upon the wood." And here let us pause a while, and by faith take a view of the place where the father has laid him. I doubt not but that blessed angels hovered round the altar, and sang.

"Glory be to God in the highest," for giving such faith to man. Come, all ye tender hearted parents, who know what it is to look over a dying child: fancy that you saw the altar erected before you, and the wood laid in order, and the beloved Isaac bound upon it: fancy that you saw the aged parent standing by weeping. (For, why may we not suppose that Abraham wept, since Jesus himself wept at the grave of Lazarus?) O what pious, endearing expressions passed now alternately between the father and the son! Joseph records a pathetic speech made by each, whether genuine I now not: but methinks I see the tears trickle down the Patriarch Abraham's cheeks; and out of the abundance of the heart, he cries, Adieu, adieu, my son; the Lord gave thee to me, and the Lord calls thee away; blessed be the name of the Lord: adieu, my Isaac, my only son, whom I love as my own soul; adieu, adieu. I see Isaac at the same time meekly resigning himself into his heavenly Father's hands, and praying to the most High to strengthen his earthly parent to strike the stroke. But why do I attempt to describe what either son or father felt? It is impossible: we may indeed form some faint idea of, but shall never full comprehend it, till we come and sit down with them in the kingdom of heaven, and hear them tell the pleasing story over again. Hasten, O Lord, that blessed time! O let thy kingdom come!

And now, the fatal blow is going to be given. "And Abraham stretched forth his hand, and took the knife to slay his son." But do you not think he intended to turn away his head, when he gave the blow? Nay, why may we not suppose he sometimes drew his hand in, after it was stretched out, willing to take another last farewell of his beloved Isaac, and desirous to defer it a little, though resolved at last to strike home? Be that is it will, his arm is now stretched out, the knife is in his hand, and he is about to put it to his dear son's throat.

But sing, O heavens! and rejoice, O earth! Man's extremity is God's opportunity: for behold, just as the knife, in all probability, was near his throat, ver. 11, "the angel of the Lord, (or rather the Lord of angels, Jesus Christ, the angel of the everlasting covenant) called unto him, (probably in a very audible manner) from heaven, and said, Abraham, Abraham. (The word is doubled, to engage his attention; and perhaps the suddenness of the call made him draw back his hand, just as he was going to strike his son.) And Abraham said, Here am I." "And he said, Lay not thine hand upon the lad, neither do thou any thing unto him: for now know I that thou fearest God, seeing thou hast not withheld thy son, thine only son from me." Here then it was that Abraham received his son Isaac from the dead in a figure. He was in effect offered upon the altar, and God looked upon him as offered and given unto him. Now it was that Abraham's faith, being tried, was found more precious than gold purified seven times in the fire.

Now as a reward of grace, though not of debt, for this signal act of obedience, by an oath, God gives and confirms the promise, "that in his seed all the nations of the earth should be blessed," ver. 17, 18. With what comfort may we suppose the good old man and his son went down from the mount, and returned unto the young men! With what joy may we imagine he went home, and related all that had passed to Sarah! And above all, with what triumph is he now exulting in the paradise of God, and adoring rich, free, distinguishing, electing, everlasting love, which alone made him to differ from the rest of mankind, and rendered him worthy of that title which he will have so long as the sun and the moon endure, "The Father of the faithful!" But let us now draw our eyes from the creature, and do what Abraham, if he was present, would direct to; I mean, fix them on the Creator, God blessed for evermore.

I see your hearts affected, I see your eyes weep. (And indeed, who can refrain weeping at the relation of such a story?) But, behold, I show you a mystery, hid under the sacrifice of Abraham's only son, which, unless your hearts are hardened, must cause you to weep tears of love, and that plentifully too. I would willingly hope you even prevent me here, and are ready to say, "It is the love of God, in giving Jesus Christ to die for our sins." Yes; that is it. And yet perhaps you find your hearts, at the mentioning of this, not so much affected. Let this convince you, that we are all fallen creatures, and that we do not love God or Christ as we ought to do: for, if you admire Abraham offering up his Isaac, how much more ought you to extol, magnify and adore the love of God, who so loved the world, as to give his only begotten Son Christ Jesus our Lord, "that whosoever believeth on Him should not perish, but have everlasting life?" May we not well cry out, Now know we, O Lord, that thou hast loved us, since thou hast not withheld thy Son, thine only Son from us! Abraham was God's creature (and God was Abraham's friend) and therefore under the highest obligation to surrender up his Isaac. But O stupendous love! Whilst we were his enemies, God sent forth his Son, made of a woman, made under the law, that he might become a curse for us. O the freeness, as well as the infinity, of the love of God our Father! It is unsearchable: I am lost in contemplating it; it is past finding out. Think, O believers, think of the love of God, in giving Jesus Christ to be a propitiation for our sins.

And when you hear how Abraham built an altar, and laid the wood in order, and bound Isaac his son, and laid him on the altar upon the wood; think how your heavenly Father bound Jesus Christ his only Son, and offered him upon the altar of his justice, and laid upon him the iniquities of us all. When you read of Abraham's stretching forth his hand to slay his son, Think, O think, how God actually suffered his Son to be slain, that we might live for evermore. Do you read of Isaac carrying the wood upon his shoulders, upon which he was to be offered? Let this lead you to mount Calvary (this very mount of Moriah where Isaac was offered, as some think) and take a view of the antitype Jesus Christ, the Son of God, bearing and ready to sink under the weight of that cross, on which he was to hang for us. Do you admire Isaac so freely consenting to die, though a creature, and therefore obliged to go when God called? O do not forget to admire infinitely more the dear Lord Jesus, that promised seed, who willingly said, "Lo, I come," though under no obligation so to do, "to do thy will," to obey and die for men, "O God!" Did you weep just now, when I bid you fancy you saw the altar, and the wood laid in order, and Isaac laid bound on the altar? Look by faith, behold the blessed Jesus, our all-glorious Emmanuel, not bound, but nailed on a accursed tree: see how he hangs crowned with thorns, and had in derision of all that are round about him: see how the thorns pierce him, and how the blood in purple streams trickle down his sacred temples!

Hark how the God of nature groans! See how he bows his head, and at length humanity gives up the ghost! Isaac is saved, but Jesus, the God of Isaac, dies; A ram is offered up in Isaac's room, but Jesus has no substitute; Jesus must bleed, Jesus must die; God the Father provided this Lamb for himself from all eternity. He must be offered in time, or man must be damned for evermore. And now, where are your tears? Shall I say, refrain your voice from weeping? No; rather let me exhort you to look to him whom you have pierced, and mourn, as a woman mourneth for her first-born: for we have been the betrayers, we have been the murderers of this Lord of glory; and shall we not bewail those sins, which brought the blessed Jesus to the accursed tree? Having so much done, so much suffered for us, so much forgiven, shall we not love much! O! let us love Him with all our hearts, and minds, and strength, and glorify him in our souls and bodies, for they are his. Which leads me to a second inference I shall draw from the foregoing discourse.

From hence we may learn the nature of true, justifying faith. Whoever understands and preaches the truth, as it is in Jesus, must acknowledge, that salvation is God's free gift, and that we are saved, not by any or all the works of righteousness which we have done or can do: no; we can neither wholly nor in part justify ourselves in the light of God. The Lord Jesus Christ is our righteousness; and if we are accepted with God, it must be only in and through the personal righteousness, the active and passive obedience, of Jesus Christ his beloved Son. This righteousness must be imputed, or counted over to us, and applied by faith to our hearts, or else we can in no wise be justified in God's sight: and that very moment a sinner is enabled to lay hold on Christ's righteousness by faith, he is freely justified from all his sins, and shall never enter into condemnation, notwithstanding he was a fire-brand of hell before. Thus is was that Abraham was justified before he did any good work: he was enabled to believe on the Lord Christ; it was accounted to him for righteousness; that is, Christ's righteousness was made over to him, and so accounted his.

This, this is the gospel; this is the only was of finding acceptance with God: good works have nothing to do with our justification in his sight. We are justified by faith alone, as saith the article of our church; agreeable to which the apostle Paul says, "By grace ye are saved, through faith; and that not of yourselves; it is the gift of God." Notwithstanding, good works have their proper place: they justify our faith, though not our persons; they follow it, and evidence our justification in the sight of men. Hence it is that the apostle James asks, was not Abraham justified by works?

(alluding no doubt to the story on which we have been discoursing) that is, did he not prove he was in a justified state, because his faith was productive of good works? This declarative justification in the sight of men, is what is directly to be understood in the words of the text; "Now know I, says God, that thou fearest me, since thou hast not withheld thy son, thine only son from me." Not but that God knew it before; but this is spoken in condescension to our weak capacities, and plainly shows, that his offering up his son was accepted with God, as an evidence of the sincerity of his faith, and for this, was left on record to future ages. Hence then you may learn, whether you are blessed with, and are sons and daughters of, faithful Abraham. You say you believe; you talk of free grace and free justification: you do well; the devils also believe and tremble. But has the faith, which you pretend to, influenced your hearts, renewed your souls, and, like Abraham's, worked by love? Are you affections, like his, set on things above? Are you heavenly-minded, and like him, do you confess yourselves strangers and pilgrims on the earth? In short, has your faith enabled you to overcome the world, and strengthened you to give up your Isaacs, your laughter, your most beloved lusts, friends, pleasures, and profits for God? If so, take the comfort of it; for justly may you say, "We know assuredly, that we do fear and love God, or rather are loved of him." But if you are only talking believers, have only a faith of the head, and never felt the power of it in your hearts, however you may bolster yourselves up, and say, "We have Abraham for our father, or Christ is our Savior," unless you get a faith of the heart, a faith working by love, you shall never sit with Abraham, Isaac, Jacob, or Jesus Christ, in the kingdom of heaven.

But I must draw one more inference, and with that I shall conclude.

Learn, O saints! From what has been said, to sit loose to all your worldly comforts; and stand ready prepared to part with everything, when God shall require it at your hand. Some of you perhaps may have friends, who are to you as your own souls; and others may have children, in whose lives your own lives are bound up: all I believe have their Isaacs, their particular delights of some kind or other. Labor, for Christ's sake, labor, ye sons and daughters of Abraham, to resign them daily in affection to God, that, when he shall require you really to sacrifice them, you may not confer with flesh and blood, any more than the blessed patriarch now before us. And as for you that have been in any measure tried like unto him, let his example encourage and comfort you. Remember, Abraham your father was tried so before you: think, O think of the happiness he now enjoys, and how he is incessantly thanking God for tempting and trying him when here below.

Look up often by the eye of faith, and see him sitting with his dearly beloved Issac in the world of spirits. Remember, it will be but a little while, and you shall sit with them also, and tell one another what God has done for your souls. There I hope to sit with you, and hear this story of his offering up his Son from his own mouth, and to praise the Lamb that sitteth upon the throne, for what he hath done for all or souls, for ever and ever.

Sermon 4 The Great Duty of Family Religion

Joshua 24:15 "As for me and my house, we will serve the Lord.

These words contain the holy resolution of pious Joshua, who having in a most moving, affectionate discourse recounted to the Israelites what great things God had done for them, in the verse immediately preceding the text, comes to draw a proper inference from what he had been delivering; and acquaints them, in the most pressing terms, that since God had been so exceeding gracious unto them, they could do not less, than out of gratitude for such uncommon favors and mercies, dedicate both themselves and families to his service. "Now therefore, fear the Lord, and serve him in sincerity and truth, and put away the Gods which your fathers served on the other side of the flood." And by the same engaging motive does the prophet Samuel afterwards enforce their obedience to the commandments of God, 1 Sam. 12:24, "Only fear the Lord, and serve him in truth, with all your heart; for consider how great things he hath done for you." But then, that they might not excuse themselves (as too many might be apt to do) by his giving them a bad example, or think he was laying heavy burdens upon them, whilst he himself touched them not with one of his fingers, he tells them in the text, that whatever regard they might pay to the doctrine he had been preaching, yet he (as all ministers ought to do) was resolved to live up to and practice it himself: "Choose you therefore, whom you will serve, whether the Gods which your fathers served, or the Gods of the Amorites, in whose land ye dwell: but as for me and my house, we will serve the Lord." A resolution this, worthy of Joshua, and no less becoming, no less necessary for every true son of Joshua, that is entrusted with the care and government of a family in our day: and, if it was ever seasonable for ministers to preach up, or people to put in practice family-religion, it was never more so than in the present age; since it is greatly to be feared, that out of those many households that call themselves Christians, there are but few that serve God in their respective families as they ought.

It is true indeed, visit our churches, and you may perhaps see something of the form of godliness still subsisting amongst us; but even that is scarcely to be met with in private houses. So that were the blessed angels to come, as in the patriarchal age, and observe our spiritual oeconomy at home, would they not be tempted to say as Abraham to Abimilech, "Surely, the fear of God is not in this place?" Gen. 20:11.

How such a general neglect of family-religion first began to overspread the Christian world, is difficult to determine. As for the primitive Christians, I am positive it was not so with them: No, they had not so learned Christ, as falsely to imagine religion was to be confined solely to their assemblies for public worship; but, on the contrary, behaved with such piety and exemplary holiness in their private families, that St. Paul often styles their house a church: "Salute such a one, says he, and the church which is in his house." And, I believe, we must for ever despair of seeing a primitive spirit of piety revived in the world, till we are so happy as to see a revival of primitive family religion; and persons unanimously resolving with good old Joshua, in the words of the text, "As for me and my house, we will serve the Lord." From which words, I shall beg leave to insist on these three things.

I. First, That it is the duty of every governor of a family to take care, that not only he himself, but also that those committed to his charge, "serve the Lord."

II. Secondly, I shall endeavor to show after what manner a governor and his household ought to serve the Lord. And, III. Thirdly, I shall offer some motives, in order to excite all governors, with their respective households, to serve the Lord in the manner that shall be recommended.

And First, I am to show that it is the duty of every governor of a family to take care, that not only he himself, but also that those committed to his charge, should serve the Lord.

And this will appear, if we consider that every governor of a family ought to look upon himself as obliged to act in three capacities as a prophet, to instruct: as a priest, to pray for and with; as a king, to govern, direct, and provide for them. It is true indeed, the latter of these, their kingly office, they are not so frequently deficient in, (nay in this they are generally too solicitous) but as for the two former, their priestly and prophetic office, like Gallio, they care for no such things.

But however indifferent some governors may be about it, they may be assured, that God will require a due discharge of these offices at their hands. For if, as the apostle argues, "He that does not provide for his own house," in temporal things, has denied the faith, and is worse than an infidel;" to what greater degree of apostasy must he have arrived, who takes no thought to provide for the spiritual welfare of his family!

But farther, persons are generally very liberal of their invectives against the clergy, and think they justly blame the conduct of that minister who does not take heed to and watch over the flock, of which the Holy Ghost has made him overseer: but may not every governor of a family, be in a lower degree liable to the same censure, who takes no thought for those souls that are committed too his charge? For every house is as it were a little parish, every governor (as was before observed) a priest, every family a flock; and if any of them perish through the governor's neglect, their blood will God require at their hands.

Was a minister to disregard teaching his people publicly, and from house to house, and to excuse himself by saying, that he had enough to do to work out his own salvation with fear and trembling, without concerning himself with that of others; would you not be apt to think such a minister, to be like the unjust judge, "One that neither feared God, nor regarded man?" And yet, odious as such a character would be, it is no worse than that governor of a family deserves, who thinks himself obliged only to have his own soul, without paying any regard to the souls of his household. For (as was above hinted) every house is as it were a parish, and every master is concerned to secure, as much as in him lies, the spiritual prosperity of every one under his rood, as any minister whatever is obliged to look to the spiritual welfare of every individual person under his charge.

What precedents men who neglect their duty in this particular, can plead for such omission, I cannot tell. Doubtless not the example of holy Job, who was so far from imagining that he had no concern, as governor of a family, with any one's soul but his own, that the scripture acquaints us, "When the days of his children's feasting were gone about, that Job sent and sanctified them, and offered burnt-offerings, according to the number of them all; for Job said, It may be that my sons have sinned and cursed God in their hearts: thus did Job continually." Nor can they plead the practice of good old Joshua, whom, in the text, we find as much concerned for his household's welfare, as his own. Nor lastly, that of Cornelius, who feared God, not only himself, but with all his house: and were Christians but of the same spirit of Job, Joshua, and the Gentile centurion, they would act as Job, Joshua, and Cornelius did.

But alas! If this be the case, and all governors of families ought not only to serve the Lord themselves, but likewise to see that their respective households do so too; what will then become of those who not only neglect serving God themselves, but also make it their business to ridicule and scoff at any of their house that do? Who are not content with "not entering into the kingdom of heaven themselves; but shoe also that are willing to enter in, they hinder." Surely such men are factors for the devil indeed. Surely their damnation slumbereth not: for although God, is in his good providence, may suffer such stumbling-blocks to be put in his children's way, and suffer their greatest enemies to be those of their own households, for a trial of their sincerity, and improvement of their faith; yet we cannot but pronounce a woe against those masters by whom such offenses come. For if those that only take care of their own souls, can scarcely be saved, where will such monstrous profane and wicked governors appear?

But hoping there are but few of this unhappy stamp, proceed we now to the

Second thing proposed: To show after what manner a governor and his household ought to serve the Lord.

1. And the first thing I shall mention, is READING THE WORD OF GOD.

This is a duty incumbent on every private person. "Search the scriptures, for in them ye think ye have eternal life," is a precept given by our blessed Lord indifferently to all: but much more so, ought every governor of a family to think it in a peculiar manner spoken to himself, because (as hath been already proved) he ought to look upon himself as a prophet, and therefore agreeably to such a character, bound to instruct those under his charge in the knowledge of the word of God.

This we find was the order God gave to his peculiar people Israel: for thus speaks his representative Moses, Deut. 6:6-7, "These words," that is, the scripture words, "which I command thee this day, shall be in thy heart, and thou shalt teach them diligently unto thy children," that is, as it is generally explained, servants, as well as children, "and shalt talk of them when thou sittest in thy house." From whence we may infer, that the only reason, why so many neglect to read the words of scripture diligently to their children is, because the words of scripture are not in their hearts: for if they were, out of the abundance of the heart their mouth would speak.

Besides, servants as well as children, are, for the generality, very ignorant, and mere novices in the laws of God: and how shall they know, unless some one teach them? And what more proper to teach them by, than the lively oracles of God, "which are able to make them wise unto salvation?" And who more proper to instruct them by these lively oracles, than parents and masters, who (as hath been more than once observed) are as much concerned to feed them with spiritual, as with bodily bread, day by day.

But if these things be so, what a miserable condition are those unhappy governors in, who are so far from feeding those committed to their care with the sincere milk of the word, to the intent they may grow thereby, that they neither search the scriptures themselves, nor are careful to explain them to others? Such families must be in a happy way indeed to do their Master's will, who take such prodigious pains to know it! Would not one imagine that they had turned converts to the Church of Rome, that they thought ignorance to be the mother of devotion; and that those were to be condemned as heretics who read their Bibles? And yet how few families are there amongst us, who do not act after this unseemly manner! But shall I praise them in this? I praise them not; Brethren, this thing ought not so to be.

2. Pass we on now to the second means whereby every governor and his household ought to serve the Lord, FAMILY-PRAYER.

This is a duty, though as much neglected, yet as absolutely necessary as the former. Reading is a good preparative for prayer, as prayer is an excellent means to render reading effectual. And the reason why every governor of a family should join both these exercises together, is plain, because a governor of a family cannot perform his priestly office (which we before observed hs is in some degree invested with) without performing this duty of family prayer.

We find it therefore remarked, when mention is made of Can and Abel's offering sacrifices, that they brought them. But to whom did they bring them? Why, in all probability, to their father Adam, who, as priest of the family, was to offer sacrifice in their names. And so ought every spiritual son of the second Adam, who is entrusted with the care of an household, to offer up the spiritual sacrifices of supplications and thanksgivings, acceptable to God through Jesus Christ, in the presence and name of all who wait upon, or eat meat at his table.

Thus we read our blessed Lord behaved, when he tabernacled amongst us: for it is said often, that he prayed with his twelve disciples, which was then his little family. And he himself has promised a particular blessing to joint supplications: "Wheresoever two or three are gathered together in my name, there am I in the midst of them." And again, "If two or three are agreed touching any thing they shall ask, it shall be given them." Add to this, that we are commanded by the Apostle to "pray always, with all manner of supplication," which doubtless includes family prayer. And holy Joshua, when he set up the good resolution in the text, that he and his household would serve the Lord, certainly resolved to pray with his family, which is one of the best testimonies they could give of their serving him.

Besides, there are no families but what have some common blessings, of which they have been all partakers, to give thanks for; some common crosses and afflictions, which they are to pray against; some common sins, which they are all to lament and bewail: but how this can be done, without joining together in one common act of humiliation, supplication, and thanksgiving, is difficult to devise.

From all which considerations put together, it is evident, that family prayer is a great and necessary duty; and consequently, those governors that neglect it, are certainly without excuse. And it is much to be feared, if they live without family prayer, they live without God in the world.

And yet, such an hateful character as this is, it is to be feared, that was God to send out an angel to destroy us, as he did once to destroy the Egyptian first-born, and withal give him a commission, as then, to spare no houses but where they saw the blood of the lintel, sprinkled on the door-post, so now, to let no families escape, but those that called upon him in morning and evening prayer; few would remain unhurt by his avenging sword. Shall I term such families Christians or heathens?

Doubtless they deserve not the name of Christians; and heathens will rise up in judgment against such profane families of this generation: for they had always their household gods, whom they worshipped and whose assistance they frequently invoked. And a pretty pass those families surely are arrived at, who must be sent to school to pagans. But will not the Lord be avenged on such profane households as these? Will he not pour out his fury upon those that call not upon his name?

3. But it is time for me to hasten to the third and last means I shall recommend, whereby every governor ought with his household to serve the Lord, CATECHIZING AND INSTRUCTING their children and servants, and bringing them up in the nurture and admonition of the Lord.

That this, as well as the two former, is a duty incumbent on every governor of an house, appears from that famous encomium or commendation God gives of Abraham: "I know that he will command his children and his household after him, to keep the way of the Lord, to do justice and judgment." And indeed scarce any thing is more frequently pressed upon us in holy writ, than this duty of catechizing. Thus, says God in a passage before cited, "Thou shalt teach these words diligently unto thy children." And parents are commanded in the New Testament, to "bring up their children in the nurture and admonition of the Lord." The holy Psalmist acquaints us, that one great end why God did such great wonders for his people, was, "to the intent that when they grew up, they should show their children, or servants, the same." And in Deut. 6 at the 20th and following verses, God strictly commands his people to instruct their children in the true nature of the ceremonial worship, when they should inquire about it, as he supposed they would do, in time to come. And if servants and children were to be instructed in the nature of Jewish rites, much more ought they now to be initiated and grounded in the doctrines and first principles of the gospel of Christ: not only, because it is a revelation, which has brought life and immortality to a fuller and clearer light, but also, because many seducers are gone abroad into the world, who do their utmost endeavor to destroy not only the superstructure, but likewise to sap the very foundation of our most holy religion.

Would then the present generation have their posterity be true lovers and honorers of God; masters and parents must take Solomon's good advice, and train up and catechize their respective households in the way wherein they should go.

I am aware but of one objection, that can, with any show of reason, be urged against what has been advanced; which is, that such a procedure as this will take up too much time, and hinder families too long from their worldly business. But it is much to be questioned, whether persons that start such an abjection, are not of the same hypocritical spirit as the traitor Judas, who had indignation against devout Mary, for being so profuse of her ointment, in anointing our blessed Lord, and asked why it might not be sold for two hundred pence, and given to the poor. For has God given us so much time to work for ourselves, and shall we not allow some small pittance of it, morning and evening, to be devoted to his more immediate worship and service? Have not people read, that it is God who gives men power to get wealth, and therefore that the best way to prosper in the world, is to secure his favor? And has not our blessed Lord himself promised, that if we seek first the kingdom of God and his righteousness, all outward necessaries shall be added unto us?

Abraham, no doubt, was a man of as great business as such objectors may be; but yet he would find time to command his household to serve the Lord. Nay, David was a king, and consequently had a great deal of business upon his hands; yet notwithstanding, he professes that he would walk in his house with a perfect heart. And, to instance but one more, holy Joshua was a person certainly engaged very much in temporal affairs; and yet he solemnly declares before all Israel, that as for him and his household, they would serve the Lord. And did persons but redeem their time, as Abraham, David, or Joshua did, they would no longer complain, that family duties kept them too long from the business of the world.

III. But my Third and Last general head, under which I was to offer some motives, in order to excite all governors, with their respective households, to serve the Lord in the manner before recommended, I hope, will serve instead of a thousand arguments, to prove the weakness and folly of any such objection.

1. And the first motive I shall mention is the duty of GRATITUDE, which you that are governors of families owe to God. Your lot, every one must confess, is cast in a fair ground: providence hath given you a goodly heritage, above many of your fellow-creatures, and therefore, bout of a principle of gratitude, you ought to endeavor, as much as in you lies, to make every person of your respective households to call upon him as long as they live: not to mention, that the authority, with which God has invested you as parents and governors of families, is a talent committed to your trust, and which you are bound to improve to your Master's honor. In other things we find governors and parents can exercise lordship over their children and servants readily, and frequently enough can say to one, Go, and he goeth; and to another, Come, and he cometh; to a third, Do this, and he doeth it. And shall this power be so often employed in your own affairs, and never exerted in the things of God? Be astonished, O heavens, at this!

Thus did not faithful Abraham; no, God says, that he knew Abraham would command his servants and children after him. Thus did not Joshua: no, he was resolved not only to walk with God himself, but to improve his authority in making all about him do so too: "As for me and my household, we will serve the Lord." Let us go and do likewise.

2. But Secondly, If gratitude to God will not, methinks LOVE AND PITY TO YOUR CHILDREN should move you, with your respective families, to serve the Lord.

Most people express a great fondness for their children: nay so great, that very often their own lives are wrapped up in those of their offspring.

"Can a woman forget her sucking child, that she should not have compassion on the son of her womb?" says God by his Prophet Isaiah. He speaks of it as a monstrous thing, and scarce credible; but the words immediately following, affirm it to be possible, "Yes, they may forget" and experience also assures us they may. Father and mother may both forsake their children: for what greater degree of forgetfulness can they express towards them, than to neglect the improvement of their better part, and not bring them up in the knowledge and fear of God?

It is true indeed, parents seldom forget to provide for their children's bodies, (though, it is to be feared, some men are so far sunk beneath the beasts that perish, as to neglect even that) but then how often do they forget, or rather, when do they remember, to secure the salvation of their immortal souls? But is this their way of expressing their fondness for the fruit of their bodies? Is this the best testimony they can give of their affection to the darling of their hearts? Then was Delilah fond of Samson, when she delivered him up into the hands of the Philistines? Then were those ruffians well affected to Daniel, when they threw him into a den of lions?

3. But Thirdly, If neither gratitude to God, nor love and pity to your children, will prevail on you; yet let a principle of COMMON HONESTY AND JUSTICE move you to set up the holy resolution in the text.

This is a principle which all men would be thought to act upon. But certainly, if any may be truly censured for their injustice, none can be more liable to such censure, than those who think themselves injured if their servants withdraw themselves from their bodily work, and yet they in return take no care of their inestimable souls. For is it just that servants should spend their time and strength in their master's service, and masters not at the same time give them what is just and equal for their service?

It is true, some men may think they have done enough when they give unto their servants food and raiment, and say, "Did not I bargain with thee for so much a year?" But if they give them no other reward than this, whet do they less for their very beasts? But are not servants better than they?

Doubtless they are: and however masters may put off their convictions for the present, they will find a time will come, when they shall know they ought to have given them some spiritual as well as temporal wages; and the cry of those that have mowed down their fields, will enter into the ears of the Lord of Sabaoth.

4. But Fourthly, If neither gratitude to God, pity to children, nor a principle for common justice to servants, are sufficient to balance all objections; yet let that darling, that prevailing motive of SELF-INTEREST turn the scale, and engage you with your respective households to serve the Lord.

This weighs greatly with you in other matters: be then persuaded to let it have a due and full influence on you in this: and if it has, if you have but faith as a grain of mustard-seed, how can you avoid believing, that promoting family-religion, will be the best means to promote your own temporal, as well as eternal welfare? For "Godliness has the promise of the life that now is, as well as that which is to come." Besides, you all, doubtless wish for honest servants, and pious children: and to have them prove otherwise, would be as great a grief to you, as it was to Elisha to have a treacherous Gehazi, or David to be troubled with a rebellious Absolom. But how can it be expected they should learn their duty, except those set over them, take care to teach it to them? Is it not as reasonable to expect you should reap where had not sewn, or gather where you had not strawed?

Did Christianity, indeed, give any countenance to children and servants to disregard their parents and masters according to the flesh, or represent their duty to them, as inconsistent with their entire obedience to their father and master who is in heaven, there might then be some pretense to neglect instructing them in the principles of such a religion.

But since the precepts of this pure and undefiled religion, are all of them holy, just, and good; and the more they are taught their duty to God, the better they will perform their duties to you; methinks, to neglect the improvement of their souls, out of a dread of spending too much time in religious duties, is acting quite contrary to your own interest as well as duty.

5. Fifthly and Lastly, If neither gratitude to God, love to your children, common justice to your servants, nor even that most prevailing motive self-interest, will excite; yet let a consideration of the terrors of the Lord persuade you to put in practice the pious resolution in the text. Remember, the time will come, and that perhaps very shortly, when we must all appear before the judgment-seat of Christ; where we must give a solemn and strict account how we have had our conversation, in our respective families in this world. How will you endure to see your children and servants (who ought to be your joy and crown of rejoicing in the day of our Lord Jesus Christ) coming out as so many swift witnesses against you; cursing the father that begot them, the womb that bare them, the paps which they have sucked, and the day they ever entered into your houses? Think you not, the damnation which men must endure for their own sins, will be sufficient, that they need load themselves with the additional guilt of being accessory to the damnation of others also? O consider this, all ye that forget to serve the Lord with your respective households, "lest he pluck you away, and there be none to deliver you!" But God forbid, brethren, that any such evil should befall you: no, rather will I hope, that you have been in some measure convinced by what has been said of the great importance of FAMILY-RELIGION; and therefore are ready to cry out in the words immediately following the text, "God forbid that we should forsake the Lord;" and again, ver. 21, "Nay, but we will (with our several households) serve the Lord." And that there may be always such a heart in you, let me exhort all governors of families, in the name of our Lord Jesus Christ, often to reflect on the inestimable worth of their own souls, and the infinite ransom, even the precious blood of Jesus Christ, which has been paid

down for them. Remember, I beseech you to remember, that you are fallen creatures; that you are by nature lost and estranged from God; and that you can never be restored to your primitive happiness, till by being born again of the Holy Ghost, you arrive at your primitive state of purity, have the image of God restamped upon your souls, and are thereby made meet to be partakers of the inheritance with the saints in light. Do, I say, but seriously and frequently reflect on, and act as persons that believe such important truths, and you will no more neglect your family's spiritual welfare than your own. No, the love of God, which will then be shed abroad in your hearts, will constrain you to do your utmost to preserve them: and the deep sense of God's free grace in Christ Jesus, (which you will then have) in calling you, will excite you to do your utmost to save others, especially those of your own household. And though, after all your pious endeavors, some may continue unreformed; yet you will have this comfortable reflection to make, that you did what you could to make your families religious: and therefore may rest assured of sitting down in the kingdom of heaven, with Abraham, Joshua, and Cornelius, and all the godly householders, who in their several generations shone forth as so many lights in their respective households upon earth. Amen.

Sermon 5 Christ the Best Husband: Or an Earnest Invitation to Young Women to come and See Christ

(Preached to a Society of Young Women, in Fetter-Lane.)

Psalm 14:10-11 Hearken, O daughter, and consider, and incline thine ear: Forget also thine own people, and thy father's house: So shall the King greatly desire thy beauty, for he is thy Lord, and worship thou him.

This psalm is called the song of loves, the most pure and spiritual, the most ear and delightful loves; namely, those which are between Christ the beloved, and his church, which is his spouse; wherein is set forth, first, the Lord Jesus Christ in regard of his majesty, power, and divinity, his truth, meekness and equity: And then the spouse is set forth, in regard of her ornaments, companions, attendants and posterity; and both in regard of their comeliness and beauty. After the description of Christ, an invitation to his espousals, is given the children of men, called by the name of daughter; and therefore, particularly applicable unto you, my dear sisters, as being the daughters of men, yet not so as excluding the sons of men.

I shall now, therefore, consider the words, as spoken to you in particular, and containing this doctrine; That the Lord Jesus Christ doth invite the daughters of men to be his spouse; and is exceeding desirous of their beauty; who, forgetting their people and father's house, do hearken, consider and incline to his invitation, and join themselves to him in this relation.

I shall show, I. How Christ doth espouse himself unto the children, but, more especially, unto the daughters of men.

The Lord Jesus Christ, doth espouse himself unto the children of men, in the world, but the public solemnization of the marriage, is reserved until the last day; when his spouse shall be brought forth to him, in white robes, and a raiment of perfect righteousness, more rich and curious, my dear sisters, than any of your needle-work; and the marriage feast will be kept in his Father's house, in heaven, when they shall be received into the nearest and closest embraces of his love. The marriage knot is tied here, in which are included four things: First; Mutual Choice, Secondly, Mutual Affection, Thirdly, Mutual Union, Fourthly, Mutual Obligation.

FIRST, my dear sisters, there is a MUTUAL CHOICE, which is not only in Christ, as Mediator, but also by Christ as the eternal Son of God, yea, God himself; notwithstanding all that the polite Arians and Socinians say to the contrary. The Lord Jesus Christ, my dear sisters, doth choose you merely by his free grace; it is freely of his own mercy, that he brings you into the marriage covenant: You, who have so grievously offended him, yet, the Lord Jesus Christ hath chosen you; you did not, you would not have chosen him; but when once, my dear sisters, he hath chosen you, then, and not till then, you make choice of him for your Lord and Husband.

The Lord Jesus Christ when he first comes to you, finds you full of sin and pollution; you are deformed, defiled, enslaved, poor, miserable and wretched, very despicable and loathsome, by reason of sin; and he maketh choice of you, not because of your holiness, nor of your beauty, nor of your being qualified for them; no, the Lord Jesus Christ puts these qualifications upon you, as may make you meet for his embrace; and you are drawn to make choice of the Lord Jesus Christ because he first chose you.

SECONDLY, In this espousal of yours, my dear sisters, there is a MUTUAL AFFECTION; this doth accompany the choice. Your hearts are drawn out after Christ; your souls pant and long for him; you cannot be at rest until you are engaged to this Jesus: You are ready to cry out continually, none but Christ, none but Christ: this is the language of your hearts, if you are truly sensible of your need of him. The more acquaintance you have of this Lord Jesus, the more pleased you are with your choice, and the more your affections are drawn towards him. And where can you place your affections better than upon that Jesus who shed his blood for your sakes?

Surely he deserves both your loves and affections: Go on, go on, my dear sisters, that your affections may grow stronger and stronger.

THIRDLY, There is not only mutual choice, and mutual affection, but likewise MUTUAL UNION: And here doth the marriage lie chiefly, in this union; Christ and souls are contracted, and the knot is tied so fast, that neither men on earth, how great soever they be, nor devils in hell, though they should combine all their wrath and rage together, still they cannot dissolve, they cannot untie it; no, my dear sisters, it is indissolvable, for the union is, by the spirit, on Christ's part, and by faith on yours: By the spirit, Christ doth lay hold on you; and by faith, you do lay hold on him; and thus the match is made; Christ becomes yours, his person, portion, and all his benefits are yours; and you become Christ's, your persons, your hearts, and all that you have is resigned up unto him, and O that they may be so more and more.

FOURTHLY, There is a MUTUAL OBLIGATION between Christ and his spouse.

Christ obliges himself to love you here, he will not, indeed he never will leave you, he will protect you from the malice of the Pharisees of this generation, he will provide for you in all difficulties; he will live with you here, and at last he will take you to himself, to live with him forever. And you are engaged to him to be loving, loyal, faithful, obedient; and you are to stick close to him as long as you live; and then you will find yourselves to be married to the best advantage, both for soul and body, for time and for eternity.

II. Christ doth invite all of you to be his spouse.

And it on this account that he sends forth his ministers to preach. It is this, that makes me thus come among you; that you would accept of this invitation, to which, in the name of the Lord Jesus Christ, I do call and entreat you to take him, on his own terms. He calls all of you, my sisters, whether elder or younger, whether married or unmarried, of higher degree, or of the meanest quality, the poorest servants, yea, the rabble of this world, as the world calls you, who are willing to be espoused unto the Lord Jesus Christ. I say, the poor are as welcome to be Christ's spouse as those that are rich. He regardeth not the rich more than the poor; he chose a mean virgin, espoused to a carpenter, to be his mother; and he chooseth and calleth all such to be his spouse; then be not discouraged at your being despised in the world; for if you are but loved by Christ, and espoused to him, it will be an over-sufficiency for all the trouble that you have met with here.

III. Those who would be espoused unto Christ, must hearken, consider, and incline to his invitation, and forget even their father's house.

Such as would be espoused unto Christ must hearken. "Hearken, O daughter." Many amongst you, my sisters, stop their ears against the calls of the gospel; they shut their ears like the deaf adder, which will not hearken unto the voice of the charmer, though he charm never so wisely. You will not hearken unto the invitations of Christ; you can hearken unto the vanities of the world, and be delighted with the espousals of the world, but never think or are delighted with the espousals of Christ.

It was by the ear, that the temptation of sin was received by the first man, when he departed from God; and by the ear, the invitation to be Christ's spouse must be received, before the heart will be opened to receive Jesus Christ in this conjugal relation.

If you would, my dear sisters, be espoused to Christ, you must consider Christ's invitation. It is not a slight or bare hearing of Christ's invitation, which will be of any service to you, or make up the match between Christ and your souls; no, you must receive Christ in the heart; you must consider the thing itself, the advantages of it, the difference between Christ's invitations and the devil's temptations, or any of the world's proffers.

Those who would be espoused to Christ, must be inclined to accept of Christ's invitation. "Hearken, O daughter, consider and incline thine ear." This is to incline your hearts: You must consent with your wills; there must be a compliance to the motion of Christ, and you must have desires after Christ, and then your hearts will say, "Lord, let us be thy spouse, and be thou our beloved." You must likewise forget your father's house. "Hearken, O daughter, and consider, and forget thy father's house." You are not here to cast off all affections unto natural relations; but you must forget all relations, so as to be ready to forgo all their favor, when it standeth in competition with that of the Lord Jesus Christ: and do not let your carnal friends and relations hinder you from closing with, and espousing the Lord Jesus. I earnestly beseech you to suffer the loss of any thing, rather than to lose his favors; you must indeed forget your own people, that is, you must forget all your evil customs which you have learned in your father's house, and forsake all your vain conversation, your reading of plays, novels, or romances; and you must keep from learning to sing the songs of the drunkard; for Christ, if you are his spouse, hath redeem you.

Such of you, my dear sisters, as are espoused to the Lord Jesus Christ are very beautiful. I do not mean in respect of your bodies; you may have less of external comeliness than others, in respect of your bodies, but as to your souls you will exceed in beauty, not so much in the eyes of man, as n the eyes of God; such have the most beautiful image of God stamped upon them; none n the world beside them, have the least spark of spiritual beauty. Such as are not married to Christ, are unregenerated, they are not born again, nor brought from sin unto God, which must be done before you be espoused to Christ.

And the Lord Jesus Christ desireth to see this beauty in his spouse, for he cries out, "O my dove, thou are in the clefts of the rock, in the secret places of the stairs, let me see thy countenance, let me hear thy voice, for sweet is thy voice, and thy countenance is comely." He calleth his spouse his love, being the dear object of his love; and he admireth her loveliness; he repeats it twice in one verse, "Behold thou art fair, my love, behold thou art fair." Thus you see he describes their beauty. And then, my sisters, we have wonderful expression of Christ to his spouse, "Thou hast ravished my heart, my sister, my spouse, thou hast ravished my heart with one of thine eyes, with one chain of thy neck." Thus you see how pleased the Lord Jesus Christ is with his spouse; and will not you, therefore, be espoused unto the Lord Jesus? I offer Jesus Christ to all of you; if you have been never so notorious for sin, if you have been as great a harlot as Mary Magdalen was, when once you are espoused to Christ, you shall be forgiven. Therefore be not discouraged, at whatever slights and contempts the world may pass upon you, but come and join yourselves to the Lord Jesus Christ, and all your sins shall be washed away in his blood; and when once you are espoused to Jesus, you are disjoined from sin, you are born again. You are now, as it were, espoused unto sin; sin is your husband, and you are too fond of it, but when once you are married to Christ, when you are born again, then you may be said to die unto sin; but till then, sin liveth in your affections; therefore, my sisters, give sin its death-wound in your hearts; you have been called by the word time after time, and it has had no effect upon you; but when you are espoused unto the Lord Jesus Christ, then you will be brought to him by his Spirit: You will then lay hold on him by faith, his Spirit will draw you unto himself; he will make you to be willing in the day of his power; he will give you faith in him. Faith is the hand of the soul which layeth hold on Christ; therefore do not rest contented till you have this grace of faith wrought in you with power; do not be contented till you have received the Lord Jesus Christ.

Embrace Christ in the arms of your dearest love; then you love the Lord Jesus Christ with sincerity, when you love and esteem him before father, mother, or all the delights and pleasures of this life, but if you do delight in any thing that this world can produce, more than in the Lord Jesus Christ, you have not true love to him.

If you are espoused to Christ, you have acquaintance and converse with him; you will endeavor to promote his interest, and advance his name in the world; when others are going to the polite and fashionable diversions of life, you will be laboring to bring honor to the Lord Jesus Christ; you will commend your beloved above all other beloveds, and endeavor to bring others into love to him. Can you, my dear sisters, who are now assembled to worship God, show such evidence of your espousals unto the Lord Jesus Christ? O! how joyful, how comfortable an estate is this! Surely this is a marriage worth seeking after; this is the only desirable marriage, and the Lord Jesus Christ is the only lover that is worth seeking after.

Now, my dear sisters, I shall speak a few words to those of you who have not yet espoused yourselves to the Lord Jesus. It is a great sin, and surely you highly affront the Lord that bought you. It is likewise your folly to refuse and neglect the gracious proffers of being the spouse of Christ; hereby you forfeit all that love which he would bestow upon you; hereby you choose rags before robes, dross before gold, pebbles before jewels, built before a pardon, wounds before healing, defilement before cleansing, deformity before comeliness, trouble before peace, slavery before liberty, the service of the devil before the service of Christ.

Hereby you choose dishonor before a crown, death before life, hell before heaven, eternal misery and torment before everlasting joy and glory. And need there a further evidence of your folly and madness, in refusing and neglecting Christ to be your spouse.

My dear sisters, I should exceed the limits of your time, should I particularize all the advantages which you would obtain by being espoused to the Lord Jesus. This is your wisdom; they are foolish virgins who refuse; but you are the wise virgins who have accepted of the Lord Jesus Christ, and have disposed of yourselves to him; you have made the wisest choice; and however the blind world may deem you fools, and despise you as being methodically mad, yet you are wise in the esteem of God, and will, one day, appear so in the esteem of them that now despise you. It is your glory that you are espoused unto the Lord Jesus; and therefore glory is your espousal; glory not in yourselves, but in the Lord who hath thus freely and graciously bestowed these favors upon you. It is your safety to be espoused unto the Lord Jesus Christ, he will protect and defend you even from sin and Satan, and eternal ruin; and therefore thus far you are safe; he hath a regard for you in times of danger from men, and these times of danger seem to be hastening; it is now arising as a black cloud no bigger than a man's hand, and by and by it will overspread the heavens, and when it is full it will burst; but if you are espoused to Christ, you are safe.

Now, my dear sisters, I shall conclude with an earnest exhortation to high and low, rich and poor, one with another, to be espoused unto Christ.

Let me speak unto you, young women, who are not yet espoused unto Christ, in an especial manner. It may be to satisfy your curiosity, has brought many of you here; though, perhaps, this may be the time when you shall be brought home to embrace the Lord Jesus, and be espoused to him.

And O, that I may persuade you, by his Spirit, to espouse yourselves unto the Lord of life.

And if you are but brought to close with the Lord Jesus Christ, I shall attain my end, and then both you and I shall rejoice that I preached this sermon to you.

Come virgins, will you give me leave to be a suitor unto you, not in my own name, but in the name of the Lord? O! that I may prevail with you for your affections, and persuade you to give them unto Christ! May I be instrumental of bringing your souls unto Christ! May I be instrumental to join you and Christ together this day!

Be not coy (bashful, shy; showing reluctance to make a definite commitment), as some of you possibly are in other loves: modesty and the virgin blush may very well come you, when proposals of another kind are made unto you; but here coyness is filly, and backwardness to accept of this motion, is shame: you have ten thousand times more reason to blush at the refusal of Christ for your beloved, than at the acceptance; when otherwise the devil and sin would ravish your virgin affections. Never had you a better motion made to you; never was such a match proffered to you as this, of being matched and espoused unto the Lord Jesus Christ.

Consider who the Lord Jesus is, whom you are invited to espouse yourselves unto; he is the best husband; there is none comparable to Jesus Christ.

Do you desire one that is great? He is of the highest dignity, he is the glory of heaven, the darling of eternity, admired by angels, dreaded by devils, and adored by saints. For you to be espoused to so great a king, what honor will you have by this espousal?

Do you desire one that is rich? None is comparable to Christ, the fullness of the earth belongs to him. If you be espoused to Christ, you shall share in his unsearchable riches; you shall receive of his fullness, even grace for grace here, and you shall hereafter be admitted to glory, and shall live with this Jesus to all eternity.

Do you desire one that is wise? There is none comparable to Christ for wisdom. His knowledge is infinite, and his wisdom is correspondent thereto.

And if you are espoused to Christ, he will guide and counsel you, and make you wise unto salvation.

Do you desire one that is potent, who may defend you against your enemies, and all the insults and reproaches of the Pharisees of this generation? There is none that can equal Christ in power; for the Lord Jesus Christ hath all power.

Do you desire one that is good? There is none like unto Christ in this regard; others may have some goodness, but it is imperfect; Christ's goodness is complete and perfect, he is full of goodness and in him dwelleth no evil.

Do you desire one that is beautiful? His eyes are most sparkling, his looks and glances of love are ravishing, his smiles are most delightful and refreshing unto the soul: Christ is the most lovely person of all others in the world.

Do you desire one that can love you? None can love you like Christ: His love, my dear sisters, is incomprehensible; his love passeth all other loves: The love of the Lord Jesus is first, without beginning; his love is free without any motive; his love is great without any measure; his love is constant without any change, and his love is everlasting.

It was the love of the Lord Jesus Christ, my dear sisters, which brought him down from heaven; and which veiled his divinity in a human soul and body; for he is God over all blessed for ever: It was love that made him subject to hunger, thirst and sorrow; he was humbled, even unto death for you; for you who are espoused to him, he underwent the painful, shameful and ignominious death of the cross: and can you, my sisters, hear this, and not be concerned to think that the blessed Jesus underwent all this for such sinful creatures as you and I are? And when out of love he had finished the redemption on earth, as to what was needful for satisfaction; it was his love that carried him back to heaven, where he was before, that he might make application of what he had purchased, that there he might make intercession for those whom he had redeemed, and prepare a place for them, even glorious mansions with himself, in the house not made with hands, which is eternal in the heavens. It is out of love that he sendeth such tokens to his people from heaven to earth, which he conveyeth through his ordinances, by his Spirit unto them. Surely then none is so deserving as the Lord Jesus Christ for you to espouse yourselves unto: if you be espoused unto Christ he is yours, all that he is, all that he hath; you shall have his heart, and share in the choicest expressions of his dearest love.

The Lord Jesus Christ, my dear sisters, doth beseech you to be his spouse. We ministers have a commission from the Lord Jesus Christ to invite you, in his name, unto this very thing; and Christ's invitations are real; general; frequent; earnest; free.

Christ's invitations of you, to be his spouse, are REAL: and as the thing is real, so you, my dear sisters, are really invited unto it. The Lord doth not mock and dissemble with you, as some pretending lovers, who dissemble love unto virgins, until they have gained their affections, and then falsely and basely relinquish them, never really intending either to espouse, or marry them: but the Lord doth really intend the thing, in his invitations of you; he never cast off any whose consent and affections he had gained. Again, Christ's invitations of you, my dear sisters, are GENERAL. All of you are invited, none of you are excluded; all sorts of sinners are invited; the most vile and abominable sinners, the most notorious transgressors are invited to be Christ's spouse, and shall be as welcome as any unto the embraces of his love.

Christ's invitations of you are FREQUENT: Jesus Christ calls on you frequently; he hath waited on you time after time, one year after another; and he doth now invite you, by me this day, to come unto Him. Do not slight this invitation, but receive it with joy and thankfulness. Come, I beseech you, to this Jesus, who thus, invites you to be his spouse. Again, Christ's invitations to be his spouse are EARNEST: he doth call upon you, and not only call, but call earnestly too; yea, he useth many arguments with you; he will press you to come unto him; he is loth (loathe) to take any denial from you: he knocks, and knocks hard at the door of your hearts for entertainment; and surely you will not deny the Lord of life and glory who died for you, and gave himself for you: O my dear sisters, let this be the evening of your espousals to the Lord Jesus Christ.

He invites you FREELY to be his spouse, for all his invitations are free; he doth not expect a portion with you, as worldly lovers do; He wants nothing of you: nay, you must have nothing, if you be espoused unto the Lord Jesus Christ. If you be poor, miserable, blind, naked, Jesus Christ will supply all these defects of his own free mercy; he will fill and supply you with all things out of his treasury; he will make you meet for himself; he will prepare you to live with him for ever.

Consider, if you be once espoused unto Christ, if once joined in this relation, you shall never be separated from him; neither men nor devils shall be able to separate you: none, none, shall disjoin you; and when death doth break all other bonds, it shall not break the conjugal bond between you and Christ, but bring you unto the most full and everlasting possession of your beloved.

And what do you now say, young women? Shall I have a grant for my master, or be sent away with a repulse and refusal; no, I cannot carry such a message to my master; I hope better things of you, my sisters, and things which accompany salvation: methinks by this time ye should begin to have a mind unto Jesus Christ; you look as if you did desire; you hearken as if you would consent. What do you say? Shall the match be made up this evening between Christ and your souls? O that I may be instrumental in joining your hands, or rather your hearts together: O that I may be instrumental to tie that knot, which never can be unloosed.

Some marry in haste, and repent at leisure; but if you were once espoused unto Jesus Christ, you would never repent; nothing would grieve you, but that you were not joined to him sooner; and you would not be disjoined again for all the world.

Shall this be the day of your espousals? Some of you have stayed a long time; and will you defer any longer? If you will not now, perhaps you may never have another opportunity; this may be the last time of asking; and therefore it is dangerous to refuse; some of you are very young, too young for other espousals; but none of you, by dear sisters, are too young to be espoused unto the Lord Jesus Christ: in other espousals, you must have the consent of your parents; but in this you are at your own disposal; you may give, and ought to match yourselves to Christ, whether parents do consent or not.

But if any of you should ask, what you must do that you may be espoused unto Christ? You must be sensible of your need of being espoused to him, and until you are sensible of your need of the Lord Jesus Christ, you cannot be espoused to him: You must have desires after this Jesus, and seek unto him for an interest in him, you must cry nightly unto him to espouse you to himself; put off the filthiness of sin and all its defilements; and then, my sisters, put on the white raiment, and clean garments, which Christ hath provided for you, the robes of his righteousness; in these garments you shall be beautiful; and in these garments you shall be accepted: you must have the wedding garment on; you must put off all your own good works, for they will be but a means to keep you from Christ; no, you must come as not having your own righteousness, which is of the law, but you must have the righteousness of Christ.

Therefore, come unto the Lord Jesus Christ, and he will give it to you; he will not send you away without it. Receive him upon his own terms, and he is yours forever: O devote yourselves to him, soul and body, and all, to be his for ever; and Christ will be yours and then happy, happy you, that ever you were born! But if any of you die before this espousal unto the Lord Jesus

Christ, then woe, woe, unto you, that ever you had a being in life; but if you go to Christ you shall be espoused unto the Lord Jesus: though your sins have been never so great, yea, the blood of Christ will cleanse you from them; the marriage covenant between Christ and your souls will dissolve all your sins; you will then be weary of your old ways, for all things will become new in your souls.

Now, my dear sisters, I shall conclude by just speaking a word or two to those of you, who are already espoused unto the Lord Jesus Christ.

O admire, admire the rich and free grace, which hath brought you to this relation: Is not this an instance of the greatest of love, that you should be the spouse of the Lord Jesus Christ? You that had no beauty, you that had no comeliness, that was full of sin, that He should embrace such as you and I are; that we should be taken into the embrace of this Lord Jesus. O infinite conde-scending kindness! O amazing love! Reverence, reverence, I beseech you, this Lord Jesus Christ.

He is you Lord, and you must reverence him, love and be faithful unto him, be subject to him, and careful to please him in every thing; en-deavor to keep up a daily communion with him; look, long and prepare for Christ's second appearance, when the nuptials between you shall be solem-nized, and you live with him in mansions of everlasting joys, where you shall love and live with this king of glory for ever and ever.

I know not how to conclude; methinks I could speak to you till mid-night, if it would bring you unto the Lord Jesus Christ, and make you be espoused to him, for indeed, that will be the espousal which will turn to the greatest advantage, as you will find by experience, if you will but make the trial; and that you may do so, my prayers and my constant endeavor shall be used.

I will, my dear sisters, spend and be spent for you, and by the assis-tance of God, will persevere in this that I have begun; and as many of you may have opportunity some evening in the week, without breaking in on the business of life; I shall therefore, my sisters, either be here, or where you shall be publicly acquainted with: I will not mind being reproached or despised: the men of this world may use what language the please; they may say I am a Methodist. Indeed, my sisters, I am resolved, by the grace of God, to use all methods I can, to pluck you from Satan, that you may be as brands plucked from the burning fire: this shall be my method, which I hope will be the means of effectually having your precious and immortal souls.

And if I am the instrument of this, I shall rejoice, yea, and I will rejoice in spite of what men, or devils, can say or do to the contrary: and may the Lord Jesus Christ direct, and assist me at all times, to act what will be most for is glory, and the welfare of your souls: and may you all say a hearty Amen thereto.

"Now the Lord Jesus Christ, who is God over all, blessed for ever, assist and watch over you, keep you from all evil and sin here, and present you before his Father faultless at the great day of account! To this Lord Jesus Christ, the Father , and the blessed Spirit, three persons and but one eternal and invisible God, be ascribed all honor, power, glory, might, majesty and dominion, now, henceforth, and for ever more. Amen, Amen." "The grace of our Lord Jesus Christ, the love of God, and the fellowship of the Holy Ghost be with you all, to comfort under, and deliver you from tribulation; to preserve you to your respective place of abode; and when there, to keep you in his fear, that you may live to his glory; that to live may be Christ's, and to die by your eternal gain; so that you may live with him through eternal ages, and sing Hallelujahs to him for ever. Amen."

Sermon 6 Britain's Mercies, and Britain's Duty

(Preached at Philadelphia, on Sunday, August 14, 1746 and occasioned by the suppression of the late unnatural rebellion.)

Psalm 55:45 "That they might observe his statutes and keep his laws."

Men, brethren, and fathers, and all ye to whom I am about to preach the kingdom of God, I suppose you need not be informed, that being indispensably obliged to be absent on your late thanksgiving day, I could not show my obedience to the governor's proclamation, as my own inclination led me, or as might justly be expected from, and demanded of me. But as the occasion of that day's thanksgiving is yet, and I trust ever will be, fresh in our memory, I cannot think that a discourse on that subject can even now be altogether unseasonable. I take it for granted, further, that you need not be informed, that among the various motives which are generally urged to enforce obedience to the divine commands, that of love is the most powerful and cogent. The terrors of the law ma affright and awe, but love dissolves and melts the heart. "The love of Christ," says the great apostle of the Gentiles, "constraineth us." Nay, love is so absolutely necessary for those that name the name of Christ, that without it, their obedience cannot truly be stiled evangelical, or be acceptable in the sight of God.

"Although, (says the apostle) I bestow all my goods to feed the poor, and though I give my body to be burnt, and have not charity," (i.e. unless unfeigned love to God, and to mankind for his great name's sake, be the principle of such actions, howsoever it may benefit others) it profiteth me nothing." This is the constant language of the lively oracles of God. And, from them it is equally plain, that nothing has a greater tendency to beget and excite such an obediential love in us, than a serious and frequent consideration of the manifold mercies we receive time after time from the bands of our heavenly Father. The royal psalmist, who had the honor of being stiled, "the man after God's own heart," had an abundant experience of this. Hence it is, that whilst he is musing on the divine goodness, the fire of divine love kindles in his soul; and, out of the abundance of his heart, his mouth speaketh such grateful and ecstatic language as this, "What shall I render unto the Lord for all his mercies? Bless the Lord, O my soul, and all that is within me, bless his holy name." And why? "who forgiveth all thine iniquities, who healeth all thy diseases, who redeemeth thy life from destruction, who crowneth thee with loving kindness and tender mercies." And when the same holy man of God had a mind to stir up the people of the Jews to set about a national reformation, as the most weighty and prevailing argument he could make use of for that purpose, he lays before them, as it were, in a draught, many national mercies, and distinguishing deliverances, which have been conferred upon and wrought out for them, by the most high God. The psalm to which the words of our text belong, is a pregnant proof of this; it being a kind of epitome or compendium of the whole Jewish history: at least it contains an enumeration of man signal and extraordinary blessings the Israelites had received from God, and also the improvement they were in duty bound to make of them, "Observe his statues and keep his laws." To run through all the particulars of the psalm, or draw a parallel (which might with great ease and justice be done) between God's dealings with us and the Israelites of old; To enumerate all the national mercies bestowed upon, and remarkable deliverances wrought out for the kingdoms of Great Britain and Ireland, from the infant state of William the Norman to their present manhood, under the auspicious reign of our rightful Sovereign King George the second; howsoever pleasing and profitable it might be at any other time, would, at this juncture, prove, if not an irksome, yet an unreasonable undertaking.

The occasion of the late solemnity, I mean the suppression of a most horrid and unnatural rebellion, will afford more than sufficient matter for a discourse of this nature, and furnish us with abundant motives to love and obey that glorious Jehovah, who giveth salvation unto kings, and delivers his people from the hurtful sword.

Need I make an apology, before this auditory, if, in order to see the greatness of our late deliverance, I should remind you of the many unspeakable blessings which we have for a course of years enjoyed, during the reign of his present Majesty, and the gentle, mile administration under which we live? Without justly incurring the censure of giving flattering titles, I believe all who have eyes to see, and ears to hear, and are but a little acquainted with our public affairs, must acknowledge, that we have one of the best of Kings. It is now above nineteen years since he began to reign over us. And yet, was he seated on a royal throne, and were all his subjects placed before him, was he to address them as Samuel once addressed the Israelites, "Behold here I am, old and gray-headed, witness against me before the Lord, whose ox have

I taken? Or whose ass have I taken? Or whom have I defrauded? Whom have I oppressed?" They must, if they would do him justice, make the same answer as was given to Samuel, "Thou hast not defrauded us, nor oppressed us." What Tertulius, by way of flattery, said to Felix, may with the strictest justice be applied to our sovereign, "By thee we enjoy great quietness, and very worthy deeds have been done unto our nation by thy providence." He has been indeed Peter Patria, a father to our country, and though old and gray-headed, has jeopardized his precious life for us in the high places of the field. Nor has he less deserved the great and glorious title, which the Lord promises, that kings should sustain in the latter days, I mean, "a nursing father of the church." For not only the Church of England, as by law established, but all denominations of Christians whatsoever, have enjoyed their religious as well as civil liberties. As there has been no authorized oppression in the state, so there has been no publicly allowed persecution in the church. We breathe indeed in free air? As free (if not better) both as to temporals and spirituals, as any nation under heaven. Nor is the prospect likely to terminate in his majesty's death, which I pray God to defer. Our princesses are disposed of to Protestant powers. And we have great reason to be assured, that the present heir apparent, and his consort, are like minded with their royal father. And I cannot help thinking, that it is a peculiar blessing vouchsafed us by the King of kings, that his present Majesty has been continued so long among us. For now, his immediate successor (though his present situation obliges him, as it were, to lie dormant) has great and glorious opportunities, which we have reason to think he daily improves, of observing and weighing the national affairs, considering the various steps and turns of government, and consequently of laying in a large fund of experience, to make him a wise and great prince, if ever God should call him to sway the British scepter. Happy art thou, O England!

Happy art thou, O America, who on every side art thus highly favored!

But, alas! How soon would this happy scene have shifted, and a melancholy gloomy prospect have succeeded in its room, had the revels gained their point, and a popish abjured pretender been forced upon the British throne! For, supposing his birth not to be spurious, (as we have great reason to think it really was) what could we expect from one, descended from a father, who, when Duke of York, put all Scotland into confusion; and afterwards, when crowned King of England, for his arbitrary and tyrannical government, both in church and state, was justly obliged to abdicate the throne, by the assertors of British liberty? Or, supposing the horrid plot, first hatched in hell, and afterwards nursed at Rome, had taken place? Supposing, I say, the old Pretender should have obtained the triple crown, and have transferred his pretended title (as it is reported he has done) to his eldest son, what was all this for, but that, by being advanced to the popedom, he might rule both son and subjects with less control, and by their united interest, keep the three kingdoms of England, Scotland, and Ireland, in greater vassalage to the see of Rome? Ever since this unnatural rebellion broke out, I have looked upon the young Pretender as the phaeton (vehicle) of the present age. He is ambitiously and presumptuously aiming to seat himself in the throne of our rightful sovereign King George, which he is no more capable of keeping, than Phaetan was to guide the chariot of the sun; and had he succeeded in his attempt, like him, would only have set the world on fire. It is true, to do him justice, he has deserved well of the Church of Rome, and, in all probability, will hereafter be canonized amongst the noble order of their fictitious saints. But, with what an iron rod we might expect to have been bruised, had his troops been victorious, may easily be gathered from these cruel orders said to be found in the pockets of some of his officers, "Give no quarters to the Elector's troops." Add to this, that there was great reason to suspect, that, upon the first news of the success of the rebels, a general massacre was intended. So that if the Lord had not been on our side, Great Britain, not to say America, would, in a few weeks or months, have been an Akeldama, a field of blood.

Besides, was a Popish pretender to rule over us, instead of being represented by a free parliament, and governed by laws made by their consent, as we now are; we should shortly have had only the shadow of one, and it may be no parliament at all. This is the native product of a Popish government, and what the unhappy family, from which this young adventurer pretends he descended, has always aimed at. Arbitrary principles he has sucked in with his mother's milk, and if he had been so honest, instead of that immature motto upon his standard, Tandem triumphant, only to have put, Sret pro ratient Vahmitat, he had given us a short, but true portrait of the nature of his intended, but blessed be God, now defeated reign. And why should I mention, that the sinking of the national debt, or rending away the funded property of the people, and the dissolution of the present happy union between the two kingdoms, would have been the immediate consequences of his success, as he himself declares in his second manifesto, dated from Holy-read House? These are evils, and great ones too; but then they are only evils of a temporary nature. They chiefly concern the body, and must necessarily terminate in the grave.

But, alas! What an inundation of spiritual mischiefs, would soon have overflowed the Church, and what unspeakable danger should we and our posterity have been reduced to in respect to our better parts, our precious and immortal souls? How soon would whole swarms of monks, dominicans and friars, like so many locusts, have overspread and plagued the nation; with what winged speed would foreign titular bishops have posted over, in order to take possession of their respective fees? How quickly would our universities have been filled with youths who have been sent abroad by their Popish parents, in order to drink in all the superstitions of the church of Rome? What a speedy period would have been put to societies of all kinds, for promoting Christian knowledge, and propagating the gospel in foreign parts? How soon would have our pulpits have every where been filled with these old antichristian doctrines, free-will, meriting by works, transubstantiation, purgatory, works of supererogation, passive-obedience, non-resistance, and all the other abominations of the whore of Babylon? How soon would our Protestant charity schools in England, Scotland and Ireland, have been pulled down, our Bibles forcibly taken from us, and ignorance every where set up as the mother of devotion? How soon should we have been deprived of that invaluable blessing, liberty of conscience, and been obliged to commence (what they falsely call) catholics, or submit to all the tortures which a bigoted zeal, guided by the most cruel principles, could possibly invent? How soon would that mother of harlots have made herself once more drunk with the blood of the saints? And the whole tribe even of free-thinkers themselves, been brought to this dilemma, either to die martyrs for (although I never yet heard of one that did so) or, contrary to all their most avowed principles, renounce their great Diana, unassisted, unenlightened reason? But I must have done, lest while I am speaking against antichrist, I should unawares fall myself, and lead my hearers into an antichristian spirit. True and undefiled religion will regulate our zeal, and teach us to treat even the man of sin with no harsher language than that which the angel gave to his grand employer Satan, "The Lord rebuke thee." Glory be to God's great name! The Lord has rebuked him; and that too at a time when we had little reason to expect such a blessing at God's hands. My dear hearers, neither the present frame of my heart, nor the occasion of your late solemn meeting, lead me to give you a detail of our public vices. Though, alas! They are so many, so notorious, and withal of such a crimson-dye, that a gospel minister would not be altogether inexcusable, was he, even on such a joyful occasion, to lift up his voice like a trumpet, to show the British nation their transgression, and the people of America their sin. However, though I would not cast a dismal shade upon the pleasing picture the cause of our late rejoicings set before us; yet thus much may, and ought to be said, that as God has not dealt so bountifully with any people as with us, so no nation under heaven has dealt more ungratefully with Him. We have been like Capernaum, lifted up to heaven in privileges, and for the abuse of them, like her, have deserved to be thrust down into hell. How well soever it may be with us, in respect to our civil and ecclesiastical constitution, yet in regard to our morals, Isaiah's description of the Jewish polity is too applicable, "The whole head is sick, the whole heart is faint; from the crown of the head to the sole of our feet, we are full of wounds and bruises, and putrifying sores." We have, Jeshurun-like, waxed fat and kicked. WE have played the harlot against God, both in regard to principles and practices. "Our gold is become dim, and our fine gold changed." We have crucified the Son of God afresh, and put him to an open shame. Nay, Christ has been wounded in the house of his friends. And every thing long ago seemed to threaten an immediate storm. But, O the long-suffering and goodness of God to us-ward!

When all things seemed ripe for destruction, and matters were come to such a crisis, that God's praying people began to think, that though Noah, Daniel and Job, were living, they would only deliver their own souls; yet then in the midst of judgment the Most High remembered mercy, and when a popish enemy was breaking in upon us like a flood, the Lord himself graciously lifted up a standard.

This to me does not seem to be one of the most unfavorable circumstances which have attended this mighty deliverance; nor do I think you will look upon it as a circumstance altogether unworthy your observation. Had this cockatrice indeed been crushed in the egg, and the young Pretender driven back upon his first arrival, it would undoubtedly have been a great blessing. But not so great as that for which you lately assembled to give God thanks; for then his Majesty would not have had so good an opportunity of knowing his enemies, or trying his friends. The British subjects would in a manner have lost the fairest occasion that ever offered to express their loyalty and gratitude to the rightful sovereign.

France would not have been so greatly humbled; nor such an effectual stop have been put, as we trust there now is, to any such further Popish plot, to rob us of all that is near and dear to us. "Out of the eater therefore hath come forth meat, and out of the strong hath come forth sweetness." The Pretender's eldest son is suffered not only to land in the North-West Highlands in Scotland, but in a little while he becomes a great band. This for a time is not believed, but treated as a thing altogether incredible.

The friends of the government in those parts, not for want of loyalty, but of sufficient authority to take up arms, could not resist him. He is permitted to pass on with his terrible banditti, and, like the comet that was lately seen, spreads his baleful influences all around him. He is likewise permitted to gain a short-lived triumph by a victory over a body of our troops at Prestan-Pans, and to take a temporary possession of the metropolis of Scotland. Of this he makes his boast, and informs the public, that "Providence had hitherto favored him with wonderful success, led him in the way to victory, and to the capital of the ancient kingdom, though he came without foreign aid." Nay, he is further permitted to press into the very heart of England. But now the Almighty interposes. Hitherto he was to go, and no further. Here were his malicious designs to be staid. His troops of s sudden are driven back. Away they post to the Highlands, and there they are suffered not only to increase, but also to collect themselves into a large body, that having, as it were, what Caligula once wished Rome had, but one neck, they might be cut off with one blow.

This time, manner, and instruments of this victory, deserves our notice. It was on a general fast-day, when the clergy and good people of Scotland were lamenting the disloyalty of their persidious countrymen, and, like Moses, lifting up their hands, that Amalek might not prevail. The victory was total and decisive. Little blood was spilt on the side of the Royalists. And, to crown all, Duke William, his Majesty's youngest son, has the honor of first driving back, and then defeating the rebel-army. A prince, who in his infancy and youth, gave early proofs of an uncommon bravery and nobleness of mind; a prince, whose courage has increased with his years. Who returned wounded from the battle of Dettingen, behaved with surprising bravery at Fontenoy, and now, by a conduct and magnanimity becoming the high office he sustains, like his glorious predecessor the Prince of Orange, has delivered three kingdoms from the dread of popish cruelty, and arbitrary power. What renders it still more remarkable is, The day on which his Highness gained this victory, was the day after his birthday, when he was entering on the 26th year of his age; and when Sullivan, one of the Pretender's privy-council, like another Abitaphel, advised the rebels to give our soldiers battle, presuming they were surfeited and over-charged with their yesterday's rejoicings, and consequently unfit to make any great stand against them. But, glory be to God, who catches the wise in their own craftiness! His counsel, like Ahitaphel's, proves abortive. Both General and soldiers were prepared to meet them. "God taught their hands to war, and their fingers to fight," and brought the Duke, after a deserved slaughter of some thousands of the rebels, with most of his brave soldiers, victorious from the field.

If we then take a distinct view of this notable transaction, and trace it in all the particular circumstances that have attended it, I believe we must with one heart and voice confess, that if it be a mercy for a state to be delivered from a worse than a Catiline's conspiracy, or a church to be rescued from a hotter than a Dioclestan persecution; if it be a mercy to be delivered from a religion that turns plough-shares into swords, and pruning-hooks into spears, and makes it meritorious to shed Protestant blood; if it be a mercy to have all our present invaluable privileges, both in church and state secured to us more than ever; if it be a mercy to have these great things done for us, at a season, when for our crying sins, both church and state justly deserved to be overturned; and if it be a mercy to have all this brought about for us, under God, by one of the blood-royal, a prince acting with an experience far above his years; if any, or all of these are mercies, then have you lately commemorated one of the greatest mercies that ever the glorious God vouchsafed to the British nation.

And shall we not rejoice and give thanks? Should we refuse, would not the stones cry out against us? Rejoice then we may and ought: but, O let our rejoicing be in the Lord, and run in a religious channel. This, we find, has been the practice of God's people in all ages. When he was pleased, with a mighty hand, and out-stretched arm to lead the Israelites through the Red Sea, as on dry ground, "Then sang Moses and the children of Israel; and Miriam the prophetess, the sister of Aaron, took a timbrel in her hand, and all the women went out after her. And Miriam answered them, Sing ye to the Lord; for he hath triumphed gloriously." When God subdued Jabin, the King of Canaan, before the children of Israel, "then sang Deborah and Barak on that day, saying, "Praise ye the Lord for the avenging of Israel." When the ark was brought back out of the hands of the Philistines, David, though a king, danced before it. And, to mention but one instance more, which may serve as a general directory to us on this and such-like occasions: when the great Head of the church had rescued his people from the general massacre intended to be executed upon them by a cruel and ambitious Haman, "Mordecai sent letters unto all the Jews that were in all the provinces of the King Ahaserus, both nigh and far, to establish among them, that they should keep the fourteenth day of the month Adar, and the fifteenth day of the same yearly, as the days wherein the Jews rested from their enemies, and the month which was turned unto them from sorrow unto joy, and from mourning into a good day: that they should make them days of feasting and joy, and of sending portions one to another, and gifts to the poor." And why should wee not to and do likewise?

And shall we not also, on such an occasion, express our gratitude to, and make honorable mention of, those worthies who have signalized themselves, and been ready to sacrifice both lives and fortunes at this critical juncture?

This would be to act the part of those ungrateful Israelites, who are branded in the book of God, for not showing kindness to the house of "Jerub-Baal, namely Gideon, according to all the goodness which he showed unto Israel." Even a Pharaoh could prefer a deserving Joseph, Ahasuerus a Mordecai, and Nebuchadnezzar a Daniel, when made instruments of signal service to themselves and people. "My heart, says Deborah, is towards (i.e.

I have a particular veneration and regard for) the Governors of Israel that offered themselves willingly. And blessed above women shall Jael the wife of Heber the Kenite be; for she put her hand to the nail, and her right hand to the workman's hammer, and with the hammer she smote Sisera, she smote off his head, when she had pierced and stricken through his temples." And shall we not say, "Blessed above men let his Royal Highness the Duke of Cumberland be; for through his instrumentality, the great and glorious Jehovah hath brought might things to pass?" Should not our hearts be towards the worthy Archbishop of Tirk, the Royal Hunters, and those other English heroes who offered themselves so willingly? Let the names of Blakeney, Bland and Rea, and all those who waxed valiant in fight on this important occasion, live for ever in the British annals. And let the name of that great, that incomparable brave soldier of the King, and a good soldier of Jesus Christ, Colonel Gardiner, (excuse me if I here drop a tear; he was my intimate friend) let his name, I say, be had in everlasting remembrance.

But, after all, is there not an infinitely greater debt of gratitude and praise due from us, on this occasion, to Him that is higher than the highest, even the King of kings and Lord of Lords, the blessed and only Potentate? Is not his arm, his strong and mighty arm, (what instruments soever may have been made use of) that hath brought us this salvation? And may I not therefore address you, in the exulting language of the beginning of this psalm, from which we have taken our text? "O give thanks unto the Lord, call upon his name, make known his deeds among the people. Sing unto Him; sing psalms unto him; talk ye of all his wondrous works; glory ye in his holy name; remember his marvelous work which he hath done." But shall we put off our good and gracious benefactor with mere lip- service? God forbid. Your worthy Governor has honored God in his late excellent proclamation, and God will honor him. But shall our thanks terminate with the day? No, in no wise. Our text reminds us of a more noble sacrifice, and points out to us the great end the Almighty Jehovah proposes, in bestowing such signal favors upon a people, "That they should observe his statutes, and keep his laws." This is the return we are all taught to pray, that we may make to the Most High God, the Father of mercies, in the daily office or our church, "That our hearts may be unfeignedly thankful, and that we may show forth his praise, not only with our lips, but in our lives, by giving up ourselves to his service, and by walking before him in holiness and righteousness all our days." O that these words were the real language of all the use them! O that these were in us such a mind! How soon would our enemies then flee before us? And God, even our own God, would yet give us more abundant blessings!

And why should not we "observe God's statutes, and keep his laws?" Dare we say, that any of his commands are grievous? Is not Christ's yoke, to a renewed soul, as far as renewed, easy; and his burden comparatively light? May I not appeal to the most refined reasoner whether the religion of Jesus Christ be not a social religion? Whether the Moral Law, as explained by the Lord Jesus in the gospel, has not a natural tendency to promote the present good and happiness of a whole commonwealth, supposing they were obedient to them, as well as the happiness of every individual?

From when come wars and fighting amongst us? From what fountain do all those evil, which the present and past ages have groaned under, flow, but from a neglect of the laws and statues of our great and all-wise lawgiver Jesus of Nazareth? Tell me, ye men of letters, whether Lycurgus or Solon, Pythagoras or Plato, Aristotle, Seneca, Cicero, or all the ancient lawgivers and heathen moralists, put them all together, ever published a system of ethics, any way worthy to be compared with the glorious system laid down in that much despised book, (to use Sir Richard Steel's expression) emphatically called, the Scriptures? Is not the divine image and superscription written upon every precept of the gospel? Do they not shine with a native intrinsic luster? And, though many things in them are above, yet, is there any thing contrary to the strictest laws of right reason? Is not Jesus Christ, in scripture, stiled the Word, the Logos, the Reason? And is not his service a reasonable service? What if there be mysteries in his religion? Are they not without all controversy great and glorious? Are they n9ot mysteries of godliness, and worthy of that God who reveals them? Nay, is it not the greatest mystery, that men, who pretend to reason, and call themselves philosophers, who search into the arcana natura, and consequently find a mystery in every blade of grass, should yet be so irrational as to decry all mysteries in religion? Where is the scribe? Where is the wise? Where is the disputer against the Christian revelation? Does not every thing without and within us, conspire to prove its divine original? And would not self-interest, if there was no other motive, excite us to observe God's statutes, and keep his laws?

Besides, considered as a Protestant people, do we not lie under the greatest obligations of any nation under heaven, to pay a cheerful, unanimous, universal, persevering obedience to the divine commands.

The wonderful and surprising manner of God's bringing about a Reformation, in the reign of King Henry the Eighth; his carrying it on in the blessed reign of King Edward the Sixth; his delivering us out of the bloody hands of Queen Mary, and destroying the Spanish invincible armads, under her immediate Protestant successor Queen Elizabeth, his discovery of the popish plot under King James; the glorious revolution by King William, and, to come nearer to our own times, his driving away four thousand five hundred Spaniards, from a weak (though important) frontier colony, when they had, in a manner, actually taken possession of it; his giving us Louisbourg, one of the strongest fortresses of our enemies, contrary to all human probability, but the other day, into our hands: these, I say, with the victory which you have lately been commemorating, are such national mercies, not to mention any more, as will render us utterly inexcusable, if they do not produce a national Reformation, and incite us all, with one heart, to keep God's statutes, and observe his laws.

Need I remind you further, in order to excite in you a greater diligence to comply with the intent of the text, that though the storm, in a great measure, is abated by his Royal Highness's late success, yet we dare not say, it is altogether blown over?

The clouds may again return after the rain; and the few surviving rebels (which I pray God avert) may yet be suffered to make head against us. We are still engaged in a bloody, and, in all probability, a tedious war, with two of the most inveterate enemies to the interests of Great- Britain. And, though I cannot help thinking, that their present intentions are so iniquitous, their conduct so persidious, and their schemes so directly derogatory to the honor of the Most High God, that he will certainly humble them in the end, yet, as all things in this life happen alike to all, they may for a time, be dreadful instruments of scourging us.

If not, God has other arrows in his quiver to smite us with, besides the French King, his Catholic Majesty, or an abjured Pretender. Not only the sword, but plague, pestilence, and famine, are under the divine command.

Who knows but he may say to them all, "Pass through these lands?" A fatal murrain has lately swept away abundance of cattle at home and abroad. A like epidemical disease may have a commission to seize our persons as well as our beasts. Thus God dealt with the Egyptians: who dare say, he will not deal so with us? Has he not already given some symptoms of it? What great numbers upon the continent have been lately taken off by the bloody-flux, small-pox, and yellow-fever? Who can tell what further judgments are yet in store? However, this is certain, the rod is yet hanging over us: and I believe it will be granted on all sides, that if such various dispensations of mercy and judgment do not teach the inhabitants of any land to learn righteousness, they will only ripen them for a greater ruin. Give my leave, therefore, to dismiss you at this time with that solemn awful warning and exhortation, with which the venerable Samuel, on a public occasion, took leave of the people of Israel: "Only fear the Lord, and serve him in truth, with all your heart: for consider how great things he hath done for you.

But if ye shall still do wickedly, (I will not say as the Prophet did, You shall be consumed; but) ye know not but you may provoke the Lord Almighty to consume both you and your king." Which God of his infinite mercy prevent, for the sake of Jesus Christ: to whom, with the Father, and the Holy Ghost, three persons, but one God, be all honor and glory, now and for evermore. Amen, Amen.

Sermon 7 Thankfulness for Mercies received, a necessary Duty

(A farewell sermon, preached on board the Whitaker, at anchor near Savannah, in Georgia, Sunday, May 17, 1738)

Psalm 108:30-31 "Then art they glad, because they are at rest, and so he bringeth them unto the haven where they would be. O that men would therefore praise the Lord for his goodness, and declare the wonders that he doeth for the children of men!

Numberless marks does man bear in his soul, that he is fallen and estranged from God; but nothing gives a greater proof thereof, than that backwardness, which every one finds within himself, to the duty of praise and thanksgiving.

When God placed the first man in paradise, his soul no doubt was so filled with a sense of the riches of the divine love, that he was continually employing that breath of life, which the Almighty had not long before breathed into him, in blessing and magnifying that all-bountiful, all gracious God, in whom he lived, moved, and had his being.

And the brightest idea we can form of the angelical hierarchy above, and the spirits of just men made perfect, is, that they are continually standing round the throne of God, and cease not day and night, saying, "Worthy art thou, O Lamb that wast slain, to receive power and riches, and wisdom, and strength, and honor, and glory, and blessing." Rev. 5:12.

That then, which was man's perfection when time first began, and will be his employment when death is swallowed up in victory, and time shall be no more, without controversy, is part of our perfection, and ought to be our frequent exercise on earth: and I doubt not but those blessed spirits, who are sent forth to minister to them who shall be heirs of salvation, often stand astonished when they encamp around us, or find our hearts so rarely enlarged, and our mouths so seldom opened, to show forth the loving- kindness of the Lord, or to speak of all his praise.

Matter for praise and adoration, can never be wanting to creatures redeemed by the blood of the Son of God; and who have such continual scenes of his infinite goodness presented to their view, that were their souls duly affected with a sense of his universal love, they could not but be continually calling on heaven and earth, men and angels, to join with them in praising and blessing that "high and lofty one, who inhabiteth eternity, who maketh his sun to shine on the evil and on the good," and daily pours down his blessings on the whole race of mankind., But few are arrived to such a degree of charity or love, as to rejoice with those that do rejoice, and to be as thankful for other mercies, as their own. This part of Christian perfection, though begun on earth, will be consummated only in heaven; where our hearts will glow with such fervent love towards God and one another, that every fresh degree of glory communicated to our neighbor, will also communicate to us a fresh topic of thankfulness and joy.

That which has the greatest tendency to excite the generality of fallen men to praise and thanksgiving, is a sense of God's private mercies, and particular benefits bestowed upon ourselves. For as these come nearer our own hearts, so they must be more affecting: and as they are peculiar proofs, whereby we may know, that God does in a more especial manner favor us above others, so they cannot but sensibly touch us; and if our hearts are not quite frozen, like coals of a refiner's fire, they must melt us down into thankfulness and love. It was a consideration of the distinguishing favor God had shown to his chosen people Israel, and the frequent and remarkable deliverance wrought by him in behalf of "hose who go down to the Sea in ships, and occupy their business in great matters," that made the holy Psalmist break out so frequently as he does in this psalm, into this moving, pathetical exclamation, "that men would therefore praise the Lord for his goodness, and declare the wonders that he doeth for the children of men!" His expressing himself in so fervent a manner, implies both the importance and neglect of the duty. As when Moses in another occasion cried out, "O that they were wise, that they understood this, that they would practically consider their latter end!" Deut. 32:29.

I say, importance and neglect of the duty; for out of those man thousands that receive blessings from the Lord, how few give thanks in remembrance of his holiness? The account given us of the ungrateful lepers, is but too lively a representation of the ingratitude of mankind in general; who like them, when under any humbling providence, can cry, "Jesus, Master, have mercy on us!" Luke 17:13. But when healed of their sickness, or delivered from their distress, scarce one in ten can be found "returning to give thanks to God." And yet as common as this sin of ingratitude is, there is nothing we ought more earnestly to pray against. For what is more absolutely condemned in holy scripture than ingratitude? Or what more peremptorily (absolutely, emphatically) required than the contrary temper? Thus says the Apostle, "Rejoice evermore; in every thing give thanks," 1 Thes. 5:16,18. "Be careful for nothing; but in every thing by prayer and supplication, with thanksgiving, let your requests be made known unto God," Phil. 4:6.

On the contrary, the Apostle mentions it as one of the highest crimes of the Gentiles, that they were not thankful. "Neither were they thankful," Rom. 1:21. As also in another place, he numbers the "unthankful," 2 Tim.

3:2 amongst those unholy, profane person, who are to have their portion in the lake of fire and brimstone.

As for our sins, God puts them behind his back; but his mercies he will have acknowledged, "There is virtue gone out of me," says Jesus Christ, Luke 8:46 and the woman who was cured of her bloody issue, must confess it. And we generally find, when God sent any remarkable punishment upon a particular person, he reminded him of the favors he had received, as so many aggravations of his ingratitude. Thus when God was about to visit Eli's house, he thus expostulates with him by his prophet: "Did I plainly appear unto the house of thy fathers, when they were in Egypt, in Pharaoh's house? And did I choose him out of all the tribes of Israel, to be my priest, to offer upon mine altar, to burn incense, and to wear an ephod before me? Wherefore kick ye at my sacrifice, and at mine offering, which I have commanded in my habitation, and honorest thy sons above me; so make yourselves fat with the chiefest of all the offerings of Israel my people?

Wherefore the Lord God of Israel saith, I said indeed, that thy house, and the house of thy father, should walk before me for ever; but now the Lord saith, Be it far from me, for them that honor me will I honor, and they that despise me shall be lightly esteemed" 2 Sam. 2:27-30.

It was this and such like instances of God's severity against the unthankful, that inclined me to choose the words of the text, as the most proper subject I could discourse on at this time.

Four months, my good friends, we have now been upon the sea in this ship, and "have occupied our business in the great waters." At God Almighty's word, we have seen "the stormy wind arise, which hath lifted up the waves thereof. We have been carried up to the heaven, and down again to the deep, and some of our souls melted away because of the trouble; but I trust we cried earnestly unto the Lord, and he delivered us out of our distress. For he made the storm to cease; so that the waves thereof were still. And now we are glad, because we are at rest, for God hath brought us to the haven where we would be. O that you would therefore praise the Lord for his goodness, and declare the wonders that he hath done for us, the unworthiest of the sons of men." Thus Moses, thus Joshua behaved. For when they were about to take their leave of the children of Israel, they recounted to them what great things God had done for them, as the best arguments and motives they could urge to engage them to obedience. And how can I copy after better examples?

What fitter, what more noble motives, to holiness and purity of living, can I lay before you, than they did?

Indeed, I cannot say, that we have seen the "pillar of a cloud by day, or a pillar of fire by night," going visibly before us to guide our course; but this I can say, that the same God who was in that pillar of a cloud, and pillar of fire, which departed not from the Israelites, and who has made the sun to rule the day, and the moon to rule the night, has, by his good providence, directed us in our right way, or else the pilot had steered us in vain.

Neither can I say, That we have seen the "sun stand still," as the children of Israel did in the days of Joshua. But surely God, during part of our voyage, has caused it to withhold some of that heat, which it usually sends forth in these warmer climates, or else it had not failed, but some of you must have perished in the sickness that has been, and does yet continue among us.

We have not seen the waters stand purposely on an heap, that we might pass through, neither have we been pursued by Pharaoh and his host, and delivered out of their hands; but we have been led through the sea as through a wilderness, and were once remarkably preserved from being run down by another ship; which had God permitted, the waters, in all probability, would immediately have overwhelmed us, and like Pharaoh and his host, we should have sunk, as stones, into the sea.

We may, indeed, atheist like, ascribe all these things to natural causes, and say, "Our own skill and foresight has brought us hither in safety." But as certainly as Jesus Christ, the angel of the covenant, in the days of his flesh, walked upon the water, and said to his sinking disciples, "Be not afraid, it is I," so surely has the same everlasting I AM, "who decketh himself with light as with a garment, who spreadeth out the heavens like a curtain, who claspeth the winds in his fist, who holdeth the waters in the hollow of his hands," and guided the wise men by a star in the east; so surely, I say, has he spoken, and at his command the winds have blown us where we are not arrived. For his providence ruleth all things; "Wind and storms obey his word:" he saith to it at one time, Go, and it goeth; at another, Come, and it cometh; and at a third time, Blow this way, and it bloweth.

It is he, my brethren; and not we ourselves, that has of late sent us such prosperous gales, and made us to ride, as it were, on the wings of the wind, into the haven where we would be.

"O that you would therefore praise the Lord for his goodness," and by your lives declare, that you are truly thankful for the wonders he had shown to us; who are less than the least of the sons of men.

I say, declare it by your lives. For to give him thanks, barely with your lips; while your hearts are far from him, is but a mock sacrifice, nay, an abomination unto the Lord.

This was the end, the royal Psalmist says, God had in view, when he showed such wonders, from time to time, to the people of Israel, "That they might keep his statutes, and observe his laws," Psalm 105:44 and this, my good friends, is the end God would have accomplished in us, and the only return he desires us to make him, for all the benefits he hath conferred upon us.

O then, let me beseech you, give to God your hearts, your whole hearts; and suffer yourselves to be drawn by the cords of infinite love, to honor and obey him.

Assure yourselves you can never serve a better master; for his service is perfect freedom, his yoke, when worn a little while, is exceeding easy, his burden light, and in keeping his commandments there is great reward; love, peace, joy in the Holy Ghost here, and a crown of glory that fadeth not away, hereafter.

You may, indeed, let other lords have dominion over you, and Satan may promise to give you all the kingdoms of the world, and the glory of them, if you will fall down and worship him; but he is a liar, and was so from the beginning; he has not so much to give you, as you may tread on with the soul of your foot; or could he give you the whole world, yea, that could not make you happy without God. It is God alone, my brethren, whose we are, in whose name I now speak, and who has of late showed us such mercies in the deep, that can give solid lasting happiness to your souls; and he for this reason only desires your hearts, because without him you must be miserable.

Suffer me not then to go away without my errand; as it is the last time I shall speak to you, let me not speak in vain; but let a sense of the divine goodness lead you to repentance.

Even Saul, that abandoned wretch, when David showed him his skirt, which he had cut off, when he might have also taken his life, was so melted down with his kindness, that he lifted up his voice and wept. And we must have hearts harder than Saul's, nay, harder than the nether millstone, if a sense of God's late loving kindnesses, notwithstanding he might so often have destroyed us, does not even compel us to lay down our arms against him, and become his faithful servants and soldiers unto our lives end.

If they have not this effect upon us, we shall, of all men, be most miserable; for God is just, as well as merciful; and the more blessings we have received here, the greater damnation, if we do not improve them, shall we incur hereafter.

But God forbid that any of those should ever suffer the vengeance of eternal fire, amongst whom, I have, for these four months, been preaching the gospel of Christ; but yet thus must it be, if you do not improve the divine mercies: and instead of your being my crown of rejoicing in the day of our Lord Jesus Christ, I must appear as a swift witness against you.

But, brethren, I am persuaded better things of you, and things that accompany salvation, though I thus speak.

Blessed be God, some marks of a partial reformation at least, have been visible amongst all you that are soldiers. And my weak, though sincere endeavors, to build you up in the knowledge and fear of God, have not been altogether in vain in the Lord.

Swearing, I hope is, in a great measure, abated with you; and God, I trust, has blessed his late visitations, by making them the means of awakening your consciences, to a more solicitous inquiry about the things which belong to your everlasting peace.

Fulfill you then my joy, by continuing thus minded, and labor to go on to perfection. For I shall have no greater pleasure than to see, or hear, that you walk in the truth.

Consider, my good friends, you are now, as it were, entering on a new world, where you will be surrounded with multitudes of heathens; and if you take not heed to "have your conversation honest amongst them," and to "walk worthy of the holy vocation wherewith you are called," you will act the hellish part of Herod's soldiers over again; and cause Christ's religion, as they did his person, to be had in derision of those that are round about you.

Consider further, what peculiar privileges you have enjoyed, above many others that are entering on the same land. They have had, as it were, a famine of the word, but you have rather been in danger of being surfeited with your spiritual manna. And, therefore, as more instructions have been given you, so from you, men will most justly expect the greater improvement in goodness.

Indeed, I cannot say, I have discharged my duty towards you as I ought. No, I am sensible of many faults in my ministerial office, and for which I have not failed, nor, I hope, ever shall fail, to humble myself in secret before God. However, this I can say, that except a few days that have been spent necessarily on other persons, whom God immediately called me to write and minister unto, and the two last weeks wherein I have been confined by sickness; all the while I have been aboard, I have been either actually engaged in, or preparing myself for instructing you. And though you are now to be committed to the care of another (whose labors I heartily beseech God to bless amongst you) yet I trust I shall, at all seasons, if need be, willingly spend, and be spent, for the good of your souls, though the more abundantly I love you, the less I should be loved.

As for your military affairs, I have nothing to do with them. Fear God, and you must honor the King. Nor am I well acquainted with the nature of that land which you are now come over to protect; only this I may venture to affirm in the general, that you must necessarily expect upon your arrival at a new colony, to meet with many difficulties. But your very profession teaches you to endure hardship; "be not, therefore, faint- hearted, but quit yourselves like men, and be strong," Numb. 14. Be not like those cowardly persons, who were affrighted at the report of the false spies, that came and said, that there were people tall as the Anakims to be grappled with, but be ye like unto Caleb and Joshua, all heart; and say, we will act valiantly, for we shall be more than conquerors over all difficulties through Jesus Christ that loved us. Above all things, my brethren, take heed, and beware of murmuring, like the perverse Israelites, against those that are set over you; and "learn, whatsoever state you shall be in, therewith to be content," Phil. 4:11.

As I have spoken to you, I hope your wives also will suffer the word of exhortation, Your behavior on shipboard especially the first part of the voyage, I choose to throw a cloak over; for to use them mildest terms, it was not such as became the gospel of our Lord Jesus Christ. However, of late, blessed be God, you have taken more heed to your ways, and some of you have walked all the while, as became "women professing godliness." Let those accept my hearty thanks, and permit me to entreat you all in general, as you are all now married, to remember the solemn vow you made at your entrance into the marriage state, and see that you be subject to your own husbands, in every lawful thing: Beg of God to keep the door of your lips, that you offend not with your tongues; and walk in love, that your prayers be not hindered. You that have children, let it be your chief concern to breed them up in the nurture and admonition of the Lord. And live all of you so holy and unblameable, that you may not so much as be suspected to be unchaste; and as some of you have imitated Mary Magdalen in her sin, strive to imitate her also in her repentance.

As for you, sailors, what shall I say? How shall I address myself to you? How shall I do that which I so much long to do; touch your hearts?

Gratitude obliges me to wish thus well to you. For you have often taught me many instructive lessons, and reminded me to put up many prayers to God for you, that you might receive your spiritual sight.

When I have seen you preparing for a storm, and reefing your sails to guard against it; how have I wished that you and I were as careful to avoid that storm of God's wrath, which will certainly, without repentance, quickly overtake us? When I have observed you catch at ever fair gale, how I secretly cried, O that we were as careful to know the things that belong to our peace, before they are forever hid from our eyes!

And when I have taken notice, how steadily you eyed your compass in order to steer aright, how have I wished, that we as steadily eyed the word of God, which alone can preserve us from "making shipwreck of faith, and a good conscience!" In short, there is scarce anything you do, which has not been a lesson of instruction to me; and, therefore, it would me ungrateful in me, did I not take this opportunity of exhorting you in the name of our Lord Jesus Christ, to be as wise in the things which concern you soul, as I have observed you to be in the affairs belonging to your ship.

I am sensible, that the sea is reckoned but an ill school to learn Christ in: and to see a devout sailor, is esteemed an uncommon a thing, as to see a Saul amongst the prophets. But whence this wondering? Whence this looking upon a godly sailor, as a man to be wondered at, as a speckled bird in the creation? I am sure, for the little time I have come in and out amongst you, and as far as I can judge from the little experience I have had of things, I scarce know any way of life, that is capable of greater improvements than yours.

The continual danger you are in of being overwhelmed by the great waters; the many opportunities you have of beholding God's wonders in the deep; the happy retirement you enjoy from worldly temptations; and the daily occasions that are offered you, to endure hardships, are such noble means of promoting the spiritual life, that were your hearts bent towards God, you would account it your happiest, that his providence has called you, to "go down to the sea in ships, and to occupy your business in the great waters." The royal Psalmist knew this, and, therefore, in the words of the text, calls more especially on men of your employ, to "praise the Lord for his goodness, and declare the wonders he doeth for the children of men." And O that you would be wise in time, and hearken to his voice today, "whilst it is called to-day!" For ye yourselves know how little is to be done on a sick bed. God has, in an especial manner, of late, invited you to repentance: two of your crew he has taken off by death, and most of you he has mercifully visited with a grievous sickness. The terrors of the Lord have been upon you, and when burnt with a scorching fever, some of you have cried out, "What shall w do to be saved?" Remember then the resolutions you made, when you thought God was about to take away your souls; and see that according to your promises, you show forth your thankfulness, not only with your lips, but in your lives. For though God may bear long, he will not forbear always; and if these signal mercies and judgments do not lead you to repentance, assure yourselves there will at last come a fiery tempest, from the presence of the Lord, which will sweep away you, and all other adversaries of God.

I am positive, neither you nor the soldiers have wanted, nor will want any manner of encouragement to piety and holiness of living, from those two persons who have here the government over you; for they have been such helps to me in my ministry, and have so readily concurred in every thing for your good, that they may justly demand a public acknowledgment of thanks both from you and me.

Permit me, my honored friends, in the name of both classes of your people, to return you hearty thanks for the ears and tenderness you have expressed for the welfare of their better parts.

As for the private favors you have shown to my person, I hope so deep a sense of them is imprinted on my heart, that I shall plead them before God in prayer, as long as I live.

But I have still stronger obligations to intercede in your behalf. For God, ever adored be his free grace in Christ Jesus! Has set his seal to my ministry in your hearts. Some distant pangs of the new birth I have observed to come upon you; and God forbid that I should sin against the Lord, by ceasing to pray, that the good work begun in your souls, may be carried on till the day of our Lord Jesus Christ.

The time of our departure from each other is not at hand, and you are going out into a world of temptations. But though absent in body, let us be present with each other in spirit; and God, I trust, will enable you to be singularly good, to be ready to be accounted fools for Christ's sake; and then we shall meet never to part again in the kingdom of our Father which is in heaven.

To you, my companions and familiar friends, who came over with me to sojourn in a strange land, do I in the next place address myself. For you I especially fear, as well as for myself, because as we take sweet counsel together oftner than others, and as you are let into a more intimate friendship with me in private life, the eyes of all men will be upon you to note even the minutest miscarriage; and, therefore, it highly concerns you to "walk circumspectly towards those that are without," I hope, that nothing but a single eye to God's glory and the salvation of your own souls, brought you from your native country. Remember than the end of your coming hither, and you can never do amiss. Be patterns of industry, as well as of piety, to those who shall be around you; and above all things let us have such fervent charity amongst ourselves, that it may be said of us, as of the primitive Christians, "See how the Christians love one another." And now I have been speaking to others particularly, I have one general request to make to all, and that with reference to myself.

You have heard, my dear friends, how I have been exhorting every one of you to show forth your thankfulness for the divine goodness, not only with your lips, but in your lives. But "physician heal thyself," may justly be retorted on me. For (without any false pretenses to humility) I find my own heart so little inclined to this duty of thanksgiving for the benefits I have received, that I had need fear sharing Hezekiah's fate, who because he was lifted up by, and not thankful enough for, the great things God had done for him, was given up a prey to the pride of his own heart.

I need, therefore, and beg your most importunate petitions at the throne of grace, that no such evil may befall me; that the more Go exalts me, the more I may debase myself; and that after I have preached to others, I myself may not be cast away.

And now, brethren, into God's hands I commend your spirits, who, I trust, through his infinite mercies in Christ Jesus, will preserve you blameless, till his second coming to judge the world.

Excuse my detaining you for long; perhaps it is the last time I shall speak to you: my heart is full, and out of the abundance of it, I could continue my discourse until midnight. But I must away to your new world; may God give you new hearts, and enable you to put in practice what you have heard from time to time, to by your duty, and I need not wish you anything better. For then God will so bless you, that "you will build you cities to dwell in; then will you sow your lands and plant vineyards, which will yield you fruits of increase," Psalm 107:37. "Then your oxen shall be strong to labor, there shall be no leading into captivity, and no complaining in your streets; then shall your sons grow up as the young plants, and your daughters be as the polished corners of the temple: then shall your garners be full and plenteous with all manner of store, and your sheep bring forth thousands, and ten thousands in your streets," Psalm 144 In short, then shall the Lord be your God; and as surely as he has now brought us to this haven, where we would be, so surely, after we have past through the storms and tempests of this troublesome world, will he bring us to the haven of eternal rest, where we shall have nothing to do, but to praise him for ever for his goodness, and declare, in never-ceasing songs of praise, the wonders he has done for us, and all the other sons of men.

"To which blessed rest, God of his infinite mercy bring us all, through Jesus Christ our Lord! To whom with the Father and Holy Ghost be all honor and glory, might, majesty, and dominion, now, henceforth, and forevermore. Amen, Amen."

Sermon 8 The Necessity and Benefits of Religious Society

Eccles. 4:9-12, "Two are better than one, because they have a good reward for their labor. For if they fall, the one will lift up his fellow: but woe be to him that is alone when he falleth; for he hath not another to help him up. Again, if two lie together, then they have heat; but how can one be warm alone? And if one prevail against him, two shall withstand him; and a threefold cord is not quickly broken.

Among the many reasons assignable for the sad decay of true Christianity, perhaps the neglecting to assemble ourselves together, in religious societies, may not be one of the least. That I may therefore do my endeavor towards promoting so excellent a means of piety, I have selected a passage of scripture drawn from the experience of the wisest of men, which being a little enlarged on and illustrated, will fully answer my present design; being to show, in the best manner I can, the necessity and benefits of society in general, and of religious society in particular.

"Two are better than one, etc." From which words I shall take occasion to prove, FIRST, The truth of the wise man's assertion, "Two are better than one," and that in reference to society in general, and religious society in particular.

SECONDLY, To assign some reasons why two are better than one, especially as to the last particular. 1. Because men can raise up one another when they chance to slip: "For if they fall, the one will lift up his fellow." 2. Because they can impart heat to each other: "Again, if tow lie together, then they have heat, but how can one be warm alone?" 3.

Because they can secure each other from those that do oppose them: "And if one prevail against him, two shall withstand him; and a threefold cord is not quickly broken." From hence, THIRDLY, I shall take occasion to show the duty incumbent on every member of a religious society.

And FOURTHLY, I shall draw an inference or two from what may be said; and then conclude with a word or two of exhortation.

FIRST, I am to prove the truth of the wise man's assertion, that "two are better than one," and that in reference to society in general, and religious societies in particular.

And how can this be done better, than by showing that it is absolutely necessary for the welfare both of the bodies and souls of men? Indeed, if we look upon man as he came out of the hands of his Maker, we imagine him to be perfect, entire, lacking nothing. But God, whose thoughts are not as our thoughts, saw something still wanting to make Adam happy. And what was that? Why, and help meet for him. For thus speaketh the scripture: "And the Lord God said, It is not good that the man should be alone, I will make an help meet for him." Observe, God said, "It is not good," thereby implying that the creation would have been imperfect, in some sort, unless an help was found out meet for Adam. And if this was the case of man before the fall; if an help was meet for him in a state of perfection; surely since the fall, when we come naked and helpless out of our mother's womb, when our wants increase with our years, and we can scarcely subsist a day without the mutual assistance of each other, well may we say, "It is not good for man to be alone." Society then, we see, is absolutely necessary in respect to our bodily and personal wants. If we carry our view farther, and consider mankind as divided into different cities, countries, and nations, the necessity of it will appear yet more evident. For how can communities be kept up, or commerce carried on, without society? Certainly not at all, since providence seems wisely to have assigned a particular product to almost each particular country, on purpose, as it were, to oblige us to be social; and hath so admirably mingled the parts of the whole body of mankind together, "that the eye cannot say to the hand, I have no need of thee; nor again, the hand to the foot, I have no need of thee." Many other instances might be given of the necessity of society, in reference to our bodily, personal, and national wants. But what are all these when weighed in the balance of the sanctuary, in comparison of the infinite greater need of it, with respect to the soul? It was chiefly in regard to this better part, no doubt, that God said, "It is not good for the man to be alone." For, let us suppose Adam to be as happy as may be, placed as the Lord of the creation in the paradise of God, and spending all his hours in adoring and praising the blessed Author of his being; yet as his soul was the very copy of the divine nature, whose peculiar property it is to be communicative, without the divine all sufficiency he could not be completely happy, because he was alone and incommunicative, nor even content in paradise, for want of a partner in his joys. God knew this, and therefore said, "It is not good that the man shall be alone, I will make a help meet for him." And though this proved a fatal means of his falling; yet that was not owing to any natural consequence of society; but partly to that cursed apostate, who craftily lies in wait to deceive; partly to Adam's own folly, in rather choosing to be miserable with one he loved, than trust in God to raise him up another spouse.

If we reflect indeed on that familiar intercourse, our first parent could carry on with heaven, in a state of innocence, we shall be apt to think he had as little need of society, as to his soul, as before we supposed him to have, in respect to his body. But yet, as God and the holy angels were so far above him on the one hand, and the beasts so far beneath him on the other, there was nothing like having one to converse with, who was "bone of his bone, and flesh of his flesh." Man, then, could not be fully happy, we see, even in paradise, without a companion of his own species, much less now he is driven out. For, let us view him a little in his natural estate now, since the fall, as "having his understanding darkened, his mind alienated from the life of God;" as no more able to see his way wherein he should go, than a blind man to describe the sun: that notwithstanding this, he must receive his sight ere he can see God: and that if he never sees him, he never can be happy. Let us view him in this light (or rather than darkness) and deny the necessity of society if we can. A divine revelation we find is absolutely necessary, we being by nature as unable to know, as we are to do our duty. And how shall we learn except one teach us? But was God to do this himself, how should we, but with Moses, exceedingly quake and fear? Nor would the ministry of angels in this affair, be without too much terror. It is necessary, therefore (at least God's dealing with us hath showed it to be so) that we should be drawn with the cords of a man. And that a divine revelation being granted, we should use one another's assistance, under God, to instruct each other in the knowledge, and to exhort one another to the practice of those things which belong to our everlasting peace. This is undoubtedly the great end of society intended by God since the fall, and a strong argument it is, why "two are better than one," and why we should "not forsake the assembling ourselves together." But further, let us consider ourselves as Christians, as having this natural veil, in some measure, taken off from our eyes by the assistance of God's Holy Spirit, and so enabled to see what he requires of us. Let us suppose ourselves in some degree to have tasted the good word of life, and to have felt the powers of the world to come, influencing and molding our souls into a religious frame: to be fully and heartily convinced that we are soldiers lifted under the banner of Christ, and to have proclaimed open war at our baptism, against the world, the flesh, and the devil; and have, perhaps, frequently renewed our obligations so to do, by partaking of the Lord's supper: that we are surrounded with millions of foes without, and infected with a legion of enemies within: that we are commanded to shine as lights in the world, in the midst of a crooked and perverse generation: that we are traveling to a long eternity, and need all imaginable helps to show, and encourage us in our way thither. Let us, I say, reflect on all this, and then how shall each of us cry out, brethren, what a necessary thing it is to meet together in religious societies?

The primitive Christians were fully sensible of this, and therefore we find them continually keeping up communion with each other: for what says the scripture? They continued steadfastly in the apostle's doctrine and fellowship, Acts 2:42. Peter and John were no sooner dismissed by the great council, than they haste away to their companions. "And being set at liberty they came to their own, and told them all these things which the high priest had said unto them," Acts 4:23. Paul, as soon as converted, "tarried three days with the disciples that were at Damascus." Acts 9:19.

And Peter afterwards, when released from prison, immediately goes to the house of Mary, where there were "great multitudes assembled, praying," Acts 12:12. And it is reported of the Christians in after ages, that they used to assemble together before day-light, to sing a psalm to Christ as God. So precious was the Communion of Saints in those days.

If it be asked, what advantages we shall reap from such a procedure now? I answer, much every way. "Two are better than one, because they have a good reward for their labor: for if they fall, the one will lift up his fellow; but woe be to him that is alone when he falleth, for he hath not another to help him up. Again, if two lie together, then they have heat; but how can one be warm alone? And if one prevail against him, two shall withstand him; and a threefold cord is not quickly broken." Which directly leads me to my SECOND general head, under which I was to assign some reasons why "two are better than one," especially in Religious Society.

1. As man in his present condition cannot always stand upright, but by reason of the frailty of his nature cannot but fall; one eminent reason why two are better than one, or, in other words, one great advantage of religious society is, "That when they fall, the one will lift up his fellow." And an excellent reason this, indeed! For alas! When we reflect how prone we are to be drawn into error in our judgments, and into vice in our practice; and how unable, at least how very unwilling, to espy or correct our own miscarriages; when w consider how apt the world is to flatter us in our faults, and how few there are so kind as to tell us the truth; what an inestimable privilege must it be to have a set of true, judicious, hearty friends about us, continually watching over our souls, to inform us where we have fallen, and to warn us that we fall not again for the future.

Surely it is such a privilege, that (to use the words of an eminent Christian) we shall never know the value thereof, till we come to glory.

But this is not all; for supposing that we could always stand upright, yet whosoever reflects on the difficulties of religion in general, and his own propensity to lukewarmness and indifference in particular, will find that he must be zealous as well as steady, if ever he expects to enter the kingdom of heaven. Here, then, the wise man points out to us another excellent reason why two are better than one. "Again, if two lie together, then they have heat; but how can one be warm alone?" Which was the next thing to be considered.

2. A Second reason why two are better than one, is because they can impart heat to each other.

It is an observation no less true than common, that kindled coals, if placed asunder, soon go out, but if heaped together, quicken and enliven each other, and afford a lasting heat. The same will hold good in the case now before us. If Christians kindled by the grace of God, unite, they will quicken and enliven each other; but if they separate and keep asunder, no marvel if they soon grow cool or tepid. If two are three meet together in Christ's name, they will have heat: but how can one be warm alone?

Observe, "How can one be warm alone?" The wise man's expressing himself by way of question, implies an impossibility, at least a very great difficulty, to be warm in religion without company, where it may be had.

Behold here, then, another excellent benefit flowing from religious society; it will keep us zealous, as well as steady, in the way of godliness.

But to illustrate this a little farther by a comparison or two. Let us look upon ourselves (as was above hinted) as soldiers listed under Christ's banner; as going out with "ten thousand, to meet one that cometh against us with twenty thousand;" as persons that are to "wrestle not only with flesh and blood, but against principalities, against powers, and spiritual wickednesses in high places." And then tell me, all ye that fear God, if it be not an invaluable privilege to have a company of fellow soldiers continually about us, animating and exhorting each other to stand our ground, to keep our ranks, and manfully to follow the captain of our salvation, though it be through a sea of blood?

Let us consider ourselves in another view before mentioned, as persons traveling to a long eternity; as rescued by the free grace of God, in some measure, from our natural Egyptian bondage, and marching under the conduct of our spiritual Joshua, through the wilderness of this world, to the land of our heavenly Canaan. Let us farther reflect how apt we are to startle at every difficulty; to cry, "There are lions! There are lions in the way!

There are the sons of Anak" to be grappled with, ere we can possess the promised land. How prone we are, with Lot's wife, to look wishfully back on our spiritual Sodom, or, with the foolish Israelites, to long again for the flesh-pots of Egypt; and to return to our former natural state of bondage and slavery. Consider this, my brethren, and see what a blessed privilege it will be to have a set of Israelites indeed about us, always reminding us of the folly of any such cowardly design, and of the intolerable misery we shall run into, if we fall in the least short of the promised land.

More might be said on this particular, did not the limits of a discourse of this nature oblige me to hasten, 3. To give a third reason, mentioned by the wise man in the text, why two are better than one; because they can secure each other from enemies without. "And if one prevail against him, yet two shall withstand him: and a threefold cord is not quickly broken." Hitherto we have considered the advantages of religious societies, as a great preservative against falling (at least dangerously falling) into sin and lukewarmness, and that too from our own corruptions. But what says the wise son of Sirach? "My son, when thou goest to serve the Lord, prepare thy soul for temptation:" and that not only from inward, but outward foes; particularly from those two grand adversaries, the world and the devil: for no sooner will thine eye be bent heavenward, but the former will be immediately diverting it another way, telling thee thou needest not be singular in order to be religious; that you may be a Christian without going so much out of the common road.

Nor will the devil be wanting in his artful insinuations, or impious suggestions, to divert or terrify thee from pressing forwards, "that thou mayst lay hold on the crown of life." And if he cannot prevail this way, he will try another; and, in order to make his temptation the more undiscerned, but withal more successful, he will employ, perhaps, some of thy nearest relatives, or most powerful friends, (as he set Peter on our blessed Master) who will always be bidding thee to spare thyself; telling thee thou needest not take so much pain; that it is not so difficult a matter to get to heaven as some people would make of it, nor the way so narrow as others imagine it to be.

But see here the advantage of religious company; for supposing thou findest thyself thus surrounded on every side, and unable to withstand such horrid (though seemingly friendly) counsels, haste away to thy companions, and they will teach thee a truer and better lesson; they will tell thee, that thou must be singular if thou wilt be religious; and that it is as impossible for a Christian, as for a city set upon a hill, to be hidden: that if thou wilt be an almost Christian (and as good be none at all) thou mayest live in the same idle, indifferent manner as thou seest most other people do: but if thou wilt be not only almost, but altogether a Christian, they will inform thee thou must go a great deal farther: that thou must not only faintly seek, but "earnestly strive to enter in at the strait gate:" that there is but one way now to heaven as formerly, even through the narrow passage of a sound conversion: and that in order to bring about this mighty work, thou must undergo a constant, but necessary discipline of fasting, watching, and prayer. And therefore, the only reason why those friends give thee such advice, is, because they are not willing to take to much pains themselves; or, as our Savior told Peter on a like occasion, because they "savor not the things that be of God, but the things that be of men." This then, is another excellent blessing arising from religious society, that friends can hereby secure each other from those who oppose them. The devil is fully sensible of this, and therefore he has always done his utmost to suppress, and put a stop to the communion of saints. This was his grand artifice at the first planting of the gospel; to persecute the professors of it, in order to separate them. Which, though God, as he always will, over-ruled for the better; yet, it shows, what an enmity he has against Christians assembling themselves together. Nor has he yet left off his old stratagem; it being his usual way to entice us by ourselves, in order to tempt us; where, by being destitute of one another's help, he hopes to lead us captive at his will.

But, on the contrary, knowing his own interest is strengthened by society, he would first persuade us to neglect the communion of saints, and then bid us "stand in the way of sinners," hoping thereby to put us into the seat of the scornful. Judas and Peter are melancholy instances of this.

The former had no sooner left his company at supper, but he went out and betrayed his master: and the dismal downfall of the latter, when he would venture himself amongst a company of enemies, plainly shows us what the devil will endeavor to, when he gets us by ourselves. Had Peter kept his own company, he might have kept his integrity; but a single cord, alas! how quickly was it broken? Our blessed Savior knew this full well, and therefore it is very observable, that he always sent out his disciples "two by two." And now, after so many advantages to be reaped from religious society, may we not very justly cry out with the wise man in my text, "Woe be to him that is alone; for when he falleth, he hath not another to lift him up!" When he is cold, he hath not a friend to warm him; when he is assaulted, he hath not a second to help him to withstand his enemy.

III. I now come to my third general head, under which was to be shown the sever duties incumbent on every member of a religious society, as such, which are three. 1. Mutual reproof; 2. Mutual exhortation; 3. Mutual assisting and defending each other.

1. Mutual reproof. "Two are better than one; for when they fall, the one will lift up his fellow." Now, reproof may be taken either in a more extensive sense, and then it signifies our raising a brother by the gentlest means,

when he falls into sin and error; or in a more restrained signification, as reaching no farther than whose miscarriages, which unavoidably happen in the most holy men living.

The wise man, in the text supposes all of us subject to both: "For when they fall (thereby implying that each of us may fall) the one will lift up his fellow." From whence we may infer, that "when any brother is overtaken with a fault, he that is spiritual (that is, regenerate, and knows the corruption and weakness of human nature) ought to restore such a one in the spirit of meekness." And why he should do so, the apostle subjoins a reason "considering thyself, lest thou also be tempted;" i.e. considering thy own frailty, lest thou also fall by the like temptation.

We are all frail unstable creatures; and it is merely owing to the free grace and good providence of God that we run not into the same excess of riot with other men. Every offending brother, therefore, claims our pity rather than our resentment; and each member should strive to be the most forward, as well as most gentle, in restoring him to his former state.

But supposing a person not to be overtaken, but to fall willfully into a crime; yet who art thou that deniest forgiveness to thy offending brother? "Let him that standeth take heed lest he fall." Take ye, brethren, the holy apostles as eminent examples for you to learn by, how you ought to behave in this matter. Consider how quickly they joined the right hand of fellowship with Peter, who had so willfully denied his master: for we find John and him together but two days after, John 20:2. And ver. 19, we find him assembled with the rest. So soon did they forgive, so soon associate with their sinful, yet relenting brother. "Let us go and do likewise." But there is another kind of reproof incumbent on every member of a religious society; namely, a gentle rebuke for some miscarriage or other, which though not actually sinful, yet may become the occasion of sin. This indeed seems a more easy, but perhaps will be found a more difficult point than the former: for when a person has really sinned, he cannot but own his brethren's reproof to be just; whereas, when it was only for some little misconduct, the pride that is in our natures will scarce suffer us to brook (endure, tolerate) it. But however ungrateful this pill may be to our brother, yet if we have any concern for his welfare, it must be administered by some friendly hand or other. By all means then let it be applied; only, like a skillful physician, gild over the ungrateful pill, and endeavor, if possible, to deceive thy brother into health and soundness. "Let all bitterness, and wrath, and malice, and evil speaking, be put away" from it. Let the patient know, his recovery is the only thing aimed at, and that thou delightest not causelessly to grieve thy brother; then thou canst not want success.

2. Mutual exhortation is the second duty resulting from the words of the text. "Again, if two lie together, then they have heat." Observe, the wise man supposes it as impossible for religious persons to meet together, and not to be the warmer for each other's company, as for two persons to lie in the same bed, and yet freeze with cold. But now, how is it possible to communicate heat to each other, without mutually stirring up the gift of God which is in us, by brotherly exhortation? Let every member then of a religious society write that zealous apostle's advice on the tables of his heart; "See that ye exhort, and provoke one another to love, and to good works; and so much the more, as you see the day of the Lord approaching." Believe me, brethren, we have need of exhortation to rouse up our sleepy souls, to set us upon our watch against the temptations of the world, the flesh, and the devil; to excite us to renounce ourselves, to take up our crosses, and follow our blessed master, and the glorious company of saints and martyrs, "who through faith have fought the good fight, and are gone before us to inherit the promises." A third part, therefore, of the time wherein a religious society meets, seems necessary to be spent in this important duty: for what avails it to have our understandings enlightened by pious reading, unless our wills are at the same time inclined, and inflamed by mutual exhortation, to put it in practice? Add also, that this is the best way both to receive and impart light, and the only means to preserve and increase that warmth and heat which each person first brought with him; God so ordering this, as all other spiritual gifts, that "to him that hath, i.e. improves and communicates what he hath, shall be given; but from him that hath not, or does not improve the heat he hath, shall be taken away even that which he seemed to have." So needful, so essentially necessary, is exhortation to the good of society.

3. Thirdly, The text points out another duty incumbent on every member of a religious society, to defend each other from those that do oppose them. "And if one prevail against him, yet two shall withstand him; and a threefold cord is not quickly broken." Here the wise man takes it for granted, that offenses will come, nay , and that they may prevail too. And this is not more than our blessed master has long since told us. Not, indeed, that there is any thing in Christianity itself that has the least tendency to give rise to, or promote such offenses: No, on the contrary, it breathes nothing but unity and love.

But so it is, that ever since the fatal sentence pronounced by God, after our first parents fall, "I will put enmity between thy seed and her seed;" he that is born after the flesh, the unregenerate unconverted sinner, has in all ages "persecuted him that is born after the spirit:" and so it always will be. Accordingly we find an early proof given of this in the instance of Cain and Abel; of Ishmael and Isaac; and of Jacob and Esau.

And, indeed, the whole Bible contains little else but an history of the great and continued opposition between the children of this world, and the children of God. The first Christians were remarkable examples of this; and though those troublesome time, blessed be God, are now over, yet the apostle has laid it down as a general rule, and all who are sincere experimentally prove the truth of it; that "they that will live godly in Christ Jesus, must (to the end of the world, in some degree or other) suffer persecution." That therefore this may not make us desert our blessed master's cause, every member should unite their forces in order to stand against it. And for the better effecting this, each would do well, from time to time, to communicate his experiences, grievances, and temptations, and beg his companions (first asking God's assistance, without which all is nothing) to administer reproof, exhortation, or comfort, as his case requires: so that "if one cannot prevail against it, yet two shall withstand it; and a threefold (much less a many-fold) cord will not be quickly broken." IV. But it is time for me to proceed to the fourth general thing proposed, to draw an inference or two from what has been said.

1. And first, if "two are better than one," and the advantages of religious society are so many and so great; then it is the duty of every true Christian to set on foot, establish and promote, as much as in him lies, societies of this nature. And I believe we may venture to affirm, that if ever a spirit of true Christianity is revived in the world, it must be brought about by some such means as this. Motive, surely, cannot be wanting, to stir us up to the commendable and necessary undertaking: for, granting all hitherto advanced to be of no force, yet methinks the single consideration, that great part of our happiness in heaven will consist in the Communion of Saints; or that the interest as well as piety of those who differ from us, is strengthened and supported by nothing more than their frequent meetings; either of these considerations, I say, one would think, should induce us to do our utmost to copy after their good example, and settle a lasting and pious communion of the saints on earth. Add to this, that we find the kingdom of darkness established daily by such like means; and shall not the kingdom of Christ be set in opposition against it? Shall the children of Belial assemble and strengthen each other in wickedness; and shall not the children of God unite, and strengthen themselves in piety? Shall societies on societies be countenanced for midnight revelings, and the promoting of vice, and scarcely one be found intended for the propagation of virtue? Be astonished, O heavens at this!

2. But this leads me to a second inference; namely, to warn persons of the great danger those are in, who either by their subscriptions, presence, or approbation, promote societies of a quite opposite nature to religion.

And here I would not be understood, to mean only those public meetings which are designed manifestly for nothing else but revellings and banquetings, for chambering and wantonness, and at which a modest heathen would blush to be present; but also those seemingly innocent entertainments and meetings, which the politer part of the world are so very fond of, and spend so much time in: but which, notwithstanding, keep as many persons from a sense of true religion, as doth intemperance, debauchery, or any other crimes whatever. Indeed, whilst we are in this world, we must have proper relaxations, to fit us both for the business of our profession, and religion. But then, for persons who call themselves Christians, that have solemnly vowed at their baptism, to renounce the vanities of this sinful world; that are commanded in scripture "to abstain from all appearance of evil, and to have their conversation in heaven:" for such persons as these to support meetings, which (to say no worse of them) are vain and trifling, and have a natural tendency to draw off our minds from God, is absurd, ridiculous, and sinful. Surely two are not better than one in this case: No; it is to be wished there was not one to be found concerned in it. The sooner we forsake the assembling ourselves together in such a manner, the better; and no matte how quickly the cord that hold such societies (was it a thousand-fold) is broken.

But you, brethren, have not so learned Christ: but, on the contrary, like true disciples of your Lord and Master, have by the blessing of God (as this evening's solemnity abundantly testifies) happily formed yourselves into such societies, which, if duly attended on, and improved, cannot but strengthen you in your Christian warfare, and "make you fruitful in every good word and work." What remains for me, but, as was proposed, in the first place, to close what has been said, in a word or two, by way of exhortation, and to beseech you, in the name of our Lord Jesus Christ, to go on in the way you have begun; and by a constant conscientious attendance on your respective societies, to discountenance vice, encourage virtue, and build each other up in the knowledge and fear of God.

Only permit me to "stir up your pure minds, by way of remembrance," and to exhort you, "if there be any consolation in Christ, any fellowship of the spirit," again and again to consider, that as all Christians in general, so all members of religious societies in particular, are in an especial manner, as houses built upon an hill; and that therefore it highly concerns you to walk circumspectly towards those that are without, and to take heed to yourselves, that your conversation, in common life, be as becometh such an open and peculiar profession of the gospel of Christ: knowing that the eyes of all men are upon you, narrowly to inspect every circumstance of your behavior: and that every notorious willful miscarriage of any single member will, in some measure, redound to the scandal and dishonor of your whole fraternity.

Labor, therefore, my beloved brethren, to let your practice correspond to your profession: and think not that it will be sufficient for you to plead at the last day, Lord have we not assembled ourselves together in thy name, and enlivened each other, by singing psalms, and hymns, and spiritual songs? For verily, I say unto you, notwithstanding this, our blessed Lord will bid you depart from him; nay, you shall receive a great damnation, if, in the mists of these great pretensions, you are found to be workers of iniquity.

But God forbid that any such evil should befall you; that there should be ever a Judas, a traitor, amongst such distinguished followers of our common master. No, on the contrary, the excellency of your rule, the regularity of your meetings, and more especially your pious zeal in assembling in such a public and solemn manner so frequently in the year, persuade me to think, that you are willing, not barely to seem, but to be in reality, Christians; and hope to be found at the last day, what you would be esteemed now, holy, sincere disciples of a crucified Redeemer.

Oh, may you always continue thus minded! And make it your daily, constant endeavor, both by precept and example, to turn all your converse with, more especially those of your own societies, into the same most blessed spirit and temper. Thus will you adorn the gospel of our Lord Jesus Christ in all things: Thus will you anticipate the happiness of a future state; and by attending on, and improving the communion of stints on earth, be made meet to join the communion and fellowship of the spirits of just men made perfect, of the holy angels, nay, of the ever blessed and eternal God in heaven.

Which God of his infinite mercy grant through Jesus Christ our Lord; to whom with the Father and the Holy Ghost, three persons and one God, be ascribed, as is most due, all honor and praise, might, majesty and dominion, now and for ever. Amen.

Sermon 9 The Folly and Danger of Being Not Righteous Enough

Ecclesiastes 7:16, "Be not righteous overmuch, neither make thyself over- wise: why shouldst thou destroy thyself?"

Nothing is more frequent, than while people are living in a course of sin, and after the fashion and manner of the world, there is not notice taken of them; neither are their ways displeasing to their companions and carnal relations: but if they set their faces Zion-ward, and begin to feel the power of God on their hearts; they then are surrounded with temptations from their friends, who thus act the devil's part. The enemies, the greatest enemies a young convert meets with, my dear brethren, are those of his own house. They that will be godly, must suffer persecution; so it was in Christ" time, and so it was in the Apostles time too; for our Lord came not to send peace, but a sword. Our relations would not have us sit in the scorner's chair; they would not have us be prodigals, consuming our substance upon harlots; neither would they have us rakes (a dissolute person) or libertines, but they would have us be contented with an almost Christianity. To keep up our reputation by going to church, and adhering to the outward forms of religion, saying our prayers, reading the word of God, and taking the sacraments; this, they imagine, is all that is necessary for to be Christians indeed; and when we go one step farther than this, their mouths are open against us, as Peter's was to Christ: "Spare thyself, do thyself no harm." And of this nature are the words of the text. They are not the words of Solomon himself, but the words of an infidel speaking to him, whom he introduces in several parts of this book; for Solomon had been showing the misfortunes which attended the truly good, as in the verse before our text.

Upon this the infidel says, "Be not righteous over-much, neither be thou over-wise; why shouldst thou destroy thyself?" i.e. Why shouldst thou bring these misfortunes upon thyself, by being over strict? Be not righteous over-much; eat, drink, and be merry, live as the world lives, and then you will avoid those misfortunes which may attend you, by being righteous over-much.

This text has another meaning; but take it which way you will, by brethren, it was spoken by an unbeliever; therefore it was no credit for the person who lately preached upon this text, to take it for granted, that these were the words of Solomon: the words of an infidel was not a proper text to a Christian congregation. But as David came out against Goliath, not armed as the champion was, with sword and spear, but with a sling and stone, and then cut off his head with his own sword; so I come out against these letter-learned men, in the strength of the Lord Jesus Christ; and, my dear brethren, I trust he will direct me to use my sling, so9 that our enemies may not gainsay us; and by the sword of God's word, cut off the heads of our Redeemer's enemies.

But though they are not the words of Solomon, yet we will take them in the same manner the late writer did; and, from the words, shall, FIRST, Show you what it is, not to be righteous over-much, that we may not destroy ourselves.

SECONDLY, I shall let you see what it is to be righteous over-much.

And then, THIRDLY, Conclude with an exhortation to all of you, high and low, rich and poor, one with another, to come to the Lord Jesus Christ.

FIRST, The first thing proposed, is to show you what it is not to be righteous over-much. And here, It is by no means to be righteous over-much, to affirm we must have the same Spirit of God as the first Apostles had, and must feel that Spirit upon our hearts.

By receiving the Spirit of God, is not to be understood, that we are to be inspired to show outward signs and wonders, to raise dead bodies, to cure leprous persons, or to give sight to the blind: these miracles were only of use in the first ages of the church; and therefore Christians (nominal Christians, for we have little else but the name) may have all the gifts of the Spirit, and yet none of the graces of it. Thou, O man, mayest be enabled by faith to remove mountains; thou, by the power of God, mayest cast out devils; thou, by that power, mayest speak with the tongues of men and angels; yes, thou mayest, by that power, hold up thy finger and stop the sun in the firmament; and if all these are unsanctified by the Spirit of God, they would be of no service to thee, but would hurry thee to hell with the greater solemnity. Saul received the spirit of prophesying, and had another heart, yet Saul was probably a cast-away. We must receive the Spirit of God in its sanctifying graces upon our souls; for Christ says, "Unless a man be born again, he cannot see the kingdom of God." We are all by nature born in sin, and at as great a distance from God, as the devils themselves. I have told you often, and now tell you again, that you are by nature a motley mixture of the beast and devil, and we cannot recover ourselves from the state wherein we have fallen, therefore must be renewed by the Holy Ghost. By the Holy Ghost, I mean, the third Person of the ever blessed Trinity, co-equal, co-essential, co-eternal, and con-substantial with the Father and the Son; and therefore, when we are baptized, it is into the nature of the Father, into the nature of the Son, and into the nature of the Holy Ghost: and we are not true Christians, till we are sanctified by the Spirit of God.

Though our modern preachers do not actually deny the Spirit of God, yet they say, "Christians must not feel him;" which is in effect to deny him. When Nicodemus came to Christ, and the Lord Jesus was instructing him, concerning the new birth, says he to our Lord, "How can these things be?" Nicodemus, though a master of Israel, acts just as our learned Rabbi's do now. The answer that Christ gave him should stop the mouths of our letter-learned Pharisees: "The wind bloweth where it listeth, and we hear the sound thereof, but cannot tell whence it cometh, nor whither it goeth." Now till the Spirit of God is felt on our souls as the wind on our bodies, indeed, my dear brethren, you have no interest in him: religion consists not in external per-formance, it must be in the heart, or else it is only a name, which cannot profit us, a name to live whilst we are dead.

A late preacher upon this text, seems to laugh at us, for talking of the Spirit in a sensible manner, and talks to us as the Jews did to Christ: They said, "How can this man give us his flesh to eat?" So he asks, "What sign or proof do we give of it?" We do not imagine, that God must appear to us, and give it us: no; but there may be, and is, a frequent receiving, when no seeing of it; and it is as plainly felt in the soul, as any impression is, or can be, upon the body. To what a damnable condition should we bring poor sinners, if they could not be sensible of the Spirit of God; namely, a reprobate mind and past feeling?

"What proof do they give?" says the writer. What sign would they have?

Do they expect us to raise the dead, to give sight to the blind, to cure lepers, to make the lame to walk, and the deaf to hear? If these are what they expect, I speak with humility, God, by us, hath done greater things than these: many, who were dead in sin, are raised to scripture-life: those, who were leprous by nature, are cleansed by the Spirit of God; those, who were lame in duty, not run in God's commands; those, who were deaf, their ears are unstopped to hear his discipline, and hearken to his advice; and the poor have the gospel preached to them. No wonder people talk at this rate, when they can tell us, "That the Spirit of God, is a good conscience, consequent there-upon." My dear brethren, Seneca, Cicera, Plato, or any of the heathen philosophers, would have given as good a definition as this. It means no more, than reflecting that we have done well. This, this is only Deism refined: Deists laugh at us, when we pretend to be against notions, and yet these men use no other reason for our differing from them, than what is agreeable to Deists principles.

This writer tell us, "It is against common-sense to talk of the feeling of the Spirit of God." Common-sense, my brethren, was never allowed to be a judge; yea, it is above its comprehension, neither are, nor can the ways of God be known by common-sense. We should never have known the things of God at all by our common sense: no; it is the revelation of God which is to be our judge; it is that we appeal to, and not to our weak and shallow concep-tions of things. Thus we may see, it is by no means to be righteous over-much, to affirm we must have the Spirit of God as the Apostles had.

Nor, SECONDLY, Is it to be righteous over-much to frequent reli-gious assemblies.

The preacher, upon this text, aims at putting aside all the religious societies that are in the kingdom: Indeed, he says, "You may go to church as often as opportunity serves, and on Sundays; say your prayers, read the word of God; and, in his opinion, every thing else had better be let alone: and as for the Spirit of God upon your souls, you are to look upon it as useless and un-necessary." If this, my brethren, is the doctrine we have now preached, Christianity is at a low ebb indeed; but God forbid you should thus learn Je-sus Christ. Do you not forbear the frequenting of religious assemblies; for as nothing helps to build up the devil's kingdom more than the societies of wicked men, nothing would be more for pulling of it down, than the people of God meeting to strengthen each others hands; and as the devil has so many friends, will none of you be friends to the blessed Jesus? Yes, I hope many of you will be of the Lord's side, and build each other up in Christian love and fellowship. This is what the primitive Christians delighted in; and shall not we follow so excellent an example?

My brethren, till Christian conversation is more agreeable to us, we cannot expect to see the gospel of Christ run and be glorified. Thus it is by no means to be righteous over-much, to frequent religious assemblies. Nor, THIRDLY, Is it to be righteous over-much, to abstain from the diversions and entertainments of the age.

We are commanded to "abstain from the appearance of evil," and that "whatsoever we do, whether we eat or drink, we shall do all to the glory of God." The writer upon this text tells us, "That it will be accounted unlawful to smell to a rose:" no, my dear brethren, you man smell to a pink and rose too if you please, but take care to avoid the appearance of sin.

They talk of innocent diversions and recreations; for my part, I know of no diversion, but that of doing good: if you can find any diversion which is not contrary to your baptismal vow, of renouncing the pomps and vanities of this wicked world; if you can find any diversion which tends to the glory of God; if you can find any diversion, which you would be willing to be found at by the Lord Jesus Christ, I give you free license to go to them and welcome; but if, on the contrary, they are found to keep sinners from coming to the Lord Jesus Christ; if they are a means to harden the heart, and such as you would not willingly be found in when you come to die, then, my dear brethren, keep from them: for, indeed, the diversions of this age are contrary to Christianity. Many of you may think I have gone too far, but I shall go a great deal farther yet: I will attack the devil in his strongest holds, and bear my testimony against our fashionable and polite entertainments. What satisfaction can it be, what pleasure is there in spending several hours at cards? Strange! That even people who are grown old, can spend whole nights in this diversion: perhaps many of you will cry out, "What harm is there in it?" My dear brethren, whatsoever is not of faith, or for the glory of God, is a sin. Now does cards tend to promote this? Is it not mispending your precious time, which should be employed in working out your salvation with fear and trembling? Do play-houses, horse- racing, balls and assemblies, tend to promote the glory of God? Would you be willing to have your soul demanded of you, while you are at one of those places? Many of these are, (I must speak, I cannot forbear to speak against these entertainments; come what will, I will declare against them) many, I say, of these are kept up by public authority; the play-houses are supported by a public fund, and our newspapers are full of horse-races all through the kingdom: these things are sinful; indeed they are exceeding sinful. What good can come from a horse-race; from abusing God Almighty's creatures, and putting them to that use he never designed for them: the play-houses, are they not nurseries of debauchery in the age? And the supporters and patrons of them, are encouragers and promoters of all the evil that is done by them; they are the bane of the age, and will be the destruction of those who frequent them. Is it not high time for the true ministers of Jesus Christ, who have been partakers of the heavenly gift, to lift up their voices as a trumpet, and cry aloud against these diversions of the age? Are they not earthly, sensual, devilish? If you have tasted of the love of God, and have felt his power upon your souls, you would no more go to a play, than you would run your head into a furnace.

And what occasions these place to be so much frequented, is the clergy's making no scruple to be at these polite places: they frequent play-houses, they go to horse-races, they go to balls and assemblies, they frequent taverns, and follow all the entertainments that the age affords; and yet these are the persons who should advise their hearers to refrain from them; but instead thereof, they encourage them by their example.

Persons are too apt to rely upon, and believe their pastors, rather than the scriptures; they think that there is no crime in going to plays or horse-races, to balls and assemblies; for if there were, they think those persons, who are their ministers, would not frequent them: but, my dear brethren, observe they always go disguised, the ministers are afraid of being seen in their gowns and cassocks; the reason thereof is plain, their consciences inform them, that it is not an example fit for the ministers of the gospel to set; thus, they are the means of giving that offense to the people of God, which I would not for ten thousand worlds: they lay a stumbling-block in the way of their weak brethren, which they will not remove, though it is a stumbling-block of offense. "Woe unto the world because of offenses, but woe unto that man by whom the offense cometh." The polite gentlemen of the age, spend their time in following those diversions, because the love of God is not in their hearts; they are void of Christ, and destitute of the Spirit of God; and not being acquainted with the delight there is in God and his ways, being strangers to these things, they run to the devil for diversions, and are pleased and delighted with the silly ones he shows them.

My dear brethren, I speak of these things, these innocent diversions, as the polite part of the world calls them, by experience; perhaps none, for my age, hath read or seen more plays than I have: I took delight in, and was pleased with them. It is true, I went to church frequently, received the sacrament, and was diligent in the use of the forms of religion, but I was all this while ignorant of the power of God on my heart, and unacquainted with the work of grace; but when God was pleased to shine with power upon my soul, I could no longer be contented to feed on husks, or what the swine die eat; the Bible then was my food; there, and there only I took delight: and till you feel this same power, you will not abstain from the earthly delights of this age, you will take no comfort in God's ways, nor receive any comfort from him; for you are void of the love of God, having only the form of godliness, while you are denying the power of it; you are nominal Christians, when you have not the power of Christianity.

The polite gentlemen say, "Are we to be always upon our knees? Would you have us be always at prayer, and reading or hearing the word of God?" My dear brethren, the fashionable ones, who take delight in hunting, are not tired of being continually on horseback after their hounds; and when once you are renewed by the Spirit of God, it will be a continua pleasure to be walking with, and talking of God, and telling what great things Jesus Christ hath done for your souls; and till you can find as much pleasure in conversing with God, as these men do of their hounds, you have no share in him; but when you have tasted how good the Lord is, you will show forth his praise; out of the abundance of your heart your mouth will speak.

This brings me to the second thing proposed, which is an extreme that very seldom happens: SECONDLY, To show what it is to be righteous over-much, And here, FIRST, When we confine the Spirit of God to this or that particular church; and are not willing to converse with any but those of the same communion; this is to be righteous over-much with a witness: and so it is, to confine our communion within church-walls, and to think that Jesus could not preach in a field as well as on consecrated ground; this is judaism, this is bigotry: this is like Peter, who would not go to preach the gospel to the Gentiles, till he had a vision from God: and when his conduct was blamed by the disciples, he could not satisfy them till he had acquainted them with the vision he had seen. And, therefore, we may justly infer, the Spirit of God is the center of unity; and wherever I see the image of my Master, I never inquire of them their opinions; I ask them not what they are, so they love Jesus Christ in sincerity and truth, but embrace them as my brother, my sister, and my spouse: and this is the spirit of Christianity. Many persons, who are bigots to this or that opinion, when one of a different way of thinking hath come where they were, have left the room or place on the account: this is the spirit of the devil; and if it was possible that these persons could be admitted into heaven with such tempers, that very place would be hell to them. Christianity will never flourish, till we are all of one heart and of one mind; and this would be the only means of seeing the gospel of Jesus to flourish, more than ever it will by persecuting those who differ from us.

This may be esteemed as enthusiasm and madness, and as a design to undermine the established church: No; God is my judge, I should rejoice to see all the world adhere to her articles; I should rejoice to see the ministers of the Church of England, preach up those very articles they have subscribed to; but those ministers who do preach up the articles, are esteemed as madmen, enthusiasts, schismatics, and underminers of the established church: and though they say these things of me, blessed be God, they are without foundation. My dear brethren, I am a friend to her articles, I am a friend to her homilies, I am a friend to her liturgy; and, if they did not thrust me out of their churches, I would read them every day; but I do not confine the Spirit of God there; for I say it again, I love all that love the Lord Jesus Christ, and esteem him my brother, my friend, my spouse; aye, my very soul is knit to that person. The spirit of persecution will never, indeed it will never make any to love Jesus Christ.

The Pharisees make this to be madness, so much as to mention persecution in a Christian country; but there is as much of the spirit of persecution now in the world, as ever there was; their will is as great, but blessed be God, they want the power; otherwise, how soon would the send me to prison, make my feet fast in the stocks, yea, would think they did God service in killing me, and would rejoice to take away my life.

This is not the Spirit of Christ, my dear brethren; I had not come to have thus preached; I had not come into the highways and hedges; I had not exposed myself to the ill treatment of these letter-learned men, but for the sake of your souls: indeed, I had no other reason, but your salvation; and for that (I speak the truth in Christ, I lie not) I would be content to go to prison; yea, I would rejoice to die for you, so I could but be a means to bring some of you to Jesus: I could not bear to see so many in the highway to destruction, and not show them their danger: I could not bear, my brethren, to see you more willing to learn, than the teachers are to instruct you: and if any of them were to come and preach to you, I should not envy them, I should not call them enthusiasts or madmen; I should rejoice to hear they had ten thousand times more success than I have met with; I would give them the right hand of fellowship; I would advise them to go on; I would wish them good luck in the name of the Lord, and say as Christ did, when the disciples informed him of some casting out devils in his name, and were for rebuking of them, "Forbid them not, for they that are not against us are for us;" or as St. Paul says, "Some preach Christ of envy, and some of good-will; notwithstanding, so Christ is but preached, I rejoice; yea, and will rejoice." The gospel of Jesus, is the gospel of peace. Thus you may see, that to be righteous over-much, is to be uncharitable, censorious, and to persecute persons for differing from us in religion.

SECONDLY, Persons are righteous over-much, when they spend so much time in religious assemblies, as to neglect their families. There is no license given by the blessed Jesus, for idleness; for in the very infancy of the world, idleness was not allowed of. In paradise, Adam and Eve dressed the garden, Cain was a tiller of the ground, and Abel was a keeper of sheep; and there is a proverb amongst the Jews, "That he who brings his son up without a business, brings him up to be a thief:" and therefore our Savior was a carpenter; "Is not this the carpenter's son," said the Jews: and St. Paul, though brought up at the feet of Gamaliel, was a tent-maker.

Labor, my brethren, is imposed on all mankind as part of the divine curse; and you are called to be useful in the society to which you belong: take care first for the kingdom of God, and all things necessary shall be added.

To labor for the meat that perisheth, is your duty; only take care, that you do not neglect getting the meat for the soul: that is the greatest consequence, for this plain reason, the things of this life are temporal, but those of the next are eternal. I would have rich men to work as well as poor; it is owing to their idleness, that the devil hurries them to his diversions; they can be in their beds all the morning, and spend the afternoon and evening in dressing, visiting, and at balls, plays, or assemblies, when they should be working out their salvation with fear and trembling. Such a life as this, occasions a spiritual numbness in the soul; and if Jesus Christ was not to stop those who thus spend their time, they would be hurried into eternity, without once thinking of their immortal souls. But Jesus Christ has compassion upon many of them, and while they are in their blood, he bids them "live." And though I preach this doctrine to you, yet I do not bid you be idle; no, they that do not work should not eat. You have two callings, a general one, and a special one: as we are to regard the one in respect of our bodies, so we are to regard the other on account of our souls. Take heed, my brethren, I beseech you, take heed, lest you labor so for the meat that perisheth, as to forget that meat which endureth for ever. Seek the things of God first; look well to obtain oil in your lamps, grace in your hearts. I am not persuading you to take no care about the things of the world, but only not to be encumbered with them, so as to neglect your duty towards God, and a proper concern for your souls.

It is meet, it is right, it is your bounden duty, to mind the calling wherein God hath placed you; and you may be said to be righteous over-much not to regard them. This brings me, THIRDLY, To give you another sign of being righteous over-much; and that is, when we fast and use corporal authorities, so as to unfit us for the service of God.

This, my brethren, you may think there is no occasion at all to caution you against, and indeed there is not a great necessity for it; however, many persons, upon their first being awakened to a sense of their sin, are tempted to use authorities to that excess which is sinful. It is our duty to fast, it is our duty to fast often, and it is what we are directed to by Jesus Christ himself; but then we are to take care to do it in a proper manner: to bring our bodies under for the service of God, is that which we are commanded by our Lord Jesus Christ.

The late preacher upon this text, runs into great extremes, and charges us with saying and acting things of which we never thought; but I do not regard what he said of me: I do not mind his bitter invectives against my ministry; I do not mind his despising my youth, and calling me novice and enthusiast; I forgive him from my very heart: but when he reflects on my Master; when he speaks against my Redeemer; when Jesus Christ is spoken against, I must speak, (I must speak indeed, or I should burst:) when he gives liberty to persons to take a cheerful glass, and alledges Christ for an example, as in the marriage-feast, saying, "Christ turned water into wine, when it is plain there had been more drank than was necessary before;" what is this, but to charge Christ with encouraging drunkenness? It is true, the Governor says, "Every man in the beginning sets forth good wine, and when men have well drank, that which is worse; but thou hast kept the good wine until now:" but it does not at all follow, that it was not necessary, or that there had been a sufficient quantity before: I would not speak thus slightingly of one of my Master's miracles, for the whole world. And we may observe, that as Christ chiefly visited poor people, they might not have wherewithal to buy a sufficient quantity of wine; for having more guests than were expected, the wine was expended sooner than they thought; then the Mother of Jesus tells him, "They have no wine;" he answers, "Woman, what have I to do with thee? My hour is not yet come." After this he commanded them to fill the water-pots with water, and they filled them to the brim, and this water he turned into wine: now it does not follow, that there was more drank than was necessary; neither would the Lord Jesus Christ have continued in the house if there had. But we have an excellent lesson to learn from this miracle: by the water-pots being empty, we may understand, the heart of man being by nature destitute of his grace, his speaking and commanding to fill them, shows, that when Christ speaks, the heart that was empty of grace before, shall be filled; and the water pots being filled to the brim, shows, that Christ will fill believers hearts brim full of the Holy Ghost: and from the Governor's observing, that the last wine was the best, learn, that a believer's best comforts, shall be the last and greatest, for they shall come with the greatest power upon the soul, and continue longest there: this, this my dear brethren, is the lesson we may learn from this miracle.

But one great inconsistency I cannot avoid taking notice of in this late learned preacher. In the beginning of his sermon, he charges us with "laying heavy burdens upon people, which they are not able to bear;" in the latter part he charges us with being Antinomians, whose tenets are, "So you say you believe in the Lord Jesus Christ, you may live the life of devils." Now, he charges us with being too strict, and by and by with being too loose. Which side, my brethren, will you take? Thus you see, when persons forsake Christ, they make strange mistakes; for here can be no greater opposition of sentiments than this letter-learned writer has made: as opposite as light and darkness, good and evil, sweet and bitter. And, on this account, to find out these lettered-learned gentlemens notions of the new-birth, I put a paragraph in my Journal; and, blessed be God, I have obtained my desires, and have plainly perceived, that the persons who have lately written concerning the new-birth, know no more of it than a blind man does of colors, nor can they have any more notion of it, (by all their learning, falsely so called) than the blind man, who was to give an account what the sun was, and, after a considerable time allowed for study, he said, "It was like the sound of a trumpet." And till they are taught of God, they will be unacquainted with the new-birth; therefore, if you have a mind to know what the devil has to say against us, read Dr. Trapp's sermons.

It is with grief I speak these things, and were not the welfare of your souls, and my Redeemer's honor at stake, I would not now open my mouth, yes I would willingly die (God is my judge) for the person who wrote such bitter things against me, so it would be a means of saving his soul.

If he had only spoken against me, I would not have answered him; but, on his making my Redeemer a pattern of vice, if I was not to speak, the very stones would cry out; therefore, the honor of my Redeemer, and love to you, constrains me to speak. It is of necessity that I speak, when the divinity of Jesus Christ is spoken against, it is the duty of ministers to cry aloud, and spare not. I cannot forbear, come what will; for I know not what kind of divinity we have not among us: we must have a righteousness of our own, and do our best endeavors, and then Christ will make up the deficiency; that is, you must be your own Savior, in part. This is not the doctrine of the gospel; this not the doctrine of Jesus: no; Christ is all in all; Jesus Christ must be your whole wisdom; Jesus Christ must be your whole righteousness. Jesus Christ must be your whole sanctification; or Jesus Christ will never be your eternal redemption and sanctification.

Inward holiness is looked on, by some, as the effect of enthusiasm and madness; and preachers of the necessity of the new-birth, are esteemed as persons fit for Bedlam. Our polite and fashionable doctrine, is, "That there is a fitness in man, and that God, seeing you a good creature, bestows upon you his grace." God forbid, my dear brethren, you should thus learn Jesus Christ!

This is not the doctrine I preach to you: I say, salvation is the free gift of God. It is God' free grace, I preach unto you, not of works, lest any one should boast. Jesus Christ justifies the ungodly; Jesus Christ passed by, and saw you polluted with your blood, and bid you live. It is not of works, it is of faith: we are not justified for our faith, for faith is the instrument, but by your faith, the active as well as the passive obedience of Christ, must be applied to you. Jesus Christ hath fulfilled the law, he hath made it honorable; Jesus Christ hath made satisfaction to his Father's justice, full satisfaction; and it is as complete as it is full, and God will not demand it again. Jesus Christ is the way; Jesus Christ is the truth; and Jesus Christ is the life. The righteousness of Jesus Christ, my brethren, must be imputed to you, or you can never have any interest in the blood of Jesus; your own works are but as filthy rags, for you are justified before God, without any respect to your works past, present, or to come. This doctrine is denied by the learned rabbi's; but if they deny these truths of the gospel, they must not offended, though a child dare speak to a doctor; and, in vindication of the cause of Jesus Christ, a child, a boy, by the Spirit of God, can speak to the learned clergy of this age.

If I had a voice so great, and could speak so loud, as that the whole world could hear me, I would cry, "Be not righteous over-much," by bringing your righteousness to Christ, and by being righteous in your own eyes. Man must be abased, that God may be exalted.

The imputed righteousness of Jesus Christ is a comfortable doctrine to all real Christians; and you sinners, who ask what you must do to be saved?

How uncomfortable would it be, to tell you by good works, when, perhaps, you have never done one good work in all your life: this would be driving you to despair, indeed: no; "Believe in the Lord Jesus Christ, and you shall be saved:" therefore none of you need go away despairing. Come to the Lord Jesus by faith, and he shall receive you. You have no righteousness of your own to depend on. If you are saved, it is by the righteousness of Christ, through his atonement, his making a sacrifice for sin: his righteousness must be imputed to you, otherwise you cannot be saved. There is no difference between you, by nature, and the greatest malefactor that ever was executed at Tyburn: the difference made, is all owing to the free, the rich, the undeserved grace of God; this has made the difference. It is true, talking at this rate, will offend the Pharisees, who do not like this leveling doctrine, (as they call it); but if ever you are brought to Jesus Christ by faith, you will experience the truth of it. Come by faith to Jesus Christ; do not come, Pharisee-like, telling God what you have done, how often you have gone to church, how often you have received the sacrament, fasted, prayed, or the like: no; come to Christ as poor, lost, undone, damned sinners; come to him in this manner, and he will accept of you: do not be rich in spirit, proud and exalted, for there is no blessing attends such; but be ye poor in spirit, for theirs is the kingdom of God; they shall be made members of his mystical body here, and shall be so of the church triumphant hereafter. Acknowledge yourselves as nothing at all, and when you have done all, say, "You are unprofitable servants." There is no salvation but by Jesus Christ; there is no other name given under heaven amongst men, whereby we may be saved, but that of the Lord Jesus. God, out of Christ, is a consuming fire; therefore strive for an interest in his Son the Lord Jesus Christ; take him on the terms offered to you in the gospel; accept of him in God's own way, lay hold on him by faith.

Do not think you are Christians; do not flatter yourselves with being righteous enough, and good enough, because you lead moral decent lives, do no one any harm, go to church, and attend upon the outward means of grace;

no, my brethren, you may do this, and a great deal more, and yet be very far from having a saving, experimental knowledge of Jesus Christ.

Beg of Christ to strike home upon your hearts, that you may feel the power of religion. Indeed, you must feel the power of God here, or the wrath of God hereafter. These are truths of the utmost consequence; therefore, do not go contradicting, do not go blaspheming away. Blessed be God, you are not such cowards to run away for a little rain. I hope good things of you; I hope you have felt the power of God; and if God should bring any of you to himself through this foolishness of preaching, you will have no reason to complain it was done by a youth, by a child; no; if I could be made an instrument to bring you to God, they may call me novice, enthusiast, or what they please, I should rejoice; yea, and I would rejoice.

O that some sinner might be brought to Jesus Christ! Do not say I preach despair; I despair of no one, when I consider God had mercy on such a wretch as I, who was running in a full career to hell: I was hastening thither, but Jesus Christ passed by and stopped me; Jesus Christ passed by me while I was in my blood, when I was polluted with filth; he passed by me, and bid me live. Thus I am a monument of God's free grace; and therefore, my brethren, I despair of none of you, when I consider, I say, what a wretch I was. I am not speaking now out of a false humility, a pretended sanctity, as the Pharisees call it: no, the truth in Christ I speak, and therefore, men and devils do your worst; I have a gracious Master will protect me; it is his work I am engaged in, and Jesus Christ will carry me above their rage.

Those who are come here this night out of curiosity to hear what the babbler says; those who come to spend an idle hour to find something for an evening-conversation at a coffee-house; or you who have stopped in your coaches as you passed by, remember that you have had Jesus Christ offered to you; I offer Jesus Christ to every one of you: perhaps you may not regard it because it is in a field. But Jesus Christ is wherever his people meet in sincerity and truth to worship him: he is not confined to church walls: he has met us here; many, very many of you know he has; and therefore you may believe on him with greater confidence.

Can you bear to think of a bleeding, panting, dying Jesus, offering himself up for sinners, and you will not accept of him? Do not say, you are poor, and therefore are ashamed to go to church, for God has sent the gospel out unto you. Do not harden your hearts: oppose not the will of Jesus.

O that I could speak to your hearts, that my words would center there.

My heart is full of love to you. I would speak, till I could speak no more, so I could but bring you to Christ. I may never meet you all, perhaps, any more. The cloud of God's providence seems to be moving. God calls me by his providence away from you, for a while. God knows whether we shall ever see each other in the flesh. At the day of judgment we shall all meet again. I earnestly desire your prayers. Pray that I may not only begin, John-like, I the spirit, but that I may continue in it. Pray that I may not fall away, that I may not decline suffering for you, if I should be called to it. Be earnest, O be earnest with God in my behalf, that while I am preaching to others, I may not be a cast-away. Put up your prayers for me, I beseech you. Go not to the throne of grace, without carrying me upon your heart; for you know not what influence your prayers may have. As for you, my dear brethren, God knows my heart. I continually bear you on my mind, when I go in and out before the Lord; and it is my earnest desire, you may not perish for lack of knowledge, but that he would send out more ministers to water what his own right-hand hath planted. May the Ancient of Days come forth upon his white horse, and may all opposition fall to the ground. As we have begun to bruise the serpent's head, we must expect he will bruise our heel.

The devil will not let his kingdom fall without raging horribly. He will not suffer the ministers of Christ to go on, without bringing his power to stop them. But fear not, my dear brethren, David, though a stripling, encountered the great Goliath; and if we pray, God will give us strength against all our spiritual enemies. Show your faith by your works. Give the world the lye. Press forward. Do not stop, do not linger in your journey, but strive for the mark set before you. Fight the good fight of faith, and God will give you spiritual mercies. I hope we shall all meet at the right- hand of God. Strive, strive to enter in at the strait gate, that we may be born to Abraham's bosom, where sin and sorrow shall cease. No scoffer will be there, but we shall see Jesus, who died for us; and not only see him, but live with him forever.

Which God, of his infinite mercy, etc.

Sermon 10 A Preservative against unsettled Notions

(A Preservative against unsettled Notions, and want of Principles, in regard to Righteousness and Christian Perfection.)

(Being a more particular answer to Doctor Trapp's Four Sermons upon the same text.)

Ecclesiastes 7:16, "Be not righteous over much; neither make thyself over wise: why shouldest thou destroy thyself?"

To all the Members of Christ's Holy Church.

Dear Fellow Christians,
The great, and indeed the only motive which prompted me to publish this sermon, was the desire of providing for your security from error, at a time when the deviators from, and false pretenders to truth, are so numerous, that the most discerning find it a matter of the greatest difficulty to avoid being led astray by one or by other into downright falsehood. There is no running divisions upon truth; like a mathematical point, it will neither admit of subtraction nor addition: And as it is indivisible in its nature, there is no splitting the difference, where truth is concerned. Irreligion and enthusiasm are diametrical opposites, and true piety between both, like the center of an infinite line, is at an equal infinite distance from the one and the other, and therefore can never admit of a coalition with either. The one erring by defect, the other by excess. But whether we err by defect, or excess, is of little importance, if we are equally wide of the mark, as we certainly are in either case. For whatever is less than truth, cannot be truth; and whatever is more than true must be false.

Wherefore, as the whole of this great nation seams now more than ever in danger of being hurried into one or the other of these equally pernicious extremes, irreligion or fanaticism, I thought myself more than ordinarily obliged to rouse your, perhaps drowsy vigilance, by warning you of the nearness of your peril; cautioning you from leaning towards either side, though but to peep at the slippery precipice; and stepping between you and error, before it comes nigh enough to grapple with you. The happy medium of true Christian piety, in which it has pleased the mercy of God to establish you, is built on a firm rock, "and the gates of hell shall never prevail against it." While then you stand steadily upright in the fullness of the faith, falsehood and sin shall labor in vain to approach you; whereas, the least familiarity with error, will make you giddy, and if once you stagger in principles, your ruin is almost inevitable.

But not I have cautioned you of the danger you are in from the enemies who threaten your subversion, I hope your own watchfulness will be sufficient to guard you from any surprise. And from their own assaults you have nothing to fear, since while you persist in the firm resolution, through God's grace, to keep them out, irreligion and enthusiasm, falsehood and vice, impiety and false piety, will combine in vain to force an entrance into your hearts.

Take then, my dearly beloved fellow members of Christ's mystical body, take the friendly caution I give you in good part, and endeavor to profit by it: attend wholly to the saving truths I here deliver to you, and per persuaded, that they are uttered by one who has your eternal salvation as much at heart as his own.

"And thou, O Lord Jesus Christ, fountain of all truth, whence all wisdom flows, open the understandings of thy people to the light of thy true faith, and touch their hearts with thy grace, that they may both be able to see, and willing to perform what thou requirest of them. Drive away from us every cloud of error and perversity; guard us alike from irreligion and false pretensions to piety; and lead us on perpetually towards that perfection to which thou hast taught us to aspire; that keeping us here in a constant imitation of thee, and peaceful union which each other, thou mayest at length bring us to that everlasting glory, which thou hast promised to all such as shall endeavor to be perfect, even as the Father who is in heaven is perfect, who with thee and the Holy Ghost lives and reigns one God, world without end! Amen, Amen.

Ecclesiastes 7:16, "Be not righteous over much; neither make thyself over wise: why shouldest thou destroy thyself?"

Righteousness over-much! May one say; Is there any danger of that? Is it even possible? Can we be too good? If we give any credit to the express word of God, we cannot be too good, we cannot be righteous over-much. The injunction given by God to Abraham is very strong: "Walk before me, and be thou perfect." The same he again lays upon all Israel, in the eighteenth of Deuteronomy: "Thou shalt be perfect, and without blemish, with the Lord thy God." And lest any should think to excuse themselves from this obligation, by saying, it ceased when the old law was abolished, our blessed Savior ratified and explained it: "Be ye, therefore, perfect, even as your Father who is in heaven is perfect." So that until our perfection surpasses that of our heavenly Father, we can never be too good nor righteous over-much; and as it is impossible we should ever surpass, or even come up to him in the perfection of goodness and righteousness, it follows in course that we never can be good or righteous in excess. Nevertheless Doctor Trapp has found out that we may be righteous over-much, and has taken no small pains, with much agitation of spirit, to prove that it is a great folly and weakness, nay, a great sin. "O Lord! Rebuke thou his spirit, and grant that this false doctrine may not be published to his confusion in the day of judgment!" But if what this hasty, this deluded man advances had been true, could there be any occasion, however, of warning against it in these times, "when the danger (as he himself to his confusion owns) is on the contrary extreme; when all manner of vice and wickedness abounds to a degree almost unheard of?" I answer for the present, that "there must be heresies amongst you, that they who are approved may be made manifest." However, this earthly-minded minister of a new gospel, has taken a text which seems to favor his naughty purpose, of weaning the well-disposed little ones of Christ from that perfect purity of heart and spirit, which is necessary to all such as mean to live to our Lord Jesus. O Lord, what shall become of thy flock, when their shepherds betray them into the hands of the ravenous wolf! When a minister of thy word perverts it to overthrow thy kingdom, and to destroy scripture with scripture!

Solomon, in the person of a desponding, ignorant, indolent liver (resident), says to the man of righteousness: "Be not righteous over-much, neither make thyself overwise: Why shouldest thou destroy thyself?" But must my angry, over-sighted brother Trapp, therefore, personate a character so unbecoming his function, merely to overthrow the express injunction of the Lord to us; which obliges us never to give over pursuing and thirsting after the perfect righteousness of Christ, until we rest in him? Father, forgive him, for he knows not what he says!

What advantage might not Satan gain over the elect, if the false construction, put upon this text by that unseeing teacher, should prevail!

Yet though he blushes not to assist Satan to bruise our heel, I shall endeavor to bruise the heads of both, by showing, I. FIRST, The genuine sense of the text in question.

II. The character of the persons, who are to be supposed speaking here: And III. The character of the persons spoken to.

From whence will naturally result these consequences.

FIRST, That the Doctor was grossly (Lord grant he was not maliciously) mistaken in his explanatory sermon on this text, as well as in the application of it.

SECONDLY, That he is a teacher and approver of worldly maxims.

THIRDLY, That he is of course an enemy to perfect righteousness in men, through Christ Jesus, and, therefore, no friend to Christ: And therefore, that no one ought to be deluded by the false doctrine he advances, to beguile the innocent, and deceive, if possible, even the elect.

I. To come at the true sense of the text in question, it will be necessary to look back, to the preceding verse, where the wise man, reflecting on the vanities of his youth, puts on for a moment his former character. "All things, have I seen in the days of my vanity: (and among the rest) there is a just man that perisheth in his righteousness, and there is a wicked man who prolongeth his life in his wickedness." Now it is very plain, that he is not here talking of a man, who is righteous over- much, in the Doctor's manner of understanding the words, that is, "faulty, and criminal by excess." For on one side he commends him for being a just man, and full of righteousness, and yet on the other tells us, that his righteousness is the shortening of his life. Whereas, had he looked upon his perishing in righteousness to be an over-righteousness, he would never have called him a just man. Neither by a wicked man, can he mean a man given up to the utmost excess of wickedness, since he tells us, that he prolongeth his life in (or by) his wickedness. Who does not know, that the excess of almost every kind of vice, is of itself a shortener of life. So that the whole opposition and contrast lies between a good man, and a bad man. A good man whose goodness shortens his life, and bad man whose iniquity lengthens his life, or at least is not excessive enough to shorten the thread of it. Solomon, absorbed in these reflections, speaks here by way of prosopopeia, not the sense of Solomon, the experienced, the learned, the wise; but of the former Solomon, a vain young fellow, full of self- love, and the strong desires of life. In the quality of such a one then, he looks with the same eye upon the righteous man, who perishes in his righteousness, as he would on a wicked one, who should perish in his wickedness. For it is neither the righteousness of the one, nor the wickedness of the other, that offends him, but the superlative degrees of both; which tending equally to shorten life, he looks upon them as equally opposite to the self-love he fondles within him. And, therefore, he deems an excess of debauchery as great an enemy to the lasting enjoyment of the pleasures of life, as an extraordinary righteousness would be. Well then might he say to the latter, in this character, "Be not over-much wicked, neither be thou foolish; why shouldst thou die before thy time?" And to the former: "Be not righteous over-much, neither make thyself over-wise: Why shouldst thou destroy thyself?" What wonder then, that a youth of sprightliness and sense, but led away by self-love to be fond of the pleasures and enjoyments of life, when attained without hurry, and possessed without risk; what wonder, I say, that such a youth should conceive an equal dislike to the superlative degrees of virtue and vice, and, therefore, advise such of his companions as give into the excess of debauchery, to refrain from it: as it must infallibly tend to clog their understandings, stupify their senses, and entail upon their constitutions a train of infirmities, which cannot but debilitate their natural vigor, and shorten their days? "Be not over-much wicked, neither be thou foolish: Why shouldst thou die before thy time?" What wonder, that the same self-love should prompt him to dissuade such of his friends or acquaintance, as he wishes to have for companions, and countenancers of his worldly-minded pursuits, from pursuing righteousness and wisdom to a degree that must destroy in them all taste of earthly pleasures, and may possibly impair their constitutions, and forward their end? "Be not righteous over-much, neither make thyself overwise: Why shouldst thou destroy thyself?" This is the sense in which Solomon (placing himself in the state of vanity of his youth) speaks to the one, and the other: to the righteous, and to the ungodly. This is the true, genuine sense of the letter; and every other sense put upon it, is false and groundless, and wrested rather to pervert than explain the truth of the text. O Christian simplicity, whither art thou fled? Why will not the clergy speak truth? And why must this false prophet suffer thy people, O Lord, to believe a lie? They have held the truth in unrighteousness. Raise up, I beseech thee, O Lord, some true pastors, who may acquaint them with the nature and necessity of perfect righteousness, and lead them to that love of Christian perfection which the angry-minded, pleasure-taking Doctor Trapp, labors to divert them from, by teaching, that "all Christians must have to do with some vanities." Is not the meaning of this text plain to the weakest capacity? I have here given it to you, as I have it from the mouth of the royal preacher himself. I have made use of no "philosophy and vain deceit after the tradition of men, after the rudiments of the world, and not after Christ," to impose a fleshly sense upon you, for the sense of the word of God. No, I have given you a natural exposition obvious from the very words themselves.

Hence you may see, my fellow-strugglers in righteousness, how grossly our angry adversary is mistaken in his explanation of this text. Lord! Open his eyes, and touch his heart; and convert him, and all those erring ministers, who have seen vain and foolish things for thy people, and have not discovered their iniquity, to turn away thy captivity. For they have erred through wine, and through strong drink are out of the way! The priest and the prophet have erred through strong drink, they are swallowed up of wine, they are out of the way through strong drink, they err in vision, they stumble in judgment.

It is plain from the words of the text, that the royal Preacher was speaking in the person of a vain worldling, when he said, "Be not righteous over-much;" whereby he meant to exhort the truly righteous not to be dismayed, terrified, or disturbed from their constant pursuit of greater and greater perfection of righteousness, until they rest in Christ; notwithstanding the derision, fleshly persuasion, ill-treatment and persecution of worldly men: Who, one day, repenting and groaning for anguish of spirit, shall say within themselves, "These were they whom we had sometimes in derision, and a proverb of reproach. We fools, accounted their lives madness; and their end to be without honor. How are they numbered among the children of God, and their lot is among the saints!" How blind then is the application (not to say perverse) which this self-wise clergyman makes from the text, to such as, following the advice of the apostle (Coloss. 3:2) "set their affections on things above, not on things on the earth." Must hastiness in anger get the better of sense and truth? Must the people be misled because the pastor cannot, or will not see? Or must the injunction of Christ, "Be perfect, even as your Father, who is in heaven, is perfect," give place to the maxim of the heathen Tully: The greatest reproach to a philosopher, is to confute his doctrine by his practice; if this be the case, alas, what a deplorable, unspeakably deplorable condition is that of some Christians? Wherefore, "thus saith the Lord concerning the prophets who make his people to err, that bite with their teeth and cry peace; and he that putteth not into their mouths, they even prepare war against him: therefore night shall be unto you, that ye shall not have a vision, and it shall be dark unto you, that ye shall not divine, and the sun shall go down over the prophets, and the day shall be dark over them.

But I will leave these lovers of darkness, and turn to you, O beloved, elect of God! I beseech you, by the bowels of Christ, suffer not yourselves to be deceived by their flattering, sin-soothing speeches. "Be not of that rebellious people, lying children, children who will not hear the law of the Lord: who say to the seers, see not; and to the prophets, prophesy not unto us right things, speak unto us smooth things, prophesy deceits." Follow not those, who flatter you in the vanities they practice themselves.

O may you never be of the number of those, in the person of whom Solomon here says, "Be not righteous over-much;" for their character is the character of the beast.

II. The character of the persons, who are to be supposed speaking here in the text, is in a word the same with the character of those whom

Solomon here personates: who, as is already shown, are a vain set of men, neither righteous enough to have an habitual desire of improving virtue to its perfection, nor quite so flagitious as to give into self-destroying vices: in a word, they are self-lovers, the sole end of whose pursuits, whether indifferent, bad, or laudable in themselves, is self-enjoyment. Insomuch that they look upon virtue and vice, righteousness and wickedness, with the same eye, and their fondness of aversion for both is alike, as their different degrees appear to be the means to enhance and prolong the enjoyment of pleasure, or to lessen and shorten those pleasures. Thus any virtue, while it is kept within such bounds as may render it subservient to the pleasurable degrees of vice, will meet with no opposition from them; on the contrary, they will even commend it. But the moment it becomes a restraint to vice in moderation (if I may be allowed to make use of terms adequate to their system) from that moment it gives offense, and they put it in their caveat, "Be not righteous over-much." In like manner, vice, while confined to certain limits, which rather improve than obstruct pleasures ,is with them a desirable good; but no sooner does it launch out into any depth, sufficient to drown and diminish the relish of those pleasures, than they declare open war against it; "Be not over- much wicked." And the reason they assign for their opposition in both cases, is the same: "why shouldst thou destroy thyself? Why shouldst thou die before thy time?" Such is the prudence of the world, the flesh, and the devil. Such the maxims of these refined libertines, so much that more dangerous as they are less obvious; so much the more insinuating, as they are removed from certain extravagancies capable of shocking every man who has the least sense and delicacy. O Lord, how true is it, that the sons of darkness are wiser in their generation than the sons of light!

You are not then, beloved in the Lord, to imagine that your greatest opposition, in struggling for perfect righteousness, is to come from profligates, from men whose enormous vices create horror even to themselves: no, your most dangerous, most formidable enemies, are the kind of men I have painted to you, who render vice relishable with a mixture of apparent virtue, and clothe wickedness in the apparel of righteousness; "Beware of them, for they come to you in the clothing of sheep, but inwardly are ravenous wolves." This perverse generation will ensnare you into ungodliness, by seeming oppositions to vice, and allow you to swallow the seemings of virtue and righteousness like an emetic, only to puke forth the reality of them. They paint black, white, and the white they convert into black. Not content with seeming what they are not, they labor to make you, what they are.

Righteousness and wickedness they interweave in an artful tissue, capable of deceiving the very elect, and difficult for the most discerning among them to unravel; as almsgiving and avarice, pride and humility, temperance and luxury, are dexterously blended together; while as mutual curbs to each other, they combine to stem the tide of impediments to worldly enjoyment, which might flow from extraordinary degrees on either side. Thus "Almsgiving (you are told) is very excellent," and you believe the proposition, without knowing the particular sense it is spoken in, which is, that almsgiving is an excellent curb upon avarice, by preserving a rich man from such a superlative love of money as deprives him of the self- enjoyment of it. And upon the strength of this belief, the worldly-minded man, who labors to deceive you, gains credit enough with you to establish this maxim, that all superlative degrees of alms-giving, are GREAT SINS, and that a man must never sell all he has and give it to the poor, because some may have families of their own, and ought to make sufficient provision for them, according to that proverb, "Charity begins at home;" when no one, at least scarce any one, is wise enough to know, when he has a sufficiency.

O Lord, which are we to believe, these worldlings, or thee? If thou dost deceive us, why dost thou threaten us with punishments, if we do not heed thee? And if the world is deceitful, shall we not flee from it to cleave to thee?

"Pride is a great sin" even with these worldlings, inasmuch as the external excesses of it, may obstruct the way to many ambitious terminations of view, and its internal agitations are the destruction of that peace, to which even self-love aspires; besides, the frequent extravagancy of its motions may not only be prejudicial to health, but a shortner of life. And, therefore, no wonder they should object against it, "Be not over much wicked: why shouldst thou die before thy time?" For this reason, they look upon a little mixture of humility to be not only commendable, but even necessary to cub the extravagant follies of an over- bearing pride. But then a superlative degree of humility, that is, humility free from the least tincture of pride or vanity, which is the same with them, as "an over-strained humility, is a fault as well as folly;" because, forsooth, it is an expediment to the self-enjoyment of the world and its pleasures; "All Christians must have to do with some vanities, or else they must needs go out of the world indeed; for the world itself is all over vanity." 'Tis nothing, therefore, surprising, my brethren, to see a man of this cast of mind making a vain ostentation (act of display, show) of his little superficial acquaintance, with the ancient Greeks and Romans. What is this but acting conformably to his own principle, that "all Christians must have to do with some vanities?" And shall we wonder to hear such a one prefer their writings, to those of an apostle; or be astonished to see him wound the apostle with raillery, (good-natured ridicule) through your sides, for wishing to know nothing but Jesus Christ, and him crucified? No, with him it is consistency to laugh and reprove you out of the perfection of righteousness, which, however he may play with terms, is with him the same as being righteousness overmuch; but with you it would be inconsistency, who ought to know no difference between being righteous, and living in a perpetual, habitual desire of being superlatively so. It is no more than, than you ought to expect to hear such advocates for the world cry out to you, "Be not righteous over-much: why should you destroy yourselves?" But, O Lord, surely this is not the same voice which tells us, that unless we humble ourselves like unto children, we shall not enter into the kingdom of heaven, and that he is greatest there, who humbles himself the most like a child! But what will not men advance who are drunk with passion, and intoxicated with self-love?

"The vice of intemperance in eating, and drinking, is plain to everybody," they own. And, therefore, they give it up as an excess which cannot but tend to the impairing of health, and shortening of life: nay, it drowns the very relish of pleasure in actual eating and drinking. Hence will every refined debauchee exclaim against it with Dr. Trapp: "Be not over much wicked: why shouldst thou destroy thyself?" Little sobriety, say they, is requisite to give a zest to luxury and worldly pleasures. But too much of it is too much, "to eat nothing but bread and herbs, and drink nothing but water, unless there be a particular reason for it (such perhaps as Doctor Cheyne may assign) is folly at best (that is, even though it be done for Christ's sake) therefore no virtue:" "Be not then righteous over- much, why shouldst thou destroy thyself?" And if you should answer those carnally-minded men with the words of the apostle, Rom. 8, "We are debtors, not to the flesh, to live after the flesh; For if we live after the flesh, we shall die: but if we, through the spirit, do mortify the deeds of the flesh, we shall live." If you answer them thus, they will tell you, this is teaching for doctrines the commandments of men." And it will be to as little purpose to answer them, with what St. Paul says elsewhere (Rom. 14:17) "The kingdom of God is not meat and drink, but righteousness, and peace, and joy in the Holy Ghost:" They will not blush to tell you, that "our blessed Savior came eating and drinking, nay worked a miracle to make wind (at an entertainment) when it is plain there had been more drank than was necessary." To such lengths does the love of the world hurry these self-fond, merry-making worldlings! Tell them of self-denial, they will not hear you, it is an encroachment upon the pleasures of life, and may shorten it of a few days, which you are never sure of possessing; it is being "righteous over-much: why shouldst thou destroy thyself?" Jesus, you will say, tells us (John 12:25) "He that loveth his life shall lose it, and he that hateth his life in this world, shall keep it unto life eternal." But this and the like, they will inform you, "are hyperbolical phrases." Now what signifies minding Jesus, when he speaks hyperbolically, that is, speaks more than is strictly true. Yet, O Lord Jesus, grant us to mind thee, whatever these worldlings may say; remind us, that if any man will come after thee, he must deny himself, and take up his cross, and follow thee! O how enlarging is it to the soul, to take up the cross of Christ and follow him!

But you are charged, ye beloved lovers of perfect righteousness, with extravagances. You allow of "no sort of recreation or diversion; nothing but an universal mortification and self-denial; no pleasure but from religion only:" you teach "that the bodily appetites must not be in the least degree gratified, any farther than is absolutely necessary to keep body and soul together, and mankind in being: No allowances are to be made for melancholy misfortunes, or human infirmity: grief must be cured only by prayer;" (a horrid grievance this, to such as think prayer burdensome at best) "To divert it by worldly amusements is carnal." A heavy charge this: but left it should seem so only to those carnal persons, who are resolved to give way to their carnal appetites; what you look upon as advisable only, these perverters of truth insinuate to be looked upon by you as indispensable duties. And lest prevarication should fail, downright falsehoods must be placed to your account, "so that to taste an agreeable fruit, or smell to a rose, must be unlawful with you," however you disown it. But O, my beloved Christians, be not discouraged from the pursuit of perfect righteousness by these or such vile misrepresentations. For "blessed are ye when men shall revile you, and shall say all manner of evil against you falsely for the sake of Christ Jesus. Rejoice, and be exceeding glad: For great is your reward in heaven: for so persecuted they the prophets who were before you." Thus far, then, may suffice to show clearly with what dangerous views the worldly-minded men, whom Solomon personates in the text before us, lay siege to your souls in fair speeches. What I have said, is enough to convince you, that their character is that of the beast, whom St. John, in the Revelations, "saw coming up from the sea (that is, the flagitious [wicked] world) with seven heads." And what shall we say of a man, a clergyman, who teaches, and is an advocate for their perverse doctrines? May we not, nay, must we not, for the glory of God, and your good, inform you, that he is a "Teacher and approver of worldly maxims." May I not, nay, must I not, give you this caution with the royal preacher: "When he speaketh fair, believer him not, for there are seven abominations in his heart?" But how different is the character I have given you, from the character of the persons to whom the text under consideration is spoken! That is, the character of all such, as, like you, are resolved never to rest, `till they rest in Christ Jesus. To show this, I shall now pass to my third point.

III. To what sort of persons does Solomon in the character of a worldling address himself, when he says, "Be not righteous over-much, neither make thyself over-wise: why shouldst thou destroy thyself?" Not to the wicked, `tis plain; for besides that it would have been an unnecessary precaution, he turns to these in the next verse with another kind of warning, which however has some analogy with this. "Be not over-much wicked, neither be thou foolish, why shouldst thou die before thy time?" Was it then to the righteous, in a common way; that is, to such as content themselves with the observance of the absolute essentials of God's laws?

Surely our adversaries will not allow this, unless they be of opinion, that to be righteous at all, is to be righteous over-much. And yet it cannot possibly be supposed that the persons spoken to, are men perfectly righteous;

since, as I proved to you, in the introduction of this discourse, till we come up to the perfection of our heavenly father, we can never be righteous enough, much less perfectly righteous: wherefore, as in this life, men cannot attain to the perfection of their heavenly father, it follows in course that the persons here spoken to, cannot be men perfectly righteous, there being no such men existing; for as St. John saith, "If we say that we have no sin, we deceive ourselves, and the truth is not in us." Alas, O Lord, when shall we be delivered from the body of this death?

It remains, that the persons spoken to, in the text, are such only, as persisting steadfastly in a firm adherence to all the essential laws of God, content not themselves with the practice of common virtues in a common degree, but live in a perpetual habitude of desires, struggles, and yearnings towards an intimate union with Christ, the perfection of righteousness. They are not of the number of those righteous with indifference, who would fain blend the service of God and mammon, would fain have Christ and the world for their masters, and halting between two, like the children of Israel of old, with their faces to heaven, and their hearts to the earth, are neither hot nor cold. Alas, would they were cold or hot! But "because they are luke-warm, and neither cold nor hot, the Lord shall spew the out of his mouth." Not so the persons spoken to in my text; not so you, O beloved in God, who having shaken off the world and worldly affection; to run the more swiftly after righteousness, hate your own lives for the sake of Christ.

Happy, happy are all you, who put on our Lord Jesus, and with him the new man! "You are the true circumcision which worship God in spirit, and rejoice in Christ Jesus, and have no confidence in the flesh." What wonder then, Christians! To you I speak, all ye lovers and strugglers after the perfect righteousness of your divine Master Christ; what wonder is it, that you should be charged with enthusiasm, with folly, with fanaticism and madness? Were not the apostles so before you, when they preached Christ Jesus? Nay were they not reputed drunk with wine? Can you be amazed at it in an age, "when all manner of vice abounds to a degree almost unheard of," when the land is full of adulterers, and because of swearing the land mourneth. O how is the faithful city become an harlot! My heart within me is broken, because of the clergy, all my bones shake? I am like a drunken man, and like a man whom wine hath overcome; because of the Lord, and because of the words of his holiness, perverted by this deluded clergyman.

When the clergy, whom Christ has appointed to teach his people "to walk before him and be perfect," become teachers of worldly maxims, what can be expected from the laity? It is notorious, that for the moralizing iniquity of the priest, the land mourns. They have preached and lived many sincere persons out of the church of England. They endeavor to make you vain: (as the prophets did in the day of Jeremiah) they speak a vision out of their own mouth, and not out of the mouth of the Lord. In a word, "both prophet and priest are profane, and do wickedness in the very house of the Lord." Nay, they say still to them who despise the Lord, The Lord hath said, Ye shall have peace; and they say to every one who walketh after the imagination of his own heart, No evil shall come upon you.

Such is the language, my beloved lovers of Christian perfection, which the indolent, earthly-minded, pleasure-taking clergy of the church of England, use to strengthen the hands of evil-doers, that none may return from his wickedness. Such is the doctrine of the letter-learned divine, who has dipped his pen in gall, to decry perfect righteousness, and to delude you from it, with a false application of that text so greatly misunderstood by him: "Be not righteous over-much, neither be thou over-wise: why shouldst thou destroy thyself?" But suffer not yourselves, my fellow- Christians, to be deluded by him. For as I have already shown to you, he is grossly (Lord grant he was not maliciously) mistaken in his manner of explaining this text; and so far from making a right application of it according to the wise, the experienced Solomon's intention, he acts the character of a vain libertine, full of self-love, and earthly desires, whom Solomon but personates, to ridicule. But the doctor by realizing that character is himself, becomes the teacher and approver of worldly maxims, which he applies to you, on purpose to destroy in you the yearnings after perfect righteousness in Christ. May I not then, nay, must I not warn you, my beloved, that this man is an enemy to perfect righteousness in men through Christ Jesus, and, therefore, no friend to Christ? O that my head was an ocean, and my eyes fountains of tears, to weep night and day for this poor creature, this hood-winked member of the clergy.

Pray you, O true Christians, pray and sigh mightily to the Lord; importune him in the behalf of this erring pastor; pray that he would vouchsafe to open the eyes, and touch the stubborn heart of this scribe, that he may become better instructed. Otherwise, as the Lord said by the mouth of his true prophet Jeremiah, "Behold, I will feed him with wormwood, and make him drink the water of gall; for from him is profaneness gone forth into all the land." This good, however, hath he done by attempting to show the folly, sin, and danger of that which he miscalls being righteous over-much, that is, being superlatively righteous, in desire and habitual struggles; he has thereby given me the occasion to show you, brethren, in the course of this sermon, the great and real folly, sin, and danger of not being righteous enough; which, perhaps, I should never have thought of doing, had not this false doctrine pointed out to me the necessity of doing it. Thus does the all-wise providence of God, make use of the very vices of men to draw good out of evil; and choose their very errors to confound falsehood and make way for truth. Though this should be more than our angry adversary intended, yet, Lord, reward him according to his works: and suffer him no longer to be hasty in his words, that we may have room to entertain better hopes of him for the future.

Blessed be God for sending you better guides! I am convinced it was his divine will: our dear fellow-creature, Doctor Trapp, falling to such errors, has given so great a shock to the sound religion of Christian perfection, that unless I had opposed him, I verily believe the whole flock who listened to his doctrine, would have been scattered abroad like sheep having no shepherd. "But woe to you scribes and Pharisees! Woe be unto the pastors that destroy and scatter the sheep of my pasture, saith the Lord." Full well I know that this sermon will not be pleasing to my poor peevish adversary; but correction is not to pleasure but to profit: few children can be brought willingly to kiss the rod which rebuketh them; though, when they become of riper understanding, they will bless the hand that guided them. Thus shall this angry man, I trust, thank me one day for reproving him, when his reason shall be restored to him by the light of the Holy Spirit. O Lord, grant thou this light unto him, and suffer him to see with what bowels of pity and tenderness I love him in thee, even while I chasten him.

Neither am I insensible, brethren, how offensive my words will be to worldlings in general, who loving falsehood better than truth, and the flesh before the spirit will still prefer the doctor's sin-soothing doctrines to the plain gospel verities preached by me. O how my soul pities them. But I have done my duty, I wash my hands, and am innocent of the blood of all. I have not fought to please my hearers, but have spoken plain truth though it should offend. For what things were gain to me, those I counted loss for Christ; and hope I shall ever do so. Not that I presume to think myself already perfect. But "I press towards the mark, for the prize of the high calling of God in Christ Jesus." None of us, as I before told you, can boast of having attained the summit of perfection; though, he is the nearest to it, who is widest from the appetites of the flesh, and he stands the highest, who is the lowliest in his own esteem: wherefore, as many of us as have made any advances towards Christ and his kingdom, "whereto we have already attained, let us walk by the same rule, let us mind the same thing." Walk not then, brethren, according to the ways of the world: but be followers of Christ together with me. And if any, even an angel of light, should presume to teach you any other gospel than that which I have here taught you, let him be accursed. "For you will find many walking, like such of whom I have told you already, and now tell you weeping, that they are the enemies of the cross of Christ: whose end is destruction, whose God is their belly: and whose glory is in their shame, for they mind worldly things. But your conversation is in heaven, from whence also you look for the Savior, the Lord Jesus Christ: who shall change your vile bodies, that they may be fashioned like unto his glorious body, according to the working whereby he is able to subdue even all things unto himself," even the stubborn heart of our perverse adversary.

FIFTY-NINE SERMONS

Which God of his infinite mercy grant, etc.

Sermon 11 The Benefits of an Early Piety

(Preached at Bow Church, London, before the Religious Societies.)

Eccelesiastes 12:1, "Remember now thy Creator in the Days of thy Youth."

The amiableness of religion in itself, and the innumerable advantages that flow from it to society in general, as well as to each sincere professor in particular, cannot but recommend it to the choice of every considerate person, and make, even wicked men, as they wish to die the death, so in their more sober intervals, to envy the life of the righteous.

And, indeed, we must do the world so much justice, as to confess, that the question about religion does not usually arise from a dispute whether it be necessary or not (for most men see the necessity of doing something for the salvation of their souls;) but when is the best time to set about it.

Persons are convinced by universal experience, that the first essays or endeavors towards the attainment of religion, are attended with some difficulty and trouble, and therefore they would willingly defer the beginning of such a seemingly ungrateful work, as long as they can. The wanton prodigal, who is spending his substance in riotous living, cries, a little more pleasure, a little more sensuality, and then I will be sober in earnest. The covetous worldling, that employs all his care and pains in "heaping up riches, though he cannot tell who shall gather them," does not flatter himself that this will do always; but hopes with the rich fool in the gospel, to lay up goods for a few more years on earth, and then he will begin to lay up treasures in heaven. And, in short, thus it is that most people are convinced of the necessity of being religious some time or another; but then, like Felix, they put off the acting suitably to their convictions, 'till, what they imagine, a more convenient season: whereas, would we be so humble as to be guided by the experience and counsel of the wisest men, we should learn that youth is the fittest season for religion; "Remember now thy creator, (says Solomon) in the days of thy youth." By the word remember, we are not to understand a bare speculative remembrance, or calling to mind, (for that, like a dead faith, will profit us nothing,) but such a remembrance as will constrain us to obedience, and oblige us out of gratitude, to perform all that the Lord our God shall require of us. F9or as the forgetting God in scripture language, implies a total neglect of our duty, in like manner remembering him signifies a perfect performance of it: so that, when Solomon says, "Remember thy Creator in the days of thy youth,: it is the same as if he had said, keep God's commandments; or, in other words, be religious in the days of thy youth, thereby implying, that youth is the most proper season for it.

I shall in the following discourse, FIRST, Endeavor to make good the wise man's proposition, implied in the words of the text, and to show that youth is the fittest season for religion.

SECONDLY, By way of motive, I shall consider the many unspeakable advantages that will arise from, "Remembering our Creator in the days of our youth." And, THIRDLY, I shall conclude with a word or two of exhortation to the younger part of this audience.

FIRST, I am to make good the wise man's proposition, implied in the words of the text, and to show that youth is the fittest season for religion: "Remember now thy Creator in the days of thy youth." But to proceed more clearly in this argument, it may not be improper, first, to explain what I mean by the word religion. By this term, then, I would not be understood to mean a bare outward profession or naming the name of Christ; for we are told, that many who have even prophesied in his name, and in his name cast out devils, shall notwithstanding be rejected by him at the last day: nor would I understand by it, barely being admitted into Christ's church by baptism; for then Simon Magus, Arius, and the heresiarchs of old,, might pass for religious persons; for these were baptized: nor yet the receiving the other seal of the covenant, for then Judas himself might be canonized for a saint; nor indeed do I mean any or all of these together, considered by themselves; but a thorough, real, inward change of nature, wrought in us by the powerful operations of the Holy Ghost, conveyed to and nourished in our hearts, by a constant use of all the means of grace, evidenced by a good life, and bringing forth the fruits of the spirit.

The attaining this real, inward religion, is a work of so great difficulty, that Nicodemus, a learned doctor and teacher in Israel, thought it altogether impossible, and therefore ignorantly asked our blessed Lord, "How this thing could be?" And, truly, to rectify a disordered nature, to mortify our corrupt passions, to turn darkness to light, to put off the old man, and put on the new, and thereby to have the image of God reinstamped upon the soul, or, in one word, "to be born again," however light some may make of it, must, after all our endeavors, be owned by man to be impossible. It is true, indeed, Christ's yoke is said to be an easy or a gracious yoke, and his burden light; but then it is to those only to whom grace has been given to bear and draw in it. For, as the wise son of Sirach observes, "At first wisdom walked with her children in crooked ways, and bring them into fear, and torments them with her discipline, and does not turn to comfort and rejoice them, 'till she has tried them and d proved their judgment." No, we must not flatter ourselves that we shall walk in wisdom's pleasant ways, unless we first submit to a great many difficulties. The spiritual birth is attended with its pangs, as well as the natural: for they that have experienced it (an they only are the proper judges,) can acquaint you, that in all things that are dear to corrupt nature, we must deny ourselves, lest, after all, when w come to the birth, we should want strength to bring forth.

But if these things are so; if there are difficulties and pangs attending our being born again; if we must deny ourselves, what season more proper than that of youth? When, if ever, our bodies are robust and vigorous, and our minds active and courageous; and, consequently, we are then best qualified to endure hardness, as good soldiers of Jesus Christ.

We find, in secular matters, people commonly observe this method, and send their children abroad among the toils and fatigues of business, in their younger years, as well knowing they are then fittest to undergo them.

And why do they not act with the same consistency in the grand affair of religion? Because, as our Savior has told us, "The children of this world are wiser in their generation than the children of light.

But, SECONDLY, If pure and undefiled religion consists in the renewal of our corrupted natures, then it is not only a work of difficulty, but, the perfection of it, of time.

And if this be the case, then it highly concerns every one to set about it betimes, and to "work their work while it is day, before the night cometh, when no man can work." Could we, indeed, live to the age of Methuselah, and had but little business to employ ourselves in, we might then be more excusable, if we made no other use of this world, than what too many do, take our pastime therein: but since our lives are so very short, and we are called to work our salvation with fear and trembling, we have no room left for trifling, lest we should be snatched away while our lamps are untrimmed, and we are entirely unprepared to meet the Bridegroom.

Did we know a friend or neighbor, who had a long journey of the utmost importance to make, and yet should stand all the day idle, neglecting to set out till the sun was about to go down, we could not but pity and condemn his egregious folly. And yet it is to be feared most men are just such fools; they have a long journey to take, nay, a journey to eternity, a journey of infinite importance, and which they are obliged to dispatch before the sun of their natural life be gone down; and yet they loiter away the time allotted them to perform their journey in, till sickness or death surprises them; and then they cry out, "What shall we do to inherit eternal life?" But leaving such to the mercies of God in Christ, who can call at the eleventh hour, I pass on to The SECOND general thing proposed, To show the advantages that will arise from remembering our Creator in the days of our youth; which may serve as so many motives to excite and quicken all persons immediately to set about it.

And the FIRST benefit resulting from thence is, that it will bring most honor and glory to God. This, I suppose, every serious person will grant, ought to be the point in which our actions should center; for to this end were we born, and to this end were we redeemed by the precious blood of Jesus Christ, that we should promote God's eternal glory. And as the glory of God is most advanced by paying obedience to his precepts, they that begin soonest to walk in his ways, act most to his glory. The common objection against the divine laws in general, and the doctrines of the gospel in particular, is, they are not practicable; that they are contrary to flesh and blood; and that all those precepts concerning self-denial, renunciation of and deadness to the world, are but so many arbitrary restraints imposed upon human nature: but when we see mere striplings not only practicing, but delighting in such religious duties, and in the days of their youth, when, if ever, they have a relish for sensual pleasures, subduing and despising the lust of the flesh, the lust of the eyes and the pride of life; this, this is pleasing to God; this vindicates his injured honor; this shows that his service is perfect freedom, "that his yoke is easy, and his burden light." But, SECONDLY, as an early piety redounds most to the honor o God, so it will bring most honor to ourselves: for those that honor God, God will honor. We find it, therefore, remarked to the praise of Obadiah, that he served the Lord from his youth: of Samuel, that he stood, when young, before God in a linen ephod: of Timothy, that from a child he had known the holy scriptures: of St. John, that he was the youngest and most beloved disciple: and of our blessed Lord himself, that at twelve years old he went up to the temple, and sat among the doctors, both hearing and asking them questions.

Nor, THIRDLY, will an early piety afford us less comfort than honor, not only because it renders religion habitual to us, but also because it gives us a well-grounded assurance of the sincerity of our profession. Was there no other argument against a death-bed repentance, but the unsatisfactoriness and anxiety of such a state, that should be sufficient to deter all thinking persons from deferring the most important business of their life to such a dreadful period of it. For supposing a man to be sincere in his profession of repentance on a death-bed (which, in most cases, is very much to be doubted) yet, he is often afraid lest his convictions and remorse proceed not from a true sorrow for sin, but a servile fear of punishment. But one, who is a young saint, need fear no such perplexity; he knows that he loves God for his own sake, and is not driven to him by a dread of impending evil; he does not decline the gratifications of sense, because he can no longer "hear the voice of singing men and singing women;" but willingly takes up his cross, and follows his blessed Master in his youth, and therefore has reason to expect greater confidence of his sincerity towards God. But further, as an early piety assures the heart of its sincerity, so, likewise, it brings its present reward with it, as it renders religion and its duties habitual and easy. A young saint, were you to ask him, would joyfully tell you the unspeakable comfort of beginning to be religious betimes: as for his part, he knows not what men mean by talking of mortification, self-denial, and retirement, as hard and rigorous duties; for he has so accustomed himself to them, that, by the grace of God, they are now become even natural, and he takes infinitely more pleasure in practicing the severest precepts of the gospel, than a luxurious Dives in a bed of state, or an ambitious Haman at a royal banquet. And O how happy must that youth be, whose duty is become a second nature, and to whom those things, which seem terrible to others, are grown both easy and delightful!

But the greatest advantage of an early piety is still behind, FOURTHLY, It lays in the best provision of comfort and support against such time as we shall stand most in need thereof, viz. All times of our tribulation, and in particular, against the time of old age, the hour of death, and the day of judgment.

This is the argument the wise man makes use of in the words immediately following the text: "Remember now your Creator in the days of thy youth, while the evil days come not, nor the years draw nigh, wherein thou shalt say, I have no pleasure in them." Observe, the time of old age, is an evil time, years wherein there is no pleasure: and ask those that are grown old, and they will inform you so. Cordials surely, then, must be exceeding proper to support our drooping spirits: and O what cordial comparable to the recollection of early piety, depending wholly on the righteousness of Christ? When the eyes, like Isaac's, are grown dim with age; when "the keepers of the house, the hands, shall tremble," as the wise man goes on to describe the infirmities of old age; when "the strong men bow themselves," or the legs grow feeble; and the "grinders," the tooth, shall cease to do their proper office, because they are few; for a person then to hear the precepts of the gospel read over to him, and to be able to lay his hand on his heart, and to say sincerely, notwithstanding a consciousness of numberless short-comings, "All these have I endeavored, through grace, to keep from my youth:" this must give him, through Christ who worketh all, comfort that I want words to express and thoughts to conceive. But, supposing it was possible for us to escape the inconveniences of old age, yet still death is a debt, since the fall, we all must pay; and, what is worse, it generally comes attended with such dreadful circumstances, that it will make even a Felix to tremble. But as for the godly, that have been enabled to serve the Lord from their youth, it is not usually so with them; no, they have faith given them to look upon death, not as a king of terrors, but as a welcome messenger, that is come to conduct them to their wished-for home. All the days of their appointed time have they waited, and it has been the business of their whole lives to study to prepare themselves for the coming of their great change; and, therefore, they rejoice to hear they are called to meet the heavenly Bridegroom. Thus dies the early pious, whose "path has been as the shining light, that shineth more and more unto the perfect day." But follow him beyond the grave, and see with what an holy triumph he enters into his Master's joy; with what an humble boldness he stands at the dreadful tribunal of Jesus Christ; and can you then forbear to cry out, "Let me die the death of the righteous, and let my latter end, and future state, be like his?" Need I then, after having shown so many advantages to arise from an early piety, use any more arguments to persuade the younger part of this audience, to whom, in the THIRD and last place, I address myself, to "remember their Creator in the days of their youth?" What! Will not all the arguments I have mentioned, prevail with them to leave their husks, and return home to eat of the fatted calf? What! Will they thus requite our Savior's love? That be far from them! Did he come down and shed his precious blood to deliver them from the power of sin; and will they spend their youthful strength and vigor in the service of it, and then think to serve Christ, when they can follow their lusts no longer? Is it fit, that many, who are endowed with excellent gifts, and are thereby qualified to be supports and ornaments of our sinking church, should, notwithstanding, forget the God who gave them, and employ them in things that will not profit? O why will they not arise, and, like so many Phineas's, be zealous for the Lord of Hosts? Doubtless, when death overtakes them, they will wish they had: and what hinders them, but that they begin now? Think you that any one yet ever repented that he began to be religious too soon? But how many, on the contrary, have repented that they began when almost too late? May we not well imagine, that young Samuel now rejoices that he waited so soon at the tabernacle of the Lord? Or young Timothy, that from a child he knew the holy scriptures? And if you wish to be partakers of their joy, let me persuade you to be partakers of their piety.

I could still go on to fill my mouth with arguments; but the circumstances and piety of those amongst whom I am now preaching "the kingdom of God," remind me to change my style; and, instead of urging any more dissuasives from sin, to fill up what is behind of this discourse, with encouragements to persevere in holiness.

Blessed, for ever blessed be the God and the Father of our Lord Jesus Christ, I am not speaking to persons inflamed with youthful lusts, but to a multitude of young professors, who by frequently assembling together, and forming themselves into religious societies, are, I hope on good ground, in a ready way to be of the number of those "young men, who have overcome the wicked-one." Believe me, it gladdens my very soul, to see so many of your faces set heaven-wards, and the visible happy effects of your uniting together, cannot but rejoice the hearts of all sincere Christians, and oblige them to wish you good luck in the name of the Lord. The many souls who are nourished weekly with the spiritual body and blood of Jesus Christ, by your means; the weekly and monthly lectures that are preached by your contributions; the daily incense of thanksgiving and prayer which is publicly sent up to the throne of grace by your subscriptions; the many children which are trained up "in the nurture and admonition of the Lord," by your charities; and, lastly, the commendable and pious zeal you exert in promoting and encouraging divine psalmody, are such plain and apparent proofs of the benefit of your religious societies, that they call for a public acknowledgment of praise and thanksgiving to our blessed Master, who has not only put into your hearts such good designs, but enabled you also to bring the same to good effect.

It is true it has been object, "That young men forming themselves into religious societies, has a tendency to make them spiritually proud, and to think more highly of themselves than they ought to think." And, perhaps, the imprudent, imperious behavior of some novices in religion, who, "though they went out from you, were not of you," may have given too much occasion for such as aspersion.

But you, brethren, have not so learned Christ. Far, far be it from you to look upon yourselves, as righteous, and despise others, because you often assemble yourselves together. No; this, instead of creating pride, ought to beget an holy fear in your hearts, lest your practice should not correspond with your profession, and that, after you have benefited and edified others, you yourselves should become cast-aways.

Worldly-mindedness, my brethren, is another rock against which we are in danger of splitting. For, if other sins have slain their thousands of professing Christians, this has slain its ten thousands. I need not appeal to past ages; your own experience, no doubt, has furnished you with many unhappy instances of young men, who, "after (as one would have imagined) they had escaped the pollutions which are in the world through lust," and "had tasted the good word of life," and endured for a season, whilst under the tuition and inspection of others; yet, when they have come to be their own masters, through a want of faith, and through too great an earnestness in "laboring for the meat which perisheth," have cast off their first love, been again entangled with the world, and "returned like the dog to his vomit, and like the sow that was washed, to her wallowing in the mire." You would, therefore, do well, my brethren, frequently to remind each other of this dangerous snare, and to exhort one another to begin, pursue, and end your Christian warfare, in a thorough renunciation of the world, and worldly tempers; so that, when you are obliged by Providence to provide for yourselves, and those of your respective households, you may continue to walk by faith, and still "seek first the kingdom of God, and his righteousness;" not doubting, but all other things, upon your honest industry and endeavors, shall be added unto you.

And now, what shall I say more? To speak unto you, fathers, who have been in Christ so many years before me, and know the malignity of worldly- mindedness, and pride in the spiritual life, would be altogether needless.

To you, therefore, O young men, (for whom I am distressed, for whom I fear as well as for myself) do I once more address myself, in the words of the beloved disciple, "Look to yourselves, that we lose not those things which we have wrought, but receive a full reward." Be ever mindful, then, of the words that have been spoken to us by the apostles of the Lord and Savior, "Give diligence to make your calling and election sure. Beware, lest ye also being led away by the error of the wicked, fall from your own steadfastness. Let him that thinketh he standeth, take heed lest he fall.

Be not high-minded, but fear. But we are persuaded better things of you, and things that accompany salvation, though we thus speak. For God is not unrighteous, to forget your works and labor of love. And we desire that every one of you do show the same diligence, to the full assurance of hope unto the end: that ye be not slothful, but followers of them, who through faith and patience inherit the promises." It is true, we have many difficulties to encounter, many powerful enemies to overcome, ere we can get possession of the promised land. WE have an artful devil, and ensnaring world, and above all, the treachery of our own hearts, to withstand and strive against. "For straight is the gate, and narrow is the way that leadeth unto eternal life." But wherefore should we fear, since he that is with us is far more powerful, than all who are against us? Have we not already experienced his almighty power, in enabling us to conquer some difficulties which seemed as insurmountable then, as those we struggle with now? And cannot he, who delivered us out of the paws of those bears and lions, preserve us also from being hurt by the strongest Goliath?

"Be steadfast therefore, my brethren, be immovable." Be not "ashamed of the gospel of Christ: for it is the power of God unto salvation." Fear not man; fear not the contempt and revilings which you must meet with in the way of duty; for one of you shall chase a thousand; and two of you put ten thousand of your enemies to flight. And if you will be contented, through grace, to suffer for a short time here; I speak the truth in Christ, I lie not; then may ye hope, according to the blessed word of promise, that ye shall be exalted to sit down with the Son of Man, when he shall come in the glory of his Father, with his holy angels, to judgment hereafter. May Almighty God give every one of us such a measure of his grace, that we may not be of the number of those that draw back unto perdition, but of them that believe and endure unto the end, to the saving of our souls, through our Lord Jesus Christ.

Which God, etc.

Sermon 12 Christ the Believer's Husband

Isaiah 54:5, "For thy Maker is thy Husband."

Although believers by nature, are far from God, and children of wrath, even as others, yet it is amazing to think how nigh they are brought to him again by the blood of Jesus Christ. Eye hath not seen, nor ear heard, neither hath it entered into the heart of any man living, fully to conceive, the nearness and dearness of that relation, in which they stand to their common head. He is not ashamed to call them brethren. Behold, says the blessed Jesus in the days of his flesh, "my mother and my brethren." And again after his resurrection, "go tell my brethren." Nay sometimes he is pleased to term believers his friends. "Henceforth call I you no longer servants, but friends." "Our friend Lazarus sleepeth." And what is a friend? Why there is a friend that is nearer than a brother, nay as near as one's own soul. And "thy friend, (says God in the book of Deuteronomy) which is as thy own soul." Kind and endearing applications these, that undoubtedly bespeak a very near and ineffably intimate union between the Lord Jesus and the true living members of his mystical body! But, methinks, the words of our text point out to us a relation, which not only comprehends, but in respect to nearness and dearness , exceeds all other relations whatsoever. I mean that of a Husband, "For thy Maker is thy husband; the Lord of Hosts is his name; and thy Redeemer the Holy One of Israel, the God of the whole earth shall he be called." These words were originally spoken to the people of the Jews, considered collectively as a peculiar people, whom our Lord had betrothed and married to himself; and they seem to be spoken, when religion was on the decline among their churches; when they had, in a great measure, lost that life and power, which they once experienced; and their enemies began to insult them with a "where is now your God?" Such a state of things must undoubtedly be very afflicting to the true mourners in Zion; and put them upon crying unto the Lord, in this their deep distress. He hears their prayer, his bowels yearn towards them; and in the preceding verse, he assures them, that though the enemy had broken in upon them like a flood, yet their extremity should be his opportunity to lift up a standard against him. "Fear not, (says the great Head and King of his church) for thou shalt not be ashamed (finally or totally); neither be thou confounded, (dissipated or dejected, giving up all for gone, as though thou never shouldst see better days, or another revival of religion) for thou shalt not (entirely) be put to shame;" though for a while, for thy humiliation, and the greater confusion of thy adversaries, I suffer them to triumph over thee: "For thou shalt forget the shame of thy youth, and shalt not remember the reproach of thy widow-hood any more;" i.e. I will vouchsafe you such another glorious gale of my blessed Spirit, that you shall quite forget your former troubled widow-state, and give your enemies no more occasion to insult you, on account of your infant-condition, but rather to envy you, and gnash their teeth, and melt away at the sight of your un-thought-of glory and prosperity. And why will the infinitely great and condescending Jesus deal thus with his people? Because the church is his spouse; "For, (as in the words just now read to you) thy Maker is thy husband; thy Redeemer, the Holy One of Israel;" and therefore he loves them too well, to let thy enemies always trample thee under foot. "The Lord of Hosts is his name, the God of the whole earth shall he be called;" and therefore he is armed with sufficient power to relieve his oppressed people, and over come and avenge himself of all their haughty and insulting foes.

This seems to be the prime and genuine interpretation of the text and context, especially if we add, that they may have a further view to the latter-day glory, and that blesses state of the church, which the people of God have been looking for in all ages, and the speedy approach of which, we undoubtedly pray for, when we put up that petition of our Lord's, "thy kingdom come." But, though the words were originally spoken to the Jews, yet they are undoubtedly applicable to all believers in all ages, and, when enlarged on in a proper manner, will afford us suitable matter of discourse both for sinners and for saints; for such as know God, as well as for such who know him not; and likewise for those, who once walked in the light of his blessed countenance, but are now backslidden from him, have their harps hung upon the willows, and are afraid that their beloved is gone, and will return to their souls no more. Accordingly, without prefacing this discourse any further, as I suppose that a mixed multitude of saints, unconverted sinners, and backsliders, are present here this day, I shall endeavor to speak from the words of the text, that each may have a proper portion, and none be went empty away.

In prosecuting this design, I will, I. Endeavor to show, what must pass between Jesus Christ and our souls before we can say, "that our Maker is our husband." II. The duties of love which they owe to our Lord, who stand in so near a relation to him, III. The miserable condition of such as cannot yet say "their Maker is their husband." And IV. I shall conclude with a general exhortation to all such unhappy souls, to come and match with the dear Lord Jesus. And O! may that God who blessed Abraham's servant, when he went out to seek a wife for his son Isaac, bless me, even me also, now I am come, I trust, relying on divine strength, to invite poor sinners, and recall backsliders, to my Master Jesus!

And FIRST, I am to show, what must pass between Jesus Christ and our souls before we can say, "Our Maker is our husband." But before I proceed to this, it may not be improper to observe, that if any of you, amongst whom I am now preaching the kingdom of God, are enemies to inward religion, and explode the doctrine of inward feelings, as enthusiasm, cant and nonsense, I shall not be surprised, if your hearts rise against me whilst I am preaching; for I am about to discourse on true, vital, internal piety; and an inspired apostle hath told us, "that the natural man discerneth not the things of the spirit, because they are spiritually discerned." But, however, be noble as the Bereans were; search the Scriptures as they did; lay aside prejudice; hear like Nathaniel, with a true Israelitish ear; be willing to do the will of God; and then you shall according to the promise of our dearest Lord, "know of the doctrine, whether it be of God, or whether I speak of myself." I would further observe, that if any here do expect fine preaching from me this day, they will, in all probability, go away disappointed. For I came not here to shoot over people's heads; but, if the Lord shall be pleased to bless me, to reach their hearts. Accordingly, I shall endeavor to clothe my ideas in such plain language, that the meanest negro or servant, if God is pleased to give a hearing ear, may understand me; for I am certain, if the poor and unlearned can comprehend, the learned and rich must.

This being premised, proceed we to show what must pass between Jesus Christ and our souls, before we can say, "our Maker is our husband." Now, that we may discourse more pertinently and intelligibly upon this point, it may not be amiss to consider, what is necessary to be done, before a marriage between two parties amongst ourselves, can be said to be valid in the sight of God and men. And that will lead us in a familiar way, to show what must be done, or what must pass between us and Jesus Christ, before we can say, "our Maker is our husband." And FIRST, in all lawful marriages, it is absolutely necessary, that the parties to be joined together in that holy and honorable estate, are actually and legally freed from all pre-engagements whatsoever. "A woman is bound to her husband, (saith the apostle) so long as her husband liveth." The same law holds good in respect to the man. And so likewise, if either party be betrothed and promised, though not actually married to another, the marriage is not lawful, till that pre-engagement and promise be fairly and mutually dissolved. Now, it is just thus between us and the Lord Jesus.

For, we are all by nature born under, and wedded to the law, as a covenant of works. Hence it is that we are so fond of, and artfully go about, in order to establish a righteousness o four own. It is as natural for us to do this, as it is to breathe. Our first parents, Adam and Eve, even after the covenant of grace was revealed to them in that promise, "the seed of the woman shall bruise the serpent's head," reached out their hands, and would again have taken hold of the tree of life, which they had forfeited, had not God drove them our of paradise, and compelled them, as it were, to be saved by grace. And thus all their descendants naturally run to, and want to be saved, partly at least, if not wholly, by their works. And even gracious souls, who are inwardly renewed, so far as the old man abides in them, find a strong propensity this way. Hence it is, that natural men are generally so fond of Arminian principles. "Do and live," is the native language of a proud, self-righteous heart. But before we can say, "our Maker is our husband," we must be delivered from our old husband the law; we must renounce our own righteousness, our own doings and performances, in point of dependence, whether in whole or part, as dung and dross, for the excellency of the knowledge of Christ Jesus our Lord. For thus speaks the apostle Paul to the Romans, chapter 7:4, "Ye also are become dead to the law (as a covenant of works) by the body of Christ, that ye should be married to another, even to him, who is raised from the dead." As he also speaketh in another place, "I have espoused you, as a chaste virgin to Jesus Christ." This was the apostle's own case. Whilst he depended on his being a Hebrew of the Hebrews, and thought himself secure, because, as to the outward observation of the law, he was blameless; he was an entire stranger to the divine life: but when he began to experience the power of Jesus Christ's resurrection, we find him, in his epistle to the Philippians, absolutely renouncing all his external privileges, and all his Pharisaical righteousness; "Yes, doubtless, and I count all things but loss, nay but dung, that I may win Christ, and be found in him, not having mine own righteousness, which is of the law, but that which is through the faith of Jesus Christ, the righteousness which is of God by faith." And thus it must be with is. Ere we can say, "our Maker is our husband." Though we may not be wrought upon in that extraordinary way in which the apostle was, yet we must be dead to the law, we must be espoused as chaste virgins to Jesus Christ, and count all external privileges, and our most splendid performances (as was before observed) only "ad dung and dross, for the excellency of the knowledge of Jesus Christ our Lord." But further; before a marriage among us can stand good in law, both parties must not only be freed from all pre-engagements, but there must be a mutual consent on both sides. We are not used to marry people against their wills. This is what the Jews called betrothing, or espousing, a thing previous to the solemnity of marriage. Thus we find, the Virgin Mary is said to be espoused to Joseph, before they actually came together, Matt.

1:18. And thus it is among us. Both parties are previously agreed, and, as it were, espoused to each other, before we publish, what we call the banns of marriage concerning them. And so it will be in the spiritual marriage, between Jesus Christ and our souls. Before we are actually married or united to him by faith; or, to keep to the terms of the text, before we assuredly can say, that "our Maker is our husband," we must be made willing people in the day of God's power, we must be sweetly and effectually persuaded by the Holy Spirit of God, that the glorious Emanuel is willing to accept of us, just as we are, and also that we are willing to accept of him upon his own terms, yea, upon any terms. And when once it comes to this, the spiritual marriage goes on apace, and there is but one thing lacking to make it complete. And what is that? An actual union.

This is absolutely necessary in every lawful marriage among men. There must be a joining of hands before witnesses, ere they can be deemed lawfully joined together. Some men indeed of corrupt minds, are apt to look upon this as a needless ceremony, and think it sufficient to be married, as they term it, in the sight of God. But whence men get such divinity, I know not. I am positive, not from the Bible; for we there read that even at the first marriage in paradise, there was something of outward solemnity; God himself (if I may speak) being there the priest. For we are told, Gen. 2:22 that, after God had made the woman, "he brought her unto the man." And indeed, to lay aside all manner of outward ceremony in marriage, would be to turn the world into a den of brute beasts. Men would then take, or forsake as many wives as they pleased, and we should soon sink into as bad and brutal a state, as those nations are, amongst whom such practices are allowed of, and who are utterly destitute of the knowledge of our Lord and Savior Jesus Christ. Whoever has experienced the power of his resurrection, I am persuaded will never plead for such a licentious practice. For the terms made us of in Scripture, to represent the mystical union between Christ and his church, such as, our being "joined to the Lord," and "married to Jesus Christ," are all metaphorical expressions, taken from some analogous practices amongst men. And as persons when married, though before twain, are now one flesh; so those that are joined to the Lord, and can truly say, "our Maker is our husband," are in the apostle's language, one spirit. This was typified in the original marriage of our first parents. When God brought Eve to Adam, he received her with joy at his hands, and said, "this is bone of my bone, and flesh of my flesh." They had there, primarily, but one name. For thus speaks the sacred Historian, Gen.

5: 1-2, "In the day that God created man, he blessed them, and called their name Adam." And why? Because they were one flesh, and were to have but one heart. The self same terms are made use of in Scripture, to express the believer's union with Jesus Christ. We are called Christians, after Christ's name, because made partakers of Christ's nature. Out of his fullness, believers receive grace for grace. And therefore, the marriage state, especially by the apostle Paul, is frequently made use of, to figure out to us the real, vital union, between Jesus Christ and regenerate souls.

This is termed by the apostle, Eph. 5:32, "A great mystery." But great as it is, we must all experience it, before we can say assuredly, that "our Maker is our husband." For what says our Lord, in that prayer he put up to his Father before his bitter passion? "Father, I will that those whom thou hast given me, shall be where I am, that they may be one with thee; even as thou, O Father, and I are one, I in them, and they in me, that we all may be made perfect in one." O infinite condescension! On ineffable union!

Hence it is, that believers are said to be members of his body, of his flesh, and of his bones. Hence it is, that the apostle speaking of himself, says, "I live, yet not I, but Christ liveth in me." What an expression is that? How much does it comprehend? And, that we might not think this was something peculiar to himself, he puts this close question to the Corinthians; "Know ye not, that Christ is in you, unless you be reprobates?" Agreeable to what he says in his epistle to the Colossians; "Christ in you, the hope of glory." And hence it is, that our church, in the communion-office, directs the minister to acquaint all those who receive the sacrament worthily, that they are one with Christ, and Christ with them; that they dwell in Christ, and Christ in them. Words that deserve to be written in letters of gold, and which evidently show, what our reformers believed all persons must experience, before they could truly and assuredly say, that "their Maker is their husband." From what has been delivered, may not the poorest and most illiterate person here present easily know whether or not he is really married to Jesus Christ. Some indeed, I am afraid, are so presumptuous as to affirm, as least to insinuate, that there is no such thing as knowing, or being fully assured, whilst here below, whether we are in Christ or not. Or at least, if there be such a thing, it is very rare, or was only the privilege of the primitive believers. Part of this is true, and part of this absolutely false. That this glorious privilege of a full assurance is very rare, is too, too true. And so it is equally too true, that real Christians, comparatively speaking, are very rare also. But that there is no such thing, or that this was only the privilege of the first followers of our blessed Lord, is directly opposite to the word of God. "We know (says St. John, speaking of believers in general) that we are his, by the spirit which he hath given us;" and, "He that believeth hath the witness of himself;" "because you are sons (saith St. Paul) God hath sent forth his Spirit into your hearts, even the spirit of adoption, whereby we cry, Abba, Father." Not that I dare affirm, that there is no real Christian, but what has this full assurance of faith, and clearly knows, that his Maker is his husband. In speaking thus, I should undoubtedly condemn some of the generation of God's dear children, who through the prevalence of unbelief, indwelling sin, spiritual sloth, or it may be, for want of being informed of the privileges of believers, may walk in darkness, and see no light; therefore, though I dare not affirm, that a full assurance of faith is absolutely necessary for the very being, yet I dare assert, that it is absolutely necessary, for the well being of a Christian. And for my own part, I cannot conceive, how any persons, that pretend to Christianity, can rest satisfied or contented without it. This is stopping short, on this side Jordan, with a witness. And gives others too much reason to suspect, that such persons, however high their profession may be, have, as yet, no true saving grace at all.

Men, whose hearts are set on this world's goods, or, to use our Lord's language, "the children of this world," act not so. I suppose there is scarce a single merchant in this great congregation, especially in these troublous times, that will venture out either his ship or cargo, without first insuring, both against the violence of an enemy, or a storm. And I suppose there is scarce a single house, of any considerable value, in any populous town or city, but the owner has taken out a policy from the fire- office, to unsure it, in case of fire. And can I be so irrational as to think, that there is such a thing as securing my goods, and my house, and that there is no such thing as insuring, what is infinitely more valuable, my precious and immortal soul? Or if there be such a thing, as undoubtedly there is, what foolishness of folly must it needs be in men, that pretend to be men of parts, of good sense, and solid reasoning, to be so anxious to secure their ships against a storm, and their houses against a fire, and at the same time, not to be unspeakably more solicitous, to take a policy out of the assurance-office of heaven; even the soul and witness of the blessed Spirit of God, to insure their souls against that storm of divine wrath, and that vengeance of eternal fire, which will at the last decisive day come upon all those, who know not God, and have not obeyed his gracious gospel? To affirm therefore, that there is no such thing as knowing, that "our Maker is our husband;" or that it was a privilege peculiar to the first Christians, to speak in the mildest terms, is both irrational and unscriptural. Not that all who can say, their Maker is their husband, can give the same clear and distinct account of the time, manner and means of their being spiritually united and married by faith, to the blessed bridegroom of the church. Some there may be now, as well as formerly, sanctified from the womb. And others in their infancy and non-age, as it were silently converted. Such perhaps may say, with a little Scotch maiden, now with God, when I asked her, whether Jesus Christ had taken away her old heart, and given her a new one? "Sir, it may be, (said she,) I cannot directly tell you the time and place, but this I know, it is done." And indeed it is not so very material, though no doubt it is very satisfactory, if we cannot relate all the minute and particular circumstances, that attended our conversion; if so be we are truly converted now, and can say, the work is done, and that, "our Maker is our husband." And I question, whether there is one single adult believer, now on earth, who lived before conversion, either in a course of secret or open sin, but can, in a good degree, give an account of the beginning and progress of a work of grace in his heart.

What think ye? Need I tell my married persons in this congregation, that they must go to the university, and learn the languages, before they can tell whether they are married or not? Or, if their marriage was to be doubted, could they not, think you, bring their certificates, to certify the time and place of their marriage; and the minister that joined them together in that holy state? And if you are adult, and are indeed married to Jesus Christ, though you may be unlearned, and what the world terms illiterate men, cannot you tell me the rise and progress, and consummation of the spiritual marriage, between Jesus Christ and your souls? Know you not the time, when you were first under the drawings of the Father, and Jesus began to woo you for himself? Tell me, O man, tell me, O woman, knowest thou not the time, or at least, knowest thou not, that there was a time, when the blessed Spirit of God stripped thee of the fig-leaves of thy own righteousness, hunted thee out of the trees of the garden of they performances, forced thee from the embraces of thy old husband the law, and made thee to abhor thy own righteousness, as so many filthy rags? Canst thou not remember, when, after a long struggle with unbelief, Jesus appeared to thee, as altogether lovely, mighty and willing to save? And canst thou not reflect upon a season, when thy own stubborn heart was made to bend; and thou wast made willing to embrace him, as freely offered to thee in the everlasting gospel? And canst thou not, with pleasure unspeakable, reflect on some happy period, some certain point of time, in which a sacred something (perhaps thou could it not then well tell what) did captivate, and fill thy heart, so that thou could say, in a rapture of holy surprise, and ecstasy of divine love, "My Lord and my God! My beloved is mine, and I am his; I know that my Redeemer liveth;" or, to keep to the words of our text, "My Maker is my husband." Surely, amidst this great and solemn assembly, there are many that can answer these questions in the affirmative. For these are transactions, not easily to be forgotten; and the day of our espousals is, generally, a very remarkable day; a day to be had in everlasting remembrance.

And can any of you indeed, upon good grounds say, that your Maker is your husband? May I not then (as it is customary to wish persons joy who are just entered into the marriage state) congratulate you upon your happy change, and wish you joy, with all my heart? Sure am I that there was joy in heaven on the day of your espousals: and why should not the blessed news occasion joy on earth? May I not address you in the language of our Lord to the women that came to visit his sepulcher, "All hail!" for ye are highly favored. Blessed are ye among men, blessed are ye among women! All generations shall call you blessed. What! "is your Maker your husband? The holy on of Israel your Redeemer?" Sing, O heavens, and rejoice, O earth!

What an amazing stoop is this! What a new thing has God created on the earth! Do not your hearts, O believers, burn within you, when meditating on this unspeakable condescension of the high and lofty one that inhabiteth eternity? Whilst you are musing, does not the sacred fire of divine love kindle in your souls? And, out of the abundance of your hearts, do you not often speak with your tongues, and call upon all that is within you, to laud and magnify your Redeemer's holy name? Is not that God-exalting, self- abasing expression frequently in your mouths, "Why me, Lord, why me?" And are you not often constrained to break out into that devout exclamation of Solomon, when the glory of the Lord filled the temple, "And will God indeed dwell with man?" ungrateful, rebellious, ill, and hell-deserving man! O, my brethren, my heart is enlarged towards you! Tears, while I am speaking, are ready to gush out. But they are tears of love and joy. How shall I give it vent? How shall I set forth thy happiness, O believer, thou bride of God!

And is thy Maker thy husband? Is his name "The Lord of hosts?" Whom then shouldst thou fear? And is thy Redeemer the holy one of Israel? The God of the whole earth should he be called! Of whom then shouldst thou be afraid?

He that toucheth thee, toucheth the very apple of God's eye. "The very hairs of thy head are all numbered;" and "it is better that a man should have a millstone tied round his neck, and be drowned in the sea, than that he should justly offend thee." All hail, (I must again repeat it) thou Lamb's bride! For thou art all glorious within, and comely, through the comeliness thy heavenly bridegroom hath put upon thee. Thy garment is indeed of wrought gold; and, ere long, the King shall bring thee forth with a raiment of needle-work, and present thee blameless before his Father, without spot, or wrinkle, or any such thing. In the mean while, well shall it be with you, and happy shall you be, who are married to Jesus Christ: for all that Christ has, is yours. "He is made of God to you, wisdom, righteousness, sanctification, and eternal redemption." "Whether Paul, or Cephas, or the world, or life, or death, or things present, or things to come; all are yours." All his attributes are engaged for your preservation, and all things shall work together for your good, who love God, and, by being thus married to the Lord Jesus, give an evident proof that you are called according to his purpose. What say you?

When you meditate on these things, are you not frequently ready to cry out, What shall we render unto the Lord for all these mercies, which, of his free unmerited grace, he hath been pleased to bestow upon us? For, though you are dead to the law, as a covenant of works, yet you are alive to the law as a rule of life, and are in, or under the law (for either expression seems to denote the same thing) to your glorious husband, Jesus Christ.

Pass we on therefore to the SECOND general head, under which I was to show, what duties of love they owe to Jesus Christ, who are so happy as to be able to say, "My Maker is my husband." I say, duties of love. For being now married to Jesus Christ, you work not for life, but from life. The love of God constrains you, so that, if there was no written law, or supposing Jesus would set you at liberty from his yoke, so far as grace prevails in your hearts, you would say, we love our blessed bridegroom, and will not go from him.

And what does the Lord require of you? That we may speak on this head as plainly as may be, we shall pursue the method we began with; and, by carrying on the allegory, and examining what is required of truly Christian wives, under the gospel, infer what our Lord may justly demand of those who are united to him by faith, and can therefore say, "our Maker is our husband." And here let us go to the law and to the testimony. What says the scripture? "Let the wife see that she REVERENCE her "husband." It is, no doubt, the duty of married women to think highly of their husbands. From whom may husbands justly command respect, if not from their wives? The apostle's expression is emphatic. "Let the wife see that she reverence her husband;" thereby implying, that women, some of them at least, are too prone to disrespect their husbands; as Michal, Saul's daughter, despised David in her heart, when she tauntingly said, 2 Sam. 6:20, "How glorious was the king of Israel to-day, who uncovered himself to-day in the eyes of the handmaids of his servants, as one of the vain fellows shamelessly uncovereth himself." This is a source and fountain, from whence many domestic evils frequently flow. Women should remember the character that husbands sustain in scripture. The are to them, what Christ is to the church. And it is mentioned to the honor of Sarah, that she called Abraham "Lord." "Shall I have a child who am old, my Lord being old also?" It is remarkable, there are but two good words in that whole sentence, "my Lord," (for all the others are the language of unbelief) and yet those two words the Holy Ghost mentions to her eternal honor, and buries, as it were, the rest in oblivion. "Even as Sarah (says St. Peter) obeyed Abraham, calling him Lord." An evident proof how pleasing it is in the sight of God, for women in the married state to reverence and respect their husbands. Not that husbands therefore should lord it over their wives, or require too much respect at their hands. This would be unchristian, as well as ungenerous, indeed. They ought rather, as God has taken such care to keep up their authority, commanding their wives to reverence and respect them; they ought, I say, to be doubly careful, that they live so holy and unblameable, as to lay their wives under no temptation to despise them. But to return from this digression. Does the apostle say, "Let the wife see that she reverence her husband?" May I not pertinently apply this caution to you who are married to Jesus Christ? See to it that you reverence and respect your husband. I say, SEE TO IT. For the devil will be often suggesting to you hard and mean thoughts against your husband. It was thus he beset our mother Eve, even in a state of innocence. He would fain persuade her to entertain hard thoughts of her glorious benefactor, "What, has God said, ye shall not eat of the trees of the garden?" Has he been so cruel to put you here in a beautiful garden only to vex and tease you? This he made use of as an inlet to all his succeeding insinuations. And this trade he is still pursuing, and will be pursuing to the very end of time. Besides, in the eyes of the world, Jesus Christ has no form or comeliness that they should desire him; and therefore, unless you "watch and pray," you will be led into temptation, and not keep up such high thoughts of your blessed Jesus as he justly deserves. In this you can never exceed. Women, perhaps may sometimes think too highly of, and, through excess of love, idolize their earthly comforts. But it is impossible for you to think too highly of your heavenly husband, Jesus Christ.

Farther, what says the apostle in his epistle to the Ephesians?

Speaking of the marriage state, he says, "The wife is the glory of her husband;" as though he had said, a Christian wife should so behave, and so walk, as to be a credit to her husband. As Abigail was an honor to Nubal, and by her sweet deportment made up, in some degree, for her husband's churlishness. This is to be a help-meet indeed. Such a woman will be praised in the gate; and her husband get glory, and meet with respect on her account. And ought a woman to be the glory of her husband? How much more ought you, that are the Lamb's bride, so to live, and so to walk, as to bring glory, and gain respect, to the cause and interest of your husband Jesus? This is what the apostle everywhere supposes, when he would draw a parallel between a temporal and spiritual marriage. "The woman, is the glory of her husband, even as the church is the glory of Christ." Agreeable to this, he tells the Corinthians, "Whether you eat or drink, or whatsoever you do, do all to the glory of God;" and as he also speaks to the Thessalonians, 1 Thess. 2:11-12, "As you know how we exhorted, and comforted, and charged every one of you (as a father doth his children) that you would walk worthy of God who hath called you to his kingdom, and his glory." What an expression is here! "That you would walk worthy of God." O! how ought this, and such like texts, to stir up your pure minds, O believers, so to have your conversation in this world, that you may be what the apostle says some particular persons were, even "the glory of Christ." You are his glory; he rejoices over you with singing; and you should so walk, that all who know and hear of you, may glorify Christ in you.

SUBJECTION, is another duty, that is enjoined married women, in the word of God. They are to "be subject to their own husbands in every thing." Every lawful thing: "For, the husband is the head of the wife, even as Christ is the head of the church." And knowing how inapt some base minds would be to submit to the husband's authority, he takes care to enforce this duty of subjection by many cogent and powerful arguments." "For Adam was first made, and not Eve. Neither was the man made for the woman, but the woman for the man." And again, "The man was not first in the transgression, but the woman." Upon which accounts, subjection was imposed on her as part of her punishment. "Thy desire (says God) shall be to thy husband, and he shall rule (though not tyrannize) over thee." So then, to use the words of pious Mr. Henry, those who attempt to usurp authority over their husbands, not only contradict a divine command, but thwart a divine curse. And if women are to be subject to their own husbands in every thing, how much more ought believers, whether men or women, to be subject to Jesus Christ: for he is the head of the church. He has bought her by his blood.

Believers therefore are not their own, but are under the highest obligations to glorify and obey Jesus Christ, in their bodies and their souls, which are his. Add to this, that his service, as it is admirably expressed in one of our collects, is perfect freedom. His commandments holy, just, and good. And therefore it is your highest privilege, O believers, to submit to, and obey them. Earthly husbands may be so mean as to impose some things upon their wives, merely to show their authority; but it is not so with Jesus Christ. He can and does impose nothing, but what immediately conduces to our present, as well as future good. In doing, nay, in suffering for Jesus Christ, there is a present unspeakable reward. And therefore I may say to believers, as the blessed Virgin said to the servants at the marriage in Cana, "Whatsoever he says unto you, do it." "For his yoke is easy, and his burden is light." And I believe it might easily be proved in a few minutes, that all the disorders which are now in the world, whether in church or state, are owing to a want of being universally, unanimously, cheerfully, and perseveringly conformed to the laws and example of our Lord and Savior Jesus Christ.

Again, FAITHFULNESS in the marriage state, is strictly enjoined in the scriptures of truth. "Marriage is honorable in all, and the bed undefiled.

But whoremongers and adulterers God will judge." Nay, adultery is an iniquity to be punished by the earthly judges; it dissolves the marriage relation. "For the man has not power over his own body, but the woman; neither has the woman power over her own body, but the man." The heathens themselves have been taught this by the light of nature; and adultery, among some of them, is punished with immediate death. And ought married persons to be thus careful to keep the marriage-bed undefiled, how carefully then ought believers to keep their souls chaste, pure, and undefiled, now they are espoused to Jesus Christ? For there is such a thing as spiritual adultery; "O ye adulterers and adulteresses," saith St. James.

And God frequently complains of his people's playing the harlot. Hence it is, that St. John, in the most endearing manner, exhorts believers to "keep themselves from idols." For the lust of the eye, the lust of the flesh, and pride of life, are always ready to steal away our hearts from Jesus Christ.

And every time we place our affections upon any thing more than Christ, we do undoubtedly commit spiritual adultery. For we admit a creature to rival the Creator, who is God over all, blessed for evermore. "Little children, therefore, keep yourselves from idols." But it is time for me to draw towards the close of this head.

FRUITFULNESS was a blessing promised by God to the first happy pair; "Increase and multiply, and replenish the earth." "Lo, children, and the fruit of the womb, (says the Psalmist) are a gift and heritage, which cometh of the Lord." And so, if we are married to Jesus Christ, we must be fruitful. In what? In every good word and work: for this speaks the Apostle, in his epistle to the Romans: "Wherefore, my brethren, ye also are become dead to the law, by the body of Christ, that ye should be married to another, even to him who is raised from the dead." What follows? "That we should bring forth fruit unto God." Glorious words, and proper to be considered in a peculiar manner, by such who would explode the doctrine of free justification, as an Antinomian doctrine, and as though it destroyed good works. No; it establishes, and lays a solid foundation, whereon to build the superstructure of good works. Titus is therefore commanded to "exhort believers to be careful to maintain good works." And "herein (says our Lord) is my Father glorified, that ye bring forth much fruit. Let your light so shine before men, that they may see your good works, and glorify your Father which is in heaven;" with a multitude of passages to the same purpose.

Moreover, it is required of wives, that they not only love and reverence their husbands, but that they also love and respect their HUSBAND'S FRIENDS. And if we are married to Jesus Christ, we shall not only reverence the bridegroom, but we shall also love and honor the bridegroom's friends. "By this, shall all men know that ye are my disciples, if ye love one another." "By this we know, (says the beloved disciple) that we have passed from death to life because we love the brethren." Observe, the brethren, indefinitely; of whatever denomination. And this love must be "without dissimulation, and with a pure heart fervently." This was the case of the primitive Christians. They were all of one heart, and of one mind.

It was said of them (O that it could be said of us!) "See how these Christians love one another!" They were of the same spirit as a good woman of Scotland was, who, when she saw a great multitude, as is customary in the country, coming from various parts to receive the blessed sacrament, saluted them with a "Come in, ye blessed of the Lord, I have an house that will hold an hundred of you, and a heart that will hold ten thousand." Let us go and do likewise.

Once more. Persons that are married, take one another FOR BETTER OR FOR WORSE, for richer or for poorer, to love and to cherish each other in sickness and in health. And if we are married to Jesus Christ, we shall be willing to bear his CROSS, as well as to wear his CROWN. "If any man will come after me, let him deny himself, take up his cross, and follow me." Neither will they be compelled to do this, as Simon of Cyrene was, but they will be volunteers in his service; they will cry out, Crown him, crown him ,when others are crying out, "Crucify him, crucify him." They will never leave or forsake him, but willingly follow the Captain of their salvation, though it be through a sea of blood.

I might run the parallel still further, and also enlarge upon the hints already given; but I fear I have said enough already to reproach most believers; I am sure I have said more than enough to abash and upbraid myself. For alas! how vilely, treacherously, and ungratefully have we behaved towards our spiritual husband, the dear Lord Jesus, ever since the day of our espousals? Had our friends, or even the wives of our own bosoms, behaved to us as we have behaved to our great and best friend, our glorious husband, we should have broken off our friendship, and sued for a bill of divorcement long ago. Under our first love, what promises did we make to him? But how frowardly have we behaved ourselves in this covenant? How little have we reverenced him? How often has our Beloved been no more to us than another beloved? How little have we lived to his glory? Have we not been a shame and reproach to his gospel? Have we not crucified him afresh, and has he not been sorely wounded in the house of his friends? Nay, has not his holy name been blasphemed through our means? For alas! how little have we obeyed him? How careless and indifferent have we been, whether we pleased him or not? We have often said, indeed, when commanded by him to go work in his vineyard, We go, Lord; but alas! we went not. Or if we did go, with what reluctance has it been? How unwilling to watch with our dear Lord and Master, only one hour? And of his sabbaths, how often have we said, What weariness is this? As for our adulteries, and spiritual fornications, how frequent, how aggravated have they been? Have not idols of all sorts, been suffered to fill up the room of the ever-blessed Jesus in our hearts?

You that love him in sincerity, will not be offended if I tell you, that the 16th chapter of Ezekiel gives, in my opinion, a lively description of our behavior towards our Lord. We were, like base-born children, cast out in the field to the loathing of our persons: no eye pitied or had compassion on us. Jesus passed by, saw us polluted in our own blood, and said unto us, "Live," i.e. preserved us, even in our natural state, from death. And when his time of love was come, he spread the skirt of his imputed righteousness over us, and covered the nakedness of our souls, entered into covenant with us, and we became his. He washed us also with water, even in the laver of regeneration, and thoroughly washed us by his precious blood, from the guild of all our sins. He clothed us also with broidered work, and decked us with ornaments, even with righteousness, and peace, and joy in the Holy Ghost. We did eat fine flour and honey at his ordinances, and we fed on Jesus Christ in our hearts by faith, with thanksgiving. In short, we were made exceeding beautiful, and the kingdom of God was erected in our hearts. We were renowned among our neighbors for our love to God, and all that know us took knowledge of us, that we had been with Jesus. But alas! how have we fallen, who were once sons of the morning! How have we trusted in our own beauty, have grown spiritually proud, and provoked our patient and unspeakably long-suffering Lord to anger? Where is that ardent love we spoke of, when we told him, that, though we should die for him, we would not deny him in any wise? How desperately wicked, and deceitful above all things, have we proved our hearts to be, since we have done all these things, even the work of an imperious woman? These are great and numerous charges; but great and numerous as they are, there is not a single believer here present, but, if he knows his own heart, may plead guilty to some, or all of them. But this is a tender point: I see you concerned: your tears, O believers, are a proof of the anguish of your souls. And can any of us give any reason, why Jesus Christ should not give us a bill of divorcement, and put us away? May he not justly speak to us as he did to his adulteress Israel, in the aforementioned 16th of Ezekiel, "Wherefore, O harlot, hear the word of the Lord; I will judge thee as women that break wedlock, and shed blood, are judged. I will give thee blood in fury and jealousy, because thou hast not remembered the days of thy youth, but hast fretted me in all these things.

Behold, therefore, I also will recompense thy way upon thy head. I will even deal with thee as thou hast done, who hast despised the oath, in breaking the covenant, the marriage contract that was between us." This, I am persuaded, you will confess to be the treatment which we all most justly deserve. But be not overwhelmed with over-much sorrow: for though the Lord our God is a jealous God, and will certainly visit our offenses with a rod, and our backslidings with a spiritual scourge, yet his loving-kindness will he not utterly take from us, nor suffer his truth to fail. Though we have changed, yet he changeth not: He abideth faithful: his loving-kindness abideth for evermore. Hark! how sweetly he speaks to his backsliding people of old; "O Israel, thou hast destroyed thyself, but in me is thy help. I will heal their backsliding, and love them freely." And in the verses immediately following the words of the text, how comfortably does he address his espoused people! "In a little wrath, I hid my face from thee for a moment; but with everlasting kindness will I have mercy on thee, saith the Lord thy Redeemer. For this is as the waters of Noah unto me; for as I have sworn, that the waters of Noah should no more go over the earth; so have I sworn, that I would not be wroth with thee, nor rebuke thee. For the mountains shall depart, and the hills be removed, but my kindness shall not depart from thee, neither shall the covenant of my peace be removed, saith the Lord that hath mercy on thee." O that this goodness may lead us to repentance! O that this unparalleled, infinite, unchangeable love, may constrain us to an universal, uniform, cheerful, unanimous, persevering obedience to all the commands of God!

Brethren, my heart is enlarged towards you, and I could dwell a long while upon the many great and precious invitations that are made to backsliders, to return to their first love, and do their first works: but it is high time for me, if, as was proposed, III. I give to every one their proper portion; to speak to those poor souls, who know nothing of this blessed Bridegroom of the church, and consequently cannot say, "My Maker is my husband." Ah! I pity you from my inmost soul; I could weep over, and for you, though perhaps you will not weep for yourselves. But surely you would weep, and howl too, did you know the miserable condition those are in, who are not married to Jesus Christ. Will you give me leave (I think I speak it in much love) to inform you, that if you are not married to Jesus Christ, you are married to the law, the world, the flesh, and the devil, neither of which can make you happy; but all, on the contrary, concur to make you miserable. Hear ye not, ye that are married to the law, and seek to be justified in the sight of God, partly, at least, if not wholly, by your own works, what the law saith to those that are under it, as a covenant of works? "Cursed is every one that continueth not in all things that are written in the book of the law, to do them." Every word breathes threatening and slaughter to poor fallen creatures. Cursed, both here and hereafter, be this man, and every one, naturally engendered of the offspring of Adam, without exception, that continueth not, even to the very end of life, in all things; not only in some, or many, but in all things, that are written in the book of the law, to do them, in the utmost perfection; for "he that offendeth in one point, is guilty of all." So that, according to the tenor of the covenant of works, whosoever is guilty of one wicked thought, word, or action, is under the curse of an angry sin- avenging God. "For a many as are under the law, are under the curse." And do you know what it is to be under the curse of God, and to have the wrath of God abide upon you? If you did, I believe you would not be so unwilling to be divorced from the law, and be espoused, as chaste virgins, to Jesus Christ.

And why are ye so wedded to the world? Did it ever prove faithful or satisfactory to any of its votaries? Has not Solomon reckoned up the sum total of worldly happiness? And what does it amount to? "Vanity, vanity, saith the preacher, all is vanity," nay he adds, "and vexation of spirit." And has not a greater than Solomon informed us, that a man's life, the happiness of a man's life, doth not consist in the things which he possesseth? Besides, "know ye not that the friendship of this world is enmity with God; so that whosoever will be a friend to the world, (to the corrupt customs and vices of it) is an enemy of God?" And what better reasons can you give for being wedded to your lusts? Might not the poor slaves in the galleys, as reasonably be wedded to their chains? For do not your lusts fetter down your souls from God? Do they not lord it, and have they not dominion over you? Do not they say, Come, and ye come; Go, and ye go; Do this, and ye do it? And is not he or she that liveth in pleasure, dead, whilst he liveth? And above all, how can ye bear the thoughts of being wedded to the devil, as every natural man is: for thus speaks the scripture, "He now ruleth in the children of disobedience." And how can ye bear to be ruled by one, who is such a professed open enemy to the most high and holy God? Who will make a drudge of you, whilst you live, and be your companion in endless and extreme torment, after you are dead? For thus will our Lord say to those on the left hand, "Depart from me, ye cursed, into everlasting fire, prepared for the devil and his angels." But, IV. Will you permit me, O sinners, that I may draw towards a close of this discourse, to propose a better match to your souls. This is a part of the discourse which I long to come to, it being my heart's desire, and earnest prayer to God, that your souls may be saved. "And now, O Lord God Almighty, thou Father of mercies, and God of all consolations, thou God and Father of our Lord Jesus Christ, who hast promised to give thy Son the heathen for his inheritance, and the uttermost parts of the earth for his possession, send me good speed this day. O Lord, send me now prosperity.

Behold, I stand here without the camp, bearing a little of thy dear Son's sacred reproach! Hear me, O Lord, hear me, and according to thy word, let thy dear, thine only begotten Son, see of the travail of his soul, and be satisfied! O help me so to speak, that many may believe on, and cleave unto thy blessed, thine holy child Jesus!

But who am I, that I should undertake to recommend the blessed Jesus to others, who am myself altogether unworthy to take his sacred name into my polluted lips? Indeed, my brethren, I do not count myself worthy of such an honor; but since it has pleased him, in whom all fullness dwells, to count me worthy, and put me into the ministry, the very stones would cry out against me, did I not attempt, at least, to lisp out his praise, and earnestly recommend the ever-blessed Jesus to the choice of all.

Thus Abraham's faithful servant behaved, when sent out to fetch a wife for his master Isaac. He spake of the riches and honors, which God had conferred on him; but what infinitely greater honors and riches, has the God and Father of our Lord Jesus, conferred on his only Son, to whom I now invite every Christless sinner! To you, therefore, I call, O ye sons of men, assuring you, there is everything in Jesus that your hearts can desire, or hunger and thirst after. Do people in disposing of themselves or their children in marriage, generally covet to be matched with PERSONS OF GREAT NAMES? Let this consideration serve as a motive to stir you up to match with Jesus. For God the Father has given him a name above every name; he has upon his vesture, and upon his thigh, a name written, "The King of kings, and the Lord of lords;" and herein the text we are told, "The Lord of Hosts is his name." Nor has he an empty title, but power equivalent; for he is a prince, as well as savior. "All power is given unto him, both in heaven and on earth;" "The God of the while earth, (says our text) he shall be called." The government of men, of the church, and of devils, is put upon his shoulders: "Thrones, principalities and powers, are made subject unto him; by him kings reign, and princes decree justice; he setteth up one, and putteth down another: and of his kingdom there shall be no end." Will RICHES be an inducement unto you to come and match with Jesus? Why then, I can tell you, the riches of Jesus are infinite: for unto me, who am less than the least of all saints, is this grace given, that I should preach to poor sinners, the unsearchable riches of Jesus Christ. I appeal to you that are his saints, whether you have not found this true, by happy experience; and though some of you, may have been acquainted with him thirty, forty, fifty years ago, do you not find his riches are yet unsearchable, and as much past finding out, as they were the very first moment in which you gave him your hearts?

Would you match with a WISE HUSBAND? Haste then, sinners, come away to Jesus: He is the fountain of wisdom, and makes all that come unto him, wise unto salvation: "He is the wisdom of the Father: the Lord possessed him in the beginning of his way, before his works of old. When he prepared the heavens, he was there; when he appointed the foundations of the earth, then was he with him, as one brought up with him; he was daily his delight, rejoicing always before him." As he is wise, so is he HOLY; and therefore, in the words of our text, he is stiled, "The Redeemer, the Holy One of Israel:" and by the angel Gabriel, "That holy Thing." The apostles, addressing God the Father, stile him his "holy child Jesus:" and the spirits of just men made perfect, and the angels in heaven, cease not day or night, saying, "Holy, holy, holy." Nor is his BEAUTY inferior to his wisdom or holiness; the seraphs veil their faces, when they appear before him: "He is the chiefest among ten thousand, nay, he is altogether lovely." And, as he is altogether lovely, so is he altogether LOVING: his name and his nature is Love. God, God in Christ is love: love in the abstract. And in this has he manifested his love, in that, whilst we were yet sinners, may open enemies, Jesus, in his own due time, died for the ungodly. He loved us so as to give himself for us. O what manner of love is this! What was Jacob's love to Rachel, in comparison of the love which Jesus bore to a perishing world! He became a curse for us. For it is written, "Cursed is every man that hangeth upon a tree." What Zipporah said to her husband improperly, Jesus may say properly to his spouse the church, "A bloody wife hast thou been to me, because of the crucifixion." For he has purchased her with his own blood. And having once loved his people, he loves them unto the end. His love, like himself, is from everlasting to everlasting. He hates putting away: though we change, yet he changeth not: he abideth faithful. When we are married here, there comes in that shocking clause, t use the words of holy Mr. Boston, "Till death us doth part:" but death itself shall not separate a true believer from the love of God, which is in Christ Jesus his Lord: for he will never cease loving his Bride, till he has loved her to heaven, and presented her before his Father, without spot or wrinkle, or any such thing. Nay, his love will, as it were, but be beginning, through the endless ages of eternity.

And now, Sirs, what say you? Shall I put that question to you, which Rebecca's relations, upon a proposal of marriage, put to her? "Will ye go with the man?" With the God-man, this infinitely great, this infinitely powerful, this all-wise, all-holy, altogether lovely, ever-loving Jesus?

What objection have you to make against such a gracious offer? One would imagine, you had not a single one; but it is to be feared, through the prevalency of unbelief, and the corruption of your desperately wicked deceitful hearts, you are ready to urge several. Methinks I hear some of you say within yourselves, "We like the proposal, but alas! we are poor." Are you so? If that be all, you may, notwithstanding, be welcome to Jesus: "For has not God chosen the poor of this world, to make them rich in faith, and heirs of his everlasting kingdom?" And what says that Savior, to whom I am now inviting you? "Blessed are the poor in Spirit, for there is the kingdom of heaven." And what says his Apostle concerning him? "Though he was rich, yet for our sakes he became poor, that we through his poverty might be made rich. But say you, "We are not only poor, but we are in debt; we owe God ten thousand talents, and have nothing to pay;" but that need not keep you back: for God the Father, from the Lord Jesus, his dearly beloved Son, has received double for all believers sins: the blood of Jesus cleanseth from them all. But you are blind, and miserable, and naked; to whom then should you fly for succor, but to Jesus, who came to open the eyes of the blind, to seek and save the miserable and lost, and clothe the naked with his perfect and spotless righteousness. And now, what can hinder your espousals with the dear and ever-blessed Lamb of God? I know but of one thing, that dreadful sin of unbelief. But this is my comfort, Jesus died for unbelief, as well as for other sins, and has promised to send down the Holy Spirit to convince the world of this sin in particular: "If I go not away, the Comforter will not come unto you; but if I go away, I will send the Comforter, and he will convince the world of son." What sin? of unbelief; "because they believe not on me." O that this promise may be so fulfilled in your hearts, and Jesus may so become the author of divine faith in your souls, that you may be able to send me the same message as a good woman in Scotland, on her dying bed, sent me by a friend: "Tell him, (says she) for his comfort, that at such a time he married me to the Lord Jesus." This would be comfort indeed. Not that we can marry you to Christ: No; the Holy Ghost must tie the marriage knot. But such honor have all God's ministers; under him they espouse poor sinners to Jesus Christ. "I have espoused you (says St. Paul) as a chaste virgin to Jesus Christ." O that you may say, We will go with the man; then will I bow my head, as Abraham's servant did, and go with joy and tell my Master, that he has not left his poor servant destitute this day: then shall I rejoice in your felicity. For I know, my Master will take you into the banqueting-house of his ordinances, and his banner over you shall be love. That this may be the happy case of you all, may the glorious God grant, for the sake of Jesus his dearly beloved Son, the glorious bridegroom of his church, to whom, with the Father, and the Holy Spirit, be all honor and glory, now and for evermore. Amen, and Amen.

Sermon 13 The Potter and the Clay

Jeremiah 18:1-6, "The word which came to Jeremiah from the LORD, saying, Arise, and go down to the potter's house, and there I will cause thee to hear my words. Then I went down to the potter's house, and, behold, he wrought a work on the wheels. And the vessel that he made of clay was marred in the hand of the potter: so he made it again another vessel, as seemed good to the potter to make. Then the word of the LORD came to me, saying, O house of Israel, cannot I do with you as this potter? saith the LORD. Behold, as the clay is in the potter's hand, so are ye in mine hand, O house of Israel."

At sundry times, and in diverse manners, God was pleased to speak to our fathers by the prophets, before he spoke to us in these last days by his Son. To Elijah, he revealed himself by a small still voice. To Jacob, by a dream. To Moses, he spoke face to face. Sometimes he was pleased to send a favorite prophet on some especial errand; and whilst he was thus employed, vouchsafed to give him a particular message, which he was ordered to deliver without reserve to all the inhabitants of the land. A very instructive instance of this kind we have recorded in the passage now read to you. The first verse informs us that it was a word, or message, which came immediately from the Lord to the prophet Jeremiah. At what time, or how the prophet was employed when it came, we are not told. Perhaps, whilst he was praying for those who would not pray for themselves. Perhaps, near the morning, when he was slumbering or musing on his bed. For the word came to him, saying, "Arise." And what must he do when risen? He must "go down to the potter's house" (the prophet knew where to find it) "and there (says the great Jehovah) I will cause thee to hear my words." Jeremiah does not confer with flesh and blood, he does not object that it was dark or cold, or desire that he might have his message given him there, but without the least hesitation is immediately obedient to the heavenly vision. "Then (says he) I went down to the potter's house, and behold he wrought a work upon the wheels." Just as he was entering into the house or workshop, the potter, it seems, had a vessel upon his wheel. And was there any thing so extraordinary in this, that it should be ushered in with the word Behold?

What a dreaming visionary, or superstitious enthusiast, would this Jeremiah be accounted, even by many who read his prophecies with seeming respect, was he alive now? But this was not the first time Jeremiah had heard from heaven in this manner. He therefore willingly obeyed; and had you or I accompanied him to the potter's house, I believe we should have seen him silently, but intensely waiting upon his great and all-wise Commander, to know wherefore he sent him thither. Methinks I see him all attention. He takes notice, that "the vessel was of clay;" but as he held it in his hand, and turned round the wheel, in order to work it into some particular form, "it was marred in the hands of the potter," and consequently unfit for the use he before intended to put it to. And what becomes of this marred vessel? Being thus marred, I suppose, the potter, without the least imputation of injustice, might have thrown it aside, and taken up another piece of clay in its room. But he did not. "He made it again another vessel." And does the potter call a council of his domestics, to inquire of them what kind of vessel they would advise him to make of it? No, in no wise. "He made it again another vessel, as seemed good to the potter to make it." "Then," adds Jeremiah, whilst he was in the way of duty _ then _ whilst he was mentally crying, Lord what wouldst thou have me to do? "Then the word of the Lord came unto me, saying, O house of Israel, cannot I do with you as this potter? Saith the Lord. Behold, as the clay is in the hands of the potter (marred, and unfit for the first designed purpose) so are ye in mine hand, O house of Israel." At length, then, Jeremiah hath his sermon given to him: short, but popular. It was to be delivered to the whole house of Israel, princes, priests, and people: short, but pungent, even sharper than a two-edged sword. What! says the sovereign Lord of heaven and earth, must I be denied the privilege of a common potter? May I not do what I will with my own? "Behold, as the clay is in the potter's hands, so are ye in mine hands, O house of Israel. I made and formed you into a people, and blessed you above any other nation under heaven: but, O Israel, thou by thy backslidings hast destroyed thyself. As the potter therefore might justly have thrown aside his marred clay, so may I justly unchurch and unpeople you. But what if I should come over the mountains of your guilt, heal your backslidings, revive my work in the midst of the years, and cause your latter end greatly to increase? Behold, as the clay is in the hands of the potter, lying at his disposal, either to be destroyed or formed into another vessel, so are ye in my hands, O house of Israel: I may either reject, and thereby ruin you, or I may revisit and revive you according to my own sovereign good will and pleasure, and who shall say unto me, what dost thou?" This seems to be the genuine interpretation, and primary intention of this beautiful part of holy writ. But waving all further inquiries about its primary design or meaning, I shall now proceed to show, that what the glorious Jehovah here says of the house of Israel in general, is applicable to every individual of mankind in particular. And as I presume this may be done, without either wire-drawing scripture on the one hand, or wrestling it from its original meaning on the other, not to detain you any longer, I shall, from the passage thus explained and paraphrased, deduce, and endeavor to enlarge on these two general heads.

FIRST, I shall undertake to prove, that every man naturally engendered of the offspring of Adam, is in the sight of the all-seeing, heart-searching God, only as a "piece of marred clay." SECONDLY, That being thus marred, he must necessarily be renewed: and under this head, we shall likewise point out by whose agency this mighty change is to be brought about.

These particulars being discussed, way will naturally be made for a short word of application.

FIRST, To prove that every man naturally engendered of the offspring of Adam, is in the sight of an all-seeing, heart-searching God, only as a piece of marred clay.

Be pleased to observe, that we say every man NATURALLY engendered of the offspring of Adam, or every man since the fall: for if we consider man as he first came out of the hands of his Maker, he was far from being in such melancholy circumstances. No; he was originally made upright; or as Moses, that sacred penman, declares, "God made him after his own image." Surely never was so much expressed in so few words; which hath often made me wonder how that great critic Longinus, who so justly admires the dignity and grandeur of Moses's account of the creation, and "God said, Let there be light, and there was light;" I say I have often wondered why he did not read a little further, and bestow as just an encomium upon this short, but withal inexpressibly august and comprehensive description of the formation of man, "so God created man in his own image." Struck with a deep sense of such amazing goodness, and that he might impress yet a deeper sense of it upon our minds too, he immediately adds, "in the image of God made he him." A council of the most adorable Trinity was called on this important occasion: God did not say, Let there be a man, and there was a man, but God said, "Let us make man in our image, after our likeness." This is the account which the lively oracles of God do give us of man in his first estate; but it is very remarkable, that the transition from the account of his creation to that of his misery, is very quick, and why? For a very good reason, because he soon fell from his primeval dignity; and by that fall, the divine image is so defaced, that he is now to be valued only as antiquarians value an ancient medal, merely for the sake of the image and superscription once stamped upon it; or of a second divine impress, which, through grace, it may yet receive.

Let us take a more particular survey of him, and see whether these things are so or not: and first, as to his UNDERSTANDING. As man was created originally "after God in knowledge," as well as righteousness and true holiness, we may rationally infer, that his understanding, in respect to things natural, as well as divine, was of a prodigious extent: for he was make but a little lower than the angels, and consequently being like them, excellent in his understanding, he knew much of God, of himself, and all about him; and in this as well as every other respect, was, as Mr.

Golter expresses it in one of his essays, a perfect major: but this is far from being our case now. For in respect to NATURAL THINGS, our understandings are evidently darkened. It is but little that we can know, and even that little knowledge which we can acquire, is with much weariness of the flesh, and we are doomed to gain it as we do our daily bread, I mean by the sweat of our brows.

Men of low and narrow minds soon commence wise in their own conceits: and having acquired a little smattering of the learned languages, and made some small proficiency in the dry sciences, are easily tempted to look upon themselves as a head taller than their fellow mortals, and accordingly too, too often put forth great swelling words of vanity. But persons of a more exalted, and extensive reach of thought, dare not boast. No: they know that the greatest scholars are in the dark, in respect to many even of the minutest things in life: and after all their painful researches into the Arcana Natura, they find such an immense void, such an unmeasurable expanse yet to be traveled over, that they are obliged at last to conclude, almost with respect to every thing, "that they know nothing yet as they ought to know." This consideration, no doubt, led Socrates, when he was asked by one of his scholars, why the oracle pronounced him the wisest man on earth, to give him this judicious answer, "Perhaps it is, because I am most sensible of my own ignorance." Would to God, that all who call themselves Christians, had learned so much as this heathen! We should then no longer hear so many learned men, falsely so called, betray their ignorance by boasting of the extent of their shallow understanding, nor by professing themselves so wise, prove themselves such arrant pedantic fools.

If we view our understandings in respect to spiritual things, we shall find that they are not only darkened, but become darkness itself, even "darkness that may be felt" by all who are not past feeling. And how should it be otherwise, since the infallible word of God assures us, that they are alienated from the light of life of God, and thereby naturally as incapable to judge of divine and spiritual things, comparatively speaking, as a man born blind is incapacitated to distinguish the various colors of the rainbow. "The natural man, (says on inspired apostle) discerneth not the things of the Spirit of God;"

so far from it, "they are foolishness unto him;" and why? Because they are only to be "spiritually discerned." Hence it was, that Nicodemus, who was blessed with an outward and divine revelation, who was a ruler of the Jews, nay a master of Israel, when our Lord told him, "he must be born again;" appeared to be quite grappled. "How (says he) can a man be born when he is old? Can he enter a second time into his mother's womb and be born? How can these things be?" Were three more absurd questions ever proposed by the most ignorant man alive? Or can there be a clearer proof of the blindness of man's understanding, in respect to divine, as well as natural things? Is not man then a piece of marred clay?

This will appear yet more evident, if we consider the PERVERSE BENT OF HIS WILL. Being made in the very image of God; undoubtedly before the fall, man had no other will but his Maker's. God's will, and Adam's, were than like unisons in music. There was not the least disunion, or discord between them. But now he hath a will, as directly contrary to the will of God, as light is contrary to darkness, or heaven to hell. We all bring into the world with us a carnal mind, which is not only an enemy to God, but "enmity itself, and which is therefore not subject unto the law of God, neither indeed can it be." A great many show much zeal in talking against the man of sin, and loudly (and indeed very justly) exclaim against the Pope for sitting in the temple, I mean the church of Christ, and "exalting himself above all that is called God." But say not within thyself, who shall go to Rome, to pull down this spiritual antichrist? As though there was no antichrist but what is without us. For know, O man, whoever thou art, an infinitely more dangerous antichrist, because less discerned, even SELF- WILL, fits daily in the temple of thy heart, exalting itself, above all that is called God, and obliging all its votaries to say of Christ himself , that Prince of peace, "we will not have this man to reign over us." God's people, whose spiritual senses, are exercised about spiritual things, and whose eyes are opened to see the abominations that are in their hearts, frequently feel this to their sorrow. Whether they will or not, this enmity from time to time bubbles up, and in spite of all their watchfulness and care, when they are under the pressure of some sharp affliction, a long desertion, or tedious night of temptation, they often find something within rising in rebellion against the all-wise disposals of divine Providence, and saying unto God their heavenly Father, "what dost thou?" This makes them to cry (and no wonder, since it constrained one of the greatest saints and apostles first to introduce the expression) "O wretched man that I am, who shall deliver me from the body of this death?" The spiritual and renewed soul groans thus, being burdened; but as for the natural and unawakened man, it is not so with him; self-will, as well as every other evil, either in a more latent or discernible manner, reigns in his unrenewed soul, and proves him, even to a demonstration to others, whether he knows, or will confess it himself or not, that in respect to the disorders of his will, as well as his understanding, man is only a piece of marred clay.

A transient view of fallen man's AFFECTIONS will yet more firmly corroborate this melancholy truth, These, at his being first placed in the paradise of God, were always kept within proper bounds, fixed upon their proper objects, and, like so many gentle rivers, sweetly, spontaneously and habitually glided into their ocean, God. But now the scene is changed. For we are not naturally full of vile affections, which like a mighty and impetuous torrent carry all before them. We love what we should hate, and hate what we should love; we fear what we should hope for, and hope for what we should fear; nay, to such an ungovernable height do our affections sometimes rise, that though our judgments are convinced to the contrary, yet we will gratify our passions though it be at the expense of our present and eternal welfare. We feel a war of our affections, warring against the law of our minds, and bringing us into captivity to the law of sin and death. So that *video meliora proboque, deteriora foquor*, I approve of better things but follow worse, is too, too often the practice of us all.

I am sensible, that many are offended, when mankind are compared to beasts and devils. And they might have some shadow of reason for being so, if we asserted in a physical sense, that they were really beasts and really devils. For then, as I once heard a very learned prelate, who was objecting against this comparison, observe, "a man being a beast would be incapable, and being a devil, would be under an impossibility of being saved." But when we make use of such shocking comparisons, as he was pleased to term them, we would be understood only in a moral sense; and in so doing, we assert no more than some of the most holy men of God have said of themselves, and others, in the lively oracles many ages ago. Holy David, the man after God's own heart, speaking of himself, says, "so foolish was I, and as a beast before thee." And holy Job, speaking of man in general, says, that "he is born as a wild ass's colt," or take away the expletive, which as some think ought to be done, and then he positively asserts, that man is a wild ass's colt. And what says our Lord, "Ye are of your father the devil;" and "the whole world is said to lie in him, the wicked one, who now rules in the children of disobedience," that is, in all unrenewed souls. Our stupidity, proneness to fix our affections on the things of the earth, and our eagerness to make provision for the flesh, to fulfill the lusts thereof, evidence us to be earthly and brutes!; and our mental passions, anger, hatred, malice, envy, and such like, prove with equal strength, that we are also devilish. Both together conspire to evince, that in respect to his affections, as well as his understanding and will, man deservedly may be termed a piece of marred clay.

The present BLINDNESS OF NATURAL CONSCIENCE makes this appear in a yet more glaring light; in the soul of the first man Adam, conscience was no doubt the candle of the Lord, and enabled him rightly and instantaneously to discern between good and evil, right and wrong. And, blessed be God!

Some remains of this are yet left; but alas, how dimly does it burn, and how easily and quickly is it covered, or put out and extinguished. I need not send you to the heathen world, to learn the truth of this; you all know it by experience. Was there no other evidence, your own consciences are instead of a thousand witnesses, that man, as to his natural conscience, as well as understanding, will and affections, is much marred clay.

Nor does that great and boasted Diana, I mean UNASSISTED UNENLIGHTENED REASON, less demonstrate the justness of such an assertion. Far be it from me to decry or exclaim against human reason. Christ himself is called the "LOGOS, the Reason;" and I believe it would not require much learning, or take up much time to prove, that so far and no farther than as we act agreeably to the laws of Christ Jesus, are we any way conformable to the laws of right reason. His service is therefore called "a reasonable service." And however his servants and followers may now be looked upon as fools and madmen; yet there will come a time, when those who despise and set themselves to oppose divine revelation, will find, that what they now call reason, is only REASON DEPRAVED, and an utterly incapable, of itself, to guide us into the way of peace, or show the way of salvation, as the men of Sodom were to find Lot's door after they were struck with blindness by the angels, who came to lead him out of the city. The horrid and dreadful mistakes, which the most refined reasoners in the heathen world ran into, both as to the object, as well as manner of divine worship, have sufficiently demonstrated the weakness and depravity of human reason: nor do our modern boasters afford us any better proofs of the greatness of its strength, since the best improvement they generally make of it, is only to reason themselves into downright willful infidelity, and thereby reason themselves out of eternal salvation. Need we now any further witness, that man, fallen man, is altogether a piece of marred clay?

But this is not all, we have yet more evidence to call; for do the blindness of our understandings, the perverseness of our will, the rebellion of our affections, the corruption our consciences, the depravity of our reason prove this charge; and does not present DISORDERED FRAME AND CONSTITUTION OF OUR BODES confirm the same also? Doubtless in this respect, man, in the most literal sense of the word, is a piece of marred clay. For God originally made him of the "dust of the earth." So that notwithstanding our boasting of our high pedigrees, and different descent, we were all originally upon a level, and a little red earth was the common substratum out of which we were all formed. Clay indeed it was, but clay wonderfully modified, even by the immediate hands of the Creator of heaven and earth.

One therefore hath observed, that it is said "God built the man;" he did not form him rashly or hastily, but built and finished him according to the plan before laid down in his own eternal mind. And though, as the great God is without body, parts, or passions, we cannot suppose when it is said "God made man after his own image," that it has any reference to his body, yet I cannot help thinking (with Doctor South) that as the eternal Logos was hereafter to appear, God manifest in the flesh, infinite wisdom was undoubtedly exerted in forming a casket into which so invaluable a pearl was in the fullness of time to be deposited. Some of the ancients are said to have asserted, that man at the first, had what we call a glory shining round him; but without attempting to be wise above what is written, we may venture to affirm, that he had a glorious body, which knowing no sin, knew neither sickness nor pain. But now on this, as well as other accounts, he may justly be called Ichabod; for its primitive strength and glory are sadly departed from it, and like the ruins of some ancient and stately fabric, only so much less as to give us some faint idea of what it was when it first appeared in its original and perfect beauty. The apostle Paul, therefore, who knew how to call things by their proper names, as well as any man living, does not scruple to term the human body, though in its original constitution fearfully and wonderfully made, a "vile body;" vile indeed! Since it is subject to such vile diseases, put to such vile, yea very vile uses, and at length is to come to so vile an end. "For dust we are, and to dust we must return." This among other considerations, we may well suppose, caused the blessed Jesus to weep at the grave of Lazarus. He wept, not only because his friend Lazarus was dead, but he wept to see human nature, through man's own default, thus laid in ruins, by being subject unto such a dissolution, made like unto the beasts that perish.

Let us here pause a while, and with our sympathizing Lord, see if we cannot shed a few silent tears at least, upon the same sorrowful occasion.

Who, who is there amongst us, that upon such a melancholy review of man' present, real, and most deplorable depravity both in body and soul, can refrain from weeping over such a piece of marred clay? Who, who can help adopting holy David's lamentation over Saul and Jonathan? "How are the mighty fallen! How are they slain in their high places!" Originally it was not so. No, "God made man after his own image; in the image of God made he man." Never was there so much expressed in so few words. He was created after God in righteousness and true holiness.

This is the account, which the sacred volume gives us of this interesting point. This, this is that blessed book, that book of books, from whence, together with an appeal to the experience of our own hearts, and the testimonies of all past ages, we have thought proper to fetch our proofs. For, after all, we must be obliged to divine revelation, to know what we were, what we are, and what we are to be. In these, as in a true glass, we may see our real and proper likeness. And from these only can we trace the source and fountain of all those innumerable evils, which like a deluge have overflowed the natural and moral world. If any should object against the authenticity of this revelation, and consequently against the doctrine this day drawn from thence, they do in my opinion thereby very much confirm it. For unless a man was very much disordered indeed, as to his understanding, will, affections, natural conscience, and his power of reasoning, he could never possibly deny such a revelation, which is founded on a multiplicity of infallible external evidences, hath so many internal evidences of a divine stamp in every page, is so suited to the common exigencies of all mankind, so agreeable to the experience of all men, and which hath been so wonderfully handed and preserved to us, hath been so instrumental to the convicting, converting, and comforting so many millions of souls, and hath stood the test of the most severe scrutinies, and exact criticisms of the most subtle and refined, as well as the most malicious and persecuting enemies, that ever lived, even from the beginning of time to this very day. Persons of such a turn of mind, I think, are rather to be prayed for, than disputed with, if so be this perverse wickedness of their hearts may be forgiven them: "They are in the very gall of bitterness, and must have their consciences seared as it were with a red-hot iron," and must have their eyes "blinded by the god of this world," otherwise they could not but see, and feel, and assent to the truth of this doctrine, of man's being universally depraved; which not only in one or two, but in one or two thousands, in every page, I could almost say, is written, in such legible characters, that runs may read. Indeed, revelation itself is founded upon the doctrine of the fall. Had we kept our original integrity, the law of God would have yet been written in our hearts, and thereby the want of a divine revelation, at least such as ours, would have been superseded; but being fallen, instead of rising in rebellion against God, we ought to be filled with unspeakable thankfulness to our all bountiful Creator, who by a few lines in his own books hath discovered more to us, than all the philosophers and most learned men in the world could, or would, have discovered, though they had studied to all eternity.

I am well aware, that some who pretend to own the validity of divine revelation, are notwithstanding enemies to the doctrine that hath this day been delivered; and would fain elude the force of the proofs generally urged in defense of it, by saying, they only bespeak the corruption of particular persons, or have reference only to the heathen world: but such persons err, not knowing their own hearts, or the power of Jesus Christ: for by nature there is no difference between Jew or Gentile, Greek or Barbarian, bond or free. We are altogether equally become abominable in God's sight, all equally fallen short of the glory of God, and consequently all alike so many pieces of marred clay.

How God came to suffer man to fall? how long man stood before he fell?

And how the corruption contracted by the fall, is propagated to every individual of his species are questions of such an abstruse and critical nature, that should I undertake to answer them, would be only gratifying a sinful curiosity, and tempting you, as Satan tempted dour first parents, to eat forbidden fruit. It will much better answer the design of this present discourse, which is practical, to pass on II. To the next thing proposed, and point out to you the absolute necessity there is of this fallen nature's being renewed.

This I have had all along in my eye, and on account of this, have purposely been so explicit on the first general head: for has Archimedes once said, "Give me a place where I may fix my foot, and I will move the world;" so without the least imputation of arrogance, with which, perhaps, he was justly chargeable, we may venture to say, grant the foregoing doctrine to be true, and then deny the necessity of man's being renewed who can.

I suppose, I may take it for granted, that all of you amongst whom I am now preaching the kingdom of God, hope after death to go to a place which we call Heaven. And my heart's desire and prayer to God for you is, that you all may have mansions prepared for you there. But give me leave to tell you, were you now to see these heavens opened, and the angel (to use the words of the seraphic Hervey clothed with all his heavenly drapery, with one foot upon the earth, and another upon the sea; nay, were you to see and hear the angel of the everlasting covenant, Jesus Christ himself, proclaiming "time shall be no more," and giving you all an invitation immediately to come to heaven; heaven would be no heaven to you, nay it would be a hell to your souls, unless you were first prepared for a proper enjoyment of it here on earth. "For what communion hath light with darkness?" Or what fellowship could unrenewed sons of Belial possibly keep up with the pure and immaculate Jesus?

The generality of people form strange ideas of heaven. And because the scriptures, in condescension to the weakness of our capacities, describe it by images taken from earthly delights and human grandeur, therefore they are apt to carry their thoughts no higher, and at the best only form to themselves a kind of Mahomitan paradise. But permit me to tell you, and God grant it may sink deep into your hearts! Heaven is rather a state than a place; and consequently, unless you are previously disposed by a suitable state of mind, you could not be happy even in heaven itself. For what is grace but glory militant? What is glory but grace triumphant? This consideration made a pious author say, that "holiness, happiness, and heaven, were only three different words for one and the self-same thing." And this made the great Preston, when he was about to die, turn to his friends, saying, "I am changing my place, but not my company." He had conversed with God and good men on earth; he was going to keep up the same, and infinitely more refined communion with God, his holy angels, and the spirits of just men made perfect, in heaven.

To make us meet to be blissful partakers of such heavenly company, this "marred clay," I mean, these depraved natures of ours, must necessarily undergo an universal moral change; our understandings must be enlightened; our wills, reason, and consciences, must be renewed; our affections must be drawn toward, and fixed upon things above; and because flesh and blood cannot inherit the kingdom of heaven, this corruptible must put on incorruption, this mortal must put on immortality. And thus old things must literally pass away, and behold all things, even the body as well as the faculties of the soul, must become new.

This moral change is what some call, repentance, some, conversion, some, regeneration; choose what name you please, I only pray God, that we all may have the thing. The scriptures call it holiness, sanctification, the new creature, and our Lord calls it a "New birth, or being born again, or born from above." These are not barely figurative expressions, or the flights of eastern language, nor do they barely denote a relative change of state conferred on all those who are admitted into Christ's church by baptism; but they denote a real, moral change of heart and life, a real participation of the divine life in the soul of man. Some indeed content themselves with a figurative interpretation; but unless they are made to experience the power and efficacy thereof, by a solid living experience in their own souls, all their learning, all their labored criticism, will not exempt them from a real damnation. Christ hath said it, and Christ will stand, "Unless a man," learned or unlearned, high or low, though he be a master of Israel as Nicodemus was, unless he "be born again, he cannot see, he cannot enter into the kingdom of God." If it be inquired, who is to be the potter? And by whose agency this marred clay is to be formed into another vessel? Or in other words, if it be asked, how this great and mighty change is to be effected? I answer, not by the mere dint and force of moral persuasion. This is good in its place. And I am so far from thinking, that Christian preachers should not make use of rational arguments and motives in their sermons, that I cannot think they are fit to preach at all, who either cannot, or will not use them. We have the example of the great God himself for such a practice; "Come (says he) and let us reason together." And St. Paul, that prince of preachers, "reasoned of temperance, and righteousness, and a judgment to come." And it is remarkable, "that whilst he was reasoning of these things, Felix trembled." Nor are the most persuasive strains of holy rhetoric less needful for a scribe ready instructed to the kingdom of God. The scriptures both of the Old and New Testament, every where abound with them. And when can they be more properly employed, and brought forth, than when we are acting as ambassadors or heaven, and beseeching poor sinners, as in Christ's stead, to be reconciled unto God. All this we readily grant. But at the same time, I would as soon go to yonder church-yard, and attempt to raise the dead carcasses, with a "come forth," as to preach to dead souls, did I not hope for some superior power to make the word effectual to the designed end. I should only be like a sounding brass for any saving purpose, or as a tinkling cymbal. Neither is this change to be wrought by the power of our own free-will. This is an idol every where set up, but we dare not fall down and worship it. "No man (says Christ) can come to me, unless the Father draw him." Our own free-will, if improved, may restrain us from the commission of many evils, and put us in the way of conversion; but, after exerting our utmost efforts (and we are bound in duty to exert them) we shall find the words of our own church article to be true, that "man since the fall hath no power to turn to God." No, we might as soon attempt to stop the ebbing and flowing of the tide, and calm the most tempestuous sea, as to imagine that we can subdue, or bring under proper regulations, our own unruly wills and affections by any strength inherent in ourselves.

And therefore, that I may keep you no longer in suspense, I inform you, that this heavenly potter, this blessed agent, is the Almighty Spirit of God, the Holy Ghost, the third person in the most adorable Trinity, coessential with the Father and the Son. This is that Spirit, which at the beginning of time moved on the face of the waters, when nature lay in one universal chaos. This was the Spirit that overshadowed the Holy Virgin, before that holy thing was born of her: and this same Spirit must come, and move upon the chaos of our souls, before we can properly be called the sons of God. This is what John the Baptist calls "being baptized with the Holy Ghost," without which, his and all other baptisms, whether infant or adult, avail nothing. This is that fire, which our Lord came to send into our earthly hearts, and which I pray the Lord of all lords to kindle in every unrenewed one this day.

As for the extraordinary operations of the Holy Ghost, such as working of miracles, or speaking with divers kinds of tongues, they are long since ceased. But as for this miracle of miracles, turning the soul to God by the more ordinary operations of the Holy Ghost, this abides yet, and will abide till time itself shall be nor more. For it is he that sanctifieth us, and all the elect people of God. On this account, true believers are said to be "born from above, to be born not of blood, nor of the will of the flesh, nor of the will of man, but of God." Their second, as well as their first creation, is truly and purely divine. It is, therefore, called "a creation;" but put ye on (says the apostle) the new man which is created" _ And how? Even as the first man was, "after God in righteousness and true holiness." These, these are the precious truths, which a scoffing world would fain rally or ridicule us out of. To produce this glorious change, this new creation, the glorious Jesus left his Father's bosom. For this he led a persecuted life; for this he died an ignominious and accursed death; for this he rose again; and for this he now sitteth at the right hand of his Father. All the precepts of his gospel, all his ordinances, all his providences, whether of an afflictive or prosperous nature, all divine revelation from the beginning to the end, all center in these two points, to show us how we are fallen, and to begin, early on, and complete a glorious and blessed change in our souls. This is an end worthy of the coming of so divine a personage. To deliver a multitude of souls of every nation, language and tongue, from so many moral evils, and to reinstate them in an incomparably more excellent condition than that from whence they are fallen, is an end worthy the shedding of such precious blood. What system of religion is there now, or was there ever exhibited to the world, any way to be compared to this? Can the deistical scheme pretend in any degree to come up to it? Is it not noble, rational, and truly divine? And why then will not all that hitherto are strangers to this blessed restoration of their fallen natures, (for my heart is too full to abstain any longer from an application) why will you any longer dispute or stand out against it? Why will you not rather bring your clay to this heavenly Potter, and say from your inmost souls, "Turn us, O good Lord, and so shall we be turned?" This, you may and can do: and if you go thus far, who knows but that this very day, yea this very hour, the heavenly Potter may take you in hand, and make you vessels of honor fit for the Redeemer's use?

Others that were once as far from the kingdom of God as you are, have been partakers of this blessedness. What a wretched creature was Mary Magdalene?

And yet out of her Jesus Christ cast seven devils. Nay, he appeared to her first, after he rose from the dead, and she became as it were an apostle to the very apostles. What a covetous creature was Zaccheus? He was a griping cheating publican; and yet, perhaps, in one quarter of an hour's time, his heart is enlarged, and he made quite willing to give half of his goods to feed the poor. And to mention no more, what a cruel person was Paul. He was a persecutor, a blasphemer, injurious; one that breathed out threatenings against the disciples of the Lord, and made havoc of the church of Christ.

And yet what a wonderful turn did he meet with, as he was journeying to Damascus? From a persecutor, he became a preacher; was afterwards made a spiritual father to thousands, and now probably sits nearest the Lord Jesus Christ in glory. And why all this? That he might be made an example to them that should hereafter believe. O then believe, repent; I beseech you, believe the gospel. Indeed, it is glad tidings, even tidings of great joy.

You will then no longer have any thing to say against the doctrine of Original Sin; or charge the Almighty foolishly, for suffering our first parents to be prevailed on to eat such sour grapes, and permitting thereby their children's teeth to be set on edge. You will then no longer cry out against the doctrine of the New Birth, as enthusiasm, or brand the assertors of such blessed truths with the opprobrious names of fools and madmen. Having felt, you will then believe; having believed, you will therefore speak; and instead of being vessels of wrath, and growing harder and harder in hell fire, like vessels in a potter's oven, you will be made vessels of honor, and be presented at the great day by Jesus, to his heavenly Father, and be translated to live with him as monuments of rich, free, distinguishing and sovereign grace, for ever and ever.

You, that have in some degree experienced the quickening influence (for I must not conclude without dropping a word or two to God's children) you know how to pity, and therefore, I beseech you also to pray for those, to whose circumstances this discourse is peculiarly adapted. But will you be content in praying for them? Will you not see reason to pray for yourselves also? Yes, doubtless, for yourselves also. For you, and you only know, how much there is yet lacking in your faith, and how far you are from being partakers in that degree, which you desire to be, of the whole mind that was in Christ Jesus. You know what a body of sin and death you carry about with you, and that you must necessarily expect many turns of God's providence and grace, before you will be wholly delivered form it. But thanks be to God, we are in safe hands. He that has been the author, will also be the finisher of our faith. Yet a little while, and we like him shall say "It is finished;" we shall bow down our heads an give up the ghost. Till then, (for to thee, O Lord, will we now direct our prayer) help us, O Almighty Father, in patience to posses our souls. Behold, we are the clay, and thou art the Potter. Let not the thing formed say to him that formed it, whatever the dispensations of thy future Will concerning us may be, Why dost thou deal with us thus? Behold, we put ourselves as blanks in thine hands, deal with us as seemeth good in thy sight, only let every cross, ever affliction, every temptation, be overruled to the stamping thy blessed image in more lively characters on our hearts; that so passing from glory to glory, by the powerful operations of they blessed Spirit, we may be made thereby more and more meet for, and at last be translated to a full, perfect, endless, and uninterrupted enjoyment of glory hereafter, with thee O Father, thee O Son, and thee O blessed Spirit; to whom, three persons but one God, be ascribed, as is most due, all honor, power, might, majesty and dominion, now and to all eternity. Amen and Amen.

Sermon 14 The Lord our Righteousness

Jeremiah 23:6, "The Lord our Righteousness."

Whoever is acquainted with the nature of mankind in general, or the propensity of his own heart in particular, must acknowledge, that self- righteousness is the last idol that is rooted out of the heart: being once born under a covenant of works, it is natural for us all to have recourse to a covenant of works, for our everlasting salvation. And we have contracted such devilish pride, by our fall from God, that we would, if not wholly, yet in part at least, glory in being the cause of our own salvation. We cry out against popery, and that very justly; but we are all Papists, at least, I am sure, we are all Arminians by nature; and therefore no wonder so many natural men embrace that scheme. It is true, we disclaim the doctrine of merit, are ashamed directly to say we deserve any good at the hands of God; therefore, as the Apostle excellently well observes, "we go about," we fetch a circuit, "to establish a righteousness of our own, and," like the Pharisees of old, "will not wholly submit to that righteousness which is of God through Jesus Christ our Lord." This is the sorest, though, alas! the most common evil that was ever yet seen under the sun. An evil, that in any age, especially in these dregs of time wherein we live, cannot sufficiently be inveighed against. For as it is with the people, so it is with the priests; and it is to be feared, even in those places, where once the truth as it is in Jesus was eminently preached, many ministers are so sadly degenerated from their pious ancestors, that the doctrines of grace, especially the personal, ALL- SUFFICIENT RIGHTEOUSNESS of Jesus, is but too seldom, too slightly mentioned. Hence the love of many waxeth cold; and I have often thought, was it possible, that this single consideration would be sufficient to raise our venerable forefathers again from their graves; who would thunder in their ears their fatal error.

The righteousness of Jesus Christ is one of those great mysteries, which the angels desire to look into, and seems to be one of the first lessons that God taught men after the fall. For, what were the coats that God made to put on our first parents, but types of the application of the merits of righteousness of Jesus Christ to believers hearts? We are told, that those coats were made of skins of beasts; and, as beasts were not then food for men, we may fairly infer, that those beasts were slain in sacrifice, in commemoration of the great sacrifice, Jesus Christ, thereafter to be offered. And the skins of the beasts thus slain, being put on Adam and Eve, they were hereby taught how their nakedness was to be covered with the righteousness of the Lamb of God.

This is it which is meant, when we are told, "Abraham believed on the Lord, and it was accounted to him for righteousness." In short, this is it of which both the law and the prophets have spoken, especially Jeremiah in the words of the text, "The Lord our righteousness." I propose, through divine grace, I. To consider who we are to understand by the word Lord.

II. How the Lord is man's righteousness.

III. I will consider some of the chief objections that are generally urged against this doctrine.

IV. I shall show some very ill consequences that flow naturally from denying this doctrine.

V Shall conclude with an exhortation to all to come to Christ by faith, that they may be enabled to say with the prophet in the text, "The Lord our righteousness." I. I am to consider who we are to understand by the word Lord. The Lord our righteousness.

If any Arians of Socinians are drawn by curiosity to hear what the babbler has to say, let them be ashamed of denying the divinity of that Lord, who has bought poor sinners with his precious blood. For the person mentioned in the text, under the character of the Lord, is Jesus Christ.

Ver. 5, "Behold, the days come, saith the Lord, that I will raise unto David a righteous branch, a king shall reign and prosper, and shall execute judgment and justice in the earth. In his days (ver. 6) Judah shall be saved, and Israel shall dwell safely; and this is his name whereby he shall be called, The Lord our righteousness." By the righteous branch, all agree, that we are to understand Jesus Christ. He it is that is called the Lord in our text. If so, if there were no other text in the Bible to prove the divinity of Christ, this is sufficient: for if the word Lord may properly belong to Jesus Christ, he must be God. And, as you have it in the margin of your Bibles, the word Lord is in the original Jehovah, which is the essential title of God himself. Come then, ye Arians, kiss the son of God, bow down before him, and honor him, even as ye honor the Father. Learn of the angels, those morning-stars, and worship him as truly God: for otherwise you are as much idolaters, as those that worship the Virgin Mary.

And as for you Socinians, who say Christ was a mere man, and yet profess that he was your Savior, according to your own principles you are accursed: for, if Christ be a mere man, then he is only an arm of flesh: and it is written, "Cursed is he that trusteth on an arm of flesh." But I would hope, there are no such monsters here; at least, that, after these considerations, they would be ashamed of broaching such monstrous absurdities any more. For it is plain, that, by the word Lord, we are to understand the Lord Jesus Christ, who here takes to himself the title Jehovah, and therefore must be very God of very God; or, as the Apostle devoutly expresses it, "God blessed for evermore." II. How the Lord is to be man's righteousness, comes next to be considered.

And that is, in one word, by IMPUTATION. For it pleased God, after he had made all things by the word of his power, to create man after his own image. And so infinite was the condescension of the high and lofty One, who inhabiteth eternity, that, although he might have insisted on the everlasting obedience of him and his posterity; yet he was pleased to oblige himself, by a covenant or agreement made with his own creatures, upon condition of an unsinning obedience, to give them immortality and eternal life. For when it is said, "The day thou eatest thereof, thou shalt surely die;" we may fairly infer, so long as he continued obedient, and did not eat thereof, he should surely live. The 3rd of Genesis gives us a full, but mournful account, how our first parents broke this covenant, and thereby stood in need of a better righteousness than their own, in order to procure their future acceptance with God. For what must they do? They were as much under a covenant of works as ever. And though, after their disobedience, they were without strength; yet they were obliged not only to do, but continue to do all things, and that too in the most perfect manner, which the Lord had required of them: and not only so, but to make satisfaction to God's infinitely offended justice, for the breach they had already been guilty of. Here then opens the amazing scene of DIVINE PHILANTHROPY; I mean, God's love to man. For behold, what man could not do, Jesus Christ, the son of his Father's love, undertakes to do for him. And that God might be just in justifying the ungodly, though "he was in the form of God, and therefore thought it no robbery to be equal with God; yet he took upon him the form of a servant," even human nature. In that nature he obeyed, and thereby fulfilled the whole moral law in our stead; and also died a painful death upon the cross, and thereby became a curse for, or instead of, those whom the Father had given to him. As God, he satisfied, at the same time that he obeyed and suffered as man; and, being God and man in one person, he wrought out a full, perfect, and sufficient righteousness for all to whom it was to be imputed.

Here then we see the meaning of the word righteousness. It implies the active as well as passive obedience of the Lord Jesus Christ. We generally, when talking of the merits of Christ, only mention the latter, -- his death; whereas, the former, -- his life and active obedience, is equally necessary. Christ is not such a Savior as becomes us, unless we join both together. Christ not only died, but lived, not only suffered, but obeyed for, or instead of, poor sinners. And both these jointly make up that complete righteousness, which is to be imputed to us, as the disobedience of our first parents was made ours by imputation. In this sense, and no other, are we to understand that parallel which the apostle Paul draws, in the 5th of the Romans, between the first and second Adam. This is what he elsewhere terms, "our being made the righteousness of God in him." This is the sense wherein the Prophet would have us to understand the words of the text; therefore, Jer. 33:16, "She (i.e. the church itself) shall be called, (having this righteousness imputed to her) The Lord our righteousness." A passage, I think, worthy of the profoundest meditation of all the sons and daughters of Abraham.

Many are the objections which the proud hearts of fallen men are continually urging against this wholesome, this divine, this soul saving doctrine. I come now, III. To answer some few of those which I think the most considerable.

And, FIRST, they say, because they would appear friends to morality, "That the doctrine of an imputed righteousness is "destructive of good works, and leads to licentiousness." And who, pray, are the persons that generally urge this objection? Are they men full of faith, and men really concerned for good works? No; whatever few exceptions there may be, if there be any at all, it is notorious, they are generally men of corrupt minds, reprobate concerning the faith. The best title I can give them is, that of PROFANE MORALISTS, or moralists false so called. For I appeal to the experience of the present as well as past ages, if iniquity did and does not most abound, where the doctrine of Christ's whole personal righteousness is most cried down, and most seldom mentioned. Arminian being antichristian principles, always did, and always will lead to antichristian practices. And never was there a reformation brought about in the church, but by the preaching the doctrine of an imputed righteousness. This, as the man of God, Luther, calls it, is "Artienlus statntis out cedentis Eichlesin," the article by which the Church stands or falls. And though the preachers of this doctrine are generally branded by those on the other side, with the opprobrious names of Antinomians, deceivers, and what not; yet, I believe, if the truth of the doctrine on both sides was to be judged of by the lives of the preachers of professors of it, on our side the question would have the advantage every way.

It is true, this, as well as every other doctrine of grace, may be abused. And perhaps the unchristian walk of some, who have talked of Christ's imputed righteousness, justification by faith, and the like, and yet never felt it imputed to their own souls, has given the enemies of the Lord thus cause to blaspheme. But this is a very unsafe, as well as a very unfair way of arguing. The only question should be, Whether or not this doctrine of an imputed righteousness, does in itself cut off the occasion of good works, or lean to licentiousness? To this we may boldly answer, In no wise. It excludes works, indeed, from being any cause of our justification in the sight of God; but it requires good works as a proof of our having this righteousness imputed to us, and as a declarative evidence of our justification in the sight of men. And then, how can the doctrine of an imputed righteousness be a doctrine leading to licentiousness?

It is all calumny. The apostle Paul introduceth an infidel making this objection, in his epistle to the Romans; and none but infidels, that never felt the power of Christ's resurrection upon their souls, will urge it over again. And therefore, notwithstanding this objection, with the Prophet in the text, we may boldly say, "The Lord is our righteousness." But Satan (and no wonder that his servants imitate him) often transforms himself into an angel of light; and therefore, (such perverse things will infidelity and Arminianism make men speak) in order to dress their objections in the best colors, some urge, "That our Savior preached no such doctrine; that in his sermon on the mount, he mentions only morality:" and consequently the doctrine of an imputed righteousness falls wholly to the ground.

But surely the men, who urge this objection, either never read, or never understood, our Lord's blessed discourse, wherein the doctrine of an imputed righteousness is so plainly taught, that he who runs, If he has eyes that see, may read.

Indeed our Lord does recommend morality and good works, (as all faithful ministers will do) and clears the moral law from many corrupt glosses put upon it by the letter-learned Pharisees. But then, before he comes to this, 'tis remarkable, he talks of inward piety, such as poverty of spirit, meekness, holy mourning, purity of heart, especially hungering and thirsting after righteousness; and then recommends good works, as an evidence of our having his righteousness imputed to us, and these graces and divine tempers wrought in our hearts. "Let your light (that is, the divine light I before have been mentioning) shine before men, in a holy life; that they, seeing your good works, may glorify your father which is in heaven." And then he immediately adds, "Think not that I am come to destroy the moral law: I came not to destroy, (to take away the force of it as a rule of life) but to fulfill, (to obey it in its whole latitude, and give the complete sense of it.") And then he goes on to show

how exceeding broad the moral law is. So that our Lord, instead of setting aside an imputed righteousness in his sermon upon the mount, not only confirms it, but also answers the foregoing objection urged against it, by making good works a proof and evidence of its being imputed to our souls. He, therefore, that hath ears to hear, let him hear what the Prophet says in the words of the text, "The Lord our righteousness." But as Satan not only quoted scripture, but backed one temptation after another with it, when he attacked Christ in the wilderness; so his children generally take the same method in treating his doctrine. And, therefore, they urge another objection against the doctrine of an imputed righteousness, from the example of the young man in the gospel.

We may state it thus: "The Evangelist Mark, say they, chapter 10, mentions a young man that came to Christ, running, and asking him what he should do to inherit eternal life? Christ referred him to the commandments, to know what he must do to inherit eternal life. It is plain, therefore, works were to be, partly at least, the cause of his justification; and consequently the doctrine of an imputed righteousness is unscriptural." This is the objection in its full strength: and little strength in all its fullness. For, was I to prove the necessity of an imputed righteousness, I scarce know how I could bring a better instance to make it good.

Let us take a nearer view of this young man, and of our Lord's behavior towards him, Mark 10:17, the Evangelist tells us, "That when Christ was gone forth into the way, there came one running (it should seem it was some nobleman; a rarity indeed to see such a one running to Christ!) and not only so, but he kneeled to him, (perhaps many of his rank now, scarce know the time when they kneeled to Christ) and asked him, saying, Good Master, what shall I do that I may inherit eternal life?" Then Jesus, to see whether or not he believed him to be what he really was, truly and properly God, said unto him, "Why callest thou me good? There is none good but one, that is God." And, that he might directly answer his question, says he, "Thou knowest the commandments: do not commit adultery, do not bear false witness, defraud not, honor thy father and thy mother." This was a direct answer to his question; namely, That eternal life was not to be attained by his doings. For our Lord, by referring him to the commandments, did not (as the objectors insinuate) in the least hint, that his morality would recommend him to the favor and mercy of God; but he intended thereby, to make the law his schoolmaster to bring him to himself; that the young man, seeing how he had broken every one of these commandments, might thereby be convinced of the insufficiency of his own, and consequently of the absolute necessity of looking out for a better righteousness, whereon he might depend for eternal life.

This was what our Lord designed. The young man being self-righteous, and willing to justify himself, said, "All these have I observed from my youth;" but had he known himself, he would have confessed, all these have I broken from my youth. For, supposing he had not actually committed adultery, had he never lusted after a woman in his heart? What, if he had not really killed another, had he never been angry without a cause, or spoken unadvisedly with his lips? If so, by breaking one of the least commandments in the least degree, he became liable to the curse of God: for "cursed is he (saith the law) that continueth not to do all things that are written in this book." And therefore, as observed before, our Lord was so far from speaking against, that he treated the young man in that manner, on purpose to convince him of the necessity of an imputed righteousness.

But perhaps they will reply, it is said, "Jesus beholding him, loved him." And what then? This he might do with a human love, and at the same time this young man have no interest in his blood. Thus Christ is said to wonder, to weep over Jerusalem, and say, "O that thou hadst known, Me." But such like passages are to be referred only to his human nature. And there is a great deal of difference between the love wherewith Christ loved this young man, and that wherewith he loved Mary, Lazarus, and their sister Martha. To illustrate this by comparison: A minister of the Lord Jesus Christ seeing many amiable dispositions, such as a readiness to hear the word, a decent behavior at public worship, and a life outwardly spotless in many, cannot but so far love them; but then there is much difference betwixt the love which a minister feels for such, and that divine love, that union and sympathy of soul, which he feels for those that he is satisfied are really born again of God. Apply this to our Lord's case, as a faint illustration of it. Consider what has been said upon the young man's case in general, and then, if before you were fond of this objection, instead of triumphing, like him you will go sorrowful away. Our Savior's reply to him more and more convinces us of the truth of the prophet's assertion in the text, that "the Lord is our righteousness." But there is a fourth, and a grand objection yet behind, which is taken from the 25th chapter of Matthew, "where our Lord is described as rewarding people with eternal life, because they fed the hungry, clothed the naked, and such-like. Their works therefore were a cause of their justification, consequently the doctrine of imputed righteousness is not agreeable to scripture." This, I confess, is the most plausible objection that is brought against the doctrine insisted on from the text; and that we may answer it in as clear and brief a manner as may be, we confess, with the Article of the Church of England, "That albeit good works do not justify us, yet they will follow after justification, as fruits of it; and though they spring from faith in Christ, and a renewed soul, they shall receive a reward of grace, though not of debt; and consequently the more we abound in such good works, the greater will be our reward when Jesus Christ shall come to judgment." Take these consideration along with us, and they will help us much to answer the objection now before us. For thus saith Matthew,

"Then shall the King say to them on his right hand, Come, ye blessed children of my Father, inherit the kingdom prepared for you from the foundation of the world. For I was an hungered, and ye gave me meat; I was thirsty, and ye gave me drink; I was a stranger, and ye took me in; naked, and ye clothed me; I was sick, and ye visited me; I was in prison, and ye came unto me. I will therefore reward you, because you have done these things out of love to me, and hereby have evidenced yourselves to be my true disciples." And that the people did not depend on these good actions for their justification in the sight of God, is evident. "For when saw we thee an hungered, say they, and fed thee? Or thirsty, and gave thee drink? When saw we thee a stranger, and took thee in, or naked, and clothed thee? Or when saw we thee sick, or in prison, and came unto thee?" Language, and questions, quite improper for persons relying on their own righteousness, for acceptance and acquittance in the sight of God.

But then they reply against thee: "In the latter part of the chapter, it is plain that Jesus Christ rejects and damns the others for not doing these things. And therefore, if he damns these for not doing, he saves those for doing; and consequently the doctrine of an imputed righteousness is good for nothing." But that is no consequence at all; for God may justly damn any man for omitting the least duty of the moral law, and yet in himself is not obliged to give to any one any reward, supposing he has done all that he can. We are unprofitable servants; we have not done near so much as it was our duty to do, must be the language of the most holy souls living; and therefore, from or in ourselves, cannot be justified in the sight of God. This was the frame of the devout souls just now referred to. Sensible of this, they were so far from depending on their works for justification in the sight of God, that they were filled, as it were, with a holy blushing, to think our Lord should condescend to mention, much more to reward them for, their poor works of faith and labors of love. I am persuaded their hearts would rise with a holy indignation against those who urge this passage, as an objection to the assertion of the prophet, that "the Lord is our righteousness." Thus, I think, we have fairly answered these grand objections, which are generally urged against the doctrine of an IMPUTED RIGHTEOUSNESS. Was I to stop here, I think I may say, "We are made more than conquerors through him that loved us." But there is a way of arguing which I have always admired, because I have thought it always very convincing, by showing the ABSURDITIES that will follow from denying any particular proposition in dispute.

IV. This is the next thing that was proposed. And never did greater or more absurdities flow from the denying any doctrine, than will flow from denying the doctrine of Christ's imputed righteousness.

And FIRST, if we deny this doctrine, we turn the truth, I mean the word of God, as much as we can, into a lie, and utterly subvert all those places of scripture which say that we are saved by grace; that it is not of works, lest any man should boast, that salvation is God's free gift, and that he who glorieth, must glory only in the Lord. For, if the whole personal righteousness of Jesus Christ be not the sole cause of my acceptance with God, if any work done by or foreseen in me, was in the least to be joined with it, or looked upon by God an in inducing, impulsive cause of acquitting my soul from guilt, then I have somewhat whereof I may glory in myself. Not boasting is excluded in the great work of our redemption; but that cannot be, if we are enemies to the doctrine of an imputed righteousness. It would be endless to enumerate how many texts of scripture must be false, if this doctrine be not true. Let it suffice to affirm in the general, that if we deny an imputed righteousness, we may as well deny a divine revelation all at once; for it is the alpha and omega, the beginning and the end of the book of God. We must either disbelieve that, or believe what the prophet has spoken in the text, "that the Lord is our righteousness." But further: I observed at the beginning of this discourse, that we are all Arminians and Papists by nature; for as one says, "Arminianism is the back way to popery." And here I venture further to affirming that if we deny the doctrine of an imputed righteousness, whatever we may stile ourselves, we are really Papists in our hearts; and deserve no other title from men.

Sirs, what think you? Suppose I was to come and tell you that you must intercede with saints, for them to intercede with God for you; would you not say, I was justly reputed a papist missionary by some, and deservedly thrust out of thy synagogues by others? I suppose you would. And why?

Because, you would say, the intercession of Jesus Christ was sufficient of itself, without the intercession of saints, and that it was blasphemous to join theirs with his, as though he was sufficient.

Suppose I went a little more round about, and told you that the death of Christ was not sufficient, without our death being added to it; that you must die as well as Christ, join your death with his, and then it would be sufficient. Might you not then, with a holy indignation, throw dust in the air, and justly call me a "setter forth of strange doctrines?" And how then, if it be not only absurd, but blasphemous to join the intercession of saints with the intercession of Christ, as though his intercession was not sufficient; or our death with the death of Christ, as though his death was not sufficient: judge ye, if it be not equally absurd, equally blasphemous, to join our obedience, either wholly or in part, with the obedience of Christ, as if that was not sufficient. And if so, what absurdities will follow the denying that the Lord, both as to his active and passive obedience, is our righteousness?

One more absurdity I shall mention, as following the denying this doctrine, and I have done.

I remember a story of a certain prelate, who, after many arguments in vain urged to convince the Earl of Rochester of the invisible realities of another world, took his leave of his lordship with some such words as these: "Well, my lord, if there be no hell, I am safe; but if there should be such a thing as hell, what will become of you?" I apply this so those that oppose the doctrine now insisted on. If there be no such thing as the doctrine of an imputed righteousness, those who hold it, and bring forth fruit unto holiness, are safe; but if there be such a thing (as there certainly is) what will become of you that deny it? It is no difficult matter to determine. Your portion must be in the lake of fire and brimstone for ever and ever. Since you will rely upon your works, by your works you shall be judged. They shall be weighed in the balance of the sanctuary; and they will be found wanting. By your works therefore shall you be condemned; and you, being out of Christ, shall find God, to your poor wretched souls, a consuming fire.

The great Stoddard or Northampton in New England, has therefore well entitled a book which he wrote (and which I would take this opportunity to recommend) "The Safety of appearing in the Righteousness of Christ." For why should I lean upon a broken reed, when I can have the rock of ages to stand upon, that never can be moved?

And now, before I come to a more particular application, give me leave, in the apostle's language, triumphantly to cry out, "Where is the scribe, where the disputer?" Where is the reasoning infidel of this generation? Can any thing appear more reasonable, even according to your own way of arguing, than the doctrine here laid down? Have you not felt a convincing power go along with the word? Why then will you not believe on the Lord Jesus Christ, that so he may become the Lord your righteousness?

But it is time for me to come a little closer to your consciences.

Brethren, though some may be offended at this doctrine, and may account it foolishness; yet, to many of you, I doubt not but it is precious, it being agreeable to the form of sound words, which from your infancy has been delivered to you; and, coming from a quarter, you would least have expected, may be received with more pleasure and satisfaction.

But give me leave to ask you one question; Can you say, the Lord our righteousness? I say, the Lord OUR righteousness. For entertaining this doctrine in your heads, without receiving the Lord Jesus Christ savingly by a lively faith into your hearts, will but increase your damnation. As I have often told you, so I tell you again, an unapplied Christ is no Christ at all. Can you then, with believing Thomas, cry our, "My Lord and my God?" Is Christ your sanctification, as well as your outward righteousness? For the word righteousness, in the text, not only implies Christ's personal righteousness imputed to us, but also holiness wrought in us. These two, God has joined together. He never did, he never dies, he never will put them asunder. If you are justified by the blood, you are also sanctified by the Spirit of our Lord. Can you then in this sense say, The Lord our righteousness? Were you ever made to abhor yourselves for your actual and original sins, and to loathe your own righteousness; for, as the prophet beautifully expresses it, "your righteousness is as filthy rags? Were you ever made to see and admire the all-sufficiency of Christ's righteousness, and excited by the Spirit of God to hunger and thirst after it? Could you ever say, my soul is athirst for Christ, yea, even for the righteousness of Christ? O when shall I come to appear before the presence of my God in the righteousness of Christ! Nothing but Christ! Nothing but Christ! Give me Christ, O god, and I am satisfied! My soul shall praise thee for ever.

Was this ever the language of your hearts? And, after these inward conflicts, were you ever enabled to reach out the arm of faith, and embrace the blessed Jesus in your souls, so that you could say, "my beloved is mine, and I am his?" If so, fear not, whoever you are. Hail, all hail, you happy souls! The Lord, the Lord Christ, the everlasting God, is your righteousness. Christ has justified you, who is he that condemneth you?

Christ has died for you, nay rather is risen again, and ever liveth to make intercession for you. Being now justified by his grace, you have peace with God, and shall, ere long, be with Jesus in glory, reaping everlasting and unspeakable fruits both in body and soul. For there is no condemnation to those that are really in Christ Jesus. "Whether Paul or Apollos, or life or death, all is yours if you are Christ's, for Christ is God's. My brethren, my heart is enlarged towards you! O think of the love of Christ in dying for you! If the Lord be your righteousness, let the righteousness of your Lord be continually in your mouth. Talk of, O talk of, and recommend the righteousness of Christ, when you lie down, and when you rise up, at your going out and coming in! Think of the greatness of the gift, as well as the giver! Show to all the world, in whom you have believed! Let all by your fruits know, that the Lord is your righteousness, and that you are waiting for your Lord from heaven! O study to be holy, even as he who has called you, and washed you in his own blood, is holy! Let not the righteousness of the Lord be evil spoken of through you. Let not Jesus be wounded in the house of his friends, but grow in grace, and in the knowledge of our Lord and Savior Jesus Christ, day by day. O think of his dying love! Let that love constrain you to obedience! Having much forgiven, love much. Be always asking, What shall I do, to express my gratitude to the Lord, for giving me his righteousness? Let that self-abasing, God-exalting question be always in your mouths; "Why me, Lord? Why me?" why am I taken, and others left?

Why is the Lord my righteousness? Why is he become my salvation, who have so often deserved damnation at his hands?

My friends, I trust I feel somewhat of a sense of God's distinguishing love upon my heart; therefore I must divert a little from congratulating you, to invite poor Christless sinners to come to him, and accept of his righteousness, that they may have life.

Alas, my heart almost bleeds! What a multitude of precious souls are now before me! How shortly must all be ushered into eternity! And yet, O cutting thought! Was God now to require all your souls, how few, comparatively speaking, could really say, the Lord our righteousness!

And think you, O sinner, that you will be able to stand in the day of judgment, if Christ be not your righteousness? No, that alone is the wedding garment in which you must appear. O Christless sinners, I am distressed for you! The desires of my soul are enlarged. O that this may be an accepted time! That the Lord may be your righteousness! For whither would you flee, if death should fine you naked? Indeed there is no hiding yourselves from his presence. The pitiful fig-leaves of your own righteousness will not cover your nakedness, when God shall call you to stand before him. Adam found them ineffectual, and so will you. O think of death! O think of judgment! Yet a little while, and time shall be no more; and then what will become of you, if the Lord be not your righteousness?

Think you that Christ will spare you? No, he that formed you, will have no mercy on you. If you are not of Christ, if Christ be not your righteousness, Christ himself shall pronounce you damned. And can you bear to think of being damned by Christ? Can you bear to hear the Lord Jesus say to you, "Depart from me, ye cursed, into everlasting fire, prepared for the devil and his angels." Can you live, think you, in everlasting burnings? Is your flesh brass, and your bones iron? What if they are? Hell-fire, that fire prepared for the devil and his angels, will heat them through and through. And can you bear to depart from Christ? O that heart-piercing thought! Ask those holy souls, who are at any time bewailing an absent God, who walk in darkness, and see no light, though but a few days or hours; ask them, what it is to lose a light and presence of Christ? See how they seek him sorrowing, and go mourning after him all the day long! And, if it is so dreadful to lose the sensible presence of Christ only for a day, what must it be to be banished from him to all eternity!

But thus it must be, if Christ be not your righteousness. For God's justice must be satisfied; and, unless Christ's righteousness is imputed and applied to you here, you must hereafter be satisfying the divine justice in hell-torments eternally; nay, Christ himself shall condemn you to that place of torment. And how cutting is that thought! Methinks I see poor, trembling, Christless wretches, standing before the bar of god, crying out, Lord, if we must be damned, let some angel, or some archangel, pronounce the damnatory sentence: but all in vain. Christ himself shall pronounce the irrevocable sentence. Knowing therefore the terrors of the Lord, let me persuade you to close with Christ, and never rest till you can say, "the Lord our righteousness." Who knows but the Lord may have mercy on, may, abundantly pardon you? Beg of God to give you faith; and, if the Lord gives you that, you will by it receive Christ, with his righteousness, and his All. You need not fear the greatness or number of your sins. For are you sinners? So am I. Are you the chief of sinners? So am I. Are you backsliding sinners? So am I. And yet the Lord (for ever adored be his rich, free and sovereign grace) the Lord is my righteousness. Come then, O young man, who (as I acted once myself) are playing the prodigal, and wandering away afar off from your heavenly Father's house, come home, come home, and leave your swines trough. Feed no longer on the husks of sensual delights: for Christ's sake arise, and come home! Your heavenly Father now calls you. See yonder the best robe, even the righteousness of his dear Son, awaits you. See it, view it again and again. Consider at how dear a rate it was purchased, even by the blood of God. Consider what great need you have of it. You are lost, undone, damned for ever, without it. Come then, poor, guilty prodigals, come home: indeed, I will not, like the elder brother in the gospel, be angry; no, I will rejoice with the angels in heaven. And O that God would now bow the heavens, and come down! Descend, O Son of God, descend; and, as thou hast shown in me such mercy, O let thy blessed Spirit apply thy righteousness to some young prodigals now before thee, and clothe their naked souls with thy best robe!

But I must speak a word to you, young maidens, as well as young men. I see many of you adorned, as to your bodies, but are not your souls naked?

Which of you can say, the Lord is my righteousness? Which of you was ever solicitous to be dressed in this robe of invaluable price, and without which you are no better than whited sepulchers in the sight of God? Let not then so many of you, young maidens, any longer forget your chief and only ornament. O seek for the Lord to be your righteousness, or otherwise burning will soon be upon you, instead of beauty!

And what shall I say to you of a middle age, you busy merchants, you cumbered Martha's, who, with all your gettings, have not yet gotten the

Lord to be your righteousness? Alas! what profit will there be of all your labor under the sun, if you do not secure this pearl of invaluable price?

This one thing, so absolutely needful, that it only can stand you in stead, when all other things shall be taken from you. Labor therefore no longer so anxiously for the meat which perisheth, but henceforward seek for the Lord to be your righteousness, a righteousness that will entitle you to life everlasting. I see also many hoary heads here, and perhaps the most of them cannot say, the Lord is my righteousness. O gray-headed sinner, I could weep over you! Your gray hairs, which ought to be your crown, and in which perhaps you glory, are now your shame. You know not that the Lord is your righteousness: O haste then, haste ye, aged sinners, and seek an interest in redeeming love! Alas, you have one foot already in the grave, your glass is just run out, your sun is just going down, and it will set and leave you in an eternal darkness, unless the Lord be your righteousness! Flee then, O flee for your lives! Be not afraid. All things are possible with God. If you come, though it be at the eleventh hour, Christ Jesus will in no wise cast you out. Seek then for the Lord to be your righteousness, and beseech him to let you know, how it is that a man may be born again when he is old!

But I must not forget the lambs of the flock. To feed them was one of my Lord's last commands. I know he will be angry with me, if I do not tell them, that the Lord may be their righteousness; and that of such is the kingdom of heaven. Come then, ye little children, come to Christ; the Lord Christ shall be your righteousness. Do not think, that you are too young to be converted. Perhaps many of you may be nine or ten years old, and yet cannot say, the Lord is our righteousness: which many have said, though younger than you. Come then, while you are young. Perhaps you may not live to be old. Do not stay for other people. If your fathers and mothers will not come to Christ, do you come without them. Let children lead them, and show them how the Lord may be their righteousness. Our Lord Jesus Christ loved little children. You are his lambs; he bids me feed you. I pray God make you willing betimes to take the Lord for your righteousness.

Here then I could conclude; but I must not forget the poor negroes; no, I must not. Jesus Christ had died for them, as well as for others. Nor do I mention you last, because I despise your souls; but because I would have what I shall say, make the deeper impression upon your hearts. O that you would seek the Lord to be your righteousness! Who knows but he may be found of you? For in Jesus Christ there is neither male nor female, bond nor free; even you may be the children of God, if you believe in Jesus. Did you never read of the eunuch belonging to the queen of Candace? A negro like yourselves. He believed. The Lord was his righteousness. He was baptized. Do you also believe, and you shall be saved. Christ Jesus is the same now as he was yesterday, and will wash you in his own blood. Go home then, turn the words of the text into a prayer, and entreat the Lord to be your righteousness. Even so, come Lord Jesus, come quickly, into all our souls! Amen, Lord Jesus, Amen and Amen!

Sermon 15 The Righteousness of Christ, an Everlasting Righteousness

Daniel 9:24, "And to bring everlasting Righteousness."

On reading these words, I cannot help addressing you in the language of the angels to the poor shepherds, who kept watch over their flocks by night, "Behold, I bring you glad tidings of great joy," such tidings, that if we have ears to hear, if we have eyes to see, and if our hearts have indeed experienced the grace of God, must cause us to cry out with the Virgin Mary, "My soul doth magnify the Lord, and my spirit doth rejoice in God my Savior." The words which I have read to you, are part of one of the most explicit revelations that was given of Jesus Christ, before he made his public entrance into this our world. It has been observed by some, and very properly too, that it is one mark of the divine goodness to his creatures, that he is pleased to let light come in gradually upon the natural world. If the sun from midnight darkness, was immediately to shine forth in his full meridian blaze, his great splendor would be apt to dazzle our eyes, and strike us blind again: but God is pleased to make light come gradually in, and by that means we are prepared to receive it. And as God is pleased to deal with the natural, so he has dealt with the moral, with the spiritual world. The Lord Jesus Christ did not appear in his full glory all at once, but as the sun rises gradually, so did the Lord Jesus, the Sun of righteousness, rise gradually upon men, with healing under his wings.

Hence it was, that our first parents had nothing to fix their faith upon, but that first promise, "The seed of the woman shall bruise the serpent's head." And in future ages, at sundry times, and after divers manners, God was pleased to speak to our fathers by the prophets, before he spake to us in these last days by his Son; and the prophets that were more peculiarly dear to God, it should seem had more peculiar and extraordinary revelations vouchsafed to them, concerning Jesus Christ.

It is plain from the accounts we have in Scripture, that the Prophet Daniel was one of these; he is stiled by the angel, not only a "man that was beloved," but a "man that was greatly beloved," or as it is in the margin of your bibles, "he was a man of desires," of large and extensive desires to promote the glory of God; he was a desirable man, a man that did much good in his generation, and therefore his life was much to be desired by those who loved God. The words which I have chosen for the subject of our present meditation, contain part of a revelation made to this man. If you look back to the beginning of this chapter, you will find how the good man was employed, when God was pleased to give him this revelation; verse 2, "In the first year of Darius's reign, I Daniel understood by books the number of the years, whereof the word of the Lord came to Jeremiah the prophet, that he would accomplish seventy years in the desolations of Jerusalem." Daniel was a great man, and withal a good man; great as he was, it seems he was not above reading his Bible; he made the Bible his constant study; for it is the Bible we are to understand by what is here termed books, and elsewhere, the scriptures of truth. He found, that the time for God's people being delivered from the captivity, was now at hand. Well, one would have thought, that therefore Daniel needed not to pray; but this, instead of retarding, quickened him in his prayers: and therefore we are told in the third verse, "I set my face unto the Lord God, to seek by prayer and supplications, with fasting and sackcloth, and ashes." It is beautifully expressed: "he set his face," as though he was resolved never to let his eye go off God, till God was pleased to give him an answer; he was resolved, Jacob-like, to wrestle with the Lord God, until God should be pleased to give him the desired blessing. We are told in the fourth verse, that "he prayed unto the Lord, and made confession," not only of his own sins, but the sins of his people. And when ye retire hence to your houses, before ye go to bed, I would recommend to you the reading of this prayer; every word of it bespeaks his exceeding concern for the public good. It would take me up too much time, was I to make such observations as indeed the prayer deserved; to bring you sooner to the words of the text, let us go forward to the twentieth verse, and there you will find the success that Daniel met with, when praying. Says he, "And whiles I was speaking, and praying, and confessing my sin and the sin of my people Israel, and presenting my supplication before the LORD my God for the holy mountain of my God; Yea, whiles I was speaking in prayer, even the man Gabriel, whom I had seen in the vision at the beginning, being caused to fly swiftly, touched me about the time of the evening oblation. The manner in which Daniel expressed himself, is very emphatical: "While I was speaking in prayer;" implying, that God suffers us, when we draw near to him by faith in prayer, to lay all our complaints before him; he suffers us to speak unto, and talk with him, as a man talketh with his friend. Daniel at this time too was making confession one part of his prayer; for we are never, never in a better frame to receive answers from above, than when we are humbling ourselves before the Lord. He was not only confessing his own sins, but he was confessing the sins of his people;

he was praying for those, who perhaps seldom prayed for themselves; "while I was speaking in prayer, the man Gabriel:" which word, by interpretation, signifies the strength of God; a very proper name, says Bishop Hall, for that angel who was to come and bring the news to the world, of the God of strength, the Lord Jesus Christ. This angel is here represented as flying, and as flying swiftly; to show us how willing, how unspeakably willing those blessed spirits are, to bring good news to men. And it is upon this account, I suppose, that we are taught by our Lord to pray, "that God's will may be done by us on earth, as it is done in heaven," that we may imitate a little of that alacrity and vigor, which angels employ, when they are sent on errands for God.

Well, here is not only mention made of the angel's flying swiftly, but there is mention made of the time that he came; "He came and touched me, about the time of the evening oblations," that is, about three o'clock in the afternoon; at this time there was a sacrifice made to God, and this sacrifice was in a peculiar manner a type of the Lord Jesus, who in the evening of the world was to become a sacrifice for sinners. We are told in the 22nd verse, what message this angel delivered, "He informed me, and talked with me, and said, O Daniel, I am now come forth to give thee skill and understanding; at the beginning of thy supplication, the commandment came forth, and I am come to show thee, for thou art greatly beloved, therefore understand the matter, and consider the vision." This passage, with such like passages of scripture, hath often comforted my soul, and may comfort the hearts of all God's people. There are a great many of you, perhaps, have prayed, and prayed again to God, and probably you do not find any answer given you: you pray for an enlarged heart, you pray for comfort, you pray for deliverance; God is pleased to withhold it for a while; then the devil strikes in, and says, God has shut out your prayers, God will never hear, God will never regard you, therefore pray no more. But, my dear friends, this is a mistake; a thousand years are with God as one day; and the Lord Jesus had bid us, "to pray always, and not faint." You may have had your prayers heard, the very moment they went out of your lips, though it may not please your God, (and it may not be proper for you) to let you know that they are heard. "At the beginning of thy supplication, the commandment went forth;" and this very angel some hundred years after, told Zecharias, that his prayer was heard;" a prayer for what? A prayer for a child: it could not be supposed that at the very time Zecharias was praying for a child; but his prayer he had put up forty years before, God was pleased to answer so long afterwards.

But to proceed with Gabriel's declaration, ver. 24, Seventy years are determined upon thy people, and upon thy holy city, to finish transgression, to make an end of sins, and to make reconciliation for iniquity, and to bring in everlasting righteousness." I do not intend to trouble you about the critical exposition of these seventy weeks; commentators are divided exceedingly upon this subject; some of them explain them one way, and some another, and perhaps we shall never know till the day of judgment, till the glorious day spoken of in the New Testament, which are right. My intention is to dwell upon this particular part of the angel's message, that some one person was to do something unspeakable for God's people, even "to bring in an everlasting righteousness." If you want to know who was the person that was to do this, look to the 26th verse, and you will find the person mentioned, the Lord Jesus Christ: "after threescore and two weeks shall the Messiah be cut off, but not for himself:" he is the person spoken of, he was "to put an end to sin, to make reconciliation for iniquity, and to bring in everlasting righteousness." From these important words, I shall endeavor, FIRST, To show you what we are to understand by the word, "Righteousness." SECONDLY, I shall endeavor to show you, upon what account it lay that the righteousness mentioned in the text, is called an "everlasting righteousness." THIRDLY, I shall show, what we are to understand by "bringing it in." And, Then speak a word to saints and sinners. And while I am speaking to your ears, may God, for the Lord Jesus Christ's sake, speak to your hearts!

FIRST, To explain what we are to understand by the word, "righteousness." If I was to ask some people what we are to understand by the word, righteousness; if the person was an Arminian, or an enemy to the doctrine of free grace, he would answer me, it signifies what we commonly call moral honesty, or doing justice between man and man. And, indeed, in various passages of scripture, the word righteousness has no other meaning, at least, it bears that meaning. I suppose, we are to understand it in this sense, when we are told, that Paul, preaching before Felix, "reasoned of temperance, of righteousness, and of a judgment to come." Felix had been a very unrighteous and unjust man, and therefore, to convince him of his wickedness, to alarm his conscience, to put him upon seeking help in the Lord Jesus, Paul preached not only of temperance, (for Felix had been a very intemperate man) but he preached to him of righteousness, of the necessity of doing justice because he had been an unjust man; and he puts before him the judgment to come, in order to make him fly to Jesus Christ for deliverance from the bad consequences of that judgment; and there are other places of scripture, where the word righteousness may be understood in this sense.

It likewise signifies inward holiness, wrought in us by the blessed Spirit of God. But, I believe, the word righteousness in my text signifies, what, I trust most, I should be glad if I could say, all who attend this night, will be glad to hear of: What is that? It is what all reformed divines, that have clear heads and clean hearts, call an imputed righteousness, or the righteousness of the Lord Jesus Christ to be imputed to poor sinners upon their believing: and, if you ask me, what I mean by an imputed righteousness, not to shoot over you heads, but rather, if God shall be pleased to make me, to reach your hearts, I will tell you by the word "righteousness," I understand all that Christ hat done, and all that Christ hath suffered: or, to make use of the term generally made use of by sound divines, "Christ's active, and Christ's passive obedience;" put those two together, and they make up the righteousness of the Lord Jesus Christ.

My dear friends, thus stood the case between God and man: at first God made man upright. Moses gives us a short, but never was so full a description of the origin and nature of man given by any other but himself. "In the image of God made he man, says the sacred historian, being inspired by the Spirit of God. God said, and it was done; God commanded, and the world arose before him; "Let there be light," and instantaneously behold light appeared: but when that lovely, that divine, that blessed creature Man, the Lord of the creation, God's vicegerent was to be made; God calls a council, and says, "Let us make man after our own image." Now, this image is to be understood, no doubt, in respect of man's soul; for God being no corporeal substance, man could not be made after his image that way. Well, in this condition God made man. Adam stood as our representative. Adam and Eve had but one name originally, "God made man, and called their name Adam. God left Adam to his own free will; he was pleased to enter into a covenant with him, which, indeed, is an amazing instance of God's condescension. God might have ordered man to do so and so, and not made him any promise of a reward: but the great Creator was pleased to promise him, that if he performed an unsinning obedience, if he abstained from eating a particular tree, that he and his posterity should live forever; but if he broke that command, in the day that he ate thereof, he and all his prosperity were to die. Now, I verily believe, had you and I been there present, however some people may object against God's severity, in imputing Adam's sin to us; yet I believe, if you and I, and all the world had been present, we should have heartily come into this agreement. Supposing God had called the whole creation together, and had said, "Ye, my creatures, I have made here a man after my own image, I have breathed into him the breath of life, I have caused him to become a living soul, I have filled him with righteousness and true holiness; he has not the least propensity to sin, only he is a fallible and mutable creature; all that I desire of this man is, that he abstain from yonder tree; I have given to him all the trees of the garden, I have made him, and planted for him a garden with mine own right hand, I desire he may abstain from plucking yonder fruit! Will ye stand or fall by this m an, will ye let him be your representative, will ye be content that his obedience or disobedience be imputed to you?" If we had been all there, every one of us would have said, "Lord God, we will let him be our representative;" the terms were so easy, the improbability of his falling was so exceeding great; that I believe every one of us should have all put our hand to the covenant. And supposing us alive, and that we had agreed to that covenant, who is that man or woman that could find fault with God's imputing Adam's sin to us. Well, my friends, God made man in this condition; the devil envied his happiness; it is supposed by some, that man was made to supply the places of the fallen angels. But the devil envied man, and had leave to tempt him; Eve soon reached out her hand and plucked of the forbidden fruit, and afterwards Adam transgressed also; and from that very moment, to make use of Mr. Beston's words, "Man's name was Ichabod," the glory of the Lord departed from him. Adam and Eve then fell; you, and I, and all their posterity (whom they represented) fell in them.

Mankind had but one neck; and God might have served mankind, as Caligula would have served Rome, according to his own words, "I wish it had but one neck, and I would cut it off with one blow." God, if he pleased, might have sent us all to hell. Here Calvin represents God's attributes as struggling one with another; Justice saying to God, seeing Justice had framed the sanction, "Is the law broken, damn the offender, and send him to hell." The mercy of God, his darling attribute, cries out, "Spare him, spare him." The wisdom of God contrives a way, that justice might be satisfied, and yet mercy be triumphant still. How was that? The Lord Jesus interposes, the days-man, the dear Redeemer! He saw God wielding his flaming sword, and his hand taking hold of vengeance; the Lord Jesus Christ saw the sword ready to be sheathed in the blood of the offender; when no eye could pity, when no angel or archangel could rescue, just as God was, as it were, about to give the fatal blow, just as the knife was put to the throat of the offender, the Son of God, the eternal Logos, says, "Father, spare the sinner; let him not die; Father, Father, O hold thy hand, withdraw thy sword, for I come to do thy will; man has broken thy law, and violated thy covenant: I do not deny but man deserves to be damned forever; but, Father, what Adam could not do, it thou wilt prepare me a body, I in the fullness of time will go, and die for him; he has broken thy law, but I will go and keep it, that thy law may be honored; I will give a perfect unsinning obedience to all thy commandments; and that thou mayst justify ungodly creatures, I will not only go down and obey thy law, but I will go down and bleed; I will go down and die: here I am; I will step in between thee and sinners, and be glad to have thy sword sheathed in my heart's blood for them." In the fullness of time descends the eternal Logos, "In the fullness of time God sent forth his Son made of a woman, made under the law, to redeem them that are under the law from the curse of it, being made a curse for us." The Lord Jesus Christ being clothed in human nature, fulfilled all righteousness; he submitted to every institution of God, and was pleased to obey the whole moral law; and afterwards, O can we think of it, O can you hear of it, without a heart leaping with joy, at last the Lord Jesus bled and died! And when he was just expiring, just as he was about to bow down his head, and give up the ghost, what do ye think he said? He said, "It is finished!" As much as to say, "Now the arduous work, the difficult task I had undertaken, blessed be God, is not completely over; all the demands of the law are finished; now God's justice is satisfied; now a new and living way is opened by my blood to the holiest of all for poor sinners." So that when Christ's righteousness is here spoken of, we are to understand "Christ's obedience and death," all that Christ has done, and all that Christ has suffered for an elect world, for all that will believe on him. And blessed be God for this righteousness! Blessed be God for the epithet which in the text is put to this righteousness; it might be called a blessed righteousness, it might be called a glorious righteousness, it might be called an invaluable righteousness; but the angel calls it an everlasting righteousness: God give you to take the comfort of it!

SECONDLY, I am to show, on what account, this righteousness is here called an everlasting righteousness; and pray why do you think is Christ's righteousness called an everlasting righteousness?

I suppose it is called an everlasting righteousness, FIRST, Because Christ's righteousness was intended by the great God to extend to mankind even from eternity. All of you know, that old love is the best love. When we have an old acquaintance, a friend, that has loved us for many years, indeed that love is sweet: though we may love new friends, yet when an old friend and a new friend meet together, we may say, that the old is better. Now this should endear God to us, to think that from all the ages of eternity God had thoughts of you; God intended the Lord Jesus Christ to save your souls and mine: hence it is, that God, to endear Jeremiah to him, tells him, I have love thee with an everlasting love.

Hence it is, that the Lord Jesus when he calls his elect people up to heaven, says, "Come, ye blessed of my Father;" what follows? "receive the kingdom prepared for you;" how long? "from the foundation of the world." All that we receive in time; all the streams that come to our souls, are but so many steams flowing from that inexhaustible fountain, God's electing, God' s sovereign, God' s distinguishing, God's everlasting love; and, therefore, the righteousness of Jesus Christ may properly be called an everlasting righteousness, because God intended it from everlasting.

SECONDLY, It is called an everlasting righteousness, because the efficacy of Christ's death took place immediately upon Adam's fall.

Christianity, in one sense, is as old as the creation. Great Professor Franck, of Germany, says, "That Christ is the sum and substance of all righteousness." Mr. Henry observes, "That the Lord Jesus Christ is the treasure hid in the field of the Old Testament, under the types and shadows of the Mosaic dispensation." We have the Sun of Righteousness shining in his full meridian in the New Testament dispensation." We have the Sun of Righteousness shining in his full meridian in the New Testament dispensation. Now the righteousness of Jesus Christ, may be called an everlasting righteousness, because all the saints that have been saved, or that ever will be saved, are all saved by the righteousness of Christ. A great many censorious people are mighty inquisitive to know, what will become of the heathens, that never heard of Jesus Christ. I would say to such persons, as the Lord Jesus Christ did to another curious inquirer, "What is that to thee? Follow thou me." Pray, for what should you and I trouble ourselves about the heathens? Are not we heathens? It is too true, that we have too much of a heathens temper and practice with us. But why should we lost our time in inquiring about what will become of the heathen, and not rather inquire what will become of our own souls? We may be sure God will deal with heathens according to their light: if he has given them no revelation, they will not be judged by a revelation; if they have not had a law, they will be judged without law. But as for the Jews and Gentiles, who have the gospel revealed to them, however Deists may argue contrary to it; however they may set up reason in opposition to divine revelation; we may be sure none were ever saved, or will be saved, but by the righteousness of Christ. It was through faith in him, that Abel was saved; it was through the sacrifice of Jesus Christ, that Abraham was accepted, and that all the prophets of old were accepted; and there is none other name given under heaven, whereby we can be saved, but that of Christ.

And therefore, since persons under the law, and under the gospel, are to be saved only through Christ; therefore, Christ's righteousness may properly be called an everlasting righteousness. But this is not all.

THIRDLY, The righteousness of Jesus Christ, is not only to be called an everlasting righteousness, because that all persons under the law and all persons under the gospel, are saved by it; but because the efficacy thereof, blessed be God for it! Is to continue till time shall be no more.

Blessed be God for Jesus Christ! The efficacy of whose blood, death, and atonement, is as great and as effectual now to the salvation of poor sinners, as when he bowed his blessed head, and gave up the ghost: "Jesus Christ is the same yesterday, today, and forever;" and whosoever believes on him, now, whosoever comes to, and accepts of him, shall now see his power, shall taste of his grace, and shall be actually saved by him, the save as if he had been in company with those who saw him expiring.

FOURTHLY, Christ's righteousness may be called an everlasting righteousness, because the benefit of it is to endure to everlasting life.

Indeed, some people tell us, that a person may be in Christ today, and go to the devil tomorrow: but, blessed be God, ye have not so learned Christ!

No, my dear friends, thanks be to God for that divine text, "There is now no condemnation to them that are in Christ Jesus." Though God's people may fall foully; and though many are full of doubts and fears, and say, "One day I shall fall by the hands of Saul;" however your poor souls may be harassed, yet no wicked devil, nor your own depraved heart, shall be able to separate you from the love of God: God has loved you, God has fixed his heart upon you, and having loved his own, he loves them unto the end. The Lord of life and of glory, the blessed Jesus, will never cease loving you, till he hath loved and brought you to heaven; when he will rejoice, and say, "Behold me, O my Father, and the dear children that thou hast given me; thou gavest them me; thine they were, I have bought them with my blood, I have won them with my sword and with my bow, and I now will wear them as so many jewels of my crown." Therefore, Jesus Christ's righteousness may be called an everlasting righteousness, because those who once take hold of, and are interested in it, shall be saved everlastingly by Christ: "It is God that justifies us, (says St. Paul) who is he that condemneth? It is Christ that died, yea rather that is risen again." He gives devils the challenge, "O death, where is thy sting, O grave, where is thy victory? Who shall separate us from the love of God? I am persuaded that neither death nor life, neither principalities nor powers, nor any other creature, shall ever be able to separate us from the love of God, which is in Christ Jesus our Lord." Those whom God justifies, he also glorifies. And because Christ lives, blessed be God, we shall live also. I know not what you may say; but though I trust I have felt the grace of Christ every day for fresh strength as if I had never believed before: and if I was to depend upon my own faithfulness, and not the faithfulness of the Son of God, I am sure I should soon desert the Lord Jesus Christ. But glory be to God, he is faithful that hath promised! Glory be to God, our salvation depends not upon our own free will, but upon God's free grace! Here is a sure bottom; the believer may build upon it; let the storms blow as long and as high as they please, they may make the poor creature tremble, but blessed be God, they never shall be able to take him off the foundation; though they may shake him, they shall only shake off his corruption: and I believe all that fear God, will be glad to part with it. ON all these accounts, Christ's righteousness may be called an everlasting righteousness.

III. It is said, in my text, that Jesus was to bring it in. What are we to understand by his bringing it in? Our Lord's promulgating and proclaiming it to the world. Indeed, it was brought in under the law, but then it was brought in under types and shadows, and most of the Jews looked no further. But Jesus Christ brought life and immortality to light by the gospel. The light of Moses was only twilight; the light of the gospel, is like the sun at noon-day, shining in his full meridian. Therefore, Jesus Christ may be said to bring in this everlasting righteousness, because he proclaimed it to the world, and commanded it to be preached, that God sent his Son into the world, that the world through him might be saved.

Again, The Lord Jesus Christ brought in this righteousness, as he wrought it out for sinners upon the cross. Some Antinomians, for want of a proper distinction, run into a grievous error, telling us, Because God intended to justify by the righteousness of Jesus Christ, therefore man is justified from all eternity: which is absurd: a person cannot be justified, till he is actually existing; therefore, though man is justified, as it lies in God's mind from all eternity, yet it was not actually brought in till the Lord Jesus Christ pronounced those blessed words, "It is finished;" the grand consummation! Then Jesus brought it in. A new and a living way was to be opened to the Holy of Holies, for poor sinners, by the blood of Christ. But I do not think that the expression, brought in, is to be limited to this sense, though I suppose it is the primary one; it implies not only Christ's bringing it into the world, as promulgating, and having it written in the word of God, and as having wrought it out for sinners in his life, and on the cross; but he brings it in, in a manner, which, I pray God may take place this night; I mean, bringing it, by his blessed Spirit, into poor believers hearts. All that Christ hath done, all that Christ hat suffered, all Christ's active obedience, all Christ's passive obedience, will do us no good, unless by the Spirit of God, it is brought into our souls. As one expresses it, "An unapplied Christ is no Christ at all." To hear of a Christ dying for sinners, will only increase your damnation, will only sink you deeper into hell, unless we have ground to say, by a work of grace wrought in our hearts, that the Lord Jesus hath brought this home to us. Hence it is, that the Apostle, speaking of Christ, says, "Who love me, and gave himself for me." O that dear, that great, that little, but important word, me. Happy they, who can adopt the Apostle's language! Happy they that can apply it to their own heart; and when they hear that Christ has brought in an everlasting righteousness, can say, Blessed be God, it is brought in by the blessed Spirit to my soul!

Are there any here that can go along with me on this doctrine? But why do I ask this question, when preaching to numbers, who, I hope, have tasted of the grace of God long ago? I do not know, I cannot distinguish you; you are just like other people, as to your looks and habits; but if I do not, and if your neighbors cannot know you, that great God, in whose presence you are, knows you; He, before whose tribunal we are shortly to appear, knows you. If Christ Jesus hath brought his everlasting righteousness into your heart; if it is applied by the Spirit of God to your soul, what shall I say to you? I will say as the Angel to John, "Come up hither," thou child of God! Come up hither, thou son, thou daughter of Abraham! Come and join with me, in calling upon angels and archangels, in calling upon the spirits of just men made perfect, to help thee to praise that loving Redeemer, that has brought in an everlasting righteousness. O was ever love like this!

When Abraham was about to offer up his son, God said, "Now I know that thou lovest me, since thou hast not withheld thy son, thine only son from me." Now may each child of God say, "Now, O God, I know that thou hast loved me, since thou hast not withheld thy Son, thy dear Son, the Lord Jesus Christ, from dying for me." If thou hast got Christ brought into thy soul by faith, O look forward, look towards a happy eternity; O look towards those everlasting mansions, into which God will bring thee after death. My dear friends, I could say much from this text to comfort God's people: But I must address myself to you, poor souls, who cannot say, that this righteousness has been brought home to your souls; but if it was never brought home before, may God, for the Lord Jesus Christ's sake, bring it home now! Are any of you depending upon a righteousness of your own? Do any of you here, think to save yourselves by your own doings? I say to you, as the Apostle said to one that offered money for a power to confer the gift of the Holy Ghost, your righteousness shall perish with you. Poor miserable creatures! What is there in your tears? What in your prayers? What in your performances, to appease the wrath of an angry God? Away from the trees of the garden; come, ye guilty wretches, come as poor, lost, undone, and wretched creatures, and accept of a better righteousness than your own. As I said before, so I tell you again, the righteousness of Jesus Christ is an everlasting righteousness: it is wrought out for the very chief of sinners.

Ho, every one that thirsteth, let him come and drink of this water of life freely. Are any of you wounded by sin? Do any of you feel you have no righteousness of your own? Are any of you perishing for hunger? Are any of you afraid ye will perish forever? Come, dear souls, in all your rags; come, thou poor man; come, thou poor, distressed woman; you, who think God will never forgive you, and that your sins are too great to be forgiven; come, thou doubting creature, who art afraid thou wilt never get comfort; arise, take comfort, the Lord Jesus Christ, the Lord of life, the Lord of glory, calls for thee: through his righteousness there is hope for the chief of sinners, for the worst of creatures. What if thou hadst committed all the sins in the world? What if thou hadst committed the sins of a thousand, what if thou hadst committed the sins of a million of worlds?

Christ's righteousness will cover, the blood of the Lord Jesus Christ will cleanse, thee from the guilt of them all. O let not one poor soul stand at a distance from the Savior. My dear friends, could my voice hold out, was my strength equal to my will, I would wrestle with you; I would strive with arguments, till you came and washed in this blood of the Lamb; till you came and accepted of this everlasting righteousness. O come, come! Now, since it is brought into the world by Christ, so in the name, in the strength, and by the assistance of the great God, I bring it now to the pulpit; I now offer this righteousness, this free, this imputed, this everlasting righteousness to all poor sinners that will accept of it. For God's sake accept it this night: you do not know but ye may die before tomorrow. How do he know, but while I am speaking, a fit of the apoplexy may seize, and death arrest you? O my dear friends, where can ye go? Where will ye appear? How will ye stand before an angry God, without the righteousness of the Lord Jesus Christ put upon your souls? Can ye stand in your own rags? Will ye dare to appear before a heart-searching God, without the apparel of your elder brother? If ye do, I know your doom: Christ will frown you into hell: "Depart, depart, ye cursed, into everlasting fire," shall be your portion. Think, I pray you, therefore, on these things; go home, go home, go home, pray over the text, and say, "Lord God, thou hast brought an everlasting righteousness into the world by the Lord Jesus Christ; by the blessed Spirit bring it into my heart!" then, die when ye will, ye are safe; if it be tomorrow, ye shall be immediately translated into the presence of the everlasting God: that will be sweet! Happy they who have got this robe on; happy they that can say, "My God hath loved me, and I shall be loved by him with an everlasting love!" That every one of you may be able to say so, may God grant, for the sake of Jesus Christ, the dear Redeemer; to whom be glory for ever. Amen.

Sermon 16 The Observation of the Birth of Christ

(The Observation of the Birth of Christ, the Duty of all Christians; or the True Way of Keeping Christmas)

Matthew 1:21, "And she shall bring forth a Son, and then shalt call his Name Jesus: For he shall save his People from their Sins."

The celebration of the birth of Christ hath been esteemed a duty by most who profess Christianity. When we consider the condescension and love of the Lord Jesus Christ, in submitting to be born of a virgin, a poor sinful creature; and especially as he knew how he was to be treated in this world; that he was to be despised, scoffed at, and at last to die a painful, shameful, and ignominious death; that he should be treated as though he was the off-scouring of all mankind; used, not like the son of man, and, therefore, not at all like the Son of God; the consideration of these things should make us to admire the love of the Lord Jesus Christ, who was so willing to offer himself as a ransom for the sins of the people, that when the fullness of time was come, Christ came, made of a woman, made under the law: he came according to the eternal counsel of the Father; he came, not in glory or in splendor, not like him who brought all salvation with him: no, he was born in a stable, and laid in a manger; oxen were his companions. O amazing condescension of the Lord Jesus Christ, to stoop to such low and poor things for our sake. What love is this, what great and wonderful love was here, that the Son of God should come into our world in so mean a condition, to deliver us from the sin and misery in which we were involved by our fall in our first parents! And as all that proceeded from the springs must be muddy, because the fountain was so, the Lord Jesus Christ came to take our natures upon him, to die a shameful, a painful, and an accursed death for our sakes; he died for our sins, and to bring us to God: he cleansed us by his blood from the guilt of sin, he satisfied for our imperfections; and now, my brethren, we have access unto him with boldness; he is a mediator between us and his offended Father.

Therefore, if we do but consider into what state, and at how great a distance from God we are fallen; how vile our natures were; what a depravity, and how incapable to restore that image of God to our souls, which we lost in our first parents: when I consider these things, my brethren, and that the Lord Jesus Christ came to restore us to that favor with God which we had lost, and that Christ not only came down with an intent to do it, but actually accomplished all that was in his heart towards us; that he raised and brought us into favor with God, that we might find kindness and mercy in his sight; surely this calls for some return of thanks on our part to our dear Redeemer, for this love and kindness to our souls. How just would it have been of him, to have left us in that deplorable state wherein we, by our guilt, had involved ourselves?

For God could not, nor can receive any additional good by our salvation; but it was love, mere love; it was free love that brought the Lord Jesus Christ into our world about 1700 years ago. What, shall we not remember the birth of our Jesus? Shall we yearly celebrate the birth of our temporal king, and shall that of the King of kings be quite forgotten? Shall that only, which ought to be had chiefly in remembrance, be quite forgotten? God forbid! No, my dear brethren, let us celebrate and keep this festival of our church, with joy in our hearts: let the birth of a Redeemer, which redeemed us from sin, from wrath, from death, from hell, be always remembered; may this Savior's love never be forgotten! But may we sing forth all his love and glory as long as life shall last here, and through an endless eternity in the world above! May we chant forth the wonders of redeeming love, and the riches of free grace, amidst angels and archangels, cherubim and seraphim, without intermission, for ever and ever! And as, my brethren, the time for keeping this festival is approaching, let us consider our duty in the true observation thereof, of the right way for the glory of God, and the good of immortal souls, to celebrate the birth of our Lord Jesus Christ; an event which ought to be had in eternal remembrance.

It is my design to lay down rules for the true keeping of that time of Christmas, which is now approaching.

I. I shall show you when you may be said, not to observe this festival aright.

II. I shall show you, when your observation and celebrating of this festival is done according to the glory of God, and to the true manner of keeping of it.

III. Shall conclude with an exhortation to all of you, high and low, rich and poor, one with another, to have a regard to your behavior at all times, but more especially, my dear brethren, on this solemn occasion.

I. My brethren, I am to show when your celebration of this festival is not of the right kind.

And FIRST, you do not celebrate this aright, when you spend most of your time in cards, dice, or gaming of any sort.

This is a season, for which there is no more allowance for wasting of your precious time in those unlawful entertainments, than any other.

Persons are apt to flatter themselves that they are free and at liberty to spend whole evenings now at cards, at dice, or any diversion whatsoever, to pass away, as they call it, a tedious evening. They can do any thing now to pass away that, which is hastening as fast as thought: time is always upon the wing; it is no sooner present but it is past, and no sooner come but it is gone. And have we so much to do, and so little time to do it in, and yet complain of time lying heavy upon our hands? Have we not the devil and the beast to get our of our souls? Are not our natures to be changed, our corruptions to be subdued, our wills to be brought over to God, or hard hearts to be softened, all old things to be done away, and all things to become new in our souls? Is there not all this to be done? And yet we have too much time upon our hands! It is well, that instead of having too much time, it be not found that we have got too little, when we come to die: then we shall wish, my brethren, that we had made more account of our time, that we had improved it for the glory of God, and the welfare of our immortal souls.

Good God! How amazing is the consideration, that many can go to church in the morning, and take the Sacrament, and come home and spend the afternoon and evening in cards. Is this, my brethren, discerning the Lord's body? Is this taking the sacrament according to its institution? Is not this a pollution thereof, and making the blood of the covenant an unholy thing.

Therefore, those of you who have made this your practice in times past, let me beseech you, in the bowels of mercy, not to do so any more; for, indeed, it is earthly, it is sensual, it is devilish. Consider what is said of those who eat and drink at the Lord's table unworthily, that they eat and drink their own damnation: And can they, my brethren, be said to eat and drink any otherwise, who no sooner go from the table of the Lord, but run to the diversions of the devil? Indeed this is exceeding sinful, and displeasing unto the Lord; then forbear those diversions which are so evil in themselves: O be not found in those exercises, and in that pleasure, which you would not be found in when you come to die. Thus, my brethren, you se it is not a right celebration of the birth of the Lord Jesus, to spend it in cards, dice, or any other diversions, which proceed so directly from the devil, and are destructive to all true goodness.

SECONDLY, They cannot be said truly to celebrate this time, who spend their time in eating and drinking to excess.

This is a season when persons are apt to indulge themselves in all manner of luxury: iniquity now abounds apace; nothing is scarcely to be seen but things of the greatest extravagance imaginable; not only for the necessities of the body, but to pamper it in lust, to feed its vices, to make it go on in sin, to be a means for gratifying our carnal appetite; and this is a means to make us forget the Lord of glory. This makes us only fit to do such drudgery, as the devil shall set us about; this is only preparing to run wheresoever the devil sends: this, instead of denying ourselves, is indulging ourselves, this is not, nor cannot be called, a celebration of the birth of our Lord Jesus Christ, when we are making ourselves worst than the beasts that perish.

I am not speaking against eating and drinking of the good things of life, but against the eating and drinking of them to excess, because, thus they unqualify us for the service of God; and to our fellow-creatures they make us unsociable, and may occasion us to be guilty of saying and acting those things, which we should be ashamed to think of, if we had only ate or drank with moderation.

Therefore, my dear brethren, let me beseech you to set a watch over yourselves; be careful that you do not run into that company which may tempt you to evil, for would a man run himself into danger on purpose?

Would a man enter himself into that company, where, before he goes, he knows he shall be exposed to great temptations; and therefore, if you have any reason to think that the company you are going into will be a temptation, I beseech you, by the mercies of God in Christ Jesus, that you would not run into it.

How can you say, "Lead us not into temptation," when you are resolved to lead yourselves into it, by running into the occasions of sins. You are commanded to keep from the appearance of evil; and do you do that, by running into the place and company where it is like to be committed? No, this is so far from avoiding, and shunning it, that it is a plain proof to the contrary; therefore, if you are for observing this time, this festival of our church, let it not be done by running to excess; for you plainly see, that those who are guilty thereof, cannot be said properly to celebrate it.

THIRDLY, Nor can they, my brethren, be said to keep, or rightly observe the commemoration of the birth of our Redeemer, the Lord Jesus Christ, who neglect their worldly callings to follow pleasures and diversions.

Alas! many, instead of keeping this time as it ought to be, run into sin with greediness; instead of devoting their time to the Lord, it is only devoted to the devil and their own lusts. How many who thus mispend their time, at this season, lay by the work of their callings for a considerable time, with no other view, but to follow earthly, sensual, and devilish pleasures. If they should go to hear a sermon, or to a society, my brethren, the mouths of all the Pharisees at once are open against them, that they are not only a going to be ruined themselves, but are going to ruin their families too; they think it needless to make so much ado; this is being righteous over-much; but you may be as wicked as you please, and they will not cry out; however, when you are wicked over-much, by serving the devil and your own pleasures for a week or a month together, then, my brethren, with them you are only taking a little recreation, spending your time in innocent diversions; no one cries out against you, there is no outcry that you are going to be ruined. Again, if you give never so small a matter among the poor people of God for their relief, then you are robbing your families, then you are going to turn madmen! And in a few days will be to methodistically mad, that you are not fit for a polite gentleman's conversation; but if you spend one hundred times the money in playhouses, etc. on your lusts and pleasures, then you are liked and esteemed as a good friend and companion; but, my dear brethren, these good companions in the world's account, are never so in the Lord Jesus Christ's. You cannot serve God and mammon; you must either lost your lusts, your pleasures, and your delights, or you cannot expect to find favor with God; for indeed, and indeed, the ways that too many follow at this time, are sinful, yea, they are exceeding sinful. You see they cannot be said to celebrate this holy time, who thus mispend their precious time to the neglect of their families; such are destroying themselves with a witness.

Thus, my dear brethren, I have shown you who they are who do not observe this holy festival.

II. I come now, in the second place, to show you, who they are who do rightly observe, and truly celebrate the birth of our Redeemer.

And I shall show you who they are in two particulars, directly opposite to the others; and then, my brethren, take your choice: you must choose the one or the other, there is no medium, you must either serve the Lord or Baal; and, therefore, my dear brethren, let me beg of you to consider, FIRST, That those spend their time aright, and truly observe this festival, who spend their hours in reading, praying, and religious conversation.

What can we do to employ our time to a more noble purpose, than reading of what our dear Redeemer has done and suffered; to read, that the King of kings, and the Lord of lords, came from his throne and took upon him the form of the meanest of his servants; and what great things he underwent. This, this is an history worth reading, this is worth employing our time about: and surely, when we read of the sufferings of our Savior, it should excite us to prayer, that we might have an interest in the Lord Jesus Christ; that the blood which he spilt upon mount Calvary, and his death and crucifixion, might make an atonement for our sins, that we might be made holy; that we might be enabled to put off the old man with his deeds, and put on the new man, even the Lord Jesus Christ; that we may throw away the heavy yoke of sin, and put on the yoke of the Lord Jesus Christ. Indeed, my brethren, these things call for prayer, and for earnest prayer too; and O do be earnest with God, that you may have an interest in this Redeemer, and that you may put on his righteousness, so that you may not come before him in your filthy rags, nor be found not having on the wedding garment. O do not, I beseech you, trust unto yourselves for justification; you cannot, indeed, you cannot be justi-fied by the works of the law. I entreat that your time may be thus spent; and if you are in company, let your time be spent in that conversation which profiteth: let it not be about your dressing, your plays, your profits, or your worldly concerns, but let it be the wonders of redeeming love: O tell, tell to each other, what great things the Lord has done for your souls; declare unto one another, how you were delivered from the hands of your common enemy, Satan, and how the Lord has brought your feet from the clay, and has set them upon the rock of ages, the Lord Jesus Christ; there, my brethren, is no slip-ping; other conversation, by often repeating, you become fully acquainted with, but of Christ there is always something new to raise your thoughts; you can never want matter when the love of the Lord Jesus Chris is the subject: then let Jesus be the subject, my brethren, of all your conversation.

Let your time be spent on him: O this, this is an employ, which if you belong to Jesus, will last you to all eternity. Let others enjoy their cards, their dice, and gaming hours; do you, my brethren, let your time be spent in reading, praying, and religious conversations. Which will stand the trial best at the last day? Which do you think will bring most comfort, most peace, in a dying hour? O live and spend your time now, as you will wish to have done, when you come to die.

SECONDLY, Let the good things of life, you enjoy, be used with moderation.

I am not, as the scoffers of this day tell you, against eating and drinking the good things of life; no, my brethren, I am only against their be-ing used to an excess; therefore, let me beseech you to avoid those great indiscretions, those sinful actions, which will give the enemies of God room to blaspheme. Let me beseech you, to have a regard, a particular regard to your behavior, at this time; for indeed the eyes of all are upon you, and they would rejoice much to find any reason to complain of you.

They can say things against us without a cause; and how would they rejoice if there was wherewith they might blame us? Then they would triumph and rejoice indeed; and all your little slips, my dear brethren, are, and would be charged upon me. O at this time, when the eyes of so many are upon you, be upon your guard; and if you use the good things of this life with moderation, you do then celebrate this festival in the manner which the institution calls for.

And instead of running into excess, let that money, which you might expend to pamper your own bodies, be given to feed the poor; now, my brethren, is the season, in which they commonly require relief; and sure you cannot act more agreeable, either to the season, to the time, or for the glory of God, than in relieving his poor distressed servants.

Therefore, if any of you have poor friends, or acquaintance, who are in distress, I beseech you to assist them; and not only those of your acquaintance, but the poor in general. O my dear brethren, that will turn to a better account another day, than all you have expended to please the lust of the flesh, the lust of the eye, or the pride of life. Consider, Christ was always willing to relieve the distressed; it is his command also; and can you better commemorate the birth of your king, your Savior, the Lord Jesus Christ, than in obeying one of his commands?

Do not, my dear brethren, be forgetful of the poor of the world; consider, if providence has smiled upon you, and blessed you with abundance of the things of this life, God calls for some returns of gratitude from you; be ye mindful of the poor, and when you are so, then you may be said to have a true regard for that time which is now approaching; if you would truly observe this festival, let it be done with moderation, and a regard to the poor of this world.

THIRDLY, Let me beg of you not to alienate too much of your time from the worldly business of this life, but have a proper regard thereunto, and then you may be said rightly to observe this festival.

God allows none to be idle: in all ages business was commended; and therefore do not think that any season will excuse us in our callings; we are not, my brethren, to labor for the things of this life inordinately, but we are to labor for them will all moderation: we are not to neglect our callings;

no, we are to regard those places and stations of life, which God in his providence has thought convenient for us; and therefore, when you neglect your business of the hurt of your families, whatever pretense you thereby make for so doing, you are guilty of sin;; you are not acting according to the doctrine of the gospel, but are breaking the commands of the Lord Jesus Christ, both according to his word, and to his own practice.

At this festival, persons are apt to take a little more liberty than usual; and if that time from our vocations is not prejudicial to ourselves or families, and is spent in the service of God, and the good of immortal souls, then I do not thing it sinful; but there is too much reason to fear, that the time spent upon our own lusts, and then it is exceeding sinful, it is against our own souls, and it is against the good of our families, and instead of commemorating the birth of our dear Redeemer, we are dishonoring him in the greatest degree possibly we can.

Therefore, inquire strictly into your end and design in spending your time; see, my brethren, whether it proceeds from a true love to your Redeemer, or whether there is not some worldly pleasure or advantage at the bottom: if there is, our end is not right; but if it proceed entirely from love to him that died, and gave himself for us, our actions will be a proof thereof; then our time will be spent, not in the polite pleasures of life, but according to the doctrine and commands of the blessed Jesus; then our conversation will be in heaven; and O that this might be found to be the end of each of you, who now hear me; then we should truly observe this festival, and have a true regard to the occasion thereof, that of Christ's coming to redeem the souls of those which were lost.

Let me now conclude, my dear brethren, with a few words of exhortation, beseeching you to think of the love of the Lord Jesus Christ.

Did Jesus come into the world to save us from death, and shall we spend no part of our time in conversing about our dear Jesus; shall we pay no regard to the birth of him, who came to redeem us from the worst of slavery, from that of sin, and the devil; and shall this Jesus not only be born on our account, but likewise die in our stead, and yet shall we be unmindful of him? Shall we spend our time in those things which are offensive to him?

Shall we not rather do all we can to promote his glory, and act according to his command? O my dear brethren, be found in the ways of God; let us not disturb our dear Redeemer by any irregular proceedings; and let me beseech you to strive to love, fear, honor and obey him, more than ever you have done yet; let not the devil engross your time, and that dear Savior who came into the world on your accounts, have so little. O be not so ungrateful to him who has been so kind to you! What could the Lord Jesus Christ have done for you more than he has? Then do not abuse his mercy, but let your time be spent in thinking and talking of the love of Jesus, who was incarnate for us, who was born of a woman, and made under the law, to redeem us from the wrath to come.

Now to God the Father, God the Son, etc.

Sermon 17 The Temptation of Christ

Matthew 4:1-11, "Then was Jesus led up of the Spirit into the wilderness to be tempted of the devil. And when he had fasted forty days and forty nights, he was afterward an hungered. And when the tempter came to him, he said, If thou be the Son of God, command that these stones be made bread.

But he answered and said, It is written, Man shall not live by bread alone, but by every word that proceedeth out of the mouth of God. Then the devil taketh him up into the holy city, and setteth him on a pinnacle of the temple, And saith unto him, If thou be the Son of God, cast thyself down: for it is written, He shall give his angels charge concerning thee: and in their hands they shall bear thee up, lest at any time thou dash thy foot against a stone. Jesus said unto him, It is written again, Thou shalt not tempt the Lord thy God. Again, the devil taketh him up into an exceeding high mountain, and sheweth him all the kingdoms of the world, and the glory of them; And saith unto him, All these things will I give thee, if thou wilt fall down and worship me. Then saith Jesus unto him, Get thee hence, Satan: for it is written, Thou shalt worship the Lord thy God, and him only shalt thou serve. Then the devil leaveth him, and, behold, angels came and ministered unto him."

Dearly beloved, today you are invited to take a walk into the wilderness, to behold, sympathize with, and get instruction and comfort from a Savior tempted. In the conflict, he approves himself to be God's beloved Son; and the Father gives demonstrable evidence, that with, and in him he is indeed well pleased. Let us with serious attention consider when, where, and how, our great Michael fought with and overcame the dragon. The Evangelist Matthew is very particular in relating the preparations for, the beginning, process, and issue of this glorious and important combat.

"Then was Jesus led up of the spirit into the wilderness, to be tempted of the devil." In the close of the foregoing chapter we are told, that the blessed Jesus had been publicly baptized, and was also solemnly inaugurated in his mediatorial office, by the opening of the heavens, by the Spirit of God descending on him like a dove, and by a voice from heaven, saying, "This is my beloved Son, in whom I am well pleased;" and then it was, when he came from the solemn ordinance of baptism; when he was about to show himself openly unto Israel; when he was full of the Holy Ghost (Luke 4:1); even then was he led, with a holy unconstrained violence, as a champion into the field, to engage an enemy, whom he was sure to conquer. But whither is this conqueror led? Into a lonesome, wide, howling wilderness; probably, says Mr. Henry, into the great wilderness of Sinai; a wilderness, not only lonesome, but inhabited by wild beasts, Mark 1:13.

Hither was our Lord led, not only that he might prepare himself by retirement and prayer, but also that he might be alone, and thereby give Satan all the advantages he could desire. In this combat, as well as that of his last agony, "of the people, there was to be none with him." Neither does he content himself with praying, but he fasts also, and that "forty days and forty nights," (verse 9): as Moses and Elias had done, many years before, it may be, in the very same place. All these fasts were miraculous; and therefore, though we are taught hereby, that fasting is a Christian duty, yet, to pretend, in an ordinary way, to imitate them, by fasting for so long a term together, in no doubt superstitious , presumptuous, and sinful; but few people, I believe, need such a caution.

During these forty days, we may suppose, our Lord felt no hunger; converse with heaven, to him was instead of meat and drink; but "afterwards he was an hungered:" exceedingly so, no doubt. And now, the important fight begins. For, then "the tempted," emphatically so called, because he first tempted our first parents to sin, and hath ever since been unwearied in tempting their descendants; then the tempter, who in an invisible manner had been attacking our blessed Lord all the whole forty days, when he saw him hungering, and in such distressing circumstances, came to him, as it should seem, in a visible shape, and probably transformed into the appearance of an angel of light. And what does he tempt him to? To nothing less, than to doubt of his being the Son of God." "If thou be the Son of God." What! Put an if to this, Satan, after the glorious Jesus had been proved to be God's son, and repeatedly too in such a glorious manner?

Surely, thou thyself couldst not but see the heavens opened, and the Spirit descending; surely, thou didst hear the voice that came to him from heaven, immediately after his baptism, saying, "This is my beloved Son:" And dost thou now say unto him, "If thou be the Son of God." Yes; but Satan knew, and believed he was full well; but he wanted to make our Lord to doubt of it. And why? Because he was in such a melancholy situation. As though he had said, "If God was thy father, he would never suffer thee to starve to death in a howling wilderness, among wild beasts. Surely, the voice thou lately didst hear, was only a delusion. If thou wast the Son of God, especially his beloved Son, in whom he was so pleased, thou wouldst be taken more care of by him." Thus he attacked our first parents, by suggesting to them hard thoughts of their all-bountiful Creator: "Yea, hath God said, Ye shall not eat of every tree in the garden?" "Hath he placed you amidst such a variety of delicious fruits, only to tease and make you miserable?" And how artfully now does he labor to insinuate himself into our Lord's affections, as he then did to ingratiate himself with our first parents. "If thou be the Son of God, says he, come, prove it, by commanding these stones (a heap of which, probably, lay very near) to be made bread: this will demonstrate thy divinity, and relieve thy pressing necessity at the same time." Thus, as in all his other temptations, Satan would fain appear to be his very kind friend; but the holy Jesus saw through the disguised enmity of his antagonist; and scorning either to distrust his righteous Father on the one hand, or to work a miracle to please and gratify the devil on the other, although he had the Spirit of God without measure, and might have made use of a thousand other ways, yet answers him with a text of scripture: "It is written, that man shall not live by bread alone, but by every word that proceedeth out of the mouth of God." This is a quotation from Deuteronomy 8:3, and contains a reason given by the great God, why he chose to feed the Israelites with manna; that they might learn thereby, man doth not live by bread alone, but by every word that proceedeth out of the mouth of God. This our blessed Lord here applies to himself; and his being in the wilderness, made the application of it still more pertinent. Israel was God's son: out of Egypt was he called to sojourn in the wilderness, where he was miraculously supported. And therefore our Lord, knowing that he was typified by this Israel, and that, like them, he was now in a wilderness, quotes this scripture as a reason why he should not, at Satan's suggestion, either despair of receiving help from his Father in his present circumstances, or distrust the validity of his late manifestations, or make use of any unwarrantable means for his present relief. For as God was his father, he would, therefore, either in an ordinary way spread a table for him in the wilderness, or support and sustain him, as he did his Israel of old, in some extraordinary way or other without it: "For man shall not live by bread alone, but by every word that proceedeth out of the mouth of God." Thus is the tempter foiled in the first onset; but he hath other arrows in his quiver, with which he will farther strive to wound the immaculate Lamb of God. Since he cannot draw him in either to distrust, or despair, he will not try if he cannot prevail on him to presume. In order to effect this, "He taketh the blessed Jesus up into the Holy City," or Jerusalem, called by our Savior, the city of the Great King, and here called holy, because the holy temple was in it, and, we would hope, many holy people. This was a populous place, and therefore, would greatly befriend the devil's design. And not only so, but "he setteth him on a pinnacle," a battlement or wing, "of the temple," the top of which was so very high, that, as Josephus observes, it would make a man's head run giddy to look down from it. And some think this was done at the time of public worship. How the holy Jesus suffered himself to be taken hither; whether he was transported through the air, or whether he followed Satan on foot, is uncertain; but certainly it was an instance of amazing condescension in our Lord, that he would permit so foul a fiend, to carry or lead his holy body about in this manner. Well! Satan hath now gotten him upon the pinnacle of the temple, and still harping upon this old string, "If thou be the Son of God, (says he) cast thyself down," and thereby show to this large worshipping assembly, (who will assuredly then believe) that thou art God's beloved Son, under the special protection of heaven, and art the Messiah, "who was to come into the world." This was artful, very artful. But he seems to improve in cunning: for he brings his Bible with him, and backs his temptation with a text of scripture; "For it is written, (says he) he shall give his angels charge concerning thee, and in their hands they shall bear thee up, lest at any time thou dash thy foot against a stone." But is Saul also among the prophets? Does the devil quote scripture, yea, and seemingly such a very apposite one too? I suspect some design, without doubt: for herein, he would mimic our Lord, who, he perceived, intended to fight him with this weapon; and not liking the sharp edge of it, he thought that if he quoted scripture, the Lord Jesus would not employ it against him any more. "It is written, (therefore said he) he shall give his angels charge concerning thee, and in their hands they shall bear thee up, lest at any time thou dash thy foot against a stone: and therefore, since thou art sure of such protection, thou needst not fear to cast thyself down." This was plausible, and by the length of it, one would be apt to imagine, it was a fair quotation; but Satan takes care, not only to misapply, but also to maim it, purposely omitting these important words, "in all thy ways." It is true, God had given charge to his angels, concerning his children in general, and his beloved Son in particular, that they should keep him in all his ways; but, if our Lord had at this time, at the devil's request, and to gratify pride, thrown himself down from the pinnacle, and thereby unnecessarily presumed on his Father's protection, he would not have been in God' s way, and therefore, would have had no right to the promised protection at all. Satan was aware of this, and therefore fitly left out what he knew would not suit his purpose. But is scripture the worse, for being abused or perverted by the devil, or his emissaries?

No, in no wise. Our Lord, therefore, lets him know, that he should not throw aside this important weapon upon this account, but puts by this home thrust, with another scripture: "It is written again, Thou shalt not tempt the Lord thy God." Still our Lord quotes something out of the book of Deuteronomy, and hath his eye upon Israel in his wilderness state.

Originally these words were directed to the Israelites in general, and accordingly are in the plural number; but here our Lord, as before, makes a particular application of them to himself: Satan bids him cast himself down, assuring him, God had promised in his word, to order his angels to take care of him. Now, says our Lord, "It is written in another part of his word, that the Israelites should not tempt the Lord their God, by distrusting his goodness on the one hand, or presuming on his protection on the other. And, therefore, as I would not command the stones to be made bread, needlessly and distrustfully set up to provide for myself; neither will I now presume unnecessarily upon God's power, by casting myself down, though placed by thee in such a dangerous situation.

Thus our great Michael comes off conqueror in the second assault. And doth not the serpent feel his head bruised enough yet? Not at all: on the contrary, being more and more enraged at such unusual opposition, and want of success, "He again taketh him up into an exceeding high mountain, (what mountain is not very material) and showeth him all the kingdoms of the world, and the glory of them," St. Luke adds, "in a moment of time:" which confirms the common conjecture, that Satan did not show our Lord really the kingdoms of the world, (for that must have taken up more time) but only took him up into an exceeding high mountain to humor the thing, and by exerting his utmost art, impressed on our Lord's imagination all at once, a very strong, and to any but innocence itself, a very striking prospect of the kingdoms of the world, and the glory of them; not the cares: that would not serve Satan's turn. He showed our Savior crowns, but never told him those crowns were gilded with thorns; "He showed him, (says Mr.

Henry, my favorite commentator) as in a landscape, or airy representation in a cloud, such as that great deceiver could easily frame and put together, the glorious and splendid appearance of princes, their robes and retinue, their equipage and lifeguards; the pomps of thrones and courts, and stately palaces; the sumptuous buildings in cities; the gardens and fields about the country feats, with the various instances of their wealth, pleasure, and gaiety; so as might be most likely to strike the fancy, and excite the admiration and affection. Such was this show." Our Savior very well knew it, only lets Satan go to the full length of his string, that his victory over him might be the more illustrious. And now, says the devil, "All these things (a mighty all indeed; a mere imaginary bubble!) will I give thee, if thou wilt fall down and worship me. He would fain have it taken for granted, that he had succeeded in the two preceding temptations: "Come, thou seest thou art not the Son of God, or if thou art, thou seest what an unkind Father he is; thou art here in a starving condition, therefore take my advice, disown thy relation to him, set up for thyself, call me father, ask of me blessings, and all these will I give thee; while all that I desire in return, is but a bow, only fall down and worship me." Here Satan discovers himself with a witness: this was a desperate parting stroke, indeed. It is not high time for thee, O thou enemy of souls, to be commanded to depart! Filled with a holy resentment at such hellish treatment, and impatient of the very thought of settling up for himself, or alienating the least part of his heart and affections from his Father, or dividing them between his God and the world; "Then said Jesus unto him, Get thee hence, Satan, (I know thee who thou art, under all thy disguises) get thee hence, thou grand adversary; for it is written, Thou shalt worship the Lord thy God, and him only shalt thou serve; this is the great commandment of the law; this is the commandment my Father gave unto his Israel of old, and wouldst thou have me, who came to fulfill the law and the prophets, thus shamefully be a transgressor of it? Get thee hence, I will bear thy insolence no longer: thy other temptations were hellish, like thyself, but this intolerably so; get thee therefore hence, Satan: my heavenly Father is the Lord my God, and him only will I serve." And now the battle is over; the important combat is ended; Jesus hath won the field: Satan is routed and totally put to flight. "Then," when the devil found that Jesus could withstand even the golden bait, the lust of the eye and pride of life, in the two last, as well as the lust of the flesh in the first temptation, despairing of the least success, and quite stunned with that all-powerful GET THEE HENC, SATAN, "he leaveth him." Hell, we may well suppose, like the Philistines of old, was confounded, and gave a horrible groan, when they saw their great Goliath, in whom they had so long trusted, thus shamefully and totally defeated in no less than three pitched battles. The first Adam was attacked but once, and was conquered; but the second Adam, though thus repeatedly assaulted, comes off without the least sin, not only conqueror, but more than conqueror. Think you not, that there was joy, joy unspeakable in heaven, upon this glorious occasion? Think you not that the angels, those sons of God, and the multitude of the heavenly host, who shouted so loud at our Lord's birth, did not repeat, if possible, with yet greater ecstasy, that heavenly anthem, "Glory be to God in the highest." For a while they were only spectators, orders, we may suppose, being issued out, that they should only wait around, but not relieve their praying, fasting, tempted Lord; but now the restraint is removed: Satan departs, and "behold, angels came and ministered unto him;" they came to administer to his bodily necessities, and to congratulate him upon the glorious and complete victory which he had gained: some of them, it may be, had done this kind office for Elijah long ago; and with unspeakably greater joy, they repeat it to the Lord of Elijah now. His Father sends him bread from heaven; and by this lets him know, that notwithstanding the horrid temptations with which he had been attacked, he is his own beloved son, in and with whom he was well pleased.

And was there joy in heaven on this happy occasion? What equal, and if possible, what infinitely greater joy ought there to be among the children of God here on earth? For we should do well to remember, that our blessed Lord in this great fight with, and conquest over the dragon, acted as a public person, as a federal head of his mystical body the church, even the common representative of all believers. We may therefore from this blessed passage gather strong consolations; since by our Lord's conquest over Satan, we are thereby assured of our own, and in the mean while can apply to him as a compassionate High Priest, who was in all things tempted as we are, that he might experimentally be enabled to succor us when we are tempted.

Who, who after hearing of or reading this, can think themselves hardly used, or utterly cast off by God, because they are tempted to self-murder, blasphemy, or any other horrid and shocking crimes? Who can wonder at wave being permitted to come upon wave, and one trial to follow upon the back of another? Who can admire, that Satan follows them to holy ordinances, and tempts them to doubt of the reality of all their manifestations, and of their being God's children, even after they have enjoyed the most intimate and delightful communion with their heavenly Father? Was not our Lord treated thus? And "shall the servant be above his Lord, or the disciple above his Master?" No, it is sufficient that the servant be as his Lord, and the disciple as his Master.

But not to dwell on a general improvement, let us see what particular lessons may be learned from this affecting portion of holy writ.

And FIRST, was our Lord thus violently beset in the wilderness? Then we may learn, that however profitable solitude and retirement may be, when used in due season, yet when carried to an extreme is hurtful, and rather befriends than prevents temptation. Woe be to him that is thus always alone; for he hath not another to lift him up when he falleth, or to advise with when he is tempted. As a hermit in America once told me, when I asked him whether he found that way of life lessened his temptations: "Dost not thou know, friend, (said he) that a tree which grows by itself, is more exposed to winds and storms than another that stands surrounded with other trees in the woods?" Our Lord knew this, and therefore he was LED BY THE SPIRIT into the wilderness to be tempted of the devil. Lord, keep us from leading ourselves into this temptation, and succor and support us whenever led by thy providence into it! Then, and then only, shall we be safe amidst the fiery darts of the grand enemy of our souls.

SECONDLY, Did our Lord by prayer, fasting, and temptation, prepare himself for his public ministry? Surely then, all those who profess to be inwardly moved by the Holy Ghost to take upon them the office and administration of the church, should be prepared in the same manner. For though the knowledge of books and men, are good in their places, yet without a knowledge of Satan's devices be superadded, a minister will be only like a physician, that undertakes to prescribe to sick people, without having studied the nature of herbs. And hence, it is to be feared, many heavy laden and afflicted souls have been sent by certain ministers, to surgeons, to be blooded in the arm, instead of being directed to apply to the blood of Christ to cleanse their hearts. Hence, conviction is looked upon as a delirium, and violent temptations censured as downright madness.

Hence, souls that are truly and earnestly repenting of their sins, and as earnestly seeking after rest in Christ, have been directed to plays, novels, romances, and merry company, to divert them from being righteous over-much. Miserable comforters are such blind guides! Surely, they deserve not better titles than that of murderers of souls! They go not into the kingdom of heaven themselves, and those who are entering in they would by this means hinder. Go not after them, all ye young men who would be able ministers of the New Testament; but on the contrary, if you would be useful in binding up the broken hearted, and pouring the oil of consolation into wounded souls, prepare yourselves for manifold temptations. For as Luther says, "prayer and meditation, reading and temptation, make a minister." If now exercised with spiritual conflicts, be not disheartened, it is a good sign that our Lord intends to make use of you. Being thus tempted like unto your brethren, you will be the better enabled to succor and advise those who shall apply to you under their temptations. What says the apostle Paul?

"If we are afflicted, it is for your sake." And if you are afflicted, it is only that you may save your own souls, and help to save the souls of those who shall be committed to your charge. Be strong therefore in the grace which is in Christ Jesus, and learn to endure hardness, like good soldiers, that are hereafter to instruct others how they must fight the good fight of faith.

THIRDLY, Did the tempter come to Christ when he saw him an hungered?

Let those of you that are reduced to a low estate, from hence learn, that an hour of poverty is an hour of temptation, not only to murmuring and doubting of our sonship and the divine favor, but also to help ourselves by unlawful means. "If thou be the Son of God, said Satan, command that these stones may be made bread." This is what Agur dreaded, "lest I be poor and steal." Learn, ye godly poor, to be upon your guard, and remember that poverty and temptations are no marks of your being cast off by God. Your Lord was an hungered; your Lord was tempted on this account to doubt his sonship, before you. Learn of him not to distrust, but rather to trust in your heavenly Father. Angels came and ministered unto Christ; and he who is Lord of the angels, will send some kind messenger or another to relieve your wants. Your extremity shall be the Redeemer's opportunity to help you.

Make your wants known unto him, he careth for you. Though in a desert, though no visible means appear at present, yet you shall in God's due time find a table spread for you and yours; "For man doth not live by bread alone, but by every word that proceedeth out of the mouth of God." And may not such among you, who are exalted, as well as those who are brought low, from Satan's taking the Lord Jesus, and placing him upon a pinnacle of the temple, learn also a lesson of holy watchfulness and caution. High places are slippery places, and are apt to make even the strongest heads and most devout hearts to turn giddy. How necessary therefore is that excellent petition in our Litany, "in all time of our wealth, (as well as in all time of our tribulation) good Lord deliver us!" Agreeably to this, Agur prays as much against riches as poverty; if he was poor, he feared he should be tempted to steal, if rich, that he should trust in uncertain riches; and say, who is the Lord?

I charge, therefore, all of you, who are rich and high in this world, to watch and pray, lest ye fall by Satan's temptation. Those especially of you, that are placed as on the pinnacle of the temple, exalted above your fellows in the church of God, take heed in an especial manner unto yourselves, lest by spiritual pride, vanity, or any other sin that doth most easily beset persons in such eminent stations, ye cast yourselves down. This is what Satan aims at. He strives to make us destroyers of ourselves. And he hath a particular enmity against such as you; he knows, that your name is Legion; and that if you cast yourselves down, he shall gain a great advantage over many others; you cannot fall alone. O that it may be said of us, as the papists use to say of Luther, "That German beast doth not love gold." May the fire of divine love burn up all the love of this present evil world, and pride of life, out of your hearts! This, Satan reserved for his last, as thinking it was the most powerful and prevailing temptation, "He took our Lord up into an exceeding high mountain, and showed him all the kingdoms of the world and the glory of them." He cares not how high he exalts us, or how high he is obliged to bid, so he can but get our hearts divided between God and the world. All this will he offer to give us, if we will only fall down and worship him. Arm us, dear Lord Jesus, with thy Spirit, and help us under all such circumstances, to learn of thee, and say unto the tempter, "Get thee hence, Satan; for it is written, thou shalt worship the Lord thy God, and him only shalt thou serve." FOURTHLY, Whether beset with this or any other temptation, let all us learn of our Lord to fight the devil with the sword of the Spirit, which is the word of God. Though he had the Spirit without measure, yet he always made use of this. We pray say of it, as David did of Goliath's sword, "none like this," none like this. And supposing Satan should be permitted to transform himself into an angel of light, and by false impressions, and delusive applications of misquoted texts, attempt to turn this weapon upon us against ourselves; let us not therefore be prevailed on to let go, but by comparing spiritual things with spiritual, as our Lord did, find out God's mind and our duty. Had Christ's children and ministers only observed this one lesson, how much strange fire would quickly have been extinguished? How much real enthusiasm been easily stopped? How may imaginary revelations have been detected? How many triumphs of Satan and his emissaries been prevented? And how much more would the comforts of Christ's people and ministers been continued and increased, not only in this present, but also in every age of the Christian church? But let us not be discouraged or think worse of Christ, his cause, or his word, because through Satan's subtlety, any of us, or others, may have been drawn in to make some wrong applications of it; others have been thus tempted and mistaken before us. However, let us be humbled before God and man, and be excited by our past ignorance of Satan's devices, to adhere more closely to the written word, and to pray more earnestly for God's holy Spirit to give us direction by it. "Then will it still be a lantern unto our feet, and a light unto our path;" we shall yet be enabled to behave more skillfully under all our future trials. Many we must yet expect; nay, perhaps our severest temptations are yet to come; Satan left our Lord, after his attacking him in the wilderness, "only for a season," as St. Luke has it, until the season of his death and passion. And thus he may be permitted to deal with us. We are not yet come to our complete rest; the King of terrors is yet to be grappled with, and the valley of the shadow of death to be passed through; long before that, we may be called to endure many a fiery trial, and be beset with manifold temptations, under which we may be as ignorant how to behave, as under those with which we have already been visited. Alas! we know not what remaining corruptions are in our hearts, which time and temptation may draw out and discover. Perhaps Satan hath not yet attacked us on our weakest side; when he does, if left to ourselves, how weak shall we be? It is said of Achilles, that he was invulnerable, except in the heel, and by a wound in that, at last he died. Let not him, therefore, that putteth on the harness, boast as though he had put it off." Neither, on the other hand, let us be faint-hearted or dismayed. Satan may tempt, but cannot force; he may sift, but Christ will pray. He who hath helped us already, will help us to the end. He who conquered for us in the wilderness, will ere long make us also more than conquerors over all trials and temptations, inward and outward, and over death and hell itself, through his almighty, everlasting and never-failing love. We now sow in tears; in a very little time, and we shall reap with joy; we may now go on our way weeping, by reason of the enemy oppressing us; but, ere long, angels shall be sent, not to minister to us in this wilderness, but to carry us to an heavenly Canaan, even to Abraham's bosom. Then shall we see this accuser and tempter of our Lord, of our brethren, and of ourselves, cast out: this wicked one, as well as the wicked world, and wicked heart, will no more be permitted to vex, disturb or annoy us.

"But woe unto you that laugh now; for you shall then lament and weep." Woe unto you, who either believer there is no devil, or never felt any of his temptations. Woe unto you that are at ease in Zion, and instead of staying to be tempted by the devil, by idleness, self-indulgence, and making continual provision for the flesh, even tempt the devil to tempt you. Woe unto you, who not content with sinning yourselves, turn factors for hell, and make a trade of tempting others to sin. Woe unto you, who either deny divine revelation, or never make use of it but to serve a bad turn. Woe unto you who sell your consciences, and pawn your souls for a little worldly wealth or honor. Woe unto you who climb up to high places, when in church or state, by corruption, bribery, extortion, cringing, flattery, or bowing down to, and soothing the vices of those by whom you expect to rise. Woe unto you! For whether you will own the relation or not, surely you are of your father the devil; for the works of your father you will do; I tremble for you. How can you escape the damnation of hell?

But I have not time to follow such as you any farther. This discourse, and the present frame of my mind, lead me rather to speak to those, who by feeling Satan's fiery darts, know assuredly that there is a devil. Comfort thou, comfort thou, these afflicted ones, O Lord. O thou all-merciful and all-bountiful God, and thou compassionate High-Priest, thou once tempted, but now triumphant Savior, as thou once didst not disdain to be ministered unto by angels, bless we pray thou this discourse, to the support and strengthening of thy tempted people, though delivered by the meanest messenger thou didst ever yet employ in thy church!

I add no more. The Lord bless you and keep you! The Lord lift up the light of his countenance, stablish, strengthen, and settle you, and bring you to his eternal kingdom!

Sermon 18 The Heinous Sin of Profane Cursing and Swearing

Matthew 5:34, "But I say unto you, Swear not at all."

Among the many heinous sins for which this nation is grown infamous, perhaps there is no one more crying, but withal more common, than the abominable custom of profane swearing and cursing. Our streets abound with persons of all degrees and qualities, who are continually provoking the holy one of Israel to anger, by their detestable oaths and blasphemies: and our very children, "out of whose mouths," the psalmist observes in his days, "was perfected praise," are now grown remarkable for the quite opposite ill quality of cursing and swearing. This cannot but be a melancholy prospect, for every sincere and honest minister of Jesus Christ, to view his fellow-creatures in; and such as will put him on contriving some means to prevent the spreading at least of so growing an evil; knowing that the Lord (without repentance) will assuredly visit for these things.

But alas! what can he do? Public animadversions are so neglected amongst us, that we seldom find a common swearer punished as the laws direct. And as for private admonition, men are now so hardened through the deceitfulness of sin, that to give them sober and pious advice, and to show them the evil of their doings, is but like "casting pearls before swine; they only turn again and rend you." Since matters then are come to this pass, all that we can do is, that as we are appointed watchmen and ambassadors of the Lord, it our duty from time to time to show the people their transgression, and warn them of their sin; so that whether they will hear, or whether they will forbear, we however may deliver our own souls.

That I therefore may discharge my duty in this particular, give me leave, in the name of God, humbly to offer to your most serious consideration, some few observations on the words of the text, in order to show the heinousness of profane cursing and swearing.

But, before I proceed directly to the prosecution of this point, it will be proper to clear this precept of our Lord from a misrepresentation that has been put on it by some, who infer from hence, that our Savior prohibits swearing before a magistrate, when required on a solemn and proper occasion. But that all swearing is not absolutely unlawful for a Christian, is evident from the writings of St. Paul, whom we often find upon some solemn occasions using several forms of imprecation, as, "I call God as witness;" "God is my judge;" "By your rejoicing in Christ Jesus," and suchlike. And that our savior does by no means forbid swearing before a magistrate, in the words now before us, is plain, if we consider the sense and design he had in view, when he gave his disciples this command. Permit me to observe to you then, that our blessed master had set himself, from the 27th verse of the chapter, out of which the text is taken, to vindicate and clear the moral law from the corrupt glosses and misconstruction of the Pharisees, who then sat in Moses's chair, but were notoriously faulty in adhering too closely to the literal expression of the law, without ever considering the due extent and spiritual meaning of it. Accordingly they imagined, that because God had said, "Thou shalt not commit adultery," that therefore, supposing a person was not guilty of the very act of adultery, he was not chargeable with the breach of the seventh commandment. And likewise in the matter of swearing, because God had forbidden his people, in the books of Exodus and Deuteronomy, "to take his name in vain," or to swear falsely by his name; they therefore judged it lawful to swear by any creature in common discourse, supposing they did not directly mention the name of God. Our blessed Savior therefore, in the words now before us, rectifies this their mistake about swearing, as he had done in the verses immediately forgoing, concerning adultery, and tells the people, that whatever allowances the Pharisees might give to swear by any creature, yet he pronounced it absolutely unlawful for any of his followers to do so.

"You have heard, that it has been said by them of old time," (namely, by the Pharisees and teachers of the Jewish law) "Thou shalt not forswear thyself, but perform unto the Lord thine oaths; but I say unto you," (I who am appointed by the Father to be the great prophet and true law-giver of his church) "Swear not at all, (in your common conversation) neither by heaven for it is God's throne; (and therefore to swear by that, is to swear by Him that sits thereon) neither by the earth, for it is his foot-stool; nor by Jerusalem, for it is the city of the great King; neither shalt thou swear by thy head, because thou canst not make one hair white or black: but let your communications (which plainly shows that Christ is here speaking of swearing, not before a magistrate, but in common conversation) let your communication be yea, yea; nay, nay, (a strong affirmation or negation at the most); for whatsoever is more than this, cometh of evil;" that is, cometh from an evil principle, from the evil one, the devil, the author of all evil.

Which by the way, methinks, should be a caution to all such persons, who, though not guilty of swearing in the gross sense of the word, yet attest the truth of what they are speaking of, though ever so trifling, by saying, Upon my life, -- as I live, -- by my faith, -- by the heavens, and such like: which expressions, however harmless and innocent they may be esteemed by some sorts of people, yet are the very oaths which our blessed Lord condemns in the words immediately following the text; and persons who use such unwarrantable forms of speaking, must expect to be convicted and condemned as swearers, at our Savior's second coming to judge the world.

But to return: It appears then from the whole tenor of our Savior's discourse, that in the words of the text he does by no means disannul or forbid swearing before a magistrate (which, as might easily be shown, is both lawful and necessary) but only profane swearing in common conversation; the heinousness and sinfulness of which I come now, more immediately to lay before you.

And here, not to mention that it is a direct breach of our blessed master's and great law-giver's command in the words of the text, as likewise of the third commandment, wherein God positively declares, "he will not hold him guiltless (that is, will assuredly punish him) that taketh his name in vain:" not to mention that it is the greatest abuse of that noble faculty of speech, whereby we are distinguished from the brute creation; or the great hazard the common swearer runs, of being perjured some time or other: not to mention those reasons against it, which of themselves would abundantly prove the folly and sinfulness of swearing: I shall at this time content myself with instancing four particulars, which highly aggravate the crime of profane swearing, and those are such as follow: I. FIRST, Because there is no temptation in nature to this sin, nor does the commission of it afford the offender the least pleasure or satisfaction.

II. SECONDLY, Because it is a sin which may be so often repeated.

III. THIRDLY, Because it hardens infidels against the Christian religion, and must give great offense, and occasion much sorrow and concern to every true disciple of Jesus Christ.

IV. FOURTHLY, Because it is an extremity of sin, which can only be matched in hell.

I. The first reason then, why swearing in common conversation is so heinous in God's sight, and why we should not swear at all, is, because it has no temptation in nature, nor does the commission of it, unless a man be a devil incarnate, afford the offender the least pleasure or satisfaction.

Now here, I presume, we may lay it down as a maxim universally agreed on, that the guilt of any crime is increased or lessened in proportion to the weakness or strength of the temptation, by which a person is carried to the commission of it. It was this consideration that extenuated and diminished the guilt of Saul's taking upon him to offer sacrifice before the Prophet Saumel came; and of Uzza's touching the ark, because it was in danger of falling: as, on the contrary, what so highly aggravated the disobedience of our first parents, and of Lot's wife, was, because the former had so little reason to eat the forbidden fruit, and the latter so small a temptation to look back on Sodom.

And now if this be granted, surely the common swearer must of all sinners be the most without excuse, since there is no manner of temptation in nature to commission of his crime. In most of the other commands, persons, perhaps, may plead the force of natural inclination in excuse for the breach of them: one, for instance, may alledge his string propensity to anger, to excuse his breaking of the sixth; another, his proneness to lust, for his violation of the seventh. But surely the common swearer has nothing of this kind to urge in his behalf; for though he may have a natural inclination to this or that crime, yet no man, it is to be presumed, can say, he is born with a swearing constitution.

But further, As there is no temptation to it, so there is no pleasure or profit to be reaped from the commission of it. Ask the drunkard why he rises up early to follow strong drink, and he will tell you, because it affords his sensual appetite some kind of pleasure and gratification, though it be no higher than that of a brute. Inquire of the covetous worldling, why he defrauds and over-reaches his neighbor, and he has an answer ready; to enrich himself, and lay up goods for many years. But it must certainly puzzle the profane swearer himself, to inform you what pleasure he reaps from swearing: for alas! it is a fruitless tasteless thing that he sells his soul for. But indeed he does not sell it at all: in this case he prodigally gives it away (without repentance) to the devil; and parts with a blessed eternity, and runs into everlasting torment, merely for nothing.

II. But SECONDLY, what increases the heinousness of profane swearing, is, that it is a sin which may so often be repeated.

This is another consideration which always serves to lessen or increase the guilt and malignity of any sin. It was some excuse for the drunkenness of Noah, and the adultery of David, that they committed these crimes but once; as, on the contrary, of the patriarch Abraham's distrust of God, that he repeated the dissembling of Sarah to be his wife, two several times. And if this be admitted as an aggravation of other profane crimes, surely much more so of the guilt of common swearing, because it is a sin which may be, and is for the generality often repeated.

In many other gross sins it cannot be so: if a man be overcome in drink, there must be a considerable time ere he can recover his debauch, and return to his cups again: or if he be accustomed to profane the sabbath, he cannot do it every day, but only one in seven. But alas! the profane swearer is ready for another oath, almost before the sound of the first is out of our ears; yea, some double and treble them in one sentence, even so as to confound the sense of what they say, by an horrid din of blasphemy!

Now if the great and terrible Jehovah has expressly declared that he will not hold him guiltless, that is, will assuredly punish him, that taketh his name but once in vain; what a vast heap of these heinous sins lies at every common swearer's door? It would be apt to sink him into an intolerable despair, did he but see the whole sum of them. And O what a seared conscience must that wretch have, that does not feel this prodigious weight!

III. But THIRDLY, what makes the sin of profane swearing appear yet more exceeding sinful, is, that it hardens infidels against the Christian religion.

It is the Apostle Peter's advice to the married persons of his time, that they should walk as became the gospel of Christ, that those who were without, might be won to embrace the Christian religion, by seeing and observing their pious conversation coupled together with fear. And what the Apostle presses on married persons, we find elsewhere enjoined on each particular member of the church. Accordingly we are commanded by our blessed Lord, to "let our light to shine before men, that they may see our good works, and glorify our Father which is in heaven;" And the Apostle Paul bids us "walk circumspectly towards them that are without, redeeming the time;" that is, embracing all opportunities to do them good, "because the days are evil." But alas! in what a direct contradiction does the profane swearer live to this and such-like precepts, who, instead of gaining proselytes to Christ from the unbelieving part of the world, does all he can to oppose it! For how can it be expected, that infidels should honor God, when Christians themselves despise him; or that any should embrace our religion, when professors of it themselves make so light of one of its strictest commands? No; to our grief and shame be it spoken, it is by reason of such impieties as these, that our holy religion (the best and purest in itself) is become a by-word among the heathen; that the sacred authority of the holy Jesus and his doctrine is despised; and "God's name (as it is written) blasphemed among the Gentiles." These cannot but be sad stumbling-blocks and offenses in the way of our brethren's conversion; "But woe be to those men by whom such offenses come." We may say of them, as our blessed Lord did of Judas, "It had been better for such men, that they had never been born;" or, as he threatens in another place, "It shall be more tolerable for Sodom and Gomorrah in the day of judgment, than for such sinners." But this is not all; As profane swearing must undoubtedly harden those in their infidelity, that are without, so must it no less grieve and give great offense to those hones and sincere persons that are within the church. We hear of David's complaining and crying out, "Woe is me, that I am constrained to dwell with Mesech, and to have my habitation amongst the tents of Kedar;" that is, that he was obliged to live and converse with a people exceedingly wicked and profane. And St. Peter tells us, that "Lot's righteous soul was grieved day by day, whilst he saw and observed the ungodly conversation of the wicked." And no doubt it was one great part of our blessed Master's sufferings whilst on earth, that he was compelled to converse with a wicked and perverse generation, and to hear his heavenly Father's sacred name profaned and scoffed at by unrighteous and wicked men.

And surely it cannot but pierce the heart of every true and sincere Christian, of every one that does in any measure partake of the spirit of his master, to hear the multitude of oaths and curses which proceed daily and hourly out of the mouths of many people, and those too, whose liberal education, and seeming regard for the welfare of religion, one would think, should teach them a more becoming behavior. To hear the great and terrible name of God polluted by men, which is adored by angels; and to consider how often that sacred name is profancd in common discourse, which we are not worthy to mention in our prayers; this, I say, cannot but make each of them cry out with holy David, "Woe is me, that I am constrained to dwell with Mesech, and to have my habitation amongst the tents of Kedar." And though the blasphemous and profane discourses of others, will not be imputed to sincere persons for sin, so long as they "have no fellowship with such hellish fruits of darkness, but rather reprove them;" yet it will greatly enhance the present guilt, and sadly increase the future punishment of every profane swearer, by whom such offenses come. For if, as our Savior tells us, "it had been better for a man to have a mill-stone tied around his neck, than that he should offend one of his little once, (that is, the weakest of his disciples) how much sorer punishment will they be thought worthy of," who not only cause God's name to be blasphemed among the Gentiles, and the religion of our dear Redeemer to be abhorred; but who make his saints to weep and mourn, and vex their righteous souls from day to day, by their ungodly, profane, and blasphemous conversation? Surely, as God will put the tears of the one into his bottle, so it will be just in him to punish the other with eternal sorrow, for all their ungodly and hard speeches, and cast them into a lake of fire and brimstone, where they shall be glad of a drop of water to cool those tongues, with which they have so often blasphemed the Lord of Hosts, and grieved the people of our God.

IV. But it is time for me to proceed to give my FOURTH and last reason, why common swearing is so exceeding sinful; and that is, Because it is such an extremity of sin, that can only be matched in hell, where all are desperate, and without hope of mercy.

The damned devils, and damned souls of men in hell, may be supposed to rave and blaspheme in their torments, because they know that the chains wherein they are held, can never be knocked off; but for men that swim in the river of God's goodness, whose mercies are renewed to them every morning, and who are visited with fresh tokens of his infinite unmerited loving-kindness every moment; for these favorite creatures to set their mouths against heaven, and to blaspheme a gracious, patient, all-bountiful God; is a height of sin which exceeds the blackness and impiety of devils and hell itself.

And now, after what has been here offered, to show the heinousness of profane cursing and swearing in common conversation, may I not very justly address myself to you in the words of the text, "Therefore I say unto you, Swear not at all;" since it is a sin that has no temptation in nature, nor brings any pleasure or profit to the committer of it; since it hardens infidels in their infidelity, and affords sad causes of grief and lamentation to every honest Christian; since it is a sin that generally grows into a habit, and lastly, such a sin that can only be matched in hell.

1. And first then, if these things be so, and the sin of profane swearing, as hath been in some measure shown, is so exceeding sinful, what shall we say to such unhappy men, who think it not only allowable, but fashionable and polite, to "take the name of God in vain;" who imagine that swearing makes them look big among their companions, and really think it a piece of honor to abound in it? But alas! little do they think that such a behavior argues the greatest degeneracy of mind and fool-hardiness, that can possibly be thought of. For what can be more base, than one hour to pretend to adore God in public worship, and the very next moment to blaspheme his name; indeed, such a behavior, from persons who deny the being of a God, (if any such fools there be) is not altogether to much to be wondered at; but for men, who not only subscribe to the belief of a Deity, but likewise acknowledge him to be a God of infinite majesty and power; for such men to blaspheme his holy name, by profane cursing and swearing, and at the same time confess, that this very God has expressly declared, he will not hold him guiltless, but will certainly and eternally punish (without repentance) him that taketh his name in vain; is such an instance of fool-hardiness, as well as baseness, that can scarcely be paralleled. This is what they presume not to do in other cases of less danger: they dare not revile a general at the head of his army, nor rouse a sleeping lion when within reach of his paw. And is the Almighty God, the

great Jehovah, the everlasting King, who can consume them by the breath of his nostrils, and frown them to hell in an instant; is he the only contemptible being in their account, that may be provoked without fear, and offended without punishment? No; though God hear long, he will not bear always; the time will come, and that too, perhaps, much sooner than such persons may expect, when God will vindicate his injured honor, when he will lay bare his almighty arm, and make those wretches feel the eternal smart of his justice, show power and name they have so often vilified and blasphemed. Alas! what will become of all their bravery then? Will they then wantonly sport with the name of their Maker, and call upon the King of all the earth to damn them any more in jest? No; their note will then be changed: indeed, they shall call, but it will be for "the rocks to fall on them, and the hills to cover them from the wrath of him that sitteth upon the throne, and from the Lamb for ever." It is true, time was when they prayed, though without thought, perhaps, for damnation both for themselves and others; and now they will find their prayers answered. "They delighted in cursing, therefore shalt it happen unto them; they loved not blessing, therefore shall it be far from them; they clothed themselves with cursing like as with a garment, and it shall come into their bowels like water, and like oil into their bones." 2. But further, if the sin of swearing is so exceeding heinous, and withal so common, then it is every particular person's duty, especially those that are in authority, to do their utmost towards discountenancing and suppressing so malignant a crime. The duty we owe both to God and our neighbor, requires this at our hands; by the one we are obliged to assert our Maker's honor; by the other to prevent our neighbor's ruin; and it is but doing as we would be done by, and as we ourselves act in cases of lesser consequence. Were we to hear either our own or our friend's good name vilified and traduced, we should think it our bounden duty to vindicate the wronged reputation of each; and shall the great, terrible, and holy name of our best and only friend, our king, our father, nay our God: shall this be daily, nay every moment, defied and blasphemed; and will no one dare to stand up in defense of his honor and holiness? Be astonished, O heavens, at this! No; let us scorn all such base and treacherous treatment; let us resolve to support the cause of religion, and with a becoming prudent courage manifest our zeal for the honor of the Lord of Hosts. Men in authority have double the advantages of ordinary Christians; their very office shows they are intended for the punishment of evil doers. And such is the degeneracy of mankind, that the generality of them will be more influenced by the power of persons in authority, than by the most labored exhortations from the pulpit. To such, therefore, if there are any here present, I humbly address myself, beseeching them, in the name of our Lord Jesus Christ, to do their utmost to put a stop to, and restrain profane cursing and swearing. And though it must be confessed, that this is a work which requires a great deal of courage and pains, yet they would do well to consider, it is for God they undertake it, who certainly will support and bear them out in a due execution of their office here, and reward them with an exceeding and eternal weight of glory hereafter. But it is time to draw towards a conclusion.

3. Let me, therefore, once more address myself to every person here present, in the name of our Lord Jesus Christ; and if any amongst them have been any way guilty of this notorious sin of swearing, let me entreat them by all that is near and dear to them, that they would neither give the magistrate the trouble to punish, nor their friends any reason for the future to warn them against committing the crime; but keep a constant and careful watch over the door of their lips, and withal implore the divine assistance (without which all is nothing) that they offend no more so scandalously with their tongues. Let them seriously lay to heart, what with great plainness and simplicity has here been delivered: and if they have any regard for themselves as men, or their reputation as Christians; if they would not be a public scandal to their profession, or a grief to all that know or converse with them: in short, if they would not be devils incarnate here, and provoke God to punish them eternally hereafter; I say unto them in the name of our Lord Jesus Christ, "Swear not at all."

Sermon 19 Christ the Support of the Tempted

Matthew 6:13, "Lead us not into temptation."

The great and important duty which is incumbent on Christians, is to guard against all appearance of evil; to watch against the first risings in the heart to evil; and to have a guard upon our actions, that they may not be sinful, or so much as seem to be so. It is true, the devil is tempting us continually, and our own evil hearts are ready to join with the tempter, to make us fall into sins, that he thereby may obtain a victory over us, and that we, my brethren, may be his subjects, his servants, his slaves; and then by-and-by he will pay us our wages, which will be death temporal, and death eternal. Our Lord Jesus Christ saw how his people would be tempted; and that the great enemy of their souls would lay hold of every opportunity, so he could but be a means of keeping poor sinners from coming to the Lord Jesus Christ; hurrying you with temptation, to drive you to some great sins; and then if he cannot gain you over, sell it to a smaller, and suit his temptations time after time; and when he finds none of these things will do, often transform himself into an angel of light, and by that means make the soul fall into sin, to the dishonor of God, and the wounding of itself; the Lord Jesus, I say, seeing how liable his disciples, and all others, would be to be overcome by temptation, therefore advises them, when they pray, to beg that they might not be led into temptation. It is so dangerous to engage so subtle and powerful an enemy as Satan is, that we shall be overcome as often as we engage, unless the Lord is on our side. My brethren, if you were left to yourselves, you would be overcome by every temptation with which you are beset.

These words are part of the prayer which Christ taught his disciples; and I shall, therefore, make no doubt, but that you all believe them to be true, since they are spoken by one who cannot lie. I shall, I. Show you who it is that tempts you.

II. Shall show, my brethren, why he tempts you.

III. Mention some of the ways and means he makes use of, to draw you over to his temptations.

IV. Let you see how earnest you ought to be to the Lord, that he may preserve you from being led into temptation.

V. I shall make some application by way of entreaty unto you, to come unto Christ, that he, my brethren, may deliver you from being tempted.

I. FIRST, We are to consider who it is that tempts us.

And the tempter is Satan, the prince of the power of the air, he that now ruleth in the children of disobedience; he is an enemy to God and goodness, he is a hater of all truth. Why else did he slander God in paradise? Why did he tell Eve, "You shall not surely die?" He is full of malice, envy, and revenge; for what reasons else could induce him to molest innocent man in paradise? The person that tempts ye, my brethren, is remarkable for his subtlety; for having not power given him from above, he is obliged to wait for opportunities to betray us, and to catch us by guile; he, therefore, made use of the serpent to tempt our first parents; and to lie in wait to deceive, is another part of his character. And though this character is given of the devil, if we were to examine our own hearts, we should find many of the tempter's characters legible in us.

Do not many of you love to make a lie? And if it is done in your trade; you therefore look on it as excusable; but whether you believe it or not, it is sinful, it is exceedingly sinful. Though you may value yourselves as fine rational creatures, and that you are noble beings; and you were so, as you first came out of God's hands; but now you are fallen, there is nothing lovely, nothing desirable in man; his heart is a sink of pollution, full of sin and uncleanness: Yet, though a man's own heart is so desperately wicked, he is told by our modern polite preachers, that there is a fitness in men, and that God seeing you a good creature, gives you his grace; but this, though it is a modern, polite, and fashionable way of talking, is very unscriptural; it is very contrary to the doctrines of the Reformation, and to our own Articles. But however contrary to the doctrines of the Church of England, yet our pulpits ring of nothing more, than doing no one any harm, living honestly, loving your neighbor as yourselves, and do what you can, and then Christ is to make up the deficiency: this is making Christ to be half a savior, and man the other part; but I say, Christ will be your whole righteousness, your whole wisdom, your whole sanctification, or else he will never be your whole redemption. How amazing is it, that the ministers of the church of England should speak quite contrary to what they have subscribed! Good God! If these are the guides of the ignorant, and esteemed to be the true ministers of Jesus, because they have a great share of letter-learning; when at the same time they are only the blind leaders of the blind; and without a special Providence, they both will fall into the ditch.

No wonder at people's talking of the fitness and unfitness of things, when they can tell us, that the Spirit of God, is a good conscience, and the comforts of the Holy Ghost are consequent thereupon. But this is wrong; for it should be said, the Spirit of God, are the comforts of the Holy Ghost, and a good conscience consequent thereupon. Seneca, Cicero, Plato, or any of the heathen philosophers, would have given as good a definition as this; it means no more than reflecting we have done well.

But let these modern, polite gentlemen, and let my letter-learned brethren, paint man in as lovely colors as they please, I will not do it; I dare not make him better than the word of God does. If I was to paint man in his proper colors, I must go to the kingdom of hell for a copy; for man is by nature full of pride, subtlety, malice, envy, revenge, and all uncharitableness; and what are these but the temper of the devil? And lust, sensuality, pleasure, these are the tempers of the beast. Thus, my brethren, man is half a beast, and half a devil, a motley mixture of the beast and devil. And this is the creature, who has made himself so obnoxious to the wrath of God, and open to his indignation, that is told, that he must be part his own savior, by doing good works, and what he cannot do Christ will do for him.

This is giving the tempter great room to come in with his temptation; he may press a soul to follow moral duties, to go to church, take the sacrament, read, pray, meditate; the devil is well content you should do all these; but if they are done in your own strength, or if you go no farther than here, you are only going a smoother way to hell.

Thus, my brethren, you may see who it is that tempts us. But II. Why he tempts you, is the second thing I am to show you.

It is our of envy to you, and to the Lord Jesus Christ, he endeavors to keep you from closing with Jesus; and if he can but keep you from laying hold by faith on Christ, he knows he has you safe enough; and the more temptations you are under, and according to their nature and greatness, you are more hurried in your minds; and the more unsettled your thoughts and affections are, the more apt you are to conclude, that if you were to go to Christ, at present, in all that hurry of mind, he would not receive you; but this is a policy of the tempter, to make you have low and dishonorable thoughts of the blessed Jesus; and so by degrees he works upon your minds, that you are careless and indifferent about Christ. This, this, my brethren, is the design of the tempter. Nothing will please him more, than to see you ruined and lost forever. He tempts you for that end, that you may lose your interest in Jesus Christ, and that you may dwell with him and apostate spirits to all eternity. He knows that Jesus Christ died for sinners, yet he would fain keep souls from seeking to this city of refuge for shelter, and from going to Gilead for the true balm.

It is he that rules in thy heart, O scoffer, O Pharisee; the devil reigns there, and endeavors to blind your eyes, that you shall not see what danger you are in, and how much evil there is in those hearts of yours; and as long as he can keep you easy and unconcerned about having your hearts changed, he will be easy; though if he can, he will tempt you to sin against him, until you are hardened in your iniquity. O, my brethren, do not give the devil a handle wherewith he may lay hold on you; alas! it is not wonder that the devil tempts you, when he finds you at a play, a ball, or masquerade; if you are doing the devil's work, it is no wonder if he presses you in the continuation thereof; and how can any say, "Lead us not into temptation," in the morning, when they are resolved to run into it at night? Good God! Are these persons members of the church of England? Alas, when you have gone to church, and read over the prayers, it is offering no more than the sacrifice of fools; you say Amen to them with your lips, when in your hearts you are either unconcerned at what you are about, or else you think that the bare saying of your prayers is sufficient, and that then God and you have balanced accounts.

But, my dear brethren, do not deceive yourselves, God is not to be mocked. You are only ruining yourselves for time and eternity. You pray, "lead us not into temptation," when you are tempting the devil to come and tempt you.

III. I shall now point out some of the ways and means, he makes use of to draw you to himself.

But this is a field so large, and I have but just begun to be a soldier of Jesus Christ, that I cannot name many unto you. I shall therefore be very short on this head.

1. He endeavors to make you think sin is not so great as it is; that there is no occasion of being so over-strict, and that you are righteous overmuch; that you are ostentatious, and will do yourself harm by it; and that you will destroy yourselves. He shows you, by brethren, the bait, but he hides the hook; he shows you the pleasure, profits, and advantages, that attend abundance of this world's goods; but he does not show you crosses, losses and vexations that you may have while you are in the enjoyment of the blessings of this world.

2. When he finds he cannot allure you by flattery, he will try you by frowns, and the terrors of this world; he will stir up people to point at you, and cry, "Here comes another troop of his followers;" He will stir them up to jeer, scoff, backbite, and hate you; but if he still finds this will not do, then he throws doubts, my brethren, and discouragement in your mind, whether the way you are in is the true way or not; or else he will suggest, What! Do you expect to be saved by Christ? Also, He did not die for you; you have been too great a sinner; you have lived in sin so long, and committed such sins against Christ, which he will not forgive. Thus he hurries poor sinners almost into despair.

And very often, when the people of God are met to worship him, he sends his agents, the scoffers, to disturb them. We saw an instance of their rage just now; they would fain have disturb us; but the Lord was on our side, and so prevented all the attempts of wicked and designing men, to disturb and disquiet us. Lord Jesus, forgive them who are thus persecuting thy truth! Jesus, show them that they are fighting against thee, and that it is hard for them to kick against the pricks! These, my brethren, are some of the ways Satan takes, in is temptations, to bring you from Christ.

Many more might be named; but these are sufficient, I hope, to keep you on your guard, against all that the enemy can do to hinder you from coming to Christ.

IV. I come to show you, how earnest you ought to be with Jesus Christ, either not to suffer you to be led into temptations, or to preserve you under them.

And here, my dear brethren, let me beseech you to go to Jesus Christ; tell him, how you are assaulted by the evil one, who lies in wait for your souls; tell him, you are not able to master him, in your own strength; beg his assistance, and you shall find him ready to help you; ready to assist you, and to be your Guide, your Comforter, your Savior, your All; He will give you strength to resist the fiery darts of the devil; and, therefore, you can no where find one so proper to relieve you, as Jesus Christ; he knows what it is to be tempted; he was tempted by Satan in the wilderness, and he will give you the assistance of his Spirit, to resist the evil one, and then he will fly from you. In Christ Jesus you shall have the strength you stand in need of, the devil shall have no power; therefore fear not, for in the name of the Lord we shall overcome all our spiritual Amalekites.

Let the devil and his agents rage, let them breathe out threatenings, yes, let them breathe out slaughters, yet we can rejoice in this, that Jesus Christ hath them in his power, they shall go no farther than he permits them;

they may rage, they may rage horribly, but they can go no farther, until they have got more power from on high.

If they could do us what mischief they would, very few of us should be permitted to see our habitations any more; but, blessed be God, we can commit ourselves to his protection; he has been our protector hitherto, he will be so still. Then earnestly entreat of the Lord to support you under those temptations, which the devil may assault you with; he is a powerful adversary, he is a cunning one too; he would be too hard for us, unless we have the strength of Christ to be with us. But let us be looking up unto Jesus, that he would send his Spirit into our hearts, and keep us from falling. O my dear brethren in Christ Jesus, how stands it now between God and your souls? Is Jesus altogether lovely to your souls? Is he precious unto you? I am sure, if you have not gone back from Christ, he will not from you; he will root out the accursed things of this world, and dwell in your hearts. You are candidates for heaven; and will you mind earth ? What are all the pleasures of earth, without an interest in the Lord Jesus Christ? And one smile from him is more to be desired than rubies, yea more than the whole world.

O you who have found Jesus Christ assisting you, and supporting you under all the temptations of this life, will you forsake him? Have you not found him a gracious master? Is he not the chiefest of ten thousand, and altogether lovely? Now you see a form and comeliness in Christ, which you never saw before. O! how do you and I wish we had known Jesus sooner, and that we had more of his love; it is condescending love, it is amazing, it is forgiving love, it is dying love, it is exalted and interceding love, and it is glorified love. Methinks when I am talking of the love of Jesus Christ, who loved me before I love him; he saw us polluted in blood, full of sores, a slave to sin, to death and hell, running to destruction, then he passed by me, and said unto my soul, "Live;" he snatched me as a brand plucked from the burning. It was love that saved me, it was all of the free grace of God, and that only. The little experience I have had of this love, makes me amazed at the condescension, the love, and mercifulness of the blessed Jesus, that he should have mercy upon such a wretch. O, my brethren, the kingdom of God is within me, and this fills me so full of love, that I would not be in my natural state again, not for millions of millions of worlds; I long to be with Jesus, to live with the Lord that bought me, to live forever with the Lamb that was slain, and to sing Hallelujah's unto him. Eternity itself will be too short to set forth the love of the Lord Jesus Christ. I cannot, indeed I cannot forbear speaking again, and again, and again, of the Lord Jesus.

And if there are any here who are strangers to this love of the Lord Jesus Christ, do not despair; come, come unto Christ, and he will have mercy upon you, he will pardon all your sins, he will heal all your backslidings, he will love you freely, and take you to be with himself.

Come therefore, O my guilty brethren, unto Jesus, and you shall find rest for your souls. You need not fear, you need not despair, when God has had mercy upon such a wretch as I; and he will save you also, if you will come unto him by faith.

Why do ye delay? What! Do you say, you are poor, and therefore ashamed to come? It is not your poverty that Christ mindeth; come in all your rags, in all your pollution, and he will save you. Do not depend upon any thing but the blood of Jesus Christ; do not stand out an hour longer, but give your hearts to Christ, give him the firstlings of the flock; come unto him now, lest he should cut you off before you are prepared, and your soul be sent to that pit from whence there is no redemption.

Do not waver, but give him that which he desires, your hearts; it is the heart the Lord Jesus Christ wanteth; and when you have an inward principle wrought in your hearts by this same Jesus, then you will feel the sweetness and pleasure of communion with God. O consider, my brethren, the love of the Lord Jesus Christ, in dying for you; and are you resolved to slight his dying love? Your sins brought Christ from heaven, and I humbly pray to the Lord that they may not be a means of sending you to hell. What language will make you leave your sins and come to Christ? O that I did but know! And that it lay in my power to give you this grace; not one of you, not the greatest scoffer here should go hence before he was changed from a natural to a spiritual life; then, then we would rejoice and take sweet council together; but all this is not in my power; but I tell you where you may have it, even of the Lord Jesus; he will give it to you, if you ask it of him, for he has told us, "Ask, and you shall receive;" therefore ask of him, and if you are repulsed again and again, entreat him more, and he will be unto you as he was to the poor Syrophoenician woman, who came to Christ on account of her daughter; and is she was so importunate to him for a body, how much more should we be solicitous for our souls? If you seek to him in faith, his answer will be to you as it was to her, "Thy faith hath saved thee, be it as thou wouldest have it." O, do not forsake the seeking of the Lord; do not, I beseech you, neglect the opportunities which may be offered to you, for the salvation of your souls; forsake not the assembling of yourselves together, to build up and confirm and strengthen those who are weak in faith; to convince sinners, that they may feel the power of God pricking them in their hearts, and make them cry out, "What must we do to be saved?" The devil and his agents have their clubs of reveling, and their societies of drunkenness; they are not ashamed to be seen and heard doing the devil their master's works; they are not ashamed to proclaim him; and sure you are not ashamed of the Lord Jesus

Christ; you dare proclaim that Jesus, who died that you might live, and who will own you before his Father and all the holy angels; Therefore, dare to be singularly good; be not afraid of the face of man; let not all the threats of the men of this world move you; what is the loss of all the grandeur, or pleasure, or reputation of this life, compared to the loss of heaven, of Christ and of your souls?

And as for the reproaches of the world, do not mind them; when they revile you, never, never revile again; do not answer railing with railing; but let love, kindness, meekness, patience, long-suffering, be found in you, as they were in the blessed Jesus; therefore, I beseech you, do not neglect the frequent coming together, and telling each other, what great things Jesus Christ hath done for your souls.

I do not now, as the Pharisees say I do, encourage you to leave your lawful callings, and your business, in which God, by his providence, hath placed you; for you have two callings, the one a general, and the other a special one; it is your duty to regard your families, and if you neglect them out of any pretense whatever, as going to church or in societies, you are out of the way of your duty, and offering that to God which he commanded you not. But then, my brethren, you are to take care that the things of this life do not hinder the preparing for that which is to come; let not the business of the world make you unmindful of your souls; but in all your moral actions, in the business of life, let all be done with a view to the glory of God, and the salvation of your souls.

The nigh draws on, and obliges me to hasten to a conclusion; though, methinks, I could speak until my tongue clave to the roof of my mouth, yes, until I could speak no more, if it was to save your souls from the paws of him who seeketh to devour you.

Therefore let me beseech you, in all love and compassion; Consider, you, who are Pharisees; you, who will not come to Christ, but are trusting to yourselves for righteousness; who think, because you lead civil, honest, decent lives, all will go well at last; but let me tell you, O ye Pharisees, that harlots, murderers, and thieves, shall enter the kingdom of God before you. Do not flatter yourselves of being in the way to heaven, when you are in the broad way to hell; but if you will throw away your righteousness and come to Christ, and be contented to let Jesus Christ do all for you, and in you, then Christ is willing to be your Savior; but if you bring your good works with you, and think to be justified on the account of them, you may seek to be justified by them forever, and never be justified; no, it is only the blood of Jesus Christ that cleanseth us from the filth and pollution of all our sins; and you must be sanctified before you are justified. As for good works, we are justified before God without any respect to them, either past, present, or to come: when w are justified, good works will follow our justification, for we can do no good works, until we are cleansed of our pollution, by the sanctification of the Spirit of God.

O ye scoffers, come and see this Jesus, this Lord of glory whom you have despised; and if you will but come to Christ, he will be willing to receive you, notwithstanding all the persecution you have used towards his members; However, if you are resolved to persist in your obstinacy, remember, salvation was offered to you, that Christ and free grace were proposed; but you refused to accept of either, and therefore your blood will be required at your own hands.

I shall only say this unto you, that however you may despise either me or my ministry, I shall not regard it, but shall frequently show you your danger, and propose to you the remedy; and shall earnestly pity and pray for you, that God would show you your error, and bring you home into his sheepfold, that you, from ravenous lions, may become peaceful lambs.

And as for you, O my brethren, who desire to choose Christ for you Lord, and to experience his power upon your souls, and as you do not find your desires and prayers answered; go on, and Christ will manifest himself unto you, as he does not unto the world; you shall be made to see and feel this love of Jesus upon your souls; you shall have a witness in your own breast, that you are the Lord's; therefore, do not fear, the Lord Jesus Christ will gather you with his elect, when he comes at that great day of accounts, to judge every one according to the deeds done in the body, whether they be good, or whether they be evil; and, O that the thought of answering to God for all our actions, would make us more mindful about the consequences that will attend it.

And now let me address all of you, high and low, rich and poor, one with another, to accept of mercy and grace while it is offered to you; Now is the accepted time, now is the day of salvation; and will you not accept it, now it is offered unto you? Do not stand out one moment longer; but come and accept of Jesus Christ in his own way, and then you shall be taken up at the last day, and be with him forever and ever; and sure this should make you desirous of being with that Jesus who has done so much for you, and is not interceding for you, and preparing mansions for you; where may we all arrive and sit down with Jesus to all eternity!

Which God of his infinite mercy grant, etc.

Sermon 20 Worldly Business no Plea for the Neglect of Religion

Matthew 8:22, "Let the dead bury their dead."

St. Paul preaching at Athens, tells them, that as he passed by and beheld their devotions, he perceived they were in all things too superstitious. But was this apostle to rise, can come publishing the glad tidings of salvation in any of our populous cities, he would see no reason why he should charge the inhabitants with this; but rather as he passed by and observed the tenor of their life, say, I perceive in all things ye are two worldly-minded; ye are too eagerly bent on pursuing your lawful business; so eagerly, as either wholly to neglect, or at least too heedlessly to attend on the one thing needful.

There cannot then be a greater charity shown to the Christian world, than to sound an alarm in their ears, and to warn them of the inexpressible danger, of continually grasping after the things of this life, without being equally, nay a thousand times more concerned for their well-being in a future state.

And there is still the more occasion for such an alarm, because worldly-mindedness so easily and craftily besets the hearts of men. For out of a specious pretense of serving God in laboring for the meat which perisheth, they are insensibly lulled into such a spiritual slumber, as scarce to perceive their neglect to secure that which endureth to everlasting life.

The words of the text, if not at first view, yet when examined and explained, will be found applicable to this case, as containing an admirable caution not to pursue the affairs of this world, at the expense of our happiness in the next.

They are the words of Jesus Christ himself: the occasion of their being spoken was this; As he was conversing with those that were gathered round about him, he gave one of them an immediate summons to follow him: but he, either afraid to go after such a persecuted master, or rather loving this present world, says, "Suffer me first to go home and bury my father," or, as most explain it, let me first go and dispatch some important business I have now in hand. But Jesus said unto him, "Let the dead bury their dead;" leave worldly business to worldly men, let thy secular business be left undone, rather than thou shouldst neglect to follow me.

Whether this person did as he was commanded, I know not; but this I know, that what Christ said here is person, he has often whispered with the small still voice of his holy Spirit, and said to many here present, that rise up early and late take rest, and eat the bread of carefulness, Come draw off your affections from the things of this life; take up your cross and follow me. But they, willing to justify themselves, make answer, Lord, suffer us first to bury our fathers, or dispatch our secular affairs. I say unto all such, "Let the dead bury their dead," let your worldly business be left undone, rather than you should neglect to follow him.

From the words thus explained, naturally arises this proposition, that no business, though ever so important, can justify a neglect of true religion.

The truth of which I shall first show, and then make an application of it.

I. FIRST then, I am to prove, that no temporal business, though ever so important, can justify a neglect of true religion.

By the word religion, I do not mean any set of moral virtues, any partial amendment of ourselves, or formal attendance on any outward duties whatsoever: but an application of Christ's whole and personal righteousness, made by faith to our hearts; a thorough real change of nature wrought in us by the invisible, yet powerful operation of the Holy Ghost, preserved and nourished in our souls by a constant use of all the means of grace, evidenced by a good life, and bringing forth the fruits of the Spirit.

This is true and undefiled religion, and for the perfecting this good work in our hearts, the eternal Son of God came down and shed his precious blood; for this end were we made, and sent into the world, and by this alone can we become the sons of God. Were we indeed to judge by the common practice of the world, we might think we were sent into it for no other purpose, than to care and toil for the uncertain riches of this life: but if we consult the lively oracles, they will inform us, that we were born for nobler ends, even to be born again from above, to be restored to the divine likeness by Jesus Christ, our second Adam, and thereby be made meet to inherit the kingdom of heaven; and consequently, there is an obligation laid upon all, even the most busy people, to secure this end; it being an undeniable truth, that all creatures ought to answer the end for which they were created.

Some indeed are for confining religion to the clergy, and think it only belongs to those who serve at the altar; but what a fatal mistake is this, seeing all persons are indifferently called by God to the same state of inward holiness. As we are all corrupt in our nature, so must we all be renewed and sanctified. And though it must be granted, that the clergy lie under double obligations to be examples to believers, in faith, zeal, charity, and whatever else s commendable and of good report, as being more immediately dedicated to the service of God; yet as we have been all baptized with one baptism into the death of Christ, we are all under the necessity of performing our baptismal covenant, and perfecting holiness in the fear of God: for the holy scriptures point out to us but one way of admission into the kingdom of Christ, through the narrow gate of a sound conversion: And he that does not enter into the sheepfold, whether clergy or lay-men, by this door, will find, to his everlasting confusion, there is no climbing up another way.

Besides, what a gross ignorance of the nature of true religion, as well as of our own happiness, does such a distinction discover? For what does our Savior, by willing us to be religious, require of us? But to subdue our corrupt passions, to root out ill habits, to engraft the heavenly graces of God's most holy Spirit in their room; and, in one word, to fill us with all the fullness of God.

And will men be so much their own enemies, as to affirm this belongs only to those who minister in holy things? Does it not equally concern the most active man living? Is it the end of religion to make men happy, and is it not every one's privilege to be as happy as he can? Do persons in business find the corruptions of their nature, and disorder of their passions, so pleasing, that they care not whether they ever regulate or root them out? Or will they consent that ministers shall be alone partakers of the inheritance of the saints in light? If not, as they desire the same end, why will they not make use of the same means? Do they think that God will create a new thing upon the earth, and, contrary to the purity of his nature, and immutability of his counsel, admit them into heaven in their natural state, because they have been encumbered about many worldly things?

Search the scriptures, and see if they give any room for such a groundless hope.

But farther, one would imagine there was something of the highest concern and utmost importance in our temporal affairs, that they should divert so many from purifying their hearts by faith which is in Christ Jesus.

A covetous miser, who neglects religion by being continually intent on seeking great things for himself and those of his own household, flatters himself he herein acts most wisely; and at the same time will censure and condemn a young prodigal, who has no time to be devout, because he is so perpetually engaged in wasting his substance by riotous living and following of harlots. But yet a little while, and men will be convinced, that they are as much without excuse who lost their souls by hunting after riches, as those who lose them by hunting after sensual pleasures. For though business may assume an air of importance, when compared with other trifling amusements, yet when put in the balance with the loss of our precious and immortal souls, it is equally frivolous, according to that of our Savior, "What shall it profit a man, if he shall gain the whole world, and lost his own soul; or what shall a man give in exchange for his soul?" And now what need we any further proof? We have heard the decision out of Christ's own mouth. But because it is so difficult to convince such of this important truth, whose hearts are blinded by the deceitfulness of riches, that we had need cry out to them in the language of the prophet, "O earth, earth, hear the word of the Lord," I shall lay before you one passage of scripture more, which I could wish were written on the tables of all our hearts. In the 14th of St. Luke, the 18th and following verses, our blessed Lord puts forth this parable, "A certain man made a great supper, and bade many, and sent his servant at supper-time, to call them that were bidden: but they all, with one consent, began to make excuse. The one said, I have bought a piece of ground, and I must needs go and see it, I pray thee have me excused. And another said, I have bought a yoke of oxen, and I must needs go and prove them, I pray thee therefore have me excused. So the servant returned, and showed his master all these things." And what follows? Did the master accept of their excuses? No, the text tells us the good man was angry, and said, "that none of those which were bidden, should taste of his supper." And what dies this parable teach, but that the most lawful callings cannot justify our neglect; nay, that they are no longer lawful when they in any wise interfere with the great concerns of religion?

For the marriage supper here spoken of, means the gospel; the master of the house is Christ; the servants sent out, are his ministers, whose duty it is, from time to time, to call the people to this marriage-feast, or, in other words, to be religious. Now we find those that were bidden, were very well and honestly employed. There was no harm in buying or seeing a piece of ground, or in going to prove a yoke of oxen; but here lay their faults, they were doing those things, when they were invited to come to the marriage feast.

Without doubt, persons may very honestly and commendably be employed in following their respective callings; but yet, if they are engaged so deeply in these, as to hinder their working our their salvation with fear and trembling, they must expect the same sentence with their predecessors in the parable, that none of them shall taste of Christ's supper: for our particular calling, as of this or that profession, must never interfere with our general and precious calling, as Christians. Not that Christianity calls us entirely out of the world, the holy scriptures warrant no such doctrine.

It is very remarkable, that in the book of life, we find some almost of all kinds of occupations, who notwithstanding served God in their respective generations, and shone as so many lights in the world. Thus we hear of a good centurion in the evangelists, and a devout Cornelius in the Acts; a pious lawyer; and some that walked with God, even of Nero's household, in the epistles; and our divine master himself, in his check to Martha, does not condemn her for minding, but for being cumbered or perplexed about many things.

No, you may, nay, you must labor, our of obedience to God, even for the meat which perisheth.

But I come, in the SECOND place, to apply what has been said.

I beseech you, by the mercies of God in Christ Jesus, let not your concern for the meat which perisheth be at the expense of that which endureth to everlasting life; for, to repeat our blessed Savior's words, "What shall it profit a man, if he shall gain the whole world, and lose his own soul; or, what shall a man give in exchange for his soul?

Were we always to live in the world, then worldly wisdom would be our highest wisdom: but forasmuch as we have here no continuing city, and were only sent into this world to have our natures changed, and to fit ourselves for that which is to come; then to neglect this important work for a little worldly gain, what is it but, with profane Esau, to sell our birth-right for a mess of pottage.

Alas! how unlike are Christians to Christianity! They are commanded to "seek first the kingdom of God and his righteousness," and all other real necessaries shall be added unto them; but they are fearful (O men of little faith!) that if they should do so, all other necessaries would be taken from them: they are strictly forbidden to be careful for the morrow, and yet they rest not night or day, but are continually heaping up riches for many years, though they know not who shall gather them. Is this acting like persons that are strangers and pilgrims upon earth? Is this keeping their baptismal vow? Or rather, is it not directly apostatizing from it, and deserting the service of Jesus Christ, to list themselves under the banner of mammon?

But what will be the hope of such worldlings, when God shall take away their souls? What if the almighty should say to each of them, as he did to the rich fool in the gospel, "this night shall thy soul be required of thee;" O then, what would all those things profit them, which they are now so busy in providing?

Was eternal life, that free gift of God in Christ Jesus, to be purchased with money; or could men carry their flocks beyond the grave, to buy oil for their lamps, i.e. grace for their hearts, when they should be called to meet the bridegroom, there might be some reason why God might well bear with them: but since their money is to perish with them; since it is certain, as they brought nothing into the world, so they can carry nothing out; or supposing they could, since there is no oil to be bought, no grace to be purchased when once the lamp of their natural life is gone out; would it not be much more prudent to spend the short time they have here allotted them, in buying oil while it may be had, and not for fear of having a little less of that which will quickly be another man's, eternally lose the true riches?

What think you? Is it to be supposed, it grieved that covetous worldling before mentioned, when his sprung into the world of spirits, that he could not stay here till he had pulled down his barns and built greater?

Or think you not that all things here below seemed equally little to him then, and he only repented that he had not employed more time in pulling down every high thought that exalted itself against the Almighty, and building up his soul in the knowledge and fear of God?

And thus it will be with all unhappy men, who like him are disquieting themselves in a vain pursuit after worldly riches, and at the same time are not rich towards God.

They may, for a season, seem excellently well employed in being solicitously careful about the important concerns of this life; but when once their eyes are opened by death, and their souls launched into eternity, they will then see the littleness of all sublunary cares, and wonder they should be so besotted to the things of another life, while they were, it may be, applauded for their great wisdom and profound sagacity in the affairs of this world.

Alas! how will they bemoan themselves for acting like the unjust steward, so very wisely in their temporal concerns, in calling their respective debtors so carefully, and asking how much every one owes to them, and yet never remembering to call themselves to an account, or inquire how much they owed to their own great Lord and master?

And now what shall I say more? The God of this world, and the inordinate desire of other things, must have wholly stifled the conscience of that man, who does not see the force of these plain reasonings.

Permit me only to add a word or two to the rich, and to persons that are freed from the business of this life.

But here I must pause a while, for I am sensible that it is but an ungrateful, and as some may imagine, an assuming thing, for such a novice in religion to take upon him to instruct men in high stations, and who perhaps would disdain to set me with the dogs of their flock.

But however, since St. Paul, who knew what best became a young preacher, commanded Timothy, young as he was, to exhort and charge the rich with all authority; I hope none here that are so, will be offended, if with humility I beg leave to remind them, though they once knew this, that if persons in the most busy employs are indispensably obliged to "work out their salvation with fear and trembling," much more ought they to do so, who are free from the toils and encumbrance of a lower way of life, and consequently have greater opportunities to leisure to prepare themselves for a future state.

But is this really the case? Or do we not find, by fatal experience, that too many of those whom God has exalted above their brethren, who are "clothed in purple and fine linen, and fare sumptuously every day," by a sad abuse of God's great bounty towards them, think that their stations set them above religion, and so let the poor, who live by the sweat of their brows, attend more constantly on the means of grace than do they?

But woe unto such rich men! For they have received their consolation.

Happy had it been if they had never been born: for if the careless irreligious tradesman cannot be saved, where will luxurious and wicked gentlemen appear?

Let me therefore, by way of conclusion, exhort all persons, high and low, rich and poor, one with another, to make the renewal of their fallen nature, the one business of their lives; and to let no worldly profit, no worldly pleasure, divert them from the thoughts of it. Let this cry, "Behold the bridegroom cometh," be ever sounding in our ears; and let us live as creatures that are every moment liable to be hurried away by death to judgment: let us remember, that this life is a state of infinite importance, a point between two eternities, and that after these few days are ended, there will remain no more sacrifice for sin; let us be often asking ourselves, how we shall wish we had lived when we leave the world?

And then we shall always live in such a state, as we shall never fear to die in. Whether we live, we shall live unto the Lord; or whether we die, we shall die unto the Lord; so that living or dying we may be the Lord's.

To which end, let us beseech God, the protector of all them that put their trust in him, without whom nothing is string, nothing is holy, to increase and multiply upon us his mercy, that he being our ruler and guide, we may so pass through things temporal, that we finally lose not the things eternal; though Jesus Christ our Lord.

Sermon 21 Christ the only Rest for the Weary and Heavy-Laden

Matthew 11:28, "Come unto me, all ye that are weary and heavy laden, and I will give you rest."

Nothing is more generally known than our duties which belong to Christianity; and yet, how amazing is it, nothing is less practiced? There is much of it in name and show, but little of it in the heart and conversation; indeed, if going to church, and to the sacrament, or, if our being called after the name of Christ, and being baptized into that name; if that will make us Christians, I believe all of us would have a claim thereto: but if it consists in the heart, that there must be an inward principle wrought in us by faith; that there must be a change of the whole nature, a putting off the old man with his deeds, a turning from sin unto God, a cleaving only unto the Son of Right-eousness; and that there must be a new birth, and we experience the pangs thereof; and that you must feel yourselves weary and heavy laden with your sins, before you will seek for deliverance from them; if this is to be the case, if there is so much in being children of God, alas! how many who please themselves with an outside show, a name to live whilst they are dead; and how few that have any share in this spiritual state, in this true and living name? How few are they who are weary and heavy laden with their sins, and seek to Christ for rest?

They say, in a formal customary manner, we are sinners, and there is no health in us; but how few feel themselves sinners, and are so oppressed in their own spirits, that they have no quiet nor rest in them, because of the burden of their sins, and the weight that is fallen and lays on their minds?

Under these burdens, these heavy burdens, they are at a loss what to do whereby they may obtain rest; they fly to their works, they go to a minis-ter, and he tells them to read, to pray, and meditate, and take the sacrament: thus they go away, and read, and pray, and meditate almost without ceasing, and never neglect the sacrament whenever there is an opportunity for the taking of it. Well, when the poor soul has done all this, it still finds no ease, there is yet no relief. Well, what must you do then? To lie still under the burden they cannot, and to get rid of it then cannot. O what must the burdened soul do! Why, goes to the clergyman again, and tells him the case, and what it has done, and that it is no better. Well, he asks, have you given alms to the poor? Why no. Then go and do that, and you will find rest. Thus the poor sinner is hurried from duty to duty, and still finds no rest: all things are uneasy and disquiet within, and there remains no rest in the soul. And if it was to go through all the duties of religion, and read over a thousand manuals of prayers, none would ever give the soul any rest; nothing will, until it goes to the Lord Jesus Christ, for there is the only true rest; that is the rest which abideth, and will continue for ever. It is not in your own works, nor in your endeavors: no; when Christ comes into your souls, he pardons you, without any respect to your works, either past, present, or to come.

From the words, my brethren, I have now read, I shall I. Show you who are the weary and heavy laden.

II. Inquire what is meant by coming to Christ. And, III. Conclude with exhorting you to accept of the invitation which the Lord Jesus Christ gives unto you to come unto him, with the assurance of finding rest.

FIRST, I am to show you, who are the weary and heavy-laden.

And here it will be necessary to consider who are not; and then, to consider who they are that are really so.

1. Those who think themselves good enough, and are pleased that they are not so bad as others, these are not weary or heavy laden.

No, these Pharisees are not thus troubled; they laugh and jest at those who talk of feeling their sins, and think there is no occasion to make so much ado about religion: it is to be righteous over-much, and the means to destroy yourselves. They think if they do but mean well, and say their prayers, as they call them, it is sufficient: though they may say a prayer, yea, thousands of prayers, and all the while be only offering up the sacrifice of fools. They may call God, Father, every day, when it is only mocking of God, and offering up false fire unto him; and it would be just for him to serve them, as he did Nadab and Abihu, destroy them, cut them off from the face of the earth: but he is waiting to be gracious, and willing to try a little longer, whether you will bring forth any thing more than the leaven of an outward profession, which is not all that the Lord requires; no, he wants the heart; and unless you honor him with that, he does not regard your mouths, when the other is far from him. You may say over your prayers all your lives, and yet you may never pray over one: therefore, while you flatter yourselves you are good enough, and that you are in a state of salvation, you are only deceiving you own souls, and hastening on your own destruction. Come unto him, not as being good enough, but as vile sinners, as poor, and blind, and naked, and miserable, and then Jesus will have compassion.

O ye Pharisees, what fruits do ye bring forth? Why, you are moral, polite creatures; you do your endeavors, you do what you can, and so Jesus is to make up the rest. You esteem yourselves fine, rational, and polite beings, and think it is too unfashionable to pray; it is not polite enough: perhaps you have read some prayers, but knew not how to pray from your hearts; no, by no means: that was being righteous over-much indeed.

But when once you are sensible of your being lost, damned creatures, and see hell gaping ready to receive you: if God was but to cut the thread of life, O then, then you would cry earnestly unto the Lord to receive you, to open the door of mercy unto you; your bones would then be changed, you would no more flatter yourselves with your abilities and good wishes; no, you would see how unable you were, how incapable to save yourselves; that there is no fitness, no free will in you; no fitness, but for eternal damnation, no free will but that of doing evil; and that when you would do good, evil is present with you, and the thing that ye would not, that do ye. He knows the secret intent of every heart; and this is a pleasure to you, my dear brethren, who come on purpose to meet with him, though it be a field. And, however some may esteem me a mountebank, and an enthusiast, one that is only going to make you methodically mad; they may breathe out their invectives against me, yet Christ knows all; he takes notice of it, and I shall leave it to him to plead my cause, for he is a gracious Master: I have already found him so, and am sure he will continue so. Vengeance is his, and he will repay it. Let them revile me; let them cast me out of their synagogues, and have my name in reproach, I shall not answer them by reviling again, or in speaking evil against them: no, that is not the Spirit of Christ, but meekness, patience, long-suffering, kindness, etc.

Ye Pharisees, who are going about to establish your own righteousness; you, who are too polite to follow the Lord Jesus Christ in sincerity and truth; you, who are all for a little show, a little outside work; who lead moral, civil, decent lives, Christ will not know you at the great day, but will say unto you, O ye Pharisees, was there any place for me in your love?

Alas! you are full of anger and malice, and self-will; yet you pretended to love and serve me, and to be my people: but, however, I despise you; I, who am God, and knoweth the secret of all hearts; I, who am truth itself, the faithful and true witness, say unto you, "Depart from me, ye workers of iniquity, into that place of torment, prepared for the devil and his angels." Good God! And must these discreet polite creatures, who never did any one harm, but led such civil, decent lives, must they suffer the vengeance of eternal fire? Cannot their righteous souls be saved? Where then must the sinner and the ungodly appear? Where wilt thou, O Sabbath- breaker, appear, thou, who canst take thy pleasure, thy recreation, on the Lord's-day, who refuseth to hear the word of God, who wilt not come to church to be instructed in the ways of the Lord? Where will you, O ye adulterers, fornicators, and such-like of this generation appear?

Whoremongers and adulterers God will judge, and them he will condemn. Then you will not call these tricks of youth: no, but you will call on the rocks and the mountains to fall on you, to hide you from the fury and anger of the Lord. Where wilt thou, O man, appear, that takes pleasure in making a mock of sin, who despiseth all reproof, who throws about thy jests as a madman does fire, and asks whether thou art not in sport? Where wilt thou, O man, appear, that makes it thy business to preach against the children of the Most High; thou, who art inventing methods in order to stop the progress of the gospel, and using thy utmost power to quash the preaching thereof; who art raising of evil reports against the disciple of Christ, and esteemest them madmen, fools, schismatics, and a parcel of rabble? Thou, O man, with all thy letter-learning, wilt surely see the judgment seat of Christ, though, perhaps, sorely against your will; to be cast by him into eternal fire, a place prepared for the devil and his angels. There is a burning tophet kindled by the fury of an avenging God, which will never, never be quenched. The devil longs to embrace you in his hellish arms, whenever the sentence is past, where you must for ever bear the weight of your sin: there is no redemption then; the day of grace is past; the door of hope is shut; mercy will be no more offered, but you must be shut out from God for ever. O who can dwell with everlasting burnings!

However you may think of hell, indeed it is not a painted fire; it is not an imagination to keep people in awe: then, then you will feel the power of the almighty arm. If you will not lay hold on his golden scepter, he will break you with his iron rod. O ye Pharisees, who are now so good, so much better than others, how will ye stand before Christ, when dressed in his glory as judge? You Arians, may now despise his divinity; then you shall have a proof of it; he will show, that he has all power, and that he was no subordinate God; he will show you that he has all power in heaven and earth; that he was King of kings, and Lord of lords; that he was the mighty God, the everlasting Father; and this power that he has, he will exercise in preserving you to no other end, but to punish you forever. Thus you, who please yourselves with being good enough now, who are not weary and heavy laden with a sense of your sins here, will be weary and heavy laden with a sense of your punishment hereafter.

2. Those, my brethren, are not weary and heavy laden with a sense of their sins, who can delight themselves in the polite entertainments of the age, and follow the sinful diversion of life.

Now they can go to balls and assemblies, play-houses and horse-racing; they have no thought of their sins; they know not what it is to weep for sin, or humble themselves under the mighty hand of God; they can laugh away their sorrows, and sing away their cares, and drive away these melancholy thoughts: they are too polite to entertain any sad thoughts; the talk of death and judgment is irksome to them, because it damps their mirth; they could not endure to think of their sin and danger; they could not go to a play, and think of hell; they could not go quietly to a masquerade, and think of their danger; they could not go to a ball or an assembly in peace, if they thought of their sins.

And so it is proved, even to a demonstration, that these are not weary and heavy laden: for if they are not thoughtful about their sins, they will never be weary and heavy laden of them. But at the day of judgment all will be over; they shall lose all their carnal mirth, all their pleasure, all their delight will be gone forever.

They will say then of their laughter, it is mad; and of mirth, What dost thou? Their merry conceits, and witty jests against the poor despised people of God, are then over. Their mirth was but as the crackling of thorns under a pot; it made a great blaze and unseemly noise for a while, but it was presently gone, and will return no more.

They think now, that if they were to fast or to pray, and meditate and mourn, they should be righteous over-much, and destroy themselves; their lives would be a continual trouble, and it would make them run mad. Alas, my brethren, what misery must that life be, where there is no more pleasant days, no more balls or plays, no cards or dice, those wasters of precious time, no horse-racing and cock-fighting, from whence no good ever came, unless abusing God Almighty's creatures, and putting them to that use which he never designed them, can be called so. How miserable will your life be, when all your joys are over, when your pleasures are all past, and no more mirth or pastime? Do you think there is one merry heart in hell? One pleasing countenance? Or jesting, scoffing, swearing tongue? A sermon now is irksome; the offer of salvation, by the blood of Jesus Christ, is now termed enthusiasm; but then you would give thousands of worlds, if in your power, for one tender of mercy, for one offer of grace, which now you so much despise.

Now, you are not weary of your diversions, nor are you heavy laden with the sins, with which they are accompanied; but then you will be weary of your punishment, and the aggravation which attends it. Your cards and dice, your hawks and hounds, and bowls, and your pleasant sports, will then be over. What mirth will you have in remembering your sports and diversions? I would not have you mistake me, and say, I am only preaching death and damnation to you; I am only showing you what will be the consequence of continuing in these sinful pleasures; and if the devil does not hurry you away with half a sermon, I shall show you how to avoid these dangers, which I now preach up as the effect of sin unrepented of. I mention this, lest you should be hurried away by the devil: but be not offended, if I point our unto you more of the terrors which will attend your following these polite and fashionable entertainments of the present age, and of not being weary and heavy laden with a sense of your sins.

They who delight in drinking wine to excess, and who are drunkards, what bitter draughts will they have instead of wine and ale? The heat of lust will be then also abated; they will no more sing the song of the drunkard; no more spend their time in courting their mistresses, in lascivious discourse, in amorous songs, in wanton dalliances, in brutish defilements: no, these are all over; and it will but prick each other to the heart to look one another in the face. Then they will wish, that instead of sinning together, they had prayed together; had frequented religious societies; had stirred up each other to love and holiness, and endeavored to convince each other of the evil of sin, and how obnoxious they are to the wrath of God; and the necessity of being weary and heavy laden with a sense thereof; that they might have escaped the punishment which they suffer, by their following the sinful an polite diversions of the age they fell into. But as it was against God himself they had sinned, so no less than God will punish them for their offenses: he hath prepared those torments for his enemies; his continual anger will still be devouring of them; his breath of indignation will kindle the flame; his wrath will be a continual burden to their souls. Woe be to him who falls under the stroke of the Almighty!

Thus they are not weary and heavy laden with their sins, who can follow the polite and fashionable entertainments of the age. But, SECONDLY, I am to show you what it is to be weary and heavy laden with sins. And 1. You may be said, my brethren, to be weary and heavy laden, when your sins are grievous unto you, and it is with grief and trouble you commit them.

You, who are awakened unto a sense of your sins, who see how hateful they are to God, and how they lay you open to his wrath and indignation, and would willingly avoid them; who hate yourselves for committing them; when you are thus convinced of sin, when you see the terrors of the law, and are afraid of his judgments; then you may be said to be weary of your sins. And O how terrible do they appear when you are first awakened to a sense of them; when you see nothing but the wrath of God ready to fall upon you, and you are afraid of his judgments! O how heavy is your sin to you then! Then you feel the weight thereof, and that it is grievous to be born.

2. When you are obliged to cry out under the burden of your sins, and know not what to do for relief; when this is your case, you are weary of your sins. It does not consist in a weariness all of a sudden; no, it is the continual burden of your soul, it is your grief and concern that you cannot live without offending God, and sinning against him; and these sins are so many and so great, that you fear they will not be forgiven.

I come, SECONDLY, to show you what is meant by coming to Christ.

It is not, my brethren, coming with your own works: no, you must come in full dependence upon the Lord Jesus Christ, looking on him as the Lord who died to save sinners: Go to him, tell him you are lost, undone, miserable sinners, and that you deserve nothing but hell; and when you thus go to the Lord Jesus Christ out of yourself, in full dependence on the Lord Jesus Christ, you will find him an able and a willing savior; he is pleased to see sinners coming to him in a sense of their own unworthiness; and when their case seems to be most dangerous, most distressed, then the Lord in his mercy steps in and gives you his grace; he puts his Spirit within you, takes away your heart of stone, and gives you a heart of flesh. Stand not out then against this Lord, but go unto him, not in your own strength, but in the strength of Jesus Christ.

And this brings me, THIRDLY, to consider the exhortation Christ gives unto all of you, high and low, rich and poor, one with another, to come unto him that you may have rest. And if Jesus Christ gives you rest, you may be sure it will be a rest indeed; it will be such a rest as your soul wants; it will be a rest which the world can neither give nor take away. O come all of ye this night, and you shall find rest: Jesus Christ hath promised it. Here is a gracious invitation, and do not let a little rain hurry you away from the hearing of it; do but consider what the devil and damned spirits would give to have the offer of mercy, and to accept of Christ, that they may be delivered from the torments they labor under, and must do so forever; or, how pleasing would this rain be to them to cool their parched tongues; but they are denied both, while you have mercy offered to you; free and rich mercy to come to Christ; here is food for your souls, and the rain is to bring forth the fruits of the earth, as food for you bodies. Here is mercy upon mercy.

Let me beseech you to come unto Christ, and he will give you rest; you shall find rest unto your souls. O you, my weary, burdened brethren, do but go to Christ in this manner, and though you go to him weary, you shall find rest before you come from him: let not anything short of the Lord Jesus Christ be your rest; for wherever you seek you will be disappointed; but if you do but seek unto the Lord Jesus Christ, there you will find a fullness of every thing which your weary soul wants. Go to him this night; here is an invitation to all you who are weary souls. He does not call you, O Pharisees; not, it is only you weary sinners; and sure you will not stay from him, but accept of his invitation; do not delay; one moment may be dangerous: death may take you off suddenly. You know not but that a fit of the apoplexy may hurry you from time into eternity; therefore, be not for staying till you have something to bring; come in all your rags, in all your filthiness, in all your distresses, and you will soon find Jesus Christ ready to help, and to relieve you; he loves you as well in your rags, as in your best garments; he regards not your dress; no, do but come unto him, and you shall soon find rest for your souls.

What say you? Shall I tell my Master you will come unto him, and that you will accept him on his own terms. Let me, my brethren, beseech you to take Jesus without anything of your own righteousness: for if you expect to mix anything of yourself with Christ, you build upon a sandy foundation; but if you take Christ for your rest, he will be that unto you. Let me beseech you to build upon this rock of ages. O my brethren, think of the gracious invitation, "Come unto me," to Jesus Christ; it is he that calls you; And will you not go?

Come, come unto him. If your souls were not immortal, and you in danger of losing them, I would not thus speak unto you; but the love of your souls constrains me to speak: methinks this would constrain me to speak unto you forever. Come then by faith, and lay hold of the Lord Jesus; though he be in heaven, he now calleth thee. Come, all ye drunkards, swearers, Sabbath-breakers, adulterers, fornicators; come, all ye scoffers, harlots, thieves, and murderers, and Jesus Christ will save you; he will give you rest, if you are weary of your sins. O come lay hold upon him. Had I less love for your souls, I might speak less; but that love of God, which is shed abroad in my heart, will not permit me to leave you, till I see whether you will come to Christ or no. O for your life receive him, for fear he may never call you any more. Behold, the Bridegroom cometh; it may be this night the cry may be made. Now would you hear this, if you were sure to die before the morning light? God grant you may begin to live, that when the king of terrors shall come, you may have nothing to do but to commit your souls into the hands of a faithful Redeemer.

Now to God the Father, God the Son, and God the Holy Ghost, be all honor, praises, dominion, and power, henceforth and for evermore. Amen, Amen.

Sermon 22 The Folly and Danger

The Folly and Danger of parting with Christ for the Pleasures and Profits of Life.

Matthew 8:23-34, "And when he was entered into a ship, his disciples followed him. And, behold, there arose a great tempest in the sea, insomuch that the ship was covered with the waves: but he was asleep. And his disciples came to him, and awoke him, saying, Lord, save us: we perish.

And he saith unto them, Why are ye fearful, O ye of little faith? Then he arose, and rebuked the winds and the sea; and there was a great calm. But the men marveled, saying, What manner of man is this, that even the winds and the sea obey him! And when he was come to the other side into the country of the Gergesenes, there met him two possessed with devils, coming out of the tombs, exceeding fierce, so that no man might pass by that way.

And, behold, they cried out, saying, What have we to do with thee, Jesus, thou Son of God? art thou come hither to torment us before the time? And there was a good way off from them an herd of many swine feeding. So the devils besought him, saying, If thou cast us out, suffer us to go away into the herd of swine. And he said unto them, Go. And when they were come out, they went into the herd of swine: and, behold, the whole herd of swine ran violently down a steep place into the sea, and perished in the waters. And they that kept them fled, and went their ways into the city, and told every thing, and what was befallen to the possessed of the devils. And, behold, the whole city came out to meet Jesus: and when they saw him, they besought him that he would depart out of their coasts."

If we were but sensible of the great necessity there is, in this our day, of being real Christians, sure we should not be contented with being nominal ones; but we are sunk into I know not what; we are no better than baptized heathen. And how amazing is it, that we should profess the name of Christ, and yet so little converse about him; surely, this name whereby we are called, should be the theme of our discourse here, and of our eternal Hallelu-jahs in a world to come. But is it not more amazing, to consider, that instead of the name of Jesus, whereby we are to have salvation, we are taught to look for it in ourselves, and that there must be a fitness in us before God bestows his grace and favor upon us. But what doctrine is this?

Not the doctrine of the scripture, not the doctrine of Jesus, not that of the primitive Christians, not that of the reformation, nor that of the articles of the church of England. No, it is the doctrine of the devil; this is making Christ but half a Savior, and driving man into an error of the greatest conse-quence, in making him go to Jesus in his own strength, and not in the name of the Lord Jesus Christ. But, my brethren, unless you go in the strength of Jesus Christ; unless you depend only upon him for salvation; unless he is your wis-dom, righteousness and sanctification, he will never be your redemption. Our salvation is the free gift of God; it is owing to his free love, and the free grace of Jesus Christ, that ever you are saved.

Do not flatter yourselves of being good enough, because you are morally so; because you go to church, say the prayers, and take the sacra-ment, therefore you think no more is required; alas, you are deceiving your own souls; and if God, in his free grace and mercy, does not show you your error, it will only be leading you a softer way to your eternal ruin; but God forbid that any of you, to whom I am now speaking, should imagine this; no, you must be abased, and God must be exalted, or you will never begin at the right end, you will never see Jesus with comfort or satisfaction, unless you go to him only on the account of what he has done and suffered.

Is it not plain to a demonstration, that we are acting the part of the Gergesenes, who came and desired Jesus to depart from them? Let us con-sider the words, and then we shall see how exactly we are performing the part of these men over again.

And when he was entered into a ship his disciples followed him.

Christ had been working of many miracles, as we may read a few verses before; and as he continually went about doing good, so now he was going to the country of the Gergesenes to dispossess two, who were possessed with devils; and his disciples followed him; No doubt they were reproached and pointed at, for following such a babbler, as the Scribes and Pharisees es-teemed the Lord Jesus Christ. Doubtless they were pointed at, jeered, scoffed, and esteemed madmen, enthusiasts, and a parcel of rabble; but still they fol-lowed the Lord Jesus Christ, they did not mind a little reproach; no, they loved their Master too well to forbear following him for the sake of a little persecution. And if you do but love the Lord Jesus Christ, love him above all, you will follow him in spite of the malice of all the Scribes and Pharisees of this generation.

And behold there arose a great tempest on the sea.

The presence of Christ in the ship, did not preserve the disciples from fears and troubles; they were filled with uneasiness, although Christ was with them: this was only for a trial of their faith, to see if they would stand fast for the Lord in a persecuting time. My dear brethren, if the Lord is trying of you, do not give out; no, stand fast in all that the Lord may call you to suffer: It is easy to follow Christ when all things are safe: but your love to Jesus Christ would be seen more, if you must lose your lives, or deny your Jesus; it would be a trial of your love, when fire and faggot was before you, if you would rush into that, rather than flie from the truth as it is in Jesus. Though all things are calm now, the storm is gathering, and by and by it will break; it is at present no bigger than a man's hand; but when it is full it will break, and then you will see whether you are found Christians or not. Persecution would scatter the hypocrites, and make nominal Christians afraid to worship God; they would then soon turn unto the world and the things of it.

And his disciples came to him, and awoke him, saying, Lord, save us: we perish. And he saith unto them, Why are ye fearful, O ye of little faith? Then he arose, and rebuked the winds and the sea; and there was a great calm. But the men marveled, saying, What manner of man is this, that even the winds and the sea obey him!

Here we may see the great compassion of the Lord Jesus Christ; no sooner had the disciples awakened him, and he saw their danger, but he rebuked the winds and seas, and all things were calm. Thus it was in a natural way, and will be so in a spiritual one; for no sooner does Jesus Christ speak peace to a troubled soul, but all is calm and quiet. Now none but God could have performed this great miracle, and therefore it is no wonder that his disciples and the men of the ship were amazed to see the wonders he performed; and they could not forbear to express their sense thereof, by inquiring, "What manner of man is this!"

And when he was come to the other side into the country of the Gergesenes, there met him two possessed with devils, coming out of the tombs, exceeding fierce, so that no man might pass by that way. And, behold, they cried out, saying, What have we to do with thee, Jesus, thou Son of God? art thou come hither to torment us before the time?

Two men, who were possessed bodily with that evil one who is going about seeking whom he may devour, met Jesus; as soon as they saw him they were afraid, and cried out: though they made every one afraid of them, yet they no sooner saw Christ, but their power left them, and they cried out, "What have we to do with thee, Jesus, thou Son of God?" We know that thou are God; we do not want thee, we have no power over thee, but thou hast over us, and we fear thou art come to torment us before our time; we know that we are to be brought to judgment, and therefore we would not be tormented until that time come.

And there was a good way off from them an herd of many swine feeding.

So the devils besought him, saying, If thou cast us out, suffer us to go away into the herd of swine.

The evil spirits were sensible that Christ was come to dispossess them, and that their time was now come, when they must leave the bodies of these two men; for when Christ comes, who is stronger than the strong man armed, all must fall before him; they could not stand against the power of Christ. And here we may observe, that though the devil is an enemy, yet he is a chained one; he cannot hurt a poor swine until he has power given him from above: and we may likewise see the malice of the devil, that he would hurt a poor swine rather than do no mischief; and the devil would, if in his power, destroy each of your souls, but Christ, by his mighty power, prevents him.

And he said unto them, Go. And when they were come out, they went into the herd of swine: and, behold, the whole herd of swine ran violently down a steep place into the sea, and perished in the waters. And they that kept them fled, and went their ways into the city, and told every thing, and what was befallen to the possessed of the devils. And, behold, the whole city came out to meet Jesus: and when they saw him, they besought him that he would depart out of their coasts.

Here observe, that no sooner had Christ given the devils permission to enter the swine, but they did, and their malice was so great, that the swine ran violently down a steep place into the sea, and were drowned.

What poor spite was here, that the devil should disturb poor swine!

And the city, therefore, was so grieved for the loss of a little wealth, that they came and besought Christ to depart; they did not want his company; they preferred a few poor swine before the company of Christ; and few worldly good, a little pleasure, or any thing rather than Christ, part with

Christ before any thing; but one, who is sensible of the love of Christ, will part with all, rather than with the Lord Jesus Christ.

Thus far the letter of the story goes; perhaps you think there is nothing to be learned herefrom, and that this is all you are to understand by it; but if so, my brethren, you are much mistaken; for here is an excellent lesson to be learned, and that you will see, by considering the words again, in a spiritual sense.

And, behold, there arose a great tempest in the sea, insomuch that the ship was covered with the waves: but he was asleep.

And do not you frequently experience great tempests in this world?

Does not the sea of temptation beat over your souls? You are afraid lest you should be overcome by them; you can see no way to escape, for your souls are covered with waves, and you expect to be swallowed up in the tempest; you are afraid lest you should fall into the hands of the evil one. O do not fear, for Jesus Christ, though he may be asleep to your thinking, yet will keep you, he will preserve you from the raging of the men, of the Pharisees of this world; they may rage and spit forth all their venom against you, still Christ will deliver, preserve and protect you; if you but seek unto him in a sense of your own helplessness and unworthiness, you will soon find he is a God ready to pardon and forgive. O that all that hear me would be persuaded to bow their knee, and their hearts, as soon as they go home: but alas, how many of our Christians go to God, day by day, and call him, Father, which is but mocking of God, when the devil is their father. None have a right to call him father, but those who have received the spirit of adoption, whereby they have a right to call him, "Abba, Father." Could the brute beasts speak, they might call God father as well as some of you; for hi is their Creator to whom they owe their being; but this will not entitle you to call God father, in a spiritual sense; no, you must be born again of God; however you may flatter yourselves, you must have an inward principle wrought in your hearts by faith. This you must experience, this, this you must feel before you are Christians indeed.

The Lord Jesus Christ takes notice of each of you, you may think the Lord does not take notice of us, because we are in a field, and our of church walls; but he does observe with what view you came this evening to hear his word; he knows whether it was to satisfy your curiosity, or to find out wherewith you might ridicule the preacher. The thoughts and intentions of all your hearts are not hidden from Jesus Christ; though he may seem to be asleep, because you are, at present, insensible of his workings upon your heart, and he may not seem to take notice of you, and regard you, no more than he did the Syrophoenician woman; yet he will turn to you and behold you with live; the Lord will be mindful of you in due time, and speak peace to your troubled soul, though the sea of troubles is beating over you, though the Pharisees of this day are scoffing at you, yet, when Christ rebukes, then they shall cease.

Do not depend on yourself; say unto him, "Save us, Lord, or we perish!" beseech him to be your guide, and your salvation: I beseech you, by the tender mercies of God, which are in Christ Jesus, that you present yourselves to him, as your reasonable service.

Awake, you that sleep, and arise from the dead, from the death of sin, and Christ then will give you the light of his righteousness. Come to Christ and you shall be welcome; O come unto this blessed Jesus, come notwithstanding your vileness; for if you come not you will perish. If Christ does not save you, your own good meaning, your own good intentions cannot; no, as you are in your blood, so you must perish in your blood; but if you come to Christ you will find mercy, you shall not perish. You cannot find salvation in any other but in Christ; if the disciples could have saved themselves, they would not have awoken Jesus Christ; but they were sensible that no one could save them but him; and therefore they cried out unto him; and so you, who are under the sense of sin, who are in fear of hell, if you seek unto your own works, you only seek your own death; for there is no fitness in you. I speak the truth in Christ Jesus, I lie not, there is not fitness in you, but a fitness for eternal damnation; for what are you by nature, but children of wrath, and your hearts are Satan's garrison. Because you have gone to church, said the prayers, gone to the sacrament, and done o one any harm, you speak peace to your souls; and all is in peace you think, and your case is good enough; but indeed, all is a false peace, and if you have no other peace than this, you must shortly lie down in everlasting flames; this is an ungrounded, self-created peace, and if you trust to this peace you will perish.

But do as the disciples did when they were in distress; they go to Christ and say to him, "Lord, save us, we perish." I offer you salvation this day; the door of mercy is not yet shut, there does yet remain a sacrifice for sins, for all that will accept of the Lord Jesus Christ; he only knows the inmost thoughts of thy heart, he will embrace you in the arms of his love; he sees the first risings of grace in you, and would willingly encourage it: the angels long for your being in the love and favor of God; they will rejoice to see you turn from sin unto him. All the ministers of the blessed Jesus would be glad to be instruments to turn you from darkness to light, and from the power of Satan unto God.

And he saith to them, why are ye fearful, O ye of little faith?

And so, my brethren, I may say to you; why are you fearful to leave you sins and turn to God? O turn to him, turn in a sense of your own unworthiness; tell him how polluted you are, how vile, and be not faithless, but believe; do not go in your own strength, and then you need not fear. Why fear ye that the Lord Jesus Christ will not accept of you?

Your sins will be no hindrance, your unworthiness will be no hindrance; if your own corrupt hearts do not keep you back, or if your own good works do not hinder you from coming, nothing will hinder Christ from receiving of you: he loves to see poor sinners coming to him, he is pleased to see them lie at his feet pleading his promises: and if you thus come to Christ, he will not send you away without his Spirit; no, but will receive and bless you.

O do not put a slight on infinite love; what would you have Christ do more? Is it not enough for him to come on purpose to save? Will you not serve God in your souls, as well as with your bodies? If not, you are only deceiving yourselves; and mocking of God; he must have the heart. O ye of little faith, why are ye fearful lest he should not accept of you? If you will not believe me, sure you will believe the Lord Jesus Christ; he has told thee that he will receive you; then why tarry ye, and do not go to him directly? Does he desire impossibilities? It is only, "Give me thy heart;" or, does he want your heart only for the same end as the devil does, to make you miserable? No, he only wants you to believe on him, that you might be saved. This, this, is all the dear Savior desires, to make you happy, that you may leave your sins, to sit down eternally with him, at the marriage supper of the Lamb.

Then he arose and rebuked the winds and the sea, and there was a great calm.

Thus, you see, it was only to the power of Christ to stop the raging of the sea; he rebuked it; the disciples might have spoken for ever, and it would not have ceased; so it is with the word preached; I may preach to you while I live; I may speak till I can speak no more; but the doctrines of Christ will never do you good, unless he impress them upon your hearts; O then, in all thy troubles look up to Christ, that he may rebuke them; and if he speaks the word, then they shall cease. If the Pharisees of this generation scoff and jeer you, if they say all manner of evil against you, do not answer them; leave it unto Christ to rebuke them; for all you can say will be of no more signification, than the disciples speaking to the sea; but when Christ speaks the word, then they shall cease; let it not discourage you, for if you will live godly in Christ Jesus, you must suffer persecution.

It is true, that those who are sincerely good, are set up for marks for every one to shoot at. There is a continual enmity between the seed of the woman and the seed of the serpent; if you were of the world, the world would love its own; but because Christ hath chosen you out of the world, therefore it hateth you.

Do not think of following Christ into glory, unless you go through the press here. Look forward, my brethren, into eternity, and behold Christ coming, and his reward with him, to give a kind recompense for all the temptations and difficulties of this present life.

But the men marveled, saying, What manner of man is this, that even the winds and the seas obey him!

The men of the ship were amazed to see the miracle that Jesus Christ wrought only by his word; they thought he was something more than a man.

And have not we as much reason to admire, that when we are overwhelmed with troubles, from within and without, that Jesus Christ, only by the word of his power, should speak peace, and then there is peace indeed. When God first awakens us with a sense of sin, and sets his terrors in array against us, then there are troubles and tempests; for Satan having got possession, before he will give place, he will fight and strive hard to keep the soul from closing with Jesus. But when Christ comes, he storms the heart, he breaks the peace, he giveth it most terrible alarms of judgment and hell, he sets all in a combustion of fear and sorrow, `till he hath forced it to yield to his mere mercy, and take him for its governor; then Satan is cast out; then the storm is rebuked, and he establishes a firm and lasting peace.

Can the sea be still while the wind is raging? No, it is impossible; so it is that there can be no peace in the soul, while it is at enmity with Christ; indeed, it may flatter itself and speak peace, but there can be no true peace; though thou, O Pharisee, may harden and fortify thy heart against fear, grief, and trouble, yet, as sure as God is true, they will batter down thy proud and fortified spirit, and seize upon it, and drive thee to amazement. This will be done here, or hereafter; here in mercy, or hereafter in wrath and judgment.

O my brethren, consider what Christ hath done, and you will be astonished that he has done so much for such wicked wretches as you and I are. If you are easy under the storm and tempest of sin, and do not cry to Christ for salvation, thou art in a dangerous condition; and it is a wonder to consider, how a man that is not sure of having made his peace with God, can eat, or drink, or live in peace; that thou art not afraid, when thou liest down, that thou should'st awake in hell: but if Christ speak peace unto thy soul, who can then speak trouble? None; no, not men or devils.

Therefore, lie down at the feet of Christ whom you have resisted, and say, Lord, what wouldst thou have me to do? And he will rebuke the winds and seas of thy troubled mind, and all things will be calm.

And when he was come to the other side into the country of the Gergesenes, there met him two possesses with devils, coming out of the tombs, exceeding fierce, so that no man might pass by that way.

The Lord Jesus Christ, who went about doing good continually, very well knew, that he should meet two poor men in this country of the Gergesenes, who were possessed with devils; and Jesus Christ went on purpose that way, that he might relieve them. The devil, where he has the power, never wants will; but as I said before, so I say again, though the devil is an enemy, yet he is a chained one; he could not destroy these two poor men, he could not hurt the people that passed that way, he could only terrify them; and thus it is with you; the devil tries his utmost skill and power to frighten you from coming to the Lord Jesus; he uses the utmost of his endeavors to keep poor sick and weary sinners from coming to Jesus; if he can but make you lose your souls, it is the end he aims at.

And how many souls does he keep from Christ, for fear of reproach?

Many thousands would willingly see Christ in his glory, in the world to come, and would be happy with him there, but they are afraid of being now laughed at, and of hearing the Pharisees say, here is another of his followers; they are afraid of losing their worldly business, or of being counted methodistically mad and fit for bedlam. I doubt not but many are kept from Jesus Christ, for fear of a little of inconveniency.

What will such say, when the Lord Jesus Christ shall appear in his glory? Would you be glad to be confessed by him then, you must now not be ashamed of confessing him before men; let not the fierceness of the devil keep you back from Christ, for fear of being counted fools; for the time will come, when it will be found who are truly wise, and who are truly mad.

Are you afraid to stand up for the cause of Christ in the world? Dare not you be singularly good? Are you afraid of being members of Jesus Christ? I tell you, such persons would crucify him afresh were he in the world. But do not you, my brethren, so learn Christ; let not the temptations of the devil keep you from coming to the Lord Jesus Christ; he may be fierce, he may hurry you from place to place, but strive with him, so that he may not drive you from Christ; and if you seek unto Christ, he will so help you that you shall resist the devil, and then he will fly from you; Christ will dispossess him, be not afraid therefore to meet Jesus Christ; tell him all that your souls want, and he will give it to you; and you shall not be any longer troubled with the fierce outrages of the devil.

And they cried out, saying, what have we to do with thee, Jesus, thou Son of God? Art thou come to torment us before the time?

As soon as the devils observed Jesus coming near, then they were afraid, lest he was come to punish them before that day of accounts, when all must be brought to judgment.

The devils themselves are enough to convince all our polite Arians and Socinians. They here own the Lord Jesus Christ to be God blessed for ever; they feel his power, and are assured of his being the God who must condemn them at the great day of accounts; and they were afraid lest the Lord Jesus Christ was come to punish them now. But though the devils believe the divinity of Christ, yet the world swarms with Arians and Socinians.

The Arians make Christ no more than a titular God, a subordinate deity, one who was more than a man, and yet less than God; that he was a prophet sent from God they own, but deny him to be equal with the Father.

But I hope, my brethren, he is to you, what our creed makes him, God of God, very God of very God, co-eternal and consubstantial with the Father; that as there was not a moment of time in which God the Father was not, so there is not a moment of time in which God the Son was not. For he says himself, "All things were made by him;" and if they were made by him, he must be God; and whoever reads but the word of God, will find divine homage is paid to him, "and that he thought it no robbery to be equal with God;" he is "the Alpha and Omega." These and a great many more places might be brought to prove the divinity of the Lord Jesus Christ; he could never have made satisfaction for our sins if he had not been God as well as Man. As Man he suffered; as God he satisfied; so was God and man in one person; he took our nature upon him, and was offered upon the cross for the sins of all those who come unto him, which if he had not been God he could never have satisfied for. It may be proved, even to a demonstration, that the Lord Jesus Christ is God, and that he is equal with the Father.

The Socinians do not go so far as the others; they look on Christ to be no more than a good man, who told the people their duty, and died in defense of the doctrines which he delivered unto them.

But I hope there are none such here, that have so low and dishonorable thoughts of the blessed Jesus, and that thus despise the divinity of the Lord who bought them. No, I hope better things of you, and things that accompany salvation. Think you, that any one who denies the deity of Christ can ever be saved by him, living and dying in that state? Surely, the time will come, when they who have denied his Deity, shall feel the power of it hereafter; they shall feel that he is God as well as man; then he will be owned as God by all those who now dare to deny his truths; but God forbid it should go undetermined till then! Woe unto the polite infidels of this generation, for the devils will rise up in judgment against them.

If any such are here, consider what you are doing of, before it is too late; return, return ye unto the Lord, and he will have mercy upon you, and to Jesus Christ, and he will abundantly pardon. O my friends, let me beseech you to consider what you are about, lest you fall into hell, and there be none to deliver you.

And the devils besought him, saying, If thou cast us out, suffer us to go away into the herd of swine. And he said unto them, Go. And when they were come out, they went into the herd of swine: and, behold, the whole herd of swine ran violently down a steep place into the sea, and perished in the waters.

Here we may see, that no sooner had the devil power, but he puts it into execution; thus, if the devil has but power to tempt, or to hurry a soul, O how grievous a tyrant he is, hurrying from one temptation to another, from one sin unto another, and would, if it were possible, hurry you all into hell with as much violence, as he did the poor swine into the sea; but Christ by his grace prevents it. Jesus Christ died for souls, and therefore the devil cannot do with them as he will; he may have the will, but he cannot get the power. It is plain, that when the devil himself, or persecuting men, get the power, they will harass the poor Christians; everything is goo good for them, and they are not worthy to be set with the dogs of the flock. My brethren, how joyful would many be, if the laws of our land would permit them to destroy us; how would the Pharisees hurry us to prison and to death; but, blessed be God, he does not say to them, as to the devil, "Go." No, he bids them stay, he hedges their way up with thorns that they cannot stir to hurt us; they would fain, but they dare not destroy us; nothing withholds them but the power of the blessed Jesus. And therefore, be not afraid of their wrath though it is cruel, and of their anger though it be fierce; let them shoot their arrows, even bitter words, against us, blessed be God, the shield of faith will be a preservative against them all.

And when you are thus preserved, it will be the occasion of joy in the Holy Ghost; though many look on the joy of the Holy Ghost as enthusiasm and madness, and say that there is no such thing; but well do I know there is, it carries its own evidence along with it. Plead therefore with God, in the name of Jesus Christ; continue to wrestle with him, until he bestows the blessing upon you, and gives you a feeling of that joy which the world intermeddles not with, and which they are strangers to; indeed the devil may stir up his agents to hurry us from one trouble to another; but it will not signify, for the Lord Jesus Christ will not suffer him to hurry us into hell; no, but will give us his Spirit, which will be a preservative against all the assaults of the devil. Now see what followed this miracle, which Jesus had wrought, by permitting the devil to enter into the herd of swine.

And they that kept them fled, and went their ways into the city, and told every thing, and what was befallen to the possessed of the devils.

The people were so amazed to see the power that Christ had, and the malice with which the devil was possessed, that they were afraid, and told all that had befallen the possessed of the devils; and so, when the spirit of God has been at work on your souls, and you are brought to feel the power of God upon your hearts, you will be so overjoyed that you will tell to every one what great things God has done for your souls; you will be so full of joy, that you will declare the whole working of God on your hearts, and you will declare how you have been enabled to overcome Satan, and how you were affected at such a sermon, in such a place, and at such a time.

You will then love to talk of Jesus; no conversation will be so pleasing as that of the Lord Jesus Christ; no, he will be altogether lovely unto you, when you have once tasted of his love, and felt the power of his grace upon your hearts.

And, behold, the whole city came out to meet Jesus: and when they saw him, they besought him that he would depart out of their coasts.

The whole city came to meet Jesus, not to worship, nor to thank him for the releasing of the two poor men who were possessed; no, but to beseech him to go from them; they valued their swine more than the Lord Jesus Christ, and had rather part from him, than them; and have we not among us, thousands who call themselves Christians, who had rather part with Christ than their pleasures? A play, a ball, or an assembly is far more agreeable to them than the company and presence of the Lord Jesus Christ: if they can but indulge their sensual appetite, please and pamper their bellies, satisfy the lust of the eye, the lust of the flesh, and the pride of life, they regard no more, but rest contented, as if they were to live here always. O my dear brethren, I hope none of you can rest contented with such proceedings as these, but that you like the company of the Lord Jesus too well to part with him for a few delights of this life: and are there not many, who part with Christ for their own good works, and think they can go to heaven, if they do but go to church and say their prayers and take the sacrament? But alas! they will be much deceived, for if they were in any thing short of the Lord Jesus, if they do not make him the chief corner-stone, they will fall infinitely short of what they flattered themselves to attain unto.

I would speak a few words to you before I part from you this evening, by way of application. Let me beseech you to come to Jesus Christ; I invite you all to come to him and receive him as your Lord and Savior; he is ready to receive you; if you are afraid to go because you are in a lost condition, he came to save such; and to such as were weary and heavy laden, such as feel the weight and burden of their sins, he has promised he will give rest: such as feel the weight and burden of their sins on their souls, a burden too heavy for them to bear, are weary of it, and know not how to obtain deliverance of it, in the name of my Lord and master, I invite you to come to him, that you may find rest for your souls.

If you will but come unto him he will not reproach you, as justly he might; he will not reflect upon you for not coming sooner unto him; no, my dear brethren, he will rejoice and be glad, and will say unto you, "Son, daughter, be of good cheer, your sins are forgiven you:" these words he said to others; and if you will but come unto him, by faith in his blood, he is ready to say the same unto you now, as he did to them formerly, for "he is the same to-day, yesterday and for ever:" though he suffered on the cross seventeen hundred years ago, yet he is the same in goodness and power as ever he was.

He calls you, by his ministers; O come unto him, beg of him to break your stubborn hearts, that you may be willing to be brought to him in his own way, to be made poor in spirit, and entitled to an inheritance among them that are sanctified.

O come and drink of the water of life; you may buy without money and without price; he is laboring to bring you back from sin, and from Satan unto himself: open the door of your hearts, and the King of glory shall enter in.

But if you are strangers to this doctrine, and account it foolishness; or, if you think you have enough of your own to recommend you to the favor of God, however you may go to church, or receive the sacrament, you have no true love to the Lord Jesus Christ; you are strangers to the truth of grace in your hearts, and are unacquainted with the new-birth; you do not know what it is to have your natures changed; and 'till you do experience these things, you never can enter into the kingdom of God.

What shall I say, my brethren, unto you? My heart is full, it is quite full, and I must speak, or I shall burst. What, do you think your souls of no value? Do you esteem them as not worth saving? Are your pleasures worth more than your souls? Had you rather regard the diversions of this life, than the salvation of your souls? If so, you will never be partakers with him in glory; but if you come unto him, he will give you a new nature, supply you with his grace here, and bring you to glory hereafter; and there you may sing praises and hallelujahs o the Lamb forever.

And may this be the happy end of all who hear me! may the Lord guide you by his counsel, until he comes to fetch you to heaven, and make you partakers of his glory!

May he direct you in his ways, and lead you in those paths which lead to everlasting life! May you be holy here, and happy hereafter: may your lives answer the profession you make, that we may all be found at the right hand of the Lord Jesus Christ, when he shall come to judge the world according to our works, whether they be good or evil! And that we then may be presented faultless before the presence of his glory with exceeding joy, God of his infinite mercy grant, etc.

Sermon 23 Marks of a True Conversion

Matthew 18:3, "Verily, I say unto you, except ye be converted, and become as little children, ye shall not enter into the kingdom of heaven."

I suppose I may take it for granted, that all of you, among whom I am now about to preach the kingdom of God, are fully convinced, that it is appointed for all men once to die, and that ye all really believe that after death comes the judgment, and that the consequences of that judgment will be, that ye must be doomed to dwell in the blackness of darkness, or ascend to dwell with the blessed God, for ever and ever. I may take it for granted also, that whatever your practice in common life may be, there is not one, though ever so profligate and abandoned, but hopes to go to that place, which the scriptures call Heaven, when he dies. And, I think, if I know any thing of mine own heart, my heart's desire, as well as my prayer to God, for you all, is, that I may see you sitting down in the kingdom of our heavenly Father. But then, though we all hope to go to heaven when we die, yet, if we may judge by people's lives, and our Lord says, "that by their fruits we may know them," I am afraid it will be found, that thousands, and ten thousands, who hope to go to this blessed place after death, are not now in the way to it while they live. Though we call ourselves Christians, and would consider it as an affront put upon us, for any one to doubt whether we were Christians or not; yet there are a great many, who bear the name of Christ, that yet do not so much as know what real Christianity is. Hence it is, that if you ask a great many, upon what their hopes of heaven are founded, they will tell you, that they belong to this, or that, or the other denomination, and part of Christians, into which Christendom is now unhappily divided. If you ask others, upon what foundation they have built their hope of heaven, they will tell you, that they have been baptized, that their fathers and mothers, presented them to the Lord Jesus Christ in their infancy; and though, instead of fighting under Christ's banner, they have been fighting against him, almost ever since they were baptized, yet because they have been admitted to church, and their names are in the Register book of the parish, therefore they will make us believe, that their names are also written in the book of life. But a great many, who will not build their hopes of salvation upon such a sorry rotten foundation as this, yet if they are, what we generally call, negatively good people; if they live so as their neighbors cannot say that they do anybody harm, they do not doubt but they shall be happy when they die; nay, I have found many such die, as the scripture speaks, "without any hands in their death." And if a person is what the world calls an honest moral man, if he does justly, and, what the world calls, love a little mercy, is not and then good-natured, reacheth out his hand to the poor, receives the sacrament once or twice a year, and is outwardly sober and honest; the world looks upon such an one as a Christian indeed, and doubtless we are to judge charitably of every such person. There are many likewise, who go on in a round of duties, a model of performances, that think they shall go to heaven; but if you examine them, though they have a Christ in their heads, they have no Christ in their hearts.

The Lord Jesus Christ knew this full well; he knew how desperately wicked and deceitful men's hearts were; he knew very well how many would go to hell even by the very gates of heaven, how many would climb up even to the door, and go so near as to knock at it, and yet after all be dismissed with a "verily I know you not." The Lord, therefore, plainly tells us, what great change must be wrought in us, and what must be done for us, before we can have any well grounded hopes of entering into the kingdom of heaven.

Hence, he tells Nicodemus, "that unless a man be born again, and from above, and unless a man be born of water and of the Spirit, he cannot enter into the kingdom of God." And of all the solemn declarations of our Lord, I mean with respect to this, perhaps the words of the text are one of the most solemn, "except, (says Christ) ye be converted, and become as little children, ye shall not enter into the kingdom of heaven." The words, if you look back to the context, are plainly directed to the disciples; for we are told, "that at the same time came the disciples unto Jesus." And I think it is plain from many parts of Scripture, that these disciples, to whom our Lord addressed himself at this time, were in some degree converted before.

If we take the words strictly, they are applicable only to those, that have already gotten some, though but weak, faith in Christ. Our Lord means, that though they had already tasted the grace of God, yet there was so much of the old man, so much indwelling sin, and corruption, yet remaining in their hearts, that unless they were more converted than they were, unless a greater change past upon their souls, and sanctification was still carried on, they could give but very little evidence of their belonging to his kingdom, which was not to be set up in outward grandeur, as they supposed, but was to be a spiritual kingdom, begun here, but completed in the kingdom of God hereafter. But though the words had a peculiar reference to our Lord's disciples; yet as our Lord makes such a declaration as this in other places of Scripture, especially in the discourse to Nicodemus, I believe the words may be justly applied to saints and sinners; and as I suppose there are two sorts of people here, some who know Christ, and some of you that do not know him, some that are converted, and some that are strangers to conversion, I shall endeavor so to speak, that if God shall be pleased to assist me, and to give you an hearing ear and an obedient heart, both saints and sinners may have their portion.

FIRST, I shall endeavor to show you in what respects we are to understand this assertion of our Lord's, "that we must be converted and become like little children." I shall then, SECONDLY, Speak to those who profess a little of this child-like temper, And LASTLY, shall speak to you, who have no reason to think that this change has ever past upon your souls. And FIRST, I shall endeavor to show you, what we are to understand by our Lord's saying, "Except ye be converted and become as little children." But I think, before I speak to this point, it may be proper to premise one or two particulars.

1. I think, that the words plainly imply, that before you or I can have any well-grounded, scriptural hope, of being happy in a future state, there must be some great, some notable, and amazing change pass upon our souls. I believe, there is not one adult person in the congregation, but will readily confess, that a great change hath past upon their bodies, since they came first into the world, and were infants dandled upon their mother's knees. It is true, ye have no more members than ye had then, but how are these altered! Though you are in one respect the same ye were, for the number of your limbs, and as to the shape of your body, yet if a person that knew you when ye were in your cradle, had been absent from you for some years, and saw you when grown up, then thousand to one if he would know you at all, ye are so altered, so different from what ye were, when ye were little ones. And as the words plainly imply, that there has a great change past upon our bodies since we were children, so before we can go to heaven, there must as great a change pass upon our souls. Our souls considered in a physical sense are still the same, there is to be no philosophical change wrought on them. But then, as for our temper, habit and conduct, we must be so changed and altered, that those who knew us the other day, when in a state of sin, and before we knew Christ, and are acquainted with us now, must see such an alteration, that they may stand as much amazed at it, as a person at the alteration wrought on any person he has not seen for twenty years from his infancy.

2. But I think it proper to premise something farther, because this text is the grand strong-hold of Arminians, and others. They learn of the devil to bring texts to propagate bad principles: when the devil had a mind to tempt Jesus Christ, because Christ quoted scripture, therefore Satan did so too. And such persons, that their doctrine and bad principles may go down the better, would fain persuade unwary and unstable souls, that they are founded upon

the word of God. Though the doctrine of original sin, is a doctrine written in such legible characters in the word of God, that he who runs may read it; and though, I think, everything without us, and everything within us, plainly proclaims that we are fallen creatures; though the very heathens, who had no other light, but the dim light of unassisted reason, complained of this, for they felt the wound, and discovered the disease, but were ignorant of the cause of it; yet there are too many persons of those who have been baptized in the name of Christ, that dare to speak against the doctrine of original sin, and are angry with those ill-natured ministers, who paint man in such black colors. Say they, "It cannot be that children come into the world with the guild of Adam's sin lying upon them." Why? Desire them to prove it from Scripture, and they will urge this very text, our Lord tells us, "Except ye be converted, and become as little children, ye shall not enter into the kingdom of heaven." Now their argument runs thus, "It is implied in the words of the text, that little children are innocent, and that they come into the world like a mere blank piece of white paper, otherwise our Lord must argue absurdly, for he could never pretend to say, that we must be converted, and be made like wicked creatures; that would be no conversion." But, my dear friends, this is to make Jesus Christ speak what he never intended, and what cannot be deduced from his words. That little children are guilty, I mean, that they are conceived and born in sin, is plain from the whole tenor of the book of God. David was a man after God's own heart, yet, says he, "I was conceived in sin." Jeremiah speaking of every one's heart, says, "the heart of man is deceitful and desperately wicked above all things." God's servants unanimously declare, (and Paul cites it from one of them) "that we are altogether now become abominable, altogether gone out of the way of original righteousness, there is not one of us that doeth good (by nature), no not one." And I appeal to any of you that are mothers and fathers, if ye do not discern original sin or corruption in your children, as soon as they come into the world; and as they grow up, if ye do not discover self-will, and an aversion to goodness. What is the reason your children are so averse to instruction, but because they bring enmity into the world with them, against a good and gracious God? So then, it is plain from scripture and fact, that children are born in sin, and consequently that they are children of wrath. And for my part, I think, that the death of every child is a plain proof of original sin; sickness and death came into the world by sin, and it seems not consistent with God's goodness and justice, to let a little child be sick or die, unless Adam's first sin was imputed to him. If any charge God with injustice for imputing Adam's sin to a little child, behold we have gotten a second Adam, to bring our children to him.

Therefore, when our Lord says, "unless ye are converted, and become as little children," we are not to understand, as though our Lord would insinuate, that little children are perfectly innocent; but in a comparative, and as I shall show you by and by, in a rational sense. Little children are innocent, compare them with grown people; but take them as they are, and as they come into the world, they have hearts that are sensual, and minds which are carnal. And I mention this with the greatest concern, because I verily believe, unless parents are convinced of this, they will never take proper care of their children's education. If parents were convinced, that children's hearts were so bad as they are, you would never be fond of letting them go to balls, assemblies, and plays, the natural tendency of which is to debauch their minds, and make them the children of the devil. If parents were convinced of this, I believe they would pray more, when they bring their children to be baptized, and would not make it a mere matter of form. And I believe, if they really were convinced, that their children were conceived in sin, they would always put up that petition, before their children came into the world, which I have heard that a good woman always did put up, "Lord Jesus, let me never bear a child for hell or the devil." O! is it not to be feared, that thousands of children will appear, at the great day, before God, and in presence of angels and men will say, Father and mother, next to the wickedness of mine own heart, I owe my damnation to your bad education of me.

Having premised these two particulars, I now proceed to show in what sense we are really to understand the words, that we must be converted and become like little children. The Evangelist tell us, "that the disciples at this time came unto Jesus, saying, Who is the greatest in the kingdom of heaven?" These disciples had imbibed the common prevailing notion, that the Lord Jesus Christ was to be a temporal prince; they dreamed of nothing but being ministers of state, of sitting on Christ' right hand in his kingdom, and lording it over God's people; they thought themselves qualified for state offices, as generally ignorant people are apt to conceive of themselves. Well, say they, "Who is the greatest in the kingdom of heaven?" Which of us shall have the chief management of public affairs? A pretty question for a few poor fishermen, who scarcely knew how to drag their nets to shore, much less how to govern a kingdom. Our Lord, therefore, in the 2nd verse, to mortify them, calls a little child, and sets him in the midst of them. This action was as much as if our Lord had said, "Poor creatures!

Your imaginations are very towering; you dispute who shall be greatest in the kingdom of heaven; I will make this little child preach to you, or I will preach to you by him. Verily I say unto you, (I who am truth itself, I know in what manner my subjects are to enter into my kingdom; I say unto you, ye are so far from being in a right temper for my kingdom, that) except ye be converted, and become as this little child, ye shall not enter into the kingdom of heaven, (unless ye are, comparatively speaking, as loose to the world, as loose to crowns, scepters, and kingdoms, and earthly things, as this poor little child I have in my hand) ye shall not enter into my kingdom." So that what our Lord is speaking of, is not the innocency of little children, if you consider the relation they stand in to God, and as they are in themselves, when brought into the world; but what our Lord means is, that as to ambition and lust after the world, we must in this sense become as little children. Is there never a little boy or girl in this congregation? Ask a poor little child, that can just speak, about a crown, scepter, or kingdom, the poor creature has no notion about it: give a little boy or girl a small thing to play with, it will leave the world to other people. Now in this sense we must be converted, and become as little children; that is, we must be as loose to the world, comparatively speaking, as a little child.

Do not mistake me, I am not going to persuade you to shut up your shops, or leave your business; I am not going to persuade you, that if ye will be Christians, ye must turn hermits, and retire out of the world; ye cannot leave your wicked hearts behind you, when you leave the world; for I find when I am alone, my wicked heart has followed me, go where I will. No, the religion of Jesus is a social religion. But though Jesus Christ does not call us to go out of the world, shut up our shops, and leave our children to be provided for by miracles; yet this must be said to the honor Christianity, if we are really converted, we shall be loose from the world.

Though we are engaged in it, and are obliged to work for our children; though we are obliged to follow trades and merchandise, and to be serviceable to the commonwealth, yet if we are real Christians, we shall be loose to the world; though I will not pretend to say that all real Christians have attained to the same degree of spiritual-mindedness. This is the primary meaning of these words, that we must be converted and become as little children; nevertheless, I suppose the words are to be understood in other senses.

When our Lord says, we must be converted and become as little children, I suppose he means also, that we must be sensible of our weakness, comparatively speaking, as a little child. Every one looks upon a little child, as a poor weak creature; as one that ought to go to school and learn some new lesson every day; and as simple and artless; one without guile, having not learned the abominable art, called dissimulation. Now in all these senses, I believe we are to understand the words of the text. _ Are little children sensible of their weakness? Must they be led by the hand? Must we take hold of them or they will fall? So, if we are converted, if the grace of God be really in our hearts, my dear friends, however we may have thought of ourselves once, whatever were our former high exalted imaginations; yet we shall now be sensible of our weakness; we shall no more say, "We are rich and increased with goods, and lack nothing;" we shall be inwardly poor; we shall feel "that we are poor, miserable, blind, and naked." And as a little child gives up its hand to be guided by a parent or a nurse, so those who are truly converted, and are real Christians, will give up the heart, their understandings, their wills, their affections, to be guided by the word, providence, and the Spirit of the Lord. Hence it is, that the Apostle, speaking of the sons of God, says, "As many as are led by the Spirit of God, they are (and to be sure he means they only are) the sons of God." And as little children look upon themselves to be ignorant creatures, so those that are converted, do look upon themselves as ignorant too. Hence it is, that John, speaking to Christians, calls them little children; "I have written unto you, little children." And Christ's flock is called a little flock, not only because little in number, but also because those who are members of his flock, are indeed little in their own eyes. Hence that great man, that great apostle of the Gentiles, that spiritual father of so many thousands of souls, that man, who in the opinion of Dr. Goodwin, "fits nearest the God-man, the Lord Jesus Christ, in glory," that chosen vessel, the Apostle Paul, when he speaks of himself, says, "Unto me, who am less than the least of all saints, is this grace given, that I should preach among the Gentiles the unsearchable riches of Christ." Perhaps some of you, when you read these words, will be apt to think that Paul did not speak true, that he did not really feel what he said; because you judge Paul's heart by your own proud hearts: but the more ye get of the grace of God, and the more ye are partakers of the divine life, the more will ye see your own meanness and vileness, and be less in your own eyes. Hence it is, that Mr. Flavel, in his book called, HUSBANDRY SPIRITUALIZED, compares young Christians to green corn; which before it is ripe, shoots up very high, but there is little solidity in it: whereas, an old Christian is like ripe corn; it doth not lift up its head so much, but then it is more weighty, and fit to be cut down, and put into the farmer's barn. Young Christians are also like little rivulets; ye know rivulets are shallow, yet make great noise; but an old Christian, he makes not much noise, he goes on sweetly, like a deep river sliding into the ocean.

And as a little child is looked upon as an harmless creature, and generally speaks true; so, if we are converted, and become as little children, we shall be guileless as well as harmless. What said the dear Redeemer when he saw Nathaniel? As though it was a rare sight he gazed upon, and would have others gaze upon it; "Behold an Israelite indeed:" Why so? "In whom is no guile." Do not mistake me; I am not saying, that Christians ought not to be prudent; they ought exceedingly to pray to God for prudence, otherwise they may follow the delusions of the devil, and by their imprudence give wrong touches to the ark of God. It was the lamentation of a great man, "God has given me many gifts, but God has not given me prudence." Therefore, when I say, a Christian must be guileless, I do not mean, he should expose himself, and lie open to every one's assault: we should pray for the wisdom of the serpent, though we shall generally learn this wisdom by our blunders and imprudence: and we must make some advance in Christianity, before we know our imprudence. A person really converted, can say, as it is reported of a philosopher, "I wish there was a window in my breast, that every one may see the uprightness of my heart and intentions:" And though there is too much of the old man in us, yet, if we are really converted, there will be in us no allowed guile, we shall be harmless. And that is the reason why the poor

Christian is too often imposed upon; he judgeth other people by himself; having an honest heart, he thinks every one as honest as himself, and therefore is a prey to every one. I might enlarge upon each of these points, it is a copious and important truth; but I do not intend to multiply many marks and heads.

And therefore, as I have something to say by way of personal application, give me leave therefore, with the utmost tenderness, and at the same time with faithfulness, to call upon you, my dear friends. My text is introduced in an awful manner, "Verily I say unto you;" and what Jesus said then, he says now to you, to me, and to as many as sit under a preached gospel, and to as many as the Lord our God shall call. Let me exhort you to see whether ye are converted; whether such a great and almighty change has passed upon any of your souls. As I told you before, so I tell you again, ye all hope to go to heaven, and I pray God Almighty ye may be all there: when I see such a congregation as this, if my heart is in a proper frame, I feel myself ready to lay down my life, to be instrumental only to save one soul. It makes my heart bleed within me, it makes me sometimes most unwilling to preach, lest that word that I hope will do good, may increase the damnation of any, and perhaps of a great part of the auditory, through their own unbelief. Give me leave to deal faithfully with your souls. I have your dead warrant in my hand: Christ has said it, Jesus will stand to it, it is like the laws of the Medes and Persians, it altereth not. Hark, O man! Hark, O woman! He that hath ears to hear, let him hear what the Lord Jesus Christ says, "Verily I say unto you, except ye be converted, and become as little children, ye shall not enter into the kingdom of heaven." Though this is Saturday night, and ye are now preparing for the Sabbath, for what you know, you may yet never live to see the Sabbath. You have had awful proofs of this lately; a woman died but yesterday, a man died the day before, another was killed by something that fell from a house, and it may be in twenty-four hours more, many of you may be carried into an unalterable state. Now then, for God's sake, for your own souls sake, if ye have a mind to dwell with God, and cannot bear the thought of dwelling in everlasting burning, before I go any further, silently put up one prayer, or say Amen to the prayer I would put in your mouths; "Lord, search me and try me, Lord, examine my heart, and let my conscience speak; O let me know whether I am converted or not!" What say ye, my dear hearers? What say ye, my fellow-sinners? What say ye, my guilty brethren? Has God by his blessed Spirit wrought such a change in your hearts? I do not ask you, whether God has made you angels? That I know will never be; I only ask you, Whether ye have any well-grounded hope to think that God has made you new creatures in Christ Jesus? So renewed and changed your natures, that you can say, I humbly hope, that as to the habitual temper and tendency of my mind, that my heart is free from wickedness; I have a husband, I have a wife, I have also children, I keep a shop, I mind my business; but I love these creatures for God' sake, and do every thing for Christ: and if God was now to call me away, according to the habitual temper of my mind, I can say, Lord, I am ready; and however I love the creatures, I hope I can say, Whom have I in heaven but thee? Whom have I in heaven, O my God and my dear Redeemer, that I desire in comparison of thee?

Can you thank God for the creatures, and say at the same time, these are not my Christ? I speak in plain language, you know my way of preaching: I do not want to play the orator, I do not want to be counted a scholar; I want to speak so as I may reach poor people's hearts. What say ye, my dear hearers? Are ye sensible of your weakness? Do ye feel that ye are poor, miserable, blind, and naked by nature? Do ye give up your hearts, your affections, your wills, your understanding to be guided by the Spirit of God, as a little child gives up its hand to be guided by its parent? Are ye little in your own eyes? Do ye think meanly of yourselves? And do you want to learn something new every day? I mention these marks, because I am apt to believe they are more adapted to a great many of your capacities. A great many of you have not that showing of affection ye sometimes had, therefore ye are for giving up all your evidences, and making way for the devil's coming into your heart. You are not brought up to the mount as ye used to be, therefore ye conclude ye have no grace at all. But if the Lord Jesus Christ has emptied thee, and humbled thee, if he is giving thee to se and know that thou art nothing; though thou are not growing upward, thou art growing downward; and though thou hast not so much joy, yet thy heart is emptying to be more abundantly replenished by and by. Can any of you follow me? Then, give God thanks, and take the comfort of it.

If thou art thus converted, and become a little child, I welcome thee, in the name of the Lord Jesus, into God's dear family; I welcome thee, in the name of the dear Redeemer, into the company of God's children. O ye dear souls, though the world sees nothing in you, though there be no outward difference between you and others, yet I look upon you in another light, even as so many kings sons and daughters: all hail! In the name of God, I wish every one of you joy from my soul, ye sons and daughters of the King of kings. Will not you henceforth exercise a child-like temper? Will not such a thought melt down your hearts, when I tell you, that the great God, who might have frowned you to hell for your secret sins, that nobody knew of but God and your own souls, and who might have damned you times without number, hath cast the mantle of his love over you; his voice hath been, Let that man, that woman live, for I have found a ransom. O will ye not cry out, Why me, Lord? Was King George to send for any of your children, and were you to hear they were to be his adopted sons, how highly honored would you think your children to be? What great condescension was it for Pharaoh's daughter to take up Moses, a poor child exposed in an ark of bulrushes, and bred him up for her child? But what is that happiness in comparison of thine, who was the other day a child of the devil, but now by converting grace art become a child of God? Are ye converted? Are ye become like little children? Then what must ye do? My dear hearers, be obedient to God, remember God is your father; and as every one of you must know what a dreadful cross it is to have a wicked, disobedient child; if ye do not want your children to be disobedient to you, for Christ's sake be not disobedient to your heavenly parent. If God be your father, obey him: if God be your father, serve him; love him with all your heart, love him with all your might, with all your soul, and with all your strength. If God be your father, fly from everything that may displease him; and walk worthy of that God, who has called you to his kingdom and glory. If ye are converted and become like little children, then behave as little children: they long for the breast, and with it will be contented. Are ye new-born babes? Then desire the sincere milk of the word, that ye may grow thereby. I do not want that Arminian husks should go down with you; ye are kings sons and daughters, and have a more refined taste; you must have the doctrines of grace; and blessed be God that you dwell in a country, where the sincere word is so plainly preached. Are ye children? Then grow in grace, and in the knowledge of your Lord and Savior Jesus Christ. Have any of you children that do not grow? Do not ye lament these children, and cry over them; do not ye say, my child will never be fit for anything in the world?

Well, doth it grieve you to see a child that will not grow; how much must it grieve the heart of Christ to see you grow so little? Will ye be always children? Will ye be always learning the first principles of Christianity, and never press forward toward the mark, for the prize of the high calling of God in Christ Jesus? God forbid. Let the language of your heart be, "Lord Jesus help me to grow, help me to learn more, learn me to live so as my progress may be known to all!" Are ye God's children? Are ye converted, and become like little children? Then deal with God as your little children do with you; as soon as ever they want any thing, or if any body hurt them, I appeal to yourselves if they do not directly run to their parent. Well, are ye God's children? Doth the devil trouble you? Doth the world trouble you? Go tell your father of it, go directly and complain to God. Perhaps you may say, I cannot utter fine words: but do any of you expect fine words from your children? If they come crying, and can speak but half words, do not your hearts yearn over them? And has not God unspeakably more pity to you? If ye can only make signs to him; "As a father pitieth his children, so will the Lord pity them that fear him." I pray you therefore be gold with your Father, saying, "Abba, Father," Satan troubles me, the world troubles me, my own mother's children are angry with me; heavenly Father, plead my cause! The Lord will then speak for you some way or other.

Are ye converted, and become as little children, have ye entered into God's family? Then assure yourselves, that your heavenly father will chasten you now and then: "for what son is there whom the father chasteneth not: if ye are without chastisement, of which all are partakers, then are ye bastards and not sons." It is recorded of bishop Latimer, that in the house where he came to lodge, he overheard the master of the house say, I thank God I never had a cross in my life: O said he, then I will not stay here. I believe there is not a child of God, when in a good frame, but has prayed for great humility; they have prayed for great faith, they have prayed for great love, they have prayed for all the graces of the Spirit: Do ye know, when ye put us these prayers, that ye did also say, Lord send us great trials: for how is it possible to know ye have great faith, humility and love, unless God put you into great trials, that ye may know whether ye have them or not. I mention this, because a great many of the children of God (I am sure it has been a temptation to me many times, when I have been under God's smarting rod) when they have great trials, think God is giving them over. If therefore ye are God's children; if ye are converted and become as little children; do not expect that God will be like a foolish parent; no, he is a jealous God, he loves his child too well to spare his rod. How did he correct Miriam? How did he correct Moses? How hath God in all ages corrected his dearest children? Therefore if ye are converted, and become as little children, if God hath taken away a child, or your substance, if God suffers friends to forsake you, and if you are forsaken as it were both by God and man, say, Lord I thank thee! I am a perverse child, or God would not strike me so often and so hard. Do not blame your heavenly Father, but blame yourselves; he is a loving God, and a tender Father, "he is afflicted in all our afflictions:" therefore when God spake to Moses, he spake out of the bush, as much as to say, "Moses, this bush represents my people; as this bush is burning with fire, so are my children to burn with affliction; but I am in the bush; if the bush burns, I will burn with it, I will be with them in the furnace, I will be with them in the water, and though the water come over them, it shall not overflow them." Are ye God's children? Are ye converted and become as little children?

Then will ye not long to go home and see your Father? O happy they that have gotten home before you; happy they that are up yonder, happy they who have ascended above this field of conflict. I know not what you may think of it, but since I heard that some, whose hearts God was pleased to work upon, are gone to glory, I am sometimes filled with grief, that God is not pleased to let me go home too. How can you see so much coldness among God's people? How can ye see God's people like the moon, waxing and waning? Who can but desire to be forever with the Lord? Thanks be to God, the time is soon coming; thanks be to God, he will come and will not tarry. Do not be impatient, God in his own time will fetch you home. And though ye may be brought to short allowance now, though some of you may be narrow in your circumstances, yet do not repine; a God, and the gospel of Christ, with brown bread, are great riches. In thy Father's house there is bread enough and to spare; though thou are now tormented, yet by and by thou shalt be comforted; the angels will look upon it as an honor to convey thee to Abraham's bosom, though thou are but a Lazarus here. By the frame of my heart, I am much inclined to speak comfortably to God's people.

But I only mention one thing more, and that is, if ye are converted, and become as little children, then for God's sake take care of doing what children often do; they are too apt to quarrel one with another. O love one another; "he that dwells in love dwells in God, and God in him." Joseph knew that his brethren were in danger of falling out, therefore when he left them, says he, "fall not out by the way." Ye are all children of the same Father, ye are all going to the same place; why should ye differ? The world has enough against us, the devil has enough against us, without our quarreling with each other; O walk in love. If I could preach no more, if I was not able to hold out to the end of my sermon, I would say as John did, when he was grown old and could not preach, "Little children, love one another:" if ye are God's children, then love one another. There is nothing grieves me more, than the differences amongst God's people. O hasten that time, when we shall either go to heaven, or never quarrel any more!

Would to God I could speak to all of you in this comfortable language; but my master tells me, I must "not give that which is holy to dogs, I must not cast pearls before swine;" therefore, though I have been speaking comfortably, yet what I have been saying, especially in this latter part of the discourse, belongs to children; it is children's bread, it belongs to God's people. If any of you are graceless, Christless, unconverted creatures, I charge you not to touch it, I fence it in the name of God; here is a flaming sword turning every way to keep you from this bread of life, till ye are turned to Jesus Christ. And therefore, as I suppose many of you are unconverted, and graceless, go home! And away to your closets, and down with your stubborn hearts before God; if ye have not done lit before, let this be the night. Or, do not stay till ye go home; begin now, while standing here; pray to God, and let the language of thy heart be, Lord convert me! Lord make me a little child, Lord Jesus let me not be banished from thy kingdom! My dear friends, there is a great deal more implied in the words, than is expressed: when Christ says, "Ye shall not enter into the kingdom of heaven," it is as much to say, "ye shall certainly go to hell, ye shall certainly be damned, and dwell in the blackness of darkness for ever, ye shall go where the worm dies not, and where the fire is not quenched." The Lord God impress it upon your souls!

May an arrow (as one lately wrote me in a letter) dipped in the blood of Christ, reach every unconverted sinner's heart! May God fulfill the text to every one of your souls! It is he alone that can do it. If ye confess your sins, and leave them, and lay hold on the Lord Jesus Christ, the Spirit of God shall be given you; if you will go and say, turn me, O my God! Thou knowest not, O man, what the return of God may be to thee. Did I think that preaching would be to the purpose, did I think that arguments would induce you to come, I would continue my discourse till midnight. And however some of you may hate me without a cause, would to God every one in this congregation was as much concerned for himself, as at present (blessed be God) I feel myself concerned for him. O that my head were waters, O that mine eyes were a fountain of tears, that I might weep over an unconverted, graceless, wicked, and adulterous generation. Precious souls, for God's sake think what will become of you when ye die, if you die without being converted; if ye go hence without the wedding garment, God will strike you speechless, and ye shall be banished from his presence for ever and ever. I know ye cannot dwell with everlasting burnings; behold then I show you a way of escape; Jesus is the way, Jesus is the truth, the Lord Jesus Christ is the resurrection and the live. It is his Spirit must convert you, come to Christ, and ye shall have it; and may God for Christ's sake give it to you all, and convert you, that we may all meet, never to part again, in his heavenly kingdom; even so Lord Jesus, Amen and Amen.

Sermon 24 What think ye of Christ?

Matthew 22:42, "What think ye of Christ?"

When it pleased the eternal Son of God to tabernacle among us, and preach the glad tidings of salvation to a fallen world, different opinions were entertained by different parties concerning him. As to his person, some said he was Moses; others that he was Elias, Jeremias, or one of the ancient prophets; few acknowledged him to be what he really was, God blessed for evermore. And as to his doctrine, though the common people, being free from prejudice, were persuaded of the heavenly tendency of his going about to do good, and for the generality, heard him gladly, and said he was a good man; yet the envious, worldly-minded, self-righteous governors and teachers of the Jewish church, being grieved at his success on the one hand, and unable (having never been taught of God) to understand the purity of his doctrine, on the other; notwithstanding our Lord spake as never man spake, and did such miracles which no man could possibly do, unless God was with him; yet they not only were so infatuated, as to say, that he deceived the people; but also were so blasphemous as to affirm, that he was in league with the devil himself, and cast out devils by Beeluzbul, the prince of devils. Nay, our Lord's own brethren and kinsmen, according to the flesh, were so blinded by prejudices and unbelief, that on a certain day; when he went out to teach the multitudes in the fields, they sent to take hold of him, urging this as a reason for their conduct, "That he was besides himself." Thus was the King and the Lord of glory judged by man's judgment, when manifest in flesh: far be it from any of his ministers to expect better treatment. No, if we come in the spirit and power of our Master, in this, as in every other part of his sufferings, we must follow his steps. The like reproaches which were cast on him, will be thrown on us also. Those that received our Lord and his doctrine, will receive and hear us for his name's sake. The poor, blessed be God, as our present meeting abundantly testifies, receive the gospel, and the common people hear us gladly; whilst those who are sitting in Moses' chair, and love to wear long robes, being ignorant of the righteousness which is of God by faith in Christ Jesus, and having never felt the power of God upon their hearts, will be continually crying our against us, as madmen, deceivers of the people, and as acting under the influence of evil spirits.

But he is unworthy the name of a minister of the gospel of peace, who is unwilling, not only to have his name cast out as evil, but also to die for the truths of the Lord Jesus. It is the character of hirelings and false prophets, who care not for the sheep, to have all men speak well of them. "Blessed are you, (says our Lord to his first apostles, and in them to all succeeding ministers) when men speak all manner of evil against you falsely for my name's sake." And indeed it is impossible but such offenses must come; for men will always judge of others, according to the principles from which they act themselves. And if they care not to yield obedience to the doctrines which we deliver, they must necessarily, in self-defense, speak against the preachers, lest they should be asked that question, which the Pharisees of old feared to have retorted on them, if they confessed that John was a prophet, "Why then did you not believe on him?" In all such cases, we have nothing to do but to search our own hearts, and if we can assure our consciences, before God, that we act with a single eye to his glory, we are cheerfully to go on in our work, and not in the least to regard what men or devils can say against, or do unto us.

But to return. You have heard what various thoughts there were concerning Jesus Christ, whilst here on earth; nor is he otherwise treated, even now he is exalted to sit down at the right hand of his Father in heaven. A stranger to Christianity, were he to hear, that we all profess to hold one Lord, would naturally infer, that we all thought and spoke one and the same thing about him. But alas! to our shame be it mentioned, though Christ be not divided in himself, yet professors are sadly divided in their thoughts about him; and that not only as to the circumstances of his religion, but also of those essential truths which must necessarily be believed and received by us, if ever we hope to be heirs of eternal salvation.

Some, and I fear a multitude which no man can easily number, there are amongst us, who call themselves Christians, and yet seldom or never seriously think of Jesus Christ at all. They can think of their shops and their farms, their plays, their balls, their assemblies, and horse-races (entertainments which directly tend to exclude religion out of the world); but as for Christ, the author and finisher of faith, the Lord who has bought poor sinners with his precious blood, and who is the only thing worth thinking of, alas! he is not in all, or at most in very few of their thoughts. But believe me, O ye earthly, sensual, carnally-minded professors, however little you may think of Christ now, or however industriously you may strive to keep him out of your thoughts, by pursuing the lust of the eye, the lust of the flesh, and the pride of life, yet there is a time coming, when you will wish you had thought of Christ more, and of your profits and pleasures less. For the gay, the polite, the rich also must die as well as others, and leave their pomps and vanities, and all their wealth behind them. And O! what thoughts will you entertain concerning Jesus Christ, in that hour?

But I must not purpose these reflections: they would carry me too far from the main design of this discourse, which is to show, what those who are truly desirous to know how to worship God in spirit and in truth, ought to think concerning Jesus Christ, whom God hath sent to be the end of the law for righteousness to all them that shall believe.

I trust, my brethren, you are more noble than to think me too strict or scrupulous, in thus attempting to regulate your thoughts about Jesus Christ: for by our thoughts, as well as our words and actions, are we to be judged at the great day. And in vain do we hope to believe in, or worship Christ aright, unless our principles, on which our faith and practice are founded, are agreeable to the form of sound words delivered to us in the scriptures of truth.

Besides, many deceivers are gone abroad into the world. Mere heathen morality, and not Jesus Christ, is preached in most of our churches. And how should people think rightly of Christ, of whom they have scarcely heard? Bear with me a little then, whilst, to inform your consciences, I ask you a few questions concerning Jesus Christ. For there is no other name given under heaven, whereby we can be saved, but his.

FIRST, What think you about the person of Christ? "Whose Son is he?" This is the question our Lord put to the Pharisees in the words following the text; and never was it more necessary to repeat this question than in these last days. For numbers that are called after the name of Christ, and I fear, many that pretend to preach him, are so far advanced in the blasphemous chair, as openly to deny his being really, truly, and properly God. But no one that ever was partaker of his Spirit, will speak thus lightly of him. No; if they are asked, as Peter and his brethren were, "But whom say ye that I am?" they will reply without hesitation, "Thou art Christ the Son of the ever-living God." For the confession of our Lord's divinity, is the rock upon which he builds his church. Was it possible to take this away, the gates of hell would quickly prevail against it. My brethren, if Jesus Christ be not very God of very God, I would never preach the gospel of Christ again. For it would not be gospel; it would be only a system of moral ethics. Seneca, Cicero, or any of the Gentile philosophers, would be as good a Savior as Jesus of Nazareth. It is the divinity of our Lord that gives a sanction to his death, and makes him such a high-priest as became us, one who by the infinite mercies of his suffering could make a full, perfect sufficient sacrifice, satisfaction and oblation to infinitely offended justice. And whatsoever minister of the church of England, makes use of her forms, and eats of her bread, and yes holds not this doctrine (as I fear too many such are crept in amongst us) such a one belongs only to the synagogue of Satan. He is not a child or minister of God: no; he is a wolf in sheep's clothing; he is a child and minister of that wicked one the devil.

Many will think these hard sayings; but I think it no breach of charity to affirm, that an Arian or Socinian cannot be a Christian. The one would make us believe Jesus Christ is only a created God, which is a self- contradiction: and the other would have us look on him only as a good man; and instead of owning his death to be an atonement for the sins of the world, would persuade us, that Christ died only to seal the truth of hid doctrine with his blood. But if Jesus Christ be no more than a mere man, if he be not truly God, he was the vilest sinner that ever appeared in the world. For he accepted of divine adoration from the man who had been born blind, as we read John 9:38, "And he said, Lord I believe, and he worshipped him." Besides, if Christ be not properly God, our faith is vain, we are yet in our sins: for no created being, though of the highest order, could possibly merit anything at God' s hands; it was our Lord's divinity, that alone qualified him to take away the sins of the world; and therefore we hear St. John pronouncing so positively, that "the Word (Jesus Christ) was not only with God, but was God." For the like reason, St. Paul says, "that he was in the form of God: That in him dwelt all the fullness of the godhead bodily." Nay, Jesus Christ assumed the title which God gave to himself, when he sent Moses to deliver his people Israel. "Before Abraham was, I AM." And again, "I and my father are one." Which last words, though our modern infidels would evade and wrest, as they do other scriptures, to their own damnation, yet it is evident that the Jews understood our Lord, when he spoke thus, as making himself equal with God; otherwise, why did they stone him as a blasphemer? And now, why should it be thought a breach of charity, to affirm, that those who deny the divinity of Jesus Christ, in the strictest sense of the word, cannot be Christians? For they are greater infidels than the devils themselves, who confessed that they knew who he was, "even the holy one of God." They not only believe, but, which is more than the unbelievers of this generation do, they tremble. And was it possible for arch-heretics, to be released from their chains of darkness, under which (unless they altered their principles before they died) they are now reserved to the judgment of the great day, I am persuaded they would inform us, how hell had convinced them of the divinity of Jesus Christ, and that they would advise their followers to abhor their principles, lest they should come into the same place, and thereby increase each others torments.

But, SECONDLY, What think you of the manhood or incarnation of Jesus Christ? For Christ was not only God, but he was God and man in one person.

Thus runs the text and context, "When the Pharisees were gathered together, Jesus asked them, saying, What think ye of Christ? Whose Son is he? They say unto him, The Son of David. How then, says our divine master, does David in spirit call him Lord?" From which passage it is evident, that we do not think rightly of the person of Jesus Christ, unless we believe him to be perfect God and perfect man, or a reasonable soul and human flesh subsisting.

For it is on this account that he is called Christ, or the anointed one, who through his own voluntary offer was set apart by the father, and strengthened and qualified by the anointing or communication of the Holy Ghost, to be a mediator between Him and offending man.

The reason why the Son of God took upon him our nature, was, the fall of our first parents. I hope there is no one present so atheistical, as to think, that man made himself; no, it was God that made us, and not we ourselves. And I would willingly think, that no one is so blasphemous as to suppose, that if God did make us, he made us such creatures as we now find ourselves to be. For this would be giving God's word the lie, which tells us, that "in the image of God (not in the image which we now bear on our souls) made he man." As God made man, so God made him perfect. He placed him in the garden of Eden, and condescended to enter into a covenant with him, promising him eternal life, upon condition of unsinning obedience; and threatening eternal death, if he broke his law, and did eat the forbidden fruit.

Man did eat; and herein acting as our representative, thereby involved both himself and us in that curse, which God, the righteous judge, had said should be the consequence of his disobedience. But here begins that mystery of godliness, God manifested in the flesh. For (sing, O heavens, and rejoice, O earth!) the eternal Father, foreseeing how Satan would bruise the heel of man, had in his eternal counsel provided a means whereby he might bruise that accursed Serpent's head. Man is permitted to fall, and become subject to death; but Jesus, the only begotten Son of God, begotten of the Father before all worlds, Light of light, very God of very God, offers to die to make an atonement for his transgression, and to fulfill all righteousness in his stead. And because it was impossible for him to do this as he was God, and yet since man had offended, it was necessary it should be done in the person of man; rather than we should perish, this everlasting God, this Prince of Peace, this Ancient of Days, in the fullness of time, had a body prepared for him by the Holy Ghost, and became an infant. In this body he performed a complete obedience to the law of God; whereby he, in our stead, fulfilled the covenant of works, and at last became subject to death, even death upon the cross; that as God he might satisfy, as man he might obey and suffer; and being God and man in one person, might once more procure a union between God and our souls.

And now, What think you of this love of Christ? Do not you think it was wondrous great? Especially when you consider, that we were Christ's bitter enemies, and that he would have been infinitely happy in himself, notwithstanding we had perished forever. Whatever you may think of it, I know the blessed angels, who are not so much concerned in this mystery of godliness as we, think most highly of it. They do, they will desire to look into, and admire it, through all eternity. Why, why O ye sinners, will you not think of this love of Christ? Surely it must melt down the most hardened heart. Whilst I am speaking, the thought of this infinite and condescending love fires and warms my soul. I could dwell on it for ever.

But it is expedient for you, that I should ask you another question concerning Jesus Christ.

THIRDLY, What think you about being justified by Christ? I believe I can answer for some of you; for many, I fear, think to be justified or looked upon as righteous in God's sight, without Jesus Christ. But such will find themselves dreadfully mistaken; for out of Christ, "God is a consuming fire." Others satisfy themselves, with believing that Christ was God and man, and that he came into the world to save sinners in general; whereas, their chief concern ought to be, how they may be assured that Jesus Christ came into the world to save them in particular. "The life that I now live in the flesh, (says the Apostle) is by faith of the Son of God, who loved me, and gave himself for me." Observe, FOR ME: it is this immediate application of Jesus Christ to our own hearts; and that they can be justified in God's sight, only in or through him: but then they make him only in part a savior. They are for doing what they can themselves, and then Jesus Christ is to make up the deficiencies of their righteousness.

This is the sum and substance of our modern divinity. And was it possible for me to know the thoughts of most that hear me this day, I believe they would tell me, this was the scheme they had laid, and perhaps depended on for some years, for their eternal salvation. Is it not then high time, my brethren, for you to entertain quite different thoughts concerning justification by Jesus Christ? For if you think thus, you are in the case of those unhappy Jews, who went about to establish their own righteousness, and would not submit to, and consequently missed of that righteousness which is of God by faith in Christ Jesus our Lord. What think you then, if I tell you, that you are to be justified freely through faith in Jesus Christ, without any regard to any work or fitness foreseen in us at all?

For salvation is the free gift of God, I know no fitness in man, but a fitness to be cast into the lake of fire and brimstone for ever. Our righteousnesses, in God's sight, are but as filthy rags; he cannot away with them. Our holiness, if we have any, is not the cause, but the effect of our justification in God's sight. "We love God, because he first loved us." We must not come to God as the proud Pharisee did, bringing in as it were a reckoning of our services; we must come in the temper and language of the poor Publican, smiting upon our breasts, and saying, "God be merciful to me a sinner;" for Jesus Christ justifies us whilst we are ungodly. He came not to call the righteous, but sinners to repentance. The poor in spirit only, they who are willing to go out of themselves, and rely wholly on the righteousness of another, are so blessed as to be members of his kingdom. The righteousness, the whole righteousness of Jesus Christ, is to be imputed to us, instead of our own: ""or we are not under the law, but under grace; and to as many as walk after this rule, peace be on them;" for they, and they only are the true Israel of God. In the great work of man" redemption, boasting is entirely excluded; which could not be, if only one of our works was to be joined with the merits of Christ. Our salvation is all of God, from the beginning to the end; it is not of works, lest any man should boast; man has no hand in it: it is Christ who is to be made to us of God the Father, wisdom, righteousness, sanctification, and eternal redemption. His active as well as his passive obedience, is to be applied to poor sinners. He has fulfilled all righteousness in our stead, that we might become the righteousness of God in him. All we have to do, is to lay hold on this righteousness by faith; and the very moment we do apprehend it by a lively faith, that very moment we may be assured, that the blood of Jesus Christ has cleansed us from all sin. "For the promise is to us and to our children, and to as many as the Lord our God shall call." If we and our whole houses believe, we shall be saved as well as the jailer and his house; for the righteousness of Jesus Christ is an everlasting, as well as a perfect righteousness. It is as effectual to all who believe in him now, as formerly; and so it will be, till time shall be no more. Search the scriptures, as the Bereans did, and see whether these things are not so.

Search St. Paul's epistles to the Romans and Galatians, and there you will find this doctrine so plainly taught you, that unless you have eyes and see not, he that runs may read. Search the Eleventh Article of our Church: "We are accounted righteous before God, only for the merits of our Lord and Savior Jesus Christ by faith, and not for our own works or deservings." This doctrine of our free justification by faith in Christ Jesus, however censured and evil spoken of by our present Masters of Israel, was highly esteemed by our wise fore-fathers; for in the subsequent words of the aforementioned article, it is called a most WHOLESOME DOCTRINE, and very full of comfort; and so it is to all that are weary and heavy laden, and are truly willing to find rest in Jesus Christ.

This is gospel, this is glad tidings of great joy to all that feel themselves poor, lost, undone, damned sinners. "Ho, every one that thirsteth, come unto the waters of life, and drink freely; come and buy without money and without price." Behold a fountain opened in your Savior's side, for sin and for all uncleanness. "Look unto him whom you have pierced;" look unto him by faith, and verily you shall be saved, though you came here only to ridicule and blaspheme, and never thought of God or of Christ before.

Not that you must think God will save you because, or on account of your faith; for faith is a work, and then you would be justified for your works; but when I tell you, we are to be justified by faith, I mean that faith is the instrument whereby the sinner applies or brings home the redemption of Jesus Christ to his heart. And to whomsoever God gives such a faith, (for it is the free gift of God) he may lift up his head with boldness, he need not fear; he is a spiritual son of our spiritual David; he is passed from death to life, he shall never come into condemnation.

This is the gospel which we preach. If any man or angel preach any other gospel, than this of our being freely justified through faith in Christ Jesus, we have the authority of the greatest Apostle, to pronounce him accursed.

And now, my brethren, what think you of this foolishness of preaching?

To you that have tasted the good word of life, who have been enlightened to see the riches of God's free grace in Christ Jesus, I am persuaded it is precious, and has distilled like the dew into your souls. And O that all were like-minded! But I am afraid, numbers are ready to go away contradicting and blaspheming. Tell me, are there not many of you saying within yourselves, "This is a licentious doctrine; this preacher is opening a door for encouragement in sin." But this does not surprise me at all, it is a stale, antiquated objection, as old a the doctrine of justification itself; and (which by the way is not much to the credit of those who urge it now) it was made by an infidel. St. Paul, in his epistle to the Romans, after he had, in the first five chapters, demonstrably proved the doctrine of justification by faith alone; in the sixth, brings in an unbeliever saying, "Shall we continue in sin then, that grace may abound?" But as he rejected such an inference with a "God forbid!" so do I: for the faith which we preach, is not a dead speculative faith, an assenting to things credible, as credible, as it is commonly defined: it is not a faith of the head only, but a faith of the heart. It is a living principle wrought in the soul, by the Spirit of the ever-living God, convincing the sinner of his lost, undone condition by nature; enabling him to apply and lay hold on the perfect righteousness of Jesus Christ, freely offered him in the gospel, and continually exciting him, out of a principle of love and gratitude, to show forth that faith, by abounding in every good word and work. This is the sum and substance of the doctrine that has been delivered. And if this be a licentious doctrine, judge ye. No, my brethren, this is not destroying, but teaching you how to do good works, from a proper principle. For to use the words of our Church in another of her Articles, "Works done before the grace of Christ, and the inspiration of the Spirit, are not pleasant to God, forasmuch as they spring not of faith in Jesus Christ; rather, for that they are not done as God has willed and commanded them to be done, we doubt not but they have the nature of sin." So that they who bid you do, and then live, are just as wise as those who would persuade you to build a beautiful magnificent house, without laying a foundation.

It is true, the doctrine of our free justification by faith in Christ Jesus, like other gospel truths, may and will be abused by men of corrupt minds, reprobates concerning the faith; but they who receive the truth of God in the love if it, will always be showing their faith by their works.

For this reason, St. Paul, after he had told the Ephesians, "By grace they were saved through faith, not of works, lest any man should boast," immediately adds, "For we are his workmanship, created in Christ Jesus unto good works." And in his epistle to Titus, having given him directions to tell the people they were justified by grace, directly subjoins, chap. 3, ver. 8, "I will that you affirm constantly, that they who have believed in God might be careful to maintain good works." Agreeable to this, we are told in our Twelfth Article, "That albeit good works, which are the fruits of faith, and follow after justification, cannot put away our sins, and endure the severity of God's judgment; yet are they pleasing and acceptable to God in Christ; and do spring necessarily out of a true and lively faith, insomuch, that a lively faith may be as evidently known by them, as a tree discerned by the fruit." What would I give, that this Article was duly understood and preached by all that have subscribed to it! The ark of the Lord would not then be driven into the wilderness, nor would so many persons dissent from the Church of England. For I am fully persuaded, that it is not so much on account of rites and ceremonies, as our not preaching the truth as it is in Jesus, that so many have been obliged to go and seek for food elsewhere.

Did not we fall from our established doctrines, few, comparatively speaking, would fall from the Established Church. Where Christ is preached, though it be in a church or on a common, dissenters of all denominations have, and do must freely come. But if our clergy will preach only the law, and not show the way of salvation by faith in Christ, the charge of schism at the day of judgment, I fear, will chiefly lie at their door. The true sheep of Christ know the voice of Christ's true shepherds, and strangers they will not hear.

Observe, my dear brethren, the words of the Article, "Good works are the fruits of faith, and follow after justification." How then can they precede, or be any way the cause of it? Our persons must be justified, before our performances can be accepted. God had respect to Abel before he had respect to his offering; and therefore the righteousness of Jesus Christ must be freely imputed to, and apprehended by us through faith, before we can offer an acceptable sacrifice to God: for out of Christ, as I hinted before, God is a consuming fire: and whatsoever is not of faith in Christ, is sin.

That people mistake the doctrine of free justification, I believe, is partly owing to their not rightly considering the different persons to whom St. Paul and St. James wrote in their epistles; as also the different kind of justification each of them writes about. The former affects in line upon line, argument upon argument, "That we are justified by faith alone:" The latter put this question, "Was not Abraham justified by works?" From whence many, not considering the different views of these holy men, and the different persons they wrote to, have blended and joined faith and works, in order to justify us in the sight of God. But this is a capital mistake; for St. Paul was writing to the Jewish proselytes, who sought righteousness by the works, not of the ceremonial only, but of the moral law. In contradistinction to that, he tells them, they were to look for justification in God's sight, only by the perfect righteousness of Jesus Christ apprehended by faith. St. James had a different set of people to deal with; such who abused the doctrines of free justification, and thought they should be saved (as numbers among us do now) upon their barely professing to believe on Jesus Christ. These the holy Apostle endeavors wisely to convince, that such a faith was only a dead and false faith; and therefore, it behooved all who would be blessed with faithful Abraham, to show forth their faith by their works, as he did. "For was not Abraham justified by works?" Did he not prove that his faith was a true justifying faith, by its being productive of good works? From whence it is plain, that St. James is talking of a declarative justification before men; show me, demonstrate, evidence to me, that thou hast a true faith, by thy works.

Whereas, St. Paul is talking only of our being justified in the sight of God; and thus he proves, that Abraham, as we also are to be, was justified before ever the moral or ceremonial law was given to the Jews, for it is written, "Abraham believed in the Lord, and it was accounted to him for righteousness." Take the substance of what has been said on this head, in the few following words. Every man that is saved, is justified three ways: FIRST, MERITORIOUSLY, by the death of Jesus Christ: "It is the blood of Jesus Christ alone that cleanses us from all sin." SECONDLY, INSTRUMENTALLY, by faith; faith is the means or instrument whereby the merits of Jesus Christ are applied to the sinner's heart: "Ye are all the children of God by faith in Christ Jesus." THIRDLY, we are justified DECLARATIVELY; namely, by good works; good works declare and prove to the world, that our faith is a true saving faith. "Was not Abraham justified by works?" And again, "Show me thy faith by thy works." It may not be improper to illustrate this doctrine by an example or two. I suppose no one will pretend to say, that there was any fitness for salvation in Zaccheus the publican, when he came to see Jesus out of no better principle, than that whereby perhaps thousands are led to hear me preach; I mean, curiosity: but Jesus Christ prevented and called him by his free grace, and sweetly, but irresistibly inclined him to obey that call; as, I pray God, he may influence all you that come only to see who the preacher is. Zaccheus received our Lord joyfully into his house, and at the same time by faith received him into his heart; Zaccheus was then freely justified in the sight of God. But behold the immediate fruits of that justification! He stands forth in the midst and as before he had believed in his heart, he now makes confession with his mouth to salvation: "Behold, Lord, the half of my goods I give unto the poor; and if I have taken any thing from any man by false accusation, I restore him four-fold." And thus it will be with thee, O believer, as soon as ever God's dear Son is revealed in thee by a living faith; thou wilt have no rest in thy spirit, till out of love and gratitude for what God has done for thy soul, thou showest forth thy faith by thy works.

Again, I suppose every body will grant there was no fitness for salvation in the persecutor Saul; no more than there is in those persecuting zealots of these last days, who are already breathing out threatenings, and, if in their power, would breathe out slaughter also, against the disciples of the Lord.

Now our Lord, we know, freely prevented him by his grace, (and O that he would thus effectually call the persecutors of this generation) and by a light from heaven struck him to the ground. At the same time, by his Spirit, he pricked him to the heart, convinced him of sin, and caused him to cry out, "Who art thou, Lord?" Christ replies, "I am Jesus whom thou persecutest." Faith then was instantaneously given to him, and behold, immediately Saul cries out, "Lord, what wouldst thou have me to do?" And so will every poor soul that believes on the Lord Jesus with his whole heart.

He will be always asking, Lord, what shall I do for thee? Lord, what wouldst thou have me to do? Not to justify himself, but only to evidence the sincerity of his love and thankfulness to his all-merciful High-priest, for plucking him as a firebrand out of the fire.

Perhaps many self-righteous persons amongst you, may flatter yourselves, that you are not so wicked as either Zaccheus or Saul was, and consequently there is a greater fitness for salvation in you than in them.

But if you think thus, indeed you think more highly of yourselves than you ought to think: for by nature we are all alike, all equally fallen short of the glory of God, all equally dead in trespasses and sins, and there needs the same almighty power to be exerted in converting any one of the most so-ber, good-natured, moral persons here present, as there was in converting the publican Zaccheus, or that notorious persecutor Saul. And was it possible for you to ascend into the highest heaven, and to inquire of the spirits of just men made perfect, I am persuaded they would tell you this doctrine is from God. But we have a more sure word of prophecy, to which we do well to give heed, as unto a light shining in a dark place. My brethren, the word is nigh you; search the scriptures; beg of God to make you willing to be saved in this day of his power; for it is not flesh and blood, but the Spirit of Jesus Christ, that alone can reveal these things unto you.

FOURTHLY and LASTLY, What think you of Jesus Christ being formed within you? For whom Christ justifies, them he also sanctifies. Al-though he finds, yet he does not leave us unholy. A true Christian may not so properly be said to live, as Jesus Christ to live in him. For they only that are led by the Spirit of Christ, are the true sons of God.

As I observed before, so I tell you again, the faith which we preach is not a dead, but a lively active faith wrought in the soul, working a thorough change, by the power of the Holy Ghost, in the whole man; and unless Christ be thus in you, notwithstanding you may be orthodox as to the foregoing principles, notwithstanding you may have good desires, and attend constantly on the means of grace; yet, in St. Paul's opinion, you are out of a state of sal-vation. "Know you not, (says that Apostle to the Corinthians, a church famous for its gifts above any church under heaven) that Christ is in you, (by his Spirit) unless you are reprobates?" For Christ came not only to save us from the guilt, but from the power of our sins; till he has done this, however he may be a Savior to others, we can have no assurance of well-grounded hope, that he has saved us; for it is by receiving his blessed Spirit into our hearts, and feeling him witnessing with our spirits, that we are the sons of God, that we can be certified of our being sealed to the day of redemption.

This is a great mystery; but I speak of Christ and the new-birth.

Marvel not at my asking you, what you think about Christ being formed within you? For either God must change his nature, or we ours. For as in Adam we all have spiritually died, so all that are effectually saved by Christ, must in Christ be spiritually made alive. His only end in and rising again, and interceding for us now in heaven, is to redeem us from the misery of our fallen nature, and, by the operation of his blessed Spirit, to make us meet to be partakers of the heavenly inheritance with the saints in light. None but those that thus are changed by his grace here, shall appear with him in glory hereafter.

Examine yourselves, therefore, my brethren, whether you are in the faith; prove yourselves; and think it not sufficient to say in your creed, I believe in Jesus Christ; many say so, who do not believe, who are reprobates, and yet in a state of death. You take God's name in vain, when you call him Father, and your prayers are turned into sin, unless you believe in Christ, so as to have your life hid with him in God, and to receive life and nourishment from him, as branches do from the vine.

I know, indeed, the men of this generation deny there is any such thing as feeling Christ within them; but alas! to what a dreadful condition would such reduce us, even to the state of the abandoned heathen, who, St.

Paul tells us, "were past feeling." The Apostle prays, that the Ephesians may abound in all knowledge and spiritual understanding, or as it might be rendered, spiritual sensation. And in the office for the visitation of the sick, the minister prays, that the Lord may make the sick person know and feel, that there is not other name under heaven given unto men, in whom and through whom they may receive health and salvation, but only the name of our Lord Jesus. For there is a spiritual, as well as a corporeal feeling; and though this is not communicated to us in a sensible manner, as outward objects affect our senses, yet it is as real as any sensible or visible sensation, and may be as truly felt and discerned by the soul, as any impression from without can be felt by the body. All who are born again of God, know that I lie not.

What think you, Sirs, did Naaman feel, when he was cured of his leprosy? Did the woman feel virtue coming out of Jesus Christ, when she touched the hem of his garment, and was cured of her bloody issue? So surely mayst thou feel, O believer, when Jesus Christ dwelleth in thy heart. I pray God to make you all know and feel this, ere you depart hence.

O my brethren, my heart is enlarge towards you. I trust I feel something of that hidden, but powerful presence of Christ, whilst I am preaching to you. Indeed it is sweet, it is exceedingly comfortable. All the harm I wish you, who without cause are my enemies, is, that you felt the like. Believe me, though it would be hell to my soul, to return to a natural state again, yet I would willingly change status with you for a little while, that you might know what it is to have Christ dwelling in your hearts by faith. Do not turn your backs; do not let the devil hurry you away; be not afraid of convictions; do not think worse of the doctrine, because preached without the church walls. Our Lord, I the days of his flesh, preached on a mount, in a ship, and a field; and I am persuaded, many have felt his gracious presence here. Indeed we speak what we know. Do not reject the kingdom of God against yourselves; be so wise as to receive our witness. I cannot, I will not let you go; stay a little, let us reason together. However lightly you may esteem your souls, I know our Lord has set an unspeakable value on them. He thought them worthy of his most precious blood. I beseech you, therefore, O sinners, be ye reconciled to God. I hope you do not fear being accepted in the beloved. Behold, he calleth you; behold, he prevents and follows you with his mercy, and hath sent forth his servants unto the highways and hedges, to compel you to come in. Remember then, that at such an hour of such a day, in such a year, in this place, you were all told what you ought to think concerning Jesus Christ. If you now perish, it will not be for lack of knowledge: I am free from the blood of you all. You cannot say I have been preaching damnation to you; you cannot say I have, like legal preachers, been requiring you to make brick without straw. I have not bidden you to make yourselves saints, and then come to God; but I have offered you salvation on as cheap terms as you can desire. I have offered you Christ's whole wisdom, Christ's whole righteousness, Christ's whole sanctification and eternal redemption, if you will but believe on him. If you say, you cannot believe, you say right; for faith, as well as every other blessing, is the gift of God; but then wait upon God, and who knows but he may have mercy on thee? Why do we not entertain more loving thoughts of Christ? Or do you think he will have mercy on others, and not on you? But are you not sinners? And did not Jesus Christ come into the world to save sinners? If you say you are the chief of sinners, I answer, that will be no hindrance to your salvation, indeed it will not, if you lay hold on him by faith. Read the Evangelists, and see how kindly he behaved to his disciples who fled from and denied him: "Go tell my brethren," says he. He did not say, Go tell those traitors; but, "Go tell my brethren in general, and poor Peter in particular, "that I am risen;" O comfort his poor drooping heart, tell him am reconciled to him; bit him weep no more so bitterly: for though with and curses he thrice denied me, yet I have died for his sins, I am risen again for his justification: I freely forgive him all. Thus slow to anger, and of great kindness, was our all-merciful High-priest. And do you think he has changed his nature, and forgets poor sinners; now he is exalted to the right hand of God? No, he is the same yesterday, today, and forever, and sitteth there only to make intercession for us. Come then, ye harlots, come ye publicans, come ye most abandoned of sinners, come and believe on Jesus Christ. Though the whole world despise you and cast you out, yet he will not disdain to take you up. O amazing, O infinitely condescending love! even you, he will not be ashamed to call his brethren. How will you escape if you neglect such a glorious offer of salvation? What would the damned spirits, now in the prison of hell, give, if Christ was so freely offered to their souls?

And why are not we lifting up our eyes in torments? Does any one out of this great multitude dare say, he does not deserve damnation? If not, why are we left, and others taken away by death? What is this but an instance of God's free grace, and a sign of his good will towards us? Let God's goodness lead us to repentance! O let there be joy in heaven over some of you repenting! Though we are in a field, I am persuaded the blessed angels are hovering now around us, and do long, "as the hart panteth after the water-brooks," to sing an anthem at your conversion. Blessed be God, I hope their joy will be fulfilled. An awful silence appears amongst us. I have good hope that the words which the Lord has enabled me to speak in your ears this day, have not altogether fallen to the ground. Your tears and deep attention, are an evidence, that the Lord God is amongst us of a truth. Come, ye Pharisees, come and see, in spite of your satanical rage and fury, the Lord Jesus is getting himself the victory. And brethren, I speak the truth in Christ, I lie not, if one soul of you, by the blessing of God, be brought to think savingly of Jesus Christ this day, I care not if my enemies were permitted to carry me to prison, and put my feet fast in the stocks, as soon as I have delivered this sermon. Brethren, my heart's desire and prayer to God is, that you may be saved. For this cause I follow my Master without the camp. I care not how much of his sacred reproach I bear, so that some of you be converted from the errors of your ways. I rejoice, yea and I will rejoice. Ye men, ye devils, do your worst: the Lord who sent, will support me. And when Christ, who is our life, and whom I have now been preaching, shall appear, I also, together with his despised little ones, shall appear with him in glory. And then, what will you think of Christ? I know what you will think of him. You will then think him to be the fairest among ten thousand: You will then think and feel him to be a just and sin-avenging judge. Be ye then persuaded to kiss him lest he be angry, and so you be banished for ever from the presence of the Lord.

Behold, I come to you as the angel did to Lot. Flee, flee, for your lives; haste, linger no longer in your spiritual Sodom, for otherwise you will be eternally destroyed. Numbers, no doubt, there are amongst you, that may regard me no more than Lot's sons-in-law regarded him. I am persuaded I seem t some of you as one that mocketh: but I speak the truth in Christ, I lie not; as sure as fire and brimstone was rained from the Lord out of heaven, to destroy Sodom and Gomorrah, so surely, at the great day, shall the vials of God's wrath be poured on you. If you do not think seriously of, and act agreeable to the gospel of the Lord's Christ. Behold, I have told you before; and I pray God, all you that forget him may seriously think of what has been said, before he pluck you away, and there be none to deliver you.

Now to God the Father, etc

Sermon 25 The Wise and Foolish Virgins

Matthew 25:13 "Watch therefore, for ye know neither the day nor the hour in which the Son of man cometh."

(Text is actually Matt. 25:1-13)

The apostle Paul, in his epistle to the Hebrews, informs us, "That it is appointed for all men once to die; after that is the judgment." And I think, if any consideration be sufficient to awaken a sleeping drowsy world, it must be this, That there will be a day wherein these heavens shall be wrapped up like a scroll, this element melt with fervent heat, the earth and all things therein be burnt up, and every soul, of every nation and language, summoned to appear before the dreadful tribunal of the righteous Judge of quick and dead, to receive rewards and punishments, according to the deeds done in their bodies. The great apostle just mentioned, when brought before Felix, could think of no better means to convert that sinful man, than to reason to temperance, righteousness, and more especially of a judgment to come. The first might in some measure affect, but, I am persuaded, it was the last consideration, a judgment to come, that made him to tremble: and so bad as the world is now grown, yet there are few have their consciences so far seared, as to deny that there will be a reckoning hereafter. The promiscuous dispensations of providence in this life, wherein we see good men afflicted, destitute, tormented, and the wicked permitted triumphantly to ride over their heads, has been always looked upon as an indisputable argument, by the generality of men, that there will be a day in which God will judge the world in righteousness, and administer equity unto his people. Some indeed are so bold as to deny it, while they are engaged in the pursuit of the lust of the eye, and the pride of life. But follow them to their death bed, ask them, when their souls are ready to launch into eternity, what they then think of a judgment to come and they will tell you, they dare not give their consciences the lie any longer. They feel a fearful looking for of judgment and fiery indignation in their hearts. Since then these things are so, does it not highly concern each of us, my brethren, before we come on a bed of sickness, seriously to examine how the account stands between God and our souls, and how it will fare with us in that day? As for the openly profane, the drunkard, the whoremonger, the adulterer, and such-like, there is no doubt of what will become of them; without repentance they shall never enter into the kingdom of God and his Christ: no; their damnation slumbereth not; a burning fiery Tophet, kindled by the fury of God's eternal wrath, is prepared for their reception, wherein they must suffer the vengeance of eternal fire. Nor is there the least doubt of the state of true believers. For though they are despised and rejected of natural men, yet being born again of God, they are heirs of God, and joint heirs with Christ. They have the earnest of the promised inheritance in their hearts, and are assured that a new and living way is made open for them, into the holy of holies, by the blood of Jesus Christ, into which an abundant entrance shall be administered to them at the great day of account. The only question is, what will become of the ALMOST CHRISTIAN, one that is content to go, as he thinks, in a middle way to heaven, without being profane on the one hand, or, as he falsely imagines, righteous over-much on the other? Many there are in every congregation, and consequently some here present, of this stamp. And what is worst of all, it is more easy to convince the most notorious publicans and sinners of their being out of a state of salvation, than any of these.

Notwithstanding, if Jesus Christ may be our judge, they shall as certainly be rejected and disowned by him at the last day, as though they lived in open defiance of all his laws. For what says our Lord in the parable of which the words of the text are a conclusion, and which I intend to make the subject of my present discourse. "Then," at the day of judgment, which he had been discoursing of in the foregoing, and prosecutes in this chapter, "shall the kingdom of heaven, (the state of professors in the gospel church) be likened unto ten virgins, who took their lamps, and went forth to meet the bridegroom." In which words, is a manifest allusion to a custom prevailing in our Lord's time among the Jews, at marriage solemnities, which were generally at night, and at which it was customary for the persons of the bride-chamber to go out in procession, with many lights, to meet the bridegroom. By the bridegroom, you are here to understand Jesus Christ. The church, i.e. true believers, are his Israel; he is united to them by one spirit, even in this life; but the solemnizing of their sacred nuptials, is reserved till the day of judgment, when he shall come to take them home to himself, and present them before men and angels, as his purchase, to his Father, without spot or wrinkle, or any such thing. By the ten virgins we are to understand, the professors of Christianity in general. All are called virgins, because all are called to be saints. Whosoever names the name of Christ, is obliged by that profession to depart from all iniquity. But the pure and chaste in heart, are the only persons that will be blessed as to see God. As Christ was born of a virgin, so he can dwell in none but virgins souls, made pure and holy by the cohabitation of his holy Spirit. What says the apostle? "All are not Israel that are of Israel," all are not Christians that are called after the name of Christ: No, says our Lord, in the 2nd verse, "Five of those virgins were wise," true believers, "and five were foolish," formal hypocrites. But why are five said to be wise, and the other five foolish?

Hear what our Lord says in the following verses; "They that were foolish took their lamps, and took no oil with them: but the wise took oil in their vessels with their lamps." They that were foolish took their lamps of an outward profession. They would go to church, say over several manuals of prayers, come perhaps into a field to hear a sermon, give at a collection, and receive the sacrament constantly, nay, oftener than once a month. But then here lay the mistake; they had no oil in their lamps, no principle of grace, no living faith in their hearts, without which, though we should give all our goods to feed the poor, and our bodies to be burnt, it would profit us nothing. In short, they were exact, nay, superstitious bigots as to the form, but all the while they were strangers to, and, in effect, denied the power of godliness in their hearts. They would go to church, but at the same time, think it no harm to go to a ball or an assembly, notwithstanding they promised at their baptism, to renounce the pomps and vanities of this wicked world. They were so exceedingly fearful of being righteous over-much, that they would even persecute those that were truly devout, if they attempted to go a step farther than themselves. In one word, they never effectually felt the power of the world to come. They thought they might be Christians without so much inward feeling, and therefore, notwithstanding their high pretensions, had only a name of live.

And now, Sirs, let pause a while, and in the name of God, whom I endeavor to serve in the gospel of his dear Son, give me leave to ask one question. Whilst I have been drawing, though in miniature, the character of these foolish virgins, have not many of your consciences made the application, and with a small, still, though articulate voice, said, Thou man, thou woman, art one of those foolish virgins, for thy sentiments and practice agree thereto? Stifle not, but rather encourage these convictions; and who knows, but that Lord who is rich in mercy to all that call upon him faithfully, may so work upon you even by this foolishness of preaching, as to make you wise virgins before you return home?

What they were you shall know immediately: "But the wise took oil in their vessels with their lamps." Observe, the wise, the true believers, had their lamps as well as the foolish virgins; for Christianity does not require us to cast off all outward forms; we may use forms, and yet not be formal: for instance, it is possible to worship God in a set form of prayer, and yet worship him in spirit and in truth. And therefore, brethren, let us not judge one another. The wise virgins had their lamps; herein did not lie the difference between them and the foolish, that one worshipped God with a form, and the other did not: No: as the Pharisee and Publican went up to the temple to pray, so these wise and foolish virgins might go to the same place of worship, and sit under the same ministry; but then the wise took oil in their vessels with their lamps; they kept up the form, but did not rest in it; their words in prayer were the language of their hearts, and they were no strangers to inward feelings; they were not afraid of searching doctrines, nor affronted when ministers told them they deserved to be damned; they were not self-righteous, but were willing that Jesus Christ should have all the glory of their salvation; they were convinced that the merits of Jesus Christ were to be apprehended only by faith; but yet were they as careful to maintain good works, as though they were to be justified by them: in short, their obedience flowed from love and gratitude, and was cheerful, constant, uniform, universal, like that obedience which the holy angels pay our Father in heaven.

Here then let me exhort you to pause again; and if any of you can faithfully apply these characters to your hearts, give God the glory, and take the comfort to your own souls; you are not false but true believers.

Jesus Christ has been made of God to you wisdom, even that wisdom, whereby you shall be made wise unto salvation. God sees a difference between you and foolish virgins, if natural men will not. You need not be uneasy, though one chance and fate in this may happen to you both. I say, once chance and fate; for, ver. 5 "while the bridegroom tarried," in the space of time which passed between our Lord's ascension and his coming again to judgment, "they all slumbered and slept." The wise as well as foolish died, for dust we are, and to dust we must return. It is no reflection at all upon the divine goodness, that believers, as well as hypocrites, must pass through the valley of the shadow of death; for Christ has taken away the sting of death, so that we need fear no evil. It is to them a passage to everlasting life: death is only terrible to those who have no hope, because they live without faith in the world. Whosoever there are amongst you, that have received the first-fruits of the spirit, I am persuaded you are ready to cry out, we would not live here always, we long to be dissolved, that we may be with Jesus Christ; and though worms must destroy our bodies as well as others, yet we are content, being assured that our Redeemer liveth, that he will stand at the latter days upon the earth, and that in our flesh we shall see God.

But it is not so with hypocrites and unbelievers beyond the grave; for what says our Lord? "And at midnight:" observe, at midnight, when all was hushed and quiet, and no one dreaming of any such thing, "a cry was made;" the voice of the arch-angel and the trump of God was heard sounding this general alarm; to things in heaven, to things in earth, and to things in the waters under the earth, "Behold!" mark how this awful summons is ushered in with the word BEHOLD, to engage our attention? "Behold the bridegroom cometh!" even Jesus Christ, the desire of nations, the bridegroom of his spouse the church: Because he tarried for a while to exercise the faith of saints, and give sinners space to repent, scoffers were apt to cry out, "Where is the promise of his coming? But the Lord is not slack concerning his promise, as these men account slackness." For behold, he that was to come, now cometh, and will not tarry any longer: he cometh to be glorified in his saints, and to take vengeance on them that know not God, and have not obeyed his gospel: he cometh not as a poor despised Galilean; not be laid in a stinking manger; not to be despised and rejected of men; not to be blindfolded, spit upon, and buffeted; not to be nailed to an accursed tree; he cometh not as the Son of man, but as he really was, the eternal Son of the eternal God: He cometh riding on the wings of the wind, in the glory of the Father and his holy angels, and to be had in everlasting reverence of all that shall be round about him. 'Go ye forth to meet him;" arise, ye dead, ye foolish, as well as wise virgin, arise and come to judgment. Multitudes, not doubt, that hear this awakening cry, would rejoice if the rocks might fall on, and the hills cover them from the presence of the Lamb: what would they give, if as they lived as beasts, they might now die like the beasts that perish? How would they rejoice, if those same excuses which they made on this side eternity for not attending on holy ordinances, would serve to keep them from appearing before the heavenly bridegroom! But as Adam, notwithstanding his fig- leaves, and the trees of the garden, could not hide himself from God, when arrested with an "Adam, where art thou?" So now the decree is gone forth, and the trump of God has given its last sound; all tongues, people, nations, and languages, both wise and foolish virgins, must come into his presence, and bow beneath his footstool; even Pontius Pilate, Annas and Caiaphas; even the proud persecuting high-priests and Pharisees of this generation, must appear before him: for says our Lord, "then, (when the cry was made, Behold, the bridegroom cometh!) in a moment, in the twinkling of an eye, the graves were opened, the sea gave up its dead, and "all those virgins, both wise and foolish, arose and trimmed their lamp," or endeavored to put themselves in a proper posture to meet the bridegroom.

But how may we imagine the foolish virgins were surprised, when, notwithstanding their high thoughts and proud imaginations of their security, they now find themselves wholly naked, and void of that inward holiness and purity of heart, without which no man living at that day shall comfortably meet the Lord! I doubt not, but may of these foolish virgins, whilst in this world, were clothed in purple and fine linen, fared sumptuously every day, and disdained to set the wise virgins, some of whom might be as poor as Lazarus, even with the dogs of their flock. These were looked upon by them as enthusiasts and madmen, as persons that were righteous over- much, and who intended to turn the world upside down: but now death hath opened their eyes, and convinced them, to their eternal sorrow, that he is not a true Christian, who is only one outwardly. Now they find (though, alas! too late) they, and not the wise virgins, had been beside themselves.

Now their proud hearts are made to stoop, their lofty looks are brought low; and as Dives entreated that Lazarus might dip the tip of his finger in water, and be sent to cool his tongue, so these foolish virgins, these formal hypocrites, are obliged to turn beggars to those whom they once despised: "Give us of your oil;" O! impart to us a little of that grace and holy spirit, for the insisting on which we fools accounted your lives madness; for alas! "our lamps are gone out;" we had only the form of godliness; we were whited sepulchers; we were heart-hypocrites; we contented ourselves with desiring to be good; and though confident of salvation whilst we lived, yet our hope is entirely gone, now God has taken away our souls: Give us therefore, O! give us, though we once despised you, give us of your oil, for our lamps of an outward profession, and transient convictions, are quite gone out. "Comfort ye, comfort ye, my people, saith the Lord." My brethren in Christ, hear what the foolish say to the wise virgins, and learn in patience to possess your souls. If you are true followers of the lowly Jesus, I am persuaded you have your names cast out, and all manner of evil spoken falsely against you, for his name's sake; for no one ever did or will live godly in Christ Jesus, without suffering persecution; nay, I doubt not but your chief foes are those of your own household: tell me, do not your carnal relations and friends vex your tender souls day by day, in bidding you spare yourselves, and take heed lest you go too far: And as you passed along to come and hear the word of God, have you not heard many a Pharisee cry out, Here comes another troop of his followers! Brethren, be not surprised, Christ's servants were always the world's fools; you know it hated him before it hated you. Rejoice and be exceeding glad. Yet a little while, and behold the bridegroom cometh, and then shall you hear these formal scoffing Pharisees saying unto you, "Give us of your oil, for our lamps are gone out." When you are reviled, revile not again: when you suffer, threaten not; commit your souls into the hands of him that judgeth righteously: for behold the day cometh, when the children of God shall speak for themselves.

The wise virgins, in the parable, no doubt endured the same cruel mockings as you may do, but as the lamb before the shearers is dumb, so in this life opened they not their mouths; but now we find they can give their enemies an answer: "Not so, lest there be not enough for us and you; but go ye rather to them that sell, and buy for yourselves." These words are not to be understood as though they were spoken in an insulting manner; for true charity teaches us to use the worst of sinners, and our most bitter enemies, with the meekness and gentleness of Christ: Though Dives was in hell, yet Abraham does not say, Thou villain, but only, "Son, remember:" and I am persuaded, had it been in the power of these wise virgins, they would have dealt with the foolish virgins, as God knows, I would willingly deal with my most inveterate enemies, not only give them of their oil, but also exalt them to the right hand of God. It was not then for want of love, but the fear of wanting a sufficiency for themselves, that made them return this answer, "Not so, lest there be not enough for us and you:" For they that have most grace, have none to spare; none but self-righteous, foolish virgins think they are good enough, or have already attained. Those who are truly wise are always most distrustful of themselves, pressing forwards to the things that are before, and think it well if after they have done all, they can make their calling and election sure. "Not so, lest there be not enough for us and you; but go ye rather to them that sell, and buy for yourselves." These words indeed seem to be spoken in a triumphant, but certainly they were uttered in the most compassionate manner; "go ye to them that sell, and buy for yourselves;" unhappy virgins! you accounted our lives folly; whilst with you in the body, how often have you condemned us for our zeal in running to hear the word of God, and looked upon us as enthusiasts, for talking and affirming, that we must be led by the spirit, and walk by the spirit, and feel the spirit of God witnessing with our spirits, that we are his children? But now you would be glad to be partakers of this privilege, but it is not ours to give. You contented yourselves with seeking, when you should have been striving to enter in at the strait gate. And now go to them that sell, if you can, and buy for yourselves.

And what say you to this, ye foolish formal professors? For I doubt not but curiosity and novelty hath brought many such, even to this despised place, to hear a sermon. Can you hear this reply to the foolish virgins, and yet not tremble? Why, yet a little while, and thus it shall be done to you. Rejoice and bolster yourselves up in your duties and forms; endeavor to cover your nakedness with the fig-leaves of an outward profession and a legal righteousness, and despise the true servants of Christ as much as you please, yet know, that all your hopes will fail you when God brings you into judgment. For not he who commendeth himself is justified, but he whom the Lord commendeth.

But to return; we do not hear of any reply the foolish virgins make: No, their consciences condemned them; like the person without a wedding-garment, they are struck dumb, and are now filled with anxious thoughts how they shall buy oil, that they may lift up their heads before the bridegroom. "But whilst they went to buy," ver. 10, whilst they were thinking what they should do, the bridegroom, the Lord Jesus, the king, the husband of his spouse the church, cometh, attended with thousands and twenty times then thousands of saints and angels, publicly to count up his jewels; "and they that were ready," the wise virgins who had oil in their lamp, and were sealed by his spirit to the day of redemption, these having on the wedding garment of an imputed righteousness, and a new nature, "went in with him to the marriage." But who can express the transports that these wise virgins felt, when they were thus admitted, in holy triumph, into the presence and full enjoyment of him, whom their souls hungered and thirsted after! No doubt they had tasted of his love, and by faith had often fed on him in their hearts, when sitting down to commemorate his last supper here on earth; but how full may we think their hearts and tongues were of his praises, when they see themselves seated together to eat bread in his heavenly kingdom.

And what was best of all, "the door was shut, and shut them in, to enjoy the ever blessed God, and the company of angels and the spirits of just men made perfect, without interruption for evermore. I say, without interruption; for in this life, their eyes often gushed out with water, because men kept not God's law; and they could never come to appear before the Lord, or to hear his word, but Satan and his emissaries would come also to disturb them; but now "the door is shut," now there is a perfect communion of saints, which they in vain longed for in this lower world; not tares no longer grow up with the wheat; not one single hypocrite or unbeliever can screen himself amongst them. "Now the wicked cease from troubling, and now their weary souls enjoy an everlasting rest." Once more, O believers, let me exhort you in patience to possess your souls. God, if he has freely justified you by faith in his son, and given you his spirit, has sealed you to be his; and has secured you, as surely as he secured Noah, when he locked him in the ark. But though heirs of God, and joint heirs with Christ, and neither men nor devils can pluck you our of your heavenly Father's hand, yet you must be tossed about with manifold temptations; however, lift up your heads, the day of your perfect, complete redemption draweth nigh. Behold the bridegroom cometh to take you to himself, the door shall be shut, and you shall be for ever with the Lord.

But I even tremble to tell you, O nominal Christians, that the door will be shut, I mean the door of mercy, never, never to be opened to give you admission, though you should continue knocking to all eternity. For thus speaks our Lord, v. 11. "Afterwards," after those that were ready went in, and the door was shut; after they had, to their sorrow, found that no oil was to be bought, no grace to be procured, "came also the other virgins;" and as Esau, after Jacob had gotten the blessing, cried with an exceeding bitter cry, "Bless me, even me also, O my father;" so they came saying, "Lord, Lord, open to us." Observe the importunity of these foolish virgins, implied in the words, "Lord, Lord." Whilst in the body, I suppose they only read, did not pray over their prayers. If you now tell them, they should "pray without ceasing," they should pray from their hearts, and feel the want of what they pray for; they would answer, they could not tell what you mean by inward feelings; that God did not require us to be always on our knees, but if a man did justly, and loved mercy, and did as the church forms required him, it was as much as the Lord required at his hands.

I fear, sirs, too many among us are of this mind: nay, I fear there are many so polite, so void of the love of God, as to think it too great a piece of self-denial, to rise early to offer up a sacrifice of praise and thanksgiving acceptable to God through Jesus Christ. If any such, by the good providence of

God, are brought hither this morning, I beseech you to consider your ways, and remember, if you are not awakened out of your spiritual lethargy, and live a life of prayer here, you shall but in vain cry out with the foolish virgins, "Lord, Lord, open unto us," hereafter.

Observe farther, the impudence, as well as importunity of these other virgins; "Lord, Lord," say they, as though they were intimately acquainted with the holy Jesus. Like numbers among us, who because they go to church, repeat their creeds, and receive the blessed sacrament, think they have a right to call Jesus their Savior, and dare call God their Father, when they put up the Lord's prayer. But Jesus is not your Savior. The devil, not God, is your father, unless your hearts are purified by faith, and you are born again from above. It is not merely being baptized by water, but being born again of the Holy Ghost that must qualify you for salvation; and it will do you no service at the great day, to say unto Christ, Lord, my name is in the register of such and such a parish. I am persuaded, the foolish virgins could say this and more; but what answer did Jesus make? He answered and said, ver. 12, "Verily, I say unto you:" He puts the VERILY, to assure them he was in earnest. "I say unto you," I who am truth itself, I whom you have owned in words, but in works denied, "verily, I say unto you, I know you not." These words must not be understood literally; for whatever Arians and Socinians may say to the contrary, yet we affirm, that Jesus Christ is God, God blessed for ever, and therefore knoweth all things. He saw Nathaniel, when under the fig-tree: he sees, and is not looking down from heaven his dwelling-place, upon us, to see how we behave in these fields. Brethren, I know nothing of the thoughts and intents of your hearts, in coming hither; but Jesus Christ knows who came like new-born babes, desirous to be fed with the sincere milk of the word; and he knows who came to hear what the babbler says, and to run away with part of a broken sentence, that they may have whereof to accuse him. This expression then, "I know you not," must not be understood literally; no, it implies a knowledge of approbation, as though Christ has said, "You call me, Lord, Lord, but you have not done the things that I have said; you desire me to open the door, but how can you come in hither not having on a wedding garment? Alas, you are naked! Where is my outward righteousness imputed to you? Where is my divine image stamped upon your souls? How dare you call me Lord, Lord, when you have not received the Holy Ghost, whereby I seal all that are truly mine? "Verily, I know you not; depart from me, ye cursed, into everlasting fire, prepared for the devil and his angels." And now, he that hath ears to hear, let him hear what manner of persons these were, whom Jesus Christ dismissed with this answer. Remember, I entreat you, remember they are not sent away for being fornicators, swearers, Sabbath-breakers, or prodigals. No, in all probability, as I observed before, they were, touching the outward observance of the moral law, blameless; they were constant as to the form of religion; and if they did no good, yet no one could say, they did any one any harm. The only thing for which they were condemned, and eternally banished from the presence of the Lord, (for so much is implied in "I know you not") was this, they had no oil in their lamps, no principle of a true living faith and holiness in their hearts. And if persons may go to church, receive the sacrament, lead honest moral lives, and yet be sent to hell at the last day, as they certainly will be if they advance no farther, Where wilt thou, O drunkard? Where wilt thou, O swearer? Where wilt thou, O Sabbath-breaker?

Where wilt thou that deniest divine revelation, and even the form of godliness? Where wilt you, and such like sinners appear? I know very well.

You must appear before the dreadful tribunal of Jesus Christ; however you may, like Felix, put off the prosecution of your convictions, yet you, as well as others, must arise after death, and appear in judgment; you will then find, to your eternal sorrow, what I just hinted at in the beginning of this discourse, that your damnation slumbereth not: sin has blinded your hearts, and hardened your foreheads now, but yet a little while, and our Lord will ease him of his adversaries. Methinks, by faith, I see the heavens opened, and the holy Jesus coming, with his face brighter than ten thousand suns, darting fury upon you from his eyes! Methinks I see you rising from your graves, trembling and astonished, and crying out, who can abide this day of his coming!

And now what inference shall I draw from what has been delivered? Our Lord, in the words of the text, has drawn one for me; "Watch therefore, for ye know neither the day nor the hour wherein the Son of man cometh." "Watch," that is, be upon your guard, and keep your graces in continual exercise. For as when we are commanded to watch unto prayer, it signifies that we should continue instant in that duty; so when we are required to watch in general, it means that we should put on the whole armor of God, and live every day as though it was our last. And O that the Lord may now enable me to lift up my voice like a trumpet! For had I a thousand tongues, or could I speak so loud that the whole world might hear me, I could not sound a more useful alarm than that which is contained in the text. Watch therefore, my brethren, I beseech you by the mercies of God in Christ Jesus, watch; be upon your guard; awake, ye that sleep in the dust: for ye know neither the day nor the hour wherein the Son of man cometh. Perhaps today, perhaps this midnight, the cry may be made: "for in a moment, in the twinkling of an eye, the trump is to sound." However, supposing the final day of judgment may yet be a great way off, the day of death is certainly near at hand: for what is our life? "It is but a vapor," but a span long, soon passeth it away, and we are gone. Blessed be God, we are all here well; but who, out of this great multitude, dares say, I shall go home to my house in safety? Who knows, but whilst I am speaking, God may commission his ministering spirits immediately to call some of you away by a sudden stroke, to give an account with what attention you have heard this sermon. You know, my brethren, some such instances we have lately had. And what angel or spirit hath assured us, that some of you shall not be the next? "Watch therefore, for ye know neither the day nor the hour wherein the Son of man will come;" And it is chiefly for this reason, that God has hidden the day of our deaths from us. For since I know not but I may die to morrow, why, O my soul, may each of us say, wilt thou not watch to day?

Since I know not but I may die the next moment, why wilt thou not prepare for dying this? Many such reflections as these, my brethren, crowd in upon my mind. At present, blessed be the Lord, who delights to magnify his strength in a poor worm's weakness, I am at a stand, not so much about what I shall say, as what I shall leave unsaid. My belly, like Elihu's, is, as it were, full of new wines; "out of the abundance of my heart my mouth speaketh." The seeing so great a multitude standing before me; a sense of the infinite majesty of that God in whose name I preach, and before whom I as well as you must appear, to give an account, and the uncertainty there is whether I shall live another day, to speak to you any more: these considerations, especially the presence of God, which I feel upon my soul, furnishes me with so much matter, that I scarce know where to begin, or where to end my application. However, for method-sake, by the divine assistance, I will branch it into three particulars.

And FIRST, I would remind you that are notoriously ungodly, of what our Lord says in the text: For though I have said that your damnation slumbereth no, whilst you continue in an impenitent state; yet that was only to set you upon your watch, to convince you of your danger, and excite you to cry out, "What shall we do to be saved?" I appeal to all that hear me, whether I have said, the door of mercy should be shut against you, if you believe on Jesus Christ: No, if you are the chief of sinners; if you are murderers of fathers, and murderers of mothers; if you are emphatically the dung and offscouring of all things; yet if you believe on Jesus Christ, and cry unto him with the same faith as the expiring thief, "Lord, remember me, now thou art in thy kingdom;" I will pawn my eternal salvation upon it, if he does not shortly translate you to his heavenly paradise. Wonder not at my speaking with so much assurance: For I know "it is a faithful and true saying, and worthy of all acceptation, that Jesus Christ came into the world to save (all truly affected and believing) sinners: Nay, so great is his love, that I am persuaded, was it necessary, he would come again into the world, and die a second time for them on the cross. But, blessed be God, when our Lord bowed down his head, and gave up the ghost, our redemption was finished. It is not our sins, but our want of a lively faith in his blood, that will prove our condemnation: if you draw near to him by faith, though ye are the worst of sinners, yet he will not say unto you, "Verily I know you not." No, a door of mercy shall be opened to you. Look then, look then, by an eye of faith, to that God-man whom ye have pierced.

Behold him bleeding, panting, dying upon the cross, with arms stretched out ready to embrace you all. Hark! How he groans! See how all nature is in agony! The rocks rend, the graves open; the sun withdraws its light, ashamed as it were to see the God of nature suffer; and all this to usher in man's great redemption. Nay, the Holy Jesus, in the very agonies and pangs of death, prays for his very murderers; "Father, forgive them, for they know not what they do." If then you have crucified the Son of God afresh, and put him to an open shame, yet do not despair, only believe, and even this shall be forgiven. You have read, at least you have heard, no doubt, how three thousand were converted at St. Peter's preaching one single sermon, after our Lord's ascension into heaven; and many of those who crucified the Lord of glory undoubtedly were amongst them, and why should you despair? For "Jesus Christ is the same yesterday, today, and for ever." The Holy Ghost shall be sent down on you, as well as on them, if you do but believe; for Christ ascended up on high to receive this gift even for the vilest of men. Come then, all ye that are weary and heavy laden with the sense of your sins, lay hold on Christ by faith, and he will give you rest; for salvation is the free gift of God to all them that believe.

And though you may think this too good news to be true, yet I speak the truth in Christ, I lie not, this is the gospel, this is the glad tidings which we are commissioned to preach to every creature. Be not faithless then, but believing. Let not the devil lead you captive at his will any longer; for all the wages he gives his servants is death, death often in this life, death everlasting in the next: But the free gift of God, is eternal life to all that believe in Jesus Christ. Pharisees are and will be offended at my coming here, and offering you salvation on such cheap terms; but the more they bid me hold my peace, the more will I cry out and proclaim to convicted sinners, that Jesus, David's Son according to the flesh, but David's Lord as he was God, will have mercy upon all that by a living faith truly turn to him. If this is to be vile, I pray God, I may be more vile. If they will not let me preach Christ crucified, and offer salvation to poor sinners in a church, I will preach him in the lanes, streets, highways and hedges; and nothing pleases me better, than to think I am now in one of the devil's strongest holds. Surely, the Lord has not sent me and all you hither for nothing; no, blessed be God, the fields are white ready unto harvest, and many souls I hope will be gathered into his heavenly garner. It is true, it is the midnight of the church, especially the poor church of England, but God has lately sent forth his servants to cry, "Behold the bridegroom cometh:" I beseech you, O sinners, hearken unto the voice! Let me espouse you by faith to my dear master; and henceforward "watch and pray," that you may be ready to go forth to meet him.

SECONDLY, I would apply myself to those amongst you, that are not openly profane, but by depending on a formal round of duties, deceive your own souls, and are only foolish virgins. But I must speak to your conviction, rather than your comfort. My dear brethren, do not deceive your own souls. You have heard how far the foolish virgins went, and yet were answered with "Verily I know you not." The reason is, because none but such who have a living faith in Jesus Christ, and are truly born again, can possibly enter into the kingdom of heaven. You may, perhaps, live honest and outwardly moral lives, but if you depend on that morality, or join your works with your faith, in order to justify you before God, you have no lot or share in Christ's redemption: For what is this but to deny the Lord that has bought you? What is this but making yourselves your own Saviors? Taking the crown from Jesus Christ, and putting it on your own heads? The crime of the devil, some have supposed, consisted in this, that he would not bow to Jesus Christ, when the Father commanded all the angels to worship him; and what do you less? You will not own and submit to his righteousness; and though you pretend to worship him with your lips, yet your hearts are far from him; besides you, in effect, deny the operations of his blessed spirit, you mistake common for effectual grace; you hope to be saved, because you have good desires, and a few short convictions; and what is this, but to give God, his word, and all his saints, the lie? A Jew, a Turk, has equally as good grounds whereon to build his hopes of salvation.

Need I not then to cry out to you, ye foolish virgins, watch. Beg of God to convince you of your self-righteousness, and the secret unbelief of your hearts; or otherwise, whensoever the cry shall be made, "Behold the bridegroom cometh," you will find yourselves utterly unprepared to go forth to meet him: You may cry "Lord, Lord;" but the answer will be, "Verily, I know you not." THIRDLY, I would speak a word or two by way of exhortation to those who are wise virgins, and are assured that they have on a wedding garment.

That there are many such amongst you, who by grace have renounced your own righteousness, and know that the righteousness of the Lord Jesus is imputed to you, I make no doubts. God has his secret ones in the worst of times; and I am persuaded he has not let so loud a gospel cry to be made amongst his people, as of late has been heard, for nothing. No, I am confident, the Holy Ghost has been given to many at the preaching of faith, and has powerfully fallen upon many, whilst they have been hearing the word. You are now then no longer foolish, but wise virgins; notwithstanding, I beseech you also to suffer the word of exhortation, for wise virgins are too apt, whilst the bridegroom tarries, to slumber and sleep. Watch therefore, my dear brethren, watch and pray, at this time especially; for perhaps a time of suffering is at hand. The ark of the Lord begins already to be driven into the wilderness. Be ye therefore upon your watch, and still persevere in following your Lord, even without the camp, bearing his reproach; the cry that has been lately made, has awakened the devil and his servants; they begin to rage horribly; and well they may; for I hope their kingdom is in danger. Watch therefore, for if we are not always upon our guard, a time of trial may overtake us unawares; and instead of owning, like Peter we may be tempted to deny our master. Set death and eternity often before you. Look unto Jesus, the author and finisher of your faith, and consider how little a while it will be, ere he comes to judgment; and then our reproach shall be wiped away; the accusers of us and our brethren shall be cast down, and we all shall be lodged in heaven for ever, with our dear Lord Jesus.

LASTLY, what I say unto you, I say unto all, watch; high and low, rich and poor, young and old, one with another, I beseech you, by the mercies of Jesus, to be upon your guard: fly, fly to Jesus Christ, that heavenly bridegroom; behold he desires to take you to himself, miserable, poor, blind and naked as you are; he is willing to clothe you with his everlasting righteousness, and make you partakers of that glory, which he enjoyed with the Father before the world began. Do not turn a deaf ear to me; do not reject the message on account of the meanness of the messenger.

I am a child; but the Lord has chosen me, that the glory might be all his own. Had he sent to invite you by a learned rabbi, you might have been tempted to think the man had done something; but now God has sent a child, that the excellency of the power may be seen not to be of man, but of God.

Let the learned Pharisees then despise my youth: I care not how vile I appear in the sight of such men; I glory in it. And I am persuaded, if any of you should be married to Christ by this preaching, you will have no reason to repent, when you come to heaven, that God sent a child to cry, "Behold the bridegroom cometh!" O! my brethren, the thought of being instrumental in bringing one of you to glory, fills me with fresh zeal.

Once more I entreat you, "Watch, watch and pray:" For the Lord Jesus will receive all that call upon him faithfully. Let that cry, "Behold the bridegroom cometh," be continually sounding in your ears; and begin now to live, as though you were assured, this night you were to "go forth to meet him." I could say more, but the other business and duties of the day oblige me o stop. May the Lord give you all an hearing ear, and obedient heart, and so closely unite you to himself by one spirit, that when he shall come in terrible majesty, to judge mankind, you may be found having on a wedding garment, and ready to go in with him to the marriage.

Grant this, O Lord, for thy dear Son's sake!

Sermon 26 "The Eternity of Hell-Torments"

Matthew 25:46 "These shall go away into everlasting punishment.

To the INHABITANTS of Savannah in Georgia.

My dear Friends, Though the following sermon has been preached elsewhere, yet as the occasion of my preaching it among you was particular, as you seemed to give an uncommon attention to it in public, and afterwards expressed your satisfaction in it to me, when I came to visit you in your own houses, I thought proper to offer it to you.

And here I cannot but bless God for the general dislike of heretical principles that I have found among you; as also for your zeal and approbation of my conduct, when the glory of God and your welfare, have obliged me to resent and publicly declare against the antichristian tenets of some lately under my charge.

I need only exhort you to beg of God to give you a true faith, and to add to your faith virtue, that you may adorn the gospel of our Lord Jesus Christ in all things.

Your constant daily attendance upon public worship, the gladness wherewith you have received me into your houses, the mildness wherewith you have submitted to my reproofs, more especially the great (though unmerited) concern you showed at my departure, induce me to hope this will be your endeavor.

How long God of his good providence will keep me from you, I know not.

However, you may assure yourselves I will return according to my promise, as soon as I have received imposition of hands, and completed the other business that called me hither.

In the mean while, accept of this, as a pledge of the undissembled love of Your affectionate though unworthy pastor, George Whitefield London, 1738.

Matthew 25:46 "These shall go away into everlasting punishment."

The excellency of the gospel dispensation, is greatly evidenced by those sanctions of rewards and punishments, which it offers to the choice of all its hearers, in order to engage them to be obedient to its precepts.

For it promises no less than eternal happiness to the good, and denounces no slighter a punishment than everlasting misery against the wicked: On the one hand, It is a favor of life unto life," on the other, "A favor of death unto death." And though one would imagine, the bare mentioning of the former would be sufficient to draw men to their duty, yet ministers in all ages have found it necessary, frequently to remind their people of the latter, and to set before them the terrors of the Lord, as so many powerful dissuasives from sin.

But whence is it that men are so disingenuous?

The reason seems to be this: The promise of eternal happiness is so agreeable to the inclinations and wishes of mankind, that all who call themselves christians, universally and willingly subscribe to the belief of it: but then there is something so shocking in the consideration of eternal torments, and seemingly such an infinite disproportion between an endless duration of pain, and short life spent in pleasure, that men (some at least of them) can scarcely be brought to confess it as an article of their faith, that an eternity of misery awaits the wicked in a future state.

I shall therefore at this time, beg leave to insist on the proof of this part of one of the Articles of our Creed; and endeavor to make good what our blessed Lord has here threatened in the words of the text, "These (that is, the wicked) shall go away into everlasting punishment." Accordingly, without considering the words as they stand in relation to the context; I shall resolve all I have to say, into this one general proposition, "That the torments reserved for the wicked hereafter, are eternal." But before I proceed to make good this, I must inform you that I take it for granted, All present do steadfastly believe, They have something within them, which we call a soul, and which is capable of surviving the dissolution of the body, and of being miserable or happy to all eternity.

I take it for granted farther, That you believe a divine revelation; that those books, emphatically called the Scriptures, were written by the inspiration of God, and that the things therein contained, are founded upon eternal truth.

I take it for granted, That you believe, that the Son of God came down to die for sinners; and that there is but one Mediator between God and man, even the man Christ Jesus.

These things being granted, (and they were necessary to be premised) proceed we now to make good the one general proposition asserted in the text, That the torments reserved for the wicked hereafter are eternal.

"These shall go away into everlasting punishment." The First argument I shall advance to prove that the torments reserved for the wicked hereafter, are eternal, is, That the word of God himself assures us, in line upon line, that it will be so.

To quote all the texts that might be produced in proof of this, would be endless. Let it suffice to instance only in a few. In the Old Testament, in the book of Daniel, chap. 12, ver. 2 we are told, that "some shall wake to everlasting life, and others to everlasting contempt." In the book of Isaiah, it is said, that "the worm of those that have transgressed God's law, and die impenitently, shall not die, nor their fire be quenched." And in another place the holy Prophet , struck, no doubt, with astonishment and horror at the prospect of the continuance of the torments of the damned, breaks out into this moving expostulation, "Who can dwell with everlasting burnings?" The New Testament is still fuller as to this point, it being a revelation which brought this and such-like particulars to a clear light.

The Apostle Jude tells us of the profane despisers of dignities in his days, that "for them was reserved the blackness of darkness forever." And in the book of the Revelation, it is written, that "the smoke of the torments of the wicked ascendeth for ever and ever." And if we believe the witness of men inspired, the witness of the Son of God, who had the Spirit given him, as Mediator, without measure, is still far greater: and in St.

Mark's gospel, He repeats this solemn declaration three several times, It is better for thee to enter into life maimed;" that is, it is better to forego the gratification of thy lust, or incur the displeasure of a friend, which may be as dear to thee as a hand, or as useful as a foot, "than having two hands and feet, (that is, for indulging the one, or disobeying God to oblige the other) to be cast into hell, where the worm dieth not, and the fire is not quenched." And here again, in the words of the text, "These (the wicked) shall go away into everlasting punishment." I know it has been objected by some who have denied the eternity of hell-torments, That the words everlasting and ever and ever, are often used in the Holy Scriptures (especially in the Old Testament) when they signify not an endless duration, but a limited term of time.

And this we readily grant: but then we reply, That when the words are used with this limitation, they either manifestly appear to be used so from the context; or are put in opposition to occasional types which God gave his people on some special occasions, as when it is said, "It shall be a perpetual or everlasting statute," or, "a statute for ever;" that is, a standing type, and not merely transient or occasional, as was the pillar of cloud, the manna, and such-like. Or, lastly, they have a relation to that covenant, God made with his spiritual Israel; which, if understood in a spiritual sense, will be everlasting, though the ceremonial dispensation be abolished.

Besides, it ought to be observed, that some of the passages just now referred to, have neither of these words so much as mentioned in them, and cannot possibly be interpreted, so as to denote only a limited term of years.

But let that be as it will, it is evident even to a demonstration, that the words of the text will not admit of such a restrained signification, as appears from their being directly opposed to the words immediately following, "That the righteous shall go into life eternal." From which words, all are ready to grant, that the life promised to the righteous will be eternal. And why the punishment threatened to the wicked should not be understood to be eternal likewise, when the very same word in the original, is used to express the duration of each, no shadow of a reason can be given.

But, Secondly, There cannot be one argument urged, why God should reward his saints with everlasting happiness, which will not equally prove that he ought to punish sinners with eternal misery.

For, since we know nothing (at least for a certainty) how he will deal with either but by a Diving Revelation; and since, as was proved by the foregoing argument, he hath as positively threatened eternally to punish the wicked, as to reward the good; it follows, that his truth will be as much impeached and called in question, did he not inflict his punishments, as it would be, if he did not confer his rewards.

To this also it has been objected, That though God is obliged by promise to give his rewards, yet his veracity could not be called in question, supposing he should not execute his threatenings, as he actually did not in the case of Nineveh; which God expressly declared by his Prophet Jonah, "should be destroyed in forty days:" notwithstanding the sequel of the story informs us, that Nineveh was spared.

But in answer to this objection we affirm, that God's threatenings, as well as promises, are without repentance; and for this reason, because they are both founded on the eternal laws of right reason. Accordingly we always find, that where the conditions were not performed, on the non-performance of which the threatenings were denounced, God always executed the punishment threatened. The driving Adam out of Eden, the destruction of the old world by a deluge of water, and the overthrow of Sodom and Gomorrah, are, and will be always so many standing monuments of God's executing his threatenings when denounced, though to our weak apprehensions, the punishment may seem far to exceed the crime.

It is true, God did spare Nineveh, and that because the inhabitants did actually repent, and therefore performed the conditions upon which it was supposed, by the Prophet's being sent to warn them, the threatened punishment should be withheld.

And so in respect to gospel threatenings. If men will so far consult their own welfare, as to comply with the gospel, God certainly will not punish them, but on the contrary, confer upon them his rewards. But to affirm that he will not punish, and that eternally to, impenitent, obstinate sinners, according as he hath threatened; what is it, in effect, but to make God like a man, that he should lie, or the son of man, that he should repent?

But the absurdity of such an opinion will appear still more evident from The Third argument I shall offer to prove, that the torments reserved for the wicked hereafter are eternal, From the nature of the christian covenant.

And here I must again observe, that it was taken for granted at the beginning of this discourse, that you believe the Son of God came down to save sinners; and that there is but one Mediator between God and men, even the Man Christ Jesus.

And here I take it for granted farther, (unless you believe the absurd and unwarrantable doctrine of purgatory) that you are fully persuaded, this life is the only time allotted by Almighty God for working out our salvation, and that after a few years are passed over, there will remain no more sacrifice for sin.

And if this be granted (and who dares deny it?) it follows, that if the wicked man dieth in his wickedness, and under the wrath of God, he must continue in that state to all eternity. For, since there is no possibility of their being delivered out of such a condition, but by and through Christ; and since, at the hour of death, the time of Christ's mediation and intercession for him is irrecoverably gone; the same reason that may be given, why God should punish a sinner that dieth under the guilt of his sins for a single day, will equally hold good, why he should continue to punish him for a year, an age, nay all eternity.

But I hasten to the Fourth and last argument, to prove, That the torments reserved for the wicked hereafter are eternal, Because the devil's punishment is to be so.

That there is such a being whom we call the devil; that he was once an angel of light, but for his pride and rebellion against God, was cast down from heaven, and is now permitted, with the rest of the spiritual wickednesses, to walk to and fro, seeking whom they may devour; that there is a place of torment reserved for them, or, to use the Apostle's words, "That they are reserved in everlasting chains under darkness unto the judgment of the great day;" are truths all here present were supposed to be convinced of, at the beginning of the discourse, you believing the Holy Scriptures to be written by the inspiration of God, wherein these truths are delivered.

But then if we allow all this, and think it no injustice in God to punish those once glorious spirits for their rebellion; how can we think it unjust in him, to punish wicked men for their impenitency to all eternity?

You will say, perhaps, that they have sinned against greater light, and therefore deserve a greater punishment. And so we grant that the punishment of the fallen angels may be greater as to degree, than that of wicked men; but then we affirm, it will be equal as to the eternal duration of it: for in that day, as the lively oracles of God inform us, shall the Son of Man say to them on his left hand, "Depart from me, ye cursed, into everlasting fire, prepared for the devil and his angels." Where we find that impenitent sinners are to be cast into the same everlasting fire, with the devil and his angels; and that too very justly. For though they may have sinned against greater light, yet christians sin against greater mercy. Since Christ took not hold of, did not die for, the fallen angels, but for men and for our salvation. So that if God spared not those excellent beings, assure thyself, O obstinate sinner, whoever thou art, he will by no means spare thee.

From what then has been said it plainly appears, that verily the torments reserved for the wicked hereafter, war eternal. And if so, brethren, how ought we to fly to Jesus Christ for refuge; how holy ought we to be in all manner of conversation and godliness, that we may be accounted worthy to escape this wrath to come!

But before I proceed to a practical exhortation, permit me to draw an inference or two from what has been said.

And First, If the torments reserved for the wicked hereafter are eternal, what shall we say to those, who make an open profession in their creed to believe a life everlasting, a life of misery as well as happiness, and yet dare to live in the actual commission of those sins which will unavoidably, without repentance, bring them into that place of torment?

Thou believest that the punishments of the impenitently wicked in another life, are eternal: "Thou dost well, the devils also believe and tremble." But know O vain man, unless this belief doth influence thy practice, and makes thee bid adieu to thy sins, every time thou repeatest thy creed, thou doest in effect say, I believe I shall be undone for ever.

But, Secondly, If the torments reserved for the wicked hereafter are eternal, then let this serve as a caution to such persons, (and it is to be feared there are some such) who go about to dissuade others from the belief of such an important truth: There being no surer way, in all probability, to encourage and promote infidelity and profaneness, than the broaching or maintaining so unwarrantable a doctrine. For if the positive threats of God concerning the eternity of hell-torments, are already found insufficient to deter men from sin, what a higher pitch of wickedness may w imagine they will quickly arrive at, when they are taught to entertain any hopes of a future recovery out of them; or, what is still worse, that their souls are hereafter to be annihilated, and become like the beasts that perish? But woe unto such blind leaders of the blind. No wonder if they both fall into that ditch. And let such corrupters of God's word know, that I testify unto every man that heareth me this day, "That if any one shall add unto, or take away from the words that are written in the book of God, God shall take his part out of the book of life, an shall add unto him all the plagues that are in that book." Thirdly and Lastly, If the torments reserved for the wicked hereafter are eternal, then this may serve as a reproof for those who quarrel with God, and say it is inconsistent with his justice, to punish a person to all eternity, only for enjoying the pleasures of sin for a season. But such persons must be told, that it is not their thinking or calling God unjust, will make him so, no more than a condemned prisoner's saying the law or judge is unjust, will render either duly chargeable with such an imputation. But knowest thou, O worm, what blasphemy thou are guilty of, in charging God with injustice? "Shall the thing formed say to him that formed it, why hast thou made me thus?" Wilt thou presume to arraign the Almighty at the bar of thy shallow reasoning? And call him unjust, for punishing thee eternally, only because thou wishest it may not be so? But hath God said it, and shall he not do it? He hath said it: and let God be true, though every man be a liar. "Shall not the judge of all the earth do right?" Assuredly he will. And if sinners will not own his justice in his threatenings here, they will be compelled ere long to own and feel them, when tormented by him hereafter.

But to come to a more practical application of what has been delivered.

You have heard, brethren, the eternity of hell-torments plainly proved, from the express declarations of holy scriptures, and consequences naturally drawn from them. And now there seems to need no great art of rhetoric to persuade any understanding person to avoid and abhor those sins, which without repentance will certainly plunge him into this eternal gulf. The disproportion between the pleasure and the pain (if there be any pleasure in sin) is so infinitely great, that supposing it was only possible, though not certain, that the wicked would be everlastingly punished, no one that has the reason of a man, for the enjoying a little momentary pleasure, would, one might imagine, run the hazard of enduring eternal pain. But since the torments of the damned are not only possible, but certain (since God himself, who cannot lie, has told us so) for men, notwithstanding, to persist in their disobedience, and then flatter themselves, that God will not make good his threatenings, is a most egregious instance of folly and presumption.

Dives himself supposed, that if one rose from the dead, his brethren would amend their lives, but Christians, it seems, will not repent, though the Son of God died and rose again, and told them what they must expect, if they continue obstinate in evil-doing.

Would we now and then draw off our thoughts from sensible objects, and by faith meditate a while on the miseries of the damned, I doubt not but we should, as it were, hear many an unhappy soul venting his fruitless sorrows, in some such piteous moans as these.

"O wretched man that I am, who shall deliver me from this body of death!" O foolish mortal that I was, thus to bring myself into these neverceasing tortures, for the transitory enjoyment of a few short-lived pleasures, which scarcely afforded me any satisfaction, even when I most indulged myself in them. Alas! Are these the wages, these the effects of sin? O damned apostate! First to delude me with pretended promises of happiness, and after several years drudgery in his service, thus to involve me in eternal woe. O that I had never hearkened to his beguiling insinuations! O that I had rejected his very first suggestions with the utmost detestation and abhorrence! O that I had taken up my cross and followed Christ! O that I had never ridiculed serious godliness; and out of a false politeness, condemned the truly pious as too severe, enthusiastic, or superstitious! For I then had been happy indeed, happy beyond expression, happy to all eternity, yonder in those blessed regions where they fit, clothed with unspeakable glory, and chanting forth their seraphic hallelujahs to the Lamb that sitteth upon the throne for ever. But, alas!

These reflections come now too late; these wishes now are vain and fruitless. I have not suffered, and therefore must not reign with them. I have in effect denied the Lord that bought me, and therefore justly am I now denied by him. But must I live for ever tormented in these flames? Must this body of mine, which not long since lay in state, was clothed in purple and fine linen, and fared sumptuously every day, must it be here eternally confined, and made the mockery of insulting devils? O eternity! That thought fills me with despair: I must be miserable for ever." Come then, all ye self-deluding, self-deluded sinners, and imagine yourselves for once in the place of that truly wretched man I have been here describing. Think, I beseech you by the mercies of God in Christ Jesus, think with yourselves, how racking, how unsupportable the never- dying worm of a self-condemning conscience will hereafter be to you. Think how impossible it will be for you to dwell with everlasting burnings.

Come, all ye christians of a lukewarm, Laodicean spirit, ye Gallie's in religion, who care a little, but not enough for the things of God; O think, think with yourselves, how deplorable it will be to lose the enjoyment of heaven, and run into endless torments, merely because you will be content to be almost, and will not strive to be altogether christians.

Consider, I beseech you consider, how you will rave and curse that fatal stupidity which made you believe any thing less than true faith in Jesus, productive of a life of strict piety, self-denial, and mortification, can keep you from those torments, the eternity of which I have been endeavoring to prove.

But I can no more. These thoughts are too melancholy for me to dwell on, as well as for you to hear; and God knows, as punishing is his strange work, so denouncing his threatenings is mine. But if the bare mentioning the torments of the damned is so shocking, how terrible must the enduring of them be!

And now, are not some of you ready to cry out, "These are hard sayings, who can bear them?" But let not sincere christians be in the least terrified at what has been delivered: No, for you is reserved a crown, a kingdom, an eternal and exceeding weight of glory. Christ never said that the righteous, the believing, the upright, the sincere, but the wicked, merciless, negatively good professors before described, shall go into everlasting punishment. For you, who love him in sincerity, a new and living way is laid open into the Holy of Holies by the blood of Jesus Christ: and an abundant entrance will be administered unto you, at the great day of account, into eternal life.

Take heed, therefore, and beware that there be not in any of you a root of bitterness springing up of unbelief: but on the contrary, steadfastly and heartily rely on the many precious promises reached out to you in the gospel, knowing that he who hath promised is faithful, and therefore will perform.

But let no obstinately wicked professors dare to apply any of the divine promises to themselves: "For it is not meet to take the children's meat and give it unto dogs:" No, to such the terrors of the Lord only belong. And as certainly as Christ will say to his true followers, "Come, ye blessed children of my Father, receive the kingdom prepared for you from the beginning of the world;" so he will unalterably pronounce this dreadful sentence against all that die in their sins, "Depart from me, ye cursed, into everlasting fire, prepared for the devil and his angels." From which unhappy state, may God of his infinite mercy deliver us all through Jesus Christ; to whom, with thee O Father, and thee O Holy Ghost, three Persons and one eternal God, be ascribed, as is most due, all honor, power, might, majesty, and dominion, now and for ever more.

Sermon 27 Blind Bartimeus

Mark 10:52, "And Jesus said unto him, Go thy way; thy faith hath made thee whole. And immediately he received his sight, and followed Jesus in the way."

When the apostle Peter was recommending Jesus of Nazareth, in one of his sermons to the Jews, he gave him a short, but withal a glorious and exalted character, "That we went about doing good." He went about, he sought occasions of doing good; it was his meat and drink to do the works of him that sent him, whilst the day of his public administration lasted.

Justly was he stiled by the prophet, the sun of righteousness. For, as the sun in the natural firmament diffuses his quickening and reviving beams through the universe, so, wherever this sun of righteousness, the blessed Jesus arose, he arose with healing under his wings. He was indeed a prophet like unto Moses, and proved that he was the Messiah which was to come into the world, by the miracles which he wrought; though with this material difference, the miracles of Moses, agreeable to the Old Testament dispensation, were miracles of judgment; the miracles of Jesus, who came to bear our sicknesses and heal our infirmities, were miracles of mercy, and were wrought, not only for the cure of people's bodies, but also for the conversion of their precious and immortal souls. Sometimes, one and the same person was the subject of both these mercies. A glorious proof of this, we have in the miraculous cure wrought upon a poor blind beggar, named Bartimeus, who is to be the subject of the following discourse, and to whom the words of the text refer. "Jesus said unto him, Go thy way, thy faith hath made thee whole. And immediately he received his sight, and followed Jesus in the way." My design is, FIRST, to make some observations on the matter of fact, as recorded by the evangelists. And then, SECONDLY, To point out the improvement that may be made thereof. May Jesus so bless this following discourse, that every spiritually blind hearer may receive his sight, and, after the example of Bartimeus, "follow Jesus in the way!" If we would take a view of the whole story, we must go back to the 46th verse of this chapter, "And they (our Lord and his disciples, who, we find by the context, had been conversing together) came to Jericho," a place devoted by Joshua to the curse of God; and yet, even this place yields converts to Jesus; Zaccheus had been called there formerly; and Bartimeus, as we shall hear by-and-by, in all probability, was called now.

For some good may come even out of Nazareth. Christ himself was born there, and his sovereign grace can reach and overcome the worst of people, in the very worst of places. Jesus came to Jericho. Let not his ministers, if providence points out their way, shun going to seemingly the most unlikely places to do good, some chosen vessels may be therein. Jesus and his disciples came to Jericho. They were itinerants; and, as I have frequently observed, seldom stayed long in a place; not that this is any argument against the stated settlement of particular pastors over particular parishes. But however, our Lord's practice, in this respect, gives a kind of a sanction to itinerant preaching, when persons are properly called to, and qualified for, such an employ. And I believe we may venture to affirm (though we would by no means prescribe or dictate to the Holy One of Israel) that, whenever there shall be a general revival of religion in any country, itinerant preaching will be more in vogue. And it is to be feared, that those who condemn it now, merely on account of the meanness of its appearances, would have joined with the self-righteous Scribes and Pharisees, in condemning even the Son of God himself, for such a practice.

"And as he went out of Jericho with his disciples, and a great number of people;" a great number of mob, or rabble, as the High-priests of that generation termed them; for these were the constant followers of Jesus of Nazareth; it was the poor that received his gospel, the common people heard him gladly, and followed him from place to place.

Not that all who followed him, were his true disciples. No, some followed him only for his loaves, others out of curiosity; though some undoubtedly followed to hear, and be edified by the gracious words that proceeded out of his mouth. Jesus knew this, and was also sensible how displeasing this crowding after him was to some of the rulers of the Jewish church, who, upon every occasion, were ready to say, "Have any of the Scribes and Pharisees believed on him?" But, notwithstanding, I do not hear of our blessed Lord's sending them home but once; and that was, after they had been with him three days, and had nothing left to eat, he saw they were as sheep having no shepherd, and therefore had compassion on them, and taught them. A sufficient warrant this for gospel-ministers to preach to poor souls that follow to hear the word, whatever principle their coming may proceed from. At the same time, they should caution people against thinking themselves Christians, because they follow Christ's ministers. This our Lord frequently did, For there are many that followed Jesus, and not follow his ministers, and hear them gladly; nay, perhaps do many things, as Herod did, who, it is to be feared, will never follow them into the kingdom of heaven. Much people followed Jesus out of Jericho, but how many of them were offended in him; and afterwards, it may be, cried out, "Crucify him, crucify him." Who would depend on popularity? It is like the morning cloud, or early dew, that passeth away. But what a press, and seemingly continued hurry of business did the blessed Jesus live in! He could not be hid; go where he would, much people followed him. He had scarce time to eat bread.

Happy is it for such who are called to act in a public station in the church, and to be more abundant in labors, that their Jesus has trodden in this dangerous path before them. Popularity is a fiery furnace, and no one, but he who kept the three children amidst Nebuchadnezzar's flames, can preserve popular ministers from being hurt by it. But we can do all things through Christ strengthening us. And I have often thought, that there is one consideration sufficient to extinguish, or moderate at least, any excess of joy and self-complacence, which the most popular preacher may feel, when followed even by the greatest multitudes; and that is this, "How many of these hearers will go "away, without receiving any saving benefit by my preaching; nay, how many, it may be, will only have their damnation increased by it!" As we find many will say at the great day, "hast thou not taught in our streets;" to whom Jesus shall answer, "Verily, I know you not." But to proceed, "As our Lord went out of Jericho with his disciples, and a great number of people, blind Bartimeus, (the son of Timeus) sat by the highway-side begging." It should seem that he was a noted, though by no means what we commonly call, a sturdy beggar; having no other way, as he had lost his sight, to get his bread; his case was still the more pitiable, if he was, as some think the name imports, the blind son of a blind father.

It may be, her begged for his father and himself too; and if so, then this may give us light into that passage of Matthew 20:22 where we are told, that "two men spake to Jesus." It might be father and son, though only one is mentioned here, because he only followed Jesus in the way. Thus that holy, judicious, and practical expositor of holy writ, Mr. Henry. But however this be, he is not blamed for begging, neither should we discommend others for so doing, when providence calls to it. It was the unjust steward that said, "To beg I am ashamed." It is our pride that often makes us unwilling to be beholden; Jesus was not thus minded, he lived, as it were, upon alms; the women that followed him, ministered to him of their substance. Bartimeus, not being able to dig, begs for his living; and, in order to make a better trade of it, sat by the highway-side, in all probability, without, or near the gate of the city, where people must necessarily pass in and out. But though he had lost his sight, he had his hearing perfect; and it should comfort us, if we have lost one sense, that we have the use of another, and that we are not deprived of the benefit of all. Happy was it for Bartimeus that he could hear, though not see. For in all probability, upon hearing the noise and clamor of the much people that followed after our Lord, his curiosity set him upon inquiring into the cause of it, and some one or another told him, "that Jesus of Nazareth was passing by;" Jesus of Nazareth, called so, because he was bred there, or out of contempt; Nazareth being either a very mean, or very wicked place, or both, which made guileless Nathaniel say, "Can any good come out of Nazareth?" And what does Bartimeus do when he hears of Jesus? We are told, ver. 47: "And when he heard that it was Jesus of Nazareth, he began to cry out." This plainly denotes, that though the eyes of his body were shut, yet the eyes of his mind were, in some degree, opened, so that he saw, perhaps, more than most of the multitude that followed after Jesus; for, as soon as he heard of him, he began to cry out; which he would not have done, had he not heard of him before, and believed also, that he was both able and willing to restore sight to the blind. "He began to cry out." This implies, that he had a deep sense of his own misery, and the need which he had of a cure; his prayers did not freeze as they went out of his lips; he began to cry out, that Jesus might hear him, notwithstanding the noise of the throng; and he began to cry out, as soon as he heard he was passing by, not knowing whether he might ever enjoy such an opportunity any more. "He began to cry out, Jesus, thou Son of David, have mercy upon me." The people called him Jesus of Nazareth. Bartimeus stiles him, "Jesus, thou Son of David." Thereby evidencing, that he believed him to be the Messiah who was to come into the world, unto whom the Lord God was to give the throne of his father David, and of whose kingdom there was to be no end. "Jesus, thou Son of David;" or, as it is in the parallel place of St. Matthew 20:30, "O Lord, thou son of David;" of whom it had been long foretold, Isaiah 35, that when he should come, "the eyes of the blind should be opened." "Have mercy upon me," the natural language of a soul brought to lie down at the feet of a sovereign God. Here is no laying claim to a cure by way of merit; no proud, self-righteous, God I thank thee that I am not as other men are: not bringing in a reckoning of performances, nor any doubting of Jesus' power or willingness to heal him, but out of the abundance of the heart, his mouth speaketh, and, in the language of the poor, broken-hearted publican, he cries out, "Jesus, thou Son of David, have mercy on me." Jesus, thou friend of sinners, thou Savior, who, though thou be the true God, wast pleased to become the Son of David, and to be made man, that thou mightest seek and save those that were lost, have mercy upon me; let thy bowels yearn towards a poor, miserable, blind beggar?

One would have thought that such a moving petition as this would have melted the whole multitude, that heard his piteous cry, into compassion, and induced some at least to turn suitors in his behalf, or help to carry him to the blessed Jesus. But instead of that, we are told, ver. 48, that "many charged him." The word in the original seems to imply a charge, attended with threatening, and spoken in an angry manner. They charged him "to hold his peace;" and it may be, threatened to beat him if he did not.

They looked upon him beneath the notice of Jesus of Nazareth, and were ready enough to ask, whether he thought Jesus Christ had nothing else to do but to wait upon him. This was, no doubt, very discouraging to blind Bartimeus. For opposition comes closest when it proceeds from those who are esteemed followers of the Lamb. The spouse complains as of something peculiarly afflicting, that her own mother's children were angry with her.

But opposition only serves to whet the edge of true devotion, and therefore Bartimeus, instead of being silenced by their charges and threatenings, "cried out the more a great deal, thou Son of David, have mercy on me." Still he breaks out into the same humble language, and, if Jesus, the Son of David, will have mercy on him, he cares not much what some of his peevish followers said of, or did unto him. This was not a vain repetition, but a devout reiteration of his request. We may sometimes repeat the same words, and yet not be guilty of that battalogia, or vain speaking , which our Lord condemns. For our Lord himself prayed in his agony, and said twice the same words; "Father, if it be possible, let this cup pass from me." Thus Bartimeus, "Jesus, thou Son of David, have mercy upon me." And how does the Son of David treat him? Does he join issue with the multitude, and charge him to hold his peace? Or does he go on, thinking him beneath his notice? no; for, says St. Mark, ver 49, "And Jesus stood still," though he was on a journey, and it may be in haste (for it is not losing time to stop now and then on a journey to do a good office by the way) "and commanded him to be called:" why so? To teach us to be condescending and kind even to poor, if real beggars, and tacitly to reprove the blind, misguided zeal of those who had charged him to hold his peace. By this also our Lord prepares the multitude the better to take the more notice of the blind man's faith, and of his own mercy and power exerted in the healing of him. For there are times and seasons when we are called to perform acts of charity in the most public manner, and that too very consistently with the injunction of our Savior, "not to let our right hand know what our left hand doeth." For there is a great deal of difference between giving alms, and exercising acts of charity, that are seen of men, and doing them, that they may be seen; the one is always sinful, the other often becomes our duty. Jesus commanded Bartimeus to be called, "and they called him." Who called him? It may be, those who a little before charged him t hold his peace. For it often happens, that our opposers and discouragers, afterwards become our friends, "When a man's ways please the Lord, he makes his enemies be at peace with him." And it is to be wished, that all who have charged poor souls, that are crying after Jesus, to hold their peace, and to spare themselves, and not be righteous over-much, would imitate the people here, and encourage those they once persecuted and maligned. "They call the blind man, saying unto him, Be of good comfort, ruse, he calleth thee." The words, and manner of speaking them, implies haste, and a kind of solicitude for the blind man's relief. O! that we might hereby learn to be patient and long-suffering, towards opposers. For it may be, that many may oppose awakened souls, not out of enmity, but through prejudice and misinformation, through ignorance and unbelief, and a real, though perhaps false, persuasion, that their relations are going in a wrong way. By and by they may be convinced, that Christ is indeed calling them, and then they may become real and open friends to the cause and work of God; if not, it is our duty to behave with meekness towards all, and not to render railing for railing, but contrary-wise blessing, knowing that we are thereunto called, that we may inherit a blessing; Jesus did not break out into harsh language against these opposers, neither did Bartimeus. "Our Lord stood still, and commanded him to be called; and they call the blind man; saying unto him, Be of good comfort, rise, he calleth thee; and he, casting away his garment, rose and came to Jesus." Had Bartimeus not been in earnest when he cried, "Jesus, thou Son of David, have mercy upon me," he might have said, why do you mock me? why bid ye me arise; rise indeed I can, but after I am risen, how can I, being blind, find my way unto him? If he will come to me, it is well; if not, all you r calling availeth nothing, it being impossible for me to find my way. Thus thousands now-a-days object to evangelical preachers, saying, Why do you bid us come to, and believe on Jesus Christ, when you tell us it is impossible of ourselves to turn to God, or to do good works; and that no one can come unto him, unless the Father draw him. Is not this like the people's calling upon Bartimeus, to arise and come to Jesus, when he could not possibly see his way before him?

True, it is so; and would to God that all who make this objection, would imitate Bartimeus, and put forth the strength they have! What if we do call you to come, and to believe on the Lord Jesus Christ, that you may be saved? Does this imply, that you have a power in yourselves to do so? No, in no wise, no more than Jesus saying unto Lazarus' dead and stinking carcass, "Come forth," implied, that Lazarus had a power to raise himself from the grave. We call to you, being commanded to preach the gospel to every creature, hoping and praying, that Christ's power may accompany the word, and make it effectual to the quickening and raising of your dead souls. We also call to you to believe, upon the same account as Jesus said unto the lawyer, "do this, and thou shalt live;" that you seeing your utter inability to come, might thereby be convinced of your unbelief, and be led to ask for faith of him, whose gift it is, and who is therefore in scripture emphatically stiled the Author, as well as Finisher, of our faith. Add to this, that it is your duty to wait at the pool, or to make us of the strength you have, in the earnest and steady performance of all commanded duty. For though you cannot do what is spiritually good, because you want spiritual principles of action, yet ye may do what is morally and materially good, inasmuch as ye are reasonable creatures; and though doing your duty as you can, no ways deserves mercy, or entitles you to it, yet it is the way in which you are required to walk, and the way in which God us usually found. While you are attempting to stretch out your withered arm, peradventure it may be restored; and who knows but Jesus may work faith in you, by his almighty power?

Bartimeus has set before such objectors an example; O that they would once submit to be taught by a poor blind beggar! For he, casting away his garment, rose, and blind as he was, came to Jesus; "casting away his garment." This seems to be a large coat or cloak, that he wore to screen himself from the rain and cold; undoubtedly, it was the most necessary and valuable vestment he had, and one would have thought, that he should have taken this along with him; but he knew very well, that if he did so, it might hang about his heels, and thereby his reaching Jesus be retarded at least, if not prevented entirely. Valuable therefore as it was to him, he cast it away. The word implies, that he threw it from off his shoulders, with great precipitancy and resolution, knowing that if he got a cure, which he now hoped for, by Christ's calling him, he should never want his garment again. And thus will all do that are in earnest about coming to Jesus here, or seeing and enjoying him in his kingdom eternally hereafter.

They will cut off a right hand, they will pluck out a right eye, they will leave father and mother, husband and wife, yes, and their own lives also, rather than not be his disciples. The apostle Paul, therefore, exhorts Christians, to "lay aside every weight, and the sin that doth most easily beset them," or hand about their heels, as the word in the original imports; alluding to the custom of the Romans, who wore long garments. Such a one was this, which Bartimeus had wrapped round him. But he, to show that he sincerely desired to recover his sight, casting it away, arose and came to Jesus. And what treatment did Jesus give him? did he say, come not nigh me, thou impudent noisy beggar? No, "he answered and said unto him, What wilt thou, that I should do unto thee?" an odd question this, seemingly.

For did not our Lord know what he wanted? Yes, he did; but the Lord Jesus dealt with him, as he deals with us. He will make us acknowledge our wants ourselves, that we thereby may confess our dependence upon him, and be made more sensible of the need we stand in, of his divine assistance. The blind man immediately replies, "Lord, (thereby intimating his belief of Christ's divinity) that I might receive my sight." Methinks, I see the poor creature listening to the voice of our Savior, and with looks and gestures bespeaking the inward earnestness of his soul, he cries out, "Lord, that I may receive my sight." As though he had said, I believe thou are that Messiah who was to come into the world. I have heard of thy fame, O Jesus!

And hearing the long-wished-for glad tidings of thy coming this way, I cry unto thee, asking not for silver and gold, but what thou, thou alone canst give me, Lord, that I might receive my sight. No sooner does he ask, but he receives. For, verse 52, "Jesus said unto him, Go thy way, thy faith hath made thee whole; and immediately he received his sight." With the word there went a power; and he that spake light out of darkness, saying, "Let there be light, and there was light," commanded light into this poor blind beggar's eyes, and behold there was light. The miracle was instantaneous; immediately he received his sight. And next to a miracle it was, that by breaking into open light all at once, he was not struck blind again: but he that gave the sight, preserved it when given. O! happy Bartimeus! Thy eyes are now opened, and the very first object thou dost behold, is the ever- loving, altogether-lovely Jesus. Methinks I see thee transported with wonder and admiration, and all the disciples, and the multitude, gazing around thee! And now, having received thy sight, why dost thou not obey the Lord's command, and go thy way? Why doest thou not haste to fetch thy garment, that thou just now in a hurry didst cast away? No, no! with his bodily eyes, I believe he received also a fresh addition of spiritual sight, and though others saw no form or comeliness in the blessed Jesus, that they should desire him; yet he by an eye of faith discovered such transcendent excellencies in his royal person, and felt at the same time such a divine attraction towards his all-bountiful benefactor, that instead of going his way to fetch his garment, "he followed Jesus in the way;" and by his actions, says with faithful, honest-hearted Ruth, "entreat me not to leave thee; for whither thou goest, I will go; where thou lodgest, I will lodge; thy people shall be my people; and thy God, my God." He followed Jesus in the way; the narrow way, the way of the cross; and I doubt not but long since he has followed him to his crown, and is at this time sitting with him at the right hand of his Father.

And now, my dear hearers, how find you your hearts affected at the relation of this notable miracle which Jesus wrought? Are you not ready to break out into the language of the song of Moses, and to say, "Who is like unto thee O Lord, glorious in holiness, fearful in praises, continually doing wonders!" Marvelous are thy works, O Jesus, and that our souls know right well! But we must not stop here, in admiring what the Lord did for Bartimeus; this, no doubt, as well as other parts of Scripture, was written for our learning, upon whom the ends of the world are come; consequently, as was proposed in the SECOND place, we should see what spiritual improvement can be made of this history, upon which we have already been making some remarks.

A natural man, indeed, goes no further than the outward court of the Scripture, and reads this, and the other miracles of our blessed Savior, just in the same manner as he reads Homer's battles, or the exploits of Alexander. But God forbid, that we should rest in only hearing this matter of fact. For I tell thee, O man, I tell thee, O woman, whoever thou art, that sittest this day under a preached gospel, that if thou art in a natural state, thou art as blind in thy soul, as Bartimeus was in his body; a blind child of a blind father, even of thy father Adam, who lost his sight when he lost his innocence, and entailed his blindness, justly inflicted, upon thee, and me, and his whole posterity. Some think indeed, that thy see; but alas! such talk only like men in their sleep, like persons beside themselves; the scriptures every where represent fallen man, not only as spiritually blind, but dead also; and we no more know, by nature, savingly the way of salvation by Jesus Christ, than Bartimeus, when he was blind, knew the colors of the rainbow. This, I trust, some of you begin to feel, I see you concerned, I see you weeping, and, was I to ask some of you, what you want to have done unto you? I know your answer would be, that we may receive our sight. And God forbid, that I should charge you to hold your peace, as though Jesus would not regard you! No, your being made sensible of your natural blindness, and crying thus earnestly after Jesus, is a sign at least, that you are awakened by his holy Spirit (though it is possible, that you may cry with an exceeding bitter cry, as Esau did, and be lost at last); however, Christian charity induces me to believe and hope the best; I will therefore, in the language of those who afterwards encouraged Bartimeus, say unto you, Arise, take comfort for, I trust, Jesus is calling you; follow therefore the example of Bartimeus; cast away your garment; lay aside every weight, and the sin which doth most easily beset you, arise, and come to Jesus. He commands me, by his written word, to call to you, and say, "Come unto him, all ye that are weary, and heavy laden, and he will refresh you, he will give you rest." Be not afraid, ye seek Jesus of Nazareth; behold, he comes forth to meet you; ye are now on the highway side, and Jesus, I trust, is passing by; I feel his presence, I hope many of you feel it too; O then, cry mightily to him, who is mighty and willing to save you; lay yourselves at the feet of sovereign grace, say unto him, "Jesus, thou Son of David, have mercy on me," in the same frame as Bartimeus did, and Jesus will answer you, he will not cast out your prayer; according to your faith, so shall it be done unto you. Blind as you are, you shall notwithstanding, receive your sight; Satan, indeed, and unbelief, will suggest many objections to you, your carnal relations will also join issue with them, and charge you to hold your peace; one will tell you, that your blindness is too inveterate to be cured; another, that it is too late; a third, that though Jesus can, yet he will not have mercy upon such poor, blind, despicable beggars, as ye are; but, the more they charge you to hold your peace, do you cry out so much the more a great deal, "Jesus, thou Son of David, have mercy on us." Jesus, thou Savior, thou friend of sinners, thou Son of David, and therefore a Son of man! Gracious words! Endearing appellations! Be encouraged by them, to draw nigh unto him. Though David's Lord, yet he is become David's Son, after the flesh, that ye through him may be made the sons of God: no matter what thou art, O woman, what thou art, O man; though thou art literally a poor beggar, think not thy condition too mean for Jesus to take notice of; he came into the highways and hedges, to call such poor beggars in; or, if you are rich, think not yourselves too high to stoop to Jesus; for his is the King of kings; and you never will be truly rich, until you are made rich in Jesus; fear not being despised, or losing a little worldly honor: one sight of Jesus will make amends for all: you will find something so inviting, so attracting, so satisfying, in the altogether lovely Lamb of God, that every sublunary enjoyment will sicken, and die, and vanish before you;

and you will o more desire your former vain and trifling amusements, than Bartimeus, after he had received his sight, desired to go back again and fetch his garment. O that there may be many such blind beggars among you this day!

Here is a great multitude of people following me, a poor worm, this day. I rejoice to see the fields thus white, ready unto harvest, and to spread the gospel-net amidst so many; but alas! I shall return home with a heavy heart, unless some of you will arise and come to my Jesus; I desire to preach Him, and not myself; rest not in hearing and following me.

Behold, believe on, and follow the Lamb of God, who came to take away the sins of the world. Indeed, I do not despair of any of you, neither am I discouraged, on account of my preaching in the highways and hedges; Jesus called Zaccheus; Jesus called Bartimeus, as he passed through Jericho; that cursed, that devoted place; and why may he not call some of you, out of these despised fields? Is his arm shortened, that he cannot save? Is he not as mighty now, and as willing to save, even to the uttermost, all that come to the father through him, as he was seventeen hundred years ago? Assuredly he is; he hath said, and he also will do it, "Whosoever cometh to me, I will in no wise cast out." In no wise, or by no means. O encouraging words!

Sinners, believe ye this? arise then, be of good comfort, for Jesus is indeed calling you. Some of you, I trust, have obeyed this invitation, and have had a sight of him long ago; I know then, you will bless and love him; and if he should say unto you, as he did unto Bartimeus, go you your way; your answer would be, we love our master, and will not go from him. But suffer ye the word of exhortation: Suffer me to stir up your pure minds by way of re-membrance, show that you have indeed seen him, and that you do indeed love him, by following him in the way; I mean, in the way of the cross, the way of his ordinances, and in the way of his holy commandments; for alas! the love of many waxeth cold, and few there are that follow Jesus rightly in the way; few there are that cast away their garments so heartily as they should; some idol or another hangs about us, and hinders us in running the race that is set before us. Awake therefore, ye sleepy, though, it may be, wise virgins.

Awake, awake, put on strength; shake yourselves from the dust; arise and follow Jesus more closely in the way, than ever you did yet. Lift up the hands that hang down, and strengthen the feeble knees. Provide right paths for your feet, lest that which is lame be turned out of the way, but rather be ye healed. For though the way be narrow, yet it is not long; "though the gate be straight, (to use the words of pious bishop Beveridge) yet it opens into everlasting life." O that ye may get a fresh sight of him again this day! That would be like oil to the wheels of your graces, and make your souls like the chariots of Aminadab. It is only owing to your losing sight of him, that you go so heavily from day to day. A sight of Jesus, like the sun rising in the morning, dispels the darkness and gloominess that lies upon the soul. Take therefore a fresh view of him, O believers, and never rest until you are translated to see him as he is, and to live with him for evermore, in the kingdom of heaven. Even so, Lord Jesus, Amen and Amen!

Sermon 28 Directions how to hear Sermons

Luke 8:18, "Take heed, therefore, how ye hear."

The occasion of our Lord's giving this caution, was this: Perceiving that much people were gathered together to hear him out of every city, and knowing (for he is God, and knoweth all things) that many, if not most of them, would be hearers only, and not doers of the word; he spake to them by a parable, wherein, under the similitude of a sower that went out to sow his seed, he plainly intimated, how few there were amongst them, who would receive any saving benefit from his doctrine, or bring forth fruit unto perfection.

The application one would imagine should have been plain and obvious; but the disciples, as yet unenlightened in any great degree by the Holy Spirit, and therefore unable to see into the hidden mysteries of the kingdom of God, dealt with our Savior, as people ought to deal with their ministers; they discoursed with him privately about the meaning of what he had taught them in public; and with a sincere desire of doing their duty, asked for an interpretation of the parable.

Our blessed Lord, as he always was willing to instruct those that were teachable, (herein setting his ministers an example to be courteous and easy of access) freely told them the signification. And withal, to make them more cautious and more attentive to his doctrine for the future, he tells them, that they were in an especial manner to be the light of the world, and were to proclaim on the house-top whatsoever he told them in secret: and as their improving the knowledge already imparted, was the only condition upon which more was to be given them, it therefore highly concerned them to "take heed how they heard." From the context then it appears, that the words were primarily spoken to the Apostles themselves. But as it is to be feared, out of those many thousands that flock to hear sermons, but few, comparatively speaking, are effectually influenced by them, I cannot but think it very necessary to remind you of the caution given by our Lord to his disciples, and to exhort you with the utmost earnestness, to "take heed how you hear." In prosecution of which design I shall, FIRST, Prove that every one ought to take all opportunities of hearing sermons. And, SECONDLY, I shall lay down some cautions and directions, in order to your hearing with profit and advantage.

FIRST, I am to prove, that every one ought to take all opportunities of hearing sermons.

That there have always been particular persons set apart by God to instruct and exhort his people to practice what he should require of them, is evident from many passages of scripture. St. Jude tells us, that "Enoch, the seventh from Adam, prophesied (or preached) concerning the Lord's coming with ten thousand of his saints to judgment." And Noah, who lived not long after, is stiled by St. Peter, "a preacher of righteousness." And though in all the intermediate space between the flood and giving of the law, we hear but of few preachers, yet we may reasonably conclude, that God never left himself without witness, but at sundry times, and after diverse manners, spoke to our fathers by the patriarchs and prophets.

But however it was before, we are assured that after the delivery of the law, God constantly separated to himself a certain order of men to preach to, as well as pray for his people; and commanded them to inquire their duty at the priests mouths. And thought the Jews were frequently led into captivity, and for their sins scattered abroad on the face of the earth, yet he never utterly forsook his church, but still kept up a remnant of prophets and preachers, as Ezekiel, Jeremiah, Daniel, and others, to reprove, instruct, and call them to repentance.

Thus was it under the law. Nor has the church been worse, but infinitely better provided for under the gospel. For when Jesus Christ, that great High-priest, had through the eternal Spirit offered himself, as a full, perfect, sufficient sacrifice and satisfaction for the sins of the whole world, and after his resurrection had all power committed to him, both in heaven and earth, he gave commission to his Apostles, and in them to all succeeding ministers, to "go and preach his gospel to every creature;" promising to "to be with them, to guide, assist, strengthen, and comfort them always, even to the end of the world." But if it be the duty of ministers to preach, (and woe be to them if they do not preach the gospel, for a necessity is laid upon them) no doubt, the people are obliged to attend to them; for otherwise, wherefore are ministers sent?

And how can we here avoid admiring the love and tender care which our dear Redeemer has expressed for his spouse the church? Who, because he could not be always with us in person, on account it was expedient he should go away, and as our forerunner take possession of that glory he had purchased by his precious blood, yet would not leave us comfortless, but first settled a sufficient number of pastors and teachers; and afterwards, according to his promise, actually did and will continue to sent down the Holy Ghost, to furnish them and their successors with proper gifts and graces "for the work of the ministry, for the perfecting of the saints, for the edifying of his body in love, till we all come in the unity of the spirit, to the fullness of the measure of the stature of Christ." O how insensible are those persons of this unspeakable gift, who do despite to the Spirit of grace, who crucify the Son of God afresh, and put him to an open shame, by willfully refusing to attend on so great a means of salvation? How dreadful will the end of such men be? How aggravating, that light should come into the world, that the glad tidings of salvation should be so very frequently proclaimed in this populous city, and that so many should loath this spiritual manna, this angels food, and call it light bread? How much more tolerable will it be for Tyre and Sidon, for Sodom and Gomorrah, than for such sinners? Better, that men had never heard of a Savior being born, than after they have heard, not to give heed to the ministry of those, who are employed as his ambassadors, to transact affairs between God and their souls.

We may, though at a distance, without a spirit of prophesy, foretell the deplorable condition of such men; behold them cast into hell, lifting up their eyes, being in torment, and crying out, How often would our ministers have gathered us, as a hen gathereth her chickens under her wings? But we would not. O that we had known in that our day, the things that belonged to our everlasting peace! But now they are for ever hid from our eyes.

Thus wretched, thus inconceivably miserable, will such be as slight and make a mock at the public preaching of the gospel. But taking it for granted, there are but few, if any, of this unhappy stamp, who think it worth their while to tread the courts of the Lord's house, I pass on not to the SECOND general thing proposed, to lay down some cautions and directions, in order to your hearing sermons with profit and advantage.

And here, if we reflect on what has been already delivered, and consider that preaching is an ordinance of God, a means appointed by Jesus Christ himself for promoting his kingdom amongst men, you cannot reasonably be offended, if, in order that you may hear sermons with profit and advantage, I 1. Direct or entreat you to come to hear them, not out of curiosity, but from a sincere desire to know and do your duty.

Formality and hypocrisy in any religious exercise, is an abomination unto the Lord. And to enter his house merely to have our ears entertained, and not our hearts reformed, must certainly be highly displeasing to the Most High God, as well as unprofitable to ourselves.

Hence it is, that so many remain unconverted, yea, unaffected with the most evangelical preaching; so that like St. Paul's companions, before his conversion, they only hear the preacher's voice with their outward ears, but do not experience the power of it inwardly in their hearts. Or, like the ground near Gideon's fleece, they remain untouched; whilst others, who came to be fed with the sincere milk of the word, like the fleece itself, are watered by the dew of God's heavenly blessing, and grow thereby.

Flee therefore, my brethren, flee curiosity, and prepare your hearts by a humble disposition, to receive with meekness the engrafted word, and then it will be a means, under God, to quicken, build up, purify, and save your souls.

2. A second direction I shall lay down for the same purpose, is, not only to prepare your hearts before you hear, but also to give diligent heed to the things that are spoken from the word of God.

If an earthly king was to issue out a royal proclamation, on performing or not performing the conditions therein contained, the life or death of his subjects entirely depended, how solicitous would they be to hear what those conditions were? And shall not we pay the same respect to the King of kings, and Lord of lords, and lend an attentive ear to his ministers, when they are declaring, in his name, how our pardon, peace, and happiness may be secured?

When God descended on mount Sinai in terrible majesty, to give unto his people the law, how attentive were they to his servant Moses? And if they were so earnest to hear the thunderings or threatenings of the law, shall not we be as solicitous to hear from the ministers of Christ, the glad tidings of the gospel?

Whilst Christ was himself on earth, it is said, that the people hung upon him to hear the gracious words that proceeded out of his mouth. And if we looked on ministers as we ought, as the sent of Jesus Christ, we should hang upon them to hear their words also.

Besides, the sacred truths that gospel ministers deliver, are not dry insipid lectures on moral philosophy, intended only to amuse us for a while; but the great mysteries of godliness, which, therefore, we are bound studiously to liken to, left through our negligence we should either not understand them, or by any other means let them slip.

But how regardless are those of this direction, who, instead of hanging on the preacher to hear him, doze or sleep whilst he is speaking to them from God? Unhappy men! Can they not watch with our blessed Lord one hour? What! Have they never read how Eutychus fell down as he was sleeping, when St. Paul continued like discourse till midnight, and was taken up dead?

But to return. Though you may prepare your hearts, as you may think, by a teachable disposition, and be attentive whilst discourses are delivering, yet this will profit you little, unless you observe a 3. A third direction, Not to entertain any the least prejudice against the minister.

For could a preacher speak with the tongue of men and angels, if his audience was prejudiced against him, he would be but as sounding brass, or tinkling cymbal.

That was the reason why Jesus Christ himself, the Eternal Word, could not do many mighty works, nor preach to any great effect among those of his own country; for they were offended at him: And was this same Jesus, this God incarnate, again to bow the heavens, and to come down speaking as never man spake, yet, if we were prejudiced against him, as the Jews were, we should harden our hearts as the Jews did theirs.

Take heed therefore, my brethren, and beware of entertaining any dislike against those whom the Holy Ghost has made overseers over you.

Consider that the clergy are men of lie passions with yourselves: and though we should even hear a person teaching others to do, what he has not learned himself; yet, that is no sufficient reason for rejecting his doctrine: for ministers speak not in their own, but Christ's name. And we know who commanded the people to do whatsoever the Scribes and Pharisees should say unto them, though they said but did not. But 4 Fourthly, As you ought not to be prejudiced against, so you should be careful not to depend too much on a preacher, or think more highly of him than you ought to think. For though this be an extreme that people seldom run into, yet preferring one teacher in apposition to another, has often been of ill consequence to the church of God. It was a fault which the great Apostle of the Gentiles condemned in the Corinthians. For whereas one said, "I am of Paul; another, I am of Apollos: are ye not carnal," says he? "For who is Paul, and who is Apollos, but instruments in God's hands by whom you believed?" And are not all ministers sent forth to be ministering ambassadors to those who shall be heirs of salvation? And are they not all therefore greatly to be esteemed for their work's sake.

The Apostle, it is true, commands us to pay double honor to those who labor in the word and doctrine: but then to prefer one minister at the expense of another, (perhaps, to such a degree, as when you have actually entered a church, to come out again because he does not preach) is earthly, sensual, devilish.

Not to mention that popularity and applause cannot but be exceedingly dangerous, even to a rightly informed mind; and must necessarily fill any thinking man with a holy jealousy, lest he should take that honor to himself, which is due only to God, who alone qualifies him for his ministerial labors, and from whom alone every good and perfect gift cometh.

5. A Fifth direction I would recommend is, to make a particular application of every thing that is delivered to your own hearts.

When our Savior was discoursing at the last supper with his beloved disciples, and foretold that one of them should betray him, each of them immediately applied it to his own heart, and said, "Lord, is it I?" And would persons, in like manner, when preachers are dissuading from any sin, or persuading to any duty, instead of crying, this was designed against such and such a one, turn their thoughts inwardly, and say, Lord, is it I?

How far more beneficial should we find discourses to be, than now they generally are?

But we are apt to wander too much abroad; always looking at the mote with is in our neighbor's eye, rather than at the beam which is in our own.

Haste we now to the 6. Sixth and last direction: If you would receive a blessing from the Lord, when you hear his word preached, pray to him, both before, in, and after every sermon, to endue the minister with power to speak, and to grant you a will and ability to put in practice, what he shall show from the book of God to be your duty.

This would be an excellent means to render the word preached effectual to the enlightening and enflaming your hearts; and without this, all the other means before prescribed will be in vain.

No doubt it was this consideration that made St. Paul so earnestly entreat his beloved Ephesians to intercede with God for him: "Praying always, with all manner of prayer and supplication in the spirit, and for me also, that I may open my mouth with boldness, to make known the mysteries of the gospel." And if so great an Apostle as St. Paul, needed the prayers of his people, much more do those ministers, who have only the ordinary gifts of the Holy Spirit.

Besides, this would be a good proof that you sincerely desired to do, as well as to know the will of God. And it must highly profit both ministers and people; because God, through your prayers, will give them a double portion of his Holy Spirit, whereby they will be enabled to instruct you more fully in the things which pertain to the kingdom of God.

And O that all who hear me this day, would seriously apply their hearts to practice what has now been told them! How would ministers see Satan, like lightning, fall from heaven, and people find the word preached sharper than a two-edged sword, and mighty, through God, to the pulling down of the devil's strong holds!

The Holy Ghost would then fall on all them that hear the word, as when St. Peter preached; the gospel of Christ would have free course, run very swiftly, and thousands again be converted by a sermon.

For "Jesus Christ is the same yesterday, today, and for ever." He has promised to be with his ministers always, even unto the end of the world.

And the reason why we do not receive larger effusions of the blessed Spirit of God, is not because our all-powerful Redeemer's hand is shortened, but because we do not expect them, and confine them to the primitive times.

It does indeed sometimes happen, that God, to magnify his free grace in Christ Jesus, is found of them that sought him not; a notorious sinner is forcibly worked upon by a public sermon, and plucked as a firebrand out of the fire. But this is not God's ordinary way of acting; No, for the generality, he only visits those with the power of his word, who humbly wait to know what he would have them to do; and sends unqualified hearers not only empty, but hardened away.

Take heed, therefore, ye careless, curious professors, if any such be here present, how you hear. Remember, that whether we think of it or not, "we must all appear before the judgment seat of Christ;" where ministers must give a strict account of the doctrine they have delivered, and you as strict a one, how you have improved under it. And, good God! How will you be able to stand at the bar of an angry, sin-avenging judge, and see so many discourses you have despised, so many ministers, who once longed and labored for the salvation of your precious and immortal souls, brought out as so many swift witnesses against you? Will it be sufficient then, think you, to alledge, that you went to hear them only out of curiosity, to pass away an idle hour, to admire the oratory, or ridicule the simplicity of the preacher? No; God will then let you know, that you ought to have come out of better principles; that every sermon has been put down to your account, and that you must then be justly punished for not improving by them.

But fear not, you little flock, who with meekness receive the ingrafted word, and bring forth the peaceable fruits of righteousness; for it shall not be so with you. No, you will be your minister's joy, and their crown of rejoicing in the day of our Lord Jesus: And they will present you in a holy triumph, faultless, and unblameable, to our common Redeemer, saying, "Behold us, O Lord, and the children which thou hast given us." But still take heed how you hear: for upon your improving the grace you have, more shall be given, and you shall have abundance. "He is faithful that ha promised, who also will do it." Nay, God from out of Zion, shall so bless you, that every sermon you hear shall communicate to you a fresh supply of spiritual knowledge. The word of God shall dwell in you richly; you shall go on from strength to strength, from one degree of grace unto another, till being grown up to be perfect men in Christ Jesus, and filled with all the fullness of God, you shall be translated by death to see him as he is, and to sing praises before his throne with angels and archangels, cherubim and seraphim, and the general assembly of the first- born, whose names are written in heaven, for ever and ever.

Which God, etc.

Sermon 29 The Extent and Reasonableness of Self-Denial

Luke 9:23, "And he said unto them all, if any man will come after me, let him deny himself."

Whoever reads the gospel with a single eye, and sincere intentions, will find, that our blessed Lord took all opportunities of reminding his disciples that his kingdom was not of this world; that his doctrine was a doctrine of the cross; and that their professing themselves to be his followers, would call them to a constant state of voluntary suffering and self-denial.

The words of the text afford us one instance, among many, of our savior's behavior in this matter: for having in the preceding verses revealed himself to Peter, and the other apostles, to be "The Christ of God;" lest they should be too much elated with such a peculiar discovery of his deity, or think that their relation to so great a personage would be attended with nothing but pomp and grandeur, he tells then, in the 22nd verse, that "the son of man was to suffer many things," in this world, though he was to be crowned with eternal glory and honor in the next: and that if any of them or their posterity would share in the same honor, they must bear a part with him in his self-denial and sufferings. For "He said unto them all, if any man will come after me, let him deny himself." From which words I shall consider these three things: I. FIRST, The nature of the self-denial recommended in the text; and in how many respects we must deny ourselves, in order to come after Jesus Christ.

II. SECONDLY, I shall endeavor to prove the universality and reasonableness of this duty of self-denial.

III. THIRDLY, I shall offer some considerations, which may serve as so man motives to reconcile us to, and quicken us in, the practice of this self-denial.

I. FIRST, I am to show you the nature of the self-denial recommended in the text; or in how many respects we must deny ourselves in order to follow Jesus Christ.

Now as the faculties of the soul are distinguished by the understanding, will and affections; so in all these must each of us deny himself. We must not lean to our own understanding, being wise in our own eyes, and prudent in our own sight; but we must submit our short-sighted reason to the light of divine revelation. There are mysteries in religion, which are above, though not contrary to our natural reason: and therefore we shall never become Christians unless we call down imaginations, "and every high thing that exalteth itself against the knowledge of God, and bring into captivity every thought to the obedience of Christ." It is in this respect, as well as others, that we must become fools for Christ's sake, and acknowledge we know nothing without revelation, as we ought to know. We must, with all humility and reverence, embrace the truths revealed to us in the holy scriptures; for thus only can we become truly wise, even "Wise unto salvation." It was matter of our blessed Lord's thanksgiving to his heavenly father, that he had "hidden these things from the wise and prudent, and had revealed them unto babes." And in this respect also we must "be converted and become as little children," teachable, and willing to follow the Lamb into whatsoever mysteries he shall be pleased to lead us; and believe and practice all divine truths, not because we can demonstrate them, but because God, "who cannot lie," has revealed them to us.

Hence then we may trace infidelity to its fountain head; for it is nothing else, but a pride of the understanding, an unwillingness to submit to the truths of God, that makes so many, professing themselves wise, to become such fools as to deny the Lord, who has so dearly bought them; and dispute the divinity of that eternal Word, "in whom they live, and move, and have their being:" Whereby it is justly to be feared, they will bring upon themselves sure, if not swift destruction.

But, as we must deny ourselves in our understandings, so must we deny, or, as it might be more properly rendered, renounce our wills; that is, we must make our own wills no principle of action, but "whether we eat or drink , or whatsoever we do, we must do all, (not merely to please ourselves, but) to the glory of God." Not that we are therefore to imagine we are to have no pleasure in any thing we do: "Wisdom's ways are ways of pleasantness;" but pleasing ourselves must not be the principal, but only the subordinate end of our actions.

And I cannot but particularly press this doctrine upon you, because it is the grand secret of our holy religion. It is this, my brethren, that distinguishes the true Christian from the mere moralist and formal professor; and without which none of our actions are acceptable in God's sight: For "if thine eye be single," says our blessed Lord, Matthew 6:22, that is, if thou aimest simply to please God, without any regard to thy own will, "thy whole body, (or all thy actions) will be full of light;" agreeable to the gospel, which is called light: "But if thine eye be evil, (if thine intention be diverted any other way) thy whole body, (all thy actions) will be full of darkness," sinful and unprofitable, we must not only do the will of God, but do it because it is his will; since we pray that "God's will may be done on earth as it is in heaven." And no doubt, the blessed angels not only do every thing that God willeth, but do it cheerfully, out of this principle, because God willeth it: And if we would live as we pray, we must go and do likewise.

But farther, as we must renounce our wills in doing, so likewise must we renounce them in suffering the will of God. Whatsoever befalls us, we must say with good old Eli, "It is the Lord, let him do what seemeth him good;": or with one that was infinitely greater than Eli, "Father, not my will, but thine be done." O Jesus, thine was an innocent will, and yet thou renouncedst it. Teach us, even us also, O our Savior! To submit our wills to thine, in all the evils which shall be brought upon us; and in every thing enable us to give thanks, since it is thy blessed will concerning us!

THIRDLY, we must deny ourselves, as in our understandings and wills, so likewise in our affections. More particularly, we must deny ourselves the pleasurable indulgence and self-enjoyment of riches: "If any man will come after me, he must forsake all and follow me." And again (to show the utter inconsistency of the love of the things of this world with the love of the Father) he tells us, "unless a man forsake all that he hath, he cannot be my disciple." Far be it from me to think that these texts are to be taken in a literal sense; as though they obliged rich persons to go sell all that they have and give to the poor, (for that would put it out of their power to be serviceable to the poor for the future) but however, they certainly imply thus much, that we are to sit loose to, sell and forsake all in affection, and be willing to part with every thing, when God shall require it at our hands: that is, as the apostle observes, we must "use the world as though we used it not;" and though we are in the world, we must not be of it. We must look upon ourselves as stewards, and not proprietors, of the manifold gifts of God; provide first what is necessary for ourselves and for our households, and expend the rest, not in indulgencies and superfluous ornaments, forbidden by the apostle, but in clothing, feeding, and relieving the naked, hungry, distressed disciples of Jesus Christ. This is what our blessed Lord would have us understand by forsaking all, and in this sense must each of us deny himself.

I am sensible that this will seem an hard saying to may, who will be offended because they are covetous, and "lovers of pleasure more than lovers of God;" but if I yet pleased such men, I should not be the servant of Christ. No, we must not, like Ahab's false prophets, have a lying spirit in our mouths, but declare faithfully the whole will of God; and like honest Micajah out of pity and compassion, tell men the truth, though they may falsely think we prophecy not good but evil concerning them.

But to proceed: As we must renounce our affection for riches, so likewise our affections for relations, when they stand in opposition to our love of, and duty to God: For thus saith the Savior of the world: "If any man will come after me, and hateth not his father and mother, his children, and brethren, and sisters, yea and his own life also, he cannot be my disciple." Strange doctrine this! What, hate our own flesh! What, hate the father that begat us, the mother that bare us! How can these things be? Can God contradict himself? Has he not bid us to honor our father and mother?

And yet we are here commanded to hate them. How can these truths be reconciled? By interpreting the word hate, not in a rigorous and absolute sense, but comparatively: not as implying a total alienation, but a less degree of affection. For thus our blessed Savior himself (the best and purest expositor of his own meaning) explains it in a parallel text, Matthew 10:37, "He that loveth father or mother more than me, is not worthy of me; He that loveth son or daughter more than me, is not worthy of me." So that when the persuasions of our friends (as for our trial they may be permitted to be) are contrary to the will of God, we must say with Levi, "we have not know them;" or, agreeably to our blessed Lord's rebuke to Peter, "Get you behind me, my adversaries; for you favor not the things that be of God, but the things that be of man." Farther, we must deny ourselves in things indifferent; for it might easily be shown, that as many, if not more, perish by an immoderate use of things in themselves indifferent, as by any gross sin whatever. A prudent Christian therefore, will consider not only what is lawful, but what is expedient also: not so much what degrees of self-denial best suit his inclinations here, as what will most effectually break his will, and fit him for greater degrees of glory hereafter.

LASTLY, To conclude this head, we must renounce our own righteousness: For, though we should give all our goods to feed the poor, and our bodies to be burned, yet, if we in the least depend on that, and do not wholly rely on the perfect all sufficient righteousness of Jesus Christ, it will profit us nothing. "Christ is the end of the law for righteousness to every one that believeth." We are complete in him, and him only. Our own righteousnesses are but as filthy rags. We must count all things but dung and dross, so that we may be found in him, not having our own righteousness, but the righteousness which is of God, through Jesus Christ our Lord.

And is this the doctrine of Christianity? Is not the Christian world then asleep? If not, whence so much self-righteousness, whence the self- indulgence, whence the reigning love of riches which we every where meet with? Above all, whence that predominant greediness after sensual pleasure, that has so over-run this sinful nation, that was a pious stranger to come amongst us, he would be tempted to think some heathen Venus was worshipped here, and that temples were dedicated to her service. But we have the authority of an inspired apostle to affirm, that they who live in a round of pleasure, "are dead while they live." Wherefore, as the Holy Ghost saith, "Awake thou that sleepeth, and arise from the dead, and Christ shall give thee light." But the power of raising the spiritually dead belongeth only unto God. Do thou therefore, O Holy Jesus, who by thy almighty word commandest Lazarus to come forth, though he had lain in the grave some days, speak also as effectually to these spiritually dead souls, whom Satan for many years hath so fast bound by sensual pleasures, that they are not so much as able to lift up their eyes or hearts to heaven.

II. But I pass on to the second general thing proposed, to consider the universal obligation and reasonableness of this doctrine of self- denial.

When our blessed master had been discoursing publicly concerning the watchfulness of the faithful and wise steward, his disciples asked him, "Speakest thou this parable to all, or only to us?" The same question I am aware has been, and will be put concerning the foregoing doctrine: for too many, unwilling to take Christ's easy yoke upon them, in order to evade the force of the gospel precepts, would pretend that all those commands concerning self-denial, and renouncing ourselves and the world, belonged to our Lord's first and immediate followers, and not to us or to our children.

But such persons greatly err, not knowing the scriptures, nor the power of godliness in their hearts. For the doctrine of Jesus Christ, like his blesses self, is "the same yesterday, today, and for ever." What he said unto one, he said unto all, even unto the ends of the world; "If any man will come after me, let him deny himself:" and in the text it is particularly mentioned that he said it unto them ALL. And lest we should still absurdly imagine that this word ALL was to be confined to his apostles, with whom he was then discoursing, it is said in another place, that Jesus turned unto the multitude and said, "If any man will come after me, and hateth not his father and mother, yea and his own life also, he cannot be my disciple." When our blessed Lord had spoken a certain parable, it is said, "the scribes and Pharisees were offended, for they knew the parable was spoken against them:" and if Christians can now read these plain and positive texts of scripture, and at the same time not think they are spoken of them, they are more hardened than Jews, and more insincere than Pharisees.

In the former part of this discourse I observed, that the precepts concerning forsaking and selling all, did not oblige us in a literal sense, because the state of the church does not demand it of us, as it did of the primitive Christians; but still the same deadness to the world, the same abstemious use of, and readiness to part with or goods for Christ's sake, is as absolutely necessary for, and as obligatory on us, as it was on them.

For though the church may differ as to the outward state of it, in different ages, yet as to the purity of its inward state, it was, is, and always will be invariably the same. And all the commands which we meet with in the epistles about "mortifying our members which are upon the earth, of setting our affections on things above, and of not being conformed to this world;" are but so many incontestable proofs that the same holiness, heavenly-mindedness, and deadness to the world, is as necessary for us, as for our Lord's immediate followers.

But farther, as such an objection argues an ignorance of the scriptures, so it is a manifest proof, that such as make it are strangers to the power of godliness in their hearts. For since the form and substance of religion consists in recovery from our fallen estate in Adam, by a new birth in Christ Jesus, there is an absolute necessity for us to embrace and practice the self-denial before spoken of. If we are alive unto God, we shall be dead to ourselves and the world. If all things belonging to the spirit live and grow in us, all things belonging to the old man must die in us. We must mourn before we are comforted, and receive the spirit of bondage before we are blessed with the unspeakable privilege of the spirit of adoption, and with a full assurance of faith can say, "Abba, Father." Were we indeed in a state of innocence, and had we, like Adam before his fall, the divine image fully stamped upon our souls, we then should have no need of self-denial; but since we are fallen, sickly, disordered, self-righteous creatures, we must necessarily deny ourselves (and count it our privilege to do so) ere we can follow Jesus Christ to glory. To reject such a salutary practice on account of the difficulty attending it at first, is but too like the obstinacy of a perverse sick child, who nauseates and refuses the portion reached out to it by a skillful physician or a tender parent, because it is a little ungrateful to the taste.

Had any of us seen Lazarus when he lay full of sores at the rich man's gate; or Job when he was smitten with ulcers, from the crown of his head to the sole of his foot: And had we at the same time prescribed to them some healing medicines, which, because they might put them to pain, they would not apply to their wounds, should we not most justly think, that they were either fond of a distempered body, or were not sensible of their distempers? But our souls, by nature, are in an infinitely more deplorable condition than the bodies of Job or Lazarus, when full of ulcers and boils: for, alas! "our whole head is sick, and our whole heart faint, from the crown of the head to the sold of the foot, we are full of wounds and bruises and putrifying sores, and there is no health in us." And if we are unwilling to deny ourselves, and come after Jesus Christ in order to be cured, it is a sign we are not sensible of the wretchedness of our state, and that we are not truly made whole.

Even Naaman's servants could say, when he refused (pursuant to Elisha's orders) to wash in the river Jordan, that he might cure his leprosy, "Father, if the prophet had bid thee do some great thing, wouldst thou not have done it? How much rather then, when he saith to thee, wash and be clean?" And may not I very properly address myself to you in the same manner, my brethren? If Jesus Christ, our great prophet, had bid you to do some far more difficult thing, would you not have done it? Much more then should you do it, when he only bids you deny yourselves what would certainly hurt you if indulged in, and he will give you a crown of life.

But to illustrate this by another comparison: In the 12th chapter of the Acts, we read, that "St. Peter was kept in prison, and was sleeping between two soldiers, bound with two chains. And behold an angel of the Lord came upon him, and smote Peter on the side, saying, arise up quickly.

And his chains fell off from his hands." But had this great apostle, instead of rising up quickly, and doing as the blessed angel commanded him, hugged his chains and begged that they might not be let fall from his hands, would not any one think that he was in love with slavery, and deserved to be executed next morning? And does not the person who refuses to deny himself, act as inconsistently, as this apostle would have done if he had neglected the means of his deliverance? For our souls, by nature, are in a spiritual dungeon, sleeping and fast bound between the world, the flesh, and the devil, not with two but ten thousand chains of lusts and corruptions. Now Jesus Christ, like St. Peter's good angel, by the power of his gospel comes and opens the prison door, and bids us "deny ourselves and follow him." But if we do not arise, gird up the loins of our mind and follow him, are we not in love with bondage, and to we not deserve never to be delivered from it?

Indeed, I will not affirm that this doctrine of self-denial appears in this just light to every one. No, I am sensible that to the natural man it is foolishness, and to the young convert an hard saying. But what says our Savior? "If any man will do my will, he shall know the doctrine, whether it be of God, or whether I speak of myself." This, my dear friends, is the best, the only way of conviction. Let us up and be doing; let us arise quickly, and deny ourselves, and the Lord Jesus will remove those scales from the eyes of our minds, which now, like so many veils, hinder us from seeing clearly the reasonableness, necessity, and inexpressible advantage of the doctrine that has been delivered. Let us but once thus show ourselves men, and then the spirit of God will move on the face of our souls, as he did once upon the face of the great deep; and cause them to emerge out of that confused chaos, in which they are most certainly now involved, if we are strangers and enemies to self-denial and the cross of Christ.

III. Proceed we therefore now to the third and last general thing proposed, to offer some considerations, which may serve as so many motives to reconcile us to, and quicken us in, the practice of this duty of self- denial.

1. And the first means I shall recommend to you, in order to reconcile you to this doctrine, is, to meditate frequently on the life of our blessed Lord and Master Jesus Christ. Follow him from his cradle to the cross, and see what a self-denying life he led! And shall not we drink of the cup that he drank of, and be baptized with the baptism that he was baptized with? Or think we, that Jesus Christ did and suffered everything in order to have us excused and exempted from sufferings? No, far be it from any sincere Christian to judge after this manner: for St. Peter tells us, "He suffered for us, leaving us an example that we should follow his steps." Had Christ, indeed, like those that sat in Moses' chair, laid heavy burdens of self- denial upon us, (supposing they were heavy, which they are not) and refused to touch them himself with one of his fingers; we might have had some pretense to complain: But since he has enjoined us nothing, but what he first put in practice himself, thou art inexcusable, O disciple, whoever thou art, who wouldst be above thy persecuted self-denying master: And thou art no good and faithful servant, who art unwilling to suffer and sympathize with thy mortified, heavenly-minded Lord.

2. Next to the pattern of our blessed master, think often on the lives of the glorious company of the apostles, the goodly fellowship of the prophets, and the noble army of martyrs; who by a constant looking to the author and finisher of our faith, have fought the good fight, and are gone before us to inherit the promises. View again and again, how holily, how self-denyingly, how unblameably they lived: And if self-denial was necessary for them, why not for us also? Are we not men of lie passions with them? Do we not live in the same wicked world as they did? Have we not the same good spirit to assist, support, and purify us, as they had? And is not the same eternal inheritance reached out to us, as was to them? And if we have the same nature to change, the same wicked world to withstand, the same good spirit to help, and the same eternal crown at the end; why should not we lead the same lives

as they did? Do we think they did works of supererogation? If not, why do not we do as they did? Or why does your own church set apart festivals to commemorate the deaths and sufferings of the saints, but in order to excite you to follow them as they did Christ.

3. Thirdly, Think often on the pains of hell; consider, whether it is not better to cut off a right hand or foot, and pull our a right eye, if they offend us (our cause us to sin) "rather than to be cast into hell, where the worm dieth not, and the fire is not quenched." Think how many thousands there are now reserved with damned spirits in chains of darkness unto the judgment of the great day. And think withal, that this, this must be our case shortly, unless we are wise in time, deny ourselves, and follow Jesus Christ. Think you, they now imagine Jesus Christ to be an hard master; or rather think you not, they would give ten thousand times ten thousand worlds, could they but return to life again, and take Christ's easy yoke upon them? And can we dwell with everlasting burnings more than they? No, if we cannot bear this precept, deny yourselves, take up your crosses; how shall we bear the irrevocable sentence, "Depart from me, ye cursed, into everlasting fire, prepared for the devil and his angels?" But I hope those, amongst whom I am now preaching the kingdom of God, are not so disingenuous as to need to be driven to their duty by the terrors of the Lord, but rather desire to be drawn by the cords of love.

Lastly, Therefore, often meditate on the joys of heaven: think, think with what unspeakable glory those happy souls are now encircled, who when on earth were called to deny themselves as well as we, and were not disobedient to that call: Lift up your hearts frequently towards the mansions of eternal bliss, and with an eye of faith, like Stephen, see the heavens opened, and the Son of man with his glorious retinue of departed saints, sitting and solacing themselves in eternal joys. Hark! Methinks I hear them chanting forth their everlasting Hallelujahs, and echoing triumphant songs of joy. And do you not long, my brethren, to join this heavenly choir? Do not your hearts burn within you? As the hart panteth after the water brooks, do not your souls so long after the blessed company of these sons of God? Behold then a heavenly ladder reached down to you, by which you may climb to this holy hill. Let us believe on the Lord Jesus Christ, and deny ourselves! By this alone, every saint that ever lived ascended into the joy of their Lord. And then, we, even we also shall ere long be lifted up into the same most blissful regions, there to enjoy an eternal rest with the people of God, and join with them in singing doxologies and songs of praise, to the everlasting, blessed, all-glorious, most adorable Trinity, for ever and ever.

Which God of his infinite mercy grant, etc.

Sermon 30 Christ's Transfiguration

Luke 9:28-36, "And it came to pass about an eight days after these sayings, he took Peter and John and James, and went up into a mountain to pray. And as he prayed, the fashion of his countenance was altered, and his raiment was white and glistering. And, behold, there talked with him two men, which were Moses and Elias: Who appeared in glory, and spake of his decease which he should accomplish at Jerusalem. But Peter and they that were with him were heavy with sleep: and when they were awake, they saw his glory, and the two men that stood with him. And it came to pass, as they departed from him, Peter said unto Jesus, Master, it is good for us to be here: and let us make three tabernacles; one for thee, and one for Moses, and one for Elias: not knowing what he said. While he thus spake, there came a cloud, and overshadowed them: and they feared as they entered into the cloud. And there came a voice out of the cloud, saying, This is my beloved Son: hear him. And when the voice was past, Jesus was found alone. And they kept it close, and told no man in those days any of those things which they had seen."

When the angel was sent to the Redeemer's beloved disciple John, we are told that the angel said unto him, "Come up hither." He was to be exalted, to be brought nearer heaven, that his mind might be better prepared for those great manifestations, which an infinitely great and condescending God intended to vouchsafe him. And on reading the verse that you have just now heard, when I also see such a great and serious assembly convened in the presence of God, I think I must address you, as the angel addressed John, and say unto you, "Come up hither;" leave your worldly thoughts, for a time forget the earth. And as it is the Lord's day, a time in which we ought more particularly to think of heaven, I must desire you to pray to God, that ye may get up on Pisgah's mount, and take a view of the promised land. It is true, indeed, eye hath not seen, ear hath not heard, nor hath it entered into the heart of any man to conceive the great and good things, which God hath prepared for his people here; much less, those infinitely greater and more glorious things, that he hath laid up for them that fear him, in the eternal world: but, blessed be God! Though we are not yet in heaven, unless to be in Christ may properly be termed heaven, and then all real Christians are there already; yet, but blessed Jesus has been pleased to leave upon record some account of himself, of what happened to him in the days of his flesh, and of some manifestations he was pleased to grant to a few of his disciples; that from what happened to them here below, we may form some faint, though but a faint idea of that happiness that awaits his people in his kingdom above. If any of you inquire, in what part of our Lord's life those instances are recorded, I have an answer ready: One of these instances, and that a very remarkable one, is recorded in the verses that I have now chosen for the subject of your meditation.

The verses give us an account of what is generally called our Lord's Transfiguration; his being wonderfully changed, and his being wonderfully owned by his Father upon the mount. Some think that this was done upon a Sabbath-day; and the particular occasion of our blessed Lord's condescending to let his servants have such a sight as this, we may gather from the 27th verse. It seems our blessed Lord had been promising a great reward to those who should not be ashamed of him: "Whosoever shall be ashamed of me and of my words, of him shall the Son of Man be ashamed, when he shall come in his own glory, and of his Father, and of the holy angels." In this threatening is implied, a reward to those who should not be ashamed of him: "But, (adds he) I tell you of a truth, there be some standing here, who shall not taste of death, till they see the kingdom of God." As much as to say, There will be a day, when I will come in the glory of my Father and of his holy angels; but I tell you there are some of my favorites; I tell you of a truth, though you may think it too good news, there are some of you that shall not taste of death, till ye shall see the kingdom of God.

Some divines think, that this promise has reference to our Lord's creating a gospel church; and if we take it in this sense, it means that the Apostles, who were then present, some of them at least, should not die, till they saw Satan's kingdom in a great measure pulled down, and the Redeemer's gospel kingdom erected. Some think it has a peculiar reference to John, who it seems survived all the other Apostles, and lived till Christ came; that is, till he came to destroy Jerusalem. But it is the opinion of Mr. Henry, of Bishop Hall, of Burkit, and others, who have written upon this passage, that our blessed Lord has a peculiar reference to the transfiguration upon the mount: "There be some of you here, that shall not taste of death, till ye see my transfiguration upon the mount; till ye see some glorified saint come down from heaven and pay me a visit, and consequently see a little of that kingdom of God, which ye shall have a full sight of when ye come to glory." This seems to be the right interpretation. If you will look to the margin of your Bibles, you will see the parallel place in Matthew, where the account of our

Lord's transfiguration is given, and there you will find it immediately follows upon this promise of our Lord.

Well, as Christ had told them, that they should not taste of death, till they had seen the kingdom of God, why the Evangelist, at the 28th verse , tells us, "It came to pass about an eight days after these sayings, he took Peter, and John, and James, and went up into a mountain to pray." About an eight days; that is, as Bishop Hall thinks, upon the Sabbath-day; or, according to some, the first day of the week, which was hereafter to be the Christian Sabbath; our blessed Lord takes Peter, John, and James: Why did not the Lord Jesus Christ take more of his disciples? Why three, and these three? And why three only? Our blessed Lord was pleased to take three and no more, to show us that he is a sovereign agent; to show us, that though he loved all his disciples, yet there are some to whom he is pleased to allow peculiar visits. He loved Peter, and all the other disciples; yet John was the disciple that he peculiarly loved. And he took three rather than one, because three were sufficient to testify the truth of his being transfigured: "Out of the mouth of two or three witnesses every word shall be established." And he took no more than three, because these three were enough. And he took these three, Peter, John, and James, in particular, because these very persons that were not to see Christ transfigured, were hereafter to see him agonizing in the garden, sweating great drops of blood falling unto the ground. And had not these three disciples seen Christ upon the mount, the seeing him afterwards in the garden, might have staggered them exceedingly: they might have doubted whether it was possible for the Son of God to be in such doleful circumstances. Well, our Lord takes these three "up into a mountain." Why so? Because Christ Jesus was to be like Moses, who was taken up into a mountain, when God intended to deliver unto him the moral law: And our blessed Lord went up into a mountain, because a mountain befriended devotion. When he had a mind to retire to pray to his Father, he went to such places where he could be most secret, and give the greatest vent to his heart. Thus we are told, that once when Peter prayed, it was upon the house-top. And if we have a mind to be near God, we should choose such places as are freest from ostentation, and that most befriend our communion with God. And what doth Christ, when he got up into a mountain? We are told, he went up into a mountain "to pray." Christ had no corruption to confess, and he had but few wants of his own to be relieved; yet we hear of Christ being much in prayer; we hear of his going up to a mountain to pray; of his rising up a great while before it was day to pray; and of his spending a whole night in prayer to God.

In the 20th verse, you have an account of the effect of our Lord's praying: "As he prayed, the fashion of his countenance was altered, and his raiment was white and glittering." I would have you take notice, that our Lord was not changed in respect of his body, while he was going up to the mount, but when he got upon the mount, and while engaged in prayer. It is sufficient that way for our souls to be transformed: the time we are more particularly to expect the influences of God's Spirit, is, when we are engaged in prayer. There seems to be a very great propriety in our Lord's being transfigured or changed upon the mount. I hope I need inform none of you, that when Moses went up to the mount of God, God was pleased to speak to him face to face; and when he came down from the mount, the people of Israel observed that Moses' face shone so, that he was obliged to have a veil put upon his face. Now the shining of Moses' face, was a proof to the people, that Moses had been conversing with God. And Moses told the people, "That the Lord would raise up unto them a prophet like unto him, whom the people were to hear." God the Father, in order to give his Son (considering him as man) a testimony that he was a prophet, was pleased not only to let his face glitter or shine; but to show that he was a prophet far superior to Moses, he was pleased to let his garment be white and glittering, and "his countenance (as we are told by another Evangelist) did shine as the sun." What change was here! What a sight! Methinks I see Peter, James, and John surprised; and, indeed, well might the Evangelist, considering what happened, usher in the following part of the story with the word Behold; "Behold, there talked with him two men, Moses and Elias:" And in the 31st verse, you have an account of their dress, "They appeared in glory;" and of their discourse, "They spake of his decease which he should accomplish at Jerusalem." "Behold, two men, which were Moses and Elias;" these were two very proper persons to come upon this embassy to the Son of God. Moses was the great lawgiver, Elias was the great restorer of the law: The body of Moses was hidden and never found, Elias' body was translated immediately, and carried up in a fiery chariot to heaven: And it may be that this was done particularly, because these two were hereafter to have the honor of waiting upon the Son of God. "They appeared in glory;" that is, their bodies were not in that glorious habit, in which the bodies of believers are to be at the morning of the resurrection. Christ was, as it were, now fitting in his royal robes; and as it is usual for ambassadors, when they are to be admitted into the king's presence, on bringing a message from one king to another, to appear in all their grandeur, to make the message more solemn; so here, these heavenly messengers being to wait upon the Lord Jesus Christ, are invested as with royal dignity, they appeared in glory, and "they spake of his decease which he should accomplish at Jerusalem," they came to tell the Redeemer of his sufferings, and of the place of his sufferings, and to acquaint him, that his sufferings, however great, however bitter, were to be accomplished; that there was o be an end put to them, as our Lord himself speaks, "The things concerning me are to have an end." What other particulars they spoke to our Lord, we are not told. But what effect this had upon the disciples, you may learn from the 32nd verse, "Peter, and they that were with him, were heavy with sleep." We are not to suppose, that Peter, James and John, were now asleep in a literal sense; no, if we compare this, with another passage of holy writ, I mean the account given us of Daniel's being impressed and overcome, when he saw the angel of the Lord, you will find that this sleep implies what we call a swoon. They were overcome with the sight of the glory of Christ's garments, the glittering of his body, and the glory in Moses and Elias appeared: these quite overcame them, sunk them down, and, like the Queen of Sheba, when she saw Solomon's glory, they had no life in them. But they recovered themselves: "when they were awake," that is, when they had recovered their strength, when God had put strength into them, as the angel put strength into Daniel, "they saw his glory, and the two men that stood with him." And how do you think they gazed upon Christ? How may we suppose they fixed their eyes upon Moses and Elias? Peter, who was always the first speaker, out of the abundance of his heart, spoke upon this occasion. Verse 33, "And it came to pass as they departed from him, Peter said unto Jesus, Master, it is good for us to be here; and let us make three tabernacles, one for thee, and one for Moses, and one for Elias, not knowing what he said." Peter, when he had drank a little of Christ's new wine, speaks like a person intoxicated; he was overpowered with the brightness of the manifestation. "Let us make three tabernacles, one for thee, and one for Moses, and one for Elias." It is well added, "not knowing what he said." That he should cry out, "Master, it is good for us to be here," in such good company, and in so glorious a condition, is no wonder; which of us all would not have been apt to have done the same? But to talk of building tabernacles, and one for Christ, and one for Moses, and one for Elias, was saying something for which Peter himself must stand reproved. Surely, Peter, thou wast not quite awake! Thou talkest like one I a dream: If thy Lord had taken thee at thy word, what a poor tabernacle wouldst thou have had, in comparison of that house not made with hands, eternal in the heavens, in which thou hast long since dwelt, now the earthly house of the tabernacle of thy body is dissolved? What! Build tabernacles below, and have the crown, before thou hast borne the cross? O Peter, Peter! "Master, spare thyself," sticks too too closely to thee: And why so selfish, Peter?

Carest thou not for thy fellow disciples that are below, who came not up with thee to the mount? Carest thou not for the precious souls, that are as sheep having no shepherd, and must perish for ever, unless thy Master descends from the mount to teach, and to die for them? Wouldst thou thus eat thy spiritual morsels alone? Besides, if thou art for building tabernacles, why must there be three of them, one for Christ, and one for Moses, and one for Elias? Are Christ and the prophets divided? Do they not sweetly harmonize and agree in one? Did they not prophesy concerning the sufferings of thy Lord, as well as of the glory that should follow? Alas, how unlike is their conversation to thine? Moses and Elias came down to talk of suffering, and thou are dreaming of building I know not what tabernacles. Surely, Peter, thou art so high upon the mount, that thy head runs giddy.

However, in the midst of these infirmities, there was something that bespoke the honesty and integrity of his heart. Though he knew not very well what he said, yet he was not so stupid as his pretended successor at Rome. He does not fall down and worship these two departed saints, neither do I hear him say to either , Ora prosobis; he had not so learnt Christ; no, he applies himself directly to the head, "he said unto Jesus, "Master, it is good for us to be here." And though he was for building, yet he would not build without his Master's leave. "Master, let us build," or, as St.

Mark words it, "wilt thou that we build three tabernacles, one for thee, and one for Moses, and one for Elias?" I do not hear him add, and one for James, and one for John, and one for Peter. No, he would willingly stay out with them upon the mount, though it was in the cold and dark night, so that Christ and his heavenly attendants were taken care of. The sweetness of such a heavenly vision, would more than compensate for any bodily suffering that might be the consequence of their longer abode there: nay farther, he does not desire that either Christ, or Moses, or Elias, should have any trouble in building; neither does he say, let my curates, James and John, build, whilst I sit idle and lord it over my brethren; but he says, "let us build;" he will work as hard, if not harder than either of them, and desire to be distinguished only by his activity, enduring hardness, and his zeal to promote the welfare of their common Lord and Master.

Doubtless, Peter had read how the glory of the Lord filled the tabernacle, and the temple of old; and now Jesus is transfigured, and Moses and Elias appear in glory, he thinks it right that new tabernacles shall be erected for them. Such a mixture of nature and grace, of short-sightedness and infirmity, is there in the most ardent and well-meant zeal of the very best of men, when nearest the throne of grace, or even upon the mount with God. Perfection in any grace must be looked for, or expected, only among the spirits of just men made perfect in heaven. Those who talk of any such thing on earth, like Peter, they know not what they say.

But how came Peter so readily to distinguish which was Moses, and which was Elias? He seems to speak without the least hesitation, "Let us build three tabernacles, one for thee, and one for Moses, and one for Elias," as though he was very well acquainted with them, whereas they had both been dead, long, long before Peter was born. Was there, do you imagine, any thing distinguishing in their apparel? Or any thing in their conversation that discovered them? Or rather, did he not know them here on the mount, as we may from hence infer, that departed saints do, and will know each other in heaven, even by intuition and immediate revelation? But alas! how transient are our views of heaven, during our sojourning here on earth: Verse 34, "Whilst he thus spake," whilst Peter was talking of building tabernacles, whilst he was saying, "it is good for us to be here," whilst he was dreaming that his mountain was s strong that it never could be moved, "there came a cloud and overshadowed them." St. Matthew observes, it was a bright cloud, not dark like that on mount Sinai, but bright, because the gospel opens to us a far more bright dispensation than that of the law. This overshadowed, and thereby not only filled them with an holy awe, but also screened them, in some measure, from the brightness of that glory with which they were now surrounded, and which otherwise would have been insupportable. This cloud was like the veil thrown on the face of Moses, and prepared them for the voice which they were soon to hear coming out of it. I am not much surprised at being informed by St. Matthew, that they feared as they entered into the cloud, or by St. Mark that "they were sore afraid." For since the fall, there is such a consciousness in us all of deserved wrath, that we cannot help fearing when we enter into a cloud, even though Jesus Christ himself be in the midst of it. Ah Peter, where is thy talk of building tabernacles now? Is thy strong mountain so quickly removed? What, come down so soon? why do we not now hear thee saying, "It is good for us to be here?" Alas! he and his fellow disciples are quite struck dumb; see how they tremble, and, like Moses upon another occasion, exceedingly quake and fear. But how quickly are those fears dispelled, how soon is the tumult of their minds hushed and calmed, with that soul- reviving voice that came from the excellent glory, verse 35, "This is my beloved Son, hear him." St. Mark and St. Matthew add "in whom I am well pleased." The same testimony that God the Father gave to the blessed Jesus at his baptism, before he entered upon his temptation, is now repeated, in order to strengthen and prepare him for his impending agony in the garden. Probably, it was a small still though articulate voice, attended neither with thunder nor lightning, nor the sound of a trumpet, but, agreeable to the blessed news which it contained, ushered in with tokens of unspeakable complacency and love. God the Father, hereby gives Moses and Elias a solemn discharge, as though they were sent from heaven on purpose to give up their commission to their rightful Lord, and like the morning star, disappear when the Sun of Righteousness himself arises to bring in a gospel day. "This is my beloved Son, hear Him." But the emphasis upon the word THIS; this Son of Man, this Jesus, whom you are shortly to see in a bloody sweat, blindfolded, spit upon, buffeted, scourged, and at length hanging upon a tree, I am not ashamed to own to be my Son, my only begotten Son, who was with me before the heavens were made, or the foundations of the earth were laid; my beloved Son, in whom I am well pleased, in whom my soul delighteth, and whom I do by these presents, publicly constitute and appoint to be the king, priest, and prophet of the church. "Hear ye Him." No longer look to Moses or Elias, no longer expect to be saved by the works of the law; but by the preaching and application of the ever-blessed gospel. Hear ye him, so as to believe on, love, serve, obey, and, if needs be, to die and lay down your very lives for him. "Hear him;" hear whathe hath to say, for he comes with a commission from above. Hear his doctrine; hear him, so as to obey him; hear him, so as to put in practice his precepts, and copy after his good example.

In the 36thverse, we have the close of his heavenly feast; "When the voice was past, Jesus was found alone; and they kept it close, and told no man in those days, any of those things which they had seen." If we compare this, with the account which the other Evangelists give of our blessed Lord's transfiguration, you will find this was done by Christ's order: Peter, James, and John, would otherwise have gone down and told the whole world, that they had seen the Lord Christ upon the mount of transfiguration; but our Lord ordered them to keep it silent. Why so? If they had gone down from the mount, and told it to the other disciples, it might have raised ill blood in the others; they might have said, Why did our Master single our Peter, James, and John? Why might not we have had the privilege of going up to the mount as well as they? Had they said, that their Lord was transfigured, people would not have believed them; they would have thought, that Peter, James, and John were only enthusiasts; but if they kept it till after his resurrection, and he had broken the gates of death, for them then to say, that they saw him upon the mount transfigured, would corroborate the evidence.

I have thus paraphrased the words for your better understanding the account the Evangelist gives of our blessed Lord's transfiguration; but I have not yet done; I have been speaking to your heads; the practical part is yet to come. O that God may reach your hearts! And though, according to order, I ought to begin with the practical inferences that might be drawn from the first part; yet, I think it best to show you, who are the people of God, especially you young converts, that have honesty, but not much prudence, what instructions our Lord would here have you to learn.

"When the voice was past, Jesus was found alone, and they kept it close, and told no man in those days any of those things which they had seen." There is nothing more common, when God vouchsafes communications to a poor soul, than for the person that enjoys them, to go and tell all that he has seen and felt, and often at improper seasons and to improper persons. I remember that Mr. Henry observes, "Joseph had more honesty than he had policy, or else he would never have told his brethren of his dreams." Young Christians are too apt to blunder thus: I am sure it is a fault of which I have been exceedingly guilty, speaking of things, which, perhaps, had better been concealed; which is a fault God's people are too apt to fall into. Though it is good for those that have seen Christ, and that have felt his love, to tell others what God hath done for their souls; yet, however you may think of it now, when you come down from the mount, and know yourselves a little, ye will find reason often to hold your tongue. Young Christians are like children, to whom if you give a little money in their pocket, they cannot be quiet till they have spent it upon something or other: young Christians, when they get a little of God, are ready to talk too much of it. They should therefore beware, and know when to speak, and when to be silent.

But, my dear friends, did our Lord Jesus Christ take Peter, James, and John into a mountain to pray? Are any of you fathers, mothers, masters and mistresses of families? Learn then from hence to take your children, your servants, and those that belong to you, from the world, at certain times, and not only pray for them, but pray with them. If Christ did thus, who had few wants of his own to be supplied, and nothing to confess and lament over; if Christ was such a lover of prayer, surely, you and I, who have so many wants to be supplied, so many corruptions to mourn over; you and I should spend much time in prayer. I do not say that you are to lock yourselves up in your closets, and not mind your shops or farms, or worldly business; I only say, that you should take care to husband all your time: and if you are God's children, you will frequently retire from the world, and seek a visit from your God.

Was the Lord Jesus transformed or transfigured, while he was praying?

Learn hence, to be much in spiritual prayer. The way to have the soul transformed, changed into, and make like unto God, is frequently to converse with God. We say, a man is as his company. Persons by conversing together, frequently catch each others tempers: and if you have a mind to imbibe the divine temper, pray much. And as Christ's garments became white and glittering, so shall your souls get a little of God's light to shine upon them.

Did Moses and Elias appear in glory? Are there any old saints here? I doubt not but there are a considerable number. And are any of you afraid of death? Do any of you carry about with you a body that weighs down your immortal soul? I am sure a poor creature is preaching to you, that every day drags a crazy load along. But come, believers, come, ye children of God, come, ye aged decrepit saints, come and trample upon that monster death. As thou goest over yonder church-yard, do as I know an old excellent Christian in Maryland did; go, sit upon the grave, and meditate on thine own dissolution. Thou mayest, perhaps, have a natural fear of dying: the body and the soul do not care to part without a little sympathy and a groan; but O look yonder, loon up to heaven, see there thy Jesus, thy Redeemer, and learn, that thy body is to be fashioned here-after like unto Christ's most glorious body; that poor body which is not subject to gout and gravel, and that thou canst scarce drag along; that poor body, which hinders thee so much in the spiritual life, will ere long hinder thee no more; it shall be put into the grave; but though it be sown in corruption, it shall be raised in incorruption; though it is sown in dishonor, it shall be raised again in glory. This consideration made blessed Paul to cry out, "O death, where is thy sting! O grave, where is thy victory!" Thy soul and body shall be united together again, and thou shalt be "forever with the Lord." Those knees of thine, which perhaps are hard by kneeling in prayer; that tongue of thine, which hath sung hymns to Christ; those hands of thine, which have wrought for God; those feet, which have ran to Christ's ordinances; shall all, in the twinkling of an eye, be changed; and thou shalt be able to stand under an exceeding and an eternal weight of glory.

Come then, ye believers in Christ, look beyond the grave; come, ye dear children of God, and however weak and sickly ye are now, say, Blessed be God, I shall soon have a body strong, full of vigor and of glory.

But as this speaks comfort to saints, it speaks terror to sinners, to all persons that live and die out of Christ. It is the opinion of Archbishop Usher, that as the bodies of the saints shall be glorified, so the bodies of the damned shall be deformed. And if this be true, alas! what a poor figure will the fine ladies cut, who die without a Christ! What a poor figure will the fine gentleman cut in the morning of the resurrection, that now dresses up his body, and at the same time neglects to secure an interest in Christ and eternal happiness! It is the opinion , likewise of Archbishop Usher, that damned souls will lose all the good tempers they had here; so that though God gave unregenerate people a constitutional meekness, good nature, and courage, for the benefit of the commonwealth; yet, the use of those blessings being over, and they having died without Christ, and it being impossible there will be an appearance of good in hell, their good tempers will be forever lost. If this be so, it is an awful consideration; and I think persons who love their bodies, should also hence take care to secure the welfare of their souls.

Did Peter know which was Moses and which Elias? Then I think, and God be praised for it, it is plain from this and other passages of scripture, that we shall know one another when we come to heaven. Dives knew Lazarus: "Father Abraham, send Lazarus:" And we are told, "he saw Lazarus sitting in Abraham's bosom." Adam knew his wife Eve; though cast into a deep sleep when God made her out of his rib, yes, by a kind of intuition he says, "This is bone of my bone, and flesh of my flesh." And it is on this account, that the Apostle, speaking to the Philippians, says, "Ye are my joy and crown of rejoicing, in the day of the Lord." What comfort will this be to a spiritual father! Says one, Here is the man, O Lord Jesus, that brought my soul to taste of thy love; says another, This is the man, that at such a time, and with such words, struck my heart: thou, O Lord knowest it. Then the spiritual father will rejoice over his children. You that have met and have prayed together, sighted and sympathized together, and told your temptations to one another, shall be forever with the Lord and with each other. There we shall see Abraham, Isaac, and Jacob sitting, with all the redeemed company; and we shall know the names of every one mentioned in the book of God. O blessed prospect! O blessed time! Who that thinks of this, of seeing the Lamb sitting upon the throne, with all God's people about him, but must desire to go to heaven, and be forever, forever with the Lord. And if there is such comfort for believers to know one another in heaven, with what comfort may any of you, that have lost fathers, mothers, or friends, think of them: we are parted for a little while, but we shall see them again. My father died in Christ, my mother died in the Lord, my husband, my wife, was a follower of Jesus; I shall see them, though not now; I shall go to them, but they shall not return to me! This may keep you from sorrowing as persons without hope; and keep you from being so cruel, as to wish them to come down to this evil world.

But O what a dreadful consideration is this for damned souls! I believe, that as glorified spirits will know one another, so will damned souls know one another too. And as the company of the blessed increases the happiness of heaven, so the company of the damned will increase their torments. What made Dives to put up that petition? "I have five brethren; send somebody to my father's house to testify unto them, lest they also come into this place of torment." One would imagine at first reading, that hell had made Dives charitable, and that though he was ill natured on earth, yet he had acquired some good nature in hell. No, no, there is not a spark of good nature in the place of torment. But Dives knew, if his five brethren came there, they might say, We may thank you, next to an evil heart, for coming hither; you made us drink healths, till we were drunk; you taught us to game, to curse, to swear, etc. He knew very well, that his five brethren being brought to hell by his example, hell would be heated five times hotter to torment his soul. One will cry out, Cursed be the day that ever I was companions with such an one in sin; cursed be the day that ever we hearkened to one another's advice, and were allured by each others example to sin against God!

But did a cloud overshadow Peter, James, and John? Were heavenly and divine visits here but short? Then wonder not, ye people of God, if ye are upon the mount one hour, and down in the valley of the shadow of death the next. There is nothing in the world more common, after you have been in a good frame, than for a cloud to overshadow you. We generally say, "It is good to be here," and often make a Christ of our graces; and therefore the Lord sends a cloud to overshadow us. But never fear; God shall speak to you out of the cloud; God will reveal himself to you; this cloud shall soon be gone; ere long we shall be in heaven, and in that glory where no cloud can possibly reach us.

I can now only mention one thing more, and that is, Did the Father say, "This is my beloved Son, hear him?" then let every one of our hearts echo to this testimony give of Christ, "This is my beloved Savior." Did God so love the world, as to send his only begotten Son, his well beloved Son to preach to us? Then, my dear friends, HEAR HIM. What God said seventeen hundred years ago, immediately by a voice from heaven, concerning his Son upon the mount, that same thing God says to you immediately by his word, "Hear him." If ye never heard him before, hear him now. Hear him so as to take him to be your prophet, priest, and your king; hear him, so as to take him to be your God and your all. Hear him today, ye youth, while it is called to-day; hear him now, lest God should cut you off before you have another invitation to hear him; hear him while he cries, "Come unto me;" hear him while he opens his hand and his heart; hear him while he knocks at the door of your souls, lest you should hear him saying, "Depart, depart, ye cursed, into everlasting fire, prepared for the devil and his angels." Hear him, ye old and gray-headed, hear him, ye that have one foot in the grave; hear him, I say; and if ye are dull of hearing, beg of God to open the ears of your hearts, and your blind eyes; beg of God that you may have an enlarged and a believing heart, and that ye may know what the Lord God saith concerning you. God will resent it, he will avenge himself on his adversaries, if you do not hear a blessed Savior. He is God's son, he is God's beloved son; he came upon a great errand, even to shed his precious blood for sinners; he came to cleanse you from all sin, and to save you with an everlasting salvation. Ye who have heard him, hear him again; still go on, believe in and obey him, and by-and-by you shall hear him saying, "Come, ye blessed of my Father, receive the kingdom prepared for you from the foundation of the world." May God grant it to you all, for the Lord Jesus Christ's sake. Amen, and Amen.

Sermon 31 The Care of the Soul urged as the one thing needful

Luke 10:42, "But one thing is needful."

It was the amiable character of our blessed Redeemer, that "he went about doing good," this great motive, which animated all his actions, brought him to the house of his friend Lazarus, at Bethany, and directed his behavior there. Though it was a season of recess from public labor, our Lord brought the sentiments and the pious cares of a preacher of righteousness into the parlor of a friend; and there his doctrine dropped as the rain, and distilled as the dew, as the little happy circle that were then surrounding him. Mary, the sister of Lazarus, with great delight made one amongst them; she seated herself at the feet of Jesus, in the posture of an humble disciple; and we have a great deal of reason to believe, that Martha, his other sister, would gladly have been with her there; but domestic cares pressed hard upon her, and "she was cumbered with much serving," being, perhaps, too solicitous to prepare a sumptuous entertainment for her heavenly master and the train that attended him.

Happy are they, who in a crowd of business do not lose something of the spirituality of their minds, and of the composure and sweetness of their tempers. This good woman comes to our Lord with too impatient a complaint; insinuating some little reflection, not only on Mary, but on himself too.

"Lord, dost thou not care that my sister hath left me to serve alone? Bid her, therefore, that she help me." Our Lord, willing to take all opportunities of suggesting useful thoughts, answers her in these words, of which the text is a part, "Martha, Martha, thou art careful and troubled about many things, but one thing is needful; and Mary, has chosen that good part, which shall not be taken away from her." Alas, Martha! The concerns of the soul are of so much greater importance than those of the body, that I cannot blame your sister on this occasion: I rather recommend her to your imitation, and caution you, and all my other friends, to be much on your guard, that in the midst of your worldly cares, you do not lose sight of what much better deserves your attention.

I shall consider these words, "One thing is needful," as a kind of aphorism, or wise and weighty sentence, which dropped from the mouth of our blessed Redeemer, and is evidently worthy of our most serious regard. I shall, I. Consider what we are to understand by "The one thing" here spoken of.

II. Show you what is intended, when it is said to be the one thing NEEDFUL.

III. I will show how justly it may be so represented, or prove that it is, indeed, the one thing needful. And then conclude with some reflections.

My friends, the words which are now before us, are to this day, as true, as they were seventeen hundred years ago. Set your hearts to attend to them. O that you may, by divine grace, be awakened to hear them with a due regard, and be so impressed with the plain and serious things which are now to be spoken, as you probably would, if I were speaking by your dying beds, and you had the near and lively view of eternity!

FIRST, I am to consider, what we are to understand by the "one thing needful." Now in a few words, it is the "Care of the soul," opposed, as you see in the text, to the care, the excessive care of the body; to which Martha was gently admonished by our Lord. This is a general answer, and it comprehends a variety of important particulars, which is the business of our ministry often to open to you at large: The care of the soul, implies a readiness to hear the words of Christ, to seat ourselves with Mary at his feet, and to receive both the law and the gospel from his mouth. It supposes, that we learn from this divine teacher the worth of our souls, their danger, and their remedy; and that we become above all things solicitous about their salvation. That, heartily repenting of all our sins, and cordially believing the everlasting gospel, we receive the Lord Jesus Christ for righteousness and life, resting our souls on the value of his atonement, and the efficacy of his grace. It imports, the sincere dedication of ourselves to the service of God, and a faithful adherence to it, notwithstanding all oppositions arising from inward corruptions, or outward temptations; and a resolute perseverance in the way of gospel dependence, 'till we receive the end of our faith in our complete salvation. This is the "one thing needful," represented indeed in various scriptures by various names. Sometimes it is called "Regeneration," or "the new creature," because it is the blessed work of God's efficacious grace.

Sometimes the "Fear of God," and sometimes "his love, and the keeping his commandments;" and very frequently in the new testament it is called "faith," or "receiving Christ, and believing on him," which therefore is represented as the "great work of God," John 6:20 the great thing which God in his glorious gospel requires, as well as by his spirit produces in us: each of these, if rightly understood and explained, comprehends all that I have said on this head. On the whole, we may say, that, as the body is one, though it has many members, and the soul is one, though it has many faculties, so in the present case, this real vital religion is "one thing," one sacred principle of divine life, bringing us to attend to the care of our souls, as of our greatest treasure. It is one thing, notwithstanding all the variety of views in which it may be considered, and of characters under which it may be described. I proceed, SECONDLY, To consider what may be intended in the representation which is here made of it, as the "one thing NEEDFUL." Now I think it naturally includes these three particulars: it is a matter of universal concern; of the highest importance; and of so comprehensive a nature, that every thing which is truly worthy of our regard, may be considered as included in, or subservient to it. Let me a little illustrate each of these particulars.

1. The care of the soul may be called the "one thing needful," as it is matter of universal concern.

Our Lord, you see, speaks of it as needful in the general. He says not, for this or that particular person; or for those of such an age, station, or circumstance in life, but needful for all. And indeed, when discoursing on such a subject, one might properly introduce it with those solemn words of the psalmist, "Give ear, all ye people, hear, all ye inhabitants of the earth, both high and low, rich and poor, together," Psalm 49:1,2. For it is the concern of all, from the king that sits upon the throne, to the servant that grindeth at the mill, or the beggar that lieth upon the dunghill. It is needful for us that are MINISTERS, for our own salvation is concerned: and woe, insupportable woe will be to our souls, if we think it enough to recommend it to others, and to talk of it in a warm, or an awful manner, in public assemblies, or in our private converse, while it does not penetrate our hearts, as our own greatest care.

Our case will then be like that of the Israelitish lord in Samaria, 2 Kings 7:2, who was employed to distribute the corn when the siege was raised; though we see it with our eyes, and dispense it with our hands, we shall ourselves die miserably, without tasting the blessings we impart. It is needful to all you that are our HEARERS, without the exception of one single person. It is needful to you that are RICH, though it may on some accounts be peculiarly difficult for you, even as difficult, comparatively speaking, as for a "Camel to go through the eye of a needle," Mat. 19:24, yet if it be neglected, you are poor in the midst of all your wealth, and miserable in all your abundance; a wretch starving for hunger, in a magnificent palace and a rich dress, would be less the object of compassion than you. It is needful for you that are POOR; though you are distressed with so many anxious cares, "what you shall eat, and what you shall drink, and wherewithal you shall be clothed." Matt. 6:31. The nature that makes you capable of such anxieties as these, argues your much greater concern in the "bread which endures to eternal life," John 6:27, than in that by which this mortal body must be supported. It is needful for you that are ADVANCED IN YEARS; though your strength be impaired so that the "grasshopper is a burthen," Eccl. 12:5, and though you have by your long continuance in sin, rendered this great work so hard, that were it less important, one would in pity let you alone without reminding you of it; yes, late as it is, it must be done, or your hoary heads will be brought down to the grave with wrath, and sink under a curse aggravated by every year and by every day of your lives. It is needful to you that are YOUNG, though solicited by so many gay vanities, to neglect it, though it may be represented as an unseasonable care at present, yet I repeat it, it is needful to you; immediately needful, unless you who walk so frequently over the dust of your brethren and companions, that died in the bloom and vigor of their days, have made some secret covenant with the grave for yourselves, and found out some wonderful method, hitherto unknown, or securing this precarious life, and of answering for days and months to come, while others cannot answer for one single moment.

2. The care of the soul is "a matter of the highest importance;" beyond any thing which can be brought into comparison with it.

As Solomon says of wisdom, that "it is more precious than rubies, and that all things which can be desired are not to be compared with her," Prov. 3:15. So I may properly say of this great and most important branch of wisdom; whatever can be laid in the balance wit it, will be found altogether lighter than vanity. This is strongly implied when it is said in the text, "one thing is needful;" one thing, and ONE THING ALONE is so.

Just as the blessed God is said to be "only wise," 1 Tim. 1:17, and "only holy," Rev. 15:4. Because the wisdom and holiness of angels and men is as nothing, when compared with his. What seems most great and most important in life, what kings and senates, what the wisest and greatest of this world are employing their time, their councils, their pens, their labors upon, are trifles, when compared with this one thing. A man may subsist, he may in some considerable measure be happy, without learning, without riches, without titles, without health, without liberty, without friends, nay, though "the life be more than meat, and the body than raiment," Matt. 6:25, yet may he be happy, unspeakably happy, without the body itself. But he cannot be so, in the neglect of the one thing needful. I must therefore bespeak your regard to it in the words of Moses, "it is not a light thing, but it is your life," Deut. 32:47.

3. The care of the soul is of so comprehensive a nature, that "every thing truly worthy of our regard may be considered as included in it, or subservient to it.

As David observes, that "the commandment of God is exceeding broad," Psalm 119:96, so we may say of this one thing needful; or as Solomon very justly and emphatically expresses it, "to fear God and to keep his commandments is the whole duty of man," Eccl. 12:13. His whole duty, and his whole interest; and every thing which is wise and rational does in its proper place and connection make a part of it. We should judge very ill concerning the nature of this care, if we imagined, that it consisted merely in acts of devotion, or religious contemplation; it comprehends all the lovely and harmonious band of social and human virtues. It requires a care of society, a care of our bodies, and of our temporal concerns; but then all is to be regulated, directed, and animated by proper regards to God, Christ, and immortality. Our food and our rest, our trades and our labors, are to be attended to, and all the offices of humanity performed in obedience to the will of God, for the glory of Christ, and in a view of improving the mind in a growing meekness for a state of complete perfection. Name anything which has not reference at all to his, and you name a worthless trifle, however it may be gilded to allure the eye, or however it may be sweetened to gratify the taste. Name a thing, which, instead of thus improving the soul, has a tendency to debase and pollute, to enslave and endanger it, and you name what is most unprofitable and mischievous, be the wages of iniquity ever so great; most foul and deformed, be it in the eyes of men ever so honorable, or in their customs ever so fashionable. Thus I have endeavored to show you what we may suppose implied in the expression of "one thing being needful." I am now, THIRDLY, To show you with how much propriety the care of the soul may be represented under this character, as the one thing needful, or as a matter of universal and most serious concern, to which every thing else is to be considered as subservient, if at all worthy of our care and pursuit.

There let me appeal to the sentiments of those who must be allowed most capable of judging, and to the evident reason of the case itself, as it must appear to every unprejudiced mind.

1. Let me argue "from the opinions of those who must be allowed most capable of judging in such an affair," and we shall quickly see that the care of the soul appears to them, the one thing needful.

Is the judgment of the blessed God "according to truth," how evidently and how solemnly is that judgment declared? I will not say merely in this or the other particular passage of his word, but in the whole series of his revelations to the children of men, and the whole tenor of his addresses to them. Is not this the language of all, from the early days of Job and Moses to the conclusion of the canon of scripture. Job 28:21, 23, 28, "If wisdom be hid from the eyes of all the living, surely God understandeth the way thereof, he knoweth the place thereof;" and if he does, it is plainly pointed out, for "unto man he still saith, behold, the fear of the Lord, that is wisdom, and to depart from evil, that is understanding." By Moses he declared to the Israelites, that "to do the commandments of the Lord would be their wisdom and their understanding in the sight of the nations, who should hear his statutes, and say, surely this is a wise and an understanding people," Deut. 4:6. When he had raised up one man on the throne of Israel, with the character of the wisest that ever lived upon the face of the earth, he chose to make him eminently a teacher of this great truth. And though now all that he spoke on the curious and less concerning subjects of natural philosophy is lost, "though he spoke of trees from the cedar to the hyssop, and of beasts, and of fowls, and of creeping things, and of fishes," 1 Kings 4:33, that saying is preserved in which he testifies, that "the fear of the Lord is the beginning of wisdom," Prov.

1:7,9,10, and those Proverbs, in almost every line of which, they who neglect God and their own souls, are spoken of as fools, as if that were the most proper signification of the word, while the religious alone are honored with the title of wise. But in this respect, as attesting this truth in the name of God and in his own, "a greater than Solomon is here." For if we inquire what it was that our Lord Jesus Christ judged to be the one thing needful, the words of the text contain as full an answer as can be imagined; and the sense of them is repeated in a very lively and emphatical manner, in that remarkable passage wherein our Lord not only declares his own judgment, but seems to appeal to the conscience of all, as obliged by their own secret convictions to subscribe to the truth of it.

"What is a man profited, is he gain the whole world, and lost his own soul; or what shall a man give in exchange for his soul?" Matt. 16:26. If it were once lost, what would he not be willing to give to redeem it? But it depends not on the words of Christ alone. Let his actions, his sufferings, his blood, his death, speak what a value he set on the souls of men. Is it to be imagined, that he would have relinquished heaven, have dwelt upon earth, have labored by night and by day, and at last have expired on the cross, for a matter of light importance? Or can we think that he, in whom "dwell all the treasures of wisdom and knowledge, and all the fullness of the Godhead bodily," Coloss. 2:3,9, was mistaken in judgment so deliberately formed, and so solemnly declared?

If after this, there were room to mention human judgment and testimonies, how easy would it be to produce a cloud of witnesses in such a cause, and to show that the wisest and best of men in all ages of the world have agreed in this point, that amidst all the diversities of opinion and profession, which succeeding generations have produced, this has been the unanimous judgment, this the common and most solicitous care of those whose characters are most truly valuable, to secure the salvation of their own souls, and to promote the salvation of others.

And let me beseech you seriously to reflect, what are the characters of those who have taken the liberty, most boldly and freely to declare their judgment on the contrary side? The number of such is comparatively few; and when you compare what you have observed of their temper and conduct, I will not say with what you read of holy men of old, but with what you have yourselves seen in the faithful, active, and zealous servants of Christ, in these latter ages, with whom you have conversed; do you on the whole find, that the rejecters and deriders of the gospel, are in other respects so much more prudent and judicious, so much wiser for themselves, and for others, that are influenced by them, as that you can be in reason obliged to pay any great deference to the authority of a few such names as these, in opposition to those to whom they are here opposed?

But you will say, and you will say it too truly, Though but a few may venture in words to declare for the neglect of the soul and its eternal interest, that the greater part of mankind do it in their actions. But are the greater part of mankind so wise, and so good, as implicitly to be followed in matters of the highest importance? And do not multitudes of these declare themselves on the other side, in their most serious moments?

When the intoxications of worldly business and pleasures are over, and some languishing sickness forces men to solitude and retirement; what have you generally observed to be the affect of such a circumstance? Have they not then declared themselves convinced of the truth we are now laboring to establish? Nay, do we not sometimes see, that a distemper which seizes the mind with violence, yet does not utterly destroy its reasoning faculties, fixes this conviction on the soul in a few hours, nay, sometimes in a few moments? Have you never seen a gay, thoughtless creature, surprised in the giddy round of pleasures and amusements, and presently brought not only to seriousness, but terror and trembling, by the near views of death? Have you never seen the man of business and care interrupted, like the rich fool in the parable, in the midst of his schemes for the present world? And have you not heard one and the other of them owning the vanity of those pleasures and cares, which but a few days ago were every thing to them?

Confessing that religion was the one thing needful, and recommending it to others with an earnestness, as if they hoped thereby to atone for their own former neglect? We that are ministers, frequently are witnesses to such things as these, and I believe few of our hearers are entire strangers to them.

Once more, what if to the testimony of the dying, we could add that of the dead? What if God were to turn aside the veil between us and the invisible world, and permit the most careless sinner in the assembly to converse for a few moments with the inhabitants of it? If you were to apply yourself to a happy Spirit, that trod the most thorny road to paradise, or passed through the most fiery trial, and to ask him, "was it worth your while to labor so much, and to endure so much for what you now possess?" Surely if the blessed in heaven were capable of indignation, it would move them to hear that it should be made a question. And, on the other hand, if you could inquire of one tormented in that flame below, though he might once be "clothed in purple and fine linen, and fare sumptuously every day," Luke 16:19. If you could ask him, "whether his former enjoyments were an equivalent for his present sufferings and despair?" What answer do you suppose he would return? Perhaps an answer of so much horror and rage, as you would not be able so much as to endure. Or if the malignity of his nature should prevent him from returning any answer at all, surely there would be a language even in that silence, a language in the darkness, and flames, and groans of that infernal prison, which would speak to your very soul what the word of God is with equal certainty, though less forcible conviction, speaking to your ear, that "one thing is needful." You see it is so in the judgment of God the Father, and the Lord Jesus Christ, of the wisest and best of men, of many, who seemed to judge most differently of it, when they come to more deliberate and serious thought, and not only of the dying, but of the dead too, of those who have experimentally known both worlds, and most surely know what is to be preferred. But I will not rest the whole argument here; therefore, 2. I appeal to the evident reason of the case itself, as it must appear to every unprejudiced mind, that the care of the soul is indeed the one thing needful.

I still consider myself as speaking not to atheists, or to deists, but to those who not only believe the existence and providence of God, and a future state of happiness and misery, but likewise who credit the truth of the Christian revelation, as many undoubtedly do, who live in a fatal neglect of God, and their own souls. Now on these principles, a little reflection may be sufficient to convince you, that it is needful to the present repose of your own mind; needful, if ever you would secure eternal happiness, and avoid eternal misery, which will be aggravated, rather than alleviated by all your present enjoyments.

1. The care of the soul is the one thing needful, because, "without it you cannot secure the peace of your own mind, nor avoid the upbraidings of your conscience." That noble faculty is indeed the vicegerent of God in the soul. It is sensible of the dignity and worth of an immortal spirit, and will sometimes cry out of the violence that is offered to it, and cry so loud, as to compel the sinner to hear, whether he will or not. Do you not sometimes find it yourselves? When you labor most to forget the concerns of your soul, do they not sometimes force themselves on your remembrance? You are afraid of the reflections of your own mind, but with all your artifice and all your resolution can you entirely avoid them? Does not conscience follow you to your beds, even if denied the opportunity of meeting you in your closets, and, though with an unwelcome voice, there warn you, "that your soul is neglected, and will quickly be lost." Does it not follow you to your shops and your fields, when you are busiest there? Nay, I will add, does it not sometimes follow you to the feast, to the club, to the dance, and perhaps, amidst all resistance, to the theater too? Does, it not sometimes mingle your sweetest draughts with wormwood, and your gayest scenes with horror? So that you are like a tradesman, who, suspecting his affairs to be in a bad posture, lays by his books and his papers, yet sometimes they will come accidentally in his way. He hardly dares to look abroad for fear of meeting a creditor or an arrest: and if he labors to forget his cares and his dangers, in a course of luxury at home, the remembrance is sometimes awakened, and the alarm increased, by those very extravagancies in which he is attempting to lose it. Such probably is the case of your minds, and it is a very painful state; and while things are thus within, external circumstances can no more make you happy, than a fine dress could relieve you under a violent fit of the stone. Whereas, if this great affair were secured, you might delight in reflection, as much as you now dread it; and conscience, of your bitterest enemy, would become a delightful friend, and the testimony of it your greatest rejoicing.

2. The care of the soul is the one thing needful, "because without this your eternal happiness will be lost." A crown of everlasting glory is not surely such a trifle as to be thrown away on a careless creature, that will not in good earnest pursue it. God doth not ordinarily deal thus, even with the bounties of his common providence, which are comparatively of little value. As to these, the hand of the diligent generally makes rich, and he would be thought distracted, rather than prudent, who should expect to get an estate merely by wishing for it, or without some resolute and continued application to a proper course of action for that purpose. Now, that we may not foolishly dream of obtaining heaven, in the midst of a course of indolence and sloth; we are expressly told in the word of God, that "the kingdom of heaven suffers violence, and the violent take it by force," Matt. 11:12, and are therefore exhorted to "strive," with the greatest intenseness, and eagerness of mind, as the word properly signifies, "to enter in at the strait gate," for this great and important reason, "because many shall another day seek to enter in, and shall not

be able," Luke 13:24. Nay, when our Lord makes the most gracious promises to the humble petitioner, he does it in such a manner as to exclude the hopes of those who are careless and indifferent. "Ask, and it shall be given you; seek, and you shall find; knock, and it shall be opened unto you, Matt. 7:7. If, therefore, you do not ask, seek, and knock, the door of mercy will not be opened, and eternal happiness will be lost.

Not that heaven is to be obtained by our own good works: no, no; for having done all, we must account ourselves unprofitable servants.

And surely if I could say no more as to the fatal consequences of your neglect, than this, that eternal happiness will be lost, I should say enough to impress every mind, that considers what ETERNITY means. To fall into a state of everlasting forgetfulness, might indeed appear a refuge to a mind filled with the apprehension of future misery. But O how dreadful a refuge is it! Surely it is such a refuge, as a vast precipice, (from which a man falling would be dashed to pieces in a moment) might appear to a person, pursued by the officers of justice, that he might be brought out to a painful and lingering execution. If an extravagant youth would have reason to look round with anguish, on some fair and ample paternal inheritance, which he had sold or forfeited merely for the riot of a few days: how much more melancholy would it be for a rational mind to think that its eternal happiness is lost for any earthly consideration whatever?

Tormenting thought! "Had I attended to that one thing which I have neglected, I might have been, through the grace of God in Christ Jesus, great and happy beyond expression, beyond conception: not merely for the little span of ten thousand thousand ages, for ever. A line reaching even to the remotest star would not have been able to contain the number of ages, nor would millions of years have been sufficient to figure them down; this is eternity, but I have lost it, and am now on the verge of being.

This lamp, which might have outlasted those of the firmament, will presently be extinguished, and I blotted out from amongst the works of God, and cut off from all the bounties of his hand." Would not this be a very miserable case, if this were all? And would it not be sufficient to prove this to be the better part, which, as our Lord observes, can "never be taken away?" But God forbid that we should be so unfaithful to him, and to the souls of men, as to rest in such a representation alone. I therefore add once more, 3. The care of the soul is the one thing needful, because "without it, you cannot avoid a state of eternal misery, which will be aggravated, rather than alleviated by all your present enjoyments." Nothing can be more evident from the word of the God of truth. It there plainly appears to be a determined case, which leaves no room for a more favorable conjecture or hope. "The wicked shall be turned into hell, even all the nations that forget God," Psalm 9:17. "They shall go away into everlasting punishment, Matt. 25:46, into a state where they shall in vain seek death, and death shall flee from them. Oh! brethren, it is a certain, but an awful truth, that your souls will be thinking and immortal beings, even in spite of themselves. They may indeed torment, but they cannot destroy themselves. They can no more suspend their power of thought and perception, than a mirror its property of reflecting rays that fall off its surface. Do you suspect the contrary? Make the trial immediately. Command your minds to create from thinking but for one quarter of an hour, or for half that time, and exclude every idea and every reflection. Can you succeed in that attempt? Or rather, does not thought press in with a more sensible violence on that resistance; as an anxious desire to sleep, makes us so much the more wakeful. Thus will thought follow you beyond the grave, thus will it, as an unwelcome guest, force itself upon you, when it can serve only to perplex and distress the mind. It will for ever upbraid you, that notwithstanding all the kind expostulations of God and man, notwithstanding all the keen remonstrances of conscience, and the pleadings of the blood of Christ, you have gone on in your folly, till heaven is lost, and damnation incurred; and all, for what for a shadow and a dream?

Oh think not, sinners, that the remembrance of your past pleasures, and of your success in your other cares, whilst that of the one thing needful was forgotten, think not that this will ease you minds. It will rather torment them the more. "Son, remember that thou in thy life-time receivedst thy good things." Bitter remembrance! Well might the heathen poets represent the unhappy spirits in the shades below, as eagerly catching at the water of forgetfulness, yet unable to reach it. Your present comforts will only serve to give you a livelier sense of your misery, as having tasted such degrees of enjoyment; and to inflame the reckoning, as you have misimproved those talents lodged in your hands for better purposes. Surely, if these things were believed, and seriously considered, the sinner would have no more heart to rejoice in his present prosperity, than a man would have to amuse himself with the curiosities of a fine garden, through which he was led to be broken upon the rack.

But I will enlarge no farther on these things. Would to God that the unaccountable stupidity of men's minds, and their fatal attachment to the pleasures and cares of the present life, did not make it necessary to insist on them so frequently and so copiously!

I now proceed to the reflections which naturally arise from hence, and shall only mention two.

1. How much reason have we to lament the follow of mankind in neglecting the one thing needful.

If religion be indeed the truest wisdom, then surely we have the justest reason to say with Solomon, "the folly and madness is in men's hearts," Eccl. 9:3. Is it the one thing needful? Look on the conduct of the generality of mankind, and you would imagine they thought it the one thing needless: the vainest dream, and the idlest amusement of the mind. God is admonishing them by ordinances, and providences, sometimes by such as are most awful, to lay it to heart;" he speaks once, yea twice, (yes a multitude of times) but man regards not, Job 33:14. They profess perhaps to believe all that I have been saying, but act as if the contrary were self- evident; they will risk their fouls and eternity for a thing of nought, for that, for the sake of which they would not risk so much as a hand, or a finger, or a joint, no, nor perhaps a toy that adorns it. Surely this is the wonder of angels, and perhaps of devils too, unless the observation of so many ages may have rendered it familiar to both. And can we, my Christian brethren, behold such a scene with indifference? If some epidemical madness had seized our country, or the places where we live, so that as we went from one place to another, we every where met with lunatics, and saw amongst the rest, some perhaps of the finest genius, in the most eminent stations in life, amusing themselves with others; surely were we ever so secure from the danger of infection or assault, the fight would cut us to the heart. A good-natured man would hardly be able to go abroad, or even be desirous to live, if it must be amongst so many sad spectacles. Yet these poor creatures might, notwithstanding this, be the children of God, and the higher their frenzy rose, the nearer might their complete happiness be. But alas! the greater part of mankind are seized with a worse kind of madness, in which they are ruining their souls; and can we behold it with indifference? The Lord awaken our compassion, our prayers, and our endeavors, in dependence on divine grace, that we may be instrumental in bringing them to their mind, and making them wise indeed, that is, wise to salvation!

2. How necessary is it that we should seriously inquire, how this one thing needful is regarded by us!

Let me entreat you to remember your own concern in it, and inquire _ Have I thought seriously of it? Have I seen the importance of it? Ha it lain with a due and abiding weight on my mind? Has it brought me to Christ, that I might lay the stress of these great eternal interests on him? And am I acting in the main of my life, as one that has these convictions? Am I willing, in fact, to give up other things, my interests, my pleasures, my passions to this? Am I conversing with God and with man, as one that believes these things; as one that has deliberately chosen the better part, and is determined to abide by that choice?

Observe the answer which conscience returns to these inquiries, and you will know your own part in that more particular application, with which I shall conclude.

1. Let me address those that are entirely unconcerned about the one thing needful.

Brethren, I have been stating the case at large, and now I appeal to your consciences, are these things so, or are they not? God and your own hearts best know for what the care of your soul is neglected; but be it what it will, the difference between one grain of sand and another, is not great, when it comes to be weighed against a talent of gold. Whatever it is, you had need to examine it carefully. You had need to view that commodity on all sides, of which you do in effect say, For this will I sell my soul; for this will I give up heaven, and venture hell, be heaven and hell whatever they may. In the name of God, brethren, is this the part of a man, of a rational creature? To go on with your eyes open towards a pit of eternal ruin, because there are a few gay flowers in the way: or what if you shut your eyes, will that prevent your fall? It signifies little to say, I will not think of these things, I will not consider them: God has said, "In the last days they shall consider it perfectly," Jer. 23:20. The revels of a drunken malefactor will not prevent nor respite his execution.

Pardon my plainness; if it were a fable or a tale, I would endeavor to amuse you with words, but I cannot do it where souls are at stake.

2. I would apply to those who are, in some sense, convinced of the importance of their souls, and yet are inclined to defer that care of them a little longer, which, in the general, they see to be necessary.

I know you that are young, are under peculiar temptations to do this; though it is strange that the death of so many of your companions, should not be an answer to some of the most specious and dangerous of those temptations. Methinks, if these were the least degree of uncertainty, the importance is too weighty to put matters to the venture. But here the uncertainty is great and apparent. You must surely know, that there are critical seasons of life for managing the concerns of it, which are of such a nature, that if once left, they may never return: here is a critical season: "Now is the accepted time, now is the day of salvation," 2 Cor.

6:2. "today, if ye will hear his voice, harden not your hearts," Heb.

3:7,8. This language may not be spoken tomorrow. Talk not of a more convenient season; none can be more convenient; and that to which you would probably refer it, is least of all so, a dying time. You would not choose then to have any important business in hand; and will you of choice refer the greatest business of all to that languishing, hurrying, amazing hour?

If a friend were then to come to you with the balance of an intricate account, or a view of a title to an estate, you would shake your fainting head, and lift up your pale trembling hand, and say, perhaps, with a feeble voice, "Alas, is this a time for these things?" And is it a time for so much greater things than these? I wish you knew, and would consider, into what a strait, we that are minister are sometime brought, when we are called to the dying beds of those who have spent their lives in the neglect of the one thing needful. On the one hand, we fear, lest if we palliate matters, and speak smooth things, we shall betray and ruin their souls; and on the other, that if we use a becoming plainness and seriousness, in warning them of their danger, we shall quite overwhelm them, and hasten the dying moments, which is advancing by such swift steps.

O let me entreat you for our sakes, and much more for your own, that you do not drive us to such sad extremities; but if you are convinced, as I hope some of you may now be, that the care of the soul is that needful thing we have represented, let the conviction work, let it drive you immediately to the throne of grace; from thence you may derive that wisdom and strength, which will direct you in all the intricacies which entangle you, and animate you in the midst of difficulty an discouragement.

3. I would in the last place address myself to those happy souls, who have in good earnest attended to the one thing needful.

I hope, that when you see how commonly it is neglected, neglected indeed, by many, whose natural capacities, improvements, and circumstances in life, appear to you superior to your own; you will humbly acknowledge, that it was distinguishing grace which brought you into this happy state, and formed you to this most necessary care. Bless the Lord, therefore, who hath given you that counsel, in virtue of which you can say, "He is your portion." Rejoice in the thought, that the great concern is secured: as it is natural for us to do, when some important affair is dispatched, which has long lain before us, and which we have been inclined to put off from one day to another, but have at length strenuously and successfully attended. Remember still to en-deavor to continue acting on these great principles, which at first determined your choice; and seriously consider, that those who desire their life may at last be given them for a prey, must continue on their guard, in all stages of their journey through a wilderness, where daily dangers are still surrounding them. Being enabled to secure the great concern, make yourselves easy as to others of smaller importance. You have chosen the kingdom of God, and his righteousness; other things, therefore, shall be added unto you: and if any which you desire should, not be added, comfort yourselves with this thought, that you have the good part, which can never be taken away. And, not to enlarge on these obvious hints, which must often occur, be very solicitous that others may be brought to a care about the one thing needful. If it be needful for you, it is so for your children, your friends, your servants. Let them, therefore, see your concern in this respect for them, as well as for yourselves. Let parents especially attend to this exhortation; whose care for their offspring often exceeds in other respects, and falls in this.

Remember that your children may never live to enjoy the effects of your labor and concern to get them estates and portions: the charges of their funerals may, perhaps, be all their share of what you are so anxiously careful to lay up for them. And O think what a sword would pierce through your very heart, if you should stand by the corpse of a beloved child with this reflection: "This poor creature has done with life, before it learnt its great business in it; and is gone to eternity, which I have seldom been warning it to prepare for, and which, perhaps, it learned of me to forget." On the whole, may this grand care be awakened in those by whom it has been hitherto neglected: may it be revived in each of our minds. And that you may be encouraged to pursue it with greater cheerfulness, let me conclude with this comfortable thought, that in proportion to the necessity of the case, through the merits of Christ Jesus, is the provision which divine grace has made for our assistance. If you are disposed to sit down at Christ's feet, he will teach you by his word and Spirit. If you commit this precious jewel, which is your eternal all, into his hand, he will preserve it unto that day, and will then produce it richly adorned, and gloriously improved to his own honor, and to your everlasting joy.

Which God of his infinite mercy grant, etc.

Sermon 32 A Penitent Heart

(A Penitent Heart, the best New Year's Gift.)

Luke 13:3, "Except ye repent, ye shall all likewise perish."

When we consider how heinous and aggravating our offenses are, in the sight of a just and holy God, that they bring down his wrath upon our heads, and occasion us to live under his indignation; how ought we thereby to be deterred from evil, or at least engaged to study to repent thereof, and not commit the same again; but man is so thoughtless of an eternal state, and has so little consideration of the welfare of his immortal soul, that he can sin without any thought that he must give an account of his actions at the day of judgment; or if he, at times, has any reflections on his behavior, they do not drive him to true repentance: he may, for a short time, refrain from falling into some gross sins which he had lately committed; but then, when the temptation comes again with power, he is carried away with the lust; and thus he goes on promising and resolving, and in breaking both his resolutions and his promises, as fast almost as he has made them. This is highly offensive to God, it is mocking of him. My brethren, when grace is given us to repent truly, we shall turn wholly unto God; and let me beseech you to repent of your sins, for the time is hastening when you will have neither time nor call to repent; there is none in the grave, whither we are going; but do not be afraid, for God often receives the greatest sinner to mercy through the merits of Christ Jesus; this magnifies the riches of his free grace; and should be an encouragement for you, who are great and notorious sinners, to repent, for he shall have mercy upon you, if you through Christ return unto him.

St. Paul was an eminent instance of this; he speaks of himself as "the chief of sinners," and he declareth how God showed mercy unto him. Christ loves to show mercy unto sinners, and if you repent, he will have mercy upon you. But as no word is more mistaken than that of repentance, I shall I. Show you what the nature of repentance is.

II. Consider the several parts and causes of repentance.

III. I shall give you some reasons, why repentance is necessary to salvation. And IV. Exhort all of you, high and low, rich and poor, one with another, to endeavor after repentance.

I. Repentance, my brethren, in the first place, as to its nature, is the carnal and corrupt disposition of men being changed into a renewed and sanctified disposition. A man that has truly repented, is truly regenerated: it is a different word for one and the same thing; the motley mixture of the beast and devil is gone; there is, as it were, a new creation wrought in your hearts. If your repentance is true, you are renewed throughout, both in soul and body; your understandings are enlightened with the knowledge of God, and of the Lord Jesus Christ; and your wills, which were stubborn, obstinate, and hated all good, are obedient and comformable to the will of God. Indeed, our deists tell us, that man now has a free will to do good, to love God, and to repent when he will; but indeed, there is no free will an any of you, but to sin; nay, your free-will leads you so far, that you would, if possible, pull God from is throne. This may, perhaps, offend the Pharisees; but (it is the truth in Christ which I speak, I lie not) every man by his own natural will hates God; but when he is turned unto the Lord, by evangelical repentance, then his will is changed; then your consciences, nor hardened and benumbed, shall be quickened and awakened; then your had hearts shall be melted, and your unruly affections shall be crucified. Thus, by that repentance, the whole soul will be changed, you will have new inclinations, new desires, and new habits.

You may see how vile we are by nature, that it requires so great a change to be made upon us, to recover us from this state of sin, and therefore the consideration of our dreadful state should make us earnest with God to change our condition, and that change, true repentance implies; therefore, my brethren, consider how hateful your ways are to God, while you continue in sin; how abominable you are unto him, while you run into evil: you cannot be said to be Christians while you are hating Christ, and his people; true repentance will entirely change you, the bias of your souls will be changed, then you will delight in God, in Christ, in his law, and in his people; you will then believe that there is such a thing as inward feeling, though now you may esteem it madness and enthusiasm; you will not then be ashamed of becoming fools for Christ's sake; you will not regard being scoffed at; it is not then their pointing after you and crying, "Here comes another troop of his followers," will dismay you; no, your soul will abhor such proceedings, the ways of Christ and his people will be your whole delight.

It is the nature of such repentance to make a change, and the greatest change as can be made here in the soul. Thus you see what repentance implies in its own nature; it denotes an abhorrence of all evil, and a forsaking of it. I shall now proceed SECONDLY, To show you the parts of it, and the causes concurring thereto.

The parts are, sorrow, hatred, and an entire forsaking of sin.

Our sorrow and grief for sin, must not spring merely from a fear of wrath; for if we have no other ground but that, it proceeds from self-love, and not from any love to God; and if love to God is not the chief motive of your repentance, your repentance is in vain, and not to be esteemed true.

Many, in our days, think their crying, God forgive me! or, Lord have mercy upon me! or, I am sorry for it! Is repentance, and that God will esteem it as such; but, indeed, they are mistaken; it is not the drawing near to God with our lips, while our hearts are far from him, which he regards. Repentance does not come by fits and starts; no, it is one continued act of our lives; for as we daily commit sin, so we need a daily repentance before God, to obtain forgiveness for those sins we commit.

It is not your confessing yourselves to be sinners, it is not knowing your condition to be sad and deplorable, so long as you continue in your sins; your care and endeavors should be, to get the heart thoroughly affected therewith, that you may feel yourselves to be lost and undone creatures, for Christ came to save such as are lost; and if you are enabled to groan under the weight and burden of your sins, then Christ will ease you and give you rest.

And till you are thus sensible of your misery and lost condition, you are a servant to sin and to your lusts, under the bondage and command of Satan, doing his drudgery: thou are under the curse of God, and liable to his judgment. Consider how dreadful thy state will be at death, and after the day of judgment, when thou wilt be exposed to such miseries which the ear hath not heard, neither can the heart conceive, and that to all eternity, if you die impenitent.

But I hope better things of you, my brethren, though I thus speak, and things which accompany salvation; go to God in prayer, and be earnest with him, that by his Spirit he would convince you of your miserable condition by nature, and make you truly sensible thereof. O be humbled, be humbled, I beseech you, for your sins. Having spent so many years in sinning, what canst thou do less, than be concerned to spend some hours in mourning and sorrowing for the same, and be humbled before God.

Look back into your lives, call to mind thy sins, as many as possible thou canst, the sins of thy youth, as well as of thy riper years; see how you have departed from a gracious Father, and wandered in the way of wickedness, in which you have lost yourselves, the favor of God, the comforts of his Spirit, and the peace of your own consciences; then go and beg pardon of the Lord, through the blood of the Lamb, for the evil thou hast committed, and for the good thou hast omitted. Consider, likewise, the heinousness of thy sins; see what very aggravating circumstances thy sins are attended with, how you have abused the patience of God, which should have led you to repentance; and when thou findest thy heart hard, beg of God to soften it, cry mightily unto him, and he will take away thy stony heart, and give thee a heart of flesh.

Resolve to leave all thy sinful lusts and pleasures; renounce, forsake, and abhor thy old sinful course of life, and serve God in holiness and righteousness all the remaining part of life. If you lament and bewail past sins, and do not forsake them, your repentance is in vain, you are mocking of God, and deceiving your own soul; you must put off the old man with his deeds, before you can put on the new man, Christ Jesus.

You, therefore, who have been swearers and cursers, you, who have been harlots and drunkards, you, who have been thieves and robbers, you, who have hitherto followed the sinful pleasures and diversions of life, let me beseech you, by the mercies of God in Christ Jesus, that you would no longer continue therein, but that you would forsake your evil ways, and turn unto the Lord, for he waiteth to be gracious unto you, he is ready, he is willing to pardon you of all your sins; but do not expect Christ to pardon you of sin, when you run into it, and will not abstain from complying with the temptations; but if you will be persuaded to abstain from evil and choose the good, to return unto the Lord, and repent of your wickedness, he hath promised he will abundantly pardon you, he will heal your back-slidings, and will love you freely. Resolve now this day to have done with your sins for ever; let your old ways and you be separated; you must resolve against it, for there can be no true repentance without a resolution to forsake it. Resolve for Christ, resolve against the devil and his works, and go on fighting the Lord's battles against the devil and his emissaries; attack him in the strongest holds he has, fight him as men, as Christians, and you will soon find him to be a coward; resist him and he will fly from you. Resolve, through grace, to do this, and your repentance is half done; but then take care that you do not ground your resolutions on your own strength, but in the strength of the Lord Jesus Christ; he is the way, he is the truth, and he is the life; without his assistance you can do nothing, but through his grace strengthening thee, thou wilt be enabled to do all things; and the more ready Christ will be to help thee; and what can all the men of the world do to thee when Christ is for thee? Thou wilt not regard what they say against thee, for you will have the testimony of a good conscience.

Resolve to cast thyself at the feet of Christ in subjection to him, and throw thyself into the arms of Christ for salvation by him. Consider, my dear brethren, the many invitations he has given you to come unto him, to be saved by him; "God has laid on him the iniquity of us all." O let me prevail with you, above all things, to make choice of the Lord Jesus Christ; resign yourselves unto him, take him, O take him, upon his own terms, and whosoever thou art, how great a sinner soever you have been, this evening, in the name of the great God, do I offer Jesus Christ unto thee; as thou valuest thy life and soul refuse him not, but stir up thyself to accept of the Lord Jesus, take him wholly as he is, for he will be applied wholly unto you, or else not at all. Jesus Christ must be your whole wisdom, Jesus Christ must be your whole righteousness, Jesus Christ must be your whole sanctification, or he will never be your eternal redemption.

What though you have been ever so wicked and profligate, yet, if you will not abandon your sins, and turn unto the Lord Jesus Christ, thou shalt have him given to thee, and all thy sins shall be freely forgiven. O why will you neglect the great work of your repentance? Do not defer the doing of it one day longer, but today, even now, take that Christ who is freely offered to you.

Now as to the causes hereof, the first cause is God; he is the author, "we are born of God," God hath begotten us, even God, the Father of our Lord Jesus Christ; it is he that stirs us up to will and to do of his own good pleasure: and another cause is, God's free grace; it is owing to the "riches of his free grace," my brethren, that we have been prevented from going down to hell long ago; it is because the compassions of the Lord fail not, they are new every morning, and fresh every evening.

Sometimes the instruments are very unlikely: a poor despised minister, or member of Jesus Christ, may, by the power of God, be made an instrument in the hands of God, of bringing you to true evangelical repentance; and this may be done to show, that the power is not in men, but that it is entirely owing to the good pleasure of God; and if there has been any good done among many of you, by preaching the word, as I trust there has, though it was preached in a field, if God has met and owned us, and blessed his word, though preached by an enthusiastic babbler, a boy, a madman; I do rejoice, yea, and will rejoice, let foes say what they will. I shall now THIRDLY, Show the reasons why repentance is necessary to salvation.

And this, my brethren, is plainly revealed to us in the word of God, "The soul that does not repent and turn unto the Lord, shall die in its sins, and their blood shall be required at their own heads." It is necessary, as we have sinned, we should repent; for a holy God could not, nor ever can, or will, admit any thing that is unholy into his presence: this is the beginning of grace in the soul; there must be a change in heart and life, before there can be a dwelling with a holy God. You cannot love sin and God too, you cannot love God and mammon; no unclean person can stand in the presence of God, it is contrary to the holiness of his nature; there is a contrariety between the holy nature of God, and the unholy nature of carnal and unregenerate men.

What communication can there be between a sinless God, and creatures full of sin, between a pure God and impure creatures? If you were to be admitted into heaven with your present tempers, in your impenitent condition, heaven itself would be a hell to you; the songs of angels would be as enthusiasm, and would be intolerable to you; therefore you must have these tempers changed, you must be holy, as God is: he must be your God here, and you must be his people, or you will never dwell together to all eternity. If you hate the ways of God, and cannot spend an hour in his service, how will you think to be easy, to all eternity, in singing praises to him that sits upon the throne, and to the Lamb for ever.

And this is to be the employment, my brethren, of all those who are admitted into this glorious place, where neither sin nor sinner is admitted, where no scoffer ever can come, without repentance from his evil ways, a turning unto God, and a cleaving unto him: this must be done, before any can be admitted into the glorious mansions of God, which are prepared for all that love the Lord Jesus Christ in sincerity and truth: repent ye then of all your sins. O my dear brethren, it makes my blood run cold, in thinking that any of you should not be admitted into the glorious mansions above. O that it was in my power, I would place all of you, yea, you my scoffing brethren, and the greatest enemy I have on earth, at the right hand of Jesus; but this I cannot do: however, I advise and exhort you, with all love and tenderness, to make Jesus your refuge; fly to him for relief; Jesus died to save such as you; he is full of compassion; and if you go to him, as poor, lost, undone sinners, Jesus will give you his spirit; you shall live and reign, and reign and live, you shall love and live, and live and love with this Jesus to all eternity.

I am, FORTHLY, to exhort all of you, high and low, rich and poor, one with another, to repent of all your sins, and turn unto the Lord.

And I shall speak to each of you; for you have either repented, or you have not, you are believers in Christ Jesus, or unbelievers.

And first, you who never have truly repented of your sins, and never have truly forsaken your lusts, be not offended if I speak plain to you; for it is love, love to your souls, that constrains me to speak: I shall lay before you your danger, and the misery to which you are exposed, while you remain impenitent in sin. And O that this may be a means of making you fly to Christ for pardon and forgiveness.

While thy sins are not repented of, thou art in danger of death, and if you should die, you would perish for ever. There is no hope of any who live and die in their sins, but that they will dwell with devils and damned spirits to all eternity. And how do we know we shall live much longer: we are not sure of seeing our own habitations this night in safety. What mean ye then being at ease and pleasure while your sins are not pardoned. As sure as ever the word of God is true, if you die in that condition, you are shut out of all hope and mercy for ever, and shall pass into ceaseless and endless misery.

What is all thy pleasures and diversions worth? They last but for a moment, they are of no worth, and but of short continuance. And sure it must be gross folly, eagerly to pursue those sinful lusts and pleasures, which war against the soul, which tend to harden the heart, and keep us from closing with the Lord Jesus; indeed, these are destructive o four peace here, and without repentance, will be of our peace hereafter.

O the folly and madness of this sensual world; sure if there were nothing in sin but present slavery, it would keep an ingenuous spirit from it. But to do the devils drudgery! And if we do that, we shall have his wages, which is eternal death and condemnation; O consider this, my guilty brethren, you that think it no crime to swear, whore, drink, or scoff and jeer at the people of God; consider how your voices will then be changed, and you that counted their lives madness, and their end without honor, shall howl and lament at your own madness and filly, that should bring you to so much woe and distress. Then you will lament and bemoan your own dreadful condition; but it will be of no signification: for he that is not your merciful Savior, will then become your inexorable Judge. Now he is easy to be entreated; but then, all your tears and prayers will be in vain: for God hath allotted to every man a day of grace, a time of repentance, which if he doth not improve, nut neglects and despises the means which are offered to him, he cannot be saved.

Consider, therefore, while you are going on in a course of sin and unrighteousness, I beseech you, my brethren, to think of the consequence that will attend your thus mispending your precious time; your souls are worth being concerned about: for if you can enjoy all the pleasures and diversions of life, at death you must leave them; that will put an end to all your worldly concerns. And will it not be very deplorable, to have your good things here, all your earthly, sensual, devilish pleasures, which you have been so much taken up with, all over: and the thought for how trifling a concern thou hast lost eternal welfare, will gnaw thy very soul.

Thy wealth and grandeur will stand in no stead; thou canst carry nothing of it into the other world: then the consideration of thy uncharitableness to the poor, and the ways thou didst take to obtain thy wealth, will be a very hell unto thee.

Now you enjoy the means of grace, as the preaching of his word, prayer, and sacraments; and God has sent his ministers out into the fields and highways, to invite, to woo you to come in; but they are tiresome to thee, thou hadst rather be at thy pleasures: ere long, my brethren, they will be over, and you will be no more troubled with them; but then thou wouldst give ten thousand worlds for one moment of that merciful time of grace which thou hast abused; then you will cry for a drop of that precious blood which now you trample under your feet; then you will wish for one more offer of mercy, for Christ and his free grace to be offered to you again; but your crying will be in vain: for as you would not repent here, God will not give you an opportunity to repent hereafter: if you would not in Christ's time, you shall not in your own. In what a dreadful condition will you then be? What horror and astonishment will possess your souls?

Then all thy lies and oaths, thy scoffs and jeers at the people of God, all thy filthy and unclean thoughts and actions, thy mispent time in balls, plays, and assemblies, thy spending whole evenings at cards, dice, and masquerades, thy frequenting of taverns and alehouses, thy worldliness, covetousness, and thy uncharitableness, will be brought at once to thy remembrance, and at once charged upon thy guilty soul. And how can you bear the thoughts of these things? Indeed I am full of compassion towards you, to think that this should be the portion of any who now hear me. These are truths, though awful ones; my brethren, these are the truths of the gospel; and if there was not a necessity for thus speaking, I would willingly forbear: for it is no pleasing subject to me, any more than it is to you; but it is my duty to show you the dreadful consequences of continuing in sin. I am only now acting the part of a skillful surgeon, that searches a wound before he heals it: I would show you your danger first, that deliverance may be the more readily accepted by you.

Consider, that however you may be for putting the evil day away from you, and are now striving to hide your sins, at the day of judgment there shall be a full discovery of all; hidden things on that day shall be brought to light; and after all thy sins have been revealed to the whole world, then you must depart into everlasting fire in hell, which will not be quenched night and day; it will be without intermission, without end. O then, what stupidity and senselessness hath possessed your hearts, that you are not frighted from your sins. The fear of Nebuchadnezzar's fiery furnace, made men do any thing to avoid it; and shall not an everlasting fire make men, make you, do any thing to avoid it?

O that this would awaken and cause you to humble yourselves for your sins, and to beg pardon for them, that you might find mercy in the Lord.

Do not go away, let not the devil hurry you away before the sermon is over; but stay, and you shall have a Jesus offered to you, who has made full satisfaction for all your sins.

Let me beseech you to cast away your transgressions, to strive against sin, to watch against it, and to beg power and strength from Christ, to keep down the power of those lusts that hurry you on in your sinful ways.

But if you will not do any of these things, if you are resolved to sin on, you must expect eternal death to be the consequence; you must expect to be seized with horror and trembling, with horror and amazement, to hear the dreadful sentence of condemnation pronounced against you: and then you will run and call upon the mountains to fall on you, to hide you from the Lord, and from the fierce anger of his wrath.

Had you now a heart to turn from your sins unto the living God, by true and unfeigned repentance, and to pray unto him for mercy, in and through the merits of Jesus Christ, there were hope; but at the day of judgment, thy prayers and tears will be of no signification; they will be of no service to thee, the Judge will not be entreated by thee: as you would not hearken to him when he called unto thee, but despised both him and his ministers, and would not leave your iniquities; therefore, on that day he will not be entreated, notwithstanding all thy cries and tears; for God himself hath said, "Because I have called, and you refused; I have stretched out my hand, and no man regarded, but ye have set at nought all my counsel, and would have one of my reproof; I will also laugh at your calamity, and mock when your fear cometh as desolation, and your destruction cometh as a whirlwind; when distress and anguish cometh upon you, then shall they call upon me, but I will not answer, they shall seek me early, but they shall not find me." Now you may call this enthusiasm and madness; but at that great day, if you repent not of your sins here, you will find, by woeful experience, that your own ways were madness indeed; but God forbid it should be left undone till then: seek after the Lord while he is to be found; call upon him while he is near, and you shall find mercy: repent this hour, and Christ will joyfully receive you.

What say you? Must I go to my Master, and tell him you will not come unto him, and will have none of his counsels? No; do not send me on so unhappy an errand: I cannot, I will not tell him any such thing. Shall not I rather tell him, you are willing to repent and to be converted, to become new men, and take up a new course of life: this is the only wise resolution you can make. Let me tell my Master, that you will come unto, and will wait upon him: for if you do not, it will be your ruin in time, and to eternity.

You will at death wish you had lived the life of the righteous, that you might have died his death. Be advised then; consider what is before you, Christ and the world, holiness and sin, life and death: choose now for your-selves; let your choice be made immediately, and let that choice be your dying choice.

If you would not choose to die in your sins, to die drunkards, to die adulterers, to die swearers and scoffers, etc. live not out this night in the dreadful condition you are in. Some of you, it may be, may say, You have not power, you have no strength: but have not you been wanting to yourselves in such things that were within your power? Have you not as much power to go to hear a sermon, as to go into a playhouse, or to a ball, or masquerade? You have as much power to read the Bible, as to read plays, novels, and romances; and you can associate as well with the godly, as with the wicked and profane: this is but an idle excuse, my brethren, to go on in your sins: and if you will be found in the means of grace, Christ hath promised he will give you strength. While Peter was preaching, the Holy Ghost fell on all that heard the word: how then should you be found in the way of your duty? Jesus Christ will then give thee strength; he will put his Spirit within thee; thou shalt find he will be thy wisdom, thy righteousness, thy sanctification, and thy redemp-tion. Do but try what a gracious, a kind, and loving Master he is; he will be a help to thee in all thy burdens: and if the burden of sin is on thy soul, go to him as weary and heavy laden, and thou shalt find rest.

Do not say, that your sins are too many and too great to expect to find mercy! No, be they ever so many, or ever so great, the blood of the Lord Jesus Christ will cleanse you from all sins. God's grace, my brethren, is free, rich, and sovereign. Manassah was a great sinner, and yet he was pardoned; Zaccheus was gone far from God, and went out to see Christ, with no other view but to satisfy his curiosity; and yet Jesus met him, and brought salvation to his house. Manassah was an idolater and murderer, yet her received mercy; the other was an oppressor and extortioner, who had gotten riches by fraud and deceit, and by grinding the faces of the poor: so did Matthew too, and yet they found mercy.

Have you been blasphemers and persecutors of the saints and servants of God? So was St. Paul, yet her received mercy: Have you been common harlots, filthy and unclean persons? So was Mary Magdalene, and yet she received mercy. Hast thou been a thief? The thief upon the cross found mercy. I despair of none of you, however vile and profligate you have been; I say, I despair of none of you, especially when God has had mercy on such a wretch as I am.

Remember the poor Publican, how he found favor with God, when the proud, self-conceited Pharisee, who, puffed up with his own righteousness, was rejected. And if you will go to Jesus, as the poor Publican did, under a sense of your own unworthiness, you shall find favor as he did: there is virtue enough in the blood of Jesus, to pardon greater sinners than he has yet pardoned. Then be not discouraged, but come unto Jesus, and you will find him ready to help in all thy distresses, to lead thee into all truth, to bring thee from darkness to light, and from the power of Satan to God.

Do not let the devil deceive you, by telling you, that then all your delights and pleasures will be over: No; this is so far from depriving you of all pleasure, that it is an inlet unto unspeakable delights, peculiar to all who are truly regenerated. The new birth is the very beginning of a life of peace and comfort; and the greatest pleasantness is to be found in the ways of holiness.

Solomon, who had experience of all other pleasures, yet saith of the ways of godliness, "That all her ways are ways of pleasantness, and all her paths are paths of peace." Then sure you will not let the devil deceive you; it is all he wants, it is that he aims at, to make religion appear to be melancholy, miserable, and enthusiastic: but let him say what he will, give not ear to him, regard him not, for he always was and will be a liar.

What words, what entreaties shall I use, to make you come unto the Lord Jesus Christ? The little love I have experienced since I have been brought from sin to God, is so great, that I would not be in a natural state for ten thousand worlds; and what I have felt is but little to what I hope to feel; but that little love which I have experienced, is a sufficient buoy against all the storms and tempests of this boisterous world: and let men and devils do their worst, I rejoice in the Lord Jesus, yea, and I will rejoice.

And O if you repent and come to Jesus, I would rejoice on your accounts too; and we should rejoice together to all eternity, when once passed on the other side of the grave. O come to Jesus. The arms of Jesus Christ will embrace you; he will sash away all your sins in his blood, and will love you freely.

Come, I beseech you to come unto Jesus Christ. O that my words would pierce to the very soul! O that Jesus Christ was formed in you! O that you would turn to the Lord Jesus Christ, that he might have mercy upon you! I would speak till midnight, yea, I would speak till I could speak no more, so it might be a means to bring you to Jesus; let the Lord Jesus but enter your souls, and you shall find peace which the world can neither give nor take away. There is mercy for the greatest sinner amongst you; go unto the Lord as sinners, helpless and undone without it, and then you shall find comfort in your souls, and be admitted at last amongst those who sing praises unto the Lord to all eternity.

Now, my brethren, let me speak a word of exhortation to those of you, who are already brought to the Lord Jesus, who are born again, who do belong to God, to whom it has been given to repent of your sins, and are cleansed from their guilt; and that is, be thankful to God for his mercies towards you. O admire the grace of God, and bless his name forever! Are you made alive in Christ Jesus? Is the life of God begun in your souls, and have you the evidence thereof? Be thankful for this unspeakable mercy to you: never forget to speak of his mercy. And as your life was formerly devoted to sin, and to the pleasures of the world, let it now be spent wholly in the ways of God; and O embrace every opportunity of doing and of receiving good. Whatsoever opportunity you have, do it vigorously, do it speedily, do not defer it. If thou seest one hurrying on to destruction, use the utmost of thy endeavor to stop him in his course; show him the need he has of repentance, and that without it he is lost for ever; do not regard his despising of you; still go on to show him his danger: and if thy friends mock and despise, do not let that discourage you; hold on, hold out to the end, so you shall have a crown which is immutable, and that fadeth not away.

Let the love of Jesus to you, keep you also humble; do not be high-minded, keep close unto the Lord, observe the rules which the Lord Jesus Christ has given in his word, and let not the instructions be lost which you which you are capable of giving. O consider what reason you have to be thankful to the Lord Jesus Christ for giving you that repentance you yourselves had need of: a repentance which worketh by love. Now you find more pleasure in walking with God one hour, than in all your former carnal delights, and all the pleasures of sin. O! the joy you feel in your own souls, which all the men of the world, and all the devils in hell, though they were to combine together, could not destroy. Then fear not their wrath or malice, for through many tribulations we must enter into glory.

A few days, or weeks, or years more, and then you will be beyond their reach, you will be in the heavenly Jerusalem; their is all harmony and love, there is all joy and delight; there the weary soul is at rest.

Now we have many enemies, but at death they are all lost; they cannot follow us beyond the grave: and this is a great encouragement to us not to regard the scoffs and jeers of the men of this world.

O let the love of Jesus be in your thoughts continually. It was his dying that brought you life; it was his crucifixion that paid the satisfaction for your sins; his death, burial, and resurrection that completed the work; and he is now in heaven, interceding for you at the right hand of his Father. And can you do too much for the Lord Jesus Christ, who has done so much for you? His love to you is unfathomable. O the height, the depth, the length and breadth of this love, that brought the King of glory from his throne, to die for such rebels as we are, when we had acted so unkindly against him, and deserved nothing but eternal damnation. He came down and took our nature upon him; he was made of flesh and dwelt among us; he was put to death on our account; he paid our ransom: surely this should make us rejoice in him, and not do as too many do, and as we ourselves have too often, crucify this Jesus afresh. Let us do all we can, my dear brethren, to honor him.

Come, all of you, come, and behold him stretched out for you; see his hands and feet nailed to the cross. O come, come, my brethren, and nail your sins thereto; come, come and see his side pierced; there is a fountain open for sin, and for uncleanness: O wash, wash and be clean: come and see his head crowned with thorns, and all for you. Can you think of a panting, bleeding, dying Jesus, and not be filled with pity towards him? He underwent all this for you. Come unto him by faith; lay hold on him: there is mercy for every soul of you that will come unto him. Then do not delay; fly unto the arms of this Jesus, and you shall be made clean in his blood.

O what shall I say unto you to make you come to Jesus: I have showed you the dreadful consequence of not repenting of your sins: and if after all I have said, you are resolved to persist, your blood will be required at your own heads; but I hope better things of you, and things that accompany salvation. Let me beg of you to pray in good earnest for the grace of repentance. I may never see your faces again; but at the day of judgment I will meet you: there you will either bless God that ever you were moved to repentance; or else this sermon, though in a field, will be as a swift witness against you. Repent, repent therefore, my dear brethren, as John the Baptist, and as our blessed Redeemer himself earnestly exhorted, and turn from your evil ways, and the Lord will have mercy on you.

Show them, O Father, wherein they have offended thee; make them to see their own vileness, and that they are lost and undone without true repentance; and O give them that repentance, we beseech of thee, that they may turn from sin unto thee the living and true God. These things, and whatever else thou seest needful for us, we entreat that thou wouldst bestow upon us, on account of what the dear Jesus Christ has done and suffered; to whom, with Thyself, and holy Spirit, three persons, and one God, be ascribed, as is most due, all power, glory, might, majesty, and dominion, now, henceforth, and for evermore. Amen.

Sermon 33 The Gospel Supper

Luke 14:22-24, "And the servant said, Lord, it is done as thou hast commanded, and yet there is room. And the lord said unto the servant, Go out into the high-ways, and hedges, and compel them to come in, that my house may be filled. For I say unto you, that none of those men which were bidden, shall taste of my supper."

Though here is a large and solemn assembly, yet I suppose you are all convinced, that you are not to live in this world always. May I not take it for granted, that even the most profane amongst you, do in your hearts believe, what the sacred oracles have most clearly revealed, "That as it is appointed for all men once to die, so after death comes the judgment?" Yes, I know you believe, that nothing is more certain, than that we are to "appear before the judgment-seat of Christ, to be rewarded according to the deeds done in the body, whether they have been good, or whether they have been evil." And, however hard the saying may seem to you at the first hearing, yet I cannot help informing you, that I am thoroughly persuaded, as many will be driven from that judgment-seat, with a "Depart ye cursed into everlasting fire," for pursuing things in themselves lawful, out of a wrong principle, and in too intense a degree; as for drunkenness, adultery, fornication, or any other gross enormity whatsoever. Bas as the world is, blessed be God, there are great numbers yet left amongst us, who either through the restraints of a religious education, or self-love, and outward reputation, abstain from gross sin themselves, and look with detestation and abhorrence upon others, who indulge themselves in it. But then, through an over-eager pursuit after the things of sense and time, their souls are insensibly lulled into a spiritual slumber, and by degrees become as dead to God, and as deaf to all the gracious invitations of the gospel, as the most abandoned prodigals. It is remarkable, therefore, that our Savior, knowing how desperately wicked and treacherous the heart of man was, in this, as well as other respects, after he had cautioned his disciples, and us in them, to "take heed that their hearts were not at any time overcharged with surfeiting and drunkenness," immediately adds, "and the cares (the immoderate anxious cares) of this life." For they are of a distracting, intoxicating nature, and soon overcharge and weigh down the hearts of the children of men. To prevent or remedy this evil, our Lord, during the time of his tabernacling here below, spake many parables, but not one more pertinent, not one, in which the freeness of the gospel-call, and the frivolous pretenses men frame to excuse themselves from embracing it, and the dreadful doom they incur by so doing, are more displayed, or set off in livelier colors, than that to which the words of the text refer. "And the lord said unto the servant, Go out into the highways and hedges, and compel them to come in, that my house may be filled: For I say unto you, that none of those that were bidden shall taste of my supper." In order to have a clear view of the occasion, scope, and contents of the parable, to which these words belong, it is necessary for us to look back to the very beginning of this chapter. "And it came to pass, as he went into the house of one of the chief Pharisees to eat bread, on the Sabbath day, that they watched him." The person here spoken of, as going into this Pharisee's house, is our blessed Savior. For as he came eating and drinking, agreeable to his character, he was free, courteous and affable to all; and therefore though it was on a Sabbath-day, he accepted an invitation, and went into the house of one of the chief Pharisees to eat bread, notwithstanding he knew the Pharisees were his professed enemies, and that they watched him, hoping to find some occasion to upbraid him, either for his discourse or behavior. If the Pharisee into whose house our Lord went, was one of this stamp, his invitation bespeaks him to be a very ill man, and may serve to teach us, that much rancor and heart-enmity against Jesus Christ, may be concealed and cloaked under a great and blazing profession of religion. However, our Savior was more than a match for all his enemies, and by accepting this invitation, hath warranted his ministers and disciples, to comply with the like invitations, and converse freely about the things of God, though those who invite them, may not have real religion at heart. For how knowest thou, O man, but thou mayest drop something, that may benefit their souls, and make them religious indeed? And supposing they should watch thee, watch thou unto prayer, whilst thou art in their company, and that same Jesus, who went into this Pharisee's house, and was so faithful and edifying in his conversation when there, will enable thee to go and do likewise.

That our Lord's conversation was not trifling, but such as tended to the use of edifying, and that he behaved among the guests as a faithful physician, rather than as a careless, indifferent companion, is evident from the 7th verse of this chapter, where we are told, that "he marked how they chose the chief rooms;" or, to speak in our common way, were desirous of sitting at the upper end of the table. And whether we think of it or not, the Lord Jesus takes notice of our behavior, even when we are going to sit down only at our common meals. Would to God, all that make a profession of real Christianity, considered this well! Religion then would not be so much confined to church, or meeting, but be brought home to our private houses, and many needless unchristian compliments be prevented. For (with grief I speak it) is it not too true, that abundance of professors love, and are too fond of the uppermost places in houses, as well as synagogues?

This was what our Lord blamed in the guests where he now was. He marked, he took notice, he looked before he spake (as we should always do, if we would speak to the purpose) how they chose out the chief rooms. Therefore, though they were rich in this world's goods, and were none of his guests, yet unwilling to suffer the least sin upon them, or lost any opportunity of giving instruction, he gave them a lecture upon humility, saying unto them, or directing his discourse to all in general, though probably he spake to one in particular, who sat near him, and whom, it may be, he took notice of, as more than ordinarily solicitous in choosing a chief room, or couch, on which they lay at meals, after the custom of the Romans; "When thou art bidden of any man to a wedding (which seems to intimate that this was a wedding-feast) sit not down in the highest room, lest a more honorable man than thou be bidden of him; and he that bade thee and him come and say to thee, Give this man place; and thou begin with shame to take the lowest room. But when thou are bidden, go and sit down in the lowest room; that when he that bade thee cometh, he may say unto thee, Friend, go up higher: then shalt thou have worship (or respect) in the presence of them who sit at meat with thee." O glorious example of faithfulness and love to souls!

How ought ministers especially, to copy after their blessed Master, and, with simplicity an godly sincerity, mildly and opportunely rebuke the faults of the company they are in, though superior to them in outward circumstances? What rightly informed person, after reading this passage, can think they teach right and agreeable to the word of God in this respect, who say, we must not, at least need not, reprove natural men?

Surely such doctrine cometh not from above! For are we not commanded, in any wise, to reprove our neighbor (whether he be a child of God or no) and not to suffer sin upon him? Is it not more than probable, that all these guests were natural men? And yet our Lord reproved them. Help us then, O Savior, in this and every other instance of thy moral conduct, to walk as thou hast set us an example!

Neither did our Lord stop here; but observing that none but the rich, the mighty, and the noble, were called to the feast, he took occasion also from thence, to give even his host (for the best return we make our friends for their kindness, is to be faithful to their souls) one of the chief Pharisees, a wholesome piece of advice. "Then said he also to him that bade him, when thou makest a dinner or a supper, call not thy friends, nor thy brethren, neither thy kinsmen nor thy rich neighbors, lest they also bid thee again, and a recompense be made thee. But when thou makest a feast, call the poor, the maimed, the lame, the blind, and thou shalt be blessed; for they cannot recompense thee. For thou shalt be recompensed at the resurrection of the just!" Thus did our Lord entertain the company.

Words spoken in such due season, how good are they! Would Christ's followers thus exert themselves, and, when in company, begin some useful discourse for their great master, they know not what good they might do, and how many might be influenced, by their good example, to second them in it.

An instance of this we have in the 14th verse: "And when one of them that sat at meat with him heard these things, he said unto him, Blessed is he that shall eat bread in the kingdom of God." Happy they who shall be recompensed at that resurrection of the just, which thou hast been speaking of. A very pertinent saying this! every way suitable to persons sitting down to eat bread on earth, which we should never do, without talking of, and longing for that time, when we shall sit down and eat bread in the kingdom of heaven. This opened to our Lord a fresh topic of conversation, and occasioned the parable, which is to be the more immediate subject of your present meditation. As though he had said to the person that spoke last, Thou sayest right: blessed are they indeed, who shall sit down to eat bread in the kingdom of God: But alas! most men, especially you Pharisees, act as if you did not believe this; and therefore he said unto him, "A certain man made a great supper, and bade many;" by the certain man making a great supper, we are to understand God the Father, who has made provision for perishing souls, by the obedience and death of his beloved Son Christ Jesus. This provision is here represented under the character of a supper, because the Caena or supper, among the ancients, was their grand meal: Men could never have made such provision for themselves, or angels for them.

No, our salvation is all from God, from the beginning to the end. He made it, and not we ourselves; and it is wholly owing to the divine wisdom, and not our own, that we are become God's people, and the sheep of his pasture.

This provision for perishing souls, may be justly called GREAT, because there is rich and ample provision made in the gospel for a great many souls. For however Christ's flock may be but a little flock, when asunder, yet when they come all together, they will be a multitude which no man can number. And it is especially called GREAT, because it was purchased at so great a price, the price of Christ's most precious blood. And therefore, when the apostle would exhort the Christians to glorify God in their souls and bodies, he makes use of this glorious motive, "That they were bought with a price." He does not say what price, but barely a PRICE, emphatically so called; as though all the prices in the world were nothing (as indeed they are not) when compared to this price of Christ's most precious blood.

For these reasons, Jesus said in the parable, "A certain man made a great supper, and bade many, and sent his servant at supper-time, to say to them that were bidden, Come, for all things are now ready." He bade many; the eternal God took the Jews for his peculiar people, under the Mosaic dispensation; and by types, shadows, and prophesies of the Old Testament, invited them to partake of the glorious privileges of the gospel. "But at supper-time," in the fullness of time, which God the Father had decreed from eternity, in the evening of the world (for which reason the gospel times are called the last times) "he sent his servant," Christ his Son, here called his servant, because acting as Mediator he was inferior to the Father; therefore says the prophet Isaiah, "Behold my servant whom I have chosen:" "to say to them that were bidden," to the professing Jews, called by St. John, "his own," that is, his peculiar professing people _ with this message, "Come;" repent and believe the gospel. Nothing is required on man's part, but to come, or accept of the gospel offer. It is not according to the old covenant, "Do and live;" but only "come, believe, and thou shalt be saved." All things are ready. Nothing is wanting on God's part. "All things are now ready." There seems to be a particular emphasis to be put upon NOE, implying, this was an especial season of grace, and God was now exerting his last efforts, to save lost man. Well then, if the great God be at so great an expense, to make so great a supper, for perishing creatures, and sends so great a person as his own Son, in the form of a servant, to invite them to come to it; one would imagine, that all who heard these glad tidings, should readily say, Lord, lo we come. But instead of this, we are told, "They all, (the greatest part of the Jews) with one consent began to make excuse." Conscience told them they ought to come, and in all probability they had some faint desire to come; and they had nothing, as we hear of, to object either against the person who prepared the supper, or the person that invited them, or the entertainment itself; neither do we hear that they treated either with contempt, as is the custom of too many in the days wherein we live. In all probability, they acknowledged all was very good, and that it was kind in that certain man, to send them such an invitation. But being very busy, and as they thought very lawfully engaged, they begun to make excuse.

But the excuses they made, rendered their refusal inexcusable. "The first said unto him, I have bought a piece of ground, and I must needs go and see it." Thou fool, buy a piece of ground, and then go see it! A prudent man would have gone and seen the ground first, and bought it afterwards. Why must he needs go? At least, why must he needs go NOW? The land was his own, could he not therefore have accepted the invitation today, and gone and seen his estate, or plantation, on the morrow? As he had bought it, he need not fear losing his bargain, by anothers buying it from him. But notwithstanding all this, there is a needs must for his going, and therefore says he, "I pray thee, have me excused," and improve thy interest with thy master in my behalf. This was a bad excuse.

The second was rather worse. For what says the evangelist, verse 19?

"And another said, I have bought five yoke of oxen, and I go to prove them:" One, it seems, had been buying an estate; another, cattle, to stock an estate already bought; and both equally foolish in making their bargains. For this second had bought five yoke of oxen, which must needs cost them a considerable sum, perhaps all he had in the world, and now he must go and prove them. A wise dealer would have proved the oxen first, and bought them afterwards: But our Savior speaks this, to show us, that we will trust one another, nay I may add, the devil himself, more than we will trust God.

The excuse which the third makes, is worst of all. "I have married a wife, and therefore I cannot come." Had he said, I will not come, he had spoken the real sentiments of his heart: for it is not so much men's impotency , as their want of a will, and inclination, that keeps them from the gospel-feast. But why cannot he come? He has "married a wife." Has he so? Why then, by all means he should come. For the supper to which he was invited, as it should seem, was a wedding-supper, and would have saved him the trouble of a nuptial entertainment. It was a great supper, and consequently there was provision enough for him, and his bride too. And it was made by a great man, who sent out his servant to bid many, so that he need not have doubted of meeting with a hearty welcome, though he should bring his wife with him. Or supposing his wife was unwilling to come, yet as the husband is the head of the wife, he ought to have laid his commands on her, to accompany him. For we cannot do better for our yoke-fellows, than to bring them to the gospel-feast. Or, supposing after all, she would not be prevailed upon, he ought to have gone without her: for "those that have wives, must be as though they had none;" and we must not let carnal affection get such an ascendancy over us, as to be kept thereby from spiritual entertainments. Adam paid dear for hearkening to the voice of his wife: and sometimes, unless we forsake wives, as well as houses and lands, we cannot be the Lord's disciples.

This then was the reception the servant met with, and such were the excuses, and answers, that were sent back. And what was the consequence?

"So that servant came (no doubt with a sorrowful heart) and showed his Lord these things." However little it be thought of, yet ministers must show the Lord, what success their ministry meets with. We must how it to our Lord here. We must spread the case before him in prayer. We must show it to our Lord hereafter, before the general assembly of the whole world. But how dreadful is it, when ministers are obliged to go upon their knees, crying, "O! my leanness, my leanness!" and Elias-like, to intercede as it were against those, to whom they would not only have imparted the gospel, but even their own lives. It is a heart-breaking consideration. But thus it must be; "The servant came and showed the Lord these things;" so must we.

Well, and what says the Lord? We are told, verse 21st, that "the master of the house was angry?" Not with the servant: for though Israel be not gathered, yet shall Christ be glorious; and faithful ministers shall be rewarded, whether people obey the gospel or not. "We are a sweet savor unto God, whether the world be a savor of life unto life, or a savor of death unto death." The master of the house therefore was angry, not with the servant, but with these worldly-minded, pleasure-taking refusers of his gracious invitation; who, in all probability, went to see and stock their estates, and attend upon their brides, not doubting, but their excuses would be taken, because they were lawfully employed. And, indeed, in one sense, their excuses were accepted. For I do not hear that they were ever invited any more. God took them at their word, though they would not take him at his. They begged to be excused, and they were excused, as we shall see in the sequel of this parable. Let us not therefore harden our hearts, as in the day of provocation; "Now is the accepted time, now is the day of salvation." But must the feast want guests? No, if they cannot, or will not come, others shall, and will. The master of the house therefore being angry, sent the servant upon a second errand. "Go out quickly into the streets, and lanes of the city, and bring in hither the poor, and the maimed, and the halt, and the blind." Every word bespeaks a spirit of resentment and importunity. Go out quickly, make no delay, dread no attempt or danger, into the streets and lanes of the city, and bring in hither, not only call them, but bring them in (for the master here, to encourage the servant, assures him of success) the poor, and the maimed, and the halt, and the blind. This was fulfilled, when Jesus Christ, after the gospel was rejected by the Jews, went and invited the Gentiles, and when the publicans and harlots took the kingdom of God by a holy violence, whilst the self- righteous scribes and Pharisees rejected the kingdom of God against themselves. This was also a home reproof of the rich Pharisee, at whose house the Lord Jesus was, as well as a cutting lesson to the other guests.

For our Savior would hereby show them, that God took a quite different method from his host, and was not above receiving the poor, and halt, and blind, and maimed, to the gospel supper, though he had called none such to sit down at his table. Whether the guests resented it or not, we are not told. But if they were not quite blind, both host and guests might easily see that the parable was spoken against them. But to proceed, The servant again returns, but with a more pleasing answer than before, "Lord, it is done as thou hast commanded, and yet there is room." The words bespeak the servant to be full of joy at the thoughts of the success he had met with. None can tell, but those who experience it, what comfort ministers have in seeing their labors blest. "Now I live, (says the apostle) if you stand fast in the Lord. Ye are our joy and crown of rejoicing in the day of the Lord Jesus." "Lord, it is done as thou hast commanded. The poor, and maimed, and halt, and blind, have been called, and have obeyed the summons, and I have brought them with me; yet, Lord, thy house, and thy supper is so great, there is room for more. Hereby he insinuated that he wanted to be employed again, in calling more souls; and the more we do, the more may we do for God: "To him that hath, shall be given;" and present success is a great encouragement to future diligence.

Such hints are pleasing to our Savior. He delights to see his ministers ready for new work, and waiting for fresh orders. "The Lord, therefore, we are told, ver. 23, said unto his servant, (the same servant,) Go out into the highways and hedges, and compel them to come in, that my house may be filled; 24. For I say unto you, that none of those who are bidden, shall taste of my supper." O cutting words to those that sat at meat, if they had hearts to make the application! But glad tidings of great joy to the publicans, harlots, and Gentiles, who were rejected by the proud Pharisees, as aliens to the commonwealth of Israel, and strangers to the covenant of promise! This was fulfilled, when our Lord sent the apostles, not only into the streets and lanes of the city, and places bordering upon Jerusalem and Judea; but when he gave them a commission to go out into all the world, and preach the gospel to every creature, Gentile as well a Jew; and not only gave them a command, but blessed their labors with such success, that three thousand were converted in one day. And I am not without hopes that it will be still further fulfilled, by the calling of some of you home this day.

For however this parable was spoken originally to the Jews, and upon a particular occasion, as at a feast, yet it is applicable to us, and to our children, and to as many as are afar off; yea, to as many as the Lord our God shall call. It gives a sanction, methinks, to preaching in the fields, and other places besides the synagogues; and points our the reception the gospel meets with in these days, in such a lively manner, that one would think it had a particular reference to the perfect age. For is it not too, too plain, that the gospel-offers, and gospel-grace, have been slighted, and made light of, by many professors of this generation? We have been in the churches, telling them, again and again, that God has made a great supper (and has invited many, even them) and sent us by his providence and his spirit, "to say unto them that were bidden, Come, for all things are now ready. Believe on the Lord Jesus, and you shall be saved." But the generality of the laity have made light of it, they have given us the hearing, but are too busy in their farms and their merchandises, their marrying and giving in marriage, to come and be blessed in the Lord of life. We have told them, again and again, that we do not want them to hide themselves from the world, but to teach them how they may live in, and yet not be of it. But all will not do. Many of the clergy also (like the letter-learned Scribes and Pharisees in our Savior's time) reject the kingdom of God against themselves, and deny us the use of the pulpits, for no other reason but because we preach the doctrine of justification in the sight of God by faith alone, and invite sinners to come and taste of the gospel feast freely, without money and without price.

Whatever they may think, we are persuaded, the great master of the house is angry with them, for being angry with us without a cause. He therefore now, by his providence, bids us "Go out quickly into the streets and lanes of the city, and bring in the poor, and the maimed, and the halt, and the blind," or call in the publicans and harlots, the common cursers and swearers, and Sabbath-breakers, and adulterers, who, perhaps, never entered a church door, or heard that Jesus Christ died for such sinners as they are. We, through grace, have obeyed the command, we have gone out, though exposed to such contempt for so doing, and, blessed be God, our labor has not been in vain in the Lord. For many have been made willing in the day of God's power; and, we would speak it with humility, we can go cheerfully to our Savior, and say, "It is done, Lord, as thou hast commanded, and yet there is room." He is therefore pleased, in spite of all opposition from men or devils, to continue, and renew, and enlarge our commission; he hath sent us literally into the highways and hedges; and, I trust, has given us a commission to compel sinners to come. For, could we speak with the tongues of men and angels, yet if the Lord did not attend the word with his power, and sweetly inclined men's wills to comply with the gospel-call, we should be as a sounding brass, or a tinkling cymbal.

But this we believe our Savior will do, for his house must be filled: every soul for whom he has shed his blood, shall finally be saved, "and all that the Father hath given him, shall come unto him, and whosoever cometh unto him he will in no wise cast out." This comforted our Lord, when his gospel was rejected by the Jews. As though he had said, Well, tho' you despise the offers of my grace, yet I shall not shed my blood in vain; for all that the Father hath given me shall come unto me.

Supported by this consideration, I am not ashamed to come out this day into the highways and hedges, and to confess that my business is to call the poor, and the maimed, and the halt, and the blind, self-condemned, helpless sinners, to the marriage-feast of the supper of the Lamb. My cry is, Come, believe on the Lord Jesus; throw yourselves at the footstool of his mercy, and you shall be saved; for all things are now ready. God the Father is ready, God the Son is ready, God the Holy Ghost is ready; the blessed angels above are ready, and the blessed saints below are ready, to welcome you to the gospel-feast. A perfect and everlasting righteousness is now wrought out by Jesus Christ. God, now, upon honorable terms, can acquit the guilty. God can now be just, and yet justify the ungodly. "For he hath made Christ to be sin for us, who knew no sin, that we might be made the righteousness of God in him." The fatted calf is now killed, and "Christ, our Passover, is sacrificed for us." Come, sinners, and feed upon him in your hearts by faith, with thanksgiving. For Jesus Christ's sake, do not with one consent begin to make excuse. Do not let a piece of ground, five yoke of oxen, or even a wife, keep you from this great supper. These you may enjoy, as the gifts of God, and make use of them for the Mediator's glory, and yet be present at the gospel feast. True and undefiled religion does not take away, but rather greatly enhances the comforts of life; and our Lord did not pray that we should be taken out of the world, but "that we should be delivered from the evil of it." O then that you would all, with one consent, say, Lo! we come. Assure yourselves here is provision enough. For it is a great supper. In our Father's house there is bread enough and to spare. And though a great God makes the supper, yet he is as good and condescending as he is great. Though he be the high and lofty one that inhabiteth eternity, yet he will dwell with the humble and contrite heart, even with the man that trembleth at his word. Neither can you complain for want of room; "for yet there is room. In our Father's house are many mansions." If it was not so, our Savior would have told us. The grace of Christ is as rich, as free, and as powerful as ever. He is "the same yesterday, today, and for ever." He is full of grace and truth, and out of his fullness, all that come to him may receive grace for grace. He giveth liberally, and upbraideth not. He willeth not the death of a sinner, but rather that he should believe and live. Come then, all ye halt, poor, maimed, and blind sinners; take comfort, the Lord Jesus has sent his servant to call you. It is now supper-time, and a day of uncommon grace.

The day may be far spent. Haste, therefore, and away to the supper of the Lamb. If you do not come, I know the master will be angry. And who can stand before him when he is angry? "Harden not therefore your hearts, as in the day of provocation, as in the day of temptation in the wilderness." Do not provoke the Lord to say, "None of those that were bidden shall taste of my supper." O dreadful words! Much more is implied in them than is expressed. It is the same with that in the psalms, "I sware in my wrath, that they should not enter into my rest." And if you do not enter into God's rest, nor taste of Christ's supper, you must lift up your eyes in torments, where you will have no rest, and must sup with the damned devils for ever more.

Knowing therefore the terrors of the Lord, we persuade you to haste away, and make no more frivolous excuses. For there is no excuse against believing. Perhaps you say, You call to the halt, and maimed, and blind, and poor. But if we are halt, and maimed, how can we come?: if we are blind, how can we see our way? If we are poor, how can we expect admission to so great a table? Ah! Happy are ye, if you are sensible, that you are halt and maimed. For if you feel yourselves so, and are lamenting it, who knows but whilst I am speaking, God may send his Spirit with the word, and fetch you home? Though you are blind, Jesus has eye salve to anoint you.

Though you are poor, yet you are welcome to this rich feast. It cost Jesus Christ a great price, but you shall have it gratis. For such as you was it designed: "Blessed are the poor in spirit, for theirs is the kingdom of heaven." Rich, self-righteous, self-sufficient sinners, I know, will scorn both the feast and its great provider. They have done so already, therefore the Lord ha sent us into the highways and hedges, to bring such poor souls as you are in. Venture then, my dear friends, and honor God, by taking him at his word. Come to the marriage-feast. Believe me, you will there partake of most delicious fare.

Tell me, ye that have been made to taste that the Lord is gracious, will you not recommend this feast to all? Are you not; whilst I am speaking, ready to cry out, Come all ye that are without, come ye, obey the call, for we have sat under the Redeemer's shadow with great delight, and his fruit has been pleasant to our taste. Whilst I am speaking, does not the fire kindle, do not your hearts burn with a desire that others may come and be blessed too? If you are Christians indeed, I know you will be thus minded, and the language of your hearts will be, Lord, whilst he is calling, let thy Spirit compel them to come in. O that the Lord may say, Amen! And why should we doubt? Surely our Savior will not let me complain this day that I have labored in vain, and spent my strength for nought.

Methinks I see many desiring to come. O how shall I compel you to come forwards. I will not use fire or sword, as the Papists do, by terribly perverting this text of scripture. But I will tell you of the love of God, the love of God in Christ, and surely that must compel you, that must constrain you, whether you will or not. Sinners, my heart is enlarged towards you. I could fill my mouth with arguments. Consider the greatness of the God who makes the supper. Consider the greatness of the price, wherewith it was purchased. Consider the greatness of the provision made for you. What would you have more? Consider God's infinite condescension, in calling you now, when you might have been in hell, "where the worm dieth not, and the fire is not quenched." And that you might be without excuse, he has sent his servant into the highways and hedges to invite you there. O that you tasted what I do now! I am sure you would not want arguments to induce you to come in: No, you would fly to the gospel-feast, as doves to the windows.

But, poor souls! many of you, perhaps, are not hungry. You do not feel yourselves halt, or maimed, or blind, and therefore you have no relish for this spiritual entertainment. Well, be not angry with me for calling you; be not offended if I weep over you, because you know not the day of your visitation. If I must appear in judgment as a swift witness against you, I must. But that thought chills my blood! I cannot bear it; I feel that I could lay down my life for you. But I am not willing to go without you.

What say you, my dear friends? I would put the question to you once more, Will you taste of Christ's supper, or will you not? You shall all be welcome. There is milk at this feast for babes, as well as meat for strong men, and for persons of riper years. There is room and provision for high and low, rich and poor, one with another; and our Savior will thank you for coming. Amazing condescension! Astonishing love! The thought of it quite overcomes me. Help me, help me, O believers, to bless and praise him.

And O! that this love may excite us to come afresh to him, as though we had never come before! For, though we have been often feasted, yet our souls will starve, unless we renew our acts of faith, and throw ourselves, as lost, undone sinners, continually at the feet of Christ. Feeding upon past experiences will not satisfy our souls, any more than what we did eat yesterday will sustain our bodies to day. No, believers must look for fresh influences of divine grace, and beg of the Lord to water them every moment.

The parable therefore speaks to saints as well as sinners. Come ye to the marriage-feast; you are as welcome now as ever. And may God set your souls a longing for that time when we shall sit down and eat bread in the kingdom of heaven! There we shall have full draughts of divine love, and enjoy the glorious Emanuel for ever more. Even so, Lord Jesus, Amen.

Sermon 34 The Pharisee and Publican

Luke 18:14, "I tell you, this man went down to his house justified rather than the other: For every one that exalteth himself, shall be abased; and he that humbleth himself, shall be exalted."

Though there be some who dare to deny the Lord Jesus, and disbelieve the revelation he has been pleased to give us, and thereby bring upon themselves swift destruction; yet I would charitably hope there are but few if any such among you, to whom I am now to preach the kingdom of God. Was I to ask you, how you expect to be justified in the sight of an offended God?

I suppose you would answer, only for the sake of our Lord Jesus Christ.

But, was I to come more home to your consciences, I fear that most would make the Lord Jesus but in part their Savior, and go about, as it were, to establish a righteousness of their own. And this is not thinking contrary to the rules of Christian charity: for we are all self-righteous by nature; it is as natural for us to turn to a covenant of works, as for the sparks to fly upwards. We have had so many legal and so few free-grace preachers, for these many years, that most professors now seem to be settled upon their lees, and rather deserve the title of Pharisees than Christians.

Thus it was with the generality of the people during the time of our Lord's public ministration: and therefore, in almost all his discourses, he preached the gospel to poor sinners, and denounced terrible woes against proud self-justiciaries. The parable, to which the words of the text belong, looks both these ways: For the evangelist informs us (ver. 9) that our Lord "spake it unto certain who trusted in themselves that they were righteous, and despised others." And a notable parable it is; a parable worthy of your most serious attention. "He that hath ears to hear, let him hear," what Jesus Christ speaks to all visible professors in it.

Ver. 10. "Two men went up to the temple to pray (and never two men of more opposite characters) the one a Pharisee and the other a Publican." The Pharisees were the strictest sect among the Jews. "I was of the strictest sect, of the Pharisees," says Paul. They prayed often; not only so, but they made long prayers; and, that they might appear extraordinary devout, they would pray at the corners of the street, where two ways met, that people going or coming, both ways, might see them. "They made broad (as our Lord informs us) the borders of their phylacteries," they had pieces of parchment sown to their long robes, on which some parts of the Scripture were written, that people might from thence infer, that they were lovers of the law of God. They were so very punctual and exact in outward purifications, that they washed at their going out and coming in. They held the washing of pots, brazen vessels and tables, and many other such-like things they did. They were very zealous for the traditions of the fathers, and for the observation of the rites and ceremonies of the church, notwithstanding they frequently made void the law of God by their traditions. And they were so exceedingly exact in the outward observation of the Sabbath, that they condemned our Lord for making a little clay with his spittle; and called him a sinner, and said, he was not of God, because he had given sight to a man born blind, on the Sabbath-day. For these reasons they were had in high veneration among the people, who were sadly misled by these blind guides: they had the uppermost places in the synagogues, and greetings in the market-places (which they loved dearly) and were called of men, Rabbi; in short, they had such a reputation for piety, that it became a proverb among the Jews, that, if there were but two men saved, the one of them must be a Pharisee.

As for the Publicans, it was not so with them. It seems they were sometimes Jews, or at least proselytes of the gate; for we find one here coming up to the temple; but for the generality, I am apt to think they were Gentiles; for they were gatherers of the Roman taxes, and used to amass much wealth (as appears by the confession of Zaccheus, one of the chief of them) by wronging men with false accusations. They were so universally infamous, that our Lord himself tells his disciples, "the excommunicated man should be to them as a heathen man, or a Publican." And the Pharisees thought it a sufficient impeachment of our Lord's character, that he was a friend to Publicans and sinners, and went to sit down with them at meat.

But, however they disagreed in other things, they agreed in this, that public worship is a duty incumbent upon all: for they both came up to the temple. The very heathens were observers of temple-worship. We have very early notice of men's sacrificing to, and calling upon the name of the Lord, in the Old Testament; and I find it no where contradicted in the New.

Our Lord, and his apostles, went up to the temple; and we are commanded by the apostle, "not to forsake the assembling ourselves together," as the manner of too many is in our days; and such too, as would have us think well of them, though they seldom or never tread the courts of the Lord's house. But, though our devotions begin in our closets, they must not end there. And, if people never show their devotions abroad, I must suspect they have little or none at home. "Two men went up to the temple." And what went they thither for? Not (as multitudes amongst us do) to make the house of God a house of merchandise, or turn it into a den of thieves; much less to ridicule the preacher, or disturb the congregation; no, they came to the temple, says our Lord, "to pray." Thither should the tribes of God's spiritual Israel go up, to talk with, and pour out their hearts before the mighty God of Jacob.

"Two men went up to the temple to pray." I fear one of them forgot his errand. I have often been at a loss what to call the Pharisee's address; it certainly does not deserve the name of a prayer: he may rather be said to come to the temple to boast, than to pray; for I do not find one word of confession of his original guilt; not one single petition for pardon of his past actual sins, or for grace to help and assist him for the time to come: he only brings to God, as it were, a reckoning of his performances; and does that, which no flesh can justly do, I mean, glory in his presence.

Ver. 11. "The Pharisee stood, and prayed thus with himself; God, I thank thee that I am not as other men are, extortioners,, unjust, adulterers, or even as this Publican." Our Lord first takes notice of his posture; "the Pharisee STOOD," he is not to be condemned for that; for standing, as well as kneeling, is a proper posture for prayer. "When you stand praying," says our Lord; though sometimes our Lord kneeled, nay, lay flat on his face upon the ground; his apostles also kneeled, as we read in the Acts, which has made me wonder at some, who are so bigoted to standing in family, as well as public prayer, that they will not kneel, notwithstanding all kneel that are around them. I fear there is something of the Pharisee in this conduct. Kneeling and standing are indifferent, if the knee of the soul be bent, and the heart upright towards God. We should study not to be particular in indifferent things, lest we offend weak minds. What the Pharisee is remarked for, is his "standing by himself:" for the words may be rendered, he stood by himself, upon some eminent place, at the upper part of the temple, near the Holy of holies, that the congregation might see what a devout man he was: or it may be understood as we read it, he prayed by himself, or of himself, out of his own heart; he did not pray by form; it was an extempore prayer: for there are many Pharisees that pray and preach too, extempore. I do not see why these may not be acquired, as well as other arts and sciences. A man, with a good elocution, ready turn of thought, and good memory, may repeat his own or other men's sermons, and, by the help of Wilkins or Henry,, may pray seemingly excellently well, and yet not have the least grain of true grace in his heart; I speak this, not to cry down extempore prayer, or to discourage those dear souls who really pray by the spirit; I only would hereby give a word of reproof to those who are so bigoted to extempore prayer, that they condemn, as least judge, all that use forms, as though not so holy and heavenly, as others who pray without them. Alas! this is wrong. Not every one that prays extempore is a spiritual, nor every one that prays with a form, a formal man. Let us not judge one another; let not him that uses a form, judge him that prays extempore, on that account; and let not him that prays extempore, despise him who uses a form.

"The Pharisee stood, and prayed thus by himself." Which may signify also praying inwardly in his heart; for there is a way (and that an excellent one too) of praying when we cannot speak; thus Anna prayed, when she spoke not aloud, only her lips moved. Thus God says to Moses, "Why criest thou?" when, it is plain, he did not speak a word. This is what the apostle means by the "spirit making intercession (for believers) with groanings which cannot be uttered." For there are times when the soul is too big to speak; when God fills it as it were, and overshadows it with his presence, so that it can only fall down, worship, adore, and lie in the dust before the Lord. Again, there is a time when the soul is benumbed, barren and dry, and the believer has not a word to say to his heavenly Father; and then the heart only can speak. And I mention this for the encouragement of weak Christians, who think they never are accepted but when they have a flow of words, and fancy they do not please God at the bottom, for no other reason but because they do not please themselves. Such would do well to consider, that God knows the language of the heart, and the mind of the spirit; and that we make use of words, not to inform God, but to affect ourselves. Whenever therefore any of you find yourselves in such a frame, be not discouraged: offer yourselves up in silence before God, as clay in the hands of the potter, for him t write and stamp his own divine image upon your souls. But I believe the Pharisee knew nothing of this way of prayer: he was self-righteous, a stranger to the divine life; and therefore either of the former explanations may be best put upon these words.

"He stood, and prayed thus with himself; God, I thank thee that I am not as other men are, extortioners, unjust, adulterer, or even as this Publican." Here is some appearance of devotion, but it is only in appearance. To thank God that we are not extortioners, unjust, adulterers, and as wicked in our practices as other men are, is certainly meet, right, and our bounden duty: for whatever degrees of goodness there may be in us, more than in others, it is owing to God's restraining, preventing, and assisting grace. We are all equally conceived and born in sin; all are fallen short of the glory of God, and liable to all the curses and maledictions of the law; so that "he who glorieth, must glory only in the Lord." For none of us have any thing which we did not receive; and whatever we have received, we did not in the least merit it, nor could we lay the least claim to it on any account whatever: we are wholly indebted to free grace for all. Had the Pharisee thought thus, when he said, "God, I thank thee that I am not as other men are," it would have been an excellent introduction to his prayer: but he was a free-willer, as well as self-righteous (for he that is one must be the other) and thought by his own power and strength, he had kept himself from these vices. And yet I do not see what reason he had to trust in himself that he was righteous, merely because he had to trust in himself that he was righteous, merely because he was not an extortioner, unjust, adulterer; for all this while he might be, as he certainly was (as is also every self-righteous person) as proud as the devil. But he not only boasts, but lies before God (as all self- justiciaries will be found liars here or hereafter.) He thanks God that he was not unjust: but is it not an act of the highest injustice to rob God of his prerogative? is it not an act of injustice to judge our neighbor? and yet of both these crimes this self-righteous vaunter is guilty. "Even as this Publican!" He seems to speak with the untmost disdain; this Publican!

Perhaps he pointed at the poor man, that others might treat him with the like contempt. Thou proud, confident boaster, what hadst thou to do with that poor Publican? supposing other Publicans were unjust, and extortioners, did it therefore follow that he must be so? or, if he had been such a sinner, how knowest thou but he has repented of those sins? His coming up to the temple to pray, is one good sign of a reformation at least. Thou art therefore inexcusable, O Pharisee, who thus judgest the Publican: for thou that judgest him to be unjust, art, in the very act of judging, unjust thyself: thy sacrifice is only the sacrifice of a fool.

We have seen what the Pharisee's negative goodness comes to; I think, nothing at all. Let us see how far his positive goodness extends; for, if we are truly religious, we shall not only eschew evil, but also do good: "I fast twice in the week, I give tithes of all that I possess." The Pharisee is not here condemned for his fasting, for fasting is a Christian duty; "when you fast," says our Lord, thereby taking it for granted that his disciples would fast. And "when the bridegroom shall be taken away, then shall they fast in those days." "In fasting often," says the apostle. And all that would not be cast-aways, will take care, as their privilege, without legal constraint, to "keep their bodies under, and bring them into subjection." The Pharisee is only condemned for making a righteousness of his fasting, and thinking that God would accept him, or that he was any better than his neighbors, merely on account of his fasting, and thinking that God would accept him, or that he was any better than his neighbors, merely on account of his fasting: this is what he was blamed for. The Pharisee was not to be discommended for fasting twice in a week; I wish some Christians would imitate him more in this: but to depend on fasting in the least, for his justification in the sight of God, was really abominable. "I give tithes of all that I possess." He might as well have said, I pay tithes. But self-righteous people (whatever they may say to the contrary) think they give something to God. "I give tithes of all that I possess:" I make conscience of giving tithes, not only of all that the law requires, but of my mint, annise, and cummin, of all things whatsoever I possess; this was well; but to boast of such things, or of fasting, is pharisaical and devilish. Now then let us sum up all the righteousness of this boasting Pharisee, and see what little reason he had to trust in himself, that he was righteous, or to despise others. He is not unjust (but we have only his bare word for that, I think I have proved the contrary;) he is no adulterer, no extortioner; he fasts twice in the week, and gives tithes of all that he possesses; and all this he might do, and a great deal more, and yet be a child of the devil: for here is no mention made of his loving the Lord his God with all his heart, which was the "first and great commandment of the law;" here is not a single syllable of inward religion; and he was not a true Jew, who was only one outwardly. It is only an outside piety at the best; inwardly he is full of pride, self- justification, free-will and great uncharitableness.

Were not the Pharisees, do you think, highly offended at this character? for they might easily know it was spoken against them. And though, perhaps, some of you may be offended at me, yet, out of love, I must tell you, I fear this parable is spoken against many of you: for are there not many of you, who go up to the temple to pray, with no better spirit than this Pharisee did? And because you fast, it may be in the Lent, or every Friday, and because you do no body any harm, receive the sacrament, pay tithes, and give an alms now and then; you think that you are safe, and trust in yourselves that you are righteous, and inwardly despise those, who do not come up to you in these outward duties? this, I am persuaded, is the case of many of you, though, alas! it is a desperate one, as I shall endeavor to show at the close of this discourse.

Let us now take a view of the Publican, ver. 13. "And the Publican standing afar off, would not lift up so much as his eyes unto heaven, but smote upon his breast, saying, God be merciful to me a sinner." "The Publican standing afar off." Perhaps in the outward court of the temple, conscious to himself that he was not worthy to approach the Holy of holies; so conscious and so weighed down with a sense of his own unworthiness, that he would not so much as lift up his eyes unto heaven, which he knew was God's throne. Poor heart! what did he feel at this time!

none but returning publicans, like himself, can tell. Methinks I see him standing afar off, pensive, oppressed, and even overwhelmed with sorrow; sometimes he attempts to look up; but then, thinks he, the heavens are unclean in God's sight, and the very angels are charged with folly; how then shall such a wretch as I dare to lift up my guilty head! And to show that his heart was full of holy self-resentment, and that he sorrowed after a godly sort, he smote upon his breast; the word in the original implies, that he struck hard upon his breast: he will lay the blame upon none but his own wicked heart. He will not, like unhumbled Adam, tacitly lay the fault of his vileness upon God, and say, The passions which thou gavest me, they deceived me, and I sinned: he is too penitent thus to reproach his Maker; he smites upon his breast, his treacherous, ungrateful, desperately wicked breast; a breast now ready to burst: and at length, out of the abundance of his heart, I doubt not, with many tears, he as last cries out, "God be merciful to me a sinner." Not, God be merciful to yonder proud Pharisee: he found enough in himself to vent his resentment against, without looking abroad upon others. Not, God be merciful to me a saint; for he knew "all his righteousnesses were but filthy rags." Not, God be merciful to such or such a one; but, God be merciful to me, even to me a sinner, a sinner by birth, a sinner in thought, word, and deed; a sinner as to my person, a sinner as to all my performances; a sinner in whom is no health, in whom dwelleth no good thing, a sinner, poor, miserable, blind and naked, from the crown of the head to the sole of the feet, full of wounds, and bruises, and putrefying sores; a self-accused, self-condemned sinner. What think you? would this Publican have been offended if any minister had told him that he deserved to be damned? would he have been angry, if any one had told him, that by nature he was half a devil and half a beast? No: he would have confessed a thousand hells to have been his due, and that he was an earthly, devilish sinner. He felt now what a dreadful thing it was to depart from the living God: he felt that he was inexcusable every way; that he could in nowise, upon account of any thing in himself, be justified in the sight of God; and therefore lays himself at the feet of sovereign mercy. "God be merciful to me a sinner." Here is no confidence in the flesh, no plea fetched from fasting, paying tithes, or the performance of any other duty; here is no boasting that he was not an extortioner, unjust, or an adulterer. Perhaps he had been guilty of all these crimes, at least he knew he would have been guilty of all these, had he been left to follow the devices and desires of his own heart; and therefore, with a broken and contrite spirit, he cries out, "God be merciful to me a sinner." This man came up to the temple to pray, and he prayed indeed. And a broken and contrite heart God will not despise. "I tell you," says our Lord, I who lay in the bosom of the Father from all eternity; I who am God, and therefore know all things; I who can neither deceive, nor be deceived, whose judgment is according to right; I tell you, whatever you may think of it, or think of me for telling you so, "this man," this Publican, this despised, sinful, but broken-hearted man, "went down to his house justified (acquitted, and looked upon as righteous in the sight of God) rather than the other." Let Pharisees take heed that they do not pervert this text: for when it is said, "This man went down to his house justified rather than the other," our Lord does not mean that both were justified, and that the Publican had rather more justification than the Pharisee: but it implies, either that the Publican was actually justified, but the Pharisee was not; or, that the Publican was in a better way to receive justification, than the Pharisee; according to our Lord's saying, "The Publicans and Harlots enter the kingdom of heaven before you." That the Pharisee was not justified is certain, for "God resisteth the proud;" and that the Publican was at this time actually justified (and perhaps went home with a sense of it in his heart) we have great reason to infer from the latter part of the text, "For every one that exalteth himself shall be abased, and he that humbleth himself shall be exalted." The parable therefore now speaks to all who hear me this day: for that our Lord intended it for our learning, is evident, from his making such a general application: "For every one that exalteth himself shall be abased, and he that humbleth himself shall be exalted." The parable of the Publican and Pharisee, is but as it were a glass, wherein we may see the different disposition of all mankind; for all mankind may be divided into two general classes. Either they trust wholly in themselves, or in part, that they are righteous, and then they are Pharisees; or they have no confidence in the flesh, are self-condemned sinners, and then they come under the character of the Publican just now described. And we may add also, that the different reception these men meet with, points out to us in lively colors, the different treatment the self- justiciary and self-condemned criminal will meet with at the terrible day of judgment: "Every one that exalts himself shall be abased, but he that humbleth himself shall be exalted." "Every one," without exception, young or old, high or low, rich or poor (for God is no respecter of persons) "every one," whosoever he be, that exalteth himself, and not free-grace; every one that trusteth in himself that he is righteous, that rests in his duties, or thinks to join them with the righteousness of Jesus Christ, for justification in the sight of God, though he be no adulterer, not extortioner, though he be not outwardly unjust, nay, though he fast twice in the week, and gives tithes of all that he possess; yet shall he be abased in the sight of all good men who know him here, and before men and angels, and God himself, when Jesus Christ comes to appear in judgment hereafter. How low, none but the almighty God can tell. He shall be abased to live with devils, and make his abode in the lowest hell for evermore.

Hear this, all ye self-justiciaries, tremble, and behold your doom! a dreadful doom, more dreadful than words can express, or thought conceive!

If you refuse to humble yourselves, after hearing this parable, I call heaven and earth to witness against you this day, that God shall visit you with all his storms, and pour all the vials of his wrath upon your rebellious heads; you exalted yourselves here, and God shall abase you hereafter; you are as proud as the devil, and with devils shall you dwell to all eternity. "Be not deceived, God is not mocked;" he sees your hearts, he knows all things. And, notwithstanding you may come up to the temple to pray, your prayers are turned into sin, and you go down to your houses unjustified, if you are self-justiciaries; and do you know what it is to be unjustified? why, if you are unjustified, the wrath of God abideth upon you; you are in your blood; all the curses of the law belong to you: cursed are you when you go out, cursed are you when you come in; cursed are your thoughts, cursed are your words, cursed are your deeds; every thing you do, say, or think, from morning to night is only one continued series of sin.

However highly you may be esteemed in the sight of men, however you may be honored with the uppermost seats in the synagogues, in the church militant, you will have no place in the church triumphant. "Humble yourselves therefore under the mighty hand of God:" pull down every self-righteous thought, and every proud imagination, that now exalteth itself against the perfect, personal, imputed righteousness of the dear Lord Jesus: "For he (and he alone) that humbleth himself shall be exalted." He that humbleth himself, whatever be he: if, instead of fasting twice in the week, he has been drunk twice in the week; if, instead of giving tithes of all that he possesses, he has cheated the minister of his tithes, and the king of his taxes; notwithstanding he be unjust, an extortioner, an adulterer, nay, notwithstanding the sins of all mankind center and unite in him; yet, if through grace, like the Publican, he is enabled to humble himself, he shall be exalted; not in a temporal manner; for Christians must rather expect to be abased, and to have their names cast out as evil, and to lay down their lives for Christ Jesus in this world: but he shall be exalted in a spiritual sense; he shall be freely justified from all his sins by the blood of Jesus; he shall have peace with God, a peace which passeth all understanding; not only peace, but joy in believing; he shall be translated from the kingdom of Satan, to the kingdom of God's dear Son: he shall dwell in Christ, and Christ in him: he shall be one with Christ, and Christ one with him: he shall drink of divine pleasures, as out of a river: he shall be sanctified throughout in spirit, soul and body; in one word, he shall be filled with all the fullness of God. Thus shall the man that humbleth himself be exalted here; but O, how high shall he be exalted hereafter! as high as the highest heavens, even to the right-hand of God: there he shall sit, happy both in soul and body, and judge angels; high, out of the reach of all sin and trouble, eternally secure from all danger of falling. O sinners, did you but know how highly God intends to exalt those who humble themselves, and believe in Jesus, surely you would humble yourselves, at least beg of God to humble you; for it is he that must strike the rock of your hearts, and cause floods of contrite tears to flow therefrom. O that God would give this sermon such a commission, as he once gave to the rod of Moses! I would strike you through and through with the rod of his word, until each of you was brought to cry out with the poor Publican, "God be merciful to me a sinner." What pleasant language would this be in the ears of the Lord of Sabbaoth!

Are there no poor sinners among you? what, are you all Pharisees?

Surely, you cannot bear the thoughts of returning home unjustified; can you? what if a fit of the apoplexy should seize you, and your souls be hurried away before the awful Judge of quick and dead? what will you do without Christ's righteousness? if you go out of the world unjustified, you must remain so for ever. O that you would humble yourselves! then would the Lord exalt you; it may be, that, whilst I am speaking, the Lord might justify you freely by his grace. I observed, that perhaps the Publican had a sense of his justification before he went from the temple, and knew that his pardon was sealed in heaven: and who knows but you may be thus exalted before you go home, if you humble yourselves? O what peace, love and joy, would you then feel in your hearts! you would have a heaven upon earth. O that I could hear any of you say (as I once heard a poor sinner, under my preaching, cry out) He is come, He is come! How would you then, like him, extol a precious, a free-hearted Christ! how would you magnify him for being such a friend to Publicans and sinners? greater love can no man show, than to lay down his life for a friend; but Christ laid down his life for his enemies, even for you, if you are enabled to humble yourselves, as the Publican did. Sinners, I know not how to leave off talking with you; I would fill my mouth with arguments, I would plead with you. "Come, let us reason together;" though your sins be as scarlet, yet, if you humble yourselves, they shall be as white as snow. One act of true faith in Christ, justifies you for ever and ever; he has not promised you what he cannot perform; he is able to exalt you: for God hath exalted, and given him a name above every name; that at the name of Jesus every knee shall bow; nay, God hath exalted him to be not only a Prince, but a Savior. May he be a Savior to you! and then I shall have reason to rejoice; in the day of judgment, that I have not preached in vain, not labored in vain.

Sermon 35 The Conversion of Zaccheus

Luke 19:9-10, "And Jesus said unto him, This day is salvation come to this house; forasmuch as he also is the Son of Abraham. For the Son of man is come to seek and to save that which was lost."

Salvation, every where through the whole scripture, is said to be the free gift of God, through Jesus Christ our Lord. Not only free, because God is a sovereign agent, and therefore may withhold it from, or confer it on, whom he pleaseth; but free, because there is nothing to be found in man, that can any way induce God to be merciful unto him. The righteousness of Jesus Christ is the sole cause of our finding favor in God's sight: this righteousness apprehended by faith (which is also the gift of God) makes it our own; and this faith, if true, will work by love.

These are parts of those glad tidings which are published in the gospel; and of the certainty of them, next to the express word of God, the experience of all such as have been saved, is the best, and, as I take it, the most undoubted proof. That God might teach us every way, he has been pleased to leave upon record many instances of the power of his grace exerted in the salvation of several persons, that we, hearing how he dealt with them, might from thence infer the manner we must expect to be dealt with ourselves, and learn in what way we must look for salvation, if we truly desire to be made partakers of the inheritance with the saints in light.

The conversion of the person referred to in the text, I think, will be of no small service to us in this matter, if rightly improved. I would hope, most of you know who the person is, to whom the Lord Jesus speaks; it is the publican Zaccheus, to whose house the blessed Jesus said, salvation came, and whom he pronounces a Son of Abraham.

It is my design (God helping) to make some remarks upon his conversion recorded at large in the preceding verses, and then to enforce the latter part of the text, as an encouragement to poor undone sinners to come to Jesus

Christ. "For the Son of man is come, to seek and to save that which was lost." The evangelist Luke introduces the account of this man's conversion thus, verse 1. "And Jesus entered and passed through Jericho." The holy Jesus made it his business to go about doing good. As the sun in the firmament is continually spreading his benign, quickening, and cheering influences over the natural; so the Son of righteousness arose with healing under his wings, and was daily and hourly diffusing his gracious influences over the moral world. The preceding chapter acquaints us of a notable miracle wrought by the holy Jesus, on poor blind Bartimeus; and in this, a greater presents itself to our consideration. The evangelist would have us take particular notice of it; for he introduces it with the word "behold:" "and behold, there was a man named Zaccheus, who was the chief among the Publicans, and he was rich." Well might the evangelist usher in the relation of this man's conversion with the word "behold!" For, according to human judgment, how many insurmountable obstacles lay in the way of it! Surely no one will say there was any fitness in Zaccheus for salvation; for we are told that he was a Publican, and therefore in all probability a notorious sinner. The Publicans were gatherers of the Roman taxes; they were infamous for their abominable extortion; their very name therefore became so odious, that we find the Pharisees often reproached our Lord, as very wicked, because he was a friend unto and sat down to meat with them. Zaccheus then, being a Publican, was no doubt a sinner; and, being chief among the Publicans, consequently was chief among sinners. Nay, "he was rich." One inspired apostle has told us, that "not many mighty, not many noble are called." Another saith, "God has chosen the poor of this world, rich in faith." And he who was the Maker and Redeemer of the apostles, assures us, "that it is easier for a camel, (or cable-rope) to go through the eye of a needle, than for a rich man to enter into the kingdom of God." Let not therefore the rich glory in the multitude of their riches.

But rich as he was, we are told, verse 3 that "he sought to see Jesus." A wonder indeed! The common people heard our Lord gladly, and the poor received the gospel. The multitude, the ocloS, the mob, the people that know not the law, as the proud high-priests called them, used to follow him on foot into the country, and sometimes stayed with him three days together to hear him preach. But did the rich believe or attend on him? No. Our Lord preached up the doctrine of the cross; he preached too searching for them, and therefore they counted him their enemy, persecuted and spoke all manner of evil against him falsely. Let not the ministers of Christ marvel, if they meet with the like treatment from the rich men of this wicked and adulterous generation. I should think it no scandal (supposing it true) to hear it affirmed, that none but the poor attended my ministry. Their souls are as precious to our Lord Jesus Christ, as the souls of the greatest men. They were the poor that attended him in the days of his flesh: these are they whom he hath chosen to rich in faith, and to be the greatest in the kingdom of heaven. Were the rich in this world's goods generally to speak well of me, woe be unto me; I should think it a dreadful sign that I was only a wolf in sheep's clothing, that I spoke peace, peace, when there was no peace, and prophesied smoother things than the gospel would allow of. Hear ye this, O ye rich. Let who will dare to do it, God forbid that I should despise the poor; in doing so, I should reproach my Maker. The poor are dear to my soul; I rejoice to see them fly to the doctrine of Christ, like the doves to their windows. I only pray, that the poor who attend, may be evangelized, and turned into the spirit of the gospel: if so, "Blessed are ye; for yours is the kingdom of heaven." But we must return to Zaccheus. "He sought to see Jesus." That is good news. I heartily wish I could say, it was out of a good principle: but, without speaking contrary to that charity which hopes and believeth all things for the best, we may say, that the same principle drew him after Christ, which now draws multitudes (to speak plainly, it may be multitudes of you) to hear a particular preacher, even curiosity: for we are told, that he came not to hear his doctrine, but to view his person, or, to use the words of the evangelist, "to see who he was." Our Lord's fame was now spread abroad through all Jerusalem, and all the country round about: some said he was a good man; others, "Nay, but he deceiveth the people." And therefore curiosity drew out this rich Publican Zaccheus, to see who this person was, of whom he had heard such various accounts. But it seems he could not conveniently get a sight of him for the press, and because he was little of stature. Alas! how many are kept from seeing Christ in glory, by reason of the press! I mean, how many are ashamed of being singularly good, and therefore follow a multitude to do evil, because they have a press or throng of polite acquaintance! And, for fear of being set an nought by those with whom they used to sit at meat, they deny the Lord of glory, and are ashamed to confess him before men. This base, this servile fear of man, is the bane of true Christianity; it brings a dreadful snare upon the soul, and is the ruin of ten thousands: for I am fully persuaded, numbers are rationally convicted of gospel-truths; but, not being able to brook contempt, they will not prosecute their convictions, nor reduce them to practice. Happy those, who in this respect, like Zaccheus, are resolved to overcome all impediments that lie in their way to a sight of Christ; for, finding he could not see Christ because of the press and the littleness of his natural stature, he did not smite upon his breast, and depart, saying, "It is in vain to seek after a sight of him any longer, I can never attain unto it." No, finding he could not see Christ, if he continued in the midst of, "he ran before the multitude, and climbed up into a sycamore-tree, to see him; for he was to pass that way." There is no seeing Christ in-Glory, unless we run before the multitude, and are willing to be in the number of those despised few, who take the kingdom of God by violence. The broad way, in which so many go, can never be that strait and narrow way which leads to life. Our Lord's flock was, and always will be, comparatively a little one; and unless we dare to run before the multitude in a holy singularity, and can rejoice in being accounted fools for Christ's sake, we shall never see Jesus with comfort, when he appears in glory. From mentioning the sycamore-tree, and considering the difficulty with which Zaccheus must climb it, we may farther learn, that those who would see Christ, must undergo other difficulties and hardships, besides contempt. Zaccheus, without doubt, went through both. Did not many, think you, laugh at him as he ran along, and in the language of Michal, Saul's daughter, cry out, "How glorious did the rich Zaccheus look today, when, forgetting the greatness of his station, he ran before a pitiful, giddy mob, and climbed up a sycamore-tree, to see an enthusiastic preacher!" But Zaccheus cares not for all that; his curiosity was strong: if he could but see who Jesus was, he did not value what scoffers said of him. Thus, and much more will it be with all those who have an effectual desire to see Jesus in heaven: they will go on from strength to strength, break through every difficulty lying in their way, and care not what men or devils say of or do unto them. May the Lord make us all thus minded, for his dear Son's sake!

At length, after taking much pains, and going (as we may well suppose) through much contempt, Zaccheus has climbed the tree; and there he sits, as he thinks, hid in the leaves of it, and watching when he should see Jesus pass by: "For he was to pass by that way." But sing, O heavens, and rejoice, O earth! Praise, magnify, and adore sovereign, electing, free, preventing love; Jesus the everlasting God, the Prince of peace, who saw Nathanael under the fig-tree, and Zaccheus from eternity, now sees him in the sycamore-tree, and calls him in time.

Verse 5. "And when Jesus came to the place, he looked up, and saw him, and said unto him, Zaccheus, make haste and come down; for this day I must abide at thy house." Amazing love! Well might Luke usher in the account with "behold!" It is worthy of our highest admiration. When Zaccheus thought of no such thing, nay, thought that Christ Jesus did not know him; behold, Christ does what we never hear he did before or after, I mean, invite himself to the house of Zaccheus, saying, "Zaccheus, make haste and come down; for this day I must abide at thy house." Not pray let me abide, but I must abide this day at thy house. He also calls him by name, as though he was well acquainted with him: and indeed well he might; for his name was written in the book of life, he was one of those whom the Father had given him from all eternity: therefore he must abide at his house that day. "For whom he did predestinate, them he also called." Here then, as through a glass, we may see the doctrine of free grace evidently exemplified before us. Here was not fitness in Zaccheus. He was a Publican, chief among the Publicans; not only so, but rich, and came to see Christ only out of curiosity: but sovereign grace triumphs over all. And if we do God justice, and are effectually wrought upon, we must acknowledge there was no more fitness in us than in Zaccheus; and, had not Christ prevented us by his call, we had remained dead in trespasses and sins, and alienated from the divine life, even as others. "Jesus looked up, and saw him, and said unto him, Zaccheus, make haste and come down; for this day I must abide at thy house." With what different emotions of heart may we suppose Zaccheus received this invitation? Think you not that he was surprised to hear Jesus Christ call him by name, and not only so, but invite himself to his house? Surely, thinks Zaccheus, I dream: it cannot be; how should he know me? I never saw him before: besides, I shall undergo much contempt, if I receive him under my rood. Thus, I say, we may suppose Zaccheus thought within himself. But what saith the scripture? "I will make a willing people in the day of my power." With this outward call, there went an efficacious power from God, which sweetly over-ruled his natural will: and therefore, verse 6, "He made haste, and came down, and received him joyfully;" not only into his house, but also into his heart.

Thus it is the great God brings home his children. He calls them by name, by his word or providence; he speaks to them also by his spirit.

Hereby they are enabled to open their hearts, and are made willing to receive the King of glory. For Zaccheus's sake, let us not entirely condemn people that come under the word, out of no better principle than curiosity.

Who knows but God may call them? It is good to be where the Lord is passing by. May all who are now present out of this principle, hear the voice of the Son of God speaking to their souls, and so hear that they ma live! Not that men ought therefore to take encouragement to come out of curiosity.

For perhaps a thousand more, at other times, came too see Christ out of curiosity, as well as Zaccheus, who were not effectually called by his grace. I only mention this for the encouragement of my own soul, and the consolation of God's children, who are too apt to be angry with those who do not attend on the word out of love to God: but let them alone. Brethren, pray for them. How do you know but Jesus Christ may speak to their hearts!

A few words from Christ, applied by his spirit, will save their souls.

"Zaccheus, says Christ, make haste and come down. And he made haste, and came down, and received him joyfully." I have observed, in holy scripture, how particularly it is remarked, that persons rejoiced upon believing in Christ. Thus the converted Eunuch went on his way rejoicing; thus the jailer rejoiced with his whole house; thus Zaccheus received Christ joyfully. And well may those rejoice who receive Jesus Christ; for with him they receive righteousness, sanctification, and eternal redemption. Many have brought up an ill report upon our good land, and would fain persuade people that religion will make them melancholy mad. So far from it, that joy is one ingredient of the kingdom of God in the heart of a believer; "The kingdom of God is righteousness, peace, and joy in the Holy Ghost." To rejoice in the Lord, is a gospel-duty. "Rejoice in the Lord always, and again I say, rejoice."

And who can be so joyful, as those who know that their pardon is sealed before they go hence and are no more seen? The godly may, but I cannot see how any ungodly men can, rejoice: they cannot be truly cheerful. What if wicked men may sometimes have laughter amongst them? It is only the laughter of fools; in the midst of it there is heaviness; At the best, it is but like the cracking of thorns under a pot; it makes a blaze, but soon goes out. But, as for the godly, it is not so with them; their joy is solid and lasting. As it is a joy that a stranger intermeddleth not with, so it is a joy that no man taketh from them: it is a joy in God, a "joy unspeakable and full of glory." It should seem that Zaccheus was under soul-distress but a little while; perhaps (says Guthrie, in his book entitled, THE TRIAL CONCERNING A SAVING INTEREST IN CHRIST) not above a quarter of an hour. I add, perhaps not so long: for, as one observes, sometimes the Lord Jesus delights to deliver speedily. God is a sovereign agent, and works upon his children in their effectual calling, according to the counsel of his eternal will. It is with the spiritual, as natural birth: all women have not the like pangs; all Christians have not the like degree of conviction. But all agree in this, that all have Jesus Christ formed in their hearts: and those who have not so many trials at first, may be visited with the greater conflicts hereafter; though they never come into bondage again, after they have once received the spirit of adoption. "We have not, (says Paul) received the spirit of bondage again unto fear." We know not what Zaccheus underwent before he died: however, this one thing I know, he now believed in Christ, and was justified, or acquitted, and looked upon as righteous in God's sight, though a Publican, chief among the Publicans, not many moments before. And thus it is with all, that, like Zaccheus, receive Jesus Christ by faith into their hearts: the very moment they find rest in him, they are freely justified from all things from which they could not be justified by the law of Moses; "for by grace are we saved, through faith, and that not of ourselves, it is the gift of God." Say not within yourselves, this is a licentious Antinomian doctrine; for this faith, if true, will work by love, and be productive of the fruits of holiness. See an instance in this convert Zaccheus; no sooner had he received Jesus Christ by faith into his heart, but he evidences it by his works; for, ver. 8, we are told, "Zaccheus stood forth, and said unto the Lord, Behold, Lord, the half of my goods I give unto the poor; and if I have taken any thing from any man by false accusation, I restore him four- fold." Having believed on Jesus in his heart, he now makes confession of him with his mouth to salvation. "Zaccheus stood forth;" he was not ashamed, but stood forth before his brother Publicans; for true faith casts out all servile, sinful fear of man; "and said, Behold, Lord." It is remarkable, how readily people in scripture have owned the divinity of Christ immediately upon their conversion. Thus the woman at Jacob's well; "Is not this the Christ?" Thus the man born blind; "Lord, I believe; and worshipped him." Thus Zaccheus, "Behold, Lord." An incontestable proof this to me, that those who deny our Lord's divinity, never effectually felt his power: if they had, they would not speak so lightly of him: they would scorn to deny his eternal power and Godhead.

"Zaccheus stood forth, and said, Behold, Lord, the half of m goods I give to the poor; and if I have taken any thing from any man by false accusation, I restore him four-fold." Noble fruits of a true living faith in the Lord Jesus! Every word calls for our notice. Not some small, not the tenth part, but the HALF. Of what? My goods; things that were valuable. MY goods, his own, not another's. I give: not, I will give when I die, when I can keep them no longer; but, I give now, even now. Zaccheus would be his own executor. For whilst we have time we should do good. But to whom would he give half of his goods? Not to the rich, not to those who were already clothed in purple and fine linen, of whom he might be recompensed again; but to the poor, the maimed, the halt, the blind, from which he could expect no recompense till the resurrection of the dead. "I give to the poor." But knowing that he must be just before he could be charitable, and conscious to himself that in his public administrations he had wronged many persons, he adds, "And if I have taken any thing from any man by false accusation, I restore him fourfold." Hear ye this, all ye that make no conscience of cheating the king of his taxes, or of buying or selling run goods. If ever God gives you true faith, you will never rest, till, like Zaccheus, you have made restitution to the utmost of your power. I suppose, before his conversion, he thought it no harm to cheat thus, no more than you may do now, and pleased himself frequently, to be sure, that he got rich by doing so: but now he is grieved for it at his heart; he confesses his injustice before men, and promises to make ample restitution. Go ye cheating Publicans, learn of Zaccheus; go away and do likewise. If you do not make restitution here, the Lord Jesus shall make you confess your sins before men and angels, and condemn you for it, when he comes in the glory of his Father to judgment hereafter.

After all this, with good reason might our Lord say unto him, "This day is salvation come to this house; forasmuch as he also is the son of Abraham;" not so much by a natural as by a spiritual birth. He was made partaker of like precious faith with Abraham: like Abraham he believed on the Lord, and it was accounted to him for righteousness: his faith, like Abraham's, worked by love; and I doubt not, but he has been long since sitting in Abraham's harbor.

And now, are you not ashamed of yourselves, who speak against the doctrines of grace, especially that doctrine of being justified by faith alone, as though it leaded to licentiousness? What can be more unjust than such a charge? Is not the instance of Zaccheus, a sufficient proof to the contrary? Have I strained it to serve my own turn? God forbid. To the best of my knowledge I have spoken the truth in sincerity, and the truth as it is in Jesus. I do affirm that we are saved by grace, and that we are justified by faith alone: but I do also affirm, that faith must be evidenced by good works, where there is an opportunity of performing them.

What therefore has been said of Zaccheus, may serve as a rule, whereby all may judge whether they have faith or not. You say you have faith; but how do you prove it? Did you ever hear the Lord Jesus call you by name?

Were you ever made to obey the call? Did you ever, like Zaccheus, receive Jesus Christ joyfully into your hearts? Are you influenced by the faith you say you have, to stand up and confess the Lord Jesus before men? Were you ever made willing to own, and humble yourselves for, your past offenses?

Does your faith work by love, so that you conscientiously lay up, according as God has prospered you, for the support of the poor? Do you give alms of all things that you possess? And have you made due restitution to those you have wronged? If so, happy are ye; salvation is come to your souls, you are sons, you are daughters of, you shall shortly be everlastingly blessed with, faithful Abraham. But, if you are not thus minded, do not deceive your own souls. Though you may talk of justification by faith, like angels, it will do you no good; it will only increase your damnation. You hold the truth, but it is in unrighteousness: your faith being without works, is dead: you have the devil, not Abraham, for your father. Unless you get a faith of the heart, a faith working by love, with devils and damned spirits shall you dwell for evermore.

But it is time now to enforce the latter part of the text; "For the Son of man is come to seek and to save that which was lost." These words are spoken by our savior in answer to some self-righteous Pharisees, who, instead of rejoicing with the angels in heaven, at the conversion of such a sinner, murmured, "That he was gone to be a guest with a man that was a sinner." To vindicate his conduct, he tells them, that this was an act agreeable to the design of his coming: "For the Son of Man is come to seek and to save that which was lost." He might have said, the Son of God. But O the wonderful condescension of our Redeemer! He delights to stile himself the Son of man. He came not only to save, but to seek and to save that which was lost. He came to Jericho to seek and save Zaccheus; for otherwise Zaccheus would never have been saved by him. But from whence came he? Even from heaven, his dwelling-place, to this lower earth, this vale of tears, to seek and save that which was lost; or all that feel themselves lost, and are willing, like Zaccheus, to receive him into their hearts to save them; with how great a salvation? Even from the guilt, and also from the power of their sins; to make them heirs of God, and joint heirs with himself, and partakers of that glory which he enjoyed with the Father before the world began. Thus will the Son of man save that which is lost. He was made the son of man, on purpose that he might save them. He had no other end but this in leaving his father's throne, in obeying the moral law, and hanging upon the cross: all that was done and suffered, merely to satisfy, and procure a righteousness for poor, lost, undone sinners, and that too without respect of persons. "That which was lost;" all of every nation and language, that feel, bewail, and are truly desirous of being delivered from their lost state, did the Son of man come down to seek and to save: for he is mighty, not only so, but willing, to save to the uttermost all that come to God through him. He will in no wise cast out: for he is the same today, as he was yesterday. He comes now to sinners, as well as formerly; and, I hope, hath sent me out this day to seek, and, under him, to bring home some of you, the lost sheep of the house of Israel.

What say you? Shall I go home rejoicing, saying, That many like sheep have went astray, but they have now believed on Jesus Christ, and so returned home to the great Shepherd and Bishop of their souls? If the Lord would be pleased thus to prosper my handy-work, I care not how many legalists and self-righteous Pharisees murmur against me, for offering salvation to the worst of sinners: for I know the Son of man came to seek and to save them; and the Lord Jesus will now be a guest to the worst Publican, the vilest sinner that is amongst you, if he does but believe on him. Make haste then, O sinners, make haste, and come by faith to Christ.

Then, this day, even this hour, nay, this moment, if you believe, Jesus Christ shall come and make his eternal abode in your hearts. Which of you is made willing to receive the King of glory? Which of you obeys his call, as Zaccheus did? Alas! why do you stand still? How know you, whether Jesus Christ may ever call you again? Come then, poor, guilty sinners; come away, poor, lost, undone publicans: make haste, I say, and come away to Jesus Christ. The Lord condescends to invite himself to come under the filthy roofs of the houses of your souls. Do not be afraid of entertaining him; he will fill you with all peace and joy in believing. Do not be ashamed to run before the multitude, and to have all manner of evil spoke against you falsely for his sake: one sight of Christ will make amends for all.

Zaccheus was laughed at; and all that will live godly in Christ Jesus, shall suffer persecution. But what of that? Zaccheus is now crowned in glory; as you also shall shortly be, if you believe on, and are reproached for Christ's sake. Do not, therefore, put me off with frivolous excuses: there's no excuse can be given for your not coming to Christ. You are lost, undone, without him; and if he is not glorified in your salvation, he will be glorified in your destruction; if he does not come and make his abode in your hearts, you must take up an eternal abode with the devil and his angels. O that the Lord would be pleased to pass by some of you at this time! O that he may call you by his Spirit, and make you a willing people in this day of his power! For I know my calling will not do, unless he, by his efficacious grace, compel you to come in. O that you once felt what it is to receive Jesus Christ into your hearts! You would soon, like Zaccheus, give him everything. You do not love Christ, because you do not know him; you do not come to him, because you do not feel your want of him: you are whole, and not broken hearted; you are not sick, at least not sensible of your sickness; and, therefore, no wonder you do not apply to Jesus Christ, that great, that almighty physician. You do not feel yourselves lost, and therefore do not seek to be found in Christ. O that God would wound you with the sword of his Spirit, and cause his arrows of conviction to stick deep in your hearts! O that he would dart a ray of divine light into your souls! For if you do not feel yourselves lost without Christ, you are of all men most miserable: your souls are dead; you are not only an image of hell, but in some degree hell itself: you carry hell about with you, and you know it not. O that I could see some of you sensible of this, and hear you cry out, "Lord, break this hard heart; Lord, deliver me from the body of this death; draw me, Lord, make me willing to come after thee; I am lost; Lord, save me, or I perish!" Was this your case, how soon would the Lord stretch forth his almighty hand, and say, Be of good cheer, it is I; be not afraid? What a wonderful calm would then possess your troubled souls! Your fellowship would then be with the Father and the Son: your life would be hid with Christ in God.

Some of you, I hope, have experienced this, and can say, I was lost, but I am found; I was dead, but am alive again: the Son of man came and sought me in the day of his power, and saved my sinful soul. And do you repent that you came to Christ? Has he not been a good master? Is not his presence sweet to your souls? Has he not been faithful to his promise? And have you not found, that even in doing and suffering for him, there is an exceeding present great reward? I am persuaded you will answer, Yes. O then, ye saints, recommend and talk of the love of Christ to others, and tell them, O tell them what great things the Lord has done for you! This may encourage others to come unto him. And who knows but the Lord may make you fishers of men? The story of Zaccheus was left on record for this purpose. No truly convicted soul, after such an instance of divine grace has been laid before him, need despair of mercy. What if you are Publicans?

Was not Zaccheus a Publican? What if you are chief among the Publicans? Was not Zaccheus likewise? What if you are rich? Was not Zaccheus rich also?

And yet almighty grace made him more than conqueror over all these hindrances. All things are possible to Jesus Christ; nothing is too hard for him: he is the Lord almighty. Our mountains of sins must all fall before this great Zerubbabel. On him God the Father has laid the iniquities of all that shall believe on him; and in his own body he bare them on the tree. There,

there, by faith, O mourners in Zion, may you see your Savior hanging with arms stretched out, and hear him, as it were, thus speaking to your souls; "Behold how I have loved you! Behold my hands and my feed!

Look, look into my wounded side, and see a heart flaming with love: love stronger than death. Come into my arms, O sinners, come wash your spotted souls in my heart's blood. See here is a fountain opened for all sin and all uncleanness! See, O guilty souls, how the wrath of God is now abiding upon you: come, haste away, and hide yourselves in the clefts of my wounds; for I am wounded for your transgressions; I am dying that you may live for evermore. Behold, as Moses lifted up the serpent in the wilderness, so am I here lifted up upon a tree. See how I am become a curse for you: the chastisement of your peace is upon me. I am thus scourged, thus wounded, thus crucified, that you by my stripes may be healed. O look unto me, all ye trembling sinners, even to the ends of the earth! Look unto me by faith, and you shall be saved: for I came thus to be obedient even unto death, that I might save that which was lost." And what say you to this, O sinners? Suppose you saw the King of glory dying, and thus speaking to you; would you believe on him? No, you would not, unless you believe on him now: for though he is dead, he yet speaketh all this in the scripture; nay, in effect, says all this in the words of the text, "The Son of man is come to seek and to save that which is lost." Do not therefore any longer crucify the Lord of glory. Bring those rebels, your sins, which will not have him to reign over them, bring them out to him: though you cannot slay them yourselves, yet he will slay them for you.

The power of his death and resurrection is as great now as formerly. Make haste therefore, make haste, O ye publicans and sinners, and give the dear Lord Jesus your hearts, your whole hearts. If you refuse to hearken to this call of the Lord, remember your damnation will be just: I am free from the blood of you all: you must acquit my Master and me at the terrible day of judgment. O that you may know the things that belong to your everlasting peace, before they are eternally hid from your eyes! Let all that love the Lord Jesus Christ in sincerity say, Amen.

Sermon 36 The Marriage of Cana

John 2:11, "This beginning of miracles did Jesus in Cana of Galilee, and manifested forth his glory; and his disciples believed on him."

I have more than once had occasion to observe, that the chief end St.

John had in view, when he wrote his gospel, was to prove the divinity of Jesus Christ, against those arch-heretics Ebion and Cerinthus, whose pernicious principles too many follow in these last days. For this purpose, you may take notice, that he is more particular than any other Evangelist, in relating our Lord's divine discourses, and also the glorious miracles which he wrought, not by a power derived from another, like Moses, and other prophets, but from a power inherent in himself.

The words of the text have a reference to a notable miracle which Christ performed, and thereby gave proof of his eternal power and Godhead.

"This beginning of miracles did Jesus in Cana of Galilee, and manifested forth his glory; and his disciples believed on him." The miracle here spoken of, is that of our Lord's turning water into wine at a marriage feast. I design, at present, by God's help, to make some observations on the circumstances and certainty of the miracle, and then conclude with some practical instructions; that you, by hearing how Jesus Christ has showed forth his glory, may, by the operation of God's Spirit upon your hearts, with the disciples mentioned in the text, be brought to believe on him.

FIRST, then, I would make some observations on the miracle itself.

Verse 1 and 2. "And the third day there was a marriage in Cana of Galilee; and the mother of Jesus was there. And both Jesus was called, and his disciples, to the marriage." By our Lord's being at a feast we may learn, that feasting upon solemn occasions is not absolutely unlawful: but then we must be exceeding careful at such seasons, that the occasion be solemn, and that we go not for the sake of eating and drinking, but to edify one another in love. Feasting in any other manner, I think absolutely unlawful for the followers of Jesus Christ: because if we eat and drink out of any other view, it cannot be to the glory of God. The Son of man, we know, "came eating and drinking." If a Pharisee asked him to come to his house, our Lord went, and sat down with him. But then we find his discourse was always such as tended to the use of edifying. We may then, no doubt, go and do likewise.

We may observe farther, that if our Lord was present at a marriage feast, then, to deny marriage to any order of men, is certainly a "doctrine of devils." "Marriage (says the Apostle) is honorable in all." Our Lord graced a marriage feast with his first public miracle. It was an institution of God himself, even in paradise: and therefore, no doubt, lawful for all Christians, even for those who are made perfect in holiness through the faith of Jesus Christ. But then, we may learn the reason why we have so many unhappy marriages in the world; it is because the parties concerned do not call Jesus Christ by prayer, nor ask the advice of his true disciples when they are about to marry. No; Christ and religion are the last things that are consulted; and no wonder then if matches of the devil's making (as all such are, which are contracted only on account of outward beauty, or for filthy lucre's sake) prove most miserable, and grievous to be borne.

I cannot but dwell a little on this particular, because I am persuaded the devil cannot lay a greater snare for young Christians, than to tempt them unequally to yoke themselves with unbelievers; as are all who are not born again of God. This was the snare wherein the sons of God were entangled before the flood, and one great cause why God brought that flood upon the world. For what says Moses, Gen 6:2,3, "The sons of God (the posterity of pious Seth) saw the daughters of men, (or the posterity of wicked Cain) that they were fair, (not that they were pious) and they took them wives of all which they chose:" not which God chose for them. What follows? "And the Lord saith, My spirit shall not always strive with man, for that he also is flesh;" that is, even the few righteous souls being now grown carnal by their ungodly marriages, the whole world was altogether become abominable, and had made themselves vessels of wrath fitted for destruction. I might instance farther, the care the ancient patriarchs took to choose wives for their children out of their own religious families, and it was one great mark of Esau's rebellion against his father, that he took unto himself wives of the daughters of the Canaanites, who were strangers to the covenant of promise made unto his fathers. But I forbear. Time will not permit me to enlarge here. Let it suffice to advise all, whenever they enter into a marriage state, to imitate the people of Cana in Galilee, to call Christ to the marriage; He certainly will hear and choose for you; and you will always find his choice to be the best. He then will direct you to such yoke-fellows as shall be helps meet for you in the great work of your salvation, and then he will also enable you to serve him without distraction, and cause you to walk, as Zachary and Elizabeth, in all his commandments and ordinances blameless.

But to proceed. Who these persons were that called our Lord and his disciples to the marriage, is not certain. Some (because it is said, that the mother of Jesus was there) have supposed that they were related to the Virgin, and that therefore our Lord and his disciples were invited on her account. However that be, it should seem they were not very rich, (for what had rich folks to do with a despised Jesus of Nazareth, and his mean followers?) because we find they were unfurnished with a sufficient quantity of wine for a large company, and therefore, "when they wanted wind, the mother of Jesus," having, as it should seem by her applying to him so readily on this occasion, even in his private life, seen some instances of his miraculous power, "saith unto him, They have no wine." She thought is sufficient only to inform him of the wants of the host, knowing that he was as ready to give as she to ask. In this light the blessed Virgin's request appears to us at the first view; but if we examine our Lord's answer, we shall have reason to think there was something which was not right; for Jesus saith unto her, ver. 4, "Woman, what have I to do with thee?" Observe, he calls her woman, not mother; to show her, that though she was his mother, as he was man, yet she was his creature, as he was God.

"What have I to do with thee?" Think you that I must work miracles at your bidding? Some have thought that she spoke as though she had an authority over him, which was a proud motion, and our Lord therefore checks her for it, And if Jesus Christ would not turn a little water into wine, whilst he was here on earth, at her command, how idolatrous is that church, and how justly do we separate from her, which prescribes forms, wherein the Virgin is desired to command her Son to have compassion on us!

But notwithstanding the holy Virgin was blamable in this respect, yet she hath herein set rich and poor an example which it is your duty to follow. You that are rich, and live in cieled houses, learn of her to go into the cottages of the poor; your Lord was not above it, and why should you? And when you do visit them, like the virgin-mother, examine their wants; and when you see they have no wine, and are ready to perish with hunger, shut not up your bowels of compassion, but bless the Lord for putting it in your power to administer to their necessities. Believe me, such visits would do you good. You would learn then to be thankful that God has given you bread enough, and to spare. And I am persuaded, every mite that you bestow on feeding the hungry and clothing the naked disciples of Jesus Christ, will afford you more satisfaction at the hour of death, and in the day of judgment, than all the thousands squandered away in balls and assemblies, and such like entertainments.

You that are poor in this world's goods, and thereby are disabled from helping, yet you may learn from the Virgin, to pray for one another. She could not turn the water into wine, but she could entreat her son to do it: and so may you; and doubt not of the Lord's hearing you; for God has chosen the poor in this world, rich in faith: and by your servant prayers, you may draw down many a blessing on your poor fellow creatures. O that I may ever be remembered by you before the throne of our dear Lord Jesus! But what shall we say? Will our Lord entirely disregard this motion of his mother?

No; though he check her with, "Woman, what have I to do with thee?" yet he intimates that he would do as she desired by-and-by; "Mine hour is not yet come." As though he had said, The wine is almost, but not quite out; when they are come to an extremity, and sensible of the want of my assistance, then will I show forth my glory, that they may behold it, and believe on me.

Thus, Sirs, hath our Lord been frequently pleased to deal with me, and, I doubt not, with many of you also. Often, often when I have found his presence as it were hidden from my soul, and his comforts well nigh gone, I have went unto him complaining that I had no visit and token of his love, as usual. Sometimes he has seemed to turn a deaf ear to my request, and as it were said, "What have I to do with thee?" which has made me go sorrowing all the day long; so foolish was I, and faithless before him: for I have always found he loved me notwithstanding, as he did Lazarus, though he stayed two days after he heard he was sick. But when my hour of extremity has been come, and my will broken, then hath he lifted up the light of his blessed countenance afresh; he has showed forth his glory, and made me ashamed for disbelieving him, who often hath turned my water into wine. Be not then discouraged, if the Lord does not immediately seem to regard the voice of your prayer, when you cry unto him. The holy Virgin we find was not; no, she was convinced his time was the best time, and therefore, verse 5, "saith unto the servants, (O that we could follow her advice!) whatsoever he saith unto you, do it." And now, behold the hour is come, when the eternal Son of God will show forth his glory. The circumstance of the miracle is very remarkable; ver. 6, "And there were set six water-pots of water, after the manner of the purifying of the Jews, containing two or three firkins a-piece." The manner of this purifying we have an account of in the other Evangelist, especially St. Mark, who informs us, that the Pharisees, and all the Jews, except they wash their hands oft, eat not; and when they come from the market, except they wash they eat not. This was a superstitious custom; but, however , we may learn from it, whenever we come in from conversing with those that are without, to purify our hearts by self-examination and prayer; for it is hard to go through the world, and to be kept unspotted from it.

Observe further, verse 7. "Jesus saith unto them," not to his own disciples, but unto the servants of the house, who were strangers to the holy Jesus, and whom the virgin had before charged to do whatsoever he said unto them; "Fill the water-pots with water. And they filled them to the brim. And he saith unto them, draw out now, and bear to the governor of the feast. And they bear it." How our Lord turned the water into wine we are not told. What have we to do with that? Why should we desire to be wise above what is written? It is sufficient for the manifestation of his glorious godhead, that we are assured he did do it. For we are told, verse 9, 10, "When the ruler of the feast had tasted the water that was made wine, and knew not whence it was (but the servants that drew the water knew) the governor of the feast called the bridegroom, and saith unto him, every man at the beginning doth set forth good wine, and when they have well drank, that which is worse; but thou hast kept the good wine until now." To explain this passage, you must observe, it was the custom of the Jews, nay even of the heathens themselves, (to the shame of our Christian baptized heathens be it spoken) at their public feasts to choose a governor, who was to ever see and regulate the behavior of the guests, and to take care that all things were carried on with decency and order. To this person then did the servants bear the wine; and we may judge how rich it was by his commendation of it, "Every man at the beginning, etc." Judge ye then, whether Jesus did not show forth his glory, and whether you have not good reason, like the disciple here mentioned, to believe on him?

Thus, my brethren, I have endeavored to make some observations on the miracle itself. But alas! this is only the outward court thereof, the veil is yet before our eyes; turn that aside, and we shall see such mysteries under it, as will make our hearts to dance for joy, and fill our mouths with praise for evermore!

But here I cannot help remarking what a sad inference one of our masters of Israel, in a printed sermon, has lately drawn from this commendation of the bridegroom. His words are these. "Our blessed Savior came eating and drinking, was present at weddings, and other entertainments, (though I hear of his being only at one;) nay, at one of them (which I suppose is that of which I am now discoursing) worked a miracle to make wine, when it is plain there had been more drank than was absolutely necessary for the support of nature, and consequently something had been indulged to pleasure and cheerfulness." I am sorry such words should come from the mouth and pen of a dignified clergyman of the Church of England. Alas! how is she fallen! or at least, in what danger must her tottering ark be, when such unhallowed hands are stretched out to support it! Well may I bear patiently to be stiled a blasphemer, and a setter forth of strange doctrine, when my dear Lord Jesus is thus traduced; and when those who pretend to preach in his name, urge this example to patronize licentiousness and excess. It is true (as I observed at the beginning of this discourse) our blessed Savior did come eating and drinking; he was present at a wedding, and other entertainments; nay, at one of them worked a miracle to make wine, (you see I have been making some observations on it) but then it is not plain there had been more wine drank than was absolutely necessary for the support of nature; much less does it appear, that something had been indulged to pleasure and cheerfulness.

The governor does indeed say, "When men have well drunken," but it no where appears that they were the men. Is it to be supposed, that the most holy and unspotted Lamb of God, who was manifested to destroy the works of the devil, and who, when at a Pharisee's house, took notice of even the gestures of those with whom he sat at meat; is it to be supposed, that our dear Redeemer, whose constant practice it was to tell people they must deny themselves, and take up their crosses daily; who bid his disciples to take heed, lest at any time their hearts might be over-charged with surfeiting and drunkenness; can it be supposed, that such a self-denying Jesus should now turn six large water-pots of water into the richest wine, to encourage excess and drunkenness in persons, who, according to this writer, had indulged to pleasure and cheerfulness already? Had our Lord sat by, and seen them indulge, without telling them of it, would it not be a sin? But to insinuate he not only did this, but also turned water into wine, to increase that indulgence; this is making Christ a minister of sin indeed.

What is this, but using him like the Pharisees of old, who called him a glutton, and a wine-bibber? Alas! how may we expect our dear Lord's enemies will treat him, when he is thus wounded in the house of his seeming friends? Sirs, if you follow such doctrine as this, you will not be righteous, but I am persuaded you will be wicked over-much.

But God forbid you should think our Lord behaved so much unlike himself in this matter. No, he had nobler ends in view, when he wrought this miracle. One, the evangelist mentions in the words of the text, "to show forth his glory," or to give a proof of his eternal power and godhead.

Here seems to be an allusion to the appearance of God in the tabernacle, which this same evangelist takes notice of in his first chapter, where he says, "The Word (Jesus Christ) was made flesh, and dwelt (or, as it is rendered in the margin, tabernacled) amongst us." Our dear Lord, though very God of very God, and also most perfect and glorious in himself as man, was pleased to throw a veil of flesh over this his great glory, when he came to make his soul an offering for sin. And that the world might know and believe

in him as the Savior of all men, he performed many miracles, and this in particular; for thus speaks the evangelist, "This first," .

This then was the chief design of our Lord's turning the water into
wine. But there are more which our Lord may be supposed to have had in
view, some of which I shall proceed to mention.

SECONDLY, he might do this to reward the hose for calling him
and his disciples to the marriage. Jesus Christ will not be behind-hand with
those who receive him or his followers, for his name's sake. Those who thus
honor him, he will honor. A cup of cold water given in the name of a disciple,
shall in no wise lose its reward. He will turn water into wine. Though those
who abound in alms-deeds, out of a true faith in, and love for Jesus, may
seem as it were to throw their bread upon the waters, yet they shall find it
again after many days. For they who give to the poor out of this principle,
lend unto the Lord; and look, whatsoever they lay out, it shall be repaid them
again. Even in this life, God often orders good measure pressed down and
running over, to be returned into his servants bosoms. It is the same in spirituals. To him that hath, and improves what he hath, for the sake of Christ and
his disciples, shall be given, and he shall have abundance. Brethren, I would
not boast; but, to my master's honor and free grace be it spoken, I can prove
this to be true by happy experience. When I have considered that I am a child,
and cannot speak, and have seen so many of you come out into the wilderness
to be fed, I have often said within myself, what can I do with my little stock
of grace and knowledge among so great a multitude? But, at my Lord's command, I have given you to eat of such spiritual food as I had, and before I
have done speaking, have had my soul richly fed with the bread which
cometh down from heaven. Thus shall it be done to all such who are willing
to spend and be spent for Christ or his disciples; for there is no respect of persons with God.

THIRDLY, Our Lord's turning the water, which was poured out so
plentifully, into wine, is a sign of the plentiful pouring out of his Spirit into
the hearts of believers. The holy Spirit is in scripture compared unto wine;
and therefore the prophet calls us to buy wine as well as milk, that is, the
spirit of love, which fills and gladdens the soul as it were with new wine. The
apostle alludes to this, when he bids the Ephesians "not to be drunk with
wine, wherein is excess, but be filled with the Spirit." And our Lord shows us
thus much by choosing wine; to show forth the strength and refreshment of
his blood, in the blessed sacrament.

I know these terms are unintelligible to natural men, they can no
more understand me, than if I spoke to them in an unknown tongue, for they
are only to be spiritually discerned. To you then that are spiritual do I speak,

to you who are justified by faith, and feel the blessed Spirit of Jesus Christ working upon your hearts, you can judge of what I say; you have already (I am persuaded) been as it were filled with new wine by the inspiration of his Holy Spirit. But alas! you have not yet had half your portion; thee are only earnests, and in comparison but shadows of good things to come; our Lord keeps his best wine for you till the last; and though you have drank deep of it already, yet he intends to give you more: He will not leave you, till he has filled you to the brim, till you are ready to cry out, Lord, stay thine hand, thy poor creatures can hold no more! Be not straitened in your own bowels, since Jesus Christ is not straitened in his. Open your hearts as wide as ever you will, the Spirit of the Lord shall fill them. Christ deals with true believers, as Elijah did with the poor woman, whose oil increased, to pay her husband's debts; as long as she brought pitchers, the oil continued. It did not cease till she ceased bringing vessels to contain it. My brethren, our hearts are like those pitchers; open them freely by faith, and the oil of God's free gift, the oil of gladness, the love of God through Christ, shall be continually pouring in; for believers are to be filled with all the fullness of God.

FOURTHLY, Our Lord's turning water into wine, and keeping the best until last, may show forth the glory of the latter days of his marriage feast with his church. Great things God has done already, whereat millions of saints have rejoiced, and do yet rejoice. Great things God is doing now, but yet, my brethren, we shall see greater things than these. It is meet, right, and our bounden duty, to give thanks unto God, even the Father; for many right-eous men have desired to see the things which we see, and have not seen them; and to hear the things which we hear, and have not heard them. But still there are more excellent things behind. Glorious things are spoken of these times, "when the earth shall be filled with the knowledge of the Lord, as the waters cover the sea." There is a general expectation among the people of God, when the partition-wall between Jew and Gentile shall be broken down, and all Israel be saved. Happy those who live when God does this. They shall see Satan, like lightning, fall from heaven. They shall not weep, as the Jews did at the building of the second temple. No, they shall rejoice with exceeding great joy. For all the former glory of the Christian church shall be nothing in comparison of that glory which shall excel. Then shall they cry out with the governor of the feast, "thou hast kept thy good wine until now!" FIFTHLY, and lastly, This shows us the happiness of that blessed state, when we shall all sit together at the marriage supper of the Lamb, and drink of the new wine in his eternal and glorious kingdom!

The rewards which Jesus Christ confers on his faithful servants, and the comforts of his love wherewith he comforts them, whilst pilgrims here on earth, are often so exceeding great, that was it not promised, it were almost presumption for them to hope for any reward hereafter. But, my brethren, all the manifestations of God that we can possibly be favored with here, when compared with the glory that is to be revealed in us, are no more than a drop of water when compared with an unbounded ocean. Though Christ frequently fills his saints even to the brim, yet their corruptible bodies weigh down their souls, and cause them to cry, "Who shall deliver us from these bodies of death?" These earthly tabernacles can hold no more: But, blessed be God, these earthly tabernacles are to be dissolved; this corruptible is to put on incorruption; this mortal is to put on immortality: and when God shall cause all his glory to pass before us, then shall we cry out, Lord, thou hast kept thy good wine until now. We have drank deeply of thy spirit; we have heard glorious things spoken of this thy city, O God! but we now find, that not the half, not the thousandth part hath been told us. O the invisible realities of the world of faith!

Eye hath not seen, ear hath not heard, neither hath it entered into the heart of the greatest saint to conceive how Christ will show forth his glory there! St. Paul, who was carried up into the third heavens, could give us little or no account of it. And well he might not -- for he heard and saw such things as is not possible for a man clothed with flesh and blood to utter. Whilst I am thinking, and only speaking of those things unto you, I am almost carried beyond myself. Methinks, I now receive some little foretastes of that new wine which I hope to drink with you in the heavenly kingdom for ever and ever.

And wherefore do you think I have been saying these things? Many, perhaps, may be ready to say, To manifest thy own vain-glory. But it is a small matter with me to be judged of man's judgment. He that judgeth me is the Lord. He knows that I have spoken of his miracle, only for the same end for which he at first performed it, and which I at first proposed, that is, "to show forth his glory," that you also may be brought to believe on him.

Did I come to preach myself, and not Christ Jesus my Lord, I would come to you, not in this plainness of speech, but with the enticing words of man's wisdom. Did I desire to please natural men, I need not preach here in the wilderness. I hope my heart aims at nothing else, than what our Lord's great fore-runner aimed at, and which ought to be the business of every gospel minister, that is, to point out to you the God-man Christ Jesus. "Behold then (by faith behold) the Lamb of God, who taketh away the sins of the world." Look unto him, and be saved. You have heard how he manifested, and will yet manifest his glory to true believers; and why then, O sinners, will you not believe in him? I say, O sinners, for now I have spoken to the saints, I have many things to say to you. And may God give you all an hearing ear, and an obedient heart!

The Lord Jesus who showed forth his glory above 1700 years ago, has made a marriage feast, and offers to espouse all sinners to himself, and to make them flesh of his flesh, and bone of his bone. He is willing to be united to you by one spirit. In every age, at sundry times, and after divers manners, he hath sent forth his servants, and they had bidden many, but yet, my brethren, there is room. The Lord therefore now has given a commission in these last days to others of his servants, even to compel poor sinners by the cords of love to come in. For our master's house must and shall be filled. He will not shed his gracious blood in vain. Come then, come to the marriage. Let this be the day of your espousals with Jesus Christ, he is willing to receive you, though other lords have had dominion over you. Come then to the marriage. Behold the oxen and fatlings are killed, and all things are ready; let me hear you say, as Rebecca did, when they asked her, whether she would go and be a wife to Isaac; O let me hear you say, we will come. Indeed you will not repent it. The Lord shall turn your water into wine. He shall fill your souls with marrow and fatness, and cause you to praise him with joyful lips.

Do not say, you are miserable, and poor, and blind, and naked, and therefore ashamed to come, for it is to such that this invitation is not sent. The polite, the rich, the busy, self-righteous Pharisees of this generation have been bidden already, but they have rejected the counsel of God against themselves. They are too deeply engaged in going, one to his country house, another to his merchandise. They are so deeply wedded to the pomps and vanities of this wicked world, that they, as it were with one consent, have made excuse. And though they have been often called in their own synagogues, yet all the return they make, is to thrust us out, and thereby in effect say, they will not come. But God forbid, my brethren, that you should learn of them; no, since our Lord condescends to call first, (because if left to yourselves you would never call after him) let me beseech you to answer him, as he answered for you, when called upon by infinite offended justice to die for you sins, "Lo! I come to do thy will, O God!" What if you are miserable, and poor, and blind, and naked, that is no excuse; faith is the only wedding garment which Christ requires; he does not call you because you already are, but because he intends to make you saints. It pities him to see you naked. He wants to cover you with his righteousness. In short, he desires to show forth his glory, that is, his free love through your faith in him. Not but that he will be glorified, whether you believe in him or not; for the infinitely free love of Jesus Christ will be ever the same, whether you believe it, or so receive it, or the contrary. But our Lord will not always send out his servants in vain, to call you; the time will come when he will say, None of those which were bidden, and would not come, shall taste of my supper. Our Lord is a God of justice, as well as of love; and if sinners will not take hold of his golden scepter, verily he will bruise them with his iron rod. It is for your sakes, O sinners, and not his own, that he thus condescends to invite you: suffer him then to show forth his glory, even the glory of the exceeding riches of his free grace, by believing on him, "For we are saved by grace through faith." It was grace, free grace, that moved the Father so to love the world, as to "give his only begotten Son, that whosoever believeth in him should not perish, but have everlasting life!" It was grace, that made the Son to come down and die. It was grace, free grace, that moved the Holy Ghost to undertake to sanctify the elect people of God: and it was grace, free grace, that moved our Lord Jesus Christ to send forth his ministers to call poor sinners this day. Let me not then, my brethren, go without my errand. Why will you not believe in him? Will the devil do such great and good things for you as Christ will? No indeed, he will not. Perhaps, he may give you to drink at first of a little brutish pleasure; but what will he give you to drink as last? a cup of fury and of trembling; a never-dying worm, a self-condemning conscience, and the bitter pains of eternal death. But as for the servants of Jesus Christ, it is not so with them. No, he keeps his best wine till the last. And though he may cause you to drink of the brook in the way to heaven, and of the cup of affliction, yet he sweetens it with a sense of his goodness, and makes it pleasant drink, such as their souls do love. I appeal to the experience of any saint here present, (as I doubt not but there are many such in this field) whether Christ has not proved faithful, ever since you have been espoused to him? Has he not showed forth his glory, ever since you have believed on him?

And now, sinners, what have you to object? I see you are all silent, and well you may. For if you will not be drawn by the cords of infinite and everlasting love, what will draw you? I could urge many terrors of the Lord to persuade you; but if the love of Jesus Christ will not constrain you, your case is desperate. Remember then this day I have invited all, even the worst of sinners, to be married to the Lord Jesus. If you perish, remember you do not perish for lack of invitation. You yourselves shall stand forth at the last day, and I here give you a summons to meet me at the judgment seat of Christ, and to clear both my master and me. Would weeping, would tears prevail on you, I could wish my head were waters, and my eyes fountains of tears, that I might weep out every argument, and melt you into love. Would any thing I could do or suffer, influence your hearts, I think I could bear to pluck out my eyes, or even to lay down my life for your sakes. Or was I sure to prevail on you by importunity, I could continue my discourse till midnight, I would wrestle with you even till the morning watch, as Jacob did with the angel, and would not go away till I had overcome. But such power belongeth only unto the Lord, I can only invite; it is He only can work in you both to will and to do after his good pleasure; it is his property to take away the heart of stone, and give you a heart of flesh; it is his spirit that must convince you of unbelief, and of the everlasting righteousness of his dear Son; it is He alone must give faith to apply his righteousness to your hearts; it is He alone can give you a wedding garment, and bring you to sit down and drink new wine in his kingdom. As to spirituals we are quite dead, and have no more power to turn to God of ourselves, than Lazarus had to raise himself, after he had lain stinking in the grave four days. If thou canst go, O man, and breathe upon all the dry bones that lie in the graves, and bid them live; if thou canst take thy mantle and divide yonder river, as Elijah did the river Jordan; then will we believe thou hast a power to turn to God of thyself: But as thou must despair of the one, so thou must despair of the other, without Christ's quickening grace; in him is thy only help; fly to him then by faith; say unto him, as the poor leper did, "Lord, if thou wilt," thou canst make me willing; and he will stretch forth the right-hand of his power to assist and relieve you: He will sweetly guide you by his wisdom on earth, and afterwards take you up to partake of his glory in heaven.

To his mercy therefore, and Almighty protection, do I earnestly, humbly, and most affectionately commit you: the Lord bless you and keep you; the Lord lift up the light of his blessed countenance upon you, and give you all peace and joy in believing, now and for evermore!

Sermon 37 The Duty of searching the Scriptures.

John 5:39, "Search the Scriptures."

When the Sadducees came to our blessed Lord, and put to him the question, "whose wife that woman should be in the next life, who had seven husbands in this," he told them "they erred, not knowing the scriptures." And if we would know whence all the errors, that have over-spread the church of Christ, first arose, we should find that, in a great measure, they flowed from the same fountain, ignorance of the word of God.

Our blessed Lord, though he was the eternal God, yet as man, he made the scriptures his constant rule and guide. And therefore, when he was asked by the lawyer, which was the great commandment of the law, he referred him to his Bible for an answer, "What readest thou?" And thus, when led by the Spirit to be tempted by the devil, he repelled all his assaults, with "it is written." A sufficient confutation this, of their opinion, who say, "the Spirit only, and not the Spirit by the Word, is to be our rule of action." If so, our Savior, who had the Spirit without measure, needed not always have referred to the written word.

But how few copy after the example of Christ? How many are there who do not regard the word of God at all, but throw the sacred oracles aside, as an antiquated book, fit only for illiterate men?

Such do greatly err, not knowing what the scriptures are, I shall, therefore, FIRST, Show, that it is every one's duty to search them.

And SECONDLY, Lay down some directions for you to search them with advantage.

I. I am to show, that it is every person's duty to search the Scriptures.

By the Scriptures, I understand the law and the prophets, and those books which have in all ages been accounted canonical, and which make up that volume commonly called the Bible.

These are emphatically stiled the Scriptures, and, in one place, the "Scriptures of Truth," as though no other books deserved the name of true writings or scripture in comparison of them.

They are not of any private interpretation, authority, or invention, but holy men of old wrote them, as they were moved by the Holy Ghost.

The fountain of God's revealing himself thus to man-kind, was our fall in Adam, and the necessity of our new birth in Christ Jesus. And if we search the scriptures as we ought, we shall find the sum and substance, the Alpha and Omega, the beginning and end of them, is to lead us to a knowledge of these two great truths.

All the threats, promises and precepts, all the exhortations and doctrines contained therein, all the rites, ceremonies and sacrifices appointed under the Jewish law; nay, almost all the historical parts of holy scripture, suppose our being fallen in Adam, and either point out to us a Mediator to come, or speak of him as already come in the flesh.

Had man continued in a state of innocence, he would not have needed an outward revelation, because the law of God was so deeply written in the tables of his heart. But having eaten the forbidden fruit, he incurred the displeasure of God, and lost the divine image, and, therefore, without an external revelation, could never tell how God would be reconciled unto him, or how he should be saved from the misery and darkness of his fallen nature.

That these truths are so, I need not refer you to any other book, than your own hearts.

For unless we are fallen creatures, whence those abominable corruptions which daily arise in our hearts? We could not come thus corrupt out of the hands of our Maker, because he being goodness itself could make nothing but what is like himself, holy, just, and good. And that we want to be delivered from these disorders of our nature, is evident, because we find an unwillingness within ourselves to own we are thus depraved, and are always striving to appear to others of a quite different frame and temper of mind than what we are.

I appeal to the experience of the most learned disputer against divine revelation, whether he does not find in himself, that he is naturally proud, angry, revengeful, and full of other passions contrary to the purity, holiness, and long suffering of God. And is not this a demonstration that some way or other he is fallen from God? And I appeal also, whether at the same time that he finds these hurtful lusts in his heart, he does not strive to seem amiable, courteous, kind and affable; and is not this a manifest proof, that he is sensible he is miserable, and wants, he knows not how, to be redeemed or delivered from it?

Here then, God by his word steps in, and opens to his view such a scene of divine love, and infinite goodness in the holy scriptures, that none but men, of such corrupt and reprobate minds as our modern deists, would shut their eyes against it.

What does God in his written word do more or less, than show thee, O man, how thou art fallen into that blindness, darkness, and misery, of which thou feelest and complainest? And, at the same time, he points out the way to what thou desirest, even how thou mayest be redeemed out of it by believing in, and copying after the Son of his love.

As I told you before, so I tell you again, upon these two truths rest all divine revelation. It being given us for no other end, but to show our misery, and our happiness; our fall and recovery; or, in one word, after what manner we died in Adam, and how in Christ we may again be made alive.

Hence, then arises the necessity of searching the scriptures: for since they are nothing else but the grand charter of our salvation, the revelation of a covenant made by God with men in Christ, and a light to guide us into the way of peace; it follows, that all are obliged to read and search them, because all are equally fallen from God, all equally stand in need of being informed how they must be restored to, and again united with him.

How foolishly then do the disputing infidels of this generation act, who are continually either calling for signs from heaven, or seeking for outward evidence to prove the truth of divine revelation? Whereas, what they so earnestly seek for is nigh unto, nay, within them. For let them but consult their own hearts, they cannot but feel what they want. Let them but consult the lively oracles of God, and they cannot but see a remedy revealed for all their wants, and that the written word does as exactly answer the wants and desires of their hearts, as face answers to face in the water. Where then is the scribe, where is the wise, where is the solidity of the reasoning of the disput-ers of this world? Has not God revealed himself unto them, as plain as their own hearts could wish? And yet they require a sign: but there shall no other sign be given them. For if they believe not a revelation which is every way so suited to their wants, neither will they be persuaded though on should rise from the dead.

But this discourse is not designed so much for them that believe not, as for them, who both know and believe that the scriptures contain a revela-tion which came from God, and that it is their duty, as being chief parties concerned, not only to read but search them also.

I pass on, therefore, in the SECOND place, to lay down some direc-tions, how you may search them with advantage.

FIRST, Have always in view, the end for which the scriptures were written, even to show us the way of salvation, by Jesus Christ.

"Search the scriptures," says our blessed Lord, "for they are they that testify of me." Look, therefore, always for Christ in the scripture.

He is the treasure hid in the field, both of the Old and New Testa-ment. In the Old, you will find him under prophesies, types, sacrifices, and shadows; in the New, manifested in the flesh, to become a propitiation for our sins as a Priest, and as a Prophet to reveal the whole will of his heavenly Fa-ther.

Have Christ, then, always in view when you are reading the word of God, and this, like the star in the east, will guide you to the Messiah, will serve as a key to every thing that is obscure, and unlock to you the wisdom and riches of all the mysteries of the kingdom of God.

SECONDLY, Search the scriptures with an humble child-like dis-position.

For whosoever does not read them with this temper, shall in no wise enter into the knowledge of the things contained in them. For God hides the sense of them, from those that are wise and prudent in their own eyes, and reveals them only to babes in Christ: who think they know nothing yet as they ought to know; who hunger and thirst after righteousness, and humbly desire to be fed with the sincere milk of the word, that they may grow thereby.

Fancy yourselves, therefore, when you are searching the scriptures, especially when you are reading the New Testament, to be with Mary sitting at the feet of the holy Jesus; and be as willing to learn what God shall teach you, as Samuel was, when he said, "Speak, Lord, for thy servant heareth." Oh that the unbelievers would pull down every high thought and imagination that exalts itself against the revealed will of God! O that they would, like new-born babes, desire to be fed with the pure milk of the word! Then we should have them no longer scoffing at Divine revelation, nor would they read the Bible any more with the same intend the Philistines brought our Samson, to make sport at it; but they would see the divine image and superscription written upon every line. They would hear God speaking unto their souls by it, and, consequently, be built up in the knowledge and fear of him, who is the Author thereof.

THIRDLY, Search the scriptures, with a sincere intention to put in practice what you read.

A desire to do the will of God is the only way to know it; if any man will do my will, says Jesus Christ, "He shall know of my doctrine, whether it be of God, or whether I speak of myself." As he also speaks in another place to his disciples, "To you, (who are willing to practice your duty) it is given to know the mysteries of the kingdom of God, but to those that are without (who only want to raise cavils against my doctrine) all these things are spoken in parables, that seeing they may see and not understand, and hearing they may hear and not perceive." For it is but just in God to send those strong delusions, that they may believe a lie, and to conceal the knowledge of himself from all such as do not seek him with a single intention.

Jesus Christ is the same now, as formerly, to those who desire to know from his word, who he is that they may believe on, and live by; and to him he will reveal himself as clearly as he did to the woman of Samaria, when he said, "I that speak to thee am he," or as he did to the man that was born blind, whom the Jews had cast out for his name's sake, "He that talketh with thee, is he." But to those who consult his word with a desire neither to know him, nor keep his commandments, but either merely for their entertainment, or to scoff at the simplicity of the manner in which he is revealed, to those, I say, he never will reveal himself, though they should search the scriptures to all eternity. As he never would tell those whether he was the Messiah or not, who put that question to him either out of curiosity, or that they might have whereof to accuse him.

FOURTHLY, In order to search the scriptures still more effectually, make an application of every thing you read to your own hearts.

For whatever was written in the book of God, was written for our learning. And what Christ said unto those aforetime, we must look upon as spoken to us also: for since the holy scriptures are nothing but a revelation from God, how fallen man is to be restored by Jesus Christ: all the precepts, threats, and promises, belong to us and to our children, as well as to those, to whom they were immediately made known.

Thus the Apostle, when he tells us that he lived by the faith of the Son of God, adds, "who died and gave himself for me." It is this application of Jesus Christ to our hearts, that makes his redemption effectual to each of us.

And it is this application of all the doctrinal and historical parts of scripture, when we are reading them over, that must render them profitable to us, as they were designed for reproof, for correction, for instruction in righteousness, and to make every child of God perfect, thoroughly furnished to every good work.

I dare appeal to the experience of every spiritual reader of holy writ, whether or not, if he consulted the word of God in this manner, he was not at all times and at all seasons, as plainly directed how to act, as though he had consulted the Urim and Thummim, which was upon the high- priest's breast. For this is the way God now reveals himself to man: not by making new revelations, but by applying general things that are revealed already to every sincere reader's heart.

And this, by the way, answers an objection made by those who say, "The word of God is not a perfect rule of action, because it cannot direct us how to act or how to determine in particular cases, or what place to go to, when we are in doubt, and therefore, the Spirit, and not the word, is to be our rule of action." But this I deny, and affirm on the contrary, that God at all times, circumstances, and places, though never so minute, never so particular, will, if we diligently seek the assistance of his Holy Spirit, apply general things to our hearts, and thereby, to use the words of the holy Jesus, will lead us into all truth, and give us the particular assistance we want. But this leads me to a FIFTH direction how to search the scriptures with profit: Labor to attain that Spirit by which they were written.

For the natural man discerneth not the words of the Spirit of God, because they are spiritually discerned; the words that Christ hath spoken, they are spirit, and they are life, and can be no more understood as to the true sense and meaning of them, by the mere natural man, than a person who never had learned a language can understand another speaking in it. The scriptures, therefore, have not unfitly been compared, by some, to the cloud which went before the Israelites, they are dark and hard to be understood by the natural man, as the cloud appeared dark to the Egyptians; but they are light, they are life to Christians indeed, as that same cloud which seemed dark to Pharaoh and his house, appeared bright and altogether glorious to the Israel of God.

It was the want of the assistance of this Spirit, that made Nicodemus, a teacher of Israel, and a ruler of the Jews, so utterly ignorant in the doctrine of regeneration: for being only a natural man, he could not tell how that thing could be; it was the want of this Spirit that made our Savior's disciples, though he so frequently conversed with them, daily mistake the nature of the doctrines he delivered; and it is because the natural veil is not taken off from their hearts, that so many who now pretend to search the scriptures, yet see no farther than into the bare letter of them, and continue entire strangers to the spiritual meaning couched under every parable, and contained in almost all the precepts of the book of God.

Indeed, how should it be otherwise, for God being a spirit, he cannot communicate himself any otherwise than in a spiritual manner to the hearts of men; and consequently if we are strangers to his Spirit, we must continue strangers to his word, because it is altogether like himself, spiritual. Labor, therefore, earnestly for to attain this blessed Spirit; otherwise, your understandings will never be opened to understand the scriptures aright: and remember, prayer is one of the most immediate means to get this Holy Spirit. Therefore, SIXTHLY, Let me advise you, before you read the scriptures, to pray, that Christ, according to his promise, would send his Spirit to guide you into all truth; intersperse short ejaculations whilst you are engaged in reading; pray over every word and verse, if possible; and when you close up the book, most earnestly beseech God, that the words which you have read, may be inwardly engrafted into your hearts, and bring forth in you the fruits of a good life.

Do this, and you will, with a holy violence, draw down God's Holy Spirit into your hearts; you will experience his gracious influence, and feel him enlightening, quickening, and inflaming your souls by the word of God; you will then not only read, but mark, learn, and inwardly digest what you read: and the word of God will be meat indeed, and drink indeed unto your souls; you then will be as Apollos was, powerful in the scriptures; be scribes ready instructed to the kingdom of God, and bring out of the good treasures of your heart, things both from the Old and New Testament, to entertain all you converse with. One Direction more, which shall be the last, SEVENTHLY, Read the scripture constantly, or, to use our Savior's expression in the text, "search the scriptures;" dig in them as for hid treasure; for here is a manifest allusion to those who dig in mines; and our Savior would thereby teach us, that we must take as much pains in constantly reading his word, if we would grow wise thereby, as those who dig for gold and silver. The scriptures contain the deep things of God, and therefore, can never be sufficiently searched into by a careless, superficial, cursory way of reading them, but by an industrious, close, and humble application.

The Psalmist makes it the characteristic of a good man, that he "meditates on God's law day and night." And "this book of the law, (says God to Joshua) shall not go out of thy mouth, but thou shalt meditate therein day and night;" for then thou shalt make thy way prosperous, and thou shalt have good success. Search, therefore, the scriptures, not only devoutly but daily, for in them are the words of eternal life; wait constantly at wisdom's gate, and she will then, and not till then, display and lay open to you her heavenly treasures. You that are rich, are without excuse if you do not; and you that are poor, ought to take heed and improve that little time you have: for by the scriptures you are to be acquitted, and by the scriptures you are to be condemned at the last day.

But perhaps you have no taste for this despised book; perhaps plays, romances, and books of polite entertainment, suit your taste better: if this be your case, give me leave to tell you, your taste is vitiated, and unless corrected by the Spirit and word of God, you shall never enter into his heavenly kingdom: for unless you delight in God here, how will you be made meet to dwell with him hereafter. Is it a sin then, you will say, to read useless impertinent books; I answer, Yes.

And that for the same reason, as it is a sin to indulge useless conversation, because both immediately tend to grieve and quench that Spirit, by which alone we can be sealed to the day of redemption. You may reply, How shall we know this? Why, put in practice the precept in the text; search the scripture in the manner that has been recommended, and then you will be convinced of the danger, sinfulness, and unsatisfacteriness of reading any others than the book of God, or such as are wrote in the same spirit. You will then say, when I was a child, and ignorant of the excellency of the word of God, I read what the world calls harmless books, as other children in knowledge, though old in years, have done, and still do; but now I have tasted the good word of life, and am come to a more perfect knowledge of Christ Jesus my Lord, I put away these childish, trifling things, and am determined to read no other books but what lead me to a knowledge of myself and of Christ Jesus.

Search, therefore, the scriptures, my dear brethren; taste and see how good the word of God is, and then you will never leave that heavenly manna, that angel's food, to feed on dry husks, that light bread, those trifling, sinful compositions, in which men of false taste delight themselves: no, you will then disdain such poor entertainment, and blush that yourselves once were fond of it. The word of God will then be sweeter to you than honey, and the honey-comb, and dearer than gold and silver; your souls by reading it, will be filled as it were, with marrow and fatness, and your hearts insensibly molded into the spirit of its blessed Author. In short, you will be guided by God's wisdom here, and conducted by the light of his divine word into glory hereafter.

Sermon 38 The Indwelling of the Spirit

(The Indwelling of the Spirit, the common Privilege of all Believers)

John 7:37-39, "In the last day, that great day of the feast, Jesus stood and cried, saying, If any man thirst, let him come unto me, and drink. He that believeth on me, as the scripture hath said, out of his belly shall flow rivers of living water. (But this spake he of the Spirit, which they that believe on him should receive."

Nothing has rendered the cross of Christ of less effect; nothing has been a greater stumbling-block and rock of offense to weak minds, that a supposition, now current among us, that most of what is contained in the gospel of Jesus Christ, was designed only for our Lord's first and immediate followers, and consequently calculated but for one or two hundred years. Accordingly, many now read the life, sufferings, death, and resurrection of Jesus Christ, in the same manner as Caesar's Commentaries, or the Conquests of Alexander are read: as things rather intended to afford matter for speculation, than to be acted over again in and by us.

As this is true of the doctrines of the gospel in general, so it is of the operation of God's Spirit upon the hearts of believers in particular; for we no sooner mention the necessity of our receiving the Holy Ghost in these last days, as well as formerly, but we are looked upon by some, as enthusiasts and madmen; and by others, represented as willfully deceiving the people, and undermining the established constitution of the church.

Judge ye then, whether it is not high time for the true ministers of Jesus, who have been made partakers of this heavenly gift, to lift up their voices like a trumpet; and if they would not have those souls perish, for which the Lord Jesus has shed his precious blood, to declare, with all boldness, that the Holy Spirit is the common privilege and portion of all believers in all ages; and that we as well as the first Christians, must receive the Holy Ghost, before we can be truly called the children of God.

For this reason, (and also that I might answer the design of our church in appointing the present festival of Whitsuntide) I have chosen the words of the text.

They were spoken by Jesus Christ, when he was at the feast of tabernacles. Our Lord attended on the temple-service in general, and the festivals of the Jewish church in particular. The festival at which he was now present, was that of the feast of tabernacles, which the Jews observed according to God's appointment in commemoration of their living in tents.

At the last day of this feast, it was customary for many pious people to fetch water from a certain place, and bring it on their heads, singing this anthem out of Isaiah, "And with joy shall they draw water out of the wells of salvation." Our Lord observing this, and it being his constant practice to spiritualize every thing he met with, cries out, "If any man thirst, let him come unto me, (rather than unto that well) and drink. He that believeth on me, as the scripture hath spoken, (where it is said, God will make water to spring out of a dry rock, and such-like) out of his belly shall flow rivers of living water." And that we might know what our Savior meant by this living water, the Evangelist immediately adds, "But this spake he of the Spirit, which they that believe on him should receive." The last words I shall chiefly insist on in the ensuing discourse: And FIRST, I shall briefly show, what is meant by the word Spirit.

SECONDLY, That this Spirit is the common privilege of all believers.

THIRDLY, I shall show the reason on which this doctrine is founded.

And LASTLY, Conclude with a general exhortation to believe on Jesus Christ, whereby alone we can receive the Spirit.

FIRST, I am to show, what is meant by the word Spirit.

By the Spirit, is evidently to be understood the Holy Ghost, the third person in the ever-blessed Trinity, consubstantial and co-eternal with the Father and the Son, proceeding from, yet equal to them both. For, to use the words of our Church in this day's office, that which we believe of the glory of the Father, the same we believe of the Son, and of the Holy Ghost, without any difference or inequality.

Thus, says St. John, in his first epistle, chap. 5, ver. 7, "There are three that bear record in heaven, the Father, the Word, and the Holy Ghost, and these three are one." And our Lord, when he gave his Apostles commission to go and teach all nations, commanded them to baptize in the name of the Holy Ghost, as well as of the Father and the Son. And St.

Peter, Acts v. 3 said to Ananias, "Why hath Satan filled thine heart to lie to the Holy Ghost?" And ver. 4 he says, "Thou hast not lied unto men, but unto God." From all which passages, it is plain, that the Holy Ghost, is truly and properly God, as well as the Father and the Son. This is an unspeakable mystery, but a mystery of God's revealing, and, therefore, to be assented to with our whole hearts: seeing God is not a man that he should lie, nor the son of man that he should deceive. I proceed, SECONDLY, To prove that the Holy Ghost is the common privilege of all believers.

But, here I would not be understood of to receiving the Holy Ghost, as to enable us to work miracles, or show outward signs and wonders. I allow our adversaries, that to pretend to be inspired, in this sense, is being wise above what is written. Perhaps it cannot be proved, that God ever interposed in this extraordinary manner, but when some new revelation was to be established, as at the first settling of the Mosaic and gospel dispensation: and as for my own part, I cannot but suspect the spirit of those who insist upon a repetition of such miracles at this time. For the world being now become nominally Christian, (though, God knows, little of the power is left among us) there need not outward miracles, but only an inward co-operation of the Holy Spirit with the word, to prove that Jesus is the Messiah which was to come into the world.

Besides, if it was possible for thee, O man, to have faith, so as to be able to remove mountains, or cast out devils; nay, couldst thou speak with the tongue of men and angels, yea, and bid the sun stand still in the midst of heaven; what would all these gifts of the Spirit avail thee, without being made partaker of his sanctifying graces? Saul had the spirit of government for a while, so as to become another man, and yet probably was a cast-away. And many, who cast out devils, in Christ's name, at the last will be disowned by him. If therefore, thou hadst only the gifts, and was destitute of the graces of the Holy Ghost, they would only serve to lead thee with so much the more solemnity to hell.

Here then we join issue with our adversaries, and will readily grant, that we are not in this sense to be inspired, as were our Lord's first Apostles. But unless men have eyes which see not, and ears that hear not, how can they read the latter part of the text, and not confess that the Holy Spirit, in another sense, is the common privilege of all believers, even to the end of the world?

"This spake he of the Spirit, which they that believe on him should receive." Observe, he does not say, they that believe on him for one or two ages, but they that believe on him in general, or, at all times, and in all places. So that, unless we can prove, that St. John was under a delusion when he wrote thee words, we must believe that even we also, shall receive the Holy Ghost, if we believe on the Lord Jesus with our whole hearts.

Again, our Lord, just before his bitter passion, when he was about to offer up his soul an offering for the sins of the elect world; when his heart was most enlarged and he would undoubtedly demand the most excellent gift for his disciples, prays, "That they all may be one, as thou, Father, art in me, and I in thee; that they also may be one in us, I in them, and thou in me; that they may be made perfect in one;" that is, that all his true followers might be united to him by his holy Spirit, by as real, vital, and mystical an union, as there was between Jesus Christ and the Father. I say all his true followers; for it is evident, from our Lord's own words, that he had us, and all believers, in view, when he put up this prayer; "Neither pray I for these alone, but for them also which shall believe on me through their word;" so that, unless we treat our Lord as the high priests did, and count him a blasphemer, we must confess, that all who believe in Jesus Christ, through the word, or ministration of his servants, are to be joined to Jesus Christ, by being made partakers of the Holy Spirit.

A great noise hath been made of late, about the word enthusiast, and it has been cast upon the preachers of the gospel, as a term of reproach; but every Christian, in the proper sense of the word, must be an enthusiast; that is, must be inspired of God or have God, by his Spirit, in him. St. Peter tells us, "we have many great and precious promises, that we may be made partakers of the divine nature;" our Lord prays, "that we may be one, as the Father and he are one;" and our own church, in conformity to these texts of Scripture, in her excellent communion-office, tells us, that those who receive the sacrament worthily, "dwell in Christ, and Christ in them; that they are one with Christ, and Christ with them." And yet, Christians must have their names cast out as evil, and ministers in particular, must be looked upon as deceivers of the people, for affirming, that we must be really united to God, by receiving the Holy Ghost. Be astonished, O heavens, at this!

Indeed, I will not say, all our letter-learned preachers deny this doctrine in express words; but however, they do in effect; for they talk professedly against inward feelings, and say, we may have God's Spirit without feeling it, which is in reality to deny the thing itself. And had I a mind to hinder the progress of the gospel, and to establish the kingdom of darkness, I would go about, telling people, they might have the Spirit of God, and yet not feel it.

But to return: When our Lord was about to ascend to his Father and our Father, to his God and our God he gave his apostles this commission, "Go and teach all nations, baptizing them in the name of the Father, and of the Son, and of the Holy Ghost." And accordingly, by authority of this commission, we do teach and baptize in this, and every age of the church.

And though we translate the words, "baptizing them in the name;" yet, as the name of God, in the Lord's prayer, and several other places, signifies his nature, they might as well be translated thus, "baptizing them into the nature of the Father, into the nature of the Son, and into the nature of the Holy Ghost." Consequently, if we are all to be baptized into the nature of the Holy Ghost, before our baptism be effectual to salvation, it is evident, that we all must actually receive the Holy Ghost, and ere we can say, we truly believe in Jesus Christ. For no one can say, that Jesus is my Lord, but he that has thus received the Holy Ghost.

Numbers of other texts might be quoted to make this doctrine, if possible, still more plain; but I am astonished, that any who call themselves members; much more, that many, who are preachers in the church of England, should dare so much as to open their lips against it. And yet, with grief I speak it, God is my Judge, persons of the established church seem more generally to be ignorant of it, than any dissenters whatsoever.

But, my dear brethren, what have you been doing? How often have your hearts given your lips the lie how often have you offered to God the sacrifice of fools, and had your prayers turned into sin, if you approve of, and use our church-liturgy, and yet deny the Holy Spirit to be the portion of all believers? In the daily absolution, the minister exhorts the people to pray, that "God would grant them repentance, and his Holy Spirit:" in the Collect for Christmas day, we beseech God, "that he would daily renew us by his Holy Spirit;" in the last week's Collect, we prayed that "we may evermore rejoice in the comforts of the Holy Ghost;" and in the concluding prayer, which we put up every day, we pray, not only that the grace of our Lord Jesus Christ, and the love of God, but that "the fellowship of the Holy Ghost" may be with us all evermore.

But further, a solemn season, to some, is not approaching; I mean the Easter-days, at the end of which, all that are to be ordained to the office of a deacon, are in the sight of God, and in the presence of the congregation, to declare, that "they trust they are inwardly moved by the Holy Ghost, to take upon them that administration;" and to those, who are to be ordained priests, the bishop is to repeat these solemn words, "Receive thou the Holy Ghost, now committed unto them, by the imposition of our hands." And yet, O that I had no reason to speak it, many that use our forms, and many who have witnessed this good confession, yet dare to both talk and preach against the necessity of receiving the Holy Ghost now; and not only so, but cry out against those, who do insist upon it, as madmen, enthusiasts, schismatics, and underminers of the established constitution.

But you are the schismatics, you are the bane of the church of England, who are always crying out, "the temple of the Lord, the temple of the Lord;" and yet starve the people out of our communion, by feeding them only with the dry husks of dead morality, and not bringing out to them the fatted calf; I mean, the doctrines of the operations of the blessed Spirit of God. But here is the misfortune; many of us are not led by, and therefore no wonder that we cannot talk feelingly of, the Holy Ghost; we subscribe to our articles, and make them serve for a key to get into church-preferment, and then preach contrary to those very articles to which we have subscribed. Far be it from me, to charge all the clergy with this hateful hypocrisy; no, blessed be God, there are some left among us, who dare maintain the doctrines of the Reformation, and preach the truth as it is in Jesus. But I speak the truth in Christ, I lie not; the generality of the clergy are fallen from our articles, and do not speak agreeable to them, or to the form of sound words delivered in the Scriptures; woe be unto such blind leaders of the blind! How can you escape the damnation of hell? It is not all your learning (falsely so called) it is not all your preferments can keep you from the just judgment of God. Yet a little while, and we shall all appear before the tribunal of Christ; there, there will I meet you; there Jesus Christ, the great Shepherd and Bishop of souls, shall determine who are the false prophets; who are the wolves in sheep's clothing. Those who say, that we must now receive and feel the Holy Ghost, or those who exclaim against it, as the doctrine of devils.

But I can no more; it is an unpleasing talk to censure any order of men, especially those who are in the ministry; nor would any thing excuse it but necessity: that necessity which extorted from our Lord himself so many woes against the Scribes and Pharisees, the letter-learned rulers and teachers of the Jewish church; and surely, if I could bear to see people perish for lack of knowledge, and yet be silent towards those who keep from them the key of true knowledge, the very stones would cry out.

Would we restore the church to its primitive dignity, the only way is to live and preach the doctrine of Christ, and the articles to which we have subscribed; then we shall find the number of dissenters will daily decrease, and the church of England become the joy of the whole earth.

I am, in the THIRD place, to show the reasonableness of this doctrine.

I say, the reasonableness of this doctrine; for however it may seem foolishness to the natural man, yet to those, who have tasted of the good word of life, and have felt the power of the world to come, it will appear to be founded on the highest reason; and is capable, to those who have eyes to see, even of a demonstration; I say of demonstration: for it stands on this self-evident truth, that we are fallen creatures, or, to use the scripture-expression, "have all died in Adam." I know indeed, it is now no uncommon thing amongst us, to deny the doctrine of original sin, as well as the divinity of Jesus Christ; but it is incumbent on those who deny it, first to disprove the authority of the holy Scriptures; if thou canst prove, thou unbeliever, that the book, which we call The Bible, odes not contain the lively oracles of God; if thou canst show, that holy men of old, did not write this book, as they were inwardly moved by the Holy Ghost, then will we give up the doctrine of original sin; but unless thou canst do this, we must insist upon it, that we are all conceived and born in sin; if for no other, yet for this one reason, because that God, who cannot lie, has told us so.

But what has light to do with darkness, or polite infidels with the Bible? Alas! as they are strangers to the power, so they are generally as great strangers to the word of God. And therefore, if we will preach to them, we must preach to and from the heart: for talking in the language of scripture, to them, is but like talking in an unknown tongue. Tell me then, O man, whosoever thou art, that deniest the doctrine of original sin, if thy conscience be not seared as with a hot iron! Tell me, if thou dost not find thyself, by nature, to be a mostly mixture of brute and devil? I know these terms will stir up the whole Pharisee in thy heart; but let not Satan hurry thee hence; stop a little, and let us reason together; dost thou not find, that by nature thou art prone to pride? Otherwise, wherefore art thou now offended? Again, dost not thou find in thyself the seeds of malice, revenge, and all uncharitableness? And what are these but the very tempers of the devil? Again, do we not all by nature follow, and suffer ourselves to be led by our natural appetites, always looking downwards, never looking upwards to that God, in whom we live, move, and have our being? And what is this but the very nature of the beasts that perish? Out of thy own heart, therefore, will I oblige thee to confess, what an inspired apostle has long since told us, that "the whole world (by nature) lies in the wicked one;" we are no better than those whom St. Jude calls "brute beasts;" for we have tempers in us all by nature, that prove to a demonstration, that we are earthly, sensual, devilish.

And this will serve as another argument, to prove the reality of the operations of the blessed Spirit on the hearts of believers, against those false professors, who deny there is any such thing as influences of the Holy Spirit, that may be felt. For if they will grant that the devil worketh, and so as to be felt in the hearts of the children of disobedience (which they must grant, unless they will give an apostle the lie) where is the wonder that the good

Spirit should have the same power over those who are truly obedient to the faith of Jesus Christ?

If it be true then; that we are all by nature, since the fall, a mixture of brute an devil, it is evident, that we all must receive the Holy Ghost, ere we can dwell with and enjoy God.

When you read, how the prodigal, in the gospel, was reduced to so low a condition, as to eat husks with swine, and how Nebachadnezzar was turned out, to graze with oxen; I am confident, you pity their unhappy state. And when you hear, how Jesus Christ will say, at the last day, to all that are not born again of God, "Depart from me, ye cursed, into everlasting fire, prepared for the devil and his angels," do not your hearts shrink within you, with a secret horror? And if creatures, with only our degree of goodness, cannot bear even the thoughts of dwelling with beasts or devils, to whose nature we are so nearly allied, how do we imagine God, who is infinite goodness, and purity itself, can dwell with us, while we are partakers of both their natures? We might as well think to reconcile heaven and hell.

When Adam had eaten the forbidden fruit, he fled and hid himself from God; why? Because he was naked; he was alienated from the life of God, the due punishment of his disobedience. Now, we are all by nature naked and void of God, as he was at that time, and consequently, until we are changed, renewed, and clothed with a divine nature again, we must fly from God also.

Hence then appears the reasonableness of our being obliged to receive the Spirit of God. It is founded on the doctrine of original sin: and, therefore, you will always find, that those who talk against feeling the operations of the Holy Ghost, very rarely, or slightly at least, mention our fall in Adam; no, they refer St. Paul's account of the depravity of unbelievers, only to those of old time. Whereas it is obvious, on the contrary, that we are all equally included under the guilt and consequences of our first parent's sin, even as others; and to use the language of our own church-article, "bring into the world with us, a corruption, which renders us liable to God's wrath, and eternal damnation." Should I preach to you any other doctrine, I should wrong my own soul; I should be found a false witness towards God and you; and he that preaches any other doctrine, howsoever dignified and distinguished, shall bear his punishment, whosoever he be.

From this plain reason then appears the necessity why we, as well as the first apostles, in this sense, must receive the Spirit of God.

For the great work of sanctification, or making us holy, is particularly reserved to the Holy Ghost; therefore, our Lord says, "Unless a man be born of the Spirit, he cannot enter into the kingdom of God." Jesus Christ came down to save us, not only from the guilt, but also from the power of sin: and however often we have repeated our creed, and told God we believe in the Holy Ghost, yet, if we have not believed in him, so as to be really united to Jesus Christ by him, we have no more concord with Jesus Christ than Belial himself.

And now, my brethren, what shall I say more? Tell me, are not many of you offended at what has been said already? Do not some of you think, though I mean well, yet I have carried the point a little too far? Are not others ready to cry out, if this be true, who then can be saved? Is not this driving people into despair?

Yes, I ingenuously confess it is; but into what despair? A despair of mercy through Christ? No, God forbid; but a despair of living with God without receiving the Holy Ghost. And I would to God, that not only all you that hear me this day, but that the whole world was filled with this despair. Believe me, I have been doing no more than you allow your bodily physicians to do every day: if you have a wound, and are in earnest about a cure, you bid the surgeon probe it to the very bottom; and shall not the physician of your souls be allowed the same freedom? What have I been doing but searching your natural wounds, that I might convince you of your danger, and put you upon applying to Jesus Christ for a remedy? Indeed I have dealt with you as gently as I could; and now I have wounded, I will attempt to heal you. For I was in the LAST place, to exhort you all to come to Jesus Christ by faith, whereby you, even you also, shall receive the Holy Ghost. "For this spake he of the Spirit, which they that believe on him should receive." This, this is what I long to come to. Hitherto I have been preaching only the law; but behold I bring you glad tidings of great joy. If I have wounded you, be not afraid; behold, I now bring a remedy for all your wounds. Notwithstanding you are sunk into the nature of the beast and devil, yet, if you truly believe on Jesus Christ, you shall receive the quickening Spirit promised in the text, and be restored to the glorious liberties of the sons of God; I say, if you believe on Jesus Christ. "For by faith we are saved; it is not of works, lest any one should boast." And, however some men may say, there is a fitness required in the creature, and that we must have a righteousness of our own, before we can lay hold on the righteousness of Christ; yet , if we believe the scripture, salvation is the free gift of God, in Christ Jesus our Lord; and whosoever believeth on him with his whole heart, though his soul be as black as hell itself, shall receive the gift of the Holy Ghost. Behold then, I stand up, and cry out in this great day of the feast, let every one that thirsteth come unto Jesus Christ and drink. "He that believeth on him, out of his belly shall flow (not only streams of rivulets, but whole) rivers of living water." This I speak of the Spirit, which they that believe on Jesus shall certainly receive. For Jesus Christ is the same yesterday, today, and for ever; he is the way, the truth, the resurrection, and the life; "whosoever believeth on him, though he were dead, yet shall he live." There is no respect of persons with Jesus Christ; high and low, rich and poor, one with another, may come to him with an humble confidence, if they draw near by faith; from him we may all receive grace upon grace; for Jesus Christ is full of grace and truth, and ready to save to the uttermost, all that by a true faith turn unto him. Indeed, the poor generally receive the gospel, and "God has chosen the poor in this world, rich in faith." But though not may mighty, not many noble are called; and though it be easier for a camel to go through the eye of a needle, than for a rich man to enter into the kingdom of God, yet, even to you that are rich, do I now freely offer salvation, by Jesus Christ, if you will renounce yourselves, and come to Jesus Christ as poor sinners; I say, as poor sinners; for the "poor in spirit" are only so blessed, as to have a right to the kingdom of God. And Jesus Christ calls none to him, but those who thirst after his righteousness, and feel themselves weary, and heavy laden with the burden of their sins. Jesus Christ justifies the ungodly; he came not to call the righteous, but sinners to repentance.

Do not then say you are unworthy, for this is a faithful and true saying, and worthy of all men to be received, "that Jesus Christ came into the world to save sinners;" and if you are the chief of sinners, if you feel yourselves such, verily Jesus Christ came into the world chiefly to save you. When Joseph was called out of the prison-house to Pharaoh's court, we are told, that he stayed some time to prepare himself; but do you come with all your prison clothes about you; come poor, and miserable, and blind, and naked, as you are, and God the Father shall receive you with open arms, as was the returning prodigal. He shall cover you nakedness with the best robe of his dear Son's righteousness, shall seal you with the signet of his Spirit, and feed you with the fatted calf, even with the comforts of the Holy Ghost. O, let there then be joy in heaven over some of you, as believing; let me not go back to my Master, and say, Lord, they will not believe my report. Harden no longer your hearts, but open them wide, and let the King of glory enter in; believe me, I am willing to go to prison or death for you; but I am not willing to go to heaven without you.

The love of Jesus Christ constrains me to lift up my voice like a trumpet.

My heart is not fill; out of the abundance of the love which I have for your precious and immortal souls, my mouth now speaketh; and I could now not only continue my discourse until midnight, but I could speak until I could speak no more. And why should I despair of any? No, I can despair of no one, when I consider Jesus Christ has had mercy on such a wretch as I am;

but the free grace of Christ prevented me; he saw me in my blood, he passed by me, and said unto me, Live; and the same grace which we sufficient for me, is sufficient for you also; behold, the same blessed Spirit is ready to breathe on all your dry bones, if you will believe on Jesus Christ, whom God has sent; indeed, you can never believe on, or serve a better master, one that is more mighty, or more willing to save; I can say, the Lord Christ is gracious, his yoke is easy, his burden exceeding light; after you have served him many years, like the servants under the law, was he willing to discharge you, you would say, we love our Master, and will not go from him. Come then, my guilty brethren, come and believe on the Lord that bought you with his precious blood; look up by faith, and see him whom you have pierced; behold him bleeding, panting, dying! Behold him with arms stretched out ready to receive you all; cry unto him as the penitent thief did, Lord, remember us now thou art in thy kingdom, and he shall say to your souls, shortly shall you be with me in paradise. For those whom Christ justified, them he also glorifies, even with that glory which he enjoyed with the Father, before the world began. Do not say, I have bought a piece of ground, and must needs go see it; or I have bought a yoke of oxen, and must needs go prove them; or I have married a wife, I am engaged in an eager pursuit after the lust of the eye, and the pride of life, that therefore cannot come. Do not fear having your name cast out as evil, or being accounted a fool for Christ's sake; yet a little while, and you shall shine like the stars in the firmament for ever. Only believe, and Jesus Christ shall be to you wisdom, righteousness, sanctification, and eternal redemption; your bodies shall be fashioned like unto his glorious body, and your souls be partakers of all the fullness of God.

Which God of his infinite mercy.

Sermon 39 The Resurrection of Lazarus

John 11:43-44, "And when he thus had spoken, he cried with a loud voice, Lazarus, come forth. And he that was dead came forth, bound hand and foot with grave clothes: and his face was bound about with a napkin. Jesus saith unto them, Loose him, and let him go."

When Jesus Christ, the eternal Word, was pleased to make all things by the word of his power, his last works were the best. When he looked back upon, and beheld the first products of his almighty power, he pronounced them "good;" but when that last, that lovely creature man, was formed, he pronounced them "very good." So, the same Jesus, when he came to tabernacle among us, and to begin and carry on a new and second creation, though all his works were miracles of wonder, and manifested forth the glory of his eternal Godhead, yet the nearer he came to the end of his public ministrations, the greater and more noble did the miracles which he wrought appear. The resurrection of Lazarus, that is to be the subject of the following discourse, I think, is a sufficient proof of this. To an eye of sense, it seems to be one of the greatest, if not the very greatest miracle of all which our blessed Lord performed. When our Savior bid John's disciple go and tell their Maser what things they had seen and heard, he commands them to inform him, that by his divine power "the dead were raised;" alluding no doubt to the Ruler's daughter, who was raised immediately after her decease; and the Widow's son, who at the command of Jesus, rose out of his coffin, as they were carrying his corpse to the burial. These were pregnant proofs, that Jesus was indeed the Messiah that was to come into the world. But his raising of Lazarus from the dead, after he had lain four days dead, and saw corruption, is still, if possible, a greater miracle; and consequently a stronger proof of his being the Anointed, the Christ of God. The evangelist John is very particular in giving us an account of this miracle; even so particular, as to spend a whole chapter in relating the circumstances which preceded, attended, and followed after it. And as he was undoubtedly directed herein by the all- wise, unerring Spirit of God, does it not point out unto us, that this miracle, with all its respective circumstances, calls for our particular and most serious meditation? It appears to me in this light; and therefore, as the Lord shall be pleased to assist, I shall go back to the beginning of this chapter, follow the evangelist step by step, and consider the particulars of this wondrous miracle, make some practical observations as I go along, and conclude with some suitable instructions and exhortations, which will naturally arise from the body of the discourse.

The evangelist in the first verse, makes mention of the sickness of Lazarus. "Now, a certain man was sick, named Lazarus of Bethany, the town of Mary, and her sister Martha." Some think these sisters were very wealthy, so as to own good part of the town, or, as the original word seems to imply, the village. But then it is probably the evangelist would have said the town of Lazarus, estates usually descending, as with us, in the male line: it means therefore no more, than that Martha and Mary lived in Bethany. The Holy Ghost pointing out to us hereby, that nothing makes a town so worthy of a gracious soul's remark of esteem, as its having many of God's dear children for its inhabitants. Bethany, though a little place, is more famous because it was the town of Martha and Mary, than if Alexander had fought in it one of his greatest battles. Both these women loved Jesus in sincerity, and were as good as they were great. But Mary, though the younger sister, seems to be the most eminent: for the evangelist in the second verse, speaks of her in a very distinguishing manner. "It was that Mary (that never-to-be-forgotten Mary) which anointed the Lord with ointment (expensive as it was) and wiped his feed, (after she had washed them with tears of love with her hair," even the hair of her head. What notice is taken of this action! With what an eulogy, and in what a high strain of commendation is it here spoken of? And such are the honors of all God's saints. Though all our good works are not recorded as Mary's are, yet God is not unmindful, that he should forget our works of faith, and labors which have proceeded of love. Every tear we shed, every sigh we fetch, every alms we give, though it be only a cup of cold water, are all recorded in the Lamb's book of remembrance, and shall be produced to our eternal honor, and rewarded with a reward of grace, though not of debt, at the great and terrible day of the Lord. "I was an hungered, and ye gave me meat, I was thirsty, and ye gave me drink, naked, and ye clothed me, sick and in prison, and ye came unto me." What reason have we then to be "steadfast and unmovable, always abounding in the work of the Lord, forasmuch as we are assured, that our labors will not be in vain or forgotten by the Lord!" It was that Mary that anointed the Lord with ointment, and wiped his feet with her hair. And what follows? "Whose brother Lazarus was sick." So that being related to Christ, or his disciples, will not exempt persons from sickness. In this life, time and chance happens to all, only with this material difference, those afflictions which harden the obstinately impenitent, soften and purify the heart of a true believer. "My son, therefore despise not the chastening of the Lord (on one hand), nor faint when thou art rebuked of him (on the other): for whom the Lord loveth he chasteneth, and scourgeth every son whom he receiveth." Jesus loved Lazarus, and yet Lazarus was sick. And what do his sisters do for him now he is sick? No doubt they applied to a physician, for it is tempting God to neglect making use of means for the recovery of our health, when it is impaired. But then they were not guilty of Asa's crime, "who sought to the physicians, but not to the Lord." No; they knew the most skillful prescriptions would be of no effect, unless attended with a blessing from Jesus the Great and Almighty Physician; and therefore his sisters sent unto him, probably at the beginning of their brother's illness. How unlike is their conduct, to that of the generality of people, especially the rich and great! How unfashionable is it not-a-days for persons to send to Jesus in behalf of their sick relations! It is so very uncustomary, that in some places, if a minister be sent for to a sick person, it is a sad symptom that the patient is almost past hopes of recovery. Thus did not Martha and her sister Mary; they sent unto Jesus, though he was now beyond Jordan, (chap. 10:40) where he abode, or chiefly resided, for some time. Hence it was that they knew where to send to him.

But what kind of message did they send? A very humble and suitable one.

"Lord, Behold, he whom thou lovest is sick." They might have said, Lord, he who loveth thee is sick. But they knew, that our love was not worth mentioning, and that we love Jesus only because he first loved us. Besides, here is no prescribing to our Lord what he should do, or what means he should use of. They do not so much as say, We pray thee to come, or only speak the word, and our sick brother shall be restored. They simply tell Jesus the case, knowing it was sufficient barely to lay it before an infinitely compassionate Redeemer, and leave it to him to act according to his own sovereign good-will and pleasure. "Lord, Behold he whom thou lovest is sick." Oh how sweet is it when the soul is brought to this! And with what a holy confidence may we pray to, and intercede with the holy Jesus, when we have reason to hope, that those we pray and intercede for, are lovers of, and are beloved of him! For his eyes are in a peculiar manner over the righteous, and his ears always open to their prayers. This was their message, and it soon reached Jesus Christ. And how does he receive it? We are told, verse 4, "When Jesus heard that, (that he whom he loved was sick) He said, this sickness is not unto death, but unto the glory of God, that the Son of God may be glorified thereby." To whom these words were spoken is not certain. In all probability, Jesus spake them to the persons that delivered Martha's and Mary's message. And if so, it was no doubt a comfortable answer for the present, though it must afterwards puzzle them as well as the disciples how to explain it, when they found that Lazarus was actually dead. "This sickness is not unto death," not unto an abiding death, because he intended to raise him again, soon after his decease. It is like that expression of our Lord in St. Mark, "The damsel is not dead, but sleepeth;" which must not be understood in a literal, but metaphorical sense. And this and such-like instances, ought to teach us to weigh carefully our blessed Lord's words, and to wait for an explication of them, by subsequent providences; otherwise we shall be in danger of misapplying them, and thereby bring our souls into unspeakable bondage.

"This sickness is not unto death, but unto the glory of God, that the Son of God may be glorified thereby." This is the end both of the afflictions and the deaths of God's people. By all that happens to them he will be glorified one way or another, and cause every thing to work together for their good. And who then but would be content to be sick, or willing to submit to death itself, if so be the Son of God may be glorified thereby?

This answer, no doubt, proceeded from love. For we are told, Verse 5 that "Jesus loved Martha and her sister, and Lazarus." Oh happy family! Three in it beloved of Jesus, with a peculiar, everlasting love. "Very often it so happens, (to use the words of the pious Bishop Beveridge) that there "is but one in a city, and two in a country of this stamp." But here are two sisters and a brother, all lovers of, and beloved by the glorious Jesus. What shall we say to these things? Why, that our savior's grace is free and sovereign, and he may do what he will with his own. They who are thus so highly favored as to have so many converted in one house, ought to be doubly thankful! Such a blessing have not all his saints. No; many, very many, go mourning over their perverse and graceless relations all their lives long; and find, even to their dying day, that their greatest foes are those of their own household. Surely these three relations lived a heaven upon earth. For what can they want, what could make them miserable, who are assured of Jesus' love? But surely if Jesus loves this dear little family, the next news one might think we should hear, would be, that he went immediately and healed Lazarus; or at least cured him at a distance. But instead of that, we are told, verse 6 "When he had heard that he was sick, he abode two days still in the same place where he was." A strange way this, in the eye of natural reason, of expressing love; but not so strange in the eye of faith: for the Lord Jesus very often showeth his love, by deferring to give immediate answers to our prayers.

Hereby he tries our faith and patience, and exercises all our passive graces. We have a proof of this in the Syrophonecian woman, upon whom the blessed Jesus frowned, and spake roughly to at first, only that he might afterwards turn unto her and say, "O woman, great is thy faith." Let not those then who believe, make too much haste; or immediately in their hearts repine against the Lord, because he may not answer their requests, in their own time and way. God's time and way is best. And we shall find it to be so in the end. Martha and Mary experienced the truth of this, though undoubtedly our Lord's seeming delay, to come and heal their brother, cost them great searchings of heart. But will the Lord Jesus forget his dear Lazarus, whom his soul loveth? "Can a woman forget her sucking child?" Indeed she may; but the

Lord never faileth those that fear him. Neither is he slack concerning his promise, as some men count slackness: for his very delays are answers. The vision is for an appointed time; in the end it will speak and not lie.

Though our Lord abode two days where he was, to try the faith of these sisters, yet after this, he said unto his disciples, verse 7, "Let us go into Judea again." With what a holy familiarity does Jesus converse with his dear children! Our Savior seems to speak to his disciples, as though he was only their brother, and as it were upon a level with them; "Let us go into Judea again." How gently, according to what was predicted of him, does he lead those that are with young! Jesus very well knew the weakness of his disciples, and also what a dangerous place Judea was: how gradually therefore does he make known unto them, his design of going thither! And how does he admit his disciples to expostulate with him on this account!

"Master, say they, the Jews of late sought to stone thee, and goest thou thither again?" They were amazed at our Lord's boldness, and were ready to call it presumption; as we generally are prone to censure and condemn other zealous and enterprising persons, as carrying matters too far; it may be for no other reason, if we examine the bottom of our hearts, but because they go before, and excel ourselves. The disciples, no doubt, thought that they spoke out of love to their Lord, and assuredly they did; but what a deal of self-love was there mixed and blended with it? They seem much concerned for their Master, but they were more concerned for themselves.

However Jesus overlooks their weakness, and mildly replies, verse 9 and 10, "Are there not twelve hours in the day? If any man walk in the day, he stumbleth not, because he seeth the light of the world; but if any man walk in the night, he stumbleth, because there is no light in him." As though our Lord had said, My dear disciples, I thank you for your care and concern for me. Judea is a dangerous place, and what you say of the treatment I met with from its inhabitants, is just and true: but be not afraid of going there upon my account. For as a man walketh safely twelve hours of the day, because he walketh in the light: so as long as the time appointed by my Father for my public administration lasts, I shall be as secure from the hands of my enemies, as a man that walks in broad-day is secure from falling. But as a man stumbleth if he walketh in the night, so when the night of my passion cometh, then, but not till then, shall I be given up into the hands of my spiteful foes. Oh what comfort have these words, by the blessing of God, frequently brought to my soul! How may all Christ's ministers strengthen themselves with this consideration, that so long as God hath work for them to do, they are immortal! And if after our work is over, our Lord should call us to lay down our lives for the brethren, and to seal the truth of our doctrine with our blood, it would certainly be the highest honor that can be put upon us. "To you it is given not only to believe, but also to suffer," says the apostle to the Philippians.

"These things (the evangelist tells us, ver. 11) said Jesus, and after that, (to satisfy them that he was not going into Judea without a proper call) he saith unto them, Our friend Lazarus sleepeth." Our friend.

Amazing! For what is a friend? As one's own soul. How dear then, and near are true believers to the most adorable Jesus! "Our friend LAZARUS." Still more amazing! Here is condescension, here is unparalleled familiarity indeed. And what of him? "He sleepeth." A figurative way of expression. For what is death to the lovers of Jesus Christ, but a sleep, and a refreshing one too? Thus it is said of Stephan when he died, that "he fell asleep." Christ indeed died, but believers only sleep. And "those that sleep in Jesus, (says the scripture) will God bring with him." "Our friend Lazarus sleepeth." For though he be dead, I shall raise him from the grave so soon, that his dying will be only like a person's taking a short sleep. "Our friend Lazarus sleepeth, but I go that I may awake him out of sleep." By this time, one would imagine, our Lord's disciples should have understood him: But how unwilling are we to believe anything that we do not like.

"Then said his disciples, Lord, if he sleep he shall do well." Oh fearful, and slow of heart to believe! How fain would they excuse themselves from going into Judea, for fear of a few stones! By this way of talking, how do they in effect impeach their blessed Master's conduct, and under a pretense of preserving his person, foster, and as it were plead for their own (though perhaps undiscerned) cowardice and unbelief? That charity, which hopeth and believeth all things for the best, teacheth us to judge thus favorably of them. For, "Howbeit Jesus spake of his death: they thought that he had spoken of taking rest in sleep." The great and compassionate High priest knowing and remembering they were but dust, throws a veil of love over their infirmity; and at length, verse 14, "Saith unto them plainly (for if we wait on Jesus, we shall know his will plainly, one way or another) Lazarus id dead." And even then, lest they should be swallowed up with overmuch sorrow, he immediately adds, verse 15, "And I am glad for your sakes that I was not there, to the intent ye may believe," or have more faith, or have that faith which you already possess increased and confirmed. A plain proof this, that all Jesus' delays to answer prayer, are only to strengthen our faith.

"Nevertheless, says our Lord, let us go unto him." This was a sufficient hint, if they knew how to improve it, that he intended to do something extraordinary, though he would not tell them directly what he intended. For the Lord Jesus will keep those whom he loves, at his foot, and dependent on him. "Let us go unto him." He still speaks as though they were his equals. Oh that Christians in general, Oh that ministers in particular, would learn of him their great exemplar, to condescend to men of low degree! Well, the secret is now out. Jesus has said unto them plainly, Lazarus is dead. And what reception does this melancholy news meet with? With great condolence, especially from Thomas; for verse 16, "Then said Thomas, who is called Didymus, unto his fellow disciples, let us also go and die with him;" i.e. according to some, with Lazarus, with whom, it may be Thomas had contracted an intimate acquaintance. But granting it was so; shall I commend him for this passionate expression? I commend him not.

Surely he spake unadvisedly with his lips; "Let us also go and die with him." As though there was no comfort henceforward to be expected in the world, now his friend Lazarus was gone. This was a great fault, and yet a fault that many of God's children run into daily, by mourning for their deceased relations over-much, like persons that have no hope. But this infirmity ought not to be indulged. For if our friends and dear relatives are dead, Jesus, that friend of sinners, is not dead. He will be better to us than seven sons, and will abundantly supply the place of all creature- comforts. But I am more inclined to think that the word HIM, refers to Jesus his dear Master; and if so, he is so far from being blamed, that he spake like a good soldier of Jesus Christ. Let us also go, that we may die with him. If our dear master will go into Judea, and hazard his precious life, let us not any longer make such frivolous excuses, but let us manfully accompany him; and if the Jews should not only be permitted to stone, but also to kill him, let us also go and die with him, we cannot die in a better cause. This was a speech worthy of a Christian hero, and Thomas herein hath set us an example, that we should follow his steps, by exciting and provoking one another closely to adhere to the blessed Jesus, especially when his cause and interest is in any immediate danger. This exhortation, it seems, had a proper effect. They all went, and as far as we know, cheerfully accompanied their glorious Master.

How their thoughts were exercised on the road, we are not told. But I am apt to believe they were a little discouraged when they came to Bethany.

For "When Jesus came, he found that Lazarus had been in the grave for four days already." And what would it avail them, to come so many miles only to see a dead man's tomb? But how wisely were all things ordered by the blessed Jesus, to manifest his glory in the most extraordinary manner, that not only his disciples might have their faiths confirmed, but many also of the Jews might believe on him. This Bethany, it seems, verse 18, "was nigh unto Jerusalem, about fifteen furlongs off;" or about two miles; and Martha and Mary, being what we may call people of fashion, and devout likewise; many of the devout, and we may suppose many of the wealthy Jews came from the metropolis, as well as other adjacent places, verse 19, to Martha and Mary;

not to pay an idle, trifling, but a serious, profitable visit, "to comfort them concerning their brother." This was kind and neighborly. To weep with those that weep, and to visit the afflicted in their distresses, is one essential branch of true and undefiled religion. And O how sweet is it when we visit surviving friends, that we have reason to think that their departed relations died in the Lord! And we can therefore give them comfort concerning them. For "blessed are the dead, that die in the Lord, even so saith the Spirit, for they rest from their labors." This and such-like arguments, no doubt, these visitors made use of, to comfort Martha and Mary. And indeed they stood in much need of consolation. For we have reason to suppose, from our Lord" answer, "This sickness is not unto death, but the glory of God;" that they had entertained thoughts of the recovery of their brother. But who can tell what these two holy souls must feel, when they found their brother did not recover, but was dead, laid out, and now stinking in the silent grave! What hard thoughts, without judging them, may we suppose they entertained concerning Jesus! Think you not that they were ready to cry out in the language of the prophet, "Thou hast deceived us, and we are deceived?" But man's extremity is Jesus' opportunity. In the multitude of the sorrows that they had in their hearts, the news of Christ's coming refreshes their souls. Somebody or another, commendably officious, privately informs Martha of it.

"Who, as soon as she heart that Jesus was come (without making any apology to the company for her rudeness) went and met him. But Mary sat still in the house." But why so, Mary? I thought thou hadst been most forward to attend on Jesus, and thy sister Martha more prone to be cumbered about the many things of this life. Why sittest thou still? It may be the news was brought only privately to Martha (for it is plain from verse 31st, that the Jews who were in the house knew not of it;) and Martha knowing how our Lord had chid her once, was resolved he should have no reason on the same account to chide her anymore; therefore when the news was brought, she would not so much as stay to inform her sister, but went out to see whether it were true or not, and if so, as the eldest sister, she would invite the blessed Jesus in. How happy is it, when Christ's reproofs for past neglects, excite our future zeal to come out and meet him! Such reproofs are an excellent oil. Or, it may be, the news reached Mary's ears, as well as Martha's, but being overcome with sorrow, the thought is too good news to be true, and therefore sat still in the house. O how careful ought believers to be, to cherish and maintain, even in the midst of tribulation, a holy confidence and joy in God! For the joy of the Lord is a believer's strength. Whereas giving way to melancholy and unbelief, raises gloom and vapors in the mind, clouds the understanding, clogs us in the way of duty, and gives the enemy, who loves to fish in troubled waters, a very great advantage over us.

Mary, perhaps, through the prevalence of this, and being also naturally of a sedentary disposition, "sat still in the house," while her sister

Martha got the start of her, and went out to meet Jesus. And how does she accost him? Why, in a language bespeaking the distress of a burdened and disordered mind. For she said unto Jesus, verse 21, "Lord, if thou hadst been here, my brother had not died." Here is a mixture of faith and unbelief. Faith made her say, "Lord, if thou hadst been here, my brother had not died." But unbelief made her confine Christ's power to his bodily presence. Besides, here was a tacit accusation of the blessed Jesus of unkindness, for not coming when they sent unto him the message, "Lord, he whom thou lovest is sick." Once she charged Jesus with want of care; "Lord, carest thou not, that my sister hath left me to serve alone?" Now she taxes him with want of kindness. "If thou hadst been here;" as much as to say, if thou hadst been so kind as to have come when we sent for thee," "my brother had not died;" and by saying thus, she does as it were lay her brother's death to Jesus Christ. O how apt are even those whom Jesus loves in a peculiar manner, to charge him foolishly! How often does the enmity of our desperately wicked hearts rise against Christ, when we are under the afflicting hand of his providence! And not the very best of us frequently tempted, in such circumstances, to say within ourselves at least, Why does God thus cruelly deal with us? Why did not he keep off this stroke, seeing it was in his power to have prevented it? How should we be ashamed and confounded before him upon this account? How should we pray and labor to be delivered from this remaining enmity of the heart, and long for that time, when mortality shall be swallowed up of life, and we shall never feel one single rising of heart, against a good and gracious, and all-wise and glorious Redeemer, any more? However, to do Martha justice, she pretty well recovers herself, verse 22, "But I know, that even now, whatsoever thou wilt ask of God, God will give it to thee." Whether these words imply an actual belief of our Lord's divinity, is not certain. To me they do; because we shall presently find, that she did believe our Lord was the Son of God, and the Messiah which was to come into the world. Therefore when she said, she knew that whatsoever he asked of God, God would give it to him, she may be understood as referring to God the Father, under whom the Lord Jesus acted as Mediator, though equal to him in respect to his eternal glory and godhead. This mystery we may well suppose her acquainted with, because Jesus had been frequently preaching at her house, and consequently, had opened that mystery unto her. O what a blessed thing must it be to have such a Mediator! Such an high-priest and intercessor at the Father's right-hand, that whatever he asks the father in our behalf, he will give unto us!

Jesus takes this kindly at Martha's hand, and passes over her infirmity.

For if the Lord was exact to mark every thing that we say or do amiss, alas! who could abide? He only calmly says unto her, verse 23, "Thy brother shall rise again." Glad tidings these of great joy. This should comfort us concerning our deceased, pious relations, that ere long they shall rise again, and soul and body be for ever with the Lord. Howbeit Jesus spake here of an immediate resurrection, though he did not speak plainly: For Christ loves to exercise the faith and patience of his disciples, and frequently leaves them to find out his meaning by degrees. It is best for us in our present state, that it should be so. In heaven it will be otherwise. "Thy brother, (says Christ to Martha) shall rise again." She might immediately have replied, When, Lord? But she fetches a circuit as it were, and labors to find out the mind of Jesus by degree. "I know, says she, that he shall rise again at the resurrection of the last day." These words seem to imply, that she had some distant thought of our Lord's design to raise her brother now, and that she spoke thus only to draw our Savior to speak, and tell her plainly whether he meant to do so or not. Those who are acquainted with Jesus, are taught an holy art by the blessed Spirit, in dealing with their blessed master. "I know, says she, he shall rise again at the resurrection of the last day," (a notable proof this, by the way, that the pious Jews believed the resurrection of the body). It is just the same as though she had said, Lord, dost thou mean that my brother shall rise again before that time? Our savior wisely keeps off from giving her a direct answer, but chooses rather to preach to her heart. "Jesus said unto her, I am the resurrection and the life: He that believeth in me, though he were dead, yet shall he live." On this Martha's faith, if in exercise, might take hold. O glorious words! How encouraging to you poor sinners lying in your blood! Though you are dead in trespasses and sins, and might justly be condemned to die the second death, yet if you believe on the Lord Jesus you shall live. He adds, "And whosoever believeth in me shall never die;" never die as to their souls, never die eternally, and consequently never finally fall away from God. This is an encouraging soul-comforting declaration for you, O believers, who are thus kept, as it were, in a garrison, by the mighty power of God, through faith, unto salvation! "Believest thou this?" says Christ to Martha, verse 26. What avail all the many great and precious promises of the gospel, unless they are applied and brought home in particular to each of our souls? The word does not profit unless it is mixed with faith. We therefore do well, when we are reading Christ's words, to put this question to ourselves; O my soul, believest thou this? And well would it be for us, if upon putting this question to ourselves, we could with the same holy confidence, and in the same delightful frame, say with Martha, verse 27, "Yea, Lord: I believe that thou art the Christ, the Son of God, which should come into the world." This I think is a direct confession of our Lord's divinity. How full was her heart when she spoke these words! I am persuaded it burnt within her. What a divine warmth had she contracted by talking with Jesus! How does she long that her sister might share in her holy joy! For when she had so said, verse 28, "she went away;" full of love, no doubt, and called Mary her sister, as all will labor to call their near relations, who have felt the Lord Jesus to be the resurrection and the life themselves. But Martha took care, in the midst of her zeal (as we should always do) to behave with prudence; and therefore "she called her sister secretly, saying, The master is come, and calleth for thee." The master is come. She need say no more; Mary knew very well whom she meant. For holy souls easily understand one another when talking of their master Jesus. The divine Herbert used to delight (when speaking of Jesus) to say, "My Master;" perhaps he learned if of Martha, who said here, "The Master is come, and calleth for thee? Surely a woman of thy exalted piety will not tell a deliberate lie, and in order to induce thy sister to come to Jesus, acquaint her that Jesus called her, when indeed he did not.

Thou needest not put thyself to such an expense, or do so much evil, that good may come of it. Only mention Jesus to Mary, and let her know for a certainty that the Master id indeed come, and I am persuaded she will sit no longer. Martha no doubt knew, and therefore I cannot judge her as some do, as though in her haste she said what was not true. For Jesus might bid her to call her sister, though it be not directly mentioned in this chapter. And it is very probably, that our Lord did inquire after Mary, because she used to take such great delight in sitting at his feet, and hearing the gracious words that proceeded our of his mouth. "The Master is come (saith Martha to her sister) and calleth for thee." And so say I to all poor sinners. Jesus, your Lord and Master, your Prince and Savior, is come, come unto this lower world, and is come this day in his word, and by me, who am less than the least of all his servants, and calleth for you. O that he may also come in the demonstration of the Spirit, and by his mighty power bow your stubborn hearts and wills to obey the call, as holy Mary did.

For we are told, verse 29, "When she heard that, she rose quickly, and came to Jesus." Sinners, when will you do so? Or why do you not do so? How know you whether Jesus will call for you any more, before he calls you by death to judgment? Linger, O linger no longer. Fly, fly for your lives.

Arise quickly, and with Mary come to Jesus. She obeyed the call so very speedily, that her haste was taken notice of by her visitors. "The Jews then, who were with her in the house, and comforted her, when they saw Mary that she rose up hastily (without any ceremony at all) and went out, followed her, saying, she goeth to the grave, to weep there." How wisely does our Lord permit and order all this, to bring the Jews out to behold the wonderful miracle that he was about to perform! Little did Mary and the Jews think for what end they were thus providentially led out. But when Jesus hath work to be done, he will bring souls to the place where he intends to call them, in spite of men or devils. But how does Mary behave when she comes to Jesus? We may be assured, not without great humility. No wonder then we are told, verse 32, that "when she saw him, she immediately fell down at his feet (a place Mary had been used to, and in an agony of grief, says, as her sister had done before her) Lord, if thou hadst been here, my brother had not died." Poor Mary! Her concern was great indeed.

Though she was a holy woman, she could not well bear the loss of her brother. She knew very well, that the world would miss him, and no doubt he had been a kind and tender brother to her. But I am afraid she was sinfully overcome with overmuch sorrow. However, had we been there, the sight must have affected us. It seems to have affected the visitors, especially the blessed Jesus. He, instead of blaming her, for her tacitly accusing him of unkindness, and for not coming to her brother's relief, pities and sympathizes both with Mary and her weeping friends! "When Jesus saw her weep, and the Jews also weeping, he groaned in his Spirit, and was troubled." Troubled: Not with any sinful perturbation we may be assured: nothing of that nature could possibly be in his sinless soul. And, therefore, some have judiciously enough compared the trouble our Lord now felt, to some crystal water shaken in a glass or bottle; you may shake it, but there will be no sediment: it will be crystal water still. "He groaned in is spirit." I do not see why this may not be understood of his praying in the spirit, which maketh intercession for the saints, with "groanings that cannot be uttered" (Rom. 8:26). Methinks I see the immaculate Lamb of God, secretly, but powerfully agonizing with his Father; his heart is big with sympathy! At length, out of the fullness of it, he said, ver. 34, "Where have ye laid him? They (I suppose Mary and Martha) say unto him, Lord, come and see." He came, he say, "He wept," ver.

35. It is put in a verse by itself, that we might pause a while, and ask, why Jesus wept?

He wept, to show us, that is was no sin to shed a tear of love and resignation at the grave of a deceased friend; he wept, so see what havoc sin had made in the world, and how it had reduced man, who was originally little lower than the angels, (by making him subject to death) to a level with the beasts that perish: but above all, he wept at the foresight of the people's unbelief; he wept, to think how many then present, would not only not believe on, but would be hardened, and have their prejudices increased more and more against him, though he should raise Lazarus from the dead before their eyes. Well then may ministers be excused, who, whilst they are preaching, now and then drop a few tears, at the consideration of their sermons being, through the perverseness and unbelief of many of their audience, a savor of death unto death, instead of a savor of life unto life. Upon a like occasion Jesus wept. What an affecting sight was here!

Let us for a while suppose ourselves placed amidst these holy mourners; let us imagine that we see the sepulcher just before us, and the Jews, and Mary, and the blessed Jesus weeping round it. Surely, the most obdurate of us all must drop a tear, or at least be affected with the sight; we find that it affected those who were really by-standers: for then said the Jews, ver. 36, "Behold, how he loved him." And did they say, Behold, how he loved him, when Jesus only shed a few tears over the grave of his departed Lazarus? Come then, O sinners, and view Christ dying and pouring out his precious heart's blood for you upon an accursed tree, and then surely you must needs cry out, Behold, how he loved us!

But alas, though all were affected, yet, it seems, all were not well affected at seeing Jesus weep! For we are told, ver. 37 that some of them said, "Could not this man, who opened the eyes of the blind, have caused that even this man should not have died?" One would imagine, that Satan himself could scarce have uttered a more perverse speech: every word is full of spite and rancor. Could not this man, this fellow, this deceiver, who pretends to say, that he opened the eyes of the blind, have caused that this man, whom he seems to love so, should not have died? Is not this a sufficient proof that he is a cheat? Have we catched him at last? Is it likely that he really helped others, when he could not help his own friend?

-- O how patient ought the servants of our Lord to be! And how may they expect to be censured, and have their good deeds questioned, and lessened, when their blessed Master has been thus treated before them! However, Jesus will do good, notwithstanding all these slights put upon him; and therefore, again groaning in himself, "he cometh to the grave; it was a cave, (or vault, as is customary in great families) and a stone lay upon it; Jesus said, ver. 39, "Take ye away the stone." How gradually does our Lord proceed, in order to engage the people's attention the more! Methinks I see them all eye, all ear, and eagerly waiting to see the issue of this affair. But Martha now returning with the rest of the company, seems to have lost that good frame which she was in when she went to call her sister; "She saith unto him, (ver. 39) Lord, by this time he stinketh: for he hath been either dead or buried for four days." O the dismal effects of carnal reasoning! How naturally do we fall into doubts and fears, when we have not our eye simply directed to the blessed Jesus! Martha, instead of looking up to him, looks down into the grace, and poring upon her brother's stinking corpse, falls into a fit of unbelief: "By this time he stinketh;" and, therefore, a sight of him will only be offensive. Perhaps she might think our Lord only wanted to take a view of her brother Lazarus; Jesus therefore, to give her yet a further hint, that he intended to do something extraordinary, saith unto her, ver. 40, "Said I not unto thee, that if thou wouldst believe, thou shouldst see the glory of God?" Our Lord speaks here with some degree of warmth: for nothing displeases him more than the unbelief of his own disciples. "Said I not unto thee, if thou wouldst believe, thou shouldst see the glory of God?" When Christ first spoke these words unto her, we are not told; it might be, this was part of their conversation upon another occasion some time before: however, he checks her openly for her unbelief now: for those whom Jesus loves, must expect to be rebuked sharply by him, whenever they dishonor him by unbelief. The reproof is taken.

Without making any more objections, "They took away the stone from the place where the dead was laid." And now behold with what solemnity the holy Jesus prepares himself to execute his gracious design! "And Jesus lift up his eyes, and said, Father, I thank thee that thou hast heard me; and I knew that thou hearest me always: but because of the people which stand by, I said it, that they may believe that thou hast sent me." Who can express with what fervor and intenseness of spirit, our glorious High-priest uttered these words! They are a thanksgiving arising from an assurance that his father had heard him: for Christ, as Mediator, was inferior to the Father. "I knew that thou hearest me always (and so may every believer in his degree say so); but because of the people which stand by, I said it." _ Said what? We do not hear that Jesus said any thing by way of prayer before; and that is true, if we mean vocally, but mentally he did say something, even when he groaned in the spirit once and again, and was troubled. There is a way of praying, even when we do not, and cannot speak.

"Why cryest thou," said God to Moses; though we do not hear that he spoke one single word: but he cried in his heart. And I observe this for the comfort of some weak, but real Christians, who think they never pray, unless they can have a great flow of words; but this is a great mistake: for we often pray best, when we can speak least. There are times when the heart is too big to speak: and the spirit itself maketh intercession for the saints, and that too according to the will of God, with groanings that cannot be uttered. Such was Hannah's prayer for a son, "She spake not, only her lips moved:" and such was our Lord's way of praying at this time. And perhaps the soul is never in a better frame, than when in a holy stillness, and unspeakable serenity, it can put itself as a blank in Jesus' hand, for him to stamp on it just what he pleases.

And now the hour of our Savior's performing this long-expected miracle, is come. Ver. 43, "When he thus had spoken, he cried with a loud voice, Lazarus, come forth." With the word there went an irresistible power: he spake, and it was done: he cried, and behold, "He that was dead came forth bound hand and foot with grave clothes; and his face was bound about with a napkin." What sight was here! Methinks I see surprise sit upon each spectator's face: as the body rises, their wonder rises too. See how they gaze! See how their looks bespeak the language of astonished hearts; and all with a kind of silent, but expressive oratory, ready to say, What manner of man is this? Surely this is the Messiah that was to come into the world. How did the hearts of Martha and Mary, as we may very well suppose, leap for joy! How were they ashamed of themselves, for charging Jesus foolishly, and taxing him with unkindness, for not coming to prevent their brother's dying! It is true, Christ suffered him to die, but behold he is not alive again! Jesus never denies us one thing, but he intends to give us something better in the stead of it. Think you not that Martha and Mary were not the most officious to obey our blessed Lord's command, "Loose him, and let him go?" That same power that raised Lazarus from the dead, might have also taken the grave-clothes from him: but Jesus Christ never did, and never will work a needless miracle. Others could unloose his grave-clothes, but Jesus could unloose the bands of death.

And now, perhaps, some may be ready to ask, What news hath Lazarus brought from the other world! But stop, O man, thy vain curiosity! It is forbidden, and therefore useless knowledge. The scriptures are silent concerning it. Why should we desire to be wise above what is written? It becomes us rather to be wholly employed in adoring the gracious hand of that mighty Redeemer who raised him from the dead, and to see (now we have heard the history) what improvement we can make of such a remarkable and instructive transaction.

Would to God that my preaching upon the resurrection of Lazarus today,, may have the same blessed effects upon you, as the sight of it had upon some of the standers-by. For we are told, ver. 45, "Then many of the Jews who came to Mary, and had seen the things which Jesus did, believed on him." A profitable visit this! the best, no doubt, that they ever paid in their lives. And this was in answer to our Savior's prayer, "But because of the people who stand by, I said it, that they may believe, that thou hast sent me." One would imagine, that all who saw this miracle, were induced thereby, really to believe on him: But alas! I could almost say, that I can tell you of a greater miracle than raising Lazarus from the dead. And what is that? Why, that some of these very persons who were on the spot, instead of believing on him, "went their way to the Pharisees, and told them what Jesus had done." Ver. 46. It was so far from convincing them, that it only excited their envy, stirred up the whole hell of their self-righteous hearts, and made them, from that day forward, "take counsel together," to execute what they had long before designed, to put the innocent Jesus to death. See how busy they are, ver 47, "Then gathered the chief priests and the Pharisees a council, and said, What do we? For this man doeth many miracles." Envy itself, it seems, could not deny that. And need they say then, "What do we," or what should we do? Believe in, to be sure, and submit to him; take up the cross, and follow him. No; on the contrary, say they, ver 48, "If we let him this alone, (which they would not have done so long, had not God put a hook in the Leviathan's jaws) all men will believe on him." And suppose they did? Then all men would be blessed indeed, and have a title to true happiness. No, say they, "then the Romans shall come and take away both our place and nation." But were not the Romans come already? Were they not at this time tributaries to Caesar? But they were afraid of the church as well as the state: "They will come and take away our place," our place of worship: and consequently, they look upon Jesus Christ and his proceedings, and adherents, as dangerous both to church and state.

This hath been always the method of Pharisees and high-priests, when they have been taking counsel against the Lord Jesus, and his dear anointed ones. But they need not have been afraid on this account: for our Savior's kingdom neither was, nor is of this world; and the only way to have preserved their place and nation, was to have countenanced, and as much as in them lay, caused all to believe on Jesus. How miserably were they out in their politics! The death of Jesus, which they thought would save, was the grand cause of the utter destruction both of their place and nation: And so will all politics formed against Christ and his gospel end at last in the destruction of those who contrived them.

O the desperate wickedness and treachery of man's deceitful heart!

Where are the scribes, where are the infidels, where are the letter-learned disputers of this world, who are daily calling for a repetition of miracles, in order to confirm and evidence the truth of the Christian religion? Surely if they believe not Moses and the prophets, neither would they believe, though one rose from the dead. Here was one raised from the dead before many witnesses, and yet all those witnesses did by no means believe on Jesus. For divine faith is not wrought in the heart by moral persuasion (though moral suasion is very often made use of as a means to convey it); faith is the peculiar gift of God: no one can come to Jesus unless the Father draw him: and, therefore, that I may draw near the close of this discourse, let me shut up all with a word of exhortation.

Come, ye dead, Christless, unconverted sinners, come and see the place where they laid the body of the deceased Lazarus; behold him laid out, bound hand and foot with grave-clothes, locked up and stinking in a dark cave, with a great stone placed on the top of it! View him again and again; go nearer to him; be not afraid; smell him, ah! How he stinketh. Stop there now, pause a while; and whilst thou art gazing upon the corpse of Lazarus, give me leave to tell thee with great plainness, but greater love, that this dead, bound, entombed, stinking carcass, is but a faint representation of thy poor soul in its natural state: for, whether thou believest it or not, thy spirit which thou bearest about with thee, sepulchered in flesh and blood, is as literally dead to God, and as truly dead in trespasses and sins, as the body of Lazarus was in the cave. Was he bound hand and foot with grave-clothes? So art thou bound hand and foot with thy corruptions: and as a stone was laid on the sepulcher, so is there a stone of unbelief upon thy stupid heart. Perhaps thou hast lain in this state,, not only four days, but many years, stinking in God's nostrils. And; what is still more affecting, thou art as unable to raise thyself out of this loathsome, dead state, to a life of righteousness and true holiness, as ever Lazarus was to raise himself from the cave in which he lay so long. Thou mayest try the power of thy own boasted free-will, and the force and energy of moral persuasion and rational arguments (which, without all doubt, have their proper place in religion); but all thy efforts, exerted with never so much vigor, will prove quite fruitless and abortive, till that same Jesus, who said, "Take away the stone," and cried, "Lazarus, come forth," comes by his mighty power, removes the stone of unbelief, speaks life to thy dead soul, looses thee from the fetters of they sins and corruptions, and by the influences of his blessed Spirit, enables thee to arise, and to walk in the way of his holy commandments. And O that he would now rend the heavens, and come down amongst you! O that there may be a stirring among the dry bones this day! O that whilst I am speaking, and saying, "Dead sinners, come forth," a power, an almighty power might accompany the word, and cause you to emerge into new life!

If the Lord should vouchsafe me such a mercy, and but one single soul in this great congregation, should arise and shake himself from the dust of his natural state; according to the present frame of my heart, I should not care if preaching this sermon here in the fields, was an occasion of hastening my death, as raising Lazarus hastened the death of my blessed Master. For methinks death, in some respects, is more tolerable, than to see poor sinners day by day lying sepulchered, dead and stinking in sin. O that you saw how loathsome you are in the sight of God, whilst you continue in your natural state! I believe you would not so contentedly hug your chains, and refuse to be set at liberty.

Methinks I see some of you affected at this part of my discourse. What say you? Are there not some ready to complain, alas! we have some relations present, who are so notoriously wicked, that they not only hug their chains, but make a mock of sin, and stink not only in the sight of God, but man. Dear souls! You are ready to urge this, as a reason why Jesus will not raise them; and think it hard, perhaps, that Jesus does not come, in answer to your repeated groans and prayers, to convert and save them. But what Jesus said unto Martha, I say unto you, "Believe, and you shall see the glory of God." Think it not a thing incredible, that God should raise their dead souls. Think not hard of Jesus for delaying an answer to your prayers: assure yourselves he heareth you always. And who knows, but this day Jesus may visit some of your dear relations hearts, upon whose account you have travailed in birth till Christ be formed in them? You have already sympathized with Martha and Mary, in their doubts and fears; who knows but you may also be partakers of that joy which their souls experienced, when they received their risen brother into their longing arms.

O Christless souls, you do not know what grief your continuance in sin occasions to your godly relations! You do not know how you grieve the heart of Jesus. I beseech you give him no fresh cause to weep over you upon account of your unbelief: let him not again groan in his spirit and be troubled. Behold how he has loved you, even so as to lay down his life for you. What could he do more? I pray you, therefore, dead sinners, come forth; arise and sup with Jesus. This was an honor conferred on Lazarus, and the same honor awaits you. Not that you shall sit down with him personally in this life, as Lazarus did, but you shall sit down with him at the table of his ordinances, especially at the table of the Lord's supper, and ere long sit down with him in the kingdom of heaven.

Happy, thrice happy ye, who are already raised from spiritual death, and have an earnest of an infinitely better and more glorious resurrection in your hearts. You know a little, how delightful it must have been to Martha and Mary and Lazarus, to sit down with the blessed Jesus here below; but how infinitely more delightful will it be, to sit down, not only with Mary and Martha, but with Abraham, Isaac, and Jacob, and all your other dear brethren and sisters, in the kingdom of heaven. Do you not long for that time, when Jesus shall say unto you, "Come up hither?" Well! Blessed be God, yet a little while, and that same Jesus, who cried with a loud voice, "Lazarus, come forth;" shall with the same voice, and with the same power, speak unto all that are in their graves, and they shall come forth.

That all who hear me this day may be then enabled to lift up their heads and rejoice, that the day of their complete redemption is indeed fully come, may Jesus Christ grant, for his infinite mercy's sake. Amen, and Amen.

Sermon 40 The Holy Spirit

(The Holy Spirit Convincing the World of Sin, Righteousness, and Judgment.)

John 16:8, "And when he is come, he will reprove the world of sin, and of righteousness, and of judgment."

These words contain part of a gracious promise, which the blessed Jesus was pleased to make to his weeping and sorrowful disciples. The time was now drawing near, in which the Son of man was first to be lifted up on the cross, and afterwards to heaven. Kind, wondrous kind! Had this merciful High-priest been to his disciples, during the time of his tabernacling amongst them. He had compassion on their infirmities, answered for them when assaulted by their enemies, and set them right when out of the way, either in principle or practice. He neither called nor used them as servants, but as friends; and he revealed his secrets to them from time to time. He opened their understandings, that they might understand the scriptures; explained to them the hidden mysteries of the kingdom of God, when he spoke to others in parables: nay, he became the servant of them all, and even condescended to wash their feet. The thoughts of parting with so dear and loving a Master as this, especially for a long season, must needs affect them much. When on a certain occasion he intended to be absent from them only for a night, we are told, he was obliged to constrain them to leave him; no wonder then, that when he now informed them he must entirely go away, and that the Pharisees in his absence should put them out of their synagogues, and excommunicate them; yea, that the time should come, that whosoever killed them, would think they did God service (a prophecy, one would imagine, in an especial manner designed for the suffering ministers of this generation); no wonder, I say, considering all this, that we are told, ver. 6. Sorrow had filled their hearts: "Because I have said these things unto you, sorrow hath filled your hearts." The expression is very emphatical; their hearts were so full of concern, that they were ready to burst. In order, therefore, to reconcile them to this mournful dispensation, our dear and compassionate Redeemer shows them the necessity he lay under to leave them; "Nevertheless I tell you the truth; it is expedient for you that I go away:" As though he had said, Think not, my dear disciples, that I leave you out of anger: no, it is for your sakes, for your profit, that I go away: for if I go not away, if I die not upon the cross for your sins, and rise again for your justification, and ascend into heaven to make intercession, and plead my merits before my Father's throne; the Comforter, the Holy Ghost, will not, cannot come unto you; but if I depart, I will send him unto you. And that they might know what he was to do, "When he is come, he will reprove the world of sin, and of righteousness, and of judgment." The person referred to in the words of the text, is plainly the Comforter, the Holy Ghost; and the promise was first made to our Lord's apostles. But though it was primarily made to them, and was literally and remarkably fulfilled at the day of Pentecost, when the Holy Ghost came down as a mighty rushing wind, and also when three thousand were pricked to the heart by Peter's preaching; yet, as the Apostles were the representatives of the whole body of believers, we must infer, that this promise must be looked upon as spoken to us, and to our children, and to as many as the Lord our God shall call.

My design from these words, is to show the manner in which the Holy Ghost generally works upon the hearts of those, who, through grace, are made vessels of mercy, and translated from the kingdom of darkness into the kingdom of God's dear Son.

I say, GENERALLY: For, as God is a sovereign agent, his sacred Spirit bloweth not only on whom, but when and how it listeth. Therefore, far be it from me to confine the Almighty to one way of acting, or say, that all undergo an equal degree of conviction: no, there is a holy variety in God's methods of calling home his elect. But this we may affirm assuredly, that, wherever there is a work of true conviction and conversion wrought upon a sinner's heart, the Holy Ghost, whether by a greater or less degree of inward soul-trouble, does that which our Lord Jesus told the disciples, in the words of the text, that he should do when he came.

If any of you ridicule inward-religion, or think there is no such thing as our feeling or receiving the Holy Ghost, I fear my preaching will be quite foolishness to you, and that you will understand me no more than if I spoke to you in an unknown tongue. But as the promise in the text, is made to the world, and as I know it will be fulfilling till time shall be no more, I shall proceed to explain the general way whereby the Holy Ghost works upon every converted sinner's heart; and I hope that the Lord, even whilst I am speaking, will be pleased to fulfill it in many of your hearts.

"And when he is come, he will reprove the world of sin, or righteousness, and of judgment." The word, which we translate reprove, ought to be rendered convince; and in the original it implies a conviction by way of argumentation, and coming with a power upon the mind equal to a demonstration. A great many scoffers of these last days, will ask such as they term pretenders to the Spirit, how they feel the Spirit, and how they know the Spirit? They might as well ask, how they know, and how they feel the sun when it shines upon the body? For with equal power and demonstration does the Spirit of God work upon and convince the soul. And, FIRST, It convinces of sin; and generally of some enormous sin, the worst perhaps the convicted person ever was guilt of. Thus, when our Lord was conversing with the woman of Samaria, he convinced her first of her adultery: "Woman, go call thy husband. The woman answered, and said, I have no husband. Jesus said unto her, Thou hast well said, I have no husband: for thou hast had five husbands, and he whom thou now hast, is not thy husband: in this saidst thou truly." With this there went such a powerful conviction of all her other actual sins, that soon after, "she left her water-pot, and went her way into the city, and saith to the men, Come, and see a man that told me all things that ever I did: is not this the Christ?" Thus our Lord also dealt with the persecutor Saul: he convinced him first of the horrid sin of persecution; "Saul, Saul, why persecutest thou me?" Such a sense of all his other sins, probably at the same time revived in his mind, that immediately he died; that is, died to all his false confidences, and was thrown into such an agony of soul, that he continued three days, and neither did eat nor drink. This is the method the Spirit of God generally takes in dealing with sinners; he first convinces them of some heinous actual sin, and at the same time brings all their other sins into remembrance, and as it were sets them in battle-array before them: "When he is come, he will reprove the world of sin.

And was it ever thus with you, my dear hearers? (For I must question you as I go along, because I intend, by the Divine help, to preach not only to your heads, but your hearts). Did the Spirit of God ever bring all your sins thus to remembrance, and make you cry out to God, "Thou writest bitter things against me?" Did your actual sins ever appear before you, as though drawn in a map? If not, you have great reason (unless you were sanctified from the womb) to suspect that you are not convicted, much more not converted, and that the promise of the text was never yet fulfilled in your hearts.

Farther: When the Comforter comes into a sinner's heart, though it generally convinces the sinner of his actual sin first, yet it leads him to see and bewail his original sin, the fountain from which all these polluted streams do flow.

Though every thing in the earth, air, and water; every thing both without and within, concur to prove the truth of that assertion in the scripture, "in Adam we all have died;" yet most are so hardened through the deceitfulness of sin, that notwithstanding they may give an assent, to the truth of the proposition in their heads, yet they never felt it really in their hearts. Nay, some in words professedly deny it, though their works too, too plainly prove them to be degenerate sons of a degenerate father.

But when the Comforter, the Spirit of God, arrests a sinner, and convinces him of sin, all carnal reasoning against original corruption, every proud and high imagination, which exalteth itself against that doctrine, is immediately thrown down; and he is made to cry out, "Who shall deliver me from the body of this death?" He now finds that concupiscence is sin; and does not so much bewail his actual sins, as the inward perverseness of his heart, which he now finds not only to be an enemy to, but also direct enmity against God.

And did the Comforter, my dear friends, ever come with such a convincing power as this unto your hearts? Were you ever made to see and feel, that in your flesh dwelleth no good thing; that you are conceived and born in sin; that you are by nature children of wrath; that God would be just if he damned you, though you never committed an actual sin in your lives? So often as you have been at church and sacrament, did you ever feelingly confess, that there was no health in you; that the remembrance of your original and actual sins was grievous unto you, and the burden of them intolerable? If not, you have been only offering to God vain oblations; you never yet prayed in your lives; the Comforter never yet came effectually into your souls: consequently you are not in the faith properly so called; no, you are at present in a state of death and damnation.

Again, the Comforter, when he comes effectually to work upon a sinner, not only convinces him of the sin of his nature, and the sin of his life, but also of the sin of his duties.

We all naturally are Legalists, thinking to be justified by the works of the law. When somewhat awakened by the terrors of the Lord, we immediately, like the Pharisees of old, go about to establish our own righteousness, and think we shall find acceptance with God, if we seek it with tears: finding ourselves damned by nature and our actual sins, we then think to recommend ourselves to God by our duties, and hope, by our doings of one kind or another, to inherit eternal life. But, whenever the Comforter comes into the heart, it convinces the soul of these false rests, and makes the sinner so see that all his righteousnesses are but filthy rags; and that, for the ;most pompous services, he deserves no better a doom than that of the unprofitable servant, "to be thrown into outer darkness, where is weeping, and wailing, and gnashing of teeth." And was this degree of conviction ever wrought in any of your souls?

Did the Comforter ever come into your hearts, so as to make you sick of your duties, as well as your sins? Were you ever, with the great Apostle of the Gentiles, made to abhor your own righteousness which is by the law, and acknowledge that you deserve to be damned, though you should give all your goods to feed the poor? Were you made to feel, that your very repentance needed to be repented of, and that every thing in yourselves is but dung and dross? And that all the arguments you can fetch for mercy, must be out of the heart and pure unmerited love of God? Were you ever made to lie at the feet of sovereign Grace, and to say, Lord, if thou wilt, thou mayest save me; if not, thou mayest justly damn me; I have nothing to plead, I can in no wise justify myself in thy sight; my best performances, I see, will condemn me; and all I have to depend upon is thy free grace? What say you?

Was this ever, or is this now, the habitual language of your hearts? You have been frequently at the temple; but did you ever approach it in the temper of the poor Publican, and, after you have done all, acknowledge that you have done nothing; and, upon a feeling experimental sense of your own unworthiness and sinfulness every way, smite upon your breasts, and say, "God be merciful to us sinners?" If you never were thus minded, the Comforter never yet effectually came into your souls, you are out of Christ; and if God should require your souls in that condition, he would be no better to you than a consuming fire.

But there is a fourth sin, of which the Comforter, when he comes, convinces the soul, and which alone (it is very remarkable) our Lord mentions, as though it was the only sin worth mentioning; for indeed it is the root of all other sins whatsoever: it is the reigning as well as the damning sin of the world. And what now do you imagine that sin may be? It is that cursed sin, that root of all other evils, I mean the sin of unbelief. Says our Lord, verse 9. "Of sin, because they believe not on me." But does the Christian world, or any of you that hear me this day, want the Holy Ghost to convince you of unbelief? Are there any infidels here? Yes, (O that I had not too great reason to think so!) I fear most are such: not indeed such infidels as professedly deny the Lord that bought us (though I fear too many even of such monsters are in every country); but I mean such unbelievers, that have no more faith than the devils themselves.

Perhaps you may think you believe, because you repeat the Creed, or subscribe to a Confession of Faith; because you go to church or meeting, receive the sacrament, and are taken into full communion. These are blessed privileges; but all this may be done, without our being true believers. And I know not how to detect your false hypocritical faith better, than by putting to you this question: How long have you believed? Would not most of you say, as long as we can remember; we never did disbelieve? Then this is a certain sign that you have no true faith at all; no, not so much as a grain of mustard-seed: for, if you believe now, &unless you were sanctified from your infancy, which is the case of some) you must know that there was a time in which you did not believe on the Lord Jesus Christ; and the Holy Ghost, if ever you received it, convinced you of this. Eternal truth has declared, "When he is come, he will convince the world of sin, because they believe not on me." None of us believe by nature: but after the Holy Ghost has convinced us of the sin of our natures, and the sin of our lives and duties, in order to convince us of our utter inability to save ourselves, and that we must be beholden to God, as for every thing else, so for faith (without which it is impossible to please, or be saved by Christ) he convinces us also, that we have no faith. "Dost thou believe on the Son of God?" is the grand question which the Holy Ghost now puts to the soul: at the same time he works with such power and demonstration, that the soul sees, and is obliged to confess, that it has no faith.

This is a thing little thought of by most who call themselves believers. They dream they are Christians, because they live in a Christian country: If they were born Turks, they would believe on Mohammed; for what is that which men commonly call faith, but an outward consent to the established religion? But do not you thus deceive your own selves; true faith is quite another thing. Ask yourselves, therefore, whether or not the Holy Ghost ever powerfully convinced you of the sin of unbelief? You are perhaps so devout (you may imagine) as to get a catalogue of sins; which you look over, and confess in a formal manner, as often as you go to the holy sacrament: but among all your suns, did you ever once confess and bewail that damning sin of unbelief? Were you ever made to cry out, "Lord, give me faith; Lord, give me to believe on thee; O that I had faith! O that I could believe!" If you never were thus distressed, at least, if you never saw and felt that you had no faith, it is a certain sign that the Holy Ghost, the Comforter, never came into and worked savingly upon your souls.

But is it not odd, that the Holy Ghost should be called a Comforter, when it is plain, by the experience of all God's children, that this work of conviction is usually attended with sore inward conflicts, and a great deal of soul-trouble? I answer, The Holy Ghost may well be termed a Comforter, even in this work; because it is the only way to, and ends in, true solid comfort. Blessed are they that are thus convicted by him, for they shall be comforted. Nay, not only so, but there is present comfort, even in the midst of these convictions: the soul secretly rejoices in the sight of its own misery, blesses God for bringing it our of darkness into light, and looks forward with a comfortable prospect of future deliverances, knowing, that, "though sorrow may endure for a night, joy will come in the morning." Thus it is that the Holy Ghost convinces the soul of sin. And, if so, how wretchedly are they mistaken, that blend the light of the Spirit with the light of conscience, as all such do, who say, that Christ lighteth every man that cometh into the world, and that light, if improved, will bring us to Jesus Christ? If such doctrine be true, the promise in the text was needless: our Lord's apostles had already that light; the world hereafter to be convinced, had that light; and, if that was sufficient to bring them to Christ, why was it expedient that Christ should go away to heaven, to send down the Holy Ghost to do this for them! Alas! all have not this Spirit: it is the special gift of God, and, without this special gift, we can never come to Christ.

The light of conscience will accuse or convince us of any common sin; but the light of natural conscience never did, never will, and never can, convince of unbelief. If it could, how comes it to pass, that not one of the heathens, who improved the light of nature in such an eminent degree, was ever convinced of unbelief? No, natural conscience cannot effect this; it is the peculiar property of the Holy Ghost the Comforter: "When he is come, he will reprove (or convince) the world of sin, or righteousness, and judgment." We have heard how he convinces of sin: we come not to show, SECONDLY, What is the righteousness, of which the Comforter convinces the world.

By the word righteousness, in some places of scripture, we are to understand that common justice which we ought to practice between man and man; as when Paul is said to reason of temperance and righteousness before a trembling Felix. But here (as in a multitude of other places in holy writ) we are to understand by the word righteousness, the active and passive obedience of the dear Lord Jesus; even that perfect, personal, all- sufficient righteousness, which he has wrought out for that world which the Spirit is to convince. "Of righteousness, (says our Lord) because I go to the Father, and ye see me no more." This is one argument that the Holy Spirit makes use of to prove Christ's righteousness, because he is gone to the Father, and we see him no more. For, had he not wrought out a sufficient righteousness, the Father would have sent him back, as not having done what he undertook; and we should have seen him again.

O the righteousness of Christ! It so comforts my soul, that I must be excused if I mention it in almost all my discourses. I would not, if I could help it, have one sermon without it. Whatever infidels may object, or Arminians sophistically argue against an imputed righteousness; yet whoever know themselves and God, must acknowledge, that "Jesus Christ is the end of the law for righteousness, (and perfect justification in the sight of God) to every one that believeth," and that we are to be made the righteousness of God in him. This, and this only, a poor sinner can lay hold of, as a sure anchor of his hope. Whatever other scheme of salvation men may lay, I acknowledge I can see no other foundation whereon to build my hopes of salvation, but on the rock of Christ's personal righteousness, imputed to my soul.

Many, I believe, have a rational conviction of, and agree with me in this: but rational convictions, if rested in, avail but little; it must be a spiritual, experimental conviction of the truth, which is saving. And therefore our Lord says, when the Holy Ghost comes in the day of his power, it convinces of this righteousness, of the reality, completeness, and sufficiency of it, to save a poor sinner.

We have seen how the Holy Ghost convinces the sinner of the sin of his nature, life, duties, and of the sin of unbelief; and what then must the poor creature do? He must, he must inevitably despair, if there be no hope but in himself. When therefore the Spirit has hunted the sinner out of all his false rests and hiding-places, taken off the pitiful fig-leaves of his own works, and driven him out of the trees of the garden (his outward reformations) and place him naked before the bar of a sovereign, holy, just, and sin-avenging God; then, then it is, when the soul, having the sentence of death within itself because of unbelief, has a sweet display of Christ's righteousness made to it by the Holy Spirit of God. Here it is, that he begins more immediately to act in the quality of a Comforter, and convinces the soul so powerfully of the reality and all-sufficiency of Christ's righteousness, that the soul is immediately set a hungering and thirsting after it. Now the sinner begins to see, that though he has destroyed himself, yet in Christ is his help; that, though he has no righteousness of his own to recommend him, there is a fullness of grace, a fullness of truth, a fullness of righteousness in the dear Lord Jesus, which, if once imputed to him, will make him happy for ever and ever.

None can tell, but those happy souls who have experienced it, with what demonstration of the Spirit this conviction comes. O how amiable, as well as all-sufficient, does the blessed Jesus now appear! With what new eyes does the soul now see the Lord its righteousness! Brethren, it is unutterable. If you were never thus convinced of Christ's righteousness in your own souls, though you may believe it doctrinally, it will avail you nothing, if the Comforter never came savingly into your souls, then you are comfortless indeed. But What will this righteousness avail, if the soul has it not in possession?

THIRDLY, The next thing therefore the Comforter, when he comes, convinces the soul of, is judgment.

By the word judgment, I understand that well-grounded peace, that settled judgment, which the soul forms of itself, when it is enabled by the

Spirit of God to lay hold on Christ's righteousness, which I believe it always does, when convinced in the matter before-mentioned. "Of judgment (says our Lord) because the Prince of this world is judged;" the soul, being enabled to lay hold on Christ's perfect righteousness by a lively faith, has a conviction wrought in it by the Holy Spirit, that the Prince of this world is judged. The soul being now justified by faith, has peace with God through our Lord Jesus Christ, and can triumphantly say, It is Christ that justifies me, who is he that condemns me? The strong man armed is now cast out; my soul is in a true peace; the Prince of this world will come and accuse, but he has now no share in me: the blessed Spirit which I have received, and whereby I am enabled to apply Christ's righteousness to my poor soul, powerfully convinces me of this: why should I fear? Or of what shall I be afraid, since God's Spirit witnesses with my spirit, that I am a child of God? The Lord is ascended up on high; he has led captivity captive; he has received the Holy Ghost the Comforter, that best of gifts for men: and that Comforter is come into my heart: he is faithful that hath promised: I, even I, am powerfully, rationally, spiritually convicted of sin, righteousness and judgment. By this I know the Prince of this world is judged.

Thus, I say, may we suppose that soul to triumph, in which the promise of the text is happily fulfilled. And though, at the beginning of this discourse, I said, most had never experienced any thing of this, and that therefore this preaching must be foolishness to such; yet I doubt not but there are some few happy souls, who, through grace, have been enabled to follow me step by step; and notwithstanding the Holy Ghost might not directly work in the same order as I have described, and perhaps they cannot exactly say the time when, yet they have a well-grounded confidence that the work is done, and that they have really been convinced of sin, righteousness and judgment in some way, or at some time or another.

And now, what shall I say to you? O thank God, thank the Lord Jesus, thank the ever-blessed Trinity, for this unspeakable gift: for you would never have been thus highly favored, had not he who first spoke darkness into light, loved you with an everlasting love, and enlightened you by his Holy Spirit, and that too, not on account of any good thing foreseen in you, but for his own name's sake.

Be humble therefore, O believers, be humble: look to the rock from whence you have been hewn: extol free grace; admire electing love, which alone has made you to differ from the rest of your brethren. Has God brought you into light? Walk as becometh children of light. Provoke not the Holy Spirit to depart from you: for though he hath sealed you to the day of redemption, and you know that the Prince of this world is judged; yet if you backslide, grow luke-warm, or forget your first love, the Lord will visit your offenses with the rod of affliction, and your sin with spiritual scourges. Be not therefore high-minded, but fear. Rejoice, but let it be with trembling. As the elect of God, put on, not only humbleness of mind, but bowels of compassion; and pray, O pray for your unconverted brethren!

Help me, help me now, O children of God, and hold up my hands, as Aaron and Hur once held up the hands of Moses. Pray, whilst I am preaching, that the Lord may enable me to say, This day is the promise in the text fulfilled in some poor sinners hearts. Cry mightily to God, and, with the cords of holy violence, pull down blessings on your neighbors heads. Christ yet lives and reigns in heaven: the residue of the Spirit is yet in his hand, and a plentiful effusion of it is promises in the latter days of the church. And O that the Holy Ghost, the blessed Comforter, would now come down, and convince those that are Christless amongst you, of sin, of righteousness, and of judgment! O that you were once made willing to be convinced!

But perhaps you had rather be filled with wine than with the Spirit, and are daily chasing that Holy Ghost from your souls. What shall I say for you to God? "Father, forgive them, for they know not what they do." What shall I say from God to you? Why? That "God was in Christ reconciling the world unto himself:" Therefore I beseech you, as in Christ's stead, be ye reconciled to God. Do not go away contradicting and blaspheming. I know Satan would have you be gone. Many of you may be uneasy, and are ready to cry out, "What a weariness is this!" But I will not let you go: I have wrestled with God for my hearers in private, and I must wrestle with you here in public. Though of myself I can do nothing, and you can no more by your own power come to and believe on Christ, than Lazarus could come forth from the grave; yet who knows but God may beget some of you again to a lively hope by this foolishness of preaching, and that you may be some of that world, which the Comforter is to convince of sin, or righteousness, and of judgment? Poor Christless souls! Do you know what a condition you are in? Why, you are lying in the wicked one, the devil; he rules in you, he walks and dwells in you, unless you dwell in Christ, and the Comforter is come into your hearts. And will you contentedly lie in that wicked one that devil? What wages will he give you? Eternal death. O that you would come to Christ! The free gift of God through him is eternal life. He will accept of you even now, if you will believe in him. The Comforter may yet come into your hearts, even yours. All that are now his living temples, were once lying in the wicked one, as well as you. This blessed gift, this Holy Ghost, the blessed Jesus received even for the rebellious.

I see many of you affected: but are your passions only a little wrought upon, or are your souls really touched with a lively sense of the heinousness of your sins, your want of faith, and the preciousness of the righteousness of Jesus Christ? If so, I hope the Lord has been gracious, and that the Comforter is coming into your hearts. Do not stifle these convictions! Do not go away, and straightway forget what manner of doctrine you have heard, and thereby show that these are only common workings of a few transient convictions, floating upon the surface of your hearts. Beg of God that you may be sincere (for he alone can make you so) and that you may indeed desire the promise of the text to be fulfilled in your souls. Who knows but the Lord may be gracious? Remember you have no plea but sovereign mercy; but, for your encouragement also, remember it is the world, such as you are, to whom the Comforter is to come, and whom he is to convince: wait therefore at wisdom's gates. The bare probability of having a door of mercy opened, is enough to keep you striving. Christ Jesus came into the world to save sinners, the chief of them: you know not but he came to save you. Do not go and quarrel with God's decrees, and say, if I am a reprobate, I shall be damned; if I am elected, I shall be saved; and therefore I will do nothing. What have you to do with God's decrees? Secret things belong to him; it is you business to "give all diligence to make your calling and election sure." If there are but few who find the way that leads to life, do you strive to be some of them: you know not but you may be in the number of those few, and that your striving may be the means which God intends to bless, to give you an entrance in. If you do not act thus, you are not sincere; and, if you do, who knows but you may find mercy? For though, after you have done all that you can, God may justly cut you off, yet never was a single person damned who did all that he could. Though therefore your hands are withered, stretch them out; though you are impotent, sick, and lame, come, lie at the pool. Who knows but by and by the Lord Jesus may have compassion on you, and send the Comforter to convince you of sin, righteousness, and of judgment? He is a God full of compassion and long- suffering, otherwise you and I had been long since lifted up our eyes in torments. But still he is patient with us!

O Christless sinners, you are alive, and who knows but God intends to bring you to repentance? Could my prayers or tears affect it, you should have vollies of the one, and floods of the other. My heart is touched with a sense of your condition: May our merciful High-priest now send down the Comforter, and make you sensible of it also! O the love of Christ! It constrains me yet to beseech you to come to him; what do you reject, if you reject Christ, the Lord of glory! Sinners, give the dear Redeemer a lodging in your souls. Do not be Bethshemites; give Christ your hearts, your whole hearts. Indeed he is worthy. He made you, and not you yourselves. You are not your own; give Christ then your bodies and souls, which are his! Is it not enough to melt you down, to think that the high and lofty One, who inhabiteth eternity, should condescend to invite you by his ministers? How soon can he frown you to hell? And how know you, but he may, this very instant, if you do not hear his voice? Did any yet harden their hearts against Christ, and prosper? Come then, do not send me sorrowful away: do not let me have reason to cry out, O my leanness, my leanness! Do not let me go weeping into my closet, and say, "Lord, they will not believe my report; Lord, I have called them, and they will not answer; I am unto them as a very pleasant song, and as one that plays upon a pleasant instrument; but their hearts are running after the lust of the eye, the lust of the flesh, and the pride of life." Would you be willing that I should give such an account of you, or make such a prayer before God? And yet I must not only do so here, but appear in judgment against you hereafter, unless you will come to Christ. Once more therefore I entreat you to come. What objections have you to make? Behold, I stand here in the name of God, to answer all that you can offer. But I know no one can come, unless the Father draw him: I will therefore address one to my God, and intercede with him to send the Comforter into your hearts.

O blessed Jesus, who art a God whose compassions fail not, and in whom all the promises are yea and amen; thou that sittest between the cherubims, show thyself amongst us. Let us now see thy outgoings! O let us now taste that thou art gracious, and reveal thy almighty arm! Get thyself the victory in these poor sinners hearts. Let not the word spoken prove like water spilt upon the ground. Send down, send down, O great High-priest, the Holy Spirit, to convince the world of sin, of righteousness, and of judgment. So will we give thanks and praise to thee, O Father, thee O Son, and thee O blessed Spirit; to whom, as three Persons, but one God, be ascribed by angels and archangels, by cherubims and seraphims, and all the heavenly hosts, all possible power, might, majesty, and dominion, now and for evermore. Amen, Amen, Amen.

Sermon 41 Saul's Conversion

Acts 9:22, "But Saul increased the more in strength, and confounded the Jews which dwelt at Damascus, proving that this is very Christ."

It is an undoubted truth, however paradoxical it may seem to natural men, that "whosoever will live godly in Christ Jesus, shall suffer persecution." And therefore it is very remarkable, that our blessed Lord, in his glorious sermon on the mount, after he had been pronouncing those blessed, who were poor in spirit, meek, pure in heart, and such like, immediately adds (and spends no less than three verses in this beatitude "Blessed are they who are persecuted for righteousness sake." No one ever was, or ever will be endowed with the forementioned graces in any degree, but he will be persuaded for it in a measure. There is an irreconcilable enmity between the seed of the woman, and the seed of the serpent. And if we are not of the world, but show by our fruits that we are of the number of those whom Jesus Christ has chosen out of this world, for that very reason the world will hate us. As this is true of every particular Christian, so it is true of every Christian church in general. For some years past we have heard but little of a public persecution: Why? Because but little of the power of godliness has prevailed amongst all denominations. The strong man armed has had full possession of most professors hearts, and therefore he has let them rest in a false peace. But we may assure ourselves, when Jesus Christ begins to gather in his elect in any remarkable manner, and opens an effectual door for preaching the everlasting gospel, persecution will flame out, and Satan and his emissaries will do their utmost (though all in vain) to stop the work of God. Thus it was in the first ages, thus it is in our days, and thus it will be, till time shall be no more.

Christians and Christian churches must then expect enemies. Our chief concern should be, to learn how to behave towards them in a Christian manner: For, unless we make good heed to ourselves, we shall embitter our spirits, and act unbecoming the followers of that Lord, "who, when he was reviled, reviled not again; when he suffered, threatened not; and, as a lamb before his shearers is dumb, so opened he not his mouth." But what motive shall we make use of to bring ourselves to this blessed lamb-like temper? Next to the immediate operation of the Holy Spirit upon our hearts, I know of no consideration more conducive to teach us long-suffering towards our most bitter persecutors, than this, "That, for all we know to the contrary, some of those very persons, who are now persecuting, may be chosen from all eternity by God, and hereafter called in time, to edify and build up the church of Christ." The persecutor Saul, mentioned in the words of the text, (and whose conversion, God willing, I propose to treat on in the following discourse) is a noble instance of this kind.

I say, a persecutor, and that a bloody one. For see how he is introduced in the beginning of this chapter; "And Saul yet breathing out threatenings and slaughter against the disciples of our Lord, went unto the high priest, and desired of him letters to Damascus tot he synagogues, that if he found any of this way, whether they were men or women, he might bring them bound to Jerusalem." "And Saul yet breathing out." This implies that he had been a persecutor before. To prove which, we need only look back to the 7th chapter, where we shall find him so very remarkably active at Stephen's death, that "the witnesses laid down their clothes at a young man's feet, whose name was Saul." He seems, though young, to be in some authority.

Perhaps, for his seal against the Christians, he was preferred in the church, and was allowed to sit in the great council or Sanhedrin: For we are told, chap. 8, ver. 1, "That Saul was consenting unto his death;" and again, at ver. 3, he is brought in as exceeding all in his opposition; for thus speaks the evangelist, "As for Saul, he made havoc of the church, entering into every house, and haling men and women, committed them to prison." One would have imagined, that this should have satisfied, at least abated the fury of this young zealot. No: being exceedingly mad against them, as he himself informs Agrippa, and having made havoc of all in Jerusalem, he now is resolved to persecute the disciples of the Lord, even to strange cities; and therefore yet breathing out threatenings. "Breathing out." The words are very emphatical, and expressive of his bitter enmity.

It was as natural to him now to threaten the Christians, as it was for him to breathe: he could scarce speak, but it was some threatenings against them. Nay, he not only breathed out threatenings, but slaughters also (and those who threaten, would also slaughter, if it were in their power) against the disciples of the Lord. Insatiable therefore as hell, finding he could not confute or stop the Christians by force of argument, he is resolved to do it by force of arms; and therefore went to the high priest (for there never was a persecution yet without a high priest at the head of it) and desired of him letters, issued out of his spiritual court, to the synagogues or ecclesiastical courts at Damascus, giving him authority, "that if he found any of this way, whether they were men or women, he might bring them bound unto Jerusalem," I suppose, there to be arraigned and condemned in the high priest's court. Observe how he speaks of the Christians. Luke, who wrote the Acts, calls them "disciples of the Lord," and Saul stiles them "Men and women of this way." I doubt not but he represented them as a company of upstart enthusiasts, that had lately gotten into a new method or way of living; that would not be content with the temple-service, but they must be righteous over-much, and have their private meetings or conventicles, and break bread, as they called it, from house to house, to the great disturbance of the established clergy, and to the utter subversion of all order and decency. I do not hear that the high priest makes any objection: no, he was as willing to grant letters, as Saul was to ask them; and wonderfully pleased within himself, to find he had such an active zealot to employ against the Christians.

Well then, a judicial process is immediately issued out, with the high priest's seal affixed to it. And now methinks I see the young persecutor finely equipped, and pleasing himself with thoughts, how triumphantly he should ride back with the "men and women of this way," dragging them after him to Jerusalem.

What a condition may we imagine the poor disciples at Damascus were in at this time! No doubt they had heard of Saul's imprisoning and making havoc of the saints at Jerusalem, and we may well suppose they were apprised of his design against them. I am persuaded this was a growing, because a trying time with these dear people. O how did they wrestle with God in prayer, beseeching him either to deliver them from, or give them grace sufficient to enable them to bear up under, the fury of their persecutors? The high priest doubtless with the rest of his reverend brethren, flattered themselves, that they should now put an effectual stop to this growing heresy, and waited with impatience for Saul's return.

But "He that sitteth in heaven laughs them to scorn, the Lord has them in derision." And therefore, ver. 3, "As Saul journeyed, and came even near unto Damascus," perhaps to the very gates, (our Lord permitting this, to try the faith of his disciples, and more conspicuously to baffle the designs of his enemies) "suddenly (at mid-day, as he acquaints Agrippa) there shined round about him a light from heaven," a light brighter than the sun; "and he fell to the earth (why not into hell?) and heard a voice saying unto him, Saul, Saul, why persecutest thou me/" The word is doubled, "Saul, Saul:" Like that of our Lord to Martha: "Martha, Martha;" or the prophet, O earth, earth, earth!" Perhaps these words came like thunder to his soul. That they were spoken audibly, we are assured from verse 7, "His companions heard the voice." Our Lord now arrests the persecuting zealot, calling him by name; for the word never does us good, till we find it spoken to us in particular. "Saul,

Saul, Why persecutest thou Me?" Put the emphasis upon the word WHY, what evil have I done? Put it upon the word PERSECUTEST, why persecutest? I suppose Saul thought he was not persecuting; no, he was only putting the laws of the ecclesiastical court into execution; but Jesus, whose eyes are as a flame of fire, saw through the hypocrisy of his heart, that, notwithstanding his specious pretenses, all this proceeded from a persecuting spirit, and secret enmity of heart against God; and therefore says, "Why persecutest thou me?" Put the emphasis upon the word ME, why persecutest thou me? alas! Saul was not persecuting Christ, was he? He was only taking care to prevent innovations in the church, and bringing a company of enthusiasts to justice, who otherwise would overturn the established constitution. But Jesus says, "Why persecutest thou me?" For what is done to Christ's disciples, he takes as done to himself, whether it be good, or whether it be evil. He that touches Christ's disciples, touches the apple of his eye; and they who persecute the followers of our Lord, would persecute our Lord himself, was he again to come and tabernacle amongst us.

I do not find that Saul gives any reason why he did persecute; no, he was struck dumb; as every persecutor will be, when Jesus Christ puts this same question to them at the terrible day of judgment. But being pricked at the heart, no doubt with a sense not only of this, but of all his other offenses against the great God, he said, ver. 5, "Who art thou, Lord?" See how soon God can change the heart and voice of his most bitter enemies. Not many days ago, Saul was not only blaspheming Christ himself, but, as much as in him lay, compelling others to blaspheme also: but not, he, who before was an impostor; is called Lord; "Who art thou; Lord?" This admirably points out the way in which God's Spirit works upon the heart: it first powerfully convinces of sin, and of our damnable state; and then puts us upon inquiring after Jesus Christ. Saul being struck to the ground, or pricked to the heart, cries out after Jesus, "Who art thou, Lord?" As many of you that were never so far made sensible of your damnable state, as to be made feelingly to seek after Jesus Christ, were never yet truly convicted by, much less converted to, God. May the Lord, who struck Saul, effectually now strike all my Christless hearers, and set them upon inquiring after Jesus, as their all in all! Saul said, "Who art thou, Lord?

And the Lord said, I am Jesus, whom thou persecutest." Never did any one inquire truly after Jesus Christ, but Christ made a saving discovery of himself, to his soul. It should seem, our Lord appeared to him in person; for Ananias, afterwards, says, "The Lord who appeared to thee in the way which thou camest;" though this may only imply Christ's meeting him in the way; it is not much matter: it is plain Christ here speaks to him, and says, "I am Jesus, whom thou persecutest." It is remarkable, how our Lord takes to himself the name of Jesus; for it is a name in which he delights: I am Jesus, a Savior of my people, both from the guilt and power of their sins; "a Jesus, whom thou persecutest." This seems to be spoken to convince Saul more and more of his sin; and I doubt not, but every word was sharper than a two-edged sword, and came like so many daggers to his heart; O how did these words affect him! a Jesus! A Savior! And yet I am persecuting him! this strikes him with horror; but then the word Jesus, though he was a persecutor, might give him some hope. However, our dear Lord, to convince Saul that he was to be saved by grace, and that he was not afraid of his power and enmity, tells him, "It is hard for thee to kick against the pricks." As much as to say, though he was persecuting, yet he could not overthrow the church of Christ: for he would sit as King upon his holy hill of Zion; the malice of men or devils should never be able to prevail against him.

Ver. 6, "And he, trembling and astonished, said, Lord, what wilt thou have me to do?" Those, who think Saul had a discovery of Jesus made to his heart before, think that this question is the result of his faith, and that he now desires to know what he shall do, out of gratitude, for what the Lord had done for his soul; in this sense it may be understood; "and I have made use of it as an instance to prove, that faith will work by love; but perhaps it may be more agreeable to the context, if we suppose, that Saul had only some distant discovery of Christ made to him, and not o full assurance of faith: for we are told, "he trembling and astonished," trembling at the thoughts of his persecuting a Jesus, and astonished at his own vileness, and the infinite condescension of this Jesus, cries out, "Lord, what wilt thou have me to do?" Persons under soul-trouble, and sore conviction, would be glad to do any thing, or comply on any terms, to get peace with God. "Arise, (says our Lord) and go into the city, and it shall be told thee what thou shalt do." And here we will leave Saul a while, and see what is become of his companions. But what shall we say? God is a sovereign agent; his sacred Spirit bloweth when and where it listeth; "he will have mercy on whom he will have mercy." Saul is taken, but, as far as we know to the contrary, his fellow-travelers are left to perish in their sins: for we are told, ver. 7, "That the men who journeyed with him stood, indeed, speechless, and hearing a confused voice;" I say, a confused voice, for so the word signifies, and must be so interpreted, in order to reconcile it with chap.

22, ver. 9, where Saul, giving an account of these men, tells Agrippa, "They heard not the voice f hi that spake to me." They heard a voice, a confused noise, but not the articulate voice of him that spake to Saul, and therefore remained unconverted. For what are all ordinances, all, even the ;most extraordinary dispensations of providence, without Christ speaks to the soul in them? Thus it is now under the word preached: many, like Saul's companions, are sometimes so struck with the outgoings of God appearing in the sanctuary, that they even stand speechless; they hear the preacher's voice, but not the voice of the Son of God, who, perhaps, at the same time is speaking effectually to many other hearts; this I have known often; and what shall we say to these things? O the depth of the sovereignty of God!

It is past finding out. Lord, I desire to adore what I cannot comprehend.

"Even so, Father, for so it seemeth good in thy sight!" But to return to Saul: the Lord bids him, "arise and go into the city;" and we are told, ver. 8, that "Saul arose from the earth; and when his eyes were opened, (he was so overpowered with the greatness of the light that shone upon them, that) he saw no man; but they led him by the hand, and brought him into Damascus," that very city which was to be the place of his executing or imprisoning the disciples of the Lord. "And he was three days without sight, and neither did eat nor drink." But who can tell what horrors of conscience, what convulsions of soul, what deep and pungent convictions of sin he underwent during these three long days? It was this took away his appetite (for who can eat or drink when under a sense of the wrath of God for sin?) and, being to be greatly employed hereafter, he must be greatly humbled now; therefore, the Lord leaves him three days groaning under the spirit of bondage, and buffeted, no doubt, with the fiery darts of the devil, that, being tempted like unto his brethren, he might be able hereafter to succor those that were tempted. Had Saul applied to any of the blind guides of the Jewish church, under these circumstances, they would have said, he was mad, or going besides himself; as many carnal teachers and blind Pharisees now deal with, and so more and more distress, poor souls laboring under awakening convictions of their damnable state. But God often at our first awakenings, visits us with sore trials, especially those who are, like Saul, to shine in the church, and to be used as instruments in bringing many sons to glory: those who are to be highly exalted, must first be deeply humbled; and this I speak for the comfort of such, who may be now groaning under the spirit of bondage, and perhaps, like Saul, can neither eat nor drink; for I have generally observed, that those who have had the deepest convictions, have afterwards been favored with the most precious communications, and enjoyed most of the divine presence in their souls. This was after wards remarkably exemplified in Saul, who was three days without sight, and neither did eat nor drink.

But will the Lord leave his poor servant in this distress? No; his Jesus (though Saul persecuted him) promised (and he will perform) that "it should be told him what he must do. And there was a certain disciple at Damascus, named Ananias; and unto him, said the Lord, in a vision, Ananias; and he said, Behold, I am here, Lord." What a holy familiarity is there between Jesus Christ and regenerate souls! Ananias had been used to such love-visits, and therefore knew the voice of his beloved. The Lord says, "Ananias;" Ananias says, "Behold, I am here, Lord." Thus it is that Christ now, as well as formerly, often talks with his children at sundry times and after divers manners, as a man talketh with his friend. But what has the Lord to say to Ananias?

Ver. 11, "And the Lord said unto him, Arise, and go into the street, which is called Straight, and inquire in the house of Judas, for one called Saul of Tarsus;" (See here for your comfort, O children of the most high God, what notice Jesus Christ takes of the street and the hose where his own dear servants lodge) "for behold, he prayeth;" but why is this ushered in with the word behold? What, was it such a wonder, to hear that Saul was praying? Why, Saul was a Pharisee, and therefore, no doubt, tasted and made long prayers: and, since we are told that he profited above many of his equals, I doubt not but he was taken notice of for his gift in prayer; and yet it seems, that before these three days, Saul never prayed in his life; and why? Because, before these three days, he never felt himself a condemned creature: he was alive in his own opinion, because without a knowledge of the spiritual meaning of the law; he felt not a want of, and therefore, before now, cried not after a Jesus; and consequently, though he might have said or made a prayer (as many Pharisees do now a-days) he never prayed a prayer; but now, "behold! He prayed indeed;" and this was urged as one reason why he was converted. None of God's children, as one observes, comes into the world still-born; prayer is the very breath of the new creature: and therefore, if we are prayerless, we are Christless; if we never had the spirit of supplication, it is a sad sign that we never had the spirit of grace in our souls: and you may be assured you never did pray, unless you have felt yourselves sinners, and seen the want of Jesus to be your Savior. May the Lord, whom I serve in the gospel of his dear Son, prick you all to the heart, and may it be said of you all, as it was of Saul, behold, they pray!

The Lord goes on to encourage Ananias to go to Saul: says he, ver. 12, "For he hath seen in a vision a man named Ananias, coming in, and putting his hand on him, that he might receive his sight." So that though Christ converted Saul immediately by himself, yet he will carry on the work, thus begun, by a minister. Happy they, who under soul-troubles have such experienced guides, and as well acquainted with Jesus Christ as Ananias was; you that have such, make much of and be thankful for them; and you who have them not, trust in God; he will carry on his own work without them.

Doubtless, Ananias was a good man; but shall I commend him for his answer to our Lord? I commend him not: for says he, ver 13, "Lord, I have heard by many of this man, how much evil he hath done to they saints at Jerusalem: And here, he hath authority from the chief priests to bind all that call upon thy name." I fear this answer proceeded from some relics of self-righteousness, as well as infidelity, that lay undiscovered in the heart of Ananias. "Arise, (said our Lord) and go into the street, which is called Straight, and inquire in the hose of Judas, for one called Saul of Tarsus; for behold, he prayeth!" One would think this was sufficient to satisfy him; but says Ananias, "Lord, I have heart by many of this man (he seems to speak of him with much contempt; for even good men are apt to think too contemptuously of those who are yet in their sins) how much evil he hath done to thy saints in Jerusalem: And here, he hath authority from the chief priests to bind all that call upon Christ's name, should bind him also, if he went unto him; but the Lord silences all objections, with a "Go thy way, for he is a chosen vessel unto me, to bear my name before the Gentiles, and kings, and the children of Israel. For I will show him how great things he must suffer for my name's sake." Here God stops his mouth immediately, by asserting his sovereignty, and preaching to him the doctrine of election. And the frequent conversion of notorious sinners to God, to me is one great proof, amongst a thousand others, of that precious, but too much exploded and sadly misrepresented, doctrine of God's electing love; for whence is it that such are taken, whilst thousands, not near so vile, die senseless and stupid? All the answer that can be given, is, they are chosen vessels; "Go thy way, (says God) for he is a chosen vessel unto me, to bear my name before the Gentiles, and kings, and the children of Israel: For I will show him how great things he must suffer for my name's sake." Observe what a close connection there is between doing and suffering for Christ. If any of my brethren in the ministry are present, let them bear what preferment we must expect, if we are called out to work remarkably for God: not great prebendaries or bishopricks, but great sufferings for our Lord's name sake; these are the fruits of our labor: and he that will not contentedly suffer great things for preaching Christ, is not worthy of him. Suffering will be found to be the best preferment, when w are called to give an account of our ministry at the great day.

I do not hear, that Ananias quarreled with God concerning the doctrine of election; no, (O that all good men would, in this, learn of him!) "He went his way, and entered into the house; and put his hands on him, and said, Brother Saul;" just now, it was THIS MAN; now it is BROTHER SAUL: it is not matter what a man has been, if he be now a Christian; the same should be our brother, our sister and mother; God blots our every convert's transgressions as with a thick cloud, and so should we; the more vile a man has been, the more should we love him when believing in Christ, because Christ will be more glorified on his behalf. I doubt not, but Ananias was wonderfully delighted to hear that so remarkable a persecutor was brought home to God: I am persuaded he felt his soul immediately united to him by love, and therefore addresses him not with, thou persecutor, thou murderer, that camest to butcher me and my friends; but, "brother Saul." It is remarkable that the primitive Christians much used the word brother and brethren; I know it is a term now much in reproach; but those who despise it, I believe, would be glad to be of our brotherhood, when they see us sitting at the right-hand of the Majesty on high. "Brother Saul, the Lord (even Jesus that appeared unto thee in the way as thou camest) hath sent me, that thou mightest receive thy sight, and be filled with the Holy Ghost." At this time, we may suppose, he laid his hands upon him. See the consequences.

Ver. 18, "Immediately there fell from his eyes as it had been scales, and he received sight forthwith;" not only bodily, but spiritual sight; he emerged as it were into a new world; he saw, and felt too, things unutterable: he felt a union of soul with God; he received the spirit of adoption; he could now, with a full assurance of faith, cry, "Abba, Father." Now was he filled with the Holy Ghost; and had the love of God shed abroad in his heart; now were the days of his mourning ended; now was Christ formed in his soul; now he could give men and devils the challenge, ,knowing that Christ had justified him; now he saw the excellencies of Christ, and esteemed him the fairest among ten thousand. You only know how to sympathize with the apostle in his joy, who, after a long night of bondage, have been set free by the Spirit, and have received joy in the Holy Ghost. May all that are now mourning, as Saul was, be comforted in like manner!

The scales are now removed from the eyes of Saul's mind; Ananias has done that for him, under God: he must now do another office, baptize him, and so receive him into the visible church of Christ; a good proof to me of the necessity of baptism where it may he had: for I find here, as well as elsewhere, that baptism is administered even to those who had received the Holy Ghost; Saul was convinced of this, and therefore arose and was baptized; and now it is time for him to recruit the outward man, which, by three days abstinence and spiritual conflicts, had been much impaired; we are therefore told, (ver. 19), "when he had received meat, he was strengthened." But O, with what comfort did the apostle now eat his food? I am sure it was with singleness, I am persuaded also with gladness of heart; and why? He knew that he was reconciled to God; and, for my own part, did I not know how blind and flinty our hearts are by nature, I should wonder how any one could eat even his common food with any satisfaction, who has not some well-grounded hope of his being reconciled to God. Our Lord intimates thus much to us: for in his glorious prayer, after he has taught us to pray for our daily bread, immediately adds that petition, "Forgive us our trespasses;" as though our daily bread would do us no service, unless we were sensible of having the forgiveness of our sins.

To proceed; Saul hath received meat, an is strengthened; and whither will he go now? To see the brethren; "then was Saul certain days with the disciples that were at Damascus." If we know and love Christ, we shall also love and desire to be acquainted with the brethren of Christ: we may generally know a man by his company. And though all are not saints that associate with saints, (for tares will be always springing up amongst the wheat till the time of harvest) yet, if we never keep company, but are shy and ashamed of the despised children of God, it is a certain sign we have not yet experimentally learned Jesus, or received him into our hearts. My dear friends, be not deceived; if we are friends to the Bridegroom, we shall be friends to the children of the Bridegroom. Saul, as soon as he was filled with the Holy Ghost, "was certain days with the disciples that were at Damascus." But who can tell what joy these disciples felt when Saul came amongst them! I suppose holy Ananias introduced him. Methinks I see the once persecuting zealot, when they came to salute him with a holy kiss, throwing himself upon each of their necks, weeping over them with floods of tears, and saying, "" my brother, O my sister, Can you forgive me? Can you give such a wretch as I the right-hand of fellowship, who intended to drag you behind me bound unto Jerusalem!" Thus, I say, we may suppose Saul addressed himself to his fellow-disciples; and I doubt not but they were as ready to forgive and forget as Ananias was, and saluted him with the endearing title of "brother Saul." Lovely was this meeting; so lovely, that it seemed Saul continued certain days with them, to communicate experiences, and to learn the way of God more perfectly; to pray for a blessing on his future ministry, and to praise Christ Jesus for what he had done for their souls.

Saul, perhaps, had sat certain years at the feet of Gamaliel, but undoubtedly learned more these certain days, than he had learned before in all his life. It pleases me to think how this great scholar is transformed by the renewing of his mind. What a mighty change was here! That so great a man as Saul was, both as to his station in life, and internal qualifications, and such a bitter enemy to the Christians; for him, I say, to go and be certain days with the people of THIS mad way, and to sit quietly, and be taught of illiterate men, as many of these disciples we may be sure were; what a substantial proof was this of the reality of his conversion!

What a hurry and confusion may we suppose the chief priests were now in! I warrant they were ready to cry out, What! Is he also deceived? As for the common people, who knew not the law, and are accursed, for them to be carried away, is no such wonder; but for a man bred up at the feet of Gamaliel, for such a scholar, such an enemy to the cause as Saul; for him to be led away with a company of silly, deceived men and women, surely it is impossible: we cannot believe it. But Saul soon convinces them of the reality of his becoming a fool for Christ's sake: for straightway, instead of going to deliver the letters from the high priests, as they expected, in order to bring the disciples that were at Damascus bound to Jerusalem, "he preached Christ n the synagogues, that he is the Son of God." This is another proof of his being converted. He not only conversed with Christians in private, but he preached Christ publicly in the synagogues; especially, he insisted on the divinity of our Lord, proving, notwithstanding his state of humiliation, that he was really the Son of God.

But why did Saul preach Christ thus? Because he had felt the power of Christ upon his own soul. And here is the reason why Christ is so seldom preached, and his divinity so slightly insisted on in our synagogues: because the generality of those that pretend to preach him, never felt a saving work of conversion upon their own souls. How can they preach, unless they are first taught of, and then sent by God? Saul did not preach Christ before he knew him; no more should any one else. An unconverted minister, though he could speak with the tongues of men and angels, will be but as a sounding brass and tinkling cymbal to those whose senses are exercised to discern spiritual things. Ministers that are unconverted, may talk and declaim of Christ, and prove from books that he is the Son of God; but they cannot preach with the demonstration of the Spirit and with power, unless they preach from experience, and have had a proof of his divinity, by a work of grace wrought upon their own souls. God forgive those, who lay hands on an unconverted man, knowing that he is such: I would not do it for a thousand worlds, Lord Jesus, keep thy own faithful servants pure, and let them not be partakers of other men's sins!

Such an instance as was Saul's conversion, we may be assured, must make a great deal of noise; and, therefore, no wonder we are told, ver. 21, "But all that heard him were amazed, and said, Is not this he that destroyed them who called on this name in Jerusalem, and came hither for that intent, that he might bring them bound to the chief priests." Thus it will be with all that appear publicly for Jesus Christ; and it is as impossible for a true Christian to be hid, as a city built upon a hill. Brethren, if you are faithful to, you must be reproached and have remarks made on you for Christ; especially of you have been remarkably wicked before your conversion. Your friends will say, is not this he, or she, who a little while ago would run to as great an excess of riot and vanity as the worst of us all? What has turned your brain? -- Or if you have been close, false, formal hypocrites, as Saul was, they will wonder that you should be so deceived, as to think you were not in a safe state before. No doubt, numbers were surprised to hear Saul, who was touching the law blameless, affirm that he was in a damnable condition (as in all probability he did) a few days before.

Brethren, you must expect to meet with many such difficulties as these. The scourge of the tongue, is generally the first cross we are called to bear for the sake of Christ. Let not, therefore, this move you: It did not intimidate, no, it rather encouraged Saul: says the text, "But Saul increased the more in strength, and confounded the Jews who dwelt at Damascus, proving that this is very Christ." Opposition never yet did, or ever will hurt a sincere convert: Nothing like opposition to make the man of God perfect. None but a hireling, who careth not for the sheep, will be affrighted at the approach or barking of wolves. Christ's ministers are as bold as lions: it is not for such men as they to flee.

And therefore (that I may draw towards a conclusion() let the ministers and disciples of Christ learn from Saul, not to fear men or their revilings; but, like him, increase in strength, the more wicked men endeavor to weaken their hands. We cannot be Christians without being opposed: no; disciples in general must suffer; ministers in particular must suffer great things. But let not this move any of us from our steadfastness in the gospel: He that stood by and strengthened Saul, will also stand by and strengthen us: He is a God mighty to save all that put their trust in him. If we look up with an eye of faith, we, as well as the first martyr Stephen, may see Jesus standing at the right hand of God, ready to assist and protect us. Though the Lord' seat is in heaven, yet he has respect to his saints in an especial manner, when suffering here on earth: then the Spirit of Christ and of glory rests upon their souls. And, if I may speak my own experience, I never enjoy more rich communications from God than when despised and rejected of men for the sake of Jesus Christ." However little they may design it, my enemies are my greatest friends. What I most fear, is a calm; but the enmity which is in the hearts of natural men against Christ, will not suffer them to be quiet long; No; as I hope the work of God will increase, so the rags of men and devils will increase also. Let us put on, therefore, the whole armor of God: let us not fear the face of men: "Let us fear him only, who can destroy both body and soul in hell." I say unto you let us fear him alone. You see how soon God can stop the fury of his enemies.

You have just now heard of a proud, powerful zealot stopped in his full career, struck down to the earth with a light from heaven, converted by the almighty power of efficacious grace, and thereupon zealously promoting, nay, resolutely suffering for, the faith, which once with threatenings and slaughters he endeavored to destroy. Let his teach us to pity and pray for our Lord's most inveterate enemies. Who knows, but in answer thereunto, our Lord may give them repentance unto life? Most think, that Christ had respect to Stephen's prayer, when he converted Saul.

Perhaps for this reason God suffers his adversaries to go on, that his goodness and power may shine more bright in their conversion., But let not the persecutors of Christ take encouragement from this to continue in their opposition. Remember, though Saul was converted, yet the high-priest, and Saul's companions, were left dead in trespasses and sins.

And, if this should be your case, you will of all men be most miserable: for persecutors have the lowest place in hell. And, if Saul was struck to the earth by a light from heaven, how will you be able to stand before Jesus Christ, when he comes in terrible majesty to take vengeance on all those who have persecuted his gospel? Then the question, "Why persecutest thou me?" will cut you through and through. The secret enmity of your hearts shall be then detected before men and angels, and you shall be doomed to dwell in the blackness of darkness for evermore. Kiss the Son, therefore, lest he be angry: for even you may yet find mercy, if you believe on the Son of God: though you persecute him, yet he will be your Jesus. I cannot despair of any of you, when I find a Saul among the disciples at ?Damascus. What though your sins are as scarlet, the blood of Christ shall wash them as white as snow. Having much to be forgiven, despair not; only believe, and like Saul, of whom I have now been speaking, love much. He counted himself the chiefest sinner of all, and therefore labored more abundantly than all.

Who is there among you fearing the Lord? Whose hearts hath the Lord now opened to hearken to the voice of his poor unworthy servant? Surely, the Lord will not let me preach in vain. Who is the happy soul that is this day to be washed in the blood of the Lamb? Will no poor sinner take encouragement from Saul to come to Jesus Christ? You are all thronging round, but which of you will touch the Lord Jesus? What a comfort will it be to Saul, and to your own souls, when you meet him in heaven, to tell him, that hearing of his, was a means, under God, of your conversion!

Doubtless it was written for the encouragement of all poor, returning sinners; he himself tells us so: for "in me God showed all long-suffering, that I might be an example to them that should hereafter believe." Was Saul here himself, he would tell you so, indeed he would; but being dead, by this account of his conversion he yet speaketh. O that God may speak by it to your hearts! O that the arrows of God might this day stick fast in your souls, and you made to cry out, "Who art thou, Lord?" Are there any such amongst you? Methinks I feel something of what this Saul felt, when he said, "I travail in birth again for you, till Christ be formed again in your hearts." O come, come away to Jesus, in whom Saul believed; and then I care not if the high-priests issue out never so many writs, or injuriously drag me to a prison. The thoughts of being instrumental in saving you, will make me sing praises even at midnight. And I know you will be my joy and crown of rejoicing, when I am delivered from this earthly prison, and meet you in the kingdom of God hereafter.

Now to God, etc.

Sermon 42 Marks of having Received the Holy Ghost

Acts 19:2, "Have ye received the Holy Ghost since ye believed?"

Two different significations have been given of these words. Some have supposed, that the question here put, is, Whether these disciples, whom St. Paul found at Ephesus, had received the Holy Ghost by imposition of hands at confirmation? Others think, these disciples had been already baptized into John's baptism; which not being attended with an immediate effusion of the Holy Spirit, the Apostle here asks them, Whether they had received the Holy Ghost by being baptized into Jesus Christ? And upon their answering in the negative, he first baptized, and then confirmed them in the name of the Lord Jesus.

Which of these interpretations is the most true, is neither easy nor very necessary to determine. However, as the words contain a most important inquiry, without any reference to the context, I shall from them, FIRST, Show who the Holy Ghost here spoken of, is; and that we must all receive him, before we can be stiled true believers.

SECONDLY, I shall lay down some scripture marks whereby we may know, whether we have thus received the Holy Ghost or not. And THIRDLY, By way of conclusion, address myself to several distinct classes of professors, concerning the doctrine that shall have been delivered.

FIRST, I am to show who the Holy Ghost spoken of in the text, is; and that we must all receive him before we can be stiled true believers.

By the Holy Ghost is plainly signified the Holy Spirit, the third Person in the ever-blessed Trinity, consubstantial and co-eternal with the Father and the Son, proceeding from, yet equal to them both. He is emphatically called Holy, because infinitely holy in himself, and the author and finisher of all holiness in us.

This blessed Spirit, who once moved on the face of the great deep; who over-shadowed the blessed Virgin before that holy child was born of her; who descended in a bodily shape, like a dove, on our blessed Lord, when he came up out of the water at his baptism; and afterwards came down in fiery tongues on the heads of all his Apostles at the day of Pentecost: this is the Holy Ghost, who must move on the faces of our souls; this power of the Most High, must come upon us, and we must be baptized with his baptism and refining fire, before we can be stiled true members of Christ" mystical body.

Thus says the Apostle Paul, "Know ye not that Jesus Christ is in you, (that is, by his Spirit) unless you are reprobates?" And, "If any man hath not the Spirit of Christ, he is none of his," And again, says St. John, "We know that we are his, by the Spirit that he hath given us." It is not, indeed, necessary that we should have the Spirit now given in that miraculous manner, in which he was at first given to our Lord's Apostles, by signs and wonders, but it is absolutely necessary, that we should receive the Holy Ghost in his sanctifying graces, as really as they did: and so will it continue to be till the end of the world.

For this stands the case between God and man: God at first made man upright, or as the sacred Penman expresses it, "In the image of God made he man;" that is, his soul was the very copy, the transcript of the divine nature. He, who before, by his almighty fiat, spoke the world into being, breathed into man the breath of spiritual life, and his soul was adorned with a resemblance of the perfections of Deity. This was the finishing stroke of the creation: the perfection both of the moral and material world. And so near did man resemble his divine Original, that God could not but rejoice and take pleasure in his own likeness: And therefore we read, that when God had finished the inanimate and brutish part of the creation, he looked upon it, and beheld it was good; but when that lovely, God-like creature man was made, behold it was very good.

Happy, unspeakably happy must man needs be, when thus a partaker of the divine nature. And thus might he have still continued, had he continued holy. But God placed him in a state of probation, with a free grant to eat of every tree in the garden of Eden, except the tree of knowledge of good and evil: the day he should eat thereof, he was surely to die; that is, not only to be subject to temporal, but spiritual death; and consequently, to lose that divine image, that spiritual life God had not long since breathed into him, and which was as much his happiness as his glory.

These, one would imagine, were easy conditions for a finite creature's happiness to depend on. But man, unhappy man, being seduced by the devil, and desiring, like him, to be equal with his Maker, did eat of the forbidden fruit; and thereby became liable to that curse, which the eternal God, who cannot lie, had denounced against his disobedience.

Accordingly we read, that soon after Adam had fallen, he complained that he was naked; naked, not only as to his body, but naked and destitute of those divine graces which, before decked and beautified his soul. The unhappy mutiny, and disorder which the visible creation fell into, the briars and thorns which not sprung up and overspread the earth, were but poor emblems, lifeless representations of that confusion and rebellion, and those divers lusts and passions which sprung up in, and quite overwhelmed the soul of man immediately after the fall. Alas! he was now no longer the image of the invisible God; but as he had imitated the devil's sin, he became as it were a partaker of the devil's nature, and from an union with, sunk into a state of direct enmity against God.

Now in this dreadful disordered condition, are all of us brought into the world: for as the root is, such must the branches be. Accordingly we are told, "That Adam beget a son in his own likeness;" or, with the same corrupt nature which he himself had, after he had eaten the forbidden fruit. And experience as well as scripture proves, that we also are altogether born in sin and corruption; and therefore incapable, whilst in such a state, to hole communion with God. For as light cannot have communion with darkness, so God can have no communion with such polluted sons of Belial.

Here then appears the end and design why Christ was manifest in the flesh; to put an end to these disorders, and to restore us to that primitive dignity in which we were at first created. Accordingly he shed his precious blood to satisfy his Father's justice for our sins; and thereby also he procured for us the Holy Ghost, who should once more re- instamp the divine image upon our hearts, and make us capable of living with and enjoying the blessed God.

This was the great end of our Lord's coming into the world; nay, this is the only end why the world itself is now kept in being. For as soon as a sufficient number are sanctified out of it, the heavens shall be wrapped up like a scroll, the elements shall melt with fervent heat, the earth, and all that therein is, shall be burnt up.

This sanctification of the Spirit, is that new birth mentioned by our blessed Lord to Nicodemus, "without which we cannot see the kingdom of

God." This is what St. Paul calls being "renewed in the spirit of our minds;" and it is the spring of that holiness, without which no man shall see the Lord.

Thus then, it is undeniably certain, we must receive the Holy Ghost ere we can be stiled true members of Christ's mystical body. I come in the SECOND place to lay down some scriptural marks, whereby we may easily judge, whether we have thus received the Holy Ghost or not. And the FIRST I shall mention, is, our having received a spirit of prayer and supplication; for that always accompanies the spirit of grace. No sooner was Paul converted, but "behold he prayeth." And this was urged as an argument, to convince Ananias that he was converted. And God's elect are also said to "cry to him day and night." And since one great work of the Holy Spirit is to convince us of sin, and to set us upon seeking pardon and renewing grace, through the all-sufficient merits of a crucified Redeemer, whosoever has felt the power of the world to come, awakening him from his spiritual lethargy, cannot but be always crying out, "Lord, what wouldst thou have me to do?" Or, in the language of the importunate blind Bartimeus, "Jesus, thou Son of David, have mercy upon me." The blessed Jesus, as he received the Holy Ghost without measure, so he evidenced it by nothing more, than his frequent addresses at the throne of grace. Accordingly we read, that he was often alone on the mountain praying; that he rose a great while before day to pray: nay, that he spent whole nights in prayer. And whosoever is made partaker of the same Spirit which the holy Jesus, will be of the same mind, and delight in nothing so much, as to "draw nigh unto God," and lift up holy hands and hearts in frequent and devout prayer.

It must be confessed, indeed, that this spirit of supplication is often as it were sensibly lost, and decays, for some time, even in those who have actually received the Holy Ghost. Through spiritual dryness and barrenness of soul, they find in themselves a listlessness and backwardness to this duty of prayer; but then they esteem it as their cross, and still persevere in seeking Jesus, though it be sorrowing: and their hearts, notwithstanding, are fixed upon God, though they cannot exert their affections so strongly as usual, on account of that spiritual deadness, which God, for wise reasons, has suffered to benumb their souls.

But as for the formal believer, it is not so with him: no; he either prays not at all, or if he does enter into his closet, it is with reluctance, out of custom, or to satisfy the checks of his conscience.

Whereas, the true believer can no more live without prayer, than without food day by day. And he finds his soul as really and perceptibly fed by the one, as his body is nourished and supported by the other. A SECOND scripture mark of our having received the Holy Ghost, is, Not committing sin.

"Whosoever is born of God, (says St. John) sinneth not, neither can he sin, because his seed remaineth in him." Neither can he sin. This expression does not imply the impossibility of a Christian's sinning: for we are told, that "in many things we offend all:" It only means thus much: that a man who is really born again of God, doth not willfully commit sin, much less live in the habitual practice of it. For how shall he that is dead to sin, as every converted person is, live any longer therein?

It is true, a man that is born again of God, may, through surprise, or the violence of a temptation, fall into an act of sin: witness the adultery of David, and Peter's denial of his Master. But then, like them, he quickly rises again, goes out from the world, and weeps bitterly; washes the guilt of sin away by the tears of sincere repentance, joined with faith in the blood of Jesus Christ; takes double heed to his ways for the future, and perfects holiness in the fear of God.

The meaning of this expression of the Apostle, that "a man who is born of God, cannot commit sin," has been fitly illustrated, by the example of a covetous worldling, to the general bent of whose inclinations, liberality and profuseness are directly opposite: but if, upon some unexpected, sudden occasion, he does play the prodigal, he immediately repents him of his fault, and returns with double care to his niggardliness again. And so is every one that is born again: to commit sin, is as contrary to the habitual frame and tendency of his mind, as generosity is to the inclinations of a miser; but if at any time, he is drawn into sin, he immediately, with double zeal, returns to his duty, and brings forth fruits meet for repentance. Whereas, the unconverted sinner is quite dead in trespasses and sins: or if he does abstain from gross acts of it, through worldly selfish motives, yet, there is some right eye he will not pluck out; some right- hand which he will not cut off; some specious Agag that he will not sacrifice for God; and thereby he is convinced that he is but a mere Saul: and consequently, whatever pretensions he may make to the contrary, he has not yet received the Holy Ghost. A THIRD mark whereby we may know, whether or not we have received the Holy Ghost, is, Our conquest over the world.

"For whosoever is born of God, (says the Apostle) overcometh the world." By the world, we are to understand, as St. John expressed it, "all that is in the world, the lust of the eye, the lust of the flesh, and the pride of life:" And by overcoming of it, is meant, our renouncing these, so as not to follow or be led by them: for whosoever is born from above, has his affections set on things above: he feels a divine attraction in his soul, which forcibly draws his mind heavenwards; and as the hart panteth after the water-brooks, so doth it make his soul so long after the enjoyment of his God.

Not that he is so taken up with the affairs of another life, as to neglect the business of this: No; a truly spiritual man dares not stand any day idle; but then he takes care, though he laboreth for the meat which perisheth, first to secure that which endureth to everlasting life. Or, if God has exalted him above his brethren, yet, like Moses, Joseph, and Daniel, he, notwithstanding, looks upon himself as a stranger and pilgrim upon earth: having received a principle of new life, he walks by faith and not by sight; and his hopes being full of immortality, he can look on all things here below as vanity and vexation of spirit: In short, though he is in, yet he is not of the world; and as he was made for the enjoyment of God, so nothing but God can satisfy his soul.

The ever-blessed Jesus was a perfect instance of overcoming the world.

For though he went about continually doing good, and always lived as in a press and throng; yet, wherever he was, his conversation tended heavenwards. In like manner, he that is joined to the Lord in one spirit, will so order his thoughts, words, and actions, that he will evidence to all, that his conversation is in heaven.

On the contrary, an unconverted man being of the earth, is earthy; and having no spiritual eye to discern spiritual things, he is always seeking for happiness in this life, where it never was, will, or can be found.

Being not born again from above, he is bowed down by a spirit of natural infirmity: the serpent's curse becomes his choice, and he eats of the dust of the earth all the days of his life. A FOURTH scripture mark of our having received the Holy Ghost, is, Our loving one another.

"We know (says St. John) we are passed from death unto life, because we love the brethren." "And by this (says Christ himself) shall all men know that ye are my disciples, if ye have love one towards another." Love is the fulfilling of the gospel, as well as of the law: for "God is love; and whosoever dwelleth in love, dwelleth in God." But by this love we are not to understand a softness and tenderness of mere nature, or a love founded on worldly motives (for this a natural man may have); but a love of our brethren, proceeding from love towards God: loving all men in general, because to their relation to God; and loving good men in particular, for the grace we see in them, and because they love our Lord Jesus in sincerity.

This is Christian charity, and that new commandment which Chris gave to his disciples. NEW, not in its object, but in the motive and example whereon it is founded, even Jesus Christ. This is that love which the primitive Christians were so renowned for, that it became a proverb, SEE HOW

THESE CHRISTIANS LOVE ONE ANOTHER. And without this love, though we should give all our goods to feed the poor, and our bodies to be burnt, it would profit us nothing.

Further, this love is not confined to any particular set of men, but is impartial and catholic: A love that embraces God's image wherever it beholds it, and that delights in nothing so much as to see Christ's kingdom come.

This is the love wherewith Jesus Christ loved mankind: He loved all, even the worst of men, as appears by his weeping over the obstinately perverse; but wherever he saw the least appearance of the divine likeness, that soul he loved in particular. Thus we read, that when he heard the young man say, "All these things have I kept from my youth," that so far he loved him. And when he saw any noble instance of faith, though in a Centurion and a Syrophonecian, aliens to the commonwealth of Israel, how is he said to marvel at, to rejoice in, speak of, and commend it? So every spiritual disciple of Jesus Christ will cordially embrace all who worship God in spirit and in truth, however they may differ as to the appendages of religion, and in things not essentially necessary to salvation.

I confess, indeed, that the heart of a natural man is not thus enlarged all at once; and a person may really have received the Holy Ghost, (as Peter, no doubt, had when he was unwilling to go to Cornelius) though he be not arrived to this: but then, where a person is truly in Christ, all narrowness of spirit decreases in him daily; the partition wall of bigotry and party zeal is broken down more and more; and the nearer he comes to heaven, the more his heart is enlarged with that love, which there will make no difference between any people, nation, or language, but we shall all, with one heart, and one voice, sing praises to him that sitteth upon the throne for ever. But I hasten to a FIFTH scripture mark, Loving our enemies.

"I say unto you, (says Jesus Christ) Love your enemies, bless them that curse you, do good to those that hate you, ad pray for them that despitefully use you and persecute you." And this duty of loving your enemies is so necessary, that without it, our righteousness does not exceed the righteousness of the Scribes and Pharisees, or even of Publicans and sinners: "For if you do good to them only, who do good to you, what do you more than others?" What do you extraordinary? "Do not even the Publicans the same?" And these precepts our Lord confirmed by his own example; when he wept over the bloody city; when he suffered himself to be led as a sheep to the slaughter; when he made that mile reply to the traitor Judas, "Judas, betrayest thou the Son of man with a kiss?" and more especially, when in the agonies and pangs of death, he prayed for his very murderers, "Father, forgive them, for they know not what they do." This is a difficult duty to the natural man; but whosoever is made partaker of the promise of the Spirit, will find it practicable and easy: for if we are born again of God, we must be like him, and consequently delight to be perfect in this duty of doing good to our worst enemies in the same manner, though not in the same degree as he is perfect: He sends his rain on the evil and the good; causeth his sun to shine on the just and unjust; and more especially commended his love towards us, that whilst we were his enemies, he sent forth his Son, born of a woman, made under the law, that he might become a curse for us.

Many other marks are scattered up and down the scriptures, whereby we may know whether or not we have received the Holy Ghost: such as, "to be carnally minded, is death, but to be spiritually minded is life and peace." "Now the fruits of the Spirit are joy, peace, long-suffering, meekness," with a multitude of texts to the same purpose. But as most, if not all of them, are comprehended in the duties already laid down, I dare affirm, whosoever upon an impartial examination, can find the aforesaid marks on his soul, may be as certain, as though an angel was to tell him, that his pardon is sealed in heaven.

As for my own part, I had rather see these divine graces, and this heavenly temper stamped upon my soul, than to hear an angel from heaven saying unto me, Son, be of good cheer, thy sins are forgiven thee.

These are infallible witnesses; these are Emmanuel, God with and in us; these make up that white stone, which none knoweth, saving he who hath receiveth it; these are the earnests of the heavenly inheritance in our hearts: In short, these are glory begun, and are that good thing, that better part, and which if you continue to stir up this gift of God, neither men nor devils shall ever be able to take from us.

I proceed, as was proposed, in the THIRD place, to make an application of the doctrine delivered, to several distinct classes of professors. And FIRST, I shall address myself to those who are dead in trespasses and sins. And, O how could I weep over you, as our Lord wept over Jerusalem?

For, alas! how distant must you be from God? What a prodigious work have you to finish, who, instead of praying day and night, seldom or never pray at all? And, instead of being born again of God, so as not to commit sin, are so deeply sunk into the nature of devils, as to make a mock at it? Or, instead of overcoming the world, so as not to follow or be led by it, are continually making provision for the flesh, to fulfill the lusts thereof.

And, instead of being endued with the god-like disposition of loving all men, even your enemies, have your hearts full of hatred, malice, and revenge, and deride those who are the sincere followers of the lowly Jesus.

But think you, O sinners, that God will admit such polluted wretches into his sight? Or should he admit you, do you imagine you could take any pleasure in him? No; heaven itself would be no heaven to you; the devilish dispositions which are in your hearts, would render all the spiritual enjoyments of those blessed mansions, ineffectual to make you happy. To qualify you to be blissful partakers of that heavenly inheritance with the saints in light, there is a meetness required: to attain which, ought to be the chief business of your lives.

It is true, you, as well as the righteous, in one sense, shall see God; (for we must all appear before the judgment-seat of Christ) but you must see him once, never to see him more. For as you carry about in you the devil's image, with devils you must dwell: being of the same nature, you must share the same doom. "Repent, therefore, and be converted, that your sins may be blotted out." See that you receive the Holy Ghost, before you go hence: for otherwise, how can you escape the damnation of hell?

SECONDLY, Let me apply myself to those who deceive themselves with false hopes of salvation. Some, through the influence of a good education, or other providential restraints, have not run into the same excess of riot with other men, and they think they have no need to receive the Holy Ghost, but flatter themselves that they are really born again.

But do you show it by bringing forth the fruits of the Spirit? Do you pray without ceasing? Do you not commit sin? Have you overcome the world?

And do you love your enemies, and all mankind, in the same manner, as Jesus Christ loved them?

If these things, brethren, be in you and abound, then may you have confidence towards God; but if not, although you may be civilized, yet you are not converted: no, you are yet in your sins. The nature of the old Adam still reigneth in your souls; and unless the nature of the second Adam be grafted in its room, you can never see God.

Think not, therefore, to dress yourselves up in the ornaments of a good nature, and civil education, and say with Agag, "surely the bitterness of death is past;" For God's justice, notwithstanding that, like Samuel, shall hew you to pieces. However you may be highly esteemed in the sight of men, yet, in the sight of God, you are but like the apples of Sodom, dunghills covered over with snow, mere whited sepulchers, appearing a little beautiful without, but inwardly full of corruption and of all uncleanness: and consequently will be dismissed at the last day with a "Verily, I know you not." But the word of God is profitable for comfort as well as correction.

THIRDLY, Therefore I address myself to those who are under the drawings of the Father, and are exercised with the Spirit of bondage, and not finding the marks before mentioned, are crying out, Who shall deliver us from the body of this death?

But fear not, little flock; for notwithstanding your present infant state of grace, it shall be your father's good pleasure to give you the kingdom. The grace of God, through Jesus Christ, shall deliver you, and give you what you thirst after: He hath promised, he will also do it. Ye shall receive the spirit of adoption, that promise of the Father, if you faint not: only persevere in seeking it; and determine not to be at rest in you soul, till you know and feel that you are thus born again from above, and God's Spirit witnesseth with your spirits that you are the children of God.

FOURTHLY and LASTLY, I address myself to those who have received the Holy Ghost in all his sanctifying graces, and are almost ripe for glory.

Hail, happy saints! For your heaven is begun on earth: you have already received the first fruits of the Spirit, and are patiently waiting till that blessed change come, when your harvest shall be complete. I see and admire you, though, alas! at so great a distance from you: your life, I know, is hid with Christ in God. You have comforts, you have meat to eat, which a sinful, carnal, ridiculing world knows nothing of. Christ's yoke is not become easy to you, and his burden light. You have passed through the pangs of the new birth, and now rejoice that Christ Jesus is spiritually formed in your hearts. You know what it is to dwell in Christ, and Christ in you. Like Jacob's ladder, although your bodies are on earth, yet your souls and hearts are in heaven: and by your faith and constant recollection, like the blessed angels, you do always behold the face of your Father which is in heaven.

I need not exhort you to press forward, for you know that in walking in the Spirit there is a great reward. Rather will I exhort you, in patience to possess your souls yet a little while, and Jesus Christ will deliver you from the burden of the flesh, and an abundant entrance shall be administered to you, into the eternal joy and uninterrupted felicity of his heavenly kingdom.

Which God of his infinite mercy grant, through Jesus Christ our Lord: To whom, with the Father, and the Holy Ghost, three Persons and one God, be ascribed all honor, power, and glory, for ever and ever.

Sermon 43 The Almost Christian

Acts 26:28, "Almost thou persuadest me to be a Christian."

The chapter, out of which the text is taken, contains an admirable account which the great St. Paul gave of his wonderful conversion from Judaism to Christianity, when he was called to make his defense before Festus a Gentile governor, and king Agrippa. Our blessed Lord had long since foretold, that when the Son of man should be lifted up, "his disciples should be brought before kings and rulers, for his name's sake, for a testimony unto them." And very good was the design of infinite wisdom in thus ordaining it; for Christianity being, from the beginning, a doctrine of the Cross, the princes and rulers of the earth thought themselves too high to be instructed by such mean teachers, or too happy to be disturbed b such unwelcome truths; and therefore would have always continued strangers to Jesus Christ, and him crucified, had not the apostles, by being arraigned before them, gained opportunities of preaching to them "Jesus and the resurrection." St. Paul knew full well that this was the main reason, why his blessed Master permitted his enemies at this time to arraign him at a public bar; and therefore, in compliance with the divine will, thinks it not sufficient, barely to make his defense, but endeavors at the same time to convert his judges. And this he did with such demonstration of the spirit, and of power, that Festus, unwilling to be convinced by the strongest evidence, cries out with a loud voice, "Paul, much earning doth make thee mad." To which the brave apostle (like a true follower of the holy Jesus) meekly replies, I am not mad, most noble Festus, but speak forth the words of truth and soberness." But in all probability, seeing king Agrippa more affected with his discourse, and observing in him an inclination to know the truth, he applies himself more particularly to him. "The king knoweth of these things; before whom also I speak freely; for I am persuaded that none of these things are hidden from him." And then, that if possible he might complete his wished-for conversion, he with an inimitable strain of oratory, addresses himself still more closely, "King Agrippa, believest thou the prophets? I know that thou believest them." At which the passions of the king began to work so strongly, that he was obliged in open court, to own himself affected by the prisoner's preaching, and ingenuously to cry out, "Paul, almost thou persuadest me to be a Christian." Which words, taken with the context, afford us a lively representation of the different reception, which the doctrine of Christ's ministers, who come in the power and spirit of St. Paul, meets with now-a-days in the minds of men. For notwithstanding they, like this great apostle, "speak forth the words of truth and soberness;" and with such energy and power, that all their adversaries cannot justly gainsay or resist; yet, too many, with the noble Festus before-mentioned, being like him, either too proud to be taught, or too sensual, too careless, or too worldly-minded to live up to the doctrine, in order to excuse themselves, cry out, that "much learning, much study, or, what is more unaccountable, much piety, hath made them mad." And though, blessed be God! All do not thus disbelieve our report; yet amongst those who gladly receive the word, and confess that we speak the words of truth and soberness, there are so few, who arrive at any higher degree of piety than that of Agrippa, or are any farther persuaded than to be almost Christians, that I cannot but think it highly necessary to warn my dear hearers of the danger of such a state. And therefore, from the words of the text, shall endeavor to show these three things: FIRST, What is meant by an almost-Christian.

SECONDLY, What are the chief reasons, why so many are no more than almost Christians.

THIRDLY, I shall consider the ineffectualness, danger, absurdity, and uneasiness which attends those who are but almost Christians; and then conclude with a general exhortation, to set all upon striving not only be almost, but altogether Christians.

I. And, FIRST, I am to consider what is meant by an almost Christians.

An almost Christian, if we consider him in respect to his duty to God, is one that halts between two opinions; that wavers between Christ and the world; that would reconcile God and Mammon, light and darkness, Christ and Belial. It is true, he has an inclination to religion, but then he is very cautious how he goes too far in it: his false heart is always crying out, Spare thyself, do thyself no harm. He prays indeed, that "God's will may be done on earth, as it is in heaven." But notwithstanding, he is very partial in his obedience, and fondly hopes that God will not be extreme to mark every thing that he willfully does amiss; though an inspired apostle has told him, that "he who offends in one point is guilty of all." But chiefly, he is one that depends much on outward ordinances, and on that account looks upon himself as righteous, and despises others; though at the same time he is as great a stranger to the divine life as any other person whatsoever. In short, he is fond of the form, but never experiences the power of godliness in his heart. He goes on year after year, attending on the means of grace, but then, like Pharaoh's lean cows, he is never the better, but rather the worse for them.

If you consider him in respect to his neighbor, he is one that is strictly just to all; but then this does not proceed from any love to God or regard to man, but only through a principle of self-love: because he knows dishonesty will spoil his reputation, and consequently hinder his thriving in the world.

He is one that depends much upon being negatively good, and contents himself with the consciousness of having done no one any harm; though he reads in the gospel, that "the unprofitable servant was cast into outer darkness," and the barren fig-tree was cursed and dried up from the roots, not for bearing bad, but no fruit.

He is no enemy to charitable contributions in public, if not too frequently recommended: but then he is unacquainted with the kind offices of visiting the sick and imprisoned, clothing the naked, and relieving the hungry in a private manner. He thinks that these things belong only to the clergy, though his own false heart tells him, that nothing but pride keeps him from exercising these acts of humility; and that Jesus Christ, in the 25th chapter of St. Matthew, condemns persons to everlasting punishment, not merely for being fornicators, drunkards, or extortioners, but for neglecting these charitable offices, "When the Son of man shall come in his glory, he shall set the sheep on his right-hand, and the goats on his left.

And then shall he say unto them on his left hand, depart from me, ye cursed, into everlasting fire prepared for the devil and his angels: for I was an hungered, and ye gave me no meat; I was thirsty, and ye gave me no drink; I was a stranger, and ye took me not in; naked, and ye clothed me not; sick and in prison, and ye visited me not. Then shall they also say, Lord, when saw we thee an hungered, or a-thirst, or a stranger, or naked, or sick, or in prison, and did not minister unto thee? Then shall he answer them, Verily I say unto you, inasmuch as ye have not done it unto one of the least of these my brethren, ye did it not unto me: and these shall go away into everlasting punishment unto me: and these shall go away into everlasting punishment." I thought proper to give you this whole passage of scripture at large, because our Savior lays such a particular stress upon it; and yet it is so little regarded, that were we to judge by the practice of Christians, one should be tempted to think there were no such verses in the Bible.

But to proceed in the character of an ALMOST CHRISTIAN: If we consider him in respect of himself; as we said he was strictly honest to his neighbor, so he is likewise strictly sober in himself: but then both his honesty and sobriety proceed from the same principle of a false self-love.

It is true, he runs not into the same excess of riot with other men; but then it is not out of obedience to the laws of God, but either because his constitution will not away with intemperance; or rather because he is cautious of forfeiting his reputation, or unfitting himself for temporal business. But though he is so prudent as to avoid intemperance and excess, for the reasons before-mentioned; yet he always goes to the extremity of what is lawful. It is true, he is no drunkard; but then he has no CHRISTIAN SELF-DENIAL. He cannot think our Savior to be so austere a Master, as to deny us to indulge ourselves in some particulars: and so by this means he is destitute of a sense of true religion, as much as if he lived in debauchery, or any other crime whatever. As to settling his principles as well as practice, he is guided more by the world, than by the word of God: for his part, he cannot think the way to heaven so narrow as some would make it; and therefore considers not so much what scripture requires, as what such and such a good man does, or what will best suit his own corrupt inclinations. Upon this account, he is not only very cautious himself, but likewise very careful of young converts, whose faces are set heavenward; and therefore is always acting the devil's part, and bidding them spare themselves, though they are doing no more than what the scripture strictly requires them to do: The consequence of which is, that "he suffers not himself to enter into the kingdom of God, and those that are entering in he hinders." Thus lives the almost Christian: not that I can say, I have fully described him to you; but from these outlines and sketches of his character, if your consciences have done their proper office, and made a particular application of what has been said to your own hearts, I cannot but fear that some of you may observe some features in his picture, odious as it is, to near resembling your own; and therefore I cannot but hope, that you will join with the apostle in the words immediately following the text, and wish yourselves "to be not only almost, but altogether Christians." II. I proceed to the second general thing proposed; to consider the reasons why so many are no more than almost Christians.

1. And the first reason I shall mention is, because so many set out with false notions of religion; though they live in a Christian country, yet they know not what Christianity is. This perhaps may be esteemed a hard saying, but experience sadly evinces the truth of it; for some place religion in being of this or that communion; more in morality; most in a round of duties, and a model of performances; and few, very few acknowledge it to be, what it really is, a thorough inward change of nature, a divine life, a vital participation of Jesus Christ, an union of the soul with God; which the apostle expresses by saying, "He that is joined to the Lord is one spirit." Hence it happens, that so many, even of the most knowing professors, when you come to converse with them concerning the essence, the life, the soul of religion, I

mean our new birth in Jesus Christ, confess themselves quite ignorant of the matter, and cry out with Nicodemus, "How can this thing be?" And no wonder then, that so many are only almost Christians, when so many know not what Christianity is: no marvel, that so many take up with the form, when they are quite strangers to the power of godliness; or content themselves with the shadow, when they know so little about the substance of it. And this is one cause why so many are almost, and so few are altogether Christians.

2. A second reason that may be assigned why so many are no more than almost Christians, is a servile fear of man: multitudes there are and have been, who, though awakened to a sense of the divine life, and have tasted and felt the powers of the world to come; yet out of a base sinful fear of being counted singular, or contemned by men, have suffered all those good impressions to wear off. It is true, they have some esteem for Jesus Christ; but then, like Nicodemus, they would come to him only by night: they are willing to serve him; but then they would do it secretly, for fear of the Jews: they have a mind to see Jesus, but then they cannot come to him because of the press, and for fear of being laughed at, and ridiculed by those with whom they used to sit at meat. But well did our Savior prophesy of such persons, "How can ye love me, who receive honor one of another?" Alas! have they never read, that "the friendship of this world is enmity with God;" and that our Lord himself has threatened, "Whosoever shall be ashamed of me or of my words, in this wicked and adulterous generation, of him shall the Son of man be ashamed, when he cometh in the glory of his Father and of his holy angels?" No wonder that so many are no more than almost Christians, since so many "love the praise of men more than the honor which cometh of God." 3. A third reason why so many are no more than almost Christians, is a reigning love of money. This was the pitiable case of that forward young man in the gospel, who came running to our blessed Lord, and kneeling before him, inquired "what he must do to inherit eternal life;" to whom our blessed Master replied, "Thou knowest the commandments, Do not kill, Do not commit adultery, Do not steal:" To which the young man replied, "All these have I kept from my youth." But when our Lord proceeded to tell him, "Yet lackest thou one thing; Go sell all that thou hast, and give to the poor; he was grieved at that saying, and went away sorrowful, for he had great possessions!" Poor youth! He had a good mind to be a Christian, and to inherit eternal life, but thought it too dear, if it could be purchased at no less an expense than of his estate! And thus many, both young and old, now-a-days, come running to worship our blessed Lord in public, and kneel before him in private, and inquire at his gospel, what they must do to inherit eternal life: but when they find they must renounce the self-enjoyment of riches, and forsake all in affection to follow him, they cry, "The Lord pardon us in this thing! We pray thee, have us excused." But is heaven so small a trifle in men's esteem, as not to be worth a little gilded earth? Is eternal life so mean a purchase, as not to deserve the temporary renunciation of a few transitory riches? Surely it is. But however inconsistent such a be-

havior may be, this inordinate love of money is too evidently the common and fatal cause, why so many are no more than almost Christians.

4. Nor is the love of pleasure a less uncommon, or a less fatal cause why so many are no more than almost Christians. Thousands and ten thousands there are, who despise riches, and would willingly be true disciples of Jesus Christ, if parting with their money would make them so; but when they are told that our blessed Lord has said, "Whosoever will come after him must deny himself;" like the pitiable young man before-mentioned, "they go away sorrowful"" for they have too great a love for sensual pleasures. They will perhaps send for the ministers of Christ, as Herod did for John, and hear them gladly: but touch them in their Herodias, tell them they must part with such or such a darling pleasure; and with wicked Ahab they cry out, "Hast thou found us, O our enemy?" Tell them of the necessity of mortification and self-denial, and it is as difficult for them to hear, as if you was to bid them "cut off a right-hand, or pluck out a right-eye." They cannot think our blessed Lord requires so much at their hands, though an inspired apostle has commanded us to "mortify our members which are upon earth." And who himself, even after he had converted thousands, and was very near arrived to the end of his race, yet professed that it was his daily practice to "keep under his body, and bring it into subjection, lest after he had preached to others, he himself should be a cast-away!" But some men would be wiser than this great apostle, and chalk out to us what they falsely imagine an easier way to happiness. They would flatter us, we may go to heaven without offering violence to our sensual appetites; and enter into the strait gate without striving against our carnal inclinations. And this is another reason why so many are only almost, and not altogether Christians.

5. The fifth and last reason I shall assign why so many are only almost Christians, is a fickleness and instability of temper.

It has been, no doubt, a misfortune that many a minister and sincere Christian has met with, to weep and wail over numbers of promising converts, who seemingly began in the Spirit, but after a while fell away, and basely ended in the flesh; and this not for want of right notions in religion, nor out of a servile fear of man, nor from the love of money, or of sensual pleasure, but through an instability and fickleness of temper.

They looked upon religion merely for novelty, as something which pleased them for a while; but after their curiosity was satisfied, they laid it aside again: like the young man that came to see Jesus with a linen cloth about his naked body, they have followed him for a season, but when temptations came to take hold on them, for want of a little more resolution, they have been stripped of all their good intentions, and fled away naked. They at first, like a tree planted by the water-side, grew up and flourished for a while; but having no root in themselves, no inward principle of holiness and piety, like Jonah's gourd, they were soon dried up and withered. Their good intentions are too like the violent motions of the animal spirits of a body newly beheaded, which, though impetuous, are not lasting. In short, they set out well in their journey to heaven, but finding the way either narrower or longer than they expected, through an unsteadiness of temper, they have made an eternal halt, and so "returned like the dog to his vomit, or like the sow that was washed to her wallowing in the more!" But I tremble to pronounce the fate of such unstable professors, who having put their hands to the plough, for want of a little more resolution, shamefully look back. How shall I repeat to them that dreadful threatening, "If any man draw back, my soul shall have no pleasure in him:" And again, "It is impossible (that is, exceeding difficult at least) for those that have been once enlightened, and have tasted of the heavenly gift, and the powers of the world to come, if they should fall away, to be renewed again unto repentance." But notwithstanding the gospel is so severe against apostates, yet many that begun well, through a fickleness of temper, (O that none of us here present may ever be such) have been by this means of the number of those that turn back unto perdition. And this is the fifth, and the last reason I shall give, why so many are only almost, and not altogether Christians.

III. Proceed we now to the general thing proposed, namely, to consider the folly of being no more than an almost Christian.

1. And the FIRST proof I shall give of the folly of such a proceeding is, that it is ineffectual to salvation. It is true, such men are almost good; but almost to hit the mark, is really to miss it. God requires us "to love him with all our hearts, with all our souls, and with all our strength." He loves us too well to admit any rival; because, so far as our hearts are empty of God, so far must they be unhappy. The devil, indeed, like the false mother that came before Solomon, would have our hearts divided, as she would have had the child; but God, like the true mother, will have all or none. "My Son, give me thy heart," thy whole heart, is the general call to all: and if this be not done, we never can expect the divine mercy.

Persons may play the hypocrite; but God at the great day will strike them dead, (as he did Ananias and Sapphira by the mouth of his servant Peter) for pretending to offer him all their hearts, when they keep back from him the greatest part. They may perhaps impose upon their fellow- creatures for a while; but he that enabled Elijah to cry out, "Come in thou wife of Jeroboam," when she came disguised to inquire about he sick son, will also discover them through their most artful dissimulations; and if their hearts are not wholly with him, appoint them their portion with hypocrites and unbelievers.

2. But, SECONDLY, What renders an half-way-piety more inexcusable is, that it is not only insufficient to our own salvation, but also very prejudicial to that of others.

An almost Christian is one of the most hurtful creatures in the world; he is a wolf in sheep's clothing: he is one of those false prophets, our blessed Lord bids us beware of in his sermon on the mount, who would persuade men, that the way to heaven is broader than it really is; and thereby, as it was observed before, "enter not into the kingdom of God themselves, and those that are entering in they hinder." These, these are the men that turn the world into a luke-warm Laodicean spirit; that hang out false lights, and so shipwreck unthinking benighted souls in their voyage to the haven of eternity. These are they who are greater enemies to the cross of Christ, than infidels themselves: for of an unbeliever every one will be aware; but an almost Christian, through his subtle hypocrisy, draws away many after him; and therefore must expect to receive the greater damnation.

3. But, THIRDLY, As it is most prejudicial to ourselves and hurtful to others, so it is the greatest instance of ingratitude we can express towards our Lord and Master Jesus Christ. For did he come down from heaven, and shed his precious blood, to purchase these hearts of ours, and shall we only give him half of them? O how can we say we love him, when our hearts are not wholly with him? How can we call him our Savior, when we will not endeavor sincerely to approve ourselves to him, and so let him see the travail of his soul, and be satisfied!

Had any of us purchased a slave at a most expensive rate, and who was before involved in the utmost miseries and torments, and so must have continued for ever, had we shut up our bowels of compassion from him; and was this slave afterwards to grow rebellious, or deny giving us but half his service; how, how should we exclaim against his base ingratitude! And yet this base ungrateful slave thou art, O man, who acknowledgest thyself to be redeemed from infinite unavoidable misery and punishment by the death of Jesus Christ, and yet wilt not give thyself wholly to him. But shall we deal with God our Maker in a manner we would not be dealt with by a man like ourselves? God forbid! No. Suffer me, therefore, To add a word or two of exhortation to you, to excite you to be not only almost, but altogether Christians. O let us scorn all base and treacherous treatment of our King and Savior, of our God and Creator. Let us not take some pains all our lives to go to haven, and yet plunge ourselves into hell as last. Let us give to God our whole hearts, and no longer halt between two opinions: if the world be God, let us serve that; if pleasure be a God, let us serve that; but if the Lord he be God, let us, O let us serve him alone. Alas! why, why should we stand out any longer?

Why should we be so in love with slavery, as not wholly to renounce the world, the flesh, and the devil, which, like so many spiritual chains, bind down our souls, and hinder them from flying up to God. Alas! what are we afraid of? Is not God able to reward our entire obedience? If he is, as the almost Christian's lame way of serving him, seems to grant, why then will we not serve him entirely? For the same reason we do so much, why do we not do more? Or do you think that being only half religious will make you happy, but that going farther, will render you miserable and uneasy? Alas!

this, my brethren, is delusion all over: for what is it but this half piety, this wavering between God and the world, that makes so many, that are seemingly well disposed, such utter strangers to the comforts of religion? They choose just so much of religion as will disturb them in their lusts, and follow their lusts so far as to deprive themselves of the comforts of religion. Whereas on the contrary, would they sincerely leave all in affection, and give their hearts wholly to God, they would then (and they cannot till then) experience the unspeakable pleasure of having a mind at unity with itself, and enjoy such a peace of God, which even in this life passes all understanding, and which they were entire strangers to before. It is true, it we will devote ourselves entirely to God, we must meet with contempt; but then it is because contempt is necessary to heal our pride. We must renounce some sensual pleasures, but then it is because those unfit us for spiritual ones, which are infinitely better. We must renounce the love of the world; but then it is that we may be filled with the love of God: and when that has once enlarged our hearts, we shall, like Jacob when he served for his beloved Rachel, think nothing too difficult to undergo, no hardships too tedious to endure, because of the love we shall then have for our dear Redeemer. Thus easy, thus delightful will be the ways of God even in this life: but when once we throw off these bodies, and our souls are filled with all the fullness of God, O! what heart can conceive, what tongue can express, with what unspeakable joy and consolation shall we then look back on our past sincere and hearty services. Think you then, my dear hearers, we shall repent we had done too much; or rather think you not, we shall be ashamed that we did no more; and blush we were so backward to give up all to God; when he intended hereafter to give us himself?

Let me therefore, to conclude, exhort you, my brethren, to have always before you the unspeakable happiness of enjoying God. And think withal, that every degree of holiness you neglect, every act of piety you omit, is a jewel taken out of your crown, a degree of blessedness lost in the vision of God. O! do but always think and act thus, and you will no longer be laboring to compound matters between God and the world; but, on the contrary, be daily endeavoring to give up yourselves more and more unto him; you will be always watching, always praying, always aspiring after farther degrees of purity and love, and consequently always preparing yourselves for a fuller sight and enjoyment of that God, in whose presence there is fullness of joy, and at whose right-hand there are pleasures for ever more. Amen! Amen!

Sermon 44 Christ, the Believer's Wisdom, Righteousness, Sanctification and Redemption

1 Corinthians 1:30, "But of him are ye in Christ Jesus, who of God is made unto us wisdom, and righteousness, and sanctification, and redemption."

Of all the verses in the book of God, this which I have now read to you, is, I believe, one of the most comprehensive: what glad tidings does it bring to believers! What precious privileges are they herein invested with! How are they here led to the fountain of them all, I mean, the love, the everlasting love of God the Father! `Of him are ye in Christ Jesus, who of God is made unto us wisdom, righteousness, sanctification, and redemption.' Without referring you to the context, I shall from the words, FIRST, Point out to you the fountain, from which all those blessings flow, that the elect of God partake of in Jesus Christ, "Who of God is made unto'. And, SECONDLY, I shall consider what these blessings are, `Wisdom, righteousness, sanctification, and redemption'.

FIRST, I would point out to you the fountain, from which all those blessings flow, that the elect of God partake of in Jesus, `who of God is made unto us', the father he it is who is spoken of here. Not as though Jesus Christ was not God also; but God the Father is the fountain of the Deity; and if we consider Jesus Christ acting as Mediator, God the Father is greater than he; there was an eternal contract between the Father and the Son: "I have made a covenant with my chosen, and I have sworn unto David my servant'; now David was a type of Christ, with whom the Father made a covenant, that if he would obey and suffer, and make himself a sacrifice for sin, he should `see his seed, he should prolong his days, and the pleasure of the Lord should prosper in his hands'. This compact our Lord refers to, in that glorious prayer recorded in the 17th chapter of John; and therefore he prays for, or rather demands with a full assurance, all that were given to him by the Father: `Father,

I will that they also whom thou hast given me, be with me where I am.' For this same reason, the apostle breaks out into praises of God, even the Father of our Lord Jesus Christ; for he loved the elect with an everlasting love, or, as our Lord expresses it, `before the foundation of the world'; and, therefore, to show them to whom they were beholden for their salvation, our Lord, in the 25th of Matthew, represents himself saying, `Come, ye blessed children of my Father, receive the kingdom prepared for you from the foundation of the world'. And thus, in reply to the mother of Zebedee's children, he says, `It is not mine to give, but it shall be given to them for whom it is prepared of the Father'. The apostle therefore, when here speaking of the Christian's privileges, lest they should sacrifice to their own drag, or think their salvation was owing to their own faithfulness, or improvement of their own free-will, reminds them to look back on the everlasting love of God the Father; `who of God is made unto us', etc.

Would to God this point of doctrine was considered more, and people were more studious of the covenant of redemption between the Father and the Son! We should not then have so much disputing against the doctrine of election, or hear it condemned (even by good men) as a doctrine of devils.

For my own part, I cannot see how true humbleness of mind can be attained without a knowledge of it; and though I will not say, that every one who denies election is a bad man, yet I will say, with that sweet singer, Mr.

Trail, it is a very bad sign: such a one, whoever he be, I think cannot truly know himself; for, if we deny election, we must, partly at least, glory in ourselves; but our redemption is so ordered that no flesh should glory in the Divine presence; and hence it is, that the pride of man opposes this doctrine, because, according to this doctrine, and no other, `he that glories, must glory only in the Lord'. But what shall I say?

Election is a mystery that shines with such resplendent brightness, that, to make use of the words of one who has drunk deeply of electing love, it dazzles the weak eyes even of some of God's dear children; however, though they know it not, all the blessings they receive, all the privileges they do or ill enjoy, through Jesus Christ, flow from the everlasting love of God the Father: `But of him are you in Christ Jesus, who of God is made unto us, wisdom, righteousness, sanctification, and redemption.' SECONDLY, I come to show what these blessings are, which are here, through Christ, made over to the elect. And, 1: FIRST, Christ is made to them WISDOM; but wherein does true wisdom consist? Were I to ask some of you, perhaps you would say, in indulging the lust of the flesh, and saying to your souls, eat, drink, and be merry: but this is only the wisdom of brutes; they have as good a gust and relish for sensual pleasures, as the greatest epicure on earth. Others would tell me, true wisdom consisted in adding house to house, and field to field, and calling lands after their own names: but this cannot be true wisdom; for riches often take to themselves wings, and fly away, like an eagle towards heaven. Even wisdom itself assures us, `that a man's life doth not consist in the abundance of the things which he possesses'; vanity, vanity, all these things are vanity; for, if riches leave not the owner, the owners must soon leave them; `for rich men must also die, and leave their riches for others'; their riches cannot procure them redemption from the grave, whither we are all hastening apace.

But perhaps you despise riches and pleasure, and therefore place wisdom in the knowledge of books: but it is possible for you to tell the numbers of the stars, and call them all by their names, and yet be mere fools; learned men are not always wise; nay, our common learning, so much cried up, makes men only so many accomplished fools; to keep you therefore no longer in suspense, and withal to humble you, I will send you to a heathen to school, to learn what true wisdom is: `Know thyself', was a saying of one of the wise men of Greece; this is certainly true wisdom, and this is that wisdom spoken of in the text, and which Jesus Christ is made to all elect sinners _ they are made to know themselves, so as not to think more highly of themselves than they ought to think. Before, they were darkness; now, they are light in the Lord; and in that light they see their own darkness; they now bewail themselves as fallen creatures by nature, dead in trespasses and sins, sons and heirs of hell, and children of wrath; they now see that all their righteousnesses are but as filthy rags; that there is no health in their souls; that they are poor and miserable, blind and naked; and that there is no name given under heaven, whereby they can be saved, but that of Jesus Christ. They see the necessity of closing with a Savior, and behold the wisdom of God in appointing him to be a Savior; they are also made willing to accept of salvation upon our Lord's own terms, and receive him as their all in all; thus Christ is made to them wisdom.

2. SECONDLY, RIGHTEOUSNESS, `Who of God is made unto us, wisdom, righteousness': Christ's whole personal righteousness is made over to, and accounted theirs. They are enabled to lay hold on Christ by faith, and God the Father blots out their transgressions, as with a thick cloud: their sins and their iniquities he remembers no more; they are made the righteousness of God in Christ Jesus, `who is the end of the law for righteousness to every one that believeth'. In one sense, God now sees no sin in them; the whole covenant of works is fulfilled in them; they are actually justified, acquitted, and looked upon as righteous in the sight of God; they are perfectly accepted in the beloved; they are complete in him; the flaming sword of God's wrath, which before moved every way, is not removed, and free access given to the tree of life; they are enabled to reach out the arm of faith, and pluck, and live for evermore. Hence it is that the apostle, under a sense of this

blessed privilege, breaks out into this triumphant language; `It is Christ that justifies, who is he that condemns?' Does sin condemn? Christ's righteousness delivers believers from the guilt of it: Christ is their Savior, and is become a propitiation for their sins: who therefore shall lay any thing to the charge of God's elect?

Does the law condemn? By having Christ's righteousness imputed to them, they are dead to the law, as a covenant of works; Christ has fulfilled it for them, and in their stead. Does death threaten them? They need not fear: the sting of death is sin, the strength of sin is the law; but God has given them the victory by imputing to them the righteousness of the Lord Jesus.

And what a privilege is here! Well might the angels at the birth of Christ say to the humble shepherds, `Behold, I bring you glad tidings of great joy'; unto you that believe in Christ `a Savior is born'. And well may angels rejoice at the conversion of poor sinners; for the Lord is their righteousness; they have peace with God through faith in Christ's blood, and shall never enter into condemnation. O believers! (for this discourse is intended in a special manner for you) lift up your heads; `rejoice in the Lord always; again I say, rejoice'. Christ is mad to you, of God, righteousness, what then should you fear? You are made the righteousness of God in him; you may be called, `The Lord our righteousness'. Of what then should you be afraid? What shall separate you henceforward from the love of Christ? `Shall tribulation, or distress, or persecution, or famine, or nakedness, or peril, or sword? No, I am persuaded, neither death, nor life, nor angels, nor principalities, nor powers, nor things present, nor things to come, nor height, nor depth, nor any other creature, shall be able to separate you from the love of God, which is in Christ Jesus our Lord', who of God is made unto you righteousness.

This is a glorious privilege, but this is only the beginning of the happiness of believers: For, 3: THIRDLY, Christ is not only made to them righteousness, but sanctification; by sanctification, I do not mean a bare hypocritical attendance on outward ordinances, though rightly informed Christians will think it their duty and privilege constantly to attend on all outward ordinances. Nor do I mean by sanctification a bare outward reformation, and a few transient convictions, or a little legal sorrow; for all this an unsanctified man may have; but, by sanctification I mean a total renovation of the whole man: by the righteousness of Christ, believers come legally, by sanctification they are made spiritually, alive; by the one they are entitled to, by the other they are made meet for, glory. They are sanctified, therefore, throughout, in spirit, soul, and body.

Their understandings, which were dark before, now become light in the Lord; and their wills, before contrary to, now become one with the will of

God; their affections are now set on things above; their memory is now filled with divine things; their natural consciences are now enlightened; their members, which were before instruments of uncleanness, and of iniquity into iniquity, are now new creatures; 'old things are passed away, all things are become new', in their hearts: sin has now no longer dominion over them; they are freed from the power, though not the indwelling of being, of it; they are holy both in heart and life, in all manner of conversation: they are made partakers of a divine nature, and from Jesus Christ, they receive grace; and every grace that is in Christ, is copied and transcribed into their souls; they are transformed into his likeness; he is formed within them; they dwell in him, and he in them; they are led by the Spirit, and bring forth the fruits thereof; they know that Chris is their Emmanuel, God with and in them; they are living temples of the Holy Ghost. And therefore, being a holy habitation unto the Lord, the whole Trinity dwells and walks in them; even here, they sit together with Christ in heavenly places, and are vitally united to him, their Head, by a living faith; their Redeemer, their Maker, is their husband; they are flesh of his flesh, bone of his bone; they talk, they walk with him, as a man talketh and walketh with his friend; in short, they are one with Christ, even as Jesus Christ and the Father are one.

Thus is Christ made to believers sanctification. And O what a privilege is this! to be changed from beasts into saints, and from a devilish, to be made partakers of a divine nature; to be translated from the kingdom of Satan, into the kingdom of God's dear Son! To put off the old man, which is corrupt, and to put on the new man, which is created after God, in righteousness and true holiness! O what an unspeakable blessing is this! I almost stand amazed at the contemplation thereof. Well might the apostle exhort believers to rejoice in the Lord; indeed they have reason always to rejoice, yea, to rejoice on a dying bed; for the kingdom of God is in them; they are changed from glory to glory, even by the Spirit of the Lord: well may this be a mystery to the natural, for it is a mystery even to the spiritual man himself, a mystery which he cannot fathom. Does it not often dazzle your eyes, O ye children of God, to look at your own brightness, when the candle of the Lord shines out, and your redeemer lifts up the light of his blessed countenance upon your souls? Are not you astonished, when you feel the love of God shed abroad in your hearts by the Holy Ghost, and God holds out the golden scepter of his mercy, and bids you ask what you will, and it shall be given you? Does not that peace of God, which keeps and rules your hearts, surpass the utmost limits of your understandings? And is not the joy you feel unspeakable? Is it not full of glory? I am persuaded it is; and in your secret communion, when the Lord's love flows in upon your souls, you are as it were swallowed up in, or, to use the apostle's phrase, 'filled with all the fullness of God'. Are not you ready to cry out with Solomon, 'And will the Lord, indeed, dwell thus with men!' How is it that we should be thus thy sons and daughters, O Lord God Almighty!

If you are children of God, and know what it is to have fellowship with the Father and the Son; if you walk by faith, and not by sight; I am assured this is frequently the language of your hearts.

But look forward, and see an unbounded prospect of eternal happiness lying before thee, O believer! what thou hast already received are only the first-fruits, like the cluster of grapes brought out of the land of Canaan; only an earnest and pledge of yet infinitely better things to come: the harvest is to follow; thy grace is hereafter to be swallowed up in glory.

Thy great Joshua, and merciful High-Priest, shall administer an abundant entrance to thee into the land of promise, that rest which awaits the children of God: for Christ is not only made to believers wisdom, righteousness, and sanctification, but also REDEMPTION.

But, before we enter upon the explanation and contemplation of this privilege, FIRSTLY, Learn hence the great mistake of those writers and clergy, who, notwithstanding they talk of sanctification and inward holiness, (as indeed sometimes they do, though in a very loose and superficial manner,) yet they generally make it the CAUSE, whereas they should consider it as the EFFECT, of our justification. 'Of him are ye in Christ Jesus, who of God is made unto us, wisdom, righteousness, (and then) sanctification.' For Christ's righteousness, or that which Christ has done in our stead without us, is the sole cause of our acceptance in the sight of God, and of all holiness wrought in us: to this, and not to the light within, or any thing wrought within, should poor sinners seek for justification in the sight of God: for the sake of Christ's righteousness alone, and not any thing wrought in us, does God look favorably upon us; our sanctification at best, in this life, is not complete: though we be delivered from the power, we are not freed from the in-being of sin; but not only the dominion, but the in-being of sin, is forbidden, by the perfect law of God: for it is not said, thou shalt not give way to lust, but 'thou shalt not lust'. So that whilst the principle of lust remains in the least degree in our hearts, though we are otherwise never so holy, yet we cannot, on account of that, hope for acceptance with God. We must first, therefore, look for a righteousness without us, even the righteousness of our Lord Jesus Christ: for this reason the apostle mentions it, and puts it before sanctification, in the words of the text. And whosoever teacheth any other doctrine, doth not preach the truth as it is in Jesus.

SECONDLY, From hence also, the Antinomians and formal hypocrites may be confuted, who talk of Christ without, but know nothing, experimentally, of a work of sanctification wrought within them. Whatever they may pretend to, since Christ is not in them, the Lord is not their righteousness, and they have no well-grounded hope of glory: for though sanctification is not the cause, yet it is the effect of our acceptance with God; 'Who of God is made unto us righteousness and sanctification'. He, therefore, that is really in Christ, is a new creature; it is not going back to a covenant of works, to look into our hearts, and, seeing that they are changed and renewed, from thence form a comfortable and well grounded assurance of the safety of our states: no, but this I what we are directed to in scripture; by our bringing forth the fruits, we are to judge whether or no we ever did truly partake of the Spirit of God. 'We know (says John) that we are passed from death unto life, because we love the brethren.' And however we may talk of Christ's right-eousness, and exclaim against legal preachers, yet, if we be not holy in heart and life, if we be not sanctified and renewed by the Spirit in our minds, we are self-deceivers, we are only formal hypocrites: for we must not put asunder what God has joined together; we must keep the medium between the two extremes; not insist so much on the one hand upon Christ without, as to ex-clude Christ within, as an evidence of our being his, and as a preparation for future happiness; nor, on the other hand, so depend on inherent righteousness or holiness wrought in us, as to exclude the righteousness of Jesus Christ without us. But, 4: FOURTHLY, Let us now go on, and take a view of the other link, or rather the end, of the believer's golden chain or privileges, REDEMPTION.

But we must look very high; for the top of it, like Jacob's ladder, reaches heaven, where all believers will ascend, and be placed at the right hand of God. 'Who of God is made unto us, wisdom, righteousness, sanctifi-cation, and REDEMPTION.' This is a golden chain indeed! and, what is best of all, not one link can ever be broken asunder from another. Was there no other text in the book of God, this single one sufficiently proves the final per-severance of true believers: or never did God yet justify a man, whom he did not sanctify; nor sanctify one, whom he did not completely redeem and glo-rify: no! as for God, his way, his works, is perfect; he always carried on and finished the work he begun; thus it was in the first, so it is in the new crea-tion; when God says, 'Let there be light', there is light, that shines more and more unto the perfect day, when believers enter into their eternal rest, as God entered into his. Those whom God has justified, he has in effect glorified: for as a man's worthiness was not the cause of God's giving him Christ's right-eousness; so neither shall his unworthiness be a cause of his taking it away; God's gifts and callings are without repentance: and I cannot think they are clear in the notion of Christ's righteousness, who deny the final perseverance of the saints; I fear they understand justification in that low sense, which I understood it in a few years ago, as implying no more than remission of sins: but it not only signifies remission of sins past, but also a FEDERAL RIGHT to all good things to come. If God has given us his only Son, how shall he not with him freely give us all things? Therefore, the apostle, after he says, 'Who of God is made unto us righteousness', does not say, perhaps he may be made to us sanctification and redemption: but, 'he is made': for there is an eternal, indissoluble connection between these blessed privileges. As the obedience of Christ is imputed to believers, so his perseverance in that obedience is to be imputed to them also; and it argues great ignorance of the covenant of grace and redemption, to object against it.

By the word REDEMPTION, we are to understand, not only a complete deliverance from all evil, but also a full enjoyment of all good both in body and soul: I say, both in body and soul; for the Lord is also for the body; the bodies of the saints in this life are temples of the Holy Ghost; God makes a covenant with the dust of believers; after death, though worms destroy them, yet, even in their flesh shall they see God. I fear, indeed, there are some Sadducees in our days, or at least heretics, who say, either, that there is no resurrection of the body, or that the resurrection is past already, namely, in our regeneration: Hence it is, that our Lord's coming in the flesh, at the day of judgment, is denied; and consequently, we must throw aside the sacrament of the Lord's supper. For why should we remember the Lord's death until he come to judgment, when he is already come to judge our hearts, and will not come a second time? But all this is only the reasoning of unlearned, unstable men, who certainly know not what they say, nor whereof they affirm. That we must follow our Lord in the regeneration, be partakers of a new birth, and that Christ must come into our hearts, we freely confess; and we hope, when speaking of these things, we speak no more than what we know and feel: but then it is plain, that Jesus Christ will come, hereafter, to judgment, and that he ascended into heaven with the body which he had here on earth; for says he, after his resurrection, 'Handle me, and see; a spirit has not flesh and bones, as you see me have'. And it is plain, that Christ's resurrection was an earnest of ours: for says the apostle, 'Christ is risen from the dead, and become the first-fruits of them that sleep; and as in Adam all die, and are subject to mortality; so all that are in Christ, the second Adam, who represented believers as their federal head, shall certainly be made alive, or rise again with their bodies at the last day'.

Here then, O believers! is one, though the lowest, degree of that redemption which you are to be partakers of hereafter; I mean, the redemption of your bodies: for this corruptible must put on incorruption, this mortal must put on immortality. Your bodies, as well as souls, were given to Jesus Christ by the Father; they have been companions in watching, and fasting, and praying: your bodies, therefore, as well as souls, shall Jesus Christ raise up at the last day. Fear not, therefore, O believers, to look into the grave: for to you it is not other than a consecrated dormitory, where your bodies shall sleep quietly until the morning of the resurrection; when the voice of the archangel shall sound, and the trump of God given the general alarm, 'Arise, ye dead, and come to judgment'; earth, air, fire, water, shall give up your scattered atoms, and both in body and soul shall you be ever with the Lord. I doubt not, but many of you are groaning under crazy bodies, and complain often that the mortal body weighs down the immortal soul; at least this is my case; but let us have a little patience, and we shall be delivered from our earthly prisons; ere long, these tabernacles of clay shall be dissolved, and we shall be clothed with our house which is from heaven; hereafter, our bodies shall be spiritualized, and shall be so far from hindering our souls through weakness, that they shall become string; so strong, as to bear up under an exceeding and eternal weight of glory; others again may have deformed bodies, emaciated also with sickness, and worn out with labor at age; but wait a little, until your blessed change by death comes; then your bodies shall be renewed and made glorious, like unto Christ's glorious body: of which we may form some faint idea, from the account given us of our Lord's transfiguration on the mount, when it is said, 'His raiment became bright and glistening, and his face brighter than the sun'. Well then may a believer break out in the apostle's triumphant language, 'O death, where is thy sting! O grave, where is thy victory!' But what is the redemption of the body, in comparison of the redemption of the better part, our souls? I must, therefore say to you believers, as the angel said to John, 'Come up higher'; and let us take as clear a view as we can, at such a distance, of the redemption Christ has purchased for, and will shortly put you in actual possession of. Already you are justified, already you are sanctified, and thereby freed from the guilt and dominion of sin: but, as I have observed, the being and indwelling of sin yet remains in you; God sees it proper to leave some Amalekites in the land, to keep his Israel in action. The most perfect Christian, I am persuaded, must agree, according to one of our Articles, 'That the corruption of nature remains even in the regenerate; that the flesh lusteth always against the spirit, and the spirit against the flesh'.

So that believers cannot do things for God with that perfection they desire; this grieves their righteous souls day by day, and, with the holy apostle, makes them cry out, 'Who shall deliver us from the body of this death!' I thank God, our Lord Jesus Christ will, but not completely before the day of our dissolution; they will the very being of sin be destroyed, and an eternal stop put to inbred, indwelling corruption. And is not this a great redemption? I am sure believers esteem it o: for there is nothing grieves the heart of a child of God so much, as the remains of indwelling sin. Again, believers are often in heaviness through manifold temptations; God sees that it is needful and good for them so to be; and though they may be highly favored, and wrapt up in communion with God, even to the third heavens; yet a messenger of Satan is often sent to buffet them, lest they should be puffed up with the abundance of revelations. But be not weary, be not faint in your minds: the time of your complete redemption draweth nigh.

In heaven the wicked one shall cease from troubling you, and your weary souls shall enjoy an everlasting rest; his fiery darts cannot reach those blissful regions: Satan will never come any more to appear with, disturb, or accuse the sons of God, when once the Lord Jesus Christ shuts the door.

Your righteous souls are now grieved, day by day, at the ungodly conversation of the wicked; tares now grow up among the wheat; wolves come in sheep's clothing: but the redemption spoken of in the text, will free your souls from all anxiety on these accounts; hereafter you shall enjoy a perfect communion of saints; nothing that is unholy or unsanctified shall enter into the holy of holies, which is prepared for you above: this, and all manner of evil whatsoever, you shall be delivered from, when your redemption is hereafter made complete in heaven; not only so, but you shall enter into the full enjoyment of all good. It is true, all saints will not have the same degree of happiness, but all will be as happy as their hearts can desire. Believers, you shall judge the evil, and familiarly converse with good, angels: you shall sit down with Abraham, Isaac, Jacob, and all the spirits of just men made perfect; and, to sum up all your happiness in one word, you shall see God the Father, Son, and Holy Ghost; and, by seeing God, be more and more like unto him, and pass from glory to glory, even to all eternity.

But I must stop the glories of the upper world crowd in so fast upon my soul, that I am lost in the contemplation of them. Brethren, the redemption spoken of is unutterable; we cannot here find it out; eye hath not seen, nor ear heard, nor has it entered into the hearts of the most holy men living to conceive, how great it is. Were I to entertain you whole ages with an account of it, when you come to heaven, you must say, with the queen of Sheba, 'Not half, no, not one thousandth part was told us'. All we can do here, is to go upon mount Pisgah, and, by the eye of faith, take a distant view of the promised land: we may see it, as Abraham did Christ, afar off, and rejoice in it; but here we only know in part. Blessed be God, there is a time coming, when we shall know God, even as we are known, and God be all in all. Lord Jesus, accomplish the number of thine elect! Lord Jesus, hasten thy kingdom!

And now, where are the scoffers of these last days, who count the lives of Christians to be madness, and their end to be without honor?

Unhappy men! you know not what you do. Were your eyes open, and had you senses to discern spiritual things, you would not speak all manner of evil against the children of God, but you would esteem them as the excellent ones of the earth, and envy their happiness: your souls would hunger and thirst after it: you also would become fools for Christ's sake. You boast of wisdom; so did the philosophers of Corinth: but your wisdom is the foolishness of folly in the sight of God. What will your wisdom avail you, if it does not make you wise unto salvation? Can you, with all your wisdom, propose a more consistent scheme to build you hopes of salvation on, than what has been now laid before you? Can you, with all the strength of natural reason, find out a better way of acceptance with God, than by the righteousness of the Lord Jesus Christ? Is it right to think your own works can in any measure deserve or procure it? If not, why will you not believe in him? Why will you not submit to his righteousness? Can you deny that you are fallen creatures? Do not you find that you are full of disorders, and that these disorders make you unhappy? Do not you find that you cannot change your own hearts? Have you not resolved many and many a time, and have not your corruptions yet dominion over you? Are you not bondslaves to your lusts, and led captive by the devil at his will? Why then will you not come to Christ for sanctification? Do you not desire to die the death of the righteous, and that your future state may be like theirs; I am persuaded you cannot bear the thoughts of being annihilated, much less of being miserable for ever. Whatever you may pretend, if you speak truth, you must confess, that conscience breaks in upon you in more sober intervals whether you will or not, and even constrains you to believe that hell is no painted fire. And why then will you not come to Christ? He alone can procure you everlasting redemption. Haste, haste away to him, poor beguiled sinners. You lack wisdom; ask it of Christ. Who knows but he may give it you? He is able: for he is the wisdom of the Father; he is that wisdom which was from everlasting. You have no righteousness; away, therefore, to Christ: 'He is the end of the law for righteousness to every one that believeth.' You are unholy: flee to the Lord Jesus: He is full of grace and truth; ;and of his fullness all may receive that believe in him. You are afraid to die; let this drive you to Christ: he has the keys of death and hell: in him is plenteous redemption; he alone can open the door which leads to everlasting life.

Let not, therefore, the deceived reasoner boast any longer of his pretended reason. Whatever you may think, it is the most unreasonable thing in the world not to believe on Jesus Christ, whom God has sent. Why, why will you die? Why will you not come unto him, that you may have life? 'Ho!

every one that thirsteth, come unto the waters of life, and drink freely: come, buy without money and without price.' Were these blessed privileges in the text to be purchased with money, you might say, we are poor, and cannot buy: or, were they to be conferred only on sinners of such a rank or degree, then you might say, how can such sinners as we, expect to be so highly favored? But they are to be freely given of God to the worst of sinners. 'To us', says the apostle, to me a persecutor, to you Corinthians, who were 'unclean, drunkards, covetous persons, idolaters.' Therefore, each poor sinner may say then, why not unto me? Has Christ but one blessing?

What if he has blessed millions already, by turning them away from their iniquities; yet he still continues the same: he lives for ever to make intercession, and therefore will bless you, even you also. Though, Esau- like, you have been profane, and hitherto despised your heavenly Father's birth-right; even now, if you believe, 'Christ will be made to you of God, wisdom, righteousness, sanctification, and redemption'.

But I must turn again to believers, for whose instruction, as I observed before, this discourse was particularly intended. You see, brethren, partakers of the heavenly calling, what great blessings are treasured up for you in Jesus Christ your Head, and what you are entitled to by believing on his name. Take heed, therefore, that ye walk worthy of the vocation wherewith ye are called. Think often how highly you are favored; and remember, you have not chosen Christ, but Christ has chosen you. Put on (as the elect of God) humbleness of mind, and glory, but let it be only in the Lord; for you have nothing but what you have received of God. By nature ye were foolish, as legal, as unholy, and in as damnable a condition, as others. Be pitiful, therefore, be courteous; and, as sanctification is a progressive work, beware of thinking you have already attained. Let him that is holy be holy still; knowing, that he who is most pure in heart, shall hereafter enjoy the clearest vision of God. Let indwelling sin be your daily burden; and not only bewail and lament, but see that you subdue it daily by the power of divine grace; and look up to Jesus continually to be the finisher, as well as author, of your faith.

Build not on your own faithfulness, but on God's unchangeableness. Take heed of thinking you stand by the power of your own free will. The everlasting love of God the Father, must be your only hope and consolation; let this support you under all trials. Remember that God's gifts and callings are without repentance; that Christ having once loved you, will love you to the end. Let this constrain you to obedience, and make you long and look for that blessed time, when he shall not only be your wisdom, and righteousness, and sanctification, but also complete and everlasting redemption.

Glory be to God in the highest!

Sermon 45 The Knowledge of Jesus Christ the best Knowledge

1 Corinthians 2:2, "I determined not to know any thing among you, save Jesus Christ, and him crucified."

The persons to whom these words were written, were the members of the church of Corinth; who, as appears by the foregoing chapter, were not only divided into different sects, by one saying, "I am of Paul, and another, I am of Apollos;" but also had man amongst them, who were so full of the wisdom of this world, and so wise in their own eyes, that they set at nought the simplicity of the gospel, and accounted the Apostle's preaching foolishness.

Never had the Apostle more need of the wisdom of the serpent, mingled with the innocency of the dove, than now. What is the sum of all his wisdom? He tells them, in the words of the text, "I determined not to know any thing amongst you, save Jesus Christ, and him crucified." A resolution this, worthy of the great St. Paul; and no less worthy, no less necessary for every minister, and every disciple of Christ, to make always, even unto the 3end of the world.

In the following discourse, I shall, FIRST, Explain what is meant by "not knowing any thing, save Jesus Christ, and him crucified." SECONDLY, Give some reasons why every Christian should determine not to know any thing else. And THIRDLY, Conclude with a general exhortation to put this determination into practice.

FIRST, I am to explain what is meant by "not knowing any thing, save Jesus Christ, and him crucified." By Jesus Christ, we are to understand the eternal Son of God. He is called Jesus, a Savior, because he was to save us from the guilt and power of our sins; and, like Joshua, by whom he was re-markably typified, to lead God's spiritual Israel through the wilderness of this world, to the heavenly Canaan, the promised inheritance of the children of God.

He is called CHRICT, which signifies anointed, because he was anointed by the Holy Ghost at his baptism, to be a prophet to instruct, a priest to make an atonement for, and a king to govern and protect his church. And he was crucified, or hung (O stupendous love!) till he was dead upon the cross, that he might become a curse for us: for it is written, "Cursed is every man that hangeth upon a tree." The foundation or first cause of his suffering, was our fall in Adam; in whom, as the living oracles of God declare, "We all died;" his sin was imputed to us all. It pleased God, after he had spoken the world into being, to create man after his own divine image, to breathe into him the breath of life, and to place him as our representative in the garden of Eden.

But he being left to his own free will, did eat of the forbidden fruit, notwithstanding God had told him, "The day in which he eat thereof, he should surely die;" and thereby he, with his whole posterity, in whose name he acted, became liable to the wrath of God, and sunk into a spiritual death.

But behold the goodness, as well as the severity of God! For no sooner had man been convicted as a sinner, but lo! A Savior is revealed to him, under the character of the seed of the woman: the merits of whose sacrifice were then immediately to take place, and who should, in the fullness of time, by suffering death, satisfy for the guilt we had contracted; by obeying the whole moral law, work out for us an everlasting righteousness; and by becoming a principle of new life in us, destroy the power of the devil, and thereby restore us to a better state than that in which we were at first created.

This is the plain scriptural account of that mystery of godliness, God manifested in the flesh; and to this our own hearts, unless blinded by the god of this world, cannot but yield an immediate assent.

For, let us but search our own hearts, and ask ourselves, if we could create our own children, whether or not we would not create them with a less mixture of good and evil, than we find in ourselves? Supposing God then only to have our goodness, he could not, at first, make us so sinful, so polluted as we are. But supposing him to be as he is, infinitely good, or goodness itself, then it is absolutely impossible that he should create any thing but what is like himself, perfect, entire, lacking nothing. Man then could not come out of the hands of his Maker, so miserably blind and naked, with such a mixture of the beast and devil, as he finds now in himself, but must have fallen from what he was; and as it does not suit with the goodness and justness of God, to punish the whole race of mankind with these disorders merely for nothing;

and since men bring these disorders into the world with them; it follows, that as they could not sin themselves, being yet unborn, some other man's sin must have been imputed to them; from whence, as from a fountain, all these evils flow.

I know this doctrine of our ORIGINAL SIN, or fall in Adam, is esteemed foolishness by the wise disputer of this world, who will reply, How does it suit the goodness of God, to impute one man's sin to an innocent posterity?

But has it not been proved to a demonstration, that it is so? And therefore, supposing we cannot reconcile it to our shallow comprehensions, that is no argument at all: for if it appears that God has done a thing, we may be sure it is right, whether we can see the reasons for it or not.

But this is entirely cleared up by what was said before, that no sooner was the sin imputed, but a Christ was revealed; and this Christ, this God incarnate, who was conceived by the Holy Ghost, that he might be freed from the guilt of our original sin; who was born of the Virgin Mary, that he might be the seed of the woman only; who suffered under Pontius Pilate, a Gentile governor, to fulfill these prophecies, which signified what death he should die: This same Jesus, who was crucified in weakness, but raised in power, is that divine person, that Emmanuel, that God with us, whom we preach, in whom ye believe, and whom alone the Apostle, in the text, was determined to know.

By which word KNOE, we are not to understand a bare historical knowledge; for to know that Christ was crucified by his enemies at Jerusalem, in this manner only, will do us no more service, than to know that Caesar was butchered by his friends at Rome; but the work KNOW, means to know, so as to approve of him; as when Christ says, "Verily, I know you not;" I know you not, so as to approve of you. It signifies to know him, so as to embrace him in all his offices; to take him to be our prophet, priest, and king; so as to give up ourselves wholly to be instructed, saved, and governed by him. It implies an experimental knowledge of his crucifixion, so as to feel the power of it, and to be crucified unto the world, as the Apostle explains himself in the epistle to the Philippians, where he says, "I count all things but dung and dross, that I may know him, and the power of his resurrection." This knowledge the Apostle was so swallowed up in, that he was determined not to know any thing else; he was resolved to make that his only study, the governing principle of his life, the point and end in which all his thoughts, words, and actions, should center.

SECONDLY, I pass on to give some reasons why every Christian should, with the Apostle, determine "not to know any thing, save Jesus Christ, and him crucified." FIRST, Without this, our persons will not be accepted in the sight of God. "This (and consequently this only) is life eternal, to know thee, the only true God, and Jesus Christ, whom thou has sent." As also St. Peter says, "There is now no other name given under heaven, whereby we can be saved, but that of Jesus Christ." Some, indeed, ma please themselves in knowing the world, others boast themselves in the knowledge of a multitude of languages; but could we speak with the tongue of men and angels, or did we know the number of the stars, and could call them all by their names, yet, without this experimental knowledge of Jesus Christ, and him crucified, it would profit us nothing.

The former, indeed, may procure us a little honor, which cometh of man; but the latter only can render us acceptable in the sight of God: for, if we are ignorant of Christ, God will be to us a consuming fire.

Christ is the way, the truth, and the life; "No one cometh to the Father, but through him;" "He is the Lamb slain from the foundation of the world;" and none ever were, or ever will be received up into glory, but by an experimental application of his merits to their hearts.

We might as well think to rebuild the tower of Babel, or reach heaven with our hands, as to imagine we could enter therein by any other door, than that of the knowledge of Jesus Christ. Other knowledge may make you wise in your own eyes, and puff you up; but this alone edifieth, and maketh wise unto salvation.

As the meanest Christian, if he knows but this, though he know nothing else, will be accepted; so the greatest master in Israel, the most letter-learned teacher, without this, will be rejected. His philosophy is mere nonsense, his wisdom mere foolishness in the sight of God.

The author of the word now before us, was a remarkable instance of this; never, perhaps, was a greater scholar, in all what the world calls fine learning, than he: for he was bred up at the feet of Gamaliel, and profited in the knowledge of books, as well as in the Jewish religion, above many of his equals, as appears by the language, rhetoric, and spirit of his writings; and yet, when he came to know what it was to be a Christian, "He accounted all things but loss, so he might win Christ." And, though he was now at Corinth, that seat of polite learning, yet he was absolutely determined not to know any thing, or to make nothing his study, but what taught him to know Jesus Christ, and him crucified.

Hence then, appears the folly of those who spend their whole lives in heaping up other knowledge; and, instead of searching the scriptures, which testify of Jesus Christ, and are alone able to make them wise unto salvation, disquiet themselves in a pursuit after the knowledge of such things, as when known, concern them no more, than to know that a bird dropped a feather upon one of the Pyrenean mountains.

Hence it is, that so many, who profess themselves wise, because they can dispute of the causes and effects, the moral fitness and unfitness of things, appear mere fools in the things of God; so that when you come to converse with them about the great work of redemption wrought out for us by Jesus Christ, and of his being a propitiation for our sins, a fulfiller of the covenant of works, and a principle of new life to our souls, they are quite ignorant of the whole matter; and prove, to a demonstration, that, with all their learning, they know nothing yet, as they ought to know.

But, alas! how must it surprise a man, when the Most High is about to take away his soul, to think that he has passed for a wise-man, and a learned disputer in this world, and yet is left destitute of that knowledge which alone can make him appear with boldness before the judgment-seat of Jesus Christ? How must it grieve him, in a future state, to see others, whom he despised as illiterate men, because they experimentally knew Christ, and him crucified, exalted to the right-hand of God; and himself, with all his fine accomplishments, because he knew every thing, perhaps, but Christ, thrust down into hell?

Well might the Apostle, in a holy triumph, cry out, "Where is the wise? Where is the scribe? Where is the disputer of this world?" For, God will then make foolish the wisdom of this world, and bring to nought the wisdom of those who were so knowing in their own eyes.

I have made this digression from the main point before us, not to condemn or decry human literature, but to show, that it ought to be used only in subordination to divine; and that a Christian, if the Holy Spirit guided the pen of the Apostle, when he wrote this epistle, ought to study no books, but such as lead him to a farther knowledge of Jesus Christ, and him crucified.

And there is the more reason for this, because of he great mischief the contrary practice has done to the church of God: for, what was it but this learning, or rather this ignorance, that kept so many of the Scribes and Pharisees from the saving knowledge of Jesus Christ? And what is it, but this human wisdom, this science, false so called, that blinds the understanding, and corrupts the hearts of so many modern unbelievers, and makes them unwilling to submit to the righteousness which is of God by faith in Christ

Jesus? But, SECONDLY, Without this knowledge our performances, as well as persons will not be acceptable in the sight of God.

"Through faith," says the Apostle, that is, through a lively faith in a Mediator to come, "Abel offered a more acceptable sacrifice than Cain." And it is through a like faith, or an experimental knowledge of the same divine Mediator, that our sacrifices of prayer, praise, and thanksgivings, come up as an incense before he throne of grace.

Two persons may go up to the temple to pray; but he only will return home justified, who, in the language of our collects, sincerely offers up his prayers through Jesus Christ our Lord.

For it is this great atonement, this all-sufficient sacrifice, which alone can give us boldness to approach with our prayers o the Holy of Holies: and he that presumes to go without this, acts Korah's crime over again; offers unto God strange fire, and, consequently, will be rejected by him.

Farther, as our devotions to God will not, so neither, without this knowledge of Jesus Christ, will our acts of charity to men be accepted by him. For did we give all our goods to feed the poor, and yet were destitute of this knowledge, it would profit us nothing.

This our blessed Lord himself intimates in the 25th of Matthew, where he tells those who had been rich in good works, "That inasmuch as they did it unto one of the least of his brethren, they did it unto him." From whence we may plainly infer, that it is seeing Christ in his members, and doing good to them out of an experimental knowledge of his love to us, that alone will render our alms-deeds rewardable at the last day.

LASTLY, As neither our acts of piety nor charity, so neither will our civil nor moral actions be acceptable to God, without this experimental knowledge of Jesus Christ.

Our modern pretenders to reason, indeed, set up another principle to act from; they talk, I know not what, Of doing moral an civil duties of life, from the moral fitness and unfitness of things. But such men are blind, however they may pretend to see; and going thus about to establish their own righteousness, are utterly ignorant of the righteousness which is of God by faith in Christ Jesus.

For though we grant that morality is a substantial part of Christianity, and that Christ came not to destroy, or take off the moral law, as a rule of action, but to explain, and so fulfill it; yet we affirm, that our moral and civil actions are now no farther acceptable in the sight of God the Father, than as they proceed from the principle of a new nature, and as experimental knowledge of, or vital faith in his dear Son.

The death of Jesus Christ has turned our whole lives into one continued sacrifice; and whether we eat or drink, whether we pray to God, or do any thing to man, it must all be done out of a love for, and knowledge of him who died and rose again, to render all, even our most ordinary deeds, acceptable in the sight of God.

If we live by this principle, if Christ be the Alpha and Omega of all our actions, then our least are acceptable sacrifices; but if this principle be wanting, our most pompous services avail nothing: we are but spiritual idolater; we sacrifice to our own net; we make an idol of ourselves, by making ourselves, and not Christ, the end of our actions: and, therefore, such actions are so far from being accepted by God, that, according to the language of one of the Articles of our Church, "We doubt not but they have the nature of sin, because they spring not from an experimental faith in, and knowledge of Jesus Christ." Were we not fallen creatures, we might then act, perhaps, from other principles; but since we are fallen from God in Adam, and are restored again only by the obedience and death of Jesus Christ, the face of things I entirely changed, and all we think, speak, or do, is only accepted in and through him.

Justly, therefore, may I, in the THIRD and LAST places, Exhort you to put the Apostle's resolution in practice, and beseech you, with him to determine, Not to know any thing, save Jesus Christ, and him crucified." I say, DETERMINE; for unless you sit down first, and count the cost, and from a well-grounded conviction of the excellency of this ,above all other knowledge whatsoever, resolve to make this your chief study, your only end, your one thing needful, every frivolous temptation will draw you aside from the pursuit after it.

Your friends and carnal acquaintance, and, above all, your grand adversary the devil, will be persuading you to determine not to know any thing, but how to lay up goods for many years, and to get a knowledge and taste of the pomps and vanities of this wicked world; but do you determine not to follow, or be led by them; and the more they persuade you to know other things, the more do you "determine snot to know any thing, save Jesus Christ, and him crucified." For, this knowledge never faileth; but whether they be riches, they shall fail; whether they be pomps, they shall cease; whether they be vanities, they shall fade away: but the knowledge of Jesus Christ, and him crucified, abideth for ever.

Whatever, therefore, you are ignorant of, be not ignorant of this. If you know Christ, and him crucified, you know enough to make you happy, supposing you know nothing else; and without this, all your other knowledge cannot keep you from being everlastingly miserable.

Value not then, the contempt of friends, which you must necessarily meet with upon your open profession to act according to this determination.

For your Master, whose you are, was despised before you; and all that will know nothing else but Jesus Christ, and him crucified, must, in some degree or other, suffer persecution.

It is necessary that offenses should come, to try what is in our hearts, and whether we will be faithful soldiers of Jesus Christ or not.

Dare ye then to confess our blessed Master before men, and to shine as lights in the world, amidst a crooked and perverse generation? Let us not be content with following him afar off; for then we shall, as Peter did, soon deny him; but let us be altogether Christians, and let our speech, and all our actions declare to the world whose disciples we are, and that we have indeed "determined not to know any thing, save Jesus Christ, and him crucified." Then, well will it be with us, and happy, unspeakably happy shall we be, even here; and what is infinitely better, when others that despised us, shall be calling for the mountains to fall on them, and the hills to cover them, we shall be exalted to sit down on the right-hand of God, and shine as the sun in the firmament, in the kingdom of our most adorable Redeemer, for ever and ever.

Which God of his infinite mercy grant, etc.

Sermon 46 Of Justification by Christ

1 Corinthians 6:11, "But ye are justified." The whole verse is: "And such were some of you; but ye are washed, but ye are sanctified, but ye are justified in the name of our Lord Jesus Christ, and by the Spirit of our God."

It has been objected by some, who dissent from, nay, I may add, by others also, who actually are friends to the present ecclesiastical establishment, that the ministers of the Church of England preach themselves, and not Christ Jesus the Lord; that they entertain their people with lectures of mere morality, without declaring to them the glad tidings of salvation by Jesus Christ. How well grounded such an objection may be, is not my business to inquire: All I shall say at present to the point is, that whenever such a grand objection is urged against the whole body of the clergy in general, every honest minister of Jesus Christ should do his utmost to cut off all manner of occasion, from those who desire an occasion to take offense at us; that so by hearing us continually sounding forth the word of truth, and declaring with all boldness and assurance of faith, "that there is no other name given under heaven, whereby they can be saved, but that of Jesus Christ," they may be ashamed of this their same confident boasting against us.

It was an eye to this objection, joined with the agreeableness and delightfulness of the subject (for who can but delight to talk of that which the blessed angels desire to look into?) that induces me to discourse a little on that great and fundamental article of our faith; namely, our being freely justified by the precious blood of Jesus Christ. "But ye are washed, but ye are sanctified, but ye are justified, in the name of our Lord Jesus Christ, and by the Spirit of our God." The words beginning with the particle BUT, have plainly a reference to something before; it may not therefore be improper, before I descend to particulars, to consider the words as they stand in relation to the context. The apostle, in the verses immediately foregoing, had been reckoning up many notorious sins, drunkenness, adultery, fornication, and such like, the commission of which, without a true and hearty repentance, he tells the Corinthians, would entirely shut them out of the kingdom of God.

But then, lest they should, on the one hand, grow spiritually proud by seeing themselves differ from their unconverted brethren, and therefore be tempted to set them at nought, and say with the self-conceited hypocrite in the prophet, "Come not nigh me, for I am holier than thou;" or, on the other hand, by looking back on the multitude of their past offenses, should be apt to think their sins were too many and grievous to be forgiven: he first, in order to keep them humble, reminds them of their sad state before conversion, telling them in plain terms, "such (or as it might be read, these things) were some of you;" not only one, but all that sad catalogue of vices I have been drawing up, some of you were once guilty of; but then, at the same time, to preserve them from despair, behold he brings them glad tidings of great joy: "But ye are washed; but ye are sanctified, but ye are justified in the name of our Lord Jesus Christ, and by the Spirit of our God." The former part of this text, our being sanctified, I have in some measure treated of already; I would not enlarge on our being freely justified by the precious obedience and death of Jesus Christ: "But ye are justified in the name of our Lord Jesus Christ." From which words I shall consider three things: FIRST, What is meant by the word justified.

SECONDLY, I shall endeavor to prove that all mankind in general, and every individual person in particular, stands in need of being justified.

THIRDLY, That there is no possibility of obtaining this justification, which we so much want, but by the all-perfect obedience, and precious death of Jesus Christ.

FIRST, I am to consider what is meant by the word justified.

"But ye are justified," says the apostle; which is, as though he had said, you have your sins forgiven, and are looked upon by God as though you never had offended him at all: for that is the meaning of the word justified, in almost all the passages of holy scripture where this word is mentioned. Thus, when this same apostle writes to the Romans, he tells them, that "whom God called, those he also justified:" And that this word justified, implies a blotting out of all our transgressions, is manifest from what follows, "them he also glorified," which could not be if a justified person was not looked upon by God, as though he never had offended him at all. And again, speaking of Abraham's faith, he tells them, that "Abraham believed on Him that justifies the ungodly," who acquits and clears the ungodly man; for it is a law-term, and alludes to a judge acquitting an accused criminal of the thing laid to his charge. Which expression the apostle himself explains by a quotation out of the Psalms: "Blessed is the man to whom the Lord imputeth no sin." From all which proofs, and many others that might be urged, it is evident, that by being justified, we are to understand, being so acquitted in the sight of God as to be looked upon as though we never had offended him at all. And in this sense we are to understand that article, which we profess to believe in our creed, when each of us declare in his own person, I believe the forgiveness of sins. This leads me to the SECOND thing proposed, to prove that all mankind in general, and every individual person in particular, stands in need of being justified.

And indeed the apostle supposes this in the words of the text: "But ye are justified," thereby implying that the Corinthians (and consequently all mankind, there being no difference, as will be shown hereafter) stood in need of being justified.

But not to rest in bare suppositions, in my farther enlargement on this head, I shall endeavor to prove, that we all stand in need of being justified on account of the sin of our natures, and the sin of our lives.

1. FIRST, I affirm that we all stand in need of being justified, on account of the sin of our natures: for we are all chargeable with original sin, or the sin of our first parents. Which, though a proposition that may be denied by a self-justifying infidel, who "will not come to Christ that he may have life;" yet can never be denied by any one who believes that St.

Paul's epistles were written by divine inspiration; where we are told, that "in Adam all died;" that is, Adam's sin was imputed to all; and lest we should forget to make a particular application, it is added in another place, "that there is none that doeth good (that is, by nature) no, not one: That we are all gone out of the way, (of original righteousness) and are by nature the children of wrath." And even David, who was a man after God's own heart, and, if any one could, might surely plead an exemption from this universal corruption, yet he confesses, that "he was shapen in iniquity, and that in sin did his mother conceive him." And, to mention but one text more, as immediately applicable to the present purpose, St. Paul, in his epistle to the Romans, says, that "Death came upon all men, for the disobedience of one, namely, of Adam, even upon those, (that is, little children) who had not sinned after the similitude of Adam's transgression;" who had not been guilty of actual sin, and therefore could not be punished with temporal death (which came into the world, as this same apostle elsewhere informs us, only by sin) had not the disobedience of our first parents been imputed to them. So that what has been said in this point seems to be excellently summed up in that article of our church, where she declares that "Original sin standeth not in the following of Adam, but it is the fault and corruption of every man, that naturally is engendered of the offspring of Adam; whereby man is very far gone from original righteousness, and is of his own nature inclined to evil, so that the flesh lusteth always contrary to the spirit; and the therefore in every person born into this world, it deserveth God's wrath and damnation." I have been more particular in treating of this point, because it is the very foundation of the Christian religion: For I am verily persuaded, that it is nothing but a want of being well grounded in the doctrine of original sin, and of the helpless, nay, I may say, damnable condition, each of us comes into the world in, that makes so many infidels oppose, and so many who call themselves Christians, so very lukewarm in their love and affections to Jesus Christ. It is this, and I could almost say, this only, that makes infidelity abound among us so much as it does. For, alas! we are mistaken if we imagine that men now commence or continue infidels, and set up corrupted reason in opposition to divine revelation merely for want of evidence, (for I believe it might easily be proved, that a modern unbeliever is the most credulous creature living;) no, it is only for want of an humble mind, of a sense of their original depravity, and a willingness to own themselves so depraved, that makes them so obstinately shut their eyes against the light of the glorious gospel of Christ.

Whereas, on the contrary, were they but once pricked to the heart with a due and lively sense of their natural corruption and liableness to condemnation, we should have them no more scoffing at divine revelation, and looking on it as an idle tale; but they would cry out with the trembling jailer, "What shall I do to be saved?" It was an error in this fundamental point, that made so many resist the evidence the Son of God himself gave of his divine mission, when he tabernacled amongst us. Every word he spake, every action he did, every miracle he wrought, proved that he came from God. And why then did so many harden their hearts, and would not believe his report? Why, he himself informs us, "They will not come unto me that they may have life:" They will obstinately stand out against those means God had appointed for their salvation: And St. Paul tells us, "that if the gospel be hid, it is hid to them that are lost; in whom the God of this world hath blinded the eyes of them which believe not, lest the light of the glorious gospel of Christ, who is the image of God, should shine upon them." 2 Cor. 4:3-4.

If it be asked, how it suits with the divine goodness, to impute the guilt of one man's sin, to an innocent posterity? I should think it sufficient to make use of the apostle's words: "Nay, but O man, who art thou that repliest against God? Shall the thing formed say to him that formed it, why hast thou made me thus?" But to come to a more direct reply: Persons would do well to consider that in the first covenant God made with man, Adam acted as a public person, as the common representative of all mankind, and consequently we must stand or fall with him. Had he continued in his obedience, and not eaten the forbidden fruit, the benefits of that obedience would doubtless have been imputed to us: But since he did not persist in it, but broke the covenant made with him, and us in him; who dares charge the righteous Judge of all the earth with injustice for imputing that to us also? I proceed, SECONDLY, To prove that we stand in need of being justified, on account of the sin of our lives.

That God, as he made man, has a right to demand his obedience, I suppose is a truth no one will deny: that he hath also given us both a natural and a written law, whereby we are to be judged, cannot be questioned by any one who believes St. Paul's epistle to the Romans to be of divine authority: For in it we are told of a law written in the heart, and a law given by Moses; and that each of us hath broken these laws, is too evident from our sad and frequent experience. Accordingly the holy scriptures inform us that "there is no man which liveth and sinneth not;" that "in many things we offend all;" that "if we say we have no sin we deceive ourselves," and such like. And if we are thus offenders against God, it follows, that we stand in need of forgiveness for thus offending Him; unless we suppose God to enact laws, and at the same time not care whether they are obeyed or no; which is as absurd as to suppose that a prince should establish laws for the proper government of his country, and yet let every violator of them come off with impunity. But God has not dealt so foolishly with his creatures: no, as he gave us a law, he demands our obedience to that law, and has obliged us universally and perseveringly to obey it, under no less a penalty than incurring his curse and eternal death for every breach of it: For thus speaks the scripture; "Cursed is he that continueth not in all things that are written in the law to do them;" as the scripture also speaketh in another place, "The soul that sinneth, it shall die." Now it has already been proved, that we have all of us sinned; and therefore, unless some means can be found to satisfy God's justice, we must perish eternally.

Let us then stand a while, and see in what a deplorable condition each of us comes into the world, and still continues, till we are translated into a state of grace. For surely nothing can well be supposed more deplorable, than to be born under the curse of God; to be charged with original guilt; and not only so, but to be convicted as actual breakers of God's law, the least breach of which justly deserves eternal damnation.

Surely this can be but a melancholy prospect to view ourselves in, and must put us upon contriving some means whereby we may satisfy and appease our offended judge. But what must those means be? Shall we repent? Alas! there is not one word of repentance mentioned in the first covenant: "The day that thou eatest thereof, thou shalt surely die." So that, if God be true, unless there be some way found out to satisfy divine justice, we must perish; and there is no room left for us to expect a change of mind in God, though we should seek it with tears. Well then, if repentance will not do, shall we plead the law of works? Alas! "By the law shall no man living be justified: for by the law comes the knowledge of sin." It is that which convicts and condemns, and therefore can by no means justify us; and "all our righteousnesses (says the prophet) are but as filthy rags." Wherewith then shall we come before the Lord, and bow down before the most high God?

Shall we come before Him with calves of a year old, with thousands of rams, or ten thousands of rivers of oil? Alas! God has showed thee, O man, that this will not avail: For he hath declared, "I will take no bullock out of thy house, nor he-goat out of thy fold: for all the beasts of the forests are mine, and so are the cattle upon a thousand hills." Will the Lord then be pleased to accept our first-born for our transgression, the fruit of our bodies for the sin of our souls? Even this will not purchase our pardon: for he hath declared that "the children shall not bear the iniquities of their parents." Besides, they are sinners, and therefore, being under the same condemnation, equally stand in need of forgiveness with ourselves.

They are impure, and will the Lord accept the blind and lame for sacrifice?

Shall some angel then, or archangel, undertake to fulfill the covenant which we have broken, and make atonement for us? Alas! they are only creatures, though creatures of the highest order; and therefore are obliged to obey God as well as we; and after they have done all, must say they have done no more than what was their duty to do. And supposing it was possible for them to die, yet how could the death of a finite creature satisfy an infinitely offended justice? O wretched men that we are! Who shall deliver us? I thank God, our Lord Jesus Christ. Which naturally leads me to the THIRD thing proposed, which was to endeavor to prove, that there is no possibility of obtaining this justification, which we so much want, but by the all-perfect obedience and precious death of Jesus Christ, "But ye are justified in the name of our Lord Jesus Christ." But this having been in some measure proved by what has been said under the foregoing head, wherein I have shown that neither our repentance, righteousness, nor sacrifice, no not the obedience and death of angels, themselves, could possibly procure justification for us, nothing remains for me to do under this head, but to show that Jesus Christ has procured it for us.

And here I shall still have recourse "to the law and to the testimony." For after all the most subtle disputations on either side, nothing but the lively oracles of God can give us any satisfaction in this momentous point: it being such an inconceivable mystery, that the eternal only-begotten Son of God should die for sinful man, that we durst not have presumed so much as to have thought of it, had not God revealed it in his holy word. It is true, reason may show us the wound, but revelation only can lead us to the means of our cure. And though the method God has been pleased to take to make us happy, may be to the infidel a stumbling-block, and to the wise opiniator and disputer of this world, foolishness; yet wisdom, that is, the dispensation of our redemption, will be justified, approved of, and submitted to, by all her truly wise and holy children, by every sincere and upright Christian.

But to come more directly to the point before us. Two things, as was before observed, we wanted, in order to be at peace with God.

1. To be freed from the guilt of the sin of our nature.

2. From the sin of our lives.

And both these (thanks be to God for this unspeakable gift) are secured to believers by the obedience and death of Jesus Christ. For what says the scripture?

1. As to the FIRST, it informs us, that "as by the disobedience of one man, (or by one transgression, namely, that of Adam) many were made sinners; so by the obedience of one, Jesus Christ (therein including his passive as well as active obedience) many were made righteous." And again, "As by the disobedience of one man, judgment came upon all men unto condemnation;" or all men were condemned on having Adam's sin imputed to them; "so by the obedience of one, that is, Jesus Christ, the free gift of pardon and peace came upon all men, (all sorts of men) unto justification of life." I say all sorts of men; for the apostle in this chapter is only drawing a parallel between the first and second Adam in this respect, that they acted both as representatives; and as the posterity of Adam had his sin imputed to them, so those for whom Christ died, and whose representative he is, shall have his merits imputed to them also. Whoever run the parallel farther, in order to prove universal redemption (whatever arguments they may draw for the proof of it from other passages of scripture,) if they would draw one from this for that purpose, I think they stretch their line of interpretation beyond the limits of scripture.

2. Pardon for the sin of our lives was another thing, which we wanted to have secured to us, before we could be at peace with God.

And this the holy scriptures inform us, is abundantly done by the death of Jesus Christ. The evangelical prophet foretold that the promised Redeemer should be "wounded for our transgressions, and bruised for our iniquities; that the chastisement of our peace should be upon him; and that by his stripes we should be healed," Isaiah 53:6. The angels at his birth said, that he should "save his people from their sins." And St. Paul declares, that "this is a faithful saying, and worthy of all acceptation, that Jesus Christ came into the world to save sinners." And here in the words of the text, "Such (or, as I observed before, these things) were some of you; but ye are washed, etc." and again, "Jesus Christ is the end of the law for righteousness to every one that believeth." And, to show us that none but Jesus Christ can do all this, the apostle St. Peter says, "Neither is their salvation in any other; for there is no other name under heaven given among men, whereby we must be saved, but the name of Jesus Christ.

How God will be pleased to deal with the Gentiles, who yet sit in darkness and under the shadow of death, and upon whom the sun of righteousness never yet arose, is not for us to inquire. "What have we to do to judge those that are without?" To God's mercy let us recommend them, and wait for a solution of this and every other difficult point, till the great day of accounts, when all God's dispensations, both of providence and grace, will be fully cleared up by methods to us, as yet unknown, because unrevealed. However, this we know, that the judge of all the earth will, most assuredly, do right.

But it is time for me to draw a conclusion.

I have now, brethren, by the blessings of God, discoursed on the words of the text in the method I proposed. Many useful inferences might be drawn from what has been delivered; but as I have detained you, I fear, too long already, permit me only to make a reflection or two on what has been said, and I have done.

If then we are freely justified by the death and obedience of Jesus Christ, let us here pause a while; and as before we have reflected on the misery of a fallen, let us now turn aside and see the happiness of the believing, soul. But alas! how am I lost to think that God the Father, when we were in a state of enmity and rebellion against Him, should notwithstanding yearn in his bowels towards us his fallen, his apostate creatures: And because nothing but an infinite ransom could satisfy an infinitely offended justice, that should send his only and dear Son Jesus Christ (who is God, blessed for ever, and who had lain in his bosom from all eternity) to fulfill the covenant of works, and die a cursed, painful, ignominious death, for us and for our salvation! who can avoid crying out, at the consideration of his mystery of godliness. "Oh the depth of the riches of God's love" to us his wretched, miserable and undone creatures!

"How unsearchable is his mercy, and his ways past finding out!" Now know we of a truth, O God, that thou hast loved us, "since thou hast not with-held thy Son, thine only Son Jesus Christ," from thus doing and dying for us.

But as we admire the Father sending, let us likewise humbly and thankfully adore the Son coming, when sent to die for man. But O! what thoughts can conceive, what words express the infinite greatness of that unparalleled love, which engaged the Son of God to come down from the mansions of his Father's glory to obey and die for sinful man! The Jews, when he only shed a tear at poor Lazarus' funeral, said, "Behold how he loved him." How much more justly then may we cry out, Behold how he loved us! When he not only fulfilled the whole moral law, but did not spare to shed his own most precious blood for us.

And can any poor truly-convicted sinner, after this, despair of mercy?

What, can they see their Savior hanging on a tree, with arms stretched out ready to embrace them, and yet, on their truly believing on him, doubt of finding acceptance with him? No, away with all such dishonorable, desponding thoughts. Look on his hands, bored with pins of iron; look on his side, pierced with a cruel spear, to let loose the sluices of his blood, and open a fountain for sin, and for all uncleanness; and then despair of mercy if you can! No, only believe in Him, and then, though you have crucified him afresh, yet will he abundantly pardon you; "though your sins be as scarlet, yet shall they be as wool; though deeper than crimson, yet shall they be whiter than snow." Which God of his infinite mercy grant, etc.

Sermon 47 The Great Duty of Charity Recommended

1 Corinthians 13:8, "Charity never faileth."

Nothing is more valuable and commendable, and yet, not one duty is less practiced, than that of charity. We often pretend concern and pity for the misery and distress of our fellow-creatures, but yet we seldom commiserate their condition so much as to relieve them according to our abilities; but unless we assist them with what they may stand in need of, for the body, as well as for the soul, all our wishes are no more than words of no value or regard, and are not to be esteemed or regarded: for when we hear of any deplorable circumstance, in which our fellow-creatures are involved, be they friends or enemies; it is our duty, as Christians, to assist them to the utmost of our power.

Indeed, we are not, my brethren, to hurt ourselves or our families; this is not that charity which is so much recommended by St. Paul; no, but if we are any ways capable of relieving them without injuring either ourselves, or families, then it is our duty to do it; and this never faileth, where it proceeds from a right end, and with a right view.

St. Paul had been showing, in the preceding chapter, that spiritual gifts were divers; that God had disposed of one blessing to one, and another to another; and though there was a diversity of blessings, God did not bestow them to one person, but gave to one a blessing which he denied to another, and gave a blessing, or a gift to the other which might make him as eminent in one way, as the other's gift made him so in another: but though there are these divers spiritual gifts, they are all given for some wise end, even to profit withal, and to that end they are thus diversely bestowed. We are not, on the one hand, to hide those gifts which God has given us: neither are we, on the other, to be so lavish of them, as to spend them upon our lusts and pleasures, to satisfy our sensual appetites, but they are to be used for the glory of God, and the good of immortal souls. After he had particularly illustrated this, he comes to show, that all gifts, however great they may be in themselves, are of no value unless we have charity, as you may see particularly, by considering from the beginning of this chapter.

But before I go any further, I shall inform you what the apostle means by charity; and that it, Love; if there is true love, there will be charity; there will be an endeavor to assist, help, and relieve according to that ability wherewith God has blessed us: and, since this is so much recommended by the apostle, let us see how valuable this charity is, and how commendable in all those who pursue it. I shall, I. Consider this blessing as relation to the bodies of men.

II. I shall show how much more valuable it is, when relating to the souls of men.

III. Shall show you when your charity is of the right kind.

IV. Why this charity, or the grace of love, never faileth.

V. Shall conclude all, with an exhortation to high and low, rich and poor, one with another, to be found in the constant practice of this valuable and commendable duty.

FIRST, I shall consider this duty, as relating to the bodies of men.

And, 1. O that the rich would consider how praise-worthy this duty is, in helping their fellow-creatures! We were created to be a help to each other; God has made no one so independent as not to need the assistance of another; the richest and most powerful man upon the face of this earth, needs the help and assistance of those who are around him; and though he may be great today, a thousand accidents may make him as low tomorrow; he that is rolling in plenty today, may be in as much scarcity tomorrow. If our rich men would be more charitable to their poor friends and neighbors, it would be a means of recommending them to the savor of others, if Providence should frown upon them; but alas, our great men had much rather spend their money in a playhouse, at a ball, an assembly, or a masquerade, than relieve a poor distressed servant of Jesus Christ. They had rather spend their estates on their hawks and hounds, on their whores, and earthly, sensual, devilish pleasures, than comfort , nourish, or relieve one of their distressed fellow-creatures. What difference is there between the king on the throne, and the beggar on the dunghill, when God demands their breaths? There is no difference, my brethren, in the grave, nor will there be any at the day of judgment. You will not be excused because you have had a great estate, a fine house, and lived in all the pleasures that earth could afford you; no, these things will be one means of your condemnation; neither will you be judged according to the largeness of your estate, but according to the use you have made of it.

Now, you may think nothing but of your pleasures and delights, of living in ease and plenty, and never consider how many thousands of your fellow-creatures would rejoice at what you are making waste of, and setting no account by. Let me beseech you, my rich brethren, to consider the poor of the world, and how commendable and praise-worthy it is to relieve those who are distressed. Consider, how pleasing this is to God, how delightful it is to man, and how many prayers you will have put up for your welfare, by those persons whom you relieve; and let this be a consideration to spare a little out of the abundance wherewith God has blessed you, or the relief of his poor. He could have placed you in their low condition, and they in your high state; it is only his good pleasure that has thus made the difference, and shall not this make you remember your distressed fellow- creatures?

Let me beseech you to consider, which will stand you best at the day of judgment, so much money expended at a horse-race, or a cockpit, at a play or masquerade, or so much given for the relief of your fellow- creatures, and for the distressed members of Jesus Christ.

I beseech you, that you would consider how valuable and com-mendable this duty is: do not be angry at my thus exhorting you to that duty, which is so much recommended by Jesus Christ himself, and by all his apos-tles: I speak particularly to you, my rich brethren, to entreat you to consider those that are poor in this world, and help them from time to time, as their necessity calls for it. Consider, that there is a curse denounced against the riches of those, who do not thus do good with them; namely, "Go to now you rich men, weep and howl for your miseries that shall come upon you; your riches are corrupted, your garments are moth-eaten, your gold and silver is cankered, and the rust of them shall be a witness against you, and shall eat your flesh, as it were fire; ye have heaped your treasure together for the last day." You see the dreadful woe pronounced against all those who hoard up the abundance of the things of this life, without relieving the distresses of those who are in want thereof: and the apostle James goes on also to speak against those who have acquired estates by fraud, as too many have in these days. "Behold the hire of the laborers, which have reaped down your fields, which is by you kept back by fraud, crieth; and the cries of them who have reaped, are entered into the ears of the Lord God of Sabbaoth. Ye have lived in pleasure on the earth, and been wanton; ye have nourished your hearts, as in the day of slaughter." Thus, if you go on to live after the lust of the flesh, to pamper your bellies, and make them a God, while the poor all around you are starving, God will make these things a witness against you, which shall be as a worm to your souls, and gnaw your consciences to all eternity; therefore, let me once more recommend charity unto the bodies of men, and beseech you to remember what a blessed Lord Jesus Christ has promised unto those who thus love his members, that "as they have done it to the least of his members, they have done it unto him." I am not now speaking for myself; I am not recommending my little flock in Georgia to you; then you might say, as many wantonly do, that I wanted the money for myself; no, my brethren, I am now recommending the poor of this land to you, your poor neighbors, poor friends, yea, your poor enemies; they are whom I am now speaking for; and when I see so many starving in the streets, and almost naked, my bowels are moved with pity and concern, to consider, that many in whose power it is, to lend their assisting hand, should shut up their bowels of compassion, and will not relieve their fellow-creatures, though in the most deplorable condition for the want thereof.

As I have thus recommended charity particularly to the rich among you; so now I would, 2. SECONDLY, Recommend this to another set of people among us, who, instead of being the most forward in acts of charity, are commonly the most backward; I mean the clergy of this land.

Good God! How amazing is the consideration, that those, whom God has called out to labor in spiritual things, should be so backward in this duty, as fatal experience teacheth. Our clergy (that is the generality thereof) are only seeking after preferment, running up and down, to obtain one benefice after another; and to heap up an estate, either to spend on the pleasures of life, or to gratify their sensual appetites, while the poor of their flock are forgotten; nay, worse, they are scorned, hated, and disdained.

I am not now, my brethren, speaking of all the clergy; no, blessed be God, there are some among them, who abhor such proceedings, and are willing to relieve the necessitous; but God knows, these are but very few, while many take no thought of the poor among them.

They can visit the rich and the great, but the poor they cannot bear in their sight; they are forgetful, willfully forgetful of the poor members of Jesus Christ.

They have gone out of the old paths, and turned into a new polite way, but which is not warranted in the word of God: they are sunk into a fine way of acting; but as fine as it is, it was not the practice of the apostles, or of the Christians in any age of the church: for they visited and relieved the poor among them; but how rare is this among us, how seldom do we find charity in a clergyman?

It is with grief I speak these things, but woeful experience is a witness to the truth thereof: and if all the clergy of this land were here, I would tell them boldly, that they did not keep in the ways of charity, but were remiss in their duty; instead of "selling all and giving to the poor," they will not sell any thing, nor give at all to the poor.

3. THIRDLY, I would exhort you who are poor, to be charitable to one another.

Though you may not have money, or the things of this life, to bestow upon one another; yet you may assist them, by comforting, and advising them not to be discouraged though they are low in the world; or in sickness you may help them according as you have time or ability: do not be unkind to one another: do not grieve, or vex, or be angry with each other; for this is giving the world an advantage over you.

And if God stirs up any to relieve you, do not make an ill use of what his providence, by the hands of some Christian, hath bestowed upon you: be always humble and wait on God; do not murmur or repine, if you see any relieved and you are not; still wait on the Lord, and help one another, according to your abilities, from time to time.

Having showed you how valuable this is to the bodies of men, I now proceed, SECONDLY, To show you how much more valuable this charity is, when it extends to the souls of men.

And is not the soul more valuable than the body? It would be of no advantage, but an infinite disadvantage, to obtain all the world, if we were to lose our souls. The soul is of infinite value, and of infinite concern, and, therefore, we should extend our charity whenever we see it needful, and likewise should reprove, rebuke, and exhort with all godliness and love.

We should, my dear brethren, use all means and opportunities for the salvation of our own souls, and of the souls of others. We may have a great deal of charity and concern for the bodies of our fellow-creatures, when we have no thought, or concern, for their immortal souls: But O how sad is it, to have thought for a mortal, but not for the immortal part; to have charity for the body of our fellow-creatures, while we have no concern for their immortal souls; it may be, we help them to ruin them, but have no concern in the saving of them.

You may love to spend a merry evening, to go to a play, or a horse-race, with them; but on the other hand, you cannot bear the thoughts of going to a sermon, or a religious society, with them; no, you would sing the songs of the drunkard, but you will not sing hymns, with them; this is not polite enough, this is unbecoming a gentleman of taste, unfashionable, and only practiced among a parcel of enthusiasts and madmen.

Thus, you will be so uncharitable as to join hand in hand with those who are hastening to their own damnation, while you will not be so charitable as to assist them in being brought from darkness t light, and from the power of Satan unto God. But this, this, my dear brethren, is the greatest charity, as can be, to save a soul from death: this is of far greater advantage, than relieving the body of a fellow-creature: for the most miserable object as could be, death would deliver it from all. But death, to those who are not born again, would be so far from being a release from all misery, that it would be an inlet to all torment, and that to all eternity. Therefore, we should assist, as much as possible, to keep a soul from falling into the hands of Satan: for he is the grand enemy of souls. How should this excite you to watch over your own and others souls?

For unless you are earnest with God, Satan will be too hard for you.

Surely, it is the greatest charity to watch over one another's words and actions, that we may forewarn each other when danger is nigh, or when the enemy of souls approaches.

And if you have once known the value of your own souls, and know what it is to be snatched as brands out of the burning fire, you will be solicitous that others may be brought out of the same state. It is not the leading of a moral life, being honest, and paying every man his just due; this is not a proof of your being in a state of grace, or of being born again, and renewed in the spirit of your minds: No, you may die honest, just , charitable, and yet not be in a state of salvation.

It is not the preaching of that morality, which most of our pulpits now bring forth, that is sufficient to bring you from sin unto God. I saw you willing to learn, and yet were ignorant of the necessity of being born again, regenerated, of having all old things done away, and all things becoming new in your souls: I could not bear, my brethren, to see you in the highway to destruction, and none to bring you back. It was love to your souls, it was a desire to see Christ formed in you, which brought me into the fields, the highways, and hedges, to preach unto you Jesus, a crucified Jesus as dying for you. It was charity, indeed it was charity to your souls, which has exposed me to the present ill treatment of my letter- learned brethren.

Therefore, let me advise you to be charitable to the souls of one another; that is, by advising them with all love and tenderness, to follow after Christ, and the things which belong to their immortal peace, before they be forever hid from their eyes.

I now proceed, in the THIRD place, to show when your charity is of the right kind.

And here, my brethren, I shall show, FIRST, When it is not; and , SECONDLY, When it is of the right kind.

1. FIRST, Your charity is not of the right kind, when it proceeds from worldly views or ends.

If it is to be seen of men, to receive any advantage from them, to be esteemed, or to gain a reputation in the world; or if you have any pride in it, and expect to reap benefit from God merely for it; if all, or each of these is the end of your charity, then it is all in vain; your charity does not proceed from a right end, but you are hereby deceiving your own souls.

If you give an alms purely to be observed by man, or as expecting favor from God, merely on the account thereof, then you have not the glory of God, or the benefit of your fellow-creatures at heart, but merely yourself: this, this is not charity. Nor, SECONDLY, Is that true charity, when we give any thing to our fellow- creatures purely to indulge them in vice: this is so far from being charity, that it is a sin, both against God, and against our fellow-creatures. And yet, this is a common, as it is sinful, to carry our friends, under a specious pretense of charity, to one or the other entertainment, with no other view, but to make them guilty of excess.

Hereby you are guilty of a double sin: we are not to sin ourselves, much less should we endeavor to make another sin likewise. But, THIRDLY, Our charity comes from a right end, when it proceeds from love to God, and for the welfare both of the body and soul of our fellow- creatures.

When this is the sole end of relieving our distressed fellow- creatures, then our charity comes from a right end, and we may expect to reap advantage by it: this is the charity which is pleasing to God. God is well pleased, when all our actions proceed from love, love to himself, and love to immortal souls.

Consider, my dear brethren, that it was love for souls, that brought the blessed Jesus down from the bosom of his Father; that made him, who was equal in power and glory, to come and take upon him our nature; that caused the Lord of life to die the painful, ignominious, and accursed death of the cross. It was love to immortal souls, that brought this blessed Jesus among us. And O that we might hence consider how great the value of souls was and is: it was that which made Jesus to bled, pant, and die. And surely souls must be of infinite worth, which made the Lamb of God to die so shameful a death.

And shall not this make you have a true value for souls? It is of the greatest worth: and this, this is the greatest charity, when it comes from love to God, and from love to souls. This will be a charity, the satisfaction of which will last to all eternity. O that this may make you have so much regard for the value of souls, as not to neglect all opportunities for the doing of them good: here is something worth having charity for, because they remain to all eternity. Therefore, let me earnestly beseech you both to consider the worth of immortal souls, and let your charity extend to them, that by your advice and admonition, you may be an instrument, in the hands of God, in bringing souls to the Lord Jesus.

I am in the next place to consider, FOURTHLY, Why this charity, or grace of love never faileth.

And it never faileth in respect of its proceeding from an unchangeable God. We are not to understand, that our charity is always the same: No, there may, and frequently are, ebbs and flowings; but still it never totally faileth: No, the grace of love remaineth for ever. There is, and will be, a charity to all who have erred and run astray from God. We cannot be easy to see souls in the highway to destruction, and not use our utmost endeavor to bring them back from sin, and show them the dreadful consequence of running into evil. Christians cannot bear to see those souls for whom Christ died, perish for want of knowledge: and if they see any of the bodies of their fellow-creatures in want, they will do the utmost in their power to relieve them.

Charity will never fail, among those who have a true love to the Lord Jesus, and know the value of souls: they will be charitable to those who are in distress. And thus you see, that true charity, if it proceeds from a right end, never faileth.

I now proceed, my brethren, in the LAST place, to exhort all of you, high and low, rich and poor, one with another, to practice this valuable and commendable duty of charity.

It is not rolling in your coaches, taking your pleasure, and not considering the miseries of your fellow-creatures, that is commendable or praiseworthy; but the relieving your distressed poor fellow-creatures, is valuable and praise-worthy wherever it is found. But alas! how very few of our gay and polite gentlemen consider their poor friends; rather they despise, and do not regard them. They can indulge themselves in the follies of life, and had much rather spend their estates in lusts and pleasures, while the poor all round them are not thought worthy to be set with the dogs of their flock. If you have an abundance of the things of this world, then you are esteemed as companions for the polite and gay in life; but if you are poor, then you must not expect to find any favor, but be hated, or not thought fit for company or conversation: and if you have an abundance of the things of this life, and do not want any assistance, then you have many ready to help you. My dear brethren, I do not doubt but your own experience is a proof of my assertions; as also, that if any come into distress, then those, who promised to give relief, quite forget what they promise, and will despise, because Providence has frowned. But this is not acting like those who are bound for the heavenly Jerusalem; thus our hearts and our actions give our lips the lie: for if we profess the name of Christ, and do not depart from all iniquity, we are not those, who are worthy of being esteemed Christians indeed.

For, if we have not charity, we are not Christians: charity is the great duty of Christians: and where is our Christianity, if we want charity? Therefore, let me beseech you to exercise charity to your distressed fellow-creatures. Indeed, my dear brethren, this is truly commendable, truly valuable; and therefore, I beseech you, in the bowels of tender mercy to Christ, to consider his poor distressed members; exercise, exercise, I beseech you, this charity: if you have no compassion, you are not true disciples of the Lord Jesus Christ. I humbly beg you to consider those who want relief, and are really destitute, and relieve them according to your abilities. Consider, that the more favorable Providence has been to you, it should make you the more earnest and solicitous to relieve those whom you may find in distress: it is of the utmost consequence, what is well pleasing to your fellow-creatures, and doing your duty to God.

When you are called from hence, then all riches and grandeur will be over; the grave will make no distinction; great estates will be of no signification in the other world; and if you have made a bad use of the talent which God hath put into your hands, it will be only an aggravation of your condemnation at the great day of account, when God shall come to demand your souls, and to call you to an account, for the use to which you have put the abundance of the things of this life.

To conclude, let me once more beseech each of you to act according to the circumstances of life, which God, in his rich and free mercy, has given you.

If you were sensible of the great consequences which would attend your acting in this charitable manner, and considered it as a proof of your love to God, the loving his members; you could not be uncharitable in your tempers, nor fail to relieve any of your distressed fellow creatures.

Consider how easy it is for many of you, by putting your mites together, to help one who is in distress; and how can you tell, but that the little you give, may be the means of bringing one from distress into flourishing circumstances; and then, if there is a true spirit of a Christian in them, they can never be sufficiently thankful to God the author, and to you as the instrument, in being so great a friend to them in their melancholy circumstances: consider also, once more, how much better your account will be at the day of judgment, and what peace of conscience you will enjoy. How satisfactory must be the thought of having relieved the widow and the fatherless? This is recommended by the Lord Jesus Christ, and has been practiced in all ages of the church: and therefore, my brethren, be ye now found in the practice of this duty.

I have been the larger upon this, because our enemies say we deny all moral actions; but, blessed be God, they speak against us without cause: we highly value them; but we say, that faith in Christ, the love of God, and being born again, are of infinite more worth; but you cannot be true Christians without having charity to your fellow-creatures, be they friends or enemies, if in distress. And, therefore, exert yourselves in this duty, as is commanded by the blessed Jesus: and if you have true charity, you shall live and reign with him for ever.

Now to God the Father, God the Son, and God the Holy Ghost, be all honor, power, glory, might, majesty, and dominion, both now and for evermore. Amen.

Sermon 48 Satan's Devices

2 Corinthians 2:11, "Lest Satan should get an advantage over us; for we are not ignorant of his devices."

The occasion of these words was as follows: In the church of Corinth there was an unhappy person, who had committed such incest, as was not so much as named among the Gentiles, in taking his father's wife; but either on account of his wealth, power, or some such reasons, like many notorious offenders now-adays, he had not been exposed to the censures of the church.

St. Paul, therefore, in his first epistle, severely chides them for this neglect of discipline, and commands them, "in the name of our Lord Jesus Christ, when they were gathered together, to deliver such a one, whoever he was, to Satan, for the destruction of the flesh, that his Spirit might be saved in the day of the Lord;" that is, they should solemnly excommunicate him; which was then commonly attended with some bodily disease. The Corinthians, being obedient to the Apostle, as dear children, no sooner received this reproof, but they submitted to it, and cast the offending party out of the church. But whilst they were endeavoring to amend one fault, they unhappily ran into another; and as they formerly had been too mild and remiss, so now they behaved towards him with too much severity and resentment. The Apostle, therefore, in this chapter, reproves this, and tells them, that "sufficient to the offender's shame, was the punishment which had been inflicted of many:" that he had now suffered enough; and that, therefore, lest he should be tempted to say with Cain, "My punishment is greater than I can bear;" or to use the Apostle's own words, "Lest he should be swallowed up with overmuch sorrow;" they ought, now he had given proof of his repentance, to forgive him, to confirm their love towards him, and to restore him in the spirit of meekness; "Lest Satan, (to whose buffetings he was now given, by tempting him to despair) should get an advantage over us:" and so, by representing you as merciless and cruel, cause that holy name to be blasphemed, by which you are called; "for we are not ignorant of his devices:" we know very well how many subtle ways he has to draw aside and beguile unguarded unthinking men.

Thus then, stand the words in relation to the context; but as Satan has many devices, and as his quiver is full of other poisonous darts, besides those which he shoots at us to drive us to despair, I shall, in the following discourse, FIRST, Briefly observe who we are to understand by Satan. And, SECONDLY, Point out to you, what are the chief devices he generally makes use of to draw off converts from Christ, and also prescribe some remedies against them.

FIRST, Who are we to understand by Satan?

The word Satan, in its original signification, meant an adversary; and in its general acceptation, is made use of, to point out to us the chief of the devils, who, for striving to be as God, was cast down from heaven, and is now permitted, "with the rest of his spiritual wickednesses in high places, to walk up and down, seeking whom he may devour." We hear of him immediately after the creation, when in the shape of a serpent, he lay in wait to deceive our first parents. He is called Satan, in the book of Job, where we are told, that "when the sons of God came to present themselves before the Lord, Satan also came amongst them." As the scripture also speaketh in the book of Chronicles; "and Satan moved David to number the people." In the New Testament he goes under different denominations; sometimes he is called the evil One, because he is evil in himself, and tempts us to evil. Sometimes, "the Prince of the power of the air;" and, "the Spirit that now ruleth in the children of disobedience;" because he resides chiefly in the air, and through the whole world: and all that are not born of God, are said to lie in him.

He is an enemy to God and goodness; he is a hater of all truth. Why else did he slander God in paradise? Why did he tell Eve, "You shall not surely die?" And why did he promise to give all the kingdoms of the world, and the glories of them, to Jesus Christ, if he would fall down and worship him?

He is full of malice, envy, and revenge: For what other motives could induce him to molest innocent man in paradise? And why is he still so restless in his attempts to destroy us, who have done him no wrong?

He is a being of great power, as appears in his being able to act on the imagination of our blessed Lord, so as to represent to him all the kingdoms of the world, and the glories of them, in a moment of time. As also in carrying his sacred body through the air up to a pinnacle of the temple; and his driving a herd of swine so furiously into the deep. Nay, so great is his might, that, I doubt not, was God to let him use his full strength, but he could turn the earth upside down, or pull the sun from its orb.

But what he is most remarkable for is, his subtlety: for not having power given him from above, to take us by force, he is obliged to wait for opportunities to betray us, and to catch us by guile. He, therefore, made use of the serpent, which was subtle above all the beasts of the field, in order to tempt our first parents; and accordingly he is said, in the New Testament, "To lie in wait to deceive;" and, in the words of the text, the Apostle says, "We are not ignorant of his devices:" thereby implying, that we are more in danger of being seduced by his policy, than over-borne by his power.

From this short description of Satan, we may easily judge whose children they are, who love to make a lie, who speak evil of, and slander their neighbor, and whose hearts are full of pride, subtlety, malice, envy, revenge, and all uncharitableness. Surely they have Satan for their father: for the tempers of Satan they know, and the works of Satan they do. But were they to see either themselves, or Satan as he is, they could not but be terrified at their own likeness, and abhor themselves in dust and ashes.

But, the justice of God in suffering us to be tempted, is vindicated from the following considerations: That we are here in a state of disorder; That he has promised not to suffer us to be tempted above what we are able to bear; and not only so, but to him that overcometh he will give a crown of life.

The holy angels themselves, it should seem, were once put to a trial whether they would be faithful or not. The first Adam was tempted, even in paradise. And Jesus Christ, that second Adam, though he was a son, yet was carried, as our representative, by the Holy Spirit, into the wilderness, to be tempted of the devil. And there is not one single saint in paradise, amongst the goodly fellowship of the prophets, the glorious company of the apostles, the noble army of martyrs, and the spirits of just men made perfect, who, when on earth, was not assaulted by the fiery darts of that wicked one, the devil.

What then has been the common lot of all God's children, and of the angels, nay, of the eternal Son of God himself, we must not think to be exempted from: No, it is sufficient if we are made perfect through temptations, as they were. And, therefore, since we cannot but be tempted, unless we could unmake human nature, instead of repining at our condition, we should rather be inquiring, at what time of our lives Satan most violently assaults us? And what those devices are, which he commonly makes use of, in order to "get an advantage over us?" As to the first question, what time of life? I answer, we must expect to be tempted by him, in some degree or other, all our lives long.

_ For this life being a continual warfare, we must never expect to have rest from our spiritual adversary the devil, or to say, our combat with him is finished, 'till, with our blessed master, we bow down our heads, and give up the ghost.

But since the time of our conversion, or first entering upon the spiritual life, is the most critical time at which he, for the most part, violently besets us, as well knowing, if he can prevent our setting out, he can lead us captive at his will; and since the wise son of Sirach particularly warns us, when we are going to serve the Lord, to prepare our souls for temptation, I shall, in answer to the other question, pass on to the SECOND general thing proposed; and point out those devices, which Satan generally makes use of at our first conversion, in order to get an advantage over us.

But let me observe to you, that whatsoever shall be delivered in the following discourse is only designed for such as have actually entered upon the divine life; and not for carnal almost Christians, who have the form of godliness, but never yet felt the power of it in their hearts. This being premised, The FIRST device I shall mention, which Satan makes use of, is, to drive us to despair.

When God the Father awakens a sinner by the terrors of the law, and by his Holy Spirit convinceth him of sin, in order to lead him to Christ, and show him the necessity of a Redeemer; then Satan generally strikes in, and aggravates those convictions to such a degree, as to make the sinner doubt of finding mercy thro' the Mediator.

Thus, in all his temptations of the Holy Jesus, he chiefly aimed to make him question, whether he was the Son of God? "If thou be the Son of God," do so and so. With many such desponding thoughts, no doubt, he filled the heart of the great St. Paul, when he continued three days, neither eating bread nor drinking water; and therefore he speaks by experience, when he says, in the words of the text, "We are not ignorant of his devices," that he would endeavor to drive the incestuous person to despair.

But let not any of you be influenced by him, to despair of finding mercy. For it is not the greatness or number of our crimes, but impenitence and unbelief, that will prove our ruin: No, were our sins more in number than the hairs of our head, or of a deeper die than the brightest scarlet; yet the merits of the death of Jesus Chris are infinitely greater, and faith in his blood shall make them white as snow.

Answer always, therefore, his despairing suggestions, as your Blessed Lord did, with an "It is written." Tell him, you know that your Redeemer liveth, ever to make intercession for you; that the Lord hath received from him double for all your crimes: And tho' you have sinned much, that is no reason why you should despair, but only why you should love much, having so much forgiven. A SECOND device that Satan generally makes use of, to get an advantage over young converts, is, to tempt them to presume, or to think more highly of themselves than they ought to think.

When a person ha for some little time tasted the good word of life, and felt the powers of the world to come, he is commonly (as indeed well he may) most highly transported with that sudden change he finds in himself.

But then, Satan will not be wanting, at such a time, to puff him up with a high conceit of his own attainments as if he was some great person; and will tempt him to set at nought his brethren, as though he was holier than they.

Take heed therefore, and let us beware of this device of our spiritual adversary; for as before honor is humility, so a haughty spirit generally goes before a fall; and God is obliged, when under such circumstances, to send us some humbling visitation, or permit us to fall, as he did Peter into some grievous sin, that we may learn not to be too high minded.

To check therefore all suggestions to spiritual pride, let us consider, that we did not apprehend Christ, but were apprehended of him.

That we have nothing but what we have received. That the free grace of God has alone made the difference between us and others; and, was God to leave us to the deceitfulness of our own hearts but one moment, we should become weak and wicked, like other men. We should farther consider, that being proud of grace, is the most ready way to lose it. "For God resisteth the proud, and giveth more grace only to the humble." And were we endowed with the perfections of the seraphim; yet if we were proud of those perfections, they would but render us more accomplished devils. Above all, we should pray earnestly to Almighty God, that we may learn of Jesus Christ, to be lowly in heart. That his grace, through the subtlety and deceivableness of Satan, may not be our poison. But that we may always think soberly of ourselves, as we ought to think. A THIRD device I shall mention, which Satan generally makes use of, "to get an advantage over us," is to tempt us to uneasiness, and to have hard thoughts of God, when we are dead and barren in prayer.

Though this is a term not understood by the natural man, yet, whosoever there are amongst you, who have passed through the pangs of the new birth, they know full well what I mean, when I talk of deadness and dryness in prayer. And, I doubt not, but many of you, amongst whom I am not preaching the kingdom of God, are at this very time laboring under it.

For, when persons are first awakened to the divine life, because grace is weak and nature strong, God is often pleased to vouchsafe them some extraordinary illuminations of his Holy Spirit; but when they are grown to be more perfect men in Christ, then he frequently seems to leave them to themselves; and not only so, but permits a horrible deadness and dread to overwhelm them; at which times Satan will not be wanting to vex and tempt them to impatience, to the great discomfort of their souls.

But be not afraid; for this is no more than your blessed Redeemer, that spotless Lamb of God, has undergone before you: witness his bitter agony in the garden, when his soul was exceeding sorrowful, even unto death. When he sweat great drops of blood, falling on the ground; when the sense of the Divinity was drawn from him; and Satan, in all probability, was permitted to set all his terrors in array before him.

Rejoice, therefore, my brethren, when you fall into the like circumstances; as knowing, that you are therein partakers of the sufferings of Jesus Christ. Consider, that it is necessary such inward trials should come, to wean us from the immoderate love of sensible devotion, and teach us to follow Christ, not merely for his loaves, but out of a principle of love and obedience. In patience, therefore, possess your souls, and be not terrified by Satan's suggestions. Still persevere in seeking Jesus in the use of means, though it be sorrowing; and though through barrenness of soul, you may go mourning all the day long. Consider that the spouse is with you, though behind the curtain; as he was with Mary, at the sepulcher, though she knew it not. That he was withdrawn but for a little while, to make his next visit more welcome. That though he may now seem to frown and look back on you, as he did on the Syrophonecian woman; yet if you, like her, or blind Bartimeus, cry out so much the more earnestly, "Jesus, thou Son of David, have mercy on us;" he will be made known unto you again, either in the temple, by breaking of bread, or some other way.

But amongst all the devices that Satan makes use of, "to get an advantage over us," there is none in which he is more successful, or by which he grieves the children of God worse, than a FOURTH device I am going to mention, his troubling you with blasphemous, profane, unbelieving thoughts; and sometimes to such a degree, that they are as tormenting as the rack.

Some indeed are apt to impute all such evil thoughts to a disorder of body. But those who know any thing of the spiritual life, can inform you, with greater certainty, that for the generality, they proceed from that wicked one, the devil; who, no doubt, has power given him from above, as well now as formerly, to disorder the body, as he did Job's, that he may, with the more secrecy and success, work upon, ruffle and torment the soul.

You that have felt his fiery darts, can subscribe to the truth of this, and by fatal experience can tell, how often he has bid you, "curse God and die," and darted into your thoughts a thousand blasphemous suggestions, even in your most secret and solemn retirements; the bar looking back on which makes your very hearts to tremble.

I appeal to your own consciences; Have not some of you, when you have been lifting up holy hands in prayer, been pestered with such a crowd of the most horrid insinuations, that you have been often tempted to rise off from your knees, and been made to believe your prayers were an abomination to the Lord? Nay, when, with the rest of your Christian brethren, you have crowded round the holy table, and taken the sacred symbols of Christ's most blessed body and blood into your hands, instead of remembering the death of your Savior, have you not employed in driving out evil thoughts, as Abraham was in driving away the birds, that came to devour his sacrifice; and thereby have been terrified, lest you have eat and drank your own damnation?

But marvel not, as though some strange thing happened unto you; for this has been the common lot of all God's children. We read, even in Job's time, "That when the sons of God came to appear before their Maker, (at public worship) Satan also came amongst them," to disturb their devotions.

And think not that God is angry with you for these distracting, though ever so blasphemous thoughts: No, he knows it is not you, but Satan working in you; and therefore, notwithstanding he may be displeased with, and certainly will punish him; yet he will both pity and reward you. And though it be difficult to make persons in your circumstances to believe so; yet I doubt not but you are more acceptable to God, when performing your holy duties in the midst of such involuntary distractions, than when you are wrapped up by devotion, as it were, into the third heavens; for you are then suffering, as well as doing the will of God at the same time; and, like Nehemiah's servants at the building of the temple, are holding a trowel in one hand, and a sword in the other. Be not driven from the use of any ordinance whatever, on account of those abominable suggestions; for then you let Satan get his desired advantage over you; it being his chief design, by these thoughts, to make you fall out with the means of grace; and to tempt you to believe, you do not please God, for no other reason, than because you do not please yourselves. Rather persevere in the use of the holy communion especially, and all other means whatever; and when these temptations have wrought that resignation in you, for which they were permitted, God will visit you with fresh tokens of his love, as he met Abraham, when he returned from the slaughter of the five kings; and will send an angel from heaven, as he did to his Son, on purpose to strengthen you.

Hitherto we have only observed such devices as Satan makes use of immediately by himself; but there is a FIFTH I shall mention, which is not the least, tempting us by our carnal friends and relatives.

This is one of the most common, as well as most artful devices he makes use of, to draw young converts from God; for when he cannot prevail over them by himself, he will try what he can do by the influence and mediation of others.

Thus he tempted Eve, that she might tempt Adam. Thus he stirred up Job's wife, to bid him "Curse God and die." And thus he made use of Peter's tongue, to persuade our blessed Lord "to spare himself," and thereby decline those sufferings, by which alone we could be preserved from suffering the vengeance of eternal fire. And thus, in these last days, he often stirs up our most powerful friends and dearest intimates, to dissuade us from going in that narrow way, which alone leadeth unto life eternal.

But our blessed Lord has furnished us with a sufficient answer to all such suggestions. "Get you behind me, my adversaries;" for otherwise they will be an offense unto you; and the only reason why they give such advice is, because they "favor not the things that be of God, but the things that be of men." Whoever, therefore, among you are resolved to serve the Lord, prepare your souls for many such temptations as these; for it is necessary that such offenses should come, to try your sincerity, to teach us to cease from man, and to see if we will forsake all to follow Christ.

Indeed our modernisers of Christianity would persuade us, that the gospel was calculated only for about two hundred years; and that now there is no need of hating father and mother, or of being persecuted for the sake of Christ and his gospel.

But such persons err, not knowing the scriptures, and the power of godliness in their hearts; for whosoever receives the love of God in the truth of it, will find, that Christ came to send not peace, but a sword upon earth, as much now as ever. That the father-in-law shall be against the daughter-in-law, in these latter, as well as in the primitive times; and that if we will live godly in Christ Jesus, we must, as then, so now, from carnal friends and relations, suffer persecution. But the devil hath a SIXTH device, which is as dangerous as any of the former, by not tempting us at all, or rather, by withdrawing himself for a while, in order to come upon us at an hour when we think not of it.

Thus it is said, that he left Jesus Christ only for a season; and our blessed Lord has bid us to watch and pray always, that we enter not into temptation; thereby implying, that Satan, whether we think of it or not, is always seeking how he may devour us.

If we would therefore behave like good soldiers of Jesus Christ, we must be always upon our guard, and never pretend to lay down our spiritual weapons of prayer and watching, till our warfare is accomplished by death; for if we do, our spiritual Amalek will quickly prevail against us. What if he has left us? It is only for a season; yet a little while, and, like a roaring lion, with double fury, he will break out upon us again. So great a coward as the devil is, he seldom leaves us at the first onset. As he followed our blessed Lord with one temptation after another, so will he treat his servants. And the reason why he does not renew his attacks, is sometimes, because God knows we are yet weak and unable to bear them, sometimes, because our grand adversary thinks to beset us at a more convenient season.

Watch carefully over thy heart, O Christian; and whenever thou perceivest thyself to be falling into a spiritual slumber, say to it, as Christ to his disciples, "Arise (my soul) why sleepest thou?" Awake, awake; put on strength, watch and pray, or otherwise the Philistines will be upon thee, and lead thee whither thou wouldst not. Alas! Is this life a time to lie down and slumber in? Arise, and call upon thy God; thy spiritual enemy is not dead, but lurketh in some secret place, seeking a convenient opportunity how he may betray thee. If thou ceasest to strive with him, thou ceasest to be a friend of God; thou ceasest to go in that narrow way which leadeth unto life.

Thus have I endeavored to point out to you some of those devices, that Satan generally makes use of "to get an advantage over us;" many others there are, no doubt, which he often uses.

But these, on account of my youth and want of experience, I cannot yet apprise you of; they who have been listed for many years in their master's service, and fought under his banner against our spiritual Amalek, are able to discover more of his artifices; and, being tempted in all things, like unto their brethren, can, in all things, advise and succor those that are tempted.

In the mean while, let me exhort my young fellow-soldiers, who, like myself, are but just entering the field, and for whose sake this was written, not to be discouraged at the fiery trial wherewith they must be tried, if they would be found faithful servants of Jesus Christ. You see, my dearly beloved brethren, by what has been delivered, that our way through the wilderness of this world to the heavenly Canaan, is beset with thorns, and that there are sons of Anak to be grappled with, ere you can possess the promised land. But let not these, like so many false spies, discourage you from going up to fight the Lord's battles, but say with Caleb and Joshua, "Nay, but we will go up, for we are able to conquer them." Jesus Christ, that great captain of our salvation, has in our stead, and as our representative, baffled the grand enemy of mankind, and we have nothing to do, but manfully to fight under his banner, and to go on from conquering to conquer. Our glory does not consist in being exempted from, but in enduring temptations. "Blessed is the man, (says the apostle) that endureth temptation;": and again, "Brethren, count it all joy, when you fall into divers temptations:" And in that perfect form our blessed Lord has prescribed to us, we are taught to pray, not so much to be delivered from all temptation, as "from the evil" of it. Whilst we are on this side eternity, it must needs be that temptations come; and, no doubt, "Satan has desired to have all of us, to sift us as wheat." But wherefore should we fear? For he that is for us, is by far more powerful, than all that are against us. Jesus Christ, our great High-priest, is exalted to the right hand of God, and there sitteth to make intercession for us, that our faith fail not.

Since then Christ is praying, whom should we fear? And since he has promised to make us more than conquerors, of whom should we be afraid? No, though an hose of devils are set in array against us, let us not be afraid; though there should rise up the hottest persecution against us, yet let us put our trust in God. What though Satan, and the rest of his apostate spirits, are powerful, when compared with us; yet, if put in competition with the Almighty, they are as weak as the meanest worms. God has them all reserved in chains of darkness unto the judgment of the great day. So far as he permits them, they shall go, but no farther; and where he pleases, there shall their proud malicious designs be stayed. We read in the gospel, that though a legion of them possessed one man, yet they could not destroy him; nor could they so much as enter into a swine, without first having leave given them from above. It is true, we often find they foil us, when we are assaulted by them; but let us be strong, and very courageous; for, though they bruise our heels, we shall, at length, bruise their heads. Yet a little while, and he that shall come, will come; and then we shall see all our spiritual enemies put under our feet. What f they do come out against us, like so many great Goliaths; yet, if we can go forth, as the stripling David, in the name and strength of the Lord of hosts, we may say, O Satan, where is thy power? O fallen spirits, where is your victory?

Once more therefore, and to conclude; let us be strong, and very courageous, and let us put on the whole armor of God, that we may be able to stand against the fiery darts of the wicked one. Let us renounce ourselves, and the world, and then we shall take away the armor in which he trusteth, and he will find nothing in us for his temptations to work upon.

We shall then prevent his malicious designs; and being willing to suffer ourselves, shall need less sufferings to be sent us form above. Let us have our loins girt about with truth; and for an helmet, the hope of salvation; "praying always with all manner of supplication." Above all things, "Let us take the sword of the spirit, which is the word of God," and "the shield of faith," looking always to Jesus, the author and finisher of our faith, who for the joy that was set before him, endured the cross, despising the shame, and is now sat down at the right hand of God.

To which happy place, may God of his infinite mercy translate us all, through our Lord Jesus Christ.

To whom, with the Father, and the Holy Ghost, three persons and one eternal God, be all honor and glory, now and for evermore. Amen.

Sermon 49 On Regeneration

2 Corinthians 5:17, "If any man be in Christ, he is a new creature."

The doctrine of our regeneration, or new birth in Christ Jesus, though one of the most fundamental doctrines of our holy religion; though so plainly and often pressed on us in sacred writ, "that he who runs may read;" nay though it is the very hinge on which the salvation of each of us turns, and a point too in which all sincere Christians, of every denomination, agree; yet it is so seldom considered, and so little experimentally understood by the generality of professors, that were we to judge of the truth of it, by the experience of most who call themselves Christians, we should be apt to imagine they had "not so much as heard" whether there be any such thing as regeneration or not. It is true, men for the most part are orthodox in the common articles of their creed; they believe "there is but one God, and one Mediator between God and men, even the man Christ Jesus;" and that there is no other name given under heaven, whereby they can be saved, besides his: But then tell them, they must be regenerated, they must be born again, they must be renewed in the very spirit, in the inmost faculties of their minds, ere they can truly call Christ, "Lord, Lord," or have an evidence that they have any share in the merits of his precious blood; and they are ready to cry out with Nicodemus, "How can these things be?" Or with the Athenians, on another occasion, "What wilt this bumbler say? He seemeth to be a setter-forth of strange doctrines;" because we preach unto them Christ, and the new-birth.

That I may therefore contribute my mite towards curing the fatal mistake of such persons, who would thus put asunder what God has inseparably joined together, and vainly think they are justified by Christ, or have their sins forgiven, and his perfect obedience imputed to them, when they are not sanctified, have not their natures changed, and made holy, I shall beg leave to enlarge on the words of the text in the following manner: FIRST, I shall endeavor to explain what is meant by being in Christ: "If any man be in Christ." SECONDLY, What we are to understand by being a new creature: "If any man be in Christ he is a new creature." THIRDLY, I shall produce some arguments to make good the apostle's assertion. And FOURTHLY, I shall draw some inferences from what may be delivered, and then conclude with a word or two of exhortation.

FIRST, I am to endeavor to explain what is meant by this expression in the text, "If any man be in Christ." Now a person may be said to be in Christ two ways.

FIRST, Only by an outward profession. And in this sense, every one that is called a Christian, or baptized into Christ's church, may be said to be in Christ. But that this is not the sole meaning of the apostle's phrase before us, is evident, because then, every one that names the name of Christ, or is baptized into his visible church, would be a new creature.

Which is notoriously false, it being too plain, beyond all contradiction, that comparatively but few of those that are "born of water," are "born of the Spirit" likewise; to use another spiritual way of speaking, many are baptized with water, which were never baptized with the Holy Ghost.

To be in Christ therefore, in the full import of the word, must certainly mean something more than a bare outward profession, or being called after his name. For, as this same apostle tells us, "All are not Israelites that are of Israel," so when applied to Christianity, all are not real Christians that are nominally such. Nay, this is so far from being the case, that our blessed Lord himself informs us, that many who have prophesied or preached in his name, and in his name cast out devils, and done many wonderful works, shall notwithstanding be dismissed at the last day, with "depart from me, I know you not, ye workers of iniquity." It remains therefore, that this expression, "if any man be in Christ," must be understood in a SECOND and closer signification, to be in him so as to partake of the benefits of his sufferings. To be in him not only by an outward profession, but by an inward change and purity of heart, and cohabitation of his Holy Spirit. To be in him, so as to be mystically united to him by a true and lively faith, and thereby to receive spiritual virtue from him, as the members of the natural body do from the head, or the branches from the vine. To be in him in such a manner as the apostle, speaking of himself, acquaints us he knew a person was, "I knew man in Christ," a true Christian; or, as he himself desires to be in Christ, when he wishes, in his epistle to the Philippians, that he might be found in him.

This is undoubtedly the proper meaning of the apostle's expression in the words of the text; so that what he says in his epistle to the Romans about circumcision, may very well be applied to the present subject; that he is not a real Christian who is only one outwardly; nor is that true baptism, which is only outward in the flesh. But he is a true Christian, who is one inwardly, whose baptism is that of the heart, in the spirit, and not merely in the water, whose praise is not of man but of God. Or, as he speaketh in another place, "Neither circumcision nor uncircumcision availeth any thing (of itself) but a new creature." Which amounts to what he here declares in the verse now under consideration, that if any man be truly and properly in Christ, he is a new creature. Which brings me to show, SECONDLY, What we are to understand by being a new creature.

And here it is evident at the first view, that this expression is not to be so explained as though there was a physical change required to be made in us; or as though we were to be reduced to our primitive nothings, and then created and formed again. For, supposing we were, as Nicodemus ignorantly imagined, to enter a "second time into our mother's womb, and be born," alas! what would it contribute towards rendering us spiritually new creatures? Since "that which was born of the flesh would be flesh still;" we should be the same carnal persons as ever, being derived from carnal parents, and consequently receiving the seeds of all manner of sin and corruption from them. No, it only means, that we must be so altered as to the qualities and tempers of our minds, that we must entirely forget what manner of persons we once were. As it may be said of a piece of gold, that was once in the ore, after it has been cleansed, purified and polished, that it is a new piece of gold; as it may be said of a bright glass that has been covered over with filth, when it is wiped, and so become transparent and clear, that it is a new glass: Or, as it might be said of Naaman, when he recovered of his leprosy, and his flesh returned unto him like the flesh of a young child, that he was a new man; so our souls, though still the same as to offense, yet are so purged, purified and cleansed from their natural dross, filth and leprosy, by the blessed influences of the Holy Spirit, that they may be properly said to be made anew.

How this glorious change is wrought in the soul, cannot easily be explained: For no one knows the ways of the Spirit save the Spirit of God himself. Not that this ought to be any argument against this doctrine; for, as our blessed Lord observed to Nicodemus, when he was discoursing on this very subject, "The wind bloweth where it listeth, and thou hearest the sound thereof, but knowest not whence it cometh, and whither it goeth;" and if we are told of natural things, and we understand them not, how much less ought we to wonder, if we cannot immediately account for the invisible workings of the Holy Spirit? The truth of the matter is this: the doctrine of our regeneration, or new birth in Christ Jesus, is hard to be understood by the natural man. But that there is really such a thing, and that each of us must be spiritually born again, I shall endeavor to show under my THIRD general head, in which I was to produce some arguments to make good the apostle's assertion.

And here one would think it sufficient to affirm, FIRST, That God himself, in his holy word, hath told us so. Many texts might be produced out of the Old Testament to prove this point, and indeed, one would wonder how Nicodemus, who was a teacher in Israel, and who was therefore to instruct the people n the spiritual meaning of the law, should be so ignorant of this grand article, as we find he really was, by his asking our blessed Lord, when he was pressing on him this topic, How can these things be? Surely, he could not forget how often the Psalmist had begged of God, to make him "a new heart," and "to renew a right spirit within him;" as likewise, how frequently the prophets had warned the people to make them "new hearts," and new minds, and so turn unto the Lord their God. But not to mention these and such like texts out of the Old Testament, this doctrine is so often and plainly repeated in the New, that, as I observed before, he who runs may read. For what says the great Prophet and Instructor of the world himself: "Except a man (every one that is naturally the offspring of Adam) be born again of water and the Spirit, he cannot enter into the kingdom of God." And lest we should be apt to slight this assertion, and Nicodemus-like, reject the doctrine, because we cannot immediately explain "How this thing can be;" our blessed Master therefore affirms it, as it were, by an oath, "Verily, verily, I say unto you, " or, as it may be read, I the Amen; I who am truth itself, say unto you, that it is the unalterable appointment of my heavenly Father, that "unless a man be born again, he cannot enter into the kingdom of God." Agreeable to this, are those many passages we meet with in the epistles, where we are commanded to be "renewed in the Spirit," or, which was before explained, in the inmost faculties of our minds; to "put off the Old Man, which is corrupt; and to put on the New Man, which is created after God, in righteousness and true holiness;" that "old things must pass away, and that all things must become new;" that we are to be "saved by the washing of regeneration, and the renewing of the Holy Ghost." Or, methinks, was there no other passage to be produced besides the words of the text, it would be full enough, since the apostle therein positively affirms, that "If any man be in Christ, he is a new creature." Now, what can be understood by all these different terms of being born again, or putting off the Old Man, and putting on the New, of being renewed in the spirit of our minds, and becoming new creatures; but that Christianity requires a thorough, real inward change of heart? Do we think these and suchlike forms of speaking, are mere metaphors, words of a bare sound, without any real solid signification? Indeed, it is to be feared, some men would have them interpreted so; but alas! unhappy men! They are not to be envied in their metaphorical interpretation: it will be well, if they do not interpret themselves out of their salvation.

Multitudes of other texts might be produced to confirm this same truth; but those already quoted are so plain and convincing, that one would imagine no one should deny it; were we not told, there are some, "who having eyes, see not, and ears, hear not, and that will not understand with their hearts, or hear with their ears, lest they should be converted, and Christ should heal them.

But I proceed to a SECOND argument; and that shall be taken from the purity of God, and the present corrupt and polluted state of man.

God is described in holy scripture (and I speak to those who profess to know the scripture) as a Spirit; as a being of such infinite sanctity, as to be of "purer eyes than to behold iniquity;" as to be so transcendently holy, that it is said "the very heavens are not clean in his sight; and the angels themselves he chargeth with folly." On the other hand, man is described (and every regenerate person will find it true by his own experience) as a creature altogether "conceived and born in sin;" as having "no good thing dwelling in him;" as being "carnal, sold under sin;" nay, as having "a mind which is at enmity with God," and such-like.

And since there is such an infinite disparity, can any one conceive how a filthy, corrupted, polluted wretch can dwell with an infinitely pure and holy God, before he is changed, and rendered, in some measure, like him?

Can he, who is of purer eyes than to behold iniquity, dwell with it? Can he, in whose sight the heavens are not clean, delight to dwell with uncleanness itself? No, we might as well suppose light to have communion with darkness, or Christ to have concord with Belial. But I pass on to a THIRD argument, which shall be founded on the consideration of the nature of that happiness God has prepared for those that unfeignedly love him.

To enter indeed on a minute and particular description of heaven, would be vain and presumptuous, since we are told that "eye hath not seen, nor ear heard, neither hath in entered into the heart of man to conceive, the things that are there prepared" for the sincere followers of the holy Jesus, even in this life, much less in that which is to come. However, this we may venture to affirm in general, that as God is a Spirit, so the happiness he has laid up for his people is spiritual likewise; and consequently, unless our carnal minds are changed, and spiritualized, we can never be made meet to partake of that inheritance with the saints in light.

It is true, we may flatter ourselves, that, supposing we continue in our natural corrupt estate, and carry all our lusts along with us, we should, notwithstanding, relish heaven, was God to admit us therein. And so we might, was it a Mahometan paradise, wherein we were to take our full swing in sensual delights. But since its joys are only spiritual, and no unclean thing can possibly enter those blessed mansions, there is an absolute necessity of our being changed, and undergoing a total renovation of our deprave natures, before we can have any taste or relish of those heavenly pleasures.

It is, doubtless, for this reason, that the apostle declares it to be the irrevocable decree of the Almighty, that "without holiness, (without being made pure by regeneration, and having the image of God thereby reinstamped upon the soul) no may shall see the Lord." And it is very observable, that our divine Master, in the famous passage before referred to, concerning the absolute necessity of regeneration, does not say, Unless a man be born again, he SHALL NOT, but "unless a man be born again, he CANNOT enter into the kingdom of God." It is founded in the very nature of things, that unless we have dispositions wrought in us suitable to the objects that are to entertain us, we can take no manner of complacency or satisfaction in them. For instance; what delight can the most harmonious music afford to a deaf, or what pleasure can the most excellent picture give to a blind man? Can a tasteless palate relish the richest dainties, or a filthy swine be pleased with the finest garden of flowers? No: and what reason can be assigned for it? An answer is ready; because they have neither of them any tempers of mind correspondent or agreeable to what they are to be diverted with. And thus it is with the soul hereafter; for death makes no more alteration in the soul, than as it enlarges its faculties, and makes it capable of receiving deeper impressions either of pleasure or pain. If it delighted to converse with God here, it will be transported with the sight of his glorious Majesty hereafter. If it was pleased with the communion of saints on earth, it will be infinitely more so with the communion and society of holy angels, and the spirits of just men made perfect in heaven. But if the opposite of all this be true, we may assure ourselves the soul could not be happy, was God himself to admit it (which he never will do) into the regions of the blessed. But it is time for me to hasten to the FOURTH argument, because Christ's redemption will not be complete in us, unless we are new creatures.

If we reflect indeed on the first and chief end of our blessed Lord's coming, we shall find it was to be a propitiation for our sins, to give his life a ransom for many. But then, if the benefits of our dear Redeemer's death were to extend no farther than barely to procure forgiveness of our sins, we should have as little reason to rejoice in it, as a poor condemned criminal that is ready to perish by some fatal disease, would have in receiving a pardon from his judge. For Christians would do well to consider, that there is not only a legal hindrance to our happiness, as we are breakers of God's law, but also a moral impurity in our natures, which renders us incapable of enjoying heaven (as hath been already proved) till some mighty change have been wrought in us. It is necessary therefore, in order to make Christ's redemption complete, that we should have a grant of God's Holy Spirit to change our natures, and so prepare us for the enjoyment of that happiness our Savior has purchased by his precious blood.

Accordingly the holy scriptures inform us, that whom Christ justifies, or whose sins he forgives, and to whom he imputes his perfect obedience, those he also sanctifies, purifies and cleanses, and totally changeth their corrupted natures. As the scripture also speaketh in another place, "Christ is to us justification, sanctification, and then redemption." But, FOURTHLY, Proceed we now to the next general thing proposed, to draw some inferences from what has been delivered, And, FIRST, If he that is in Christ be a new creature, this may serve as a reproof for those who rest in a bare performance of outward duties, without perceiving any real inward change of heart.

We may observe a great many persons to be very punctual in the regular returns of public and private prayer, as likewise of receiving the holy communion, and perhaps now and then too in keeping a fast. But here is the misfortune, they rest barely in the use of the means, and think all is over, when they have thus complied with those sacred institutions; whereas, were they rightly informed, they would consider, that all the instituted means of grace, as prayer, fasting, hearing and reading the word of God, receiving the blessed sacrament, and such-like, are no farther serviceable to us, than as they are found to make us inwardly better, and to carry on the spiritual life in the soul.

It is true, they are means; but then they are only means; they are part, but not the whole of religion: for if so, who more religious than the Pharisee? He fasted twice in the week, and gave tithes of all that he possessed, and yet was not justified, as our Savior himself informs us, in the sight of God.

You perhaps, like the Pharisee, may fast often, and make long prayers; you may, with Herod, hear good sermons gladly. But yet, if you continue vain and trifling, immoral or worldly-minded, and differ from the rest of your neighbors barely in going to church, or in complying with some outward performances, are you better than they? No, in no wise; you are by far much worse: for if you use them, and at the same time abuse them, you thereby encourage others to think there is nothing in them and therefore must expect to receive the greater damnation. But, SECONDLY, If he that is in Christ be a new creature, then this may check the groundless presumption of another class of professors, who rest in the attainment of some moral virtues, and falsely imagine they are good Christians, if they are just in their dealings, temperate in their diet, and do not hurt or violence to any man.

But if this was all that is requisite to make us Christians, why might not the heathens of old be good Christians, who were remarkable for these virtues? Or St. Paul before his conversion, who tells us, that he lived in all good conscience? But we find he renounces all dependence on works of this nature, and only desires to be found in Christ, and to know the power of his resurrection, or have an experimental proof of receiving the Holy Ghost, purchased for him by the death, and ensured and applied to him by the resurrection of Jesus Christ.

The sum of the matter is this: Christianity includes morality, as grace does reason; but if we are only mere Moralists, if we are not inwardly wrought upon, and changed by the powerful operations of the Holy Spirit, and our moral actions, proceed from a principle of a new nature, however we may call ourselves Christians, we shall be found naked at the great day, and in the number of those, who have neither Christ's righteousness imputed to them for their justification in the sight, nor holiness enough in their souls as the consequence of that, in order to make them meet for the enjoyment, of God. Nor, THIRDLY, Will this doctrine less condemn those, who rest in a partial amendment of themselves, without experiencing a thorough, real, inward change of heart.

A little acquaintance with the world will furnish us with instances, of no small number of persons, who, perhaps, were before openly profane; but seeing the ill consequences of their vices, and the many worldly inconveniencies it has reduced them to, on a sudden, as it were, grow civilized; and thereupon flatter themselves that they are very religious, because they differ a little from their former selves, and are not so scandalously wicked as once they were: whereas, at the same time, they shall have some secret darling sin or other, some beloved Delilah or Herodias, which they will no part with; some hidden lust, which they will not mortify; some vicious habit, which they will not take pains to root out. But wouldst thou know, O vain man! Whoever thou art, what the Lord thy God requires of thee? Thou must be informed, that nothing short of a thorough sound conversion will fit thee for the kingdom of heaven. It is not enough to turn from profaneness to civility; but thou must turn from civility to godliness. Not only some, but "all things must become new" in thy soul. It will profit thee but little to do many things, if yet some one thing thou lackest. In short, thou must not only be an almost, but altogether a new creature, or in vain thou boasteth that thou art a Christian.

FOURTHLY, If he that is in Christ be a new creature, then this may be prescribed as an infallible rule for every person of whatever denomination, age, degree or quality, to judge himself by; this being the only solid foundation, whereon we can build a well-grounded assurance of pardon, peace, and happiness.

We may indeed depend on the broken reed of an external profession; we may think we are good enough, if we lead such sober, honest, moral lives, as many heathens did. We may imagine we are in a safe condition, if we attend on the public offices of religion, and are constant in the duties of our closets. But unless all these tend to reform our lives, and change our hearts, and are only used as so many channels of divine grace; as I told you before, so I tell you again, Christianity will profit you nothing.

Let each of us therefore seriously put this question to our hearts: Have we received the Holy Ghost since we believed? Are we new creatures in Christ, or no? At least, if we are not so yet, is it our daily endeavor to become such? Do we constantly and conscientiously use all the means of grace required thereto? Do we fast, watch and pray? Do we, not lazily seek, but laboriously strive to enter in at the strait gate? In short, do we renounce our own righteousness, take up our crosses and follow Christ? If so, we are in that narrow way which leads to life; the good seed is sown in our hearts, and will, if duly watered and nourished by a regular persevering use of all the means of grace, grow up to eternal life. But on the contrary, if we have only heard, and know not experimentally, whether there be any Holy Ghost; if we are strangers to fasting, watching and prayer, and all the other spiritual exercises of devotion; if we are content to go in the broad way, merely because we see most other people do so, without once reflecting whether it be the right one or not; in short, if we are strangers, nay enemies to the cross of Christ, by lives of worldly-mindedness, and sensual pleasure, and thereby make others think, that Christianity is but an empty name, a bare formal profession; if this be the case, I say, Christ is as yet dead in vain, to us; we are under the guilt of our sins; and are unacquainted with a true and thorough conversion.

But beloved, I am persuaded better things of you, and things that accompany salvation, though I thus speak; I would humbly hope that you are sincerely persuaded, that he who hath not the Spirit of Christ is none of his; and that, unless the Spirit, which raised Jesus from the dead, dwell in you here, neither will your mortal bodies be quickened by the same Spirit to dwell with him hereafter.

Let me therefore (as was proposed in the LAST place) earnestly exhort you, in the name of our Lord Jesus Christ, to act suitable to those convictions, and to live as Christians, that are commanded in holy writ, to "put off their former conversation concerning the Old Man, and to put on the New Man, which is created after God in righteousness and true holiness." It must be owned indeed, that this is a great and difficult work; but, blessed be God, it is not impossible. Many thousands of happy souls have been assisted by a divine power to bring it about, and why should we despair of success? Is God's hand shortened, that it cannot save? Was he the God of our Fathers, is he not the God of their children also? Yes, doubtless, of their children also. It is a task likewise, that will put us to some pain; it will oblige us to part with some lust, to break with some friend, to mortify some beloved passion, which may be exceeding dear to us, and perhaps as hard to leave, as to cut off a right-hand, or pluck out a right-eye. But what of all this? Will not the being made a real living member of Christ, a child of God, and an inheritor of the kingdom of heaven, abundantly make amends for all this trouble? Undoubtedly it will.

The setting about and carrying on the great and necessary work, perhaps may, nay assuredly will expose us also to the ridicule of the unthinking part of mankind, who will wonder, that we run not into the same excess of riot with themselves; and because we deny our sinful appetites, and are not conformed to this world, being commanded in scripture to do the one, and to have our conversation in heaven, in opposition to the other, they may count our lives folly, and our end to be without honor. But will not the being numbered among the saints, and shining as the stars for ever and ever, be a more than sufficient recompense for all the ridicule, calumny, or reproach, we can possibly meet with here?

Indeed, was there no other reward attended a thorough conversion, but that peace of God, which is the unavoidable consequence of it, and which, even in this life, "passeth all understanding," we should have great reason to rejoice. But when we consider, that this is the least of those mercies God has prepared for those that are in Christ, and become new creatures; that, this is but the beginning of an eternal succession of pleasures; that the day of our deaths, which the unconverted, unrenewed sinner must so much dread, will be, as it were, but the first day of our new births, and open to us an everlasting scene of happiness and comfort; in short, if we remember, that they who are regenerate and born again, have a real title to all the glorious promises of the gospel, and are infallibly certain of being as happy, both here and hereafter, as an all-wise, all-gracious, all- powerful God can make them; methinks, every one that has but the least concern for the salvation of his precious and immortal soul, having such promises, such an hope, such an eternity of happiness set before him, should never cease watching, praying, and striving, till he find a real, inward, saving change wrought in his heart, and thereby doth know of a truth, that he dwells in Christ, and Christ in him; that he is a new creature, therefore a child of God; that he is already an inheritor, and will ere long be an actual possessor of the kingdom of heaven.

Which God of his infinite mercy grant, through Jesus Christ our Lord.

To whom, etc.

Sermon 50 Christians, Temples of the Living God

2 Corinthians 6:16, "Ye are the Temple of the living God."

Isaiah, speaking of the glory of gospel days, said, "Men have not heard nor perceived by the ear, neither hath the eye seen, O God, besides thee, what he hath prepared for him that waiteth for him." Chap. 64:4.

Could a world lying in the wicked one, be really convinced of this, they would need no other motive to induce them to renounce themselves, take up their cross, and follow Jesus Christ. And had believers this truth always deeply impressed upon their souls, they could not but abstain from every evil, be continually aspiring after every good; and in a word, use all diligence to walk worthy of Him who hath called them to his kingdom and glory. If I mistake not, that is the end purposed by the apostle Paul, in the words of the text, "Ye are the temple of the living God." Words originally directed to the church of Corinth, but which equally belong to us, and to our children, and to as many as the Lord our God shall call. To give you the true meaning of, and then practically to improve them, shall be my endeavor in the following discourse.

FIRST, I shall endeavor to give you the meaning of these words, "Ye are the temple of the living God." The expression undoubtedly is metaphorical, or figurative: but under the metaphor, something real, and of infinite importance, is to be understood. And there seems to be a manifest allusion, not only to what we call temples or churches in general, but to the Jewish temple in particular. I trust, that but few, if any here, need be informed, that the preparations for this edifice were exceedingly grand, that it was modeled and built by a divine order, and when completed was separated from common uses, and dedicated to the service of the incomprehensible Jehovah, with the utmost solemnity.

It is thus that Christians are "the temple of the living God," of Father, Son, and Holy Ghost; they who once held a consultation to create, are all equally concerned in making preparations for, and effectually bringing about the redemption of man. The Father creates, the Son redeems, and the Holy Ghost sanctifies all the elect people of God. Being loved from eternity, they are effectually called in time, they are chosen out of the world, and not only by an external formal dedication at baptism, or at the Lord's supper, but by a free, voluntary, unconstrained oblation, they devote themselves, spirit, soul, and body, to the entire service of Him, who hath loved and given himself for them.

This is true and undefiled religion before God our heavenly Father: This is the real Christian's reasonable service, or, as some think the word imports, this is the service required of us in the word of God. It implies no less than a total renunciation of the world; in short, turns the Christian's whole life into one continued sacrifice of love to God; so that, "whether he eats or drinks, he does all to his glory." Not that I would hereby insinuate, that to be Christians, or to keep to the words of our text, in order to be temples of the living God, we must become hermits, or shut ourselves up in nunneries or cloysters; this be far from me! No.

The religion, which this bible in my hand prescribes, is a social religion, a religion equally practicable by high and low, rich and poor, and which absolutely requires a due discharge of all relative duties, in whatsoever state of life God shall be pleased to place and continue us.

That some, in all ages of the church, have literally separated themselves from the world, and from a sincere desire to save their souls, and attain higher degrees of Christian perfection, have wholly devoted themselves to solitude and retirement, is what I make no doubt of. But then such a zeal is in no wise according to knowledge; for private Christians, as well as ministers, are said to be "the salt of the earth, and the lights of the world, and are commanded to "let their light shine before men." But how can this be done, if we shut ourselves up, and thereby entirely exclude ourselves from all manner of conversation with the world? Or supposing we could take the wings of the morning, and fly into the most distant and desolate parts of the earth, what would this avail us, unless we could agree with a wicked heart and wicked tempter not to pursue and molest us there?

So far should we be from thus getting ease and comfort, that I believe we should on the contrary soon find by our experience the truth of what a hermit himself once told me, that a tree which stands by itself, is most exposed and liable to the strongest blasts. When our Savior was to be tempted by the devil, he was led by the Spirit into the wilderness. How contrary this to their practice, who go into a wilderness to avoid temptation! Surely such are unmindful of the petition put up for us by our blessed Lord, "Father, I pray not that thou wouldst take them out of the world, but that thou wouldst keep them from the evil." This then is to be a Christian indeed; to be in the world, and yet not of it; to have our hands, according to our respective stations in life, employed on earth, and our hearts at the same time fixed on things above. Then, indeed, are we "temples of the living God," when with a humble boldness, we can say with a great and good soldier of Jesus Christ, we are the same in the parlor, as we are in the closet; and can at night throw off our cares, as we throw off our clothes; and being at peace with the world, ourselves, and God, are indifferent whether we sleep or die.

Farther, the Jewish temple was a house of prayer. "My house (says the Great God) shall be called a house of prayer:" and implies that the hearts of true believers are the seats of prayer. For this end was it built, and adorned with such furniture. Solomon, in that admirable prayer which he put up to God at the dedication of the temple, saith, "Hearken therefore unto the supplication of thy servant, and of they people Israel, which they shall make towards this place." And hence I suppose it was that Daniel, that man greatly beloved, in the time of captivity, "prayed as aforetime three times a day with his face towards the temple." And what was said of the first, our Lord applies to the second temple, "My house shall be called a house of prayer." On this account also, true believers may be stiled, "the temple of the living God." For being wholly devoted and dedicated to God, even a God in Christ, their heart becomes the seats of prayer, from whence, as to many living altars, a perpetual sacrifice of prayer and praise (like unto, tho' infinitely superior to the perpetual oblation under the Mosaic dispensation) is continually ascending, and offered up, to the Father of Mercies, the God of all Consolations. Such, and such only, who thus worship God in the temple of their hearts, can truly be said to be made priests unto God, or be stiled a royal priesthood; such, and such only, can truly be stiled, "the temple of the living God," because such only pray to him, as one expresses it, in the temple of their hearts, and consequently worship him in spirit and in truth.

Let no one say that such a devotion is impracticable, or at least only practicable by a few, and those such who have nothing to do with the common affairs of life; for this is the common duty and privilege of all true Christians. "To pray without ceasing," and "to rejoice in the Lord always," are precepts equally obligatory on all that name the name of Christ. And though it must be owned, that it is hard for persons that are immersed in the world, to serve the Lord without distraction; and though we must confess, that the lamp of devotion, even in the best of saints, sometimes burns too dimly, yet those who are the temple of the living God, find prayer to be their very element: And when those who make this objection, once come to love prayer, as some unhappy men love swearing, they will find no more difficulty in praying to, and praising God always, than these unhappy creatures do in cursing and swearing always. What hath been advanced, is far from being a state peculiar to persons wholly retired from the world.

My brethren, the love of God is all in all. When once possessed of this, as we certainly must be, if e are "the temple of the loving God," meditation, prayer, praise, and other spiritual exercises, become habitual and delightful. When once touched with this divine magnet, for ever after the soul feels a divine attraction, and continually turns to its center, God; and if diverted therefrom, by any sudden or violent temptation, yet when that obstruction is removed, like as a needle touched by a lodestone when your finger is taken away, turns to its rest, ins center, its God, its All, again.

The Jewish temple was also a place where the Great Jehovah was pleased in a more immediate manner to reside. Hence, he is said to put and record his name there, and to sit or dwell between the cherubims; and when Solomon first dedicated it, we are told, "the house was filled with a cloud, so that the priests could not stand to minister by reason of the cloud, for the glory of the Lord had filled the house." And wherefore all this amazing manifestation of the Divine Glory? Even for this, O man, to show thee how the High and Lofty One that inhabiteth eternity, would make believers hearts his living temple, and dwell and make his abode in all those that tremble at his word.

To this, the apostle more particularly alludes in the words immediately following our text; for having called the Corinthians "the temple of the living God," he adds, "as God hath said, I will dwell in them, and I will walk in them, and I will be their God, and they shall be my people." Strange and string expressions these! But strange and strong as they are, must be experienced by all who are indeed "the temple of the loving God." For they are said, to be "chosen to be a holy habitation through the Spirit; to dwell in God and God in them; to have the witness in themselves, and to have God's Spirit witnessing with their spirits that they are the children of God." Which expressions import no more or less, than that prayer of our Lord which he put up for his church and people a little before his bitter passion, "That they may be one, even as we are one, I in them, and thou in me, that they may be made perfect in one:" This glorious passage our church adopts in her excellent communion office, and is so far from thinking that this was only the privilege of apostles, that she asserts in the strongest terms, that it is the privilege of every worthy communicant. For then (says she) if we receive the sacrament worthily, we are one with Christ, and Christ is one with us; we dwell in Christ, and Christ in us. And what is it, but that inspiration of the Holy Spirit, which we pray for in the beginning of that office, and that fellowship of the Holy

Ghost, which the minister, in the conclusion of every day's public prayer, entreats the Lord to be with us all evermore?

Brethren, the time would fail me to mention all the scriptures, and the various branches of our liturgy, articles, and homilies, that speak of this inestimable blessing, the indwelling of the blessed Spirit, whereby we do indeed become, "the temples of the living God." If you have eyes that see, or ears that hear, you may view it almost in every page of the lively oracles, and every part of those offices, which some of you daily use, and hear read to you, in the public worship of Almighty God. In asserting therefore this doctrine, we do not vent the whimsies of a disordered brain, and heated imagination; neither do we broach any new doctrines, or set up the peculiar opinions of any particular sect or denomination of Christians whatsoever; but we speak the words of truth and soberness, we show you the right and good old way, even that, in which the articles of all the reformed churches, and all sincere Christians of all parties, however differing in other respects, do universally agree. We are now insisting upon a point, which may properly be termed the Christian shibboleth, something which is the grand criterion of our most holy religion; and on account of which, the holy Ignatius, one of the first fathers of the church, was used to stile himself a bearer of God, and the people to whom he wrote, bearers of God: For this, as it is recorded of him, he was arraigned before Trajan, who imperiously said, Where is this man, that says, he carries God about with him. With an humble boldness he answered, I am he, and then quoted the passage in the text, "Ye are the temple of the living God; as God hath said, I will dwell in them, and walk in them, and I will be their God, and they shall be my people." Upon this, to cure him of his enthusiast, he was condemned to be devoured by lions.

Blessed be God! We are not in danger of being called before such persecuting Trajans now: under our present mild and happy administration, the scourge of the tongue is all that they can legally lash us with. But if permitted to go farther, we need not be ashamed of witnessing this good confession. Suffering grace will be given for suffering times; and if, like Ignatius, we are bearers of God, we also shall be enabled to say with him, when led to the devouring lions, Now I begin to be a disciple of Christ.

But it is time for me, SECONDLY, To make some practical improvement of what has been delivered. You have heard in what sense it is that real Christians are "the temple of the living God." Shall I ask, Believe ye these things? I know and am persuaded that some of you do indeed believe them, not because I have told you, but because you yourselves have experienced the same.

I congratulate you from my inmost soul. O that your hearts may be in tune this day to "magnify the Lord," and your spirits prepared to "rejoice in God your Savior." Like the Virgin Mary, you are highly favored, and from henceforth all the generations of God's people shall call you blessed. You can call Christ, Lord, by the Holy Ghost, and thereby have an internal, as well as external evidence of the divinity, both of his person, and of his holy word. You can now prove that despised book, emphatically called The Scriptures, doth contain the perfect and acceptable will of God. You have found the second Adam to be a quickening spirit; He hath raised you from death to life. And being thus taught, and born of God, however unlearned in other respects, you can say, "Is not this the Christ?" O ineffable blessing! Inconceivable privilege! God's spirit witnesseth with your spirits, that you are the children of God. When you think of this, are you not ready to cry out with the beloved disciple, "What manner of love is this, that we should be called the children of God!" I believe that holy man was in an ecstasy when he wrote these words; and tho' he has been in heaven so long, yet his ecstatic surprise is but now beginning, and will be but as beginning through the ages of eternity. Thus shall it be with all you likewise, whom the high and lofty One, that inhabiteth eternity, hath made his living temples. For He hath sealed you to the day of redemption, and hath given you the earnest of your future inheritance. His eyes and heart shall therefore be upon you continually: and in spite of all opposition from men or devils, the top-stone of this spiritual building shall be brought forth, and you shall shout Grace, grace unto it: your bodies shall be fashioned like unto the Redeemer's glorious body, and your souls, in which (O infinite condescension!) He now delights to dwell, shall be filled with all the fullness of God. You shall then go no more out; you shall then no more need the light of the sun or the light of the moon, for the Lord himself will be your temple, and the Lamb in the midst thereof shall be your glory. Dearly beloved in the Lord, what say you to these things? Do not your hearts burn within you whilst thinking of these deep, but glorious truths of God. Whilst I am musing, and speaking of them, methinks a fire kindles even in this cold, icy heart of mine: O what shall we render unto the Lord for all these mercies? Surely He hath done great things for us: How great is his goodness, and his bounty! O the height, the depth, the length, and the breadth of the love of God! Surely it passeth knowledge. O for humility! And a soul-abasing, God-exalting sense of these things! When the blessed virgin went into the hill country, to pay a visit to her cousin Elizabeth, amazed at such a favor, she cried out, "Whence is it that the mother of my Lord vouchsafes to come to me?" And when the great Jehovah filled the temple with his glory, out of the abundance of his heart, king Solomon burst forth into this pathetic exclamation, "But will God in very deed dwell with men on the earth?" With how much greater astonishment ought we to say, And will the Lord himself in very deed come to us? Will the high and lofty One that inhabiteth eternity, dwell in, and make our earthly hearts his living temples? My brethren, whence is this?

From any fitness in us foreseen? No, I know you disclaim such an unbecoming thought. Was it then from the improvement of our own free-will? No, I am persuaded you will not thus debase the riches of God's free grace. Are you not all ready to say, Not unto us, not unto us, but unto thy free, thy unmerited, thy sovereign, distinguishing love and mercy, O Lord, be all the glory. It is this, and this alone, hath made the difference between us and others. We have nothing but what is freely given us from above: if we love God, it is because God first loved us. Let us look then unto the rock from whence we have been hewn, and the hole of the pit from whence we have been digged. And if there be any consolation in Christ, if any comfort of love, if any fellowship of the spirit, if any bowels and mercies, let us study and strive to walk as becometh those who are made the temples of the loving God, or, as the apostle elsewhere expresseth himself, "a holy temple unto the Lord." What manner of persons ought such to be in all holy conversation and godliness? How holily and how purely should we live! As our apostle argues in another place, "For what fellowship hath righteousness and unrighteousness? What communion hath light with darkness? Or what concord hath Christ with Belial?" Shall those who are temples of the living God, suffer themselves to be dens of thieves and cages of unclean birds? Shall vain unchaste thoughts be suffered to dwell within them? Much less shall any thing that is impure be conceived or acted by them? Shall we provoke the Lord to jealousy? God forbid! We all know with what distinguished ardor our blessed Redeemer purged an earthly temple; a zeal for his father's house even eat him up: with what a holy vehemence did he overturn the tables of the money-changers, and scourge the buyers and sellers out before him! Why? They made his father's house a house of merchandise: they had turned the house of prayer into a den of thieves.

O my brethren, how often have you and I been guilty of this great evil? How often have the lust of the flesh, the lust of the eye, and the pride of life, insensibly stolen away our hearts from God? Once they were indeed houses of prayer; faith, hope, love, peace, joy, and all the other fruits of the blessed Spirit lodged within them; but now, O now, it may be, thieves and robbers. Hinc illa lachryma. Hence those hidings of God's face, that dryness, and deadness, and barrenness of soul, those wearisome nights and days, which many of us have felt from time to time, and have been made to groan under. Hence those dolorous and heart-breaking complaints, "O that I knew where I might find him! O that it was with me as in days of old, when the candle of the Lord shone bright upon my soul!" Hence those domestic trials, those personal losses and disappointments: and to this perhaps some of us may add, hence all those public rebukes with which we have been visited: they are all only as so many scourges of small cords in the loving Redeemer's hands, to scourge the buyers and sellers out of the temple of our hearts. O that we may know the rod and who hath appointed it!

He hath chastised us with whips: may we be wise, and by a more close and circumspect walk prevent his chastising us in time to come with scorpions!

But who is sufficient for this thing? None but thou, O Lord, to whom alone all hearts are open, all desires known, and from whom no secrets are hidden! Cleanse thou therefore the thoughts of our hearts by the inspiration of thy blessed Spirit, that henceforward we may more perfectly love thee and more worthily magnify thy holy name!

But are not some of you ready to object, and to fear, that the Lord hath forgotten to be gracious, that he hath shut up his loving kindness in displeasure, and that he will be no more entreated? Thus the psalmist once thought, when visited for his backslidings with God's heave hand. But he acknowledged this to be his infirmity; and whether you think of it or no, I tell you, this is your infirmity. O ye dejected, desponding, distrustful souls, hear ye the word of the Lord, and call to mind his wonderful declarations of old to his people. "I, even I am He that blotteth out thy transgressions: for a small moment have I forsaken thee, but with everlasting mercies will I gather thee. Can a woman forget her sucking child? Yes she may, but the Lord will not forget you, O ye of little faith.

For as a father pitieth his own children, so doth the Lord pity them that fear him. How shall I give thee up, O Ephraim? How shall I make thee as Admah? How shall I set thee as Zeboim?" And what is the result of all these interrogations? "My repentings are kindled together: I will not return to execute the fierceness of my anger against Ephraim: For I am God, and not man." And is not the language of all these endearing passages, like that of Joseph to his self-convicted, troubled brethren? "Come near to me." O that it may be said of you, as it is said of them, "And they came near unto him." Then should you find by happy experience, that the Lord, the Lord God, merciful ad gracious, is indeed slow to anger and of great kindness, and repenteth him of the evil. Who knows but he may come down this day, this hour, nay this moment, and suddenly revisit the temple of your hearts?

Who knows but he may revive his work in your precious souls, cause you to return to your first love, help you to do your first works, and even exceed your hopes, and cause the glory of this second visitation even to surpass that glory which filled your hearts, in that happy, never to be forgotten day, in which he first vouchsafed to make you his living temples? Even so, Father, let it seem good in thy sight!

But the improvement of our subject must not end here. Hitherto I have been giving bread to the children; and it is my meat and drink so to do:

but must nothing be said to those of you who are without? I mean to such who cannot yet say, that they are "the temple of the living God." And O how great, put you all together, may the number of you be: by far, in all probability, the greatest part of this auditory. Say not I am uncharitable; the God of truth, hath said it, "Strait is the gate, and narrow is the way, which leadeth unto life, and few there be that find it." Suffer me to speak plainly to you, my brethren; you have heard what has been said upon the words of our text, and what must be wrought in us, ere we can truly say that we are "the temple of the loving God." Is it so with you? Are ye separated from the world and worldly tempers? Are your hearts become houses of prayer? Doth the Spirit of God dwell in your souls? And whether you eat or drink, or whatsoever you do, as to the habitual bent of your minds, do you do all to the glory of God? These are short, but plain, and let me tell you very important questions. What answer can you make to them? Say not, "Go thy way, and at a more convenient season I will call for thee." I will not, I must not suffer you to put me off so; I demand an answer in the name of the Lord of Hosts. What say ye? Me-thinks, I hear you say, We have been dedicated to God in baptism, we go to church or meeting, we say our prayers, repeat our creeds, or have subscribed the articles, and the confession of faith; we are quite orthodox, and great friends to the doctrines of grace; we do no body any harm, we are honest moral people, we are church-members, we keep up family-prayer, and constantly go to the table of the Lord." All these things are good in their places. But thus far, nay much farther may you go, and yet be far from the kingdom of God.

The unprofitable servant did no one any harm; and the foolish virgins had a lamp of an outward profession, and went up even to heaven's gate, calling Christ, "Lord, Lord." These things may make you whited sepulchers, but not "the temples of the loving God." Alas! Alas! one thing you yet lack, the one chief thing, and without which all is nothing; I mean the indwelling of God's blessed Spirit, without which you can never become "the temples of the loving God." Awake therefore, ye deceived formalists, awake; who, vainly puffed up with your model of performances, boastingly cry out, "The temple of the Lord, the temple of the Lord, the temple of the Lord we are." Awake, ye outward-court worshippers: ye are building on a sandy foundation: take heed lest you also go to hell by the very door of heaven. Behold, and remember, I have told you before.

And as for you who have done none of these things, who instead of making an outward profession of religion, have as it were renounced your baptism, proclaim your sin like Sodom, and willfully and daringly live a without God in the world; I ask you, how can you think to escape, if you persist in neglecting such a great salvation. Verily, I should utterly despair of your ever attaining the blessed privilege of being temples of the living God, did I not hear of thousands, who through the grace of God have been translated from a like state of darkness into his marvelous light. Such, says the apostle Paul, writing to these very Corinthians who were now God's living temples, (drunkards, whoremongers, adulterers, and such like) "such were some of you. But ye are washed, but ye are sanctified, but ye are justified in the name of the Lord Jesus, and by the Spirit of our God." O that the same blessed Spirit may this day vouchsafe to come and pluck you also as brands out of the burning! Behold, I warn you to flee from the wrath to come. Go home, and meditate on these things; and think whether it is not infinitely better, even here, to be temples of the living God, than to be bondslaves to every brutish lust, and to be led captive by the devil at his will. The Lord Jesus can, and if you fly to him for refuge, he will set your souls at liberty. He hath led captivity captive, he hath ascended up on high, on purpose to receive this gift of the blessed Spirit of God for men, "even for the rebellious," that he might dwell in your hearts by faith here, and thereby prepare you to dwell with Him and all the heavenly host in his kingdom hereafter.

That this may be the happy lot of you all, may God of his infinite mercy grant, for the sake of his dear Son Christ Jesus our Lord; to whom with the father, and the blessed Spirit, three persons, but one God, be ascribed all power, might, majesty, and dominion, now and for evermore.

Amen! And Amen!

Sermon 51 Christ the only Preservative against a Reprobate Spirit

2 Corinthians 13:5, "Know ye not your ownselves, how that Jesus Christ is in you, except ye be Reprobates."

The doctrines of the gospel are doctrines of peace, and they bring comfort to all who believe in them; they are not like the law given by Moses, which consisted of troublesome and painful ceremonies; neither do they carry with them that terror which the law did; as, "cursed is every one who continueth not to do all things which are written in the book of the law:" If you were to keep the whole law, and break but in one point, you are guilty of the breach of all. The law denounces threatenings against all who do not conform to her strict commands; but the gospel is a declaration of grace, peace and mercy; here you have an account of the blood of Christ, blood which speaketh better things than that of Abel; for Abel's blood cried aloud from vengeance, vengeance. But Jesus Christ's crieth mercy, mercy, mercy upon the guilty sinner. If he comes to Christ, confesses and forsakes his sin, then Jesus will have mercy upon him: And if, my brethren, you are but sensible of your sins, convinced of your iniquities, and feel yourselves lost, undone sinners, and come and tell Christ of your lost condition, you will soon find how ready he is to help you; he will give you his spirit; and if you have his spirit you cannot be reprobates: you will find his spirit to be quickening and refreshing; not like the spirit of the world, a spirit of reproach, envy, and all uncharitableness.

Most of your own experiences will confirm the truth hereof; for are not you reproached and slandered, and does not the world say all manner of evil against you, merely because you follow Jesus Christ; because you will not go to the same excess of riot with them? While they are singing the songs of the drunkard, you are singing psalms and hymns: while they are at a playhouse, you are hearing a sermon: while they are drinking, reveling and misspending their precious time, and hastening on their own destruction, you are reading, praying, meditating, and working out your salvation with fear and trembling. This is matter enough for a world to reproach you; you are not

polite and fashionable enough for them. If you will live godly, you must suffer persecution; you must not expect to go through this world without being
persecuted and reviled. If you were of the world, the world would love you;
for it always loves its own; but if you are not of the world, it will hate you; it
has done so in all ages, it never loved any but those who were pleased with its
vanities and allurements. It has been the death of many a lover of Jesus,
merely because they have loved him: And, therefore, my brethren, do not be
surprised if you meet with a fiery trial, for all those things will be a means of
sending you to your master the sooner.

The spirit of the world is hatred; that of Christ is love; the spirit of
the world is vexation; that of Christ is pleasure: the spirit of the world is sorrow; that of Christ is joy: the spirit of the world is evil, and that of Christ is
good: the spirit of the world will never satisfy us, but Christ's spirit is all satisfaction: the spirit of the world is misery; that of Christ is ease. In one word,
the spirit of the world has nothing lasting; but the spirit of Christ is durable,
and will last though an eternity of ages: the spirit of Christ will remove every
difficulty, satisfy every doubt, and be a means of bringing you to himself, to
live with him for ever and ever.

From the words of my text, I shall show you, I. The necessity of receiving the spirit of Christ.

II. Who Christ is, whose spirit you are to receive. And then Shall
conclude with an exhortation to all of you, high and low, rich and poor, to
come unto the Lord Jesus Christ; and to beg that you may receive his spirit,
so that you may not be reprobates.

FIRST, I am to show you the necessity there is of receiving the
spirit of Christ.

And here, my brethren, it will be necessary to consider you as in
your first state; that is, when God first created Adam, and placed him in the
garden of Eden, and gave him a privilege of eating of all the trees in the garden, except the tree of knowledge of good and evil, which stood in the midst
thereof. Our first parents had not been long in this state of innocence, before
they fell from it, they broke the divine commands, and involved all their posterity in guilt; for as Adam was our representative, so we were to stand or fall
in him; and as he was our federal head, his falling involved all our race under
the power of death, for death came into the world by sin; and we all became
liable to the eternal punishment due from God, for man's disobedience to the
divine command.

Now as man had sinned, and a satisfaction was demanded, it was impossible for a finite creature to satisfy him, who was a God of so strict purity as not to behold iniquity: And man by the justice of God would have been sent down into the pit, which was prepared of old for the devil and his angels; but when justice was going to pass the irrevocable sentence, then the Lord Jesus Christ came and offered himself a ransom for poor sinners. Here was admirable condescension of the Lord Jesus Christ! That he who was in the bosom of his father, should come down from all that glory, to die for such rebels as you and I are, who if it lay in our power, would pull the Almighty from his throne: Now can you think that if there was no need of Christ's death, can you think that if there could have been any other ransom found, whereby poor sinners might have been saved, God would not have spared his only begotten Son, and not have delivered him up for all that believe in him?

This, my brethren, I think proves to a demonstration, that it was necessary for Christ to die: But consider, it will be of no service to know that Christ died for sinners, if you do not accept of his spirit, that you may be sanctified, and fitted for the reception of that Jesus, who died for all those who believe in him. The sin of your nature, your original sin, is sufficient to sink you into torments, of which there will be no end; therefore unless you receive the spirit of Christ you are reprobates, and you cannot be saved: Nothing short of the blood of Jesus applied to your souls, will make you happy to all eternity: Then, seeing this is so absolutely necessary, that you cannot be saved without having received the spirit of Christ, but that ye are reprobates, do not rest contented 'till you have good hopes, through grace, that the good work is begun in your souls; that you have received a pardon for your sins; that Christ came down from heaven, died, and made satisfaction for your sins. Don't flatter yourselves that a little morality will be sufficient to save you; that going to church, or prayers, and sacrament, and doing all the duties of religion in an external manner, will ever carry you to heaven; no, you must have grace in your hearts; there must be a change of the whole man.

You must be born again, and become new creatures, and have the spirit of Christ within you: And until you have that spirit of Christ, however you may think to the contrary, and please yourselves in your own imagination, I say, you are no better than reprobates. You may content yourselves with leading civil, outward decent lives, but what will that avail you, unless you have the spirit of the Lord Jesus Christ in your hearts: His kingdom must be set up in your souls; there must be the life of God in the soul of man, else you belong not to the Lord Jesus Christ; and until you belong to him, you are reprobates.

This may seem as enthusiasm to some of you, but if it is so, it is what the apostle Paul taught; and therefore, my brethren, they are the words of truth. I beseech you, in the mercies of God in Christ Jesus, not to despise these words, as if they do not concern you, but were only calculated for the first ages of Christianity, and, therefore, of no signification: If you think thus, you are wronging your own souls; for whatever is written, was written for you in these times, as well as for the Christians in the first ages of the church.

For the case stands thus between God and man: God, at first, made man upright, or, as the sacred penman expresses it, "In the image of God made he man;" his soul was the very copy, the transcript of the divine nature.

He who had, by his almighty power, spoken the world into being, breathed into man the breath of spiritual life; and his soul became adorned with purity and perfection. This was the finishing stroke of the creation; the perfection both of the moral and material world; and it so resembled the divine Original, that God could not but rejoice and take pleasure in his own likeness: Therefore, we read, that when God had finished the inanimate and brutish part of the creation, "he looked, and behold it was good." But when that lovely, god-like creature man was made, "behold it was very good." Happy, unspeakably happy, to be thus partaker of a divine Nature; and thus man might have continued still, had he continued holy; but God placed him in a state of probation, with a free grant to eat of every tree in the garden, except the tree of knowledge of good and evil. The day he did eat thereof he was not only to become subject to temporal, but spiritual death; and so lost that divine image, that spiritual life which God had breathed into him, and which was as much his happiness as his glory.

But man, unhappy man, being seduced by the devil, did eat of the forbidden fruit, and thereby became liable to that curse which the eternal God had pronounced on him for his disobedience. And we read, that soon after Adam was fallen, he complained that he was naked; naked, not only as to his body, but naked and destitute of those divine graces which before beautified his soul.

An unhappy mutiny and disorder then fell upon this world; those briars and thorns which now spring up and overspread the earth, were but poor emblems, lifeless representations of that confusion and rebellion which sprung up in, and overwhelmed, the soul of man, immediately after the fall.

He now sunk into the temper of a beast and devil.

In this dreadful and disordered condition are all of us brought into the world: We are told, my brethren, that "Adam had a son in his own likeness," or with the same corrupt nature which he himself had sunk into, after eating the forbidden fruit: And experience, as well as scripture, proves, that we are altogether born in sin, and, therefore, incapable, whilst in such a state, to have communion with God.

For as light cannot have communion with darkness, so God can have no communion with such polluted sons of Belial. Here, here, appears the great and glorious end, why Christ was manifest in the flesh, to put an end to these disorders, and to restore us unto the savor of God. He came down from heaven and shed his precious blood upon the cross, to satisfy the divine justice of his Father, for our sins; and so, he purchased this Holy Ghost, who must once more re-stamp the divine image on our hearts, and make us capable of living with, and enjoying of God. We must be renewed by the spirit of God; he must dwell in us before we can be new creatures, and be freed from a reprobate spirit: the spirit of Christ must bring us home unto that fold where all his sheep are, and implant his grace in our hearts, and take from us that spirit of sin which reigns in us: And till this is rooted out of our hearts, however we may flatter ourselves with being good Christians, because we are good moralists, and lead civil, moral, decent lives, yet if we live and die, my brethren, in this way, we are only flattering ourselves into hell.

I think I have proved, to a demonstration, the necessity there is of receiving the spirit of Christ. I now come to show you, SECONDLY, Who Christ is, whose spirit you are to receive.

My brethren, (Jesus Christ is coequal, coessential, coeternal, and consubstantial with the Father, very God of very God; and as there was not a moment of time in which God the Father was not, so there was not a moment of time in which God the Son was not.

Arians and Socinians deny this godhead of Christ, and esteem him only as a creature: The Arians look on him as a titular Deity, as a created and subordinate God; but, if they would humbly search the scriptures they would find divine homage paid to Christ. He is called God in scripture, particularly when the great evangelical Prophet says, "He shall be called the mighty God, the everlasting Father, and the government shall be upon his shoulders:" And Jesus Christ himself says, that he is the Alpha and Omega;" and that "the world was made by him:" But though this be ever so plain, our gay airy sparks of this age will not believe the Lord Jesus Chris to be equal with his Father, and that for no other reason, but because it is a fashionable and polite doctrine to deny his divinity, and esteem him only as a created God.

Our Socinians do not go so far they look upon Christ only to be a good man sent from God, to show the people the way they should go, on their forsaking of Judaism; that he was to be also an example to the world, and that his death was only to prove the truth of his doctrines.

Many of those who call themselves members, yea, teachers of the church of England, have got into this polite scheme. Good God! My very soul shudders at the thoughts of the consequence that will attend such a belief.

O my brethren, do not think so dishonorably of the Lord who bought you; of the Jesus who dies for you: he must be all in all unto your souls, if ever you are saved by him: Christ must be your active, as well as passive obedience; his righteousness must be imputed to you. The doctrine of Christ's righteousness being imputed, is a comfortable, a desirable doctrine to all real Christians: And to you, sinners, who are inquiring what you must do to be saved? How uncomfortable would it be to tell you, by your own good works, when, perhaps, you have never done one good work in all your lives: This would be driving you to despair indeed; no, "believe in the Lord Jesus Christ and you shall be saved;" come to the Lord Jesus by faith, and he shall receive you. He is able and willing to save you.

This second person in the Trinity, who is God-man, the mediator of the new covenant; he, my brethren, hath virtue enough, in his blood, to atone for the sins of millions of worlds. As man he died, he was crucified, nailed to, and pierced on the accursed tree: This was the love of the Lord Jesus Christ for you; and will you then have low and dishonorable thoughts of Jesus Christ, after his having done so much for you? O my dear brethren, don't be so polite as to deny the Deity of Christ; though you may be counted fools in the eye of the world, yet in God's account, you shall be esteemed wise, wise for salvation.

You may now be looked upon as fools and madmen, as a parcel of rabble, and, in a short time, fit for Bedlam. They may say you are going to undermine the established church; but God knows the secrets of all hearts, knows our innocency; and I speak the truth in Christ, I lie not, I should rejoice to see all the world adhere to her articles; I should rejoice to see the teachers, the ministers of the church of England, preach up those very articles they have subscribed to; but those ministers who do preach them up, they esteem as madmen, and look on them as the off-scouring of the earth, unfit for company and conversation.

The evil things they say of me, blessed be God, are without foundation; I am a friend to the church homilies; I am a friend to her liturgy, and if they did not thrust me out of their churches, I would read it every day.

My brethren, I am not for limiting the spirit of God, but am for uniting all in the bonds of love; I love all that love the Lord Jesus Christ: This will make more Christians, than will the spirit of persecution.

The Pharisees may think it madness to mention persecution in a Christian country, but the spirit of persecution resides in many: their will is as great, but blessed be God, they want the power; if they had that, my brethren, fire and faggot is what we must expect, for the devil's temple is shaken. Many are coming unto Jesus, I hope many of you are already come, and many more coming; this must make Satan rage, to see his kingdom weakened; he will stir up all his malice against the people of God.

We must expect, that a suffering time will certainly come; it is now hastening on, it is ripening a-pace; then it will be proved, to a demonstration, whether you are hypocrites or not; for suffering times are always trying times. O my brethren, do not be afraid of a little reproach, but look on it as a forerunner of what will be the attendant upon it: Therefore let me, by way of application, Exhort all of you, high and low, rich and poor, one with another, to come unto the Lord Jesus Christ, that he may give you strength to undergo whatsoever he, in his wisdom, calls you to. Come, come, my brethren, to Jesus Christ, and he will give you grace, which will make you willing and ready to suffer all things for Jesus Christ.

It is not being pointed at; it is not being despised and looked on as mad, and a deluded people: Alas! what does this signify to a soul who has Jesus Christ? Do not be afraid to confess the blessed Jesus; dare to be singularly good: Don't be afraid of singing of hymns, or of meeting together to build each other up in the ways of the Lord: Shine ye as lights in the world amidst a crooked and perverse generation.

It is necessary that offenses should come, to try what is in our hearts, and whether we will be faithful soldiers of Jesus Christ or not: Be not content with following Christ afar off, for then we shall, as Peter did, soon deny him; but let us be altogether Christians. Let our speech and all our actions declare to the whole world, whose disciples we are, and that we have determined to know nothing but Jesus Christ, and him crucified. O then, then, will it be well with us, happy, unspeakably happy, shall we be, even here; and what is infinitely better, when others that despised us shall be calling for the mountains to fall on them, and the hills to cover them, we shall be exalted to sit down on the right hand of God, and shine as the sun in the firmament, and live for ever with our Redeemer. And will not this be a sufficient recompense for all the sufferings you have undergone here? Therefore, do not strive to have the greatness, the riches, the honor, and pleasures of this world, but strive to have Jesus Christ.

Your friends and carnal acquaintance, and, above all, your grand adversary the devil, will be persuading you not to have Christ until you are grown old; he would have you lay up goods for many years; to see plays, play at cards; go to balls, and masquerades; and to make you the more willing, to draw you in, he calls sinful pleasures, innocent diversions.

A late learned Rabbi of our church, told the people, in a sermon, which I myself heart, that if people went to church of a Sunday, and said the prayers while there, that it was no harm, neither would God count it a sin, to take their recreation, after the service of the church was over: But I say, my brethren, and the command of God says so too, that the whole Sabbath must be kept holy; and that as God has allowed you six days for yourselves, to do the duties in those several stations wherein Providence has place you, he expects you should give him one day to himself; and will you waste that Sabbath which should be spent in gathering provisions for your souls? God forbid!

You had ten thousand times better be ignorant of all the polite diversions of the age, than to be ignorant of the spirit of Christ's being within you, and that it must be, before you are new creatures, and are in Christ; and if you have not an interest in Christ, you are lost, your damnation is hastening on. "He that believeth shall be saved, and he that believeth not shall be damned." If you stand out against Christ, you are fighting against yourselves.

O come unto him, do not stay to bring good works with you, for they will be of no service; all your works will never carry you to heaven, they will never pardon one sin, nor give you the least comfort in a dying hour; if you have nothing more than your own works to recommend you to God, they will not prevent your sinking in that eternal abyss, where there is no bottom.

But come unto Christ, and he will give you that righteousness which will stand you in good account at the great day of the Lord, when he shall come to take notice of them that love him, and of those who have the wedding garment on.

Let all your actions spring from the love of Jesus; let him be the Alpha and Omega of all your actions; then, my brethren, our indifferent ones are acceptable sacrifices; but if this principle be wanting, our most pompous services avail nothing; we are only spiritual idolaters; we sacrifice to our own net, and make an idol of ourselves, by making ourselves and not Christ, the spring of our actions; and therefore, my brethren, such actions are so far from being accepted by God, that according to the language of one of the articles of our church, "We doubt not but that they have the nature of sin, because they spring not from an experimental faith in, and knowledge of Jesus Christ.

Were we not fallen creatures, we might then act upon other principles; but since we are fallen in Adam, and are restored again only by the death of Jesus Christ, the face of things in entirely changed, and all we think, speak, or do, is only accepted in and through him.

Therefore, my brethren, I beseech you, in the bowels of love and compassion, that you would come unto Jesus: Do not go away scoffing, offended, or blaspheming. Indeed, all I say is in love to your souls; and if I could be but an instrument of bringing you to Jesus Christ, if you were to be never so much exalted, I should not envy, but rejoice in your happiness: If I was to make up the last of the train of the companions of the blessed Jesus, it would rejoice me to see you above me in glory. I do not speak out of a false humility, a pretended sanctity; no, God is my judge, I speak the truth in Christ, I lie not, I would willingly go to prison, or to death for you, so I could but bring one soul from the devil's strong holds, into the salvation which is by Christ Jesus.

Come then unto Christ every one that hears me this night; I offer Jesus Christ, pardon, and salvation to all you, who will accept thereof.

Come, O ye drunkards, lay aside your cups, drink no more to excess; come and drink of the water which Christ will give you, and then you will thirst no more: come, O ye thieves; let him that has stolen, steal no more, but fly unto Christ and he will receive you. Come unto him, O ye harlots; lay aside your lusts and turn unto the Lord, and he will have mercy upon you, he will cleanse you of all your sins, and wash you in his blood. Come, all ye liars; come, all ye Pharisees; come, all ye fornicators, adulterers, swearers, and blasphemers, come to Christ, and he will take away all your filth, he will cleanse you from your pollution, and your sins shall be done away. Come, come, my guilty brethren; I beseech you for Christ's sake, and for your immortal soul's sake, to come unto Christ: Do not let me knock at the door of your hearts in vain, but open and let the King of Glory in, and he will dwell with you, he will come and sup with you this night; this hour, this moment he is ready to receive you, therefore come unto him.

Do not consult with flesh and blood, let not the world hinder you from coming to the Lord of life: What are a few transitory pleasures of this life worth? They are not worth your having, but Jesus Christ is a pearl of great price, he is worth the laying out all you have, to buy.

And if you are under afflictions, fly not to company to divert you, neither read what the world calls harmless books; they only tend to harden the heart, and to keep you from closing with the Lord Jesus Christ.

When I was a child, yea, when I came to riper years, God knows, it is with grief I speak it, when ignorant of the excellency of the word of God, I read as many of these harmless books as any one; but now I have tasted the good word of life, and am come to a more perfect knowledge of Christ Jesus my Lord; I put away these childish, trifling things, and am determined to read no other books but what lead me to a knowledge of myself, and Jesus Christ.

Methinks I could speak till midnight unto you, my brethren; I am full of love towards you; let me beseech you to fly to Christ for succor: "Now is the accepted time, now is the day of salvation;" therefore delay not, but strive to enter in at the strait gate; do not go the broad way of the polite world, but choose to suffer affliction with the people of God, rather than to enjoy the pleasures of sin for a season: You will have a reward afterwards, that will make amends for all the taunts, jeers, and calamities you may undergo here.

And will not the presence of Christ be a sufficient reward for all you have suffered for his name's sake? Why will you not accept of the Lord of glory? Do not say you have not heard of Christ, for he is now offered to you, and you will not accept of him; do not blame my master, he is willing to save you, if you will but lay hold on him by faith; and if you do not, your blood will be required of your own heads.

But I hope that you will not let the blood of Jesus be shed in vain, and that you will not let my preaching be of no signification. Would you have me go and tell my master, you will not come, and that I have spent my strength in vain; I cannot bear to carry so unpleasing a message unto him, I would not, indeed, I would not be a swift witness against any of you at the great day of accounts; but if you will refuse these gracious invitations, and not accept of them, I must do it: and will it not move your tender hearts to see your friends taken up into heaven, and you yourselves thrust down into hell? But I hope better things of most of you, even that you will turn unto the Lord of love, the Jesus who died for you, that in the day when he shall come to take his people to the mansions of everlasting rest, you may hear his voice, "Come, ye blessed of my Father, enter into the kingdom prepared for you before the foundation of the world." And that we may all enter into that glory, do thou, O Jesus, prepare us, by thy grace; give us thy spirit; and may our hearts be united to thee: May the word that has now been spoken, take deep root in thy people's hearts, that it may spring up and bring forth fruit, in some thirty, in some forty, and in some an hundred fold; do thou preserve them while in this life from all evil, and keep them from falling, and at last present them faultless before thy Father, when thou comest to judge the world, that where thou art, they may be also. Grant this, O Lord Jesus Christ, with whatever else thou seest needful for us, both at this time and for evermore.

Now to God the Father, God the Son, and God the Holy Ghost, be ascribed all honor, power, glory, might, majesty and dominion, both now and for evermore, Amen.

Sermon 52 The Heinous Sin of Drunkenness

Ephesians 5:18, "Be not drunk with Wine, wherein is Excess; but be filled with the Spirit."

The persons to whom these words were written, were the inhabitants of Ephesus, as we are told in the Acts, had been worshippers of the great goddess Diana, and, in all probability, worshipped the God Baccbus also; at the celebration of whose festivals, it was always customary, nay, part of their religion, to get drunk; as though there was no other way to please their God, but by turning themselves into brutes.

The apostle therefore in this chapter, amongst many other precepts more especially applicable to them, lays down this in the text; and exhorts them, as they had now, by the free grace of God, been turned from heathenish darkness to the light of the gospel, to walk as children of light, and no longer make it part of their religion or practice to be "drunk with wine, wherein is excess;" but, on the contrary, strive to "be filled with the Spirit" of that Savior, after whose name they were called, and whose religion taught them to abstain from a filthy sin, and to live soberly as they ought to live.

The world being now Christian, and the doctrines of the gospel every where received, one would imagine, there should be no reason for repeating the precept now before us. But alas, Christians! I mean Christians falsely so called, are led captive by all sin in general, and by this or drunkenness in particular; that was St. Paul to rise again from the dead, he might be tempted to think most of us were turned back to the worship of dumb idols; had set up temples in honor of Baccbus; and made it part of our religion, as the Ephesians did of theirs, "to be drunk with wine, wherein is excess." Some of our civil magistrates have not been wanting to use the power given them from above, for the punishment and restraint of such evil doings; and I wish it could be said this plague of drinking, by what they have done, had been stayed amongst us. But alas! though their labor, we trust, has not been altogether in vain in the Lord, yet thousands, and I could almost say ten thousands, fall daily at our right-hand, by this sin of drunkenness, in our streets; nay, men seem to have made a covenant with hell, and though the power of the civil magistrate is exerted against them, nay, though they cannot but daily see the companions of their riot hourly, by this sin, brought to the grave, yet "they will rise up early to follow strong drink, and cry, To-morrow shall be as today, and so much the more abundantly; when we awake, we will seek it yet again." It is high time therefore, for thy ministers, O God, to lift up their voices like a trumpet; and since human threats cannot prevail, to set before them the terrors of the Lord, and try if these will not persuade them to cease from the evil of their doings.

But alas! how shall I address myself to them? I fear excess of drinking has made them such mere Nabals, that there is no speaking to them.

And many of God's servants have toiled all their life-time in dissuading them from this sin of drunkenness, yet they will not forbear. However, at thy command, I will speak also, though they be a rebellious house. Magnify thy strength, O Lord, in my weakness, and grant that I may speak with such demonstration of the Spirit, and power, that from henceforward they may cease to act so unwisely, and this sin of drunkenness may not be their ruin.

Believe me, ye unhappy men of Belial, (for such, alas! this sin has made you) it is not without the strongest reasons, as well as utmost concern for your precious and immortal souls, that I now conjure you, in the Apostle's words, "Not to be drunk with wine, or any other liquor, wherein is excess." For, FIRST, Drunkenness is a sin which must be highly displeasing to God; because it is an abuse of his good creatures.

When God first made man, and had breathed into him the breath of life, he gave him dominion over the works of his hands; and every herb bearing seed, and every tree, in which was the fruit of a tree yielding seed, to him was given for meat: but when Adam had tasted the forbidden fruit, which was the only restraint laid upon him, he forfeited this privilege, and had no right, after he had disobeyed his Creator, to the use of any one of the creatures.

But, blessed be God, this charter, as well as all other privileges, is restored to us by the death of the second Adam, our Lord and Master Jesus Christ. Of every beast of the field, every fish of the sea, and whatsoever flieth in the air, or moveth on the face of the earth, that is fit for food, "we may freely eat," without scruple take and eat; but then, with this limitation, that we use them moderately. For God, by the death of Jesus, has given no man license to be intemperate; but, on the contrary, has laid us under the strongest obligations to live soberly, as well as godly, in this present world.

But the drunkard, despising the goodness and bounty of God, in restoring to us what we had so justly forfeited, turns his grace into wantonness; and as though the creature was not of itself enough subject to vanity, by being cursed for our sake, he abuses it still more, by making it administer to his lusts; and turns that wine which was intended to make glad his heart, into a deadly poison.

But thinkest thou, O drunkard, whosoever thou art, thou shalt escape the righteous judgment of God? No, the time will shortly come that thou must be no longer steward, and then the Sovereign Lord of all the earth will reckon with thee for thus wasting his goods. Alas! wilt thou then wrest scripture any longer to thy own damnation? And because Jesus Christ turned water into wine at the marriage-feast, to supply the wants of his indigent host, say, that it is therefore meet to make merry, and be drunken. No, thou shalt be silent before him; and know, that though thou hast encouraged thyself in drunkenness by such-like arguments, yet for all these things God will bring thee into judgment. But, SECONDLY, What makes drunkenness more exceedingly sinful, is, that a man, by falling into it, sinneth against his own body.

When the apostle would dissuade the Corinthians from fornication, he urges this as an argument, "Flee fornication, brethren; for he that committeth fornication, sinneth against his own body." And may not I as justly cry out, Flee drunkenness, my brethren, since he that committeth that crime, sinneth against his own body? For, from whence come so many diseases and distempers in your bodies? Come they not from hence, even from your intemperance in drinking? Who hath pains in the head? Who hath rottenness in the bones? Who hath redness of eyes? He that tarries long at the wine, he that rises early to seek new wine. How many walking skeletons have you seen, whose bodies were once exceeding fair to look upon, fat and well-favored; but, by this sin of drinking, how has their beauty departed from them, and how have they been permitted to walk to and fro upon the earth, as though God intended to set them up, as he did Lot's wife, for monuments of his justice, that others might learn not to get drunk? Nay, I appeal to yourselves: are not many, for this cause, even now sickly among you? And have not many of your companions, whom you once saw so flourishing, like green bay trees, been brought by it with sorrow to their graves?

We might, perhaps, think ourselves hardly dealt with by God, was he to send us, as he did the royal Psalmist, to choose one plague out of three, whereby we should be destroyed. But had the Almighty decreed to cut off man from the face of the earth, and to shorten his days, he could not well send a more effectual plague, than to permit men, as they pleased, to over- charge themselves with drunkenness; for though it be a slot, yet it is a certain poison.

And if the sword has slain its thousands, drunkenness has slain its ten thousands.

And will not this alarm you, O ye transgressors? Will not this persuade you to spare yourselves, and to do your bodies no harm? What, have you lost the first principles of human nature, the fundamental law of self-preservation? You seem to have a great fondness for your bodies; why, otherwise, to gratify the inordinate appetites, do you drink to excess? But surely, if you truly loved them, you would not thus destroy them; and was there no other argument to be urged against drunkenness, the consideration that it will destroy those live you are so fond of, one would imagine, should be sufficient.

I know, indeed, that it is a common answer, which drunkards make to those, who, out of love, would pull them as firebrands out of the fire, we are no body's enemy but our own. But this, instead of being an excuse for, is an aggravation of their guilt: for (not to mention that the drunkenness of one man has clothes many a family with rags, and that it is scarce possible for a person to be drunk, without tempting his neighbor also) not to mention these, and many other ill consequences, which would prove such an excuse to be entirely false: yet what is dearer to a man than himself?

And if he himself be lost, what would all the whole world avail him? But how wilt thou stand, O man, before the judgment-seat of Christ, and make such an excuse, when thou shalt be arraigned before him as a self-murderer?

Will it then be sufficient, thinkest thou, to say, I was no man's enemy but my own? No; God will then tell thee, that thou oughtest to have glorified him with thy spirit, and with thy body, which were his; and since thou hast, by intemperance, destroyed thy body, he will destroy both thy body and soul in hell. But, THIRDLY, What renders drunkenness more inexcusable, is, that it robs a man of his reason.

Reason is the glory of a man; the chief thing whereby God has made us to differ from the brute creation. And our modern unbelievers have exalted it to such a high degree, as even to set it in opposition to revelation, and so deny the Lord that bought them. But though, in doing this, they greatly err, and whilst they profess themselves wise, become real fools; yet we must acknowledge, that reason is the candle of the Lord, and whosoever puts it out, shall bear his punishment, whosoever he be.

But yet, this the drunkard does. Nebuchadnezzar's curse he makes his choice, his reason departeth from him; and then what is he better than a brute?

The very heathen kings were so sensible of this, that, in order to deter their young princes from drinking, they used to make their slaves get drunk, and be exposed before them. And didst thou but see thine own picture, O drunkard, when, after having drowned thy reason, thou staggerest to and fro, like one of the fools in Israel, and seest thy very companions making songs upon thee, surely thou wouldst not return to thy vomit again, but abhor thyself in dust and ashes!

When David, in a holy ecstasy, was dancing before the ark, Michal, Saul's daughter, despised him in her heart; and when he came home, she said, "How glorious was the king of Israel today, who uncovered himself today in the eyes of the hand-maids of his servants, as one of the vain fellows shamelessly uncovereth himself." But may not every one that meets a drunkard, more justly say, How glorious does he, that was made a little lower than the angels, look today, when, unmindful of his dignity, he has by drinking robbed himself of his reason, and reduced himself to a level with the beasts that perish.

But what if God, in the midst of one of these drunken fits, should arrest thee by death, and say unto thee, "Thou fool, this moment shall thy soul be required of thee." O! how shouldst thou appear in those filthy garments before that God, in whose sight the heavens are not clean. And how knowest thou, O man, but this may be thy lit? Hast thou not known many summoned at such an unguarded hour? And what assurance hast thou, that thou shalt not be the next? Because God has forborn thee so long, thinkest thou he will forbear always? No, this is rather a sign that he will come at an hour thou lookest not for him; and since his goodness and long-suffering has not led thee to repentance, he will cut thee down, and not permit thee to cumber the ground any longer. Consider this then, all ye that count it a pleasure to turn yourselves into brutes, lest God pluck you away by a sudden death, and there be none to deliver you.

FOURTHLY, There is a farther aggravation of this crime, that it is an inlet to, and forerunner of many other sins; for it seldom comes alone.

We may say of drunkenness, as Solomon does in strife, that it is like the letting out of water; for we know not what will be the end thereof. Its name is Legion; behold a troop of sins cometh after it. And, for my own part, when I see a drunkard, with the holy Prophet, when he looked in Hazael's face, I can hardly forbear weeping, to consider how many vices he may fall into, ere he comes to himself again.

What horrid incest did righteous Lot commit with his own daughters, when they had made him drunk? And, I doubt not, but there are many amongst you, who have committed such crimes when you have deprived yourselves of your reason by drinking, that were you to hear of them, your heart, like Nabal's, after he was told how he had abused David when he was drunk, would die within you. And, had any one told you, when you were sober, that you would have been guilty of such crimes, you would have cried out, with Hazael before-mentioned, "Are thy servants so many dogs, that they should do that?" But no marvel that drunkards commit such crimes; for drunkenness drives the Holy Spirit from them; they become mere machines for the devil to work up to what he pleases; he enters into them, as he entered into the herd of swine; and no wonder if they then commit all uncleanness, and any other crime, with greediness. But this leads me to a FIRTH consideration, which highly aggravates the sin of drunkenness, it separates the Holy Spirit from us.

It is to be hoped, that no one here present need be informed, that before we can be assured we are Christians indeed, we must receive the Holy Ghost, must be born again from above, and have the Spirit of God witnessing with our spirits, that we are the sons of God. This, this alone is true Christianity; and without the cohabitation of this blessed Spirit in our hearts, our righteousness does not exceed the righteousness of the Scribes and Pharisees, and we shall in no wise enter into the kingdom of God.

But now, drunkards do in effect bid this blessed Spirit to depart from them: for what has he to do with such filthy swine? They have no log of share in the Spirit of the Son of David. They have chased him out of their hearts, by defiling his temple; I mean their bodies. And he can no more hold communion with them, than light can have communion with darkness, or Christ have concord with Belial.

The apostle, therefore, in the words of the text, exhorts the Ephesians, "not to be drunk with wine, wherein is excess, but to be filled with the Spirit;" thereby implying, that drunkenness and the Spirit of God could never dwell in the same heart. And in another epistle, he bids them to avoid unprofitable conversation, as a thing which grieved the Holy Spirit: whereby alone they could be sealed to the day of redemption. And if unprofitable conversation grieves the Holy Spirit, at what an infinite distance must drunkenness drive him from the hearts of men?

O that you were wise! That you would consider what a dreadful thing it is to have the Sprit of the loving God depart from you! For, assure yourselves, if you live without him, you will live without God in the world. You are in the same miserable forlorn condition as Saul was, when an evil spirit of the Lord came upon him; and you are only so many vessels of wrath fitted for destruction. But this brings me to a SIXTH reason against the sin of drunkenness; it absolutely unfits a man for the enjoyment of God in heaven, and exposes him to his eternal wrath.

To see and enjoy God, and to be like the blessed angels, always beholding the face of our heavenly Father, in the glories of his kingdom, is such an unspeakable happiness, that even wicked men, though they will not live the life of the righteous, cannot but wish their future state to be like his.

But think you, O ye drunkards, that you shall ever be partakers of this inheritance with the saints in light? Do you flatter yourselves, that you, who have made them often the subject of your drunken songs, shall now be exalted to sing with them the heavenly songs of Zion? No, as by drunkenness you have made your hearts cages of unclean birds, with impure and unclean spirits must you dwell.

A burning Tophet, kindled by God's wrath, is prepared for you reception, where you must suffer the vengeance of eternal fire, and in vain cry out for a drop of water to cool your tongues. Indeed you shall drink, but it shall be a cup of God's fury: for in the hand of the Lord there will be a cup of fury, it will be full mixed, and as for the dregs thereof, all the drunkards of the land shall suck them out.

But perhaps you may not believe this report. These words may be looked upon by you as idle tales, and I may seem to you as Lot did to his sons-in- law, when he came to warn them to get up out of Sodom, "as one that mocketh." But if you believe not me, believe eternal truth itself, which has positively declared, that no drunkard shall ever enter into his kingdom.

And I call heaven and earth to witness against you this day, that as surely as the Lord rained fire and brimstone, as soon as Lot went out of Sodom, so surely will God cast you into a lake of fire and brimstone, when he shall come to take vengeance on them that know not God, and have not obeyed the gospel of our Lord Jesus Christ.

Behold then I have told you before; remember, that you this day were informed what the end of drunkenness would be. And I summon you, in the name of that God whom I serve, to meet me at the judgment-seat of Christ, that you may acquit both my Master and me; and confess, with your own mouths, that your damnation was of yourselves, and that we are free from the blood of you all.

But, Lord, has no one believed our report? Wilt thou suffer so many words to be spoken in vain, if it be yet in vain? No, methinks I see some pricked to the heart, and ready to cry out, in the language of David to Abigail, "Blessed be the Lord God of Israel, which sent thee this day to speak unto us." For surely, unless he had sent thee, this sin of drunkenness had been our ruin: but now, since we find whither it will lead us, we are resolved to drink no liquor to excess while the world stands, lest we should be tormented in the flames of hell.

But alas! how shall we be delivered from the power of this sin? Can the Ethiopian change his skin, or the leopard his spots? So hard, almost, will it be for you who have been accustomed to be intemperate, to learn to live sober.

But do not despair; for what is impossible with man, is possible with God. Of whom then should you seek for succor, but of him your Lord? Who, though for this sin of drunkenness, he might justly turn away his face from you; yet observe, FIRST, If you pour out your hearts before him in DAILY PRAYER, and ask assistance from above, it may be God will endue you with power from on high, and make you more than conquerors through Jesus Christ. Had you kept up communion with him in prayer, you would not so long, by drunkenness, have had communion with devils. But, like the Prodigal, you have desired to be your own masters; you have lived without prayer, depended on your own strength; and now see, alas! on what a broken reed you have leaned. How soon have you made yourselves like the beasts that have no understanding?

But turn ye, turn ye from your evil ways. Come to him with the repenting Prodigal saying, "Father we have sinned;" we beseech thee, let not this sin of drunkenness have any longer dominion over us. Lay hold on Christ by faith, and lo! It shall happen to you even as you will. A SECOND means I would recommend to you, in order to get the better or drunkenness, is to AVOID EVIL COMPANY. For it is the evil communication of wicked men, that has drawn many thousands into this sin, and so corrupted their good manners.

But you may say, If I leave my companions, I must expect contempt: for they will certainly despise me for being singular. And thinkest thou, O man, ever to enter in at the strait gate by a true conversion, without being had in derision of them that are round about thee? No; though thou mayst be despised, and not go to heaven, yet thou canst not go to heaven without being despised: "For the friendship of the world is enmity with God." And they that are born after the flesh, will persecute those that are born after the Spirit. Let not, therefore, a servile fear of being despised by a man that shall die, hinder thy turning unto the living God. For what is a little contempt? It is but a vapor which vanisheth away, and cometh not again. Better be derided by a few companions here, than be made ashamed before men and angels hereafter. Better be the song of a few drunkards on earth, than dwell with them, where they will be eternally reproaching and cursing each other in hell. Yet a little while, and they themselves shall praise thy doings, and shall say, We, fools, counted his leaving us to be folly, and his end to be without honor: but how is he numbered among the sons of God, and his lot among the saints!

But I hasten to lay down a THIRD means for those who would overcome the sin of drunkenness, to enter upon a life of STRICT SELF-DENIAL and mortification: for this kind of sin goeth not forth but by prayer and fasting. It is true, this may seem a difficult task; but then, we must thank ourselves for it; for had we begun sooner, our work would have been the easier. And even now, if you will but strive, the yoke of mortification will grow lighter and lighter every day.

And now, by way of conclusion, I cannot but exhort all persons, high and low, rich and poor, to practice a strict self-denial in eating and drinking. For though "the kingdom of God consists not in meats and drinks," yet an abstemious use of God's good creatures, greatly promotes the spiritual life. And perhaps there are more destroyed by living in a regular sensuality, than even by the very sin I have been warning you of. I know indeed, that many, who are only almost Christians, and who seek, but do not strive to enter into the kingdom of God, urge a text of scripture to justify their indulgence, saying, that "it is not what entereth into the man defileth the man." And so we grant, when taken moderately; but then they should consider, that it is possible, nay, it is proved by daily experience, that a person may eat and drink so much as not to hurt his body, and yet do infinite prejudice to his soul: for self-indulgence lulls the soul into a spiritual slumber, as well as direct intemperance; and though the latter may expose us to more contempt among men, yet the former, if continued in, will as certainly shut us out from the presence of God. St. Paul knew this full well; and therefore, though he was the spiritual father of thousands, and was near upon finishing his course, yet he says, it was his daily practice to "keep his body under, and bring it into subjection, lest after he had preached to others, he himself should be a cast-away," or disapproved of, or do something that might make him an offense or stumbling-block to any of God's children: for of his own, and all other saints final perseverance, he makes no doubt, as is evident from many of his epistles; and the word ajdovkimo" bears this sense, 2 Cor.

13:5 and sundry other places. But why urge I the apostle's example, to excite you to a strict temperance in eating and drinking? Rather let me exhort you only to put in practice the latter part of the text, to labor to "be filled with the Spirit of God," and then you will no longer search the scriptures to find arguments for self-indulgence; but you will seal sincerely with yourselves, and eat and drink no more at any time, than what is consistent with the strictest precepts of the gospel. O beg of God, that you may see, how you are fallen in Adam, and the necessity of being renewed, ere you can be happy, by the Spirit of Jesus Christ! Let us beseech him to enlighten us to see the treachery of our corrupt hearts, and how pure and holy these bodies ought to be, that they ought to be living temples of the Holy Ghost, and then we shall show ourselves men. And being made temples of the Holy Ghost, by his dwelling in our bodies here, though after death, worms may destroy them, yet shall they be raised by the same Spirit at the general resurrection of the last day, to be fashioned like unto Christ's glorious body hereafter.

Which God of his infinite mercy grant, etc.

Sermon 53 The Power of Christ's Resurrection

Philippians 3:10, "That I may know Him, and the power of his resurrection."

The apostle, in the verses before the text, had been cautioning the Philippians to "beware of the concision," Judaizing teachers, who endeavored to subvert them from the simplicity of the gospel, by telling them, they still ought to be subject to circumcision, and all the other ordinances of Moses. And that they might not think he spoke out of prejudice, and condemned their tenets, because he himself was a stranger to the Jewish dispensation, he acquaints them, that if any other man thought he had whereof he might trust in the flesh, or seek to be justified by the outward privileges of the Jews, he had more: For he was "circumcised the eighth day; of the stock of Israel (not a proselyte, but a native Israelite); of the tribe of Benjamin (the tribe which adhered to Judah when the others revolted); an Hebrew of the Hebrews (a Jew both on the father's and mother's side); and as touching the law, a Pharisee," the strictest sect amongst all Israel. To show that he was no Gallio in religion, through his great, though misguided zeal, he had persecuted the church of Christ; and "as touching the righteousness of the law (as far as the Pharisees exposition of it went, he was) blameless," and had kept it from his youth.

But, when it pleased God, who separated him from his mother's womb, to reveal his Son in him, "What things were gain to me," (he says) those privileges I boasted myself in, and sought to be justified by, "I counted loss for Christ." And that they might not think he repented that he had done so, he tells them, he was now more confirmed than ever in his judgment. For, says he, "yea doubtless (the expression in the original rises with a holy triumph) and I do count all things but loss for the excellency of the knowledge of Christ Jesus my Lord." And that they might not object that he said, and did not, he acquaints them, he had given proofs of the sincerity of these professions, because for the sake of them, he had suffered the loss of all his worldly things, and still was willing to do more; for, "I count them but dung (no more than offals thrown out to dogs) so that I may win, (or have a saving interest in) Christ, and be found in him(as the manslayer in the city of refuge) not having my own righteousness which is of the law, (not depending on having Abraham for my father, or on any works of righteousness which I have done, either to atone or serve as a balance for my evil deeds) but that which is through the faith of Christ, the righteousness which is of God by faith," a righteousness of God's appointing, and which will be imputed to me, if I believe in Christ, "that I may know him, and the power of his resurrection;" that I may have an experimental knowledge of the efficacy of his resurrection, by feeling the influences of his blessed Spirit on my soul. In which words two things are implied.

FIRST, That Jesus Christ did rise from the dead.

SECONDLY, That it highly concerns us to know the power of his rising again.

Accordingly, in the following discourse I shall endeavor to show, FIRST, That Christ is risen indeed from the dead; and that it was necessary for him so to do; and, SECONDLY, That it highly concerns us to know and experience the power of his resurrection.

FIRST, Christ is indeed risen.

That Jesus should rise from the dead was absolutely necessary; 1. FIRST, On his own account. He had often appealed to this as the last and most convincing proof he would give them that the was the Messiah, "There shall no other sign be given you, than the sign of the prophet Jonas." And again, "Destroy this temple of my body, and in three days I will build it up." Which words his enemies remembered, and urged it as an argument, to induce Pilate to grant them a watch, to prevent his being stolen out of the grave. "We know that deceiver said, whilst he was yet alive, after three days I will rise again." So that had he not risen again, they might have justly said, we know that this man was an impostor.

2. SECONDLY, It was necessary on our account. "He rose again" (says the apostle) for our justification;" or that the debt we owed to God for our sins, might be fully satisfied and discharged.

It had pleased the Father (for ever adored be his infinite love and free grace) to wound his only Son for our transgressions, and to arrest and confine him in the prison of the grave, as our surety for the guilt we had contracted by setting at nought his commandments. Now had Christ continued always in the grave, we could have had no more assurance that our sins were satisfied for, than any common debtor can have of his creditor's being satisfied, whilst his surety is kept confined. But he being released from the power of death, we are thereby assured, that with his sacrifice God was well pleased, that our atonement was finished on the cross, and that he hath made a full, perfect, and sufficient sacrifice, oblation, and satisfaction for the sins of the world.

3. THIRDLY, It was necessary that our Lord Jesus should rise again from the dead, to assure us of the certainty of the resurrection of our own bodies.

The doctrine of the resurrection of the body was entirely exploded and set at nought among the Gentiles, as appears from the Athenians mocking at, and calling St. Paul "a babbler and a setter forth of strange doctrines," when he preached to them Jesus, and the resurrection. And though it was believed by most of the Jews, as is evident from many passages of scripture, yet not by all; the whole sect of the Sadducees denied it. But the resurrection of Jesus Christ put it out of dispute. For as he acted as our representative, if he our head be risen, then must we also, who are his members, rise with him. And as in the first Adam we all died, even so in him our second Adam we must all, in this sense, be made alive.

As it was necessary, upon these accounts, that our blessed Lord should rise from the dead; so it is plain beyond contradiction, that he did. Never was any matter of fact better attested; never were more precautions made use of to prevent a cheat. He was buried in a sepulcher, hewn out of a rock, so that it could not be said that any digged under, and conveyed him away. It was a sepulcher also wherein never man before was laid; so that if any body did rise from thence, it must be the body of Jesus of Nazareth.

Besides, the sepulcher was sealed; a great stone rolled over the mouth of it; and a band of soldiers (consisting not of friends, but of his professed enemies) was set to guard it. And as for his disciples coming by night and stealing him away, it was altogether improbable: For it was not long since, that they had all forsaken him, and they were the most backward in believing his resurrection. And supposing it was true, that they came whilst the soldiers slept; yet the soldiers must be cast into a deep sleep indeed, that the rolling away so great a stone did not awake some of them.

And our blessed Lord's afterwards appearing at sundry times, and in divers manners, to his disciples, as when they were assembled together, when they were walking to Emmaus, when they were fishing: nay, and condescending to show them his hands and feet, and his appearing to above five hundred brethren at once, put the truth of his resurrection out of all dispute.

Indeed, there is one objection that may be made against what has been said, that the books wherein these facts are recorded were written by his disciples.

And who more proper persons than those who were eye-witnesses of what they related, and eat and drank with him after his resurrection? "But they were illiterate and ignorant men." Yet as good witnesses of a plain matter of fact, as the most learned masters in Israel. Nay, this rendered them more proper witnesses. For being plain men, they were therefore less to be suspected of telling or making a lie, particularly, since they laid down their lives for a testimony of the truth of it. We read indeed of Jacob's telling a lie, though he was a plain man, in order to get his father's blessing. But it was never heard since the world began, that any man, much less a whole set of men, died martyrs, for the sake of an untruth, when they themselves were to reap no advantage from it.

No, this single circumstance proves them to Israelites indeed, in whom was no guile. And the wonderful success God gave to their ministry afterwards, when three thousand were converted by one sermon; and twelve poor fishermen, in a very short time enabled to be more than conquerors over all the opposition men or devils could make, was as plain a demonstration, that Christ was risen, according to their gospel, as that a divine power, at the sound of a few ram's horns, causes the walls of Jericho to fall down.

But what need we any farther witnesses? Believe you the resurrection of our blessed Lord? I know that you believe it, as your gathering together on this first day of the week in the courts of the Lord's house abundantly testifies.

What concerns us most to be assured of, and which is the SECOND thin I was to speak to, is, Whether we have experimentally known the power of his resurrection; that is, Whether or not we have received the Holy Ghost, and by his powerful operations on our hearts have been raised from the death of sin, to a life of righteousness and true holiness.

It was this, the great apostle was chiefly desirous to know. The resurrection of Christ's body he was satisfied would avail him nothing, unless he experienced the power of it in raising his dead soul.

For another, and that a chief end of our blessed Lord's rising from the dead, was to enter heaven as our representative, and to send down the Holy Ghost to apply that redemption he had finished on the cross, to our hearts, by working an entire change in them.

Without this, Christ would have died in vain. For it would have done us no service to have had his outward righteousness imputed to us, unless we had an inward inherent righteousness wrought in us. Because, being altogether conceived and born in sin, and consequently unfit to hold communion with an infinitely pure and holy God, we cannot possibly be made meet to see or enjoy him, till a thorough renovation has passed upon our hearts.

Without this, we leave out the Holy Ghost in the great work of our redemption. But as we were made by the joint concurrence and consultation of the blessed trinity; and as we were baptized in their name, so must all of them concur in our salvation: As the Father made, and the Son redeemed, so must the Holy Ghost sanctify and seal us, or otherwise we have believed in vain.

This then is what the apostle means by the "Power of Christ's resurrection," and this is what we are as much concerned experimentally to know, as that He rose at all.

Without this, though we may be moralists, though we may be civilized, good-natured people, yet we are no Christians. For he is not a true Christian, who is only one outwardly; nor have we therefore a right, because we daily profess to believe that Christ rose again the third day from the dead. But he is a true Christian who is one inwardly; and then only can we be stiled true believers, when we not only profess to believe, but have felt the power of our blessed Lord's rising from the dead, by being quickened and raised by his Spirit, when dead in trespasses and sins, to a thorough newness both of heart and life.

The devils themselves cannot but believe the doctrine of the resurrection, and tremble; but yet they continue devils, because the benefits of this resurrection have not been applied to them, nor have they received a renovating power from it, to change and put off their diabolical nature. And so, unless we not only profess to know, but also feel that Christ is risen indeed, by being born again from above, we shall be as far from the kingdom of God as they: our faith will be as ineffectual as the faith of devils.

Nothing has done more harm to the Christian world, nothing has rendered the cross of Christ of less effect, than a vain supposition, that religion is something without us. Whereas we should consider, that every thing that Christ did outwardly, must be done over again in our souls; or otherwise, the believing there was such a divine person once on earth, who triumphed over hell and the grave, will profit us no more, than believing there was once such a person as Alexander, who conquered the world.

As Christ was born of the Virgin's womb, so must he be spiritually formed in our hearts. As he died for sin, so must we die to sin. And as he rose again from the dead, so must we also rise to a divine life.

None but those who have followed him in this regeneration, or new-birth, shall sit on thrones as approvers of his sentence, when he shall come in terrible majesty to judge the twelve tribes of Israel.

It is true, as for the outward work of our redemption, it was a transient act, and was certainly finished on the cross, but the application of that redemption to our hearts, is a work that will continue always, even unto the end of the world.

So long as there is an elect man breathing on the earth, who is naturally engendered of the offspring of the first Adam, so long must the quickening spirit, which was purchased by the resurrection of the second Adam, that Lord from heaven, be breathing upon his soul.

For though we may exist by Christ, yet we cannot be said to exist in him, till we are united to him by one spirit, and enter into a new state of things, as certainly as he entered into a new state of things, after that he rose from the dead.

We may throng and crowd about Christ, and call him "Lord, Lord," when we come to worship before his footstool; but we have not effectually touched him, till by a lively faith in his resurrection, we perceive a divine virtue coming out of him, to renew and purify our souls.

How greatly then do they err who rest in a bare historical faith of our Savior's resurrection, and look only for external proofs to evidence it? Whereas were we the most learned disputers of this world, and could speak of the certainty of this fact with the tongue of men and angels, yet without this inward testimony of it in our hearts, though we might convince others, yet we should never be saved by it ourselves.

For we are but dead men, we are like so many carcasses wrapt up in grave clothes, till that same Jesus who called Lazarus from his tomb, and at whose own resurrection many that slept arose, doth raise us also by his quickening Spirit from our natural death, in which we have so long lain, to a holy and heavenly life.

We might think ourselves happy, if we had seen the Holy Jesus after He was risen from the dead, and our hands had handled that Lord of life. But more happy are they who have not seen him, and yet having felt the power of his resurrection, therefore believe in him. For many saw our divine master, who were not saved by him; but whosoever has thus felt the power of his resurrection, has the earnest of his inheritance in his heart, he has passed from death to life, and shall never fall into final condemnation.

I am very sensible that this is foolishness to the natural man, as were many such like truths to our Lord's own disciples, when only weak in faith, before he rose again. But when these natural men, like them, have fully felt the power of his resurrection, they will then own that this doctrine is from God, and say with the Samaritans, "Now we believe not because of thy saying," for we ourselves have experienced it in our hearts.

And O that all unbelievers, all letter-learned masters of Israel, who now look upon the doctrine of the power of Christ's resurrection, or our new birth, as an idle tale, and condemn the preachers of it as enthusiasts and madmen, did but thus feel the power of it in their souls, they would no longer ask, how this thing could be? But they would be convinced of it, as much as Thomas was, when he saw the Lord's Christ; and like him, when Jesus bud him reach out his hands and thrust them into his side, in a holy confession they would cry out, "My Lord and my God!" But how shall an unbeliever, how shall the formal Christian come thus to "know Christ, and the power of his resurrection?" God, who cannot lie, has told us, "I am the resurrection and the life, whosoever liveth and believeth in me, though he were dead, yet shall he live." Again, says the apostle, "By faith we are saved, and that not of ourselves, it is the gift of God." This, this is the way, walk in it. Believe, and you shall live in Christ, and Christ in you; you shall be one with Christ, and Christ one with you. But without this, your outward goodness and professions will avail you nothing.

But then, by this faith we are not to understand a dead speculative faith, a faith in the head; but a living principle wrought in the heart by the powerful operations of the Holy Ghost, a faith that will enable us to overcome the world, and forsake all the affection for Jesus Christ. For thus speaks our blessed Master, "Unless a man forsake all that he hath, he cannot be my disciple." And so the apostle, in the words immediately following the text, says, "being made conformable to his death;" thereby implying, that we cannot know the power of Christ's resurrection, unless we are made conformable to him in his death.

If we can reconcile light and darkness, heaven and hell, then we may hope to know the power of Christ's resurrection without dying to ourselves and the world. But till we can do this, we might as well expect that Christ will have concord with Belial.

For there is such a contrariety between the spirit of this world, and the Spirit of Jesus Christ, that he who will be at friendship with the one, must be at enmity with the other: "We cannot serve God and mammon." This may, indeed, seem a hard saying; and many, with the young man in the gospel, may be tempted to go away sorrowful. But wherefore should this offend them? For what is all that is in the world, the lust of the eye, the lust of the flesh, and the pride of life, but vanity and vexation of spirit?

God is love; and therefore, could our own wills, or the world, have made us happy, he never would have sent his own dear Son Jesus Christ to die and rise again, to deliver us from the power of them. But because they only torment, and cannot satisfy, therefore God bids us to renounce them.

Had any one persuaded profane Esau not to lose so glorious a privilege, merely for the sake of gratifying a present corrupt inclination, when he saw him about to sell his birth-right for a little red pottage, would not one think that man to have been Esau's friend? And just thus stands the case between God and us. By the death and resurrection of Jesus Christ, we are new-born to an heavenly inheritance amongst all them which are sanctified; but our own corrupt wills, would tempt us to sell this glorious birth-right for the vanities of the world, which, like Esau's red pottage, may please us for a while, but will soon be taken away from us.

God knows this, and therefore rather bids us renounce them for a reason, than for the short enjoyment of them lost the privilege of that glorious birth-right, to which, by knowing the power of the resurrection of Jesus Christ, we are entitled.

O the depth of the riches and excellency of Christianity! Well might the great St. Paul count all things but dung and dross for the excellency of the knowledge of it. Well might he desire so ardently to know Jesus, and the power of his resurrection. For even on this side eternity it raises us above the world, and makes us to sit in heavenly places in Christ Jesus.

Well might that glorious company of worthies, recorded in the Holy scriptures, supported with a deep sense of their heavenly calling, despise the pleasures and profits of this life, and wander about in sheep-skins, and goat-skins, in dens and caves of the earth, being destitute, afflicted, tormented.

And O that we were all like minded! That we felt the power of Christ's resurrection as they did! How should we then "count all things as dung and dross for the excellency of the knowledge of Christ Jesus our Lord!" How should we then recover our primitive dignity, trample the earth under our feet, and with our souls be continually gasping after God?

And what hinders but we may be thus minded? Is Jesus Christ, our great High Priest, altered from what he was? No, "he is the same yesterday, today, and for ever." And though he is exalted to the right hand of God, yet he is not ashamed to call us brethren. The power of his resurrection is as great now as formerly, and the Holy Spirit, which was assured to us by his resur-rection, as ready and able to quicken us who are dead in trespasses and sins, as any saint that ever lived. Let us but cry, and that instantly, to Him that is mighty and able to save; let us, in sincerity and truth, without secretly keeping back the least part, renounce ourselves and the world; then we shall be Chris-tians indeed. And though the world may cast us out, and separate from our company, yet Jesus Christ will walk with, and abide in us. And at the general resurrection of the last day, when the voice of the archangel and trump of God shall bid the sea and the graves to give up their dead, and all nations shall appear before him, then will he confess us before his Father and the holy an-gels, and we shall receive that invitation which he shall then pronounce to all who love and fear him, "Come, ye blessed children of my Father, inherit the kingdom prepared for you from the beginning of the world.

Grand this, O Father, for thy dear Son's sake, Jesus Christ our Lord; to whom, with Thee and the Holy Ghost, etc.

Sermon 54 Intercession every Christian's Duty

1 Thessalonians 5:25, "Brethren, pray for us."

If we inquire, why there is so little love to be found amongst Christians, why the very characteristic, by which every one should know that we are disciples of the holy Jesus, is almost banished out of the Christian world, we shall find it, in a great measure, owing to a neglect or superficial performance of that excellent part of prayer, INTERCESSION, or imploring the divine grace and mercy in behalf of others.

Some forget this duty of praying for others, because they seldom remember to pray for themselves: and even those who are constant in praying to their Father who is in heaven, are often so selfish in their addresses to the throne of grace, that they do not enlarge their petitions for the welfare of their fellow Christians as they ought; and thereby fall short of attaining that Christian charity, that unfeigned love to their brethren, which their sacred profession obliges them to aspire after, and without which, though they should bestow all their goods to feed the poor, and even give their bodies to be burned, yet it would profit them nothing.

Since these things are so, I shall from the words of the text (though originally intended to be more confined) endeavor, to show, I. FIRST, That it is every Christian's duty to pray for others as well as for himself.

II. SECONDLY, Show, whom we ought to pray for, and in what manner we should do it. And, III. THIRDLY, I shall offer some motives to excite all Christians to abound in this great duty of intercession.

I. FIRST, I shall endeavor to show, That it is every Christian's duty to pray for others, as well as for himself.

Now PRAYER is a duty founded on natural religion; the very heathens never neglected it, though many Christian heathens amongst us do: and it is so essential to Christianity, that you might as reasonably expect to find a living man without breath, as a true Christian without the spirit of prayer and supplication. Thus, no sooner was St. Paul converted, but "behold he prayeth," saith the Lord Almighty. And thus will it be with every child of God, as soon as he becomes such: prayer being truly called, The natural cry of the new-born soul.

For in the heart of every true believer there is a heavenly tendency, a divine attraction, which as sensibly draws him to converse with God, as the lodestone attracts the needle.

A deep sense of their own weakness, and of Christ's fullness; a strong conviction of their natural corruption, and of the necessity of renewing grace; will not let them rest from crying day and night to their Almighty Redeemer, that the divine image, which they lost in Adam, may through his all-powerful mediation, and the sanctifying operation of his blessed spirit, be begun, carried on, and fully perfected both in their souls and bodies.

Thus earnest, thus importunate, are all sincere Christians in praying for themselves: but then, not having so lively, lasting, and deep a sense of the wants of their Christian brethren, they are for the most part too remiss and defective in their prayers for them. Whereas, was the love of God shed abroad in our hearts, and did we love our neighbor in that manner, in which the Son of God our savior loved us, and according to his command and example, we could not but be as importunate for their spiritual and temporal welfare, as for our own; and as earnestly desire and endeavor that others should share in the benefits of the death and passion of Jesus Christ, as we ourselves.

Let not any one think, that this is an uncommon degree of charity; an high pitch of perfection, to which not every one can attain: for, if we are all commanded to "love our neighbor (that is every man) even as ourselves," nay to "lay down our lives for the brethren;" then, it is the duty of all to pray for their neighbors as much as for themselves, and by all possible acts and expressions of love and affection towards them, at all times, to show their readiness even to lay down their lives for them, if ever it should please God to call them to it.

Our blessed Savior, as "he hath set us an example, that we should follow his steps" in every thing else, so hath he more especially in this: for in that divine, that perfect and inimitable prayer (recorded in the 17th of St. John) which he put up just before his passion, we find but few petitions for his own, though many for his disciples welfare: and in that perfect form which he has been pleased to prescribe us, we are taught to say, not MY, but "OUR Father," thereby to put us in mind, that, whenever we approach the throne of grace, we ought to pray not for ourselves alone, but for all our brethren in Christ.

Intercession then is certainly a duty incumbent upon all Christians.

II. Whom we are to intercede for, and how this duty is to be performed, comes next to be considered.

1. And first, our intercession must be UNIVERSAL. "I will, (says the apostle) that prayers, supplications and intercessions be made for all men." For as God's mercy is over all his works, as Jesus Christ died to redeem a people out of all nations and languages; so we should pray, that "all men may come to the knowledge of the truth, and be saved." Many precious promises are made in holy writ, that the gospel shall be published through the whole world, that "the earth shall be covered with the knowledge of the Lord, as the waters cover the sea:" and therefore it is our duty not to confine our petitions to our own nation, but to pray that all those nations, who now sit in darkness and in the shadow of death, may have the glorious gospel shine out upon them, as well as upon us. But you need not that any man should teach you this, since ye yourselves are taught of God, and of Jesus Christ himself, to pray, that his kingdom may come; part of the meaning of which petition is, that "God's ways may be known upon earth, and his saving health among all nations." 2. Next to the praying for all men, we should, according to St. Paul's rule, pray for KINGS; particularly for our present sovereign King George, and all that are put in authority under him: that we may lead quiet lives, in all godliness and honesty. For, if we consider how heavy the burden of government is, and how much the welfare of any people depends on the zeal and godly conversation of those that have the rule over them: if we set before us the many dangers and difficulties, to which governors by their station are exposed, and the continual temptations they be under to luxury and self-indulgence; we shall not only pity, but pray for them: that he who preserved Esther, David, and Josiah, "unspotted from the world," amidst the grandeur of a court, and gave success to their designs, would also preserve them holy and unblameable, and prosper all the works of their hands upon them. But 3. THIRDLY, you ought, in a more especial manner, to pray for those, whom "the Holy Ghost hath made OVERSEERS over you." This is what St. Paul begs, again and again, of the churches to whom he writes: Says he in the text, "Brethren, pray for us;" and again, in his epistle to the Ephesians, "praying always, with all manner of supplication; and for me also, that I may open my mouth boldly, to declare the mystery of the gospel." And in another place, to express his earnestness in this request, and the great importance of their prayers for him, he bids the church "strive, (or, as the original word signifies,

be in a agony) together with him in their prayers." And surely, if the great St. Paul, that chosen vessel, that favorite of heaven, needed the most importunate prayers of his Christian converts; much more do the ordinary ministers of the gospel stand in need of the intercession of their respective flocks.

And I cannot but in a more especial manner insist upon this branch of your duty, because it is a matter of such importance: for, no doubt, much good is frequently withheld from many, by reason of their neglecting to pray for their ministers, and which they would have received, had they prayed for them as they ought. Not to mention, that people often complain of the want of diligent and faithful pastors. But how do they deserve good pastors, who will not earnestly pray to God for such? If we will not pray to the Lord of the harvest, can it be expected he will send forth laborers into his harvest?

Besides, what ingratitude is it, not to pray for your ministers! For shall they watch and labor in the word and doctrine for you, and your salvation, and shall not you pray for them in return? If any bestow favors on your bodies, you think it right, meet, and your bounden duty, to pray for them; and shall not they be remembered in your prayers, who daily feed and nourish your souls? Add to all this, that praying for your ministers, will be a manifest proof of your believing, that though Paul plant, and Apollos water, yet it is God alone who giveth the increase. And you will also find it the best means you can use, to promote your own welfare; because God, in answer to your prayers, may impart a double portion of his Holy Spirit to them, whereby they will be qualified to deal out to you larger measures of knowledge in spiritual things, and be enabled more skillfully to divide the word of truth.

Would men but constantly observe this direction, and when their ministers are praying in their name to God, humbly beseech him to perform all their petitions: or, when they are speaking in God's name to them, pray that the Holy Ghost may fall on all them that hear the word; we should find a more visible good effect of their doctrine, and a greater mutual love between ministers and their people. For ministers hands would then be hold up by the people's intercessions, and the people will never dare to villify or traduce those who are the constant subjects of their prayers.

4. Next to our ministers, OUR FRIENDS claim a place in our intercessions; but then we should not content ourselves with praying in general terms for them, but suit our prayers to their particular circumstances. When Miriam was afflicted with a leprosy from God, Moses cried and said, "Lord, heal her." And when the nobleman came to apply to Jesus Christ, in behalf of his child, he said, "Lord, my little daughter lieth at the point of death, I pray thee to come and heal her." In like manner, when our friends are under any

afflicting circumstances, we should endeavor to pray for them, with a particular regard to those circumstances.

For instance, is a friend sick? We should pray, that if it be God's good pleasure, it may not be unto death; but is otherwise, that he would give him grace so to take his visitation, that, after this painful life ended, he may dwell with him in life everlasting. Is a friend in doubt in an important matter? We should lay his case before God, as Moses did that of the daughters of Zelophehad, and pray, that God's Holy Spirit may lead him into all truth, and give all seasonable direction. Is he in want? We should pray, that his faith may never fail, and that in God's due time he may be relieved. And in all other cases, we should not pray for our friends only in generals, but suit our petitions to their particular sufferings and afflictions; for otherwise, we may never ask perhaps for the things our friends most want.

It must be confessed, that such a procedure will oblige some often to break from the forms they use; but if we accustom ourselves to it, and have a deep sense of what we ask for, the most illiterate will want proper words to express themselves.

We have many noble instances in holy scripture of the success of this kind of particular intercession; but none more remarkable than that of Abraham's servant, in the book of Genesis, who being sent to seek a wife for his son Isaac, prayed in a most particular manner in his behalf. And the sequel of the story informs us, how remarkably his prayer as answered.

And did Christians now pray for their friends in the same particular manner, and with the same faith as Abraham's servant did for his master; they would, no doubt, in many instances, receive as visible answers, and have as much reason to bless God for them, as he had. But 5. As we ought thus to intercede for our friends, so in like manner must we also pray for OUR ENEMIES. "Bless them that curse you, (says Jesus Christ) and pray for them that despitefully use you, and persecute you." Which commands he enforced in the strongest manner by his own example: in the very agonies and pangs of death, he prayed even for his murderers, "Father, forgive them, for they know not what they do!" This, it must needs be confessed, is a difficult duty, yet not impracticable, to those who have renounced the things of this present life, (from an inordinate love of which all enmities arise) and who knowing the terrible woes denounced against those who offend Christ's little ones, can, out of real pity, and a sense of their danger, pray for those by whom such offenses come.

6. Lastly, and to conclude this head, we should intercede for all that are any ways AFFLICTED in mind, body, or estate; for all who desire, and stand in need of our prayers, and for all who do not pray for themselves.

And Oh! That all who hear me, would set apart some time every day for the due performance of this most necessary duty! In order to which, I shall now proceed, III. To show the advantages, and offer some considerations to excite you to the practice of daily intercession. And 1. FIRST, It will fill your hearts with love one to another. He that every day heartily intercedes at the throne of grace for all mankind, cannot but in a short time be filled with love and charity to all: and the frequent exercise of his love in this manner, will insensibly enlarge his heart, and make him partaker of that exceeding abundance of it which is in Christ Jesus our Lord! Envy, malice, revenge, and such like hellish tempers, can never long harbor in a gracious intercessor's breast; but he will be filled with joy, peace, meekness, long-suffering, and all other graces of the Holy Spirit. By frequently laying his neighbor's wants before God, he will be touched with a fellow-feeling of them; he will rejoice with those that do rejoice, and weep with those that weep. Every blessing bestowed on others, instead of exciting envy in him, will be looked on as an answer to his particular intercession, and fill his soul with joy unspeakable and full of glory.

Abound therefore in acts of general and particular intercessions; and when you hear of your neighbor's faults, instead of relating them to, and exposing them before others, lay them in secret before God, and beg of him to correct and amend them. When you hear of a notorious sinner, instead of thinking you do well to be angry, beg of Jesus Christ to convert, and make him a monument of his free grace; you cannot imagine what a blessed alteration this practice will make in your heart, and how much you will increase day by day in the spirit of love and meekness towards all mankind!

But farther, to excite you to the constant practice of this duty of intercession, consider the many instances in holy scripture, of the power and efficacy of it. Great and excellent things are there recorded as the effects of this divine employ. It has stopped plagues, it has opened and shut heaven; and has frequently turned away God's fury from his people. How was Abimelech's house freed from the disease God sent amongst them, at the intercession of Abraham! When "Phineas stood up and prayed," how soon did the plague cease! When Daniel humbled and afflicted his soul, and interceded for the Lord's inheritance, how quickly was an angel dispatched to tell him, "his prayer was heard!" And, to mention but one instance more, how does God own himself as it were overcome with the importunity of Moses, when he was interceding for his idolatrous people, "Let me alone," says God!

This sufficiently shows, I could almost say, the omnipotency of intercession, and how we may, like Jacob, wrestle with God, and by an holy violence prevail both for ourselves and others. And no doubt it is owing to the secret and prevailing intercessions of the few righteous souls who still remain among us, that God has yet spared this miserably sinful nation: for were there not some such faithful ones, like Moses, left to stand in the gap, we should soon be destroyed, even as was Sodom, and reduced to ashes like unto Gomorrah.

But, to stir you up yet farther to this exercise of intercession, consider, that in all probability, it is the frequent employment even of the glorified saints: for though they are delivered from the burden of the flesh, and restored to the glorious liberty of the sons of God, yet as their happiness cannot be perfectly consummated till the resurrection of the last day, when all their brethren will be glorified with them, we cannot but think they are often importunate in beseeching our heavenly Father, shortly to accomplish the number of his elect, and to hasten his kingdom. And shall now we, who are on earth, be often exercised in this divine employ with the glorious company of the spirits of just men made perfect? Since our happiness is so much to consist in the communion of saints in the church triumphant above, shall we not frequently intercede for the church militant here below; and earnestly beg, that we may all be one, even as the Holy Jesus and his Father are one, that we may also be made perfect in one?

To provoke you to this great work and labor of love, remember, that it is the never ceasing employment of the holy and highly exalted Jesus himself, who sits at the right hand of God, to hear all our prayers, and to make continual intercession for us! So that he who is constantly employed in interceding for others, is doing that on earth, which the eternal Son of God is always doing in heaven.

Imagine therefore, when you are lifting up holy hands in prayer for one another, that you see the heavens opened, and the Son of God in all his glory, as the great high-priest of your salvation, pleading for you the all-sufficient merit of his sacrifice before the throne of his heavenly Father! Join then your intercessions with his, and beseech him, that they may, through him, come up as incense, and be received as a sweet-smelling favor, acceptable in the sight of God! This imagination will strengthen your faith, excite a holy earnestness in your prayers, and make you wrestle with God, as Jacob did, when he saw him face to face, and his life was preserved; as Abraham, when he pleaded for Sodom; and as Jesus Christ himself, when he prayed, being in an agony, so much the more earnestly the night before his bitter passion.

And now, brethren, what shall I say more, since you are taught of Jesus Christ himself, to abound in love, and in this good work of praying one for another. Though ever so mean, though as poor as Lazarus, you will then become benefactors to all mankind; thousands, and twenty times ten thousands, will then be blessed for your sakes! And after you have employed a few years in this divine exercise here, you will be translated to that happy place, where you have so often wished others might be advanced; and be exalted to sit at the right hand of our All-powerful, All-prevailing Intercessor, in the kingdom of his heavenly Father hereafter.

However, I cannot but in an especial manner press this upon you now, because all ye, amongst whom I have now been preaching, in all probability will see me no more: for I am now going (I trust under the conduct of God's most Holy Spirit) from you, knowing not what shall befall me: I need therefore your most importunate intercessions, that nothing may move me from my duty, and that I may not "count even my life dear unto myself, so that I may finish my course with joy, and the ministry I have received of the Lord Jesus, to testify the gospel of the grace of God!" Whilst I have been here, to the best of my knowledge, I have not failed to declare unto you the whole will of God: and though my preaching may have been a savor of death unto death to some; yet I trust it has been also a savor of life unto life to others; and therefore I earnestly hope that those will not fail to remember me in their prayers. As for my own part, the many unmerited kindnesses I have received from you, will not suffer me to forget you: out of the deep, therefore, I trust shall my cry come unto God; and whilst the winds and storms are blowing over me, unto the Lord will I make my supplication for you. For it is but a little while, and "we must all appear before the judgment seat of Christ;" where I must give a strict account of the doctrine I have preached, and you of your improvement under it. And O that I may never be called out as a swift witness, against any of those, for whose salvation I have sincerely, though too faintly, longed and labored!

It is true, I have been censured by some as acting out of sinister and selfish views; "but it is a small matter with me to be judged by man's judgment; I hope my eye is single; but I beseech you, brethren, by the mercies of God in Christ Jesus, pray that it may be more so! And that I may increase with the increase of grace in the knowledge and love of God through Jesus Christ our Lord.

And now, brethren, what shall I say more? I could wish to continue my discourse much longer; for I can never fully express the desire of my soul towards you! Finally, therefore, brethren, "whatsoever things are holy, whatsoever things are pure, whatsoever things are honest, what soever things are of good report: if there be any consolation in Christ, if any fellowship of the spirit," if any hopes of our appearing to the comfort of each other at the awful tribunal of Jesus Christ, "think of the things that you have heard," and of those which your pastors have declared, and will yet declare unto you; and continue under their ministry to "work out your own salvation with fear and trembling:" so that whether I should never see you any more, or whether it shall please God to bring me back again at any time, I may always have the satisfaction of knowing that your conversation is such "as becometh the gospel of Christ." I almost persuade myself, that I could willingly suffer all things, so that it might any ways promote the salvation of your precious and immortal souls; and I beseech you, as my last request, "obey them that have the rule over you in the Lord;" and be always ready to attend on their ministry, as it is your bounden duty. Think not that I desire to have myself exalted at the expense of another's character; but rather think this, not to have any man's person too much in admiration; but esteem all your ministers highly in love, as they justly deserve for their work's sake.

And now, "brethren, I commend you to god, and to the word of his grace, which is able to build you up, and give you an inheritance amongst all them that are sanctified." May God reward you for all your works of faith, and labors of love, and make you to abound more and more in every good word and work towards all men. May he truly convert all that have been convinced, and awaken all that are dead in trespasses and sins! May he confirm all that are wavering! And may you all go on from one degree of grace unto another, till you arrive unto the measure of the stature of the fullness of Christ; and thereby be made meet to stand before that God, "in whose presence is the fullness of joy, and at whose right-hand there are pleasures for evermore!" Amen! Amen!

Sermon 55 Persecution every Christian's Lot

2 Timothy 3:12, "Yes, and all that will live godly in Christ Jesus, shall suffer persecution."

When our Lord was pleased to take upon himself the form of a servant, and to go about preaching the kingdom of God; he took all opportunities in public, and more especially in private, to caution his disciples against seeking great things for themselves, and also to forewarn them of the many distresses, afflictions and persecutions, which they must expect to endure for his name's sake. The great apostle Paul therefore, the author of this epistle, in this, as in all other things, following the steps of his blessed Master, takes particular care, among other apostolical admonitions, to warn young Timothy of the difficulties he must expect to meet with in the course of his ministry: "This know also, that in the last days perilous times shall come. For men shall be lovers of their ownselves, covetous, proud, blasphemers, disobedient to parents, unthankful, unholy, without natural affection, truce-breakers, false accusers, incontinent, fierce, despisers of those that are good, traitors, heady, high-minded, lovers of pleasure more than lovers of God; having a form of godliness, but denying the power thereof: from such turn away. For of this sort are they who creep into houses, and lead captive silly women laden with sins, led away with divers lusts, ever learning, and never able to come to the knowledge of the truth. Now, as Jannes and Jambres (two of the Egyptian magicians) withstood Moses (by working sham miracles) so do they also resist the truth; and (notwithstanding they keep up the form of religion) are men of corrupt minds, reprobate concerning the faith." But, in order to keep him from sinking under their opposition, he tells him, that though God, for wise ends, permitted these false teachers, as he did the magicians, to oppose for some time, yet they should now proceed no farther: "For their folly (says he) shall be made manifest unto all men, as theirs (the Magicians) also was," when they could not stand before Moses because of the boil; for the boil was upon the Magicians, as well as upon all the Egyptians. And then, to encourage Timothy yet the more, he propounds to him his own example; "But thou hast fully known my doctrine, manner of life, purpose, faith, long-suffering, charity, patience, persecutions, afflictions, which came unto me at Antioch, at Iconium, at Lystra; what persecutions I endured; but out of them all the Lord delivered me." And then, lest Timothy might think that this was only the particular case of Paul, says he, in the words of the text, "Yea, and all that will live godly in Christ Jesus, shall suffer persecution." The words, without considering them as they stand in relation to the context, contain an important truth, that persecution is the common lot of every godly man. This is a hard saying, How few can bear it? I trust God, in the following discourse, will enable me to make it good, by showing, I. What it is to live godly in Christ Jesus.

II. The different kinds of persecution to which they, who live godly, are exposed.

III. Why it is, that godly men must expect to suffer persecution.

LASTLY, We shall apply the whole.

I. FIRST, Let us consider what it is to live godly in Christ Jesus.

This supposes, that we are made the righteousness of God in Christ, that we are born again, and are one with Christ by a living faith, and a vital union, even as Jesus Christ and the Father are One. Unless we are thus converted, and transformed by the renewing of our minds, we cannot properly be said to be in Christ, much less to live godly in him. To be in Christ merely by baptism, and an outward profession, is not to be in Him in the strict sense of the word: no; "They that are in Christ, are new creatures; old things are passed away, and all things are become new" in their hearts.

Their life is hid with Christ in God; their souls daily feed on the invisible realities of another world. To "live godly in Christ," is to make the divine will, and not our own, the sole principle of all our thoughts, words, and actions; so that, "whether we eat or drink, or whatsoever we do, we do all to the glory of God." Those who live godly in Christ, may not so much be said to live, as Christ to live in them: He is their Alpha and Omega, their first and last, their beginning and end. They are led by his Spirit, as a child is led by the hand of its father; and are willing to follow the Lamb withersoever he leads them. They hear, know, and obey his voice. Their affections are set on things above; their hopes are full of immortality; their citizenship is in heaven. Being born again of God, they habitually live to, and daily walk with, God. They are pure in heart; and, from a principle of faith in Christ, are holy in all manner of conversation and godliness.

This is to "live godly in Christ Jesus:" and hence we may easily learn, why so few suffer persecution? Because, so few live godly in Christ Jesus. You may live formally in Christ, you may attend on outward duties; you may live morally in Christ, you may (as they term it) do no one an harm, and avoid persecution: but they "that will live godly in Christ Jesus, shall suffer persecution." 2. SECONDLY, What is the meaning of the word Persecution, and how many kinds there are of it, I come now to consider.

The word Persecution, is derived from a Greek word signifying to pursue, and generally implies pursuing a person for the sake of his goodness, or God's good-will to him. The FIRST kind of it, is that of the HEART. We have an early example of this in the wicked one Cain, who, because the Lord had respect to Abel and his offering, and not to him and his offering, was very wroth, his countenance fell, and at length he cruelly slew his envied brother. Thus the Pharisees hated and persecuted our Lord long before they laid hold on him: and our Lord mentions being inwardly hated of men, as one kind of Persecution his disciples were to undergo. This heart-enmity (if I may so term it) is the root of all other kinds of Persecution, and is, in some degree or other, to be found in the soul of every unregenerated man; and numbers are guilty of this persecution, who never have it in their power to persecute any other way. Nay, numbers would actually put in practice all other degrees of persecution, was not the name of Persecution become odious amongst mankind, and did they not hereby run the hazard of losing their reputation. Alas! how many at the great day, whom we know not now, will be convicted and condemned, that all their life harbored a secret evil-will against Zion! They may now screen it before men; but God seeth the enmity of their hearts, and will judge them as Persecutors at the great and terrible day of judgment.

SECOND degree of Persecution is that of the tongue; "out of the abundance of the heart, the mouth speaketh." Many, I suppose, think it no harm to shoot out arrows, even bitter words, against the disciples of the Lord: they scatter their firebrands, arrows and death, saying, "Are we not in sport?" But, however they may esteem it, in God's account evil-speaking is a high degree of Persecution. Thus Ishmael's mocking Isaac, is termed persecuting him. "Blessed are ye (says out Lord) when men shall revile you and persecute you, and shall say all manner of evil against you falsely for my name's sake." From whence we may gather, that reviling, and speaking all manner of evil for Christ's sake, is a high degree of persecution. For "a good name, *says the wise man) is better than precious ointment," and, to many, is dearer than life itself. It is a great breach of the sixth commandment, to slander any one; but to speak evil of and slander the disciples of Christ, merely because they are his disciples, must be highly provoking in the sight of God; and such who are guilty of it (without repentance) will find that Jesus Christ will call them to an account, and punish them for all their ungodly and hard speeches in a lake of fire and brimstone. This shall be their portion to drink. The THIRD and

LAST kind of Persecution, is that which expresses itself in ACTIONS: as when wicked men separate the children of God from their company; "Blessed are ye, (says our Lord) when they shall separate you from their company:" or expose them to church-censures. "They shall put you out of their synagogues;" threatening and prohibiting them from making an open profession of his religion or worship; or interdicting ministers for preaching his word, as the high-priests threatened the apostles, and "forbad them any more to speak in the name of Jesus;" and Paul breathed out threatenings and slaughters against the disciples of the Lord: or when they call them into courts; "You shall be called before governors," says our Lord: or when they fine, imprison, or punish them, by confiscation of goods, cruel scourging, and, lastly, death itself.

It would be impossible to enumerate in what various shapes persecution has appeared. It is a many-headed monster, cruel as the grave, insatiable as hell; and, what is worse, it generally appears under the cloak of religion. But, cruel, insatiable, and horrid as it is, they that live godly in Christ Jesus, must expect to suffer and encounter with it in all its forms.

This is what we are to make good under our next general head.

3. THIRDLY, Why is it that godly men must expect to suffer persecution? And, FIRST, This appears from the whole tenor of our Lord's doctrine. We will begin with his divine sermon on the mount. "Blessed are they who are persecuted for righteousness sake; for theirs is the kingdom of heaven." So that, if our Lord spoke truth, we are not so blessed as to have an interest in the kingdom of heaven, unless we are or have been persecuted for righteousness sake. Nay, our Lord (it is remarkable) employs three verses in this beatitude, and only one in each of the others; not only to show that it was a thing which men (as men) are unwilling to believe, but also the necessary consequence of it upon our being Christians. This is likewise evident from all those passages, wherein our Lord informs us, that he came upon the earth, "not to send peace, but a sword;" and that the father-in- law should be against the mother-in-law, and a man's foes should be those of his own household. Passages, which though confined by false prophets to the first, I am persuaded will be verified by the experience of all true Christians in this, and every age of the church. It would be endless to recount all the places, wherein our Lord forewarns his disciples, that they should be called before rulers, and thrust out of synagogues, nay, that the time would come, wherein men should think they did God service to kill them. For this reason he so frequently declared, that "unless a man forsake all that he had, and even hated life itself, he could not be his disciple." And therefore it is worthy our observation, that in the remarkable passage, wherein our Lord makes such an extensive promise to those who left all for him, he cautiously inserts persecution. "And Jesus

answered and said, Verily I say unto you, there is no man that hath left house, or brethren, or sisters, or father, or mother, or wife, or children, or lands, for my sake and the gospel's, but he shall receive an hundred-fold now in this time; houses and brethren, and sisters and mothers, and children and lands, with persecutions; (the word is in the plural number, including all kinds of persecution) and in the world to come eternal life." He that hath ears to hear, let him hear what Christ says in all these passages, and then confess, that all who will godly in Christ Jesus shall suffer persecution.

As this is proved from our Lord's doctrine, so it is no less evident from his life. Follow him from the manger to the cross, and see whether any persecution was like that which the Son of God, the Lord of glory, underwent whilst here on earth. How was he hated by wicked men? How often would that hatred have excited them to lay hold of him, had it not been for fear of the people? How was he reviled, counted and called a Blasphemer, a Wine-bibber, a Samaritan, nay, a Devil, and, in one word, had all manner of evil spoken against him falsely? What contradiction of sinners did he endure against himself? How did men separate from his company, and were ashamed to walk with him openly? Insomuch that he once said to his own disciples, "Will you also go away?" Again, How was he stoned, thrust out of the syna-gogues, arraigned as a deceiver of the people, a seditious and pestilent fellow, an enemy of Caesar, and as such scourged, blind-folded, spit upon, and at length condemned, and nailed to an accursed tree? Thus was the Master per-secuted, thus did the Lord suffer; and the servant is not above his Master, nor the disciple above his Lord: "If they have persecuted me, they will also perse-cute you," says the blessed Jesus. And again, "Every man that is perfect (a true Christian) must be as his Master," or suffer as he did. For in all these things our Lord has set us an example, that we should follow his steps: and therefore, far be it that any, who live godly in Christ Jesus, should hencefor-ward expect to escape suffering persecution.

But farther: not only our Lord's example, but the example of all the saints that ever lived, evidently demonstrates the truth of the apostle's asser-tion in the text. How soon was Abel made a martyr for his religion?

How was Isaac mocked by the son of the bond-woman? And what a large catalogue of suffering Old Testament saints, have we recorded in the 11th chapter of the Hebrews! Read the Acts of the Apostles, and see how the first Christians were threatened, stoned, imprisoned, scourged, and persecuted even unto death. Examine Church History in after-ages, and you will find the murder of the innocents by Herod, was but an earnest of the innocent blood which should be shed for the sake of Jesus. Examine the experience of saints now living on earth; and, if it were possible to consult the spirits of just men made perfect, I am persuaded each would concur with the apostle in asserting, that "all who will live godly in Christ Jesus, shall suffer persecution." How can it be otherwise in the very nature of things? Ever since the fall, there has been a irreconcilable enmity between the seed of the woman and the seed of the serpent. Wicked men hat God, and therefore cannot but hate those who are like him: they hate to be reformed, and therefore must hate and persecute those, who, by a contrary behavior, testify of them, that their deeds are evil. Besides, pride of heart leads men to persecute the servants of Jesus Christ. If they commend them, they are afraid of being asked, Why do not you follow them? And therefore because they dare not imitate, though they may sometimes be even forced to approve their way, yet pride and envy make them turn persecutors. Hence it is, that as it was formerly, so it is now, and so will it be to the end of time; "He that is born after the flesh, (the natural man, does and) will persecute him that is born after the Spirit," the regenerate man. Because Christians are not of the world, but Christ hath chosen them out of the world, therefore the world will hate them. If it be objected against this doctrine, that we now live in a Christian world, and therefore must not expect such persecution as formerly; I answer, All are not Christians that are called so; and, till the heart is changed, the enmity against God (which is the root of all persecution) remains: and consequently Christians, falsely so called, will persecute as well as others. I observed therefore, in the beginning of this discourse, that Paul mentions those that had a form of religion, as persons of whom Timothy had need be chiefly aware: for, as our Lord and his apostles were mostly persecuted by their countrymen the Jews, so we must expect the like usage from the Formalists of our own nation, the Pharisees, who seem to be religious. The most horrid and barbarous persecutions have been carried on by those who have called themselves Christians; witness the days of queen Mary; and the fines, banishments and imprisonments of the children of God in the last century, and the bitter, irreconcilable hatred that appears in thousands who call themselves Christians, even in the present days wherein we live.

Persons, who argue against persecution, are not sufficiently sensible of the bitter enmity of the heart of every unregenerate man against God.

For my own part, I am so far from wondering that Christians are persecuted, that I wonder our streets do not run with the blood of the saints: was mens power equal to their wills, such a horrid spectacle would soon appear. But, Persecution is necessary in respect to the godly themselves. If we have not all manner of evil spoken of us, how can we know whether we seek only that honor which cometh from above? If we have no persecutors, how can our passive graces be kept in exercise? How can many Christian precepts be put into practice? How can we love; pray for; and do good to; those who despitefully use us? How can we overcome evil with good? In short, how can we know we love God better than life itself? Paul was sensible of all this, and therefore so positively and peremptorily asserts, that "all who live godly in Christ Jesus, shall suffer persecution." Not that I affirm, all are persecuted in a like degree. No: this would be contrary both to scripture and experience. But though all Christians are not really called to suffer every kind of persecution, yet all Christians are liable thereto: and notwithstanding some may live in more peaceful times of the church than others, yet all Christians, in all ages, will find by their own experience, that, whether they act in a private or public capacity, they must, in some degree or other, suffer persecution.

Here then I would pause, and, LASTLY, by way of application, exhort all persons, FIRST, To stand a while and examine themselves. For, by what has been said, you may gather one mark, whereby you may judge whether you are Christians or not. Were you ever persecuted for righteousness sake? If not, you never yet lived godly in Christ our Lord. Whatever you may say to the contrary, the inspired apostle, in the words of the text (the truth of which, I think, I have sufficiently proved) positively asserts, that all who will live godly in Him, shall suffer persecution. Not that all who are persecuted are real Christians; for many sometimes suffer, and are persecuted, on other accounts than for righteousness sake. The great question therefore is, Whether you were ever persecuted for living godly?

You may boast of your great prudence and sagacity (and indeed these are excellent things) and glory because you have not run such lengths, and made yourselves so singular, and liable to such contempt, as some others have.

But, alas! this is not a mark of your being of a Christian, but of a Laodicean spirit, neither how nor cold, and sit only to be spewed out of the mouth of God. That which you call prudence, is often, only cowardice, dreadful hypocrisy, pride of heart, which makes you dread contempt, and afraid to give up your reputation for God. You are ashamed of Christ and his gospel; and in all probability, was he to appear a second time upon earth, in words, as well as works, you would deny him. Awake therefore, all ye that live only formally in Christ Jesus, and no longer seek that honor which cometh of man. I do not desire to court you, but I entreat you to live godly, and fear not contempt for the sake of Jesus Christ. Beg of God to give you his Holy Spirit, that you may see through, and discover the latent hypocrisy of your hearts, and no longer deceive your own souls.

Remember you cannot reconcile two irreconcilable differences, God and Mammon, the friendship of this world with the favor of God. Know you not who hath told you, that "the friendship of this world is enmity with God?" If therefore you are in friendship with the world, notwithstanding all your specious pretenses to piety, you are at enmity with God: you are only heart-hypocrites; and, "What is the hope of the hypocrite, when God shall take away his soul?" Let the words of the text sound an alarm in your ears; O let them sink deep into your hearts; "Yea, and all that will live godly in Christ Jesus, shall suffer persecution." SECONDLY, From the words of the text, I would take occasion to speak to those, who are about to list themselves under the banner of Christ's cross. What say you? Are you resolved to live godly in Christ Jesus, notwithstanding the consequence will be, that you must suffer persecution?

You are beginning to build; but have you taken our Lord's advice, to "sit down first and count the cost?" Have you well weighed with yourselves that weighty declaration, "He that loveth father or mother more than Me, is not worthy of Me;" and again, "Unless a man forsake all that he hath he cannot be my disciple?" Perhaps some of you have great possessions; will not you go away sorrowful, if Christ should require you to sell all that you have!

Others of you again may be kinsmen, or some way related, or under obligations, to the high-priests, or other great personages, who may be persecuting the church of Christ: What say you? Will you, with Moses, "rather choose to suffer affliction with the people of God, than enjoy the pleasures of sin for a season?" Perhaps you may say, my friends will not oppose me. That is more than you know: in all probability your chief enemies will be those of your own household. If therefore they should oppose you, are you willing naked to follow a naked Christ? And to wander about in sheep-skins and goats-skins, in dens and caves of the earth; being afflicted, destitute, tormented, rather than not be Christ's disciples? You are now all following with zeal, as Ruth and Orpah did Naomi, and may weep under the word; but are not your tears crocodiles tears? And, when difficulties come, will you not go back form following your Lord, as Orpah departed form following Naomi? Have you really the root of grace in your hearts? Or, are you only stony-ground hearers? You receive the word with joy; but, when persecution arises because of the word, will you not be immediately offended? Be not angry with me for putting these questions to you. I am jealous over you, but it is with a godly jealousy: for, alas! how many have put their hands to the plough, and afterwards have shamefully looked back? I only deal with you, as our Lord did with the person that said, "Lord, I will follow thee withersoever thou wilt. The foxes have holes, and the birds of the air have nests, but the son of man, (says he) hath not where to lay his head." What say you? Are you willing to endure hardness, and thereby approve yourselves good soldiers of Jesus Christ? You now come on foot out of the towns and villages to hear the word, and receive me as a messenger of God: but will you not by and by cry out, Away with him, away with him; it is not fit such a fellow should live upon the earth? Perhaps some of you, like Hazael, may say, "Are we dogs, that we should do this?" But, alas! I have met with many unhappy souls, who have drawn back unto perdition, and have afterwards accounted me their enemy, for dealing faithfully with them; though once, if it were possible, they would have plucked out their own eyes, and have given them unto me. Sit down therefore, I beseech you, and seriously count the cost, and ask yourselves again and again, whether you count all things but dung and dross, and are willing to suffer the loss of all things, so that you may win Christ, and be found in him: for you may assure yourselves, the apostle hath not spoken in vain, "All that will live godly in Christ Jesus, shall suffer persecution." THIRDLY, The text speaks to you that are patiently suffering for the truth's sake: "Rejoice, and be exceeding glad; great shall be your reward in heaven." For to you it is given, not only to believe, but also to suffer, and perhaps remarkably too, for the sake of Jesus! This is a mark of your discipleship, an evidence that you do live godly in Christ Jesus.

Fear not, therefore, neither be dismayed. O be not weary and faint in your minds! Jesus, your Lord, your life, cometh, and his reward is with him.

Though all men forsake you, yet will not he: no; the Spirit of Christ and of glory shall rest upon you. In patience therefore possess your souls.

Sanctify the Lord God in your hearts. Be in nothing terrified by your adversaries: on their part Christ is evil spoken of; on your part his is glorified. Be not ashamed of your glory, since others can glory in their shame. Think it not strange concerning the fiery trial, wherewith you are or may be tried. The Devil rages, knowing that he hath but a short time to reign. He or his emissaries have no more power than what is given them from above: God sets them their bounds, which they cannot pass; and the very hairs of your head are all numbered. Fear not; no one shall set upon you to hurt you, without your heavenly Father's knowledge. Do your earthly friends and parents forsake you? Are you cast out of the synagogues? The Lord shall reveal himself to you, as to the man that was born blind. Jesus Christ shall take you up. If they carry you to prison, and load you with chains, so that the iron enter into your souls, even there shall Chris send an angel from heaven to strengthen you, and enable you, with Paul and Silas, to "sing praises at midnight." Are you threatened to be thrown into a den of lions, or cast into a burning fiery furnace, because you will not bow down and worship the beast? Fear not; the God, whom you serve, is able to deliver you: or, if he should suffer the flames to devour your bodies, they would only serve, as so many fiery chariots, to carry your souls to God.

Thus it was with the martyrs of old; so that once, when he was burning, cried out, "Come, you Papists, if you want a miracle, here, behold one!

This bed of flames is to me a bed of down." Thus it was with almost all that suffered in former times: for Jesus, notwithstanding he withdrew his own divinity from himself, yet has always lifted up the light of his countenance upon the souls of suffering saints. "Fear not therefore those that can kill the body, and after that have no more that they can do; but fear Him only, who is able to destroy both body and soul in hell." Dare, dare to live godly in Christ Jesus, though you suffer all manner of persecution. But, FOURTHLY, Are there any true ministers of Jesus Christ here? You will not be offended if I tell you, that the words of the text are, in an especial manner, applicable to you. Paul wrote them to Timothy; and we, of all men, that live godly in Christ Jesus, must expect to suffer the severest persecution. Satan will endeavor to bruise our heels, let who will escape: and it has been the general way of God's providence, in times of persecution, to permit the shepherds first to be smitten, before the sheep are scattered. Let us not therefore show that we are only hirelings, who care not for the sheep; but, like the great Shepherd and Bishop of souls, let us readily lay down our lives for the sheep. Whilst others are boasting of their great perferments, let us rather glory in our great afflictions and persecutions for the sake of Christ. Paul rejoiced that he suffered afflictions and persecutions at Iconium and Lystra: out of all, the Lord delivered him; out of all, the Lord will deliver us, and cause us hereafter to sit down with him on thrones, when he comes to judge the twelve tribes of Israel.

I could proceed; but I am conscious, in this part of my discourse, I ought more particularly to speak to myself, knowing that Satan has desired to have me, that he may sift me as wheat. Without a spirit of prophecy, we may easily discern the signs of the times. Persecutions even at the doors: the tabernacle of the Lord is already driven into the wilderness: the ark of the Lord is fallen into the unhallowed hands of uncircumcised Philistines. They have long since put us out of their synagogues, and high- priests have been calling on civil magistrates to exert their authority against the disciples of the Lord. Men in power have been breathing out threatenings: we may easily guess what will follow, imprisonment and slaughter. The storm has been gathering some time; it must break shortly.

Perhaps it may fall on me first.

Brethren therefore, whether in the ministry or not, I beseech you, "pray for me," that I may never suffer justly, as an evil-doer, but only for righteousness sake. O pray that I may not deny my Lord in any wise, but that I may joyfully follow him, both to prison and to death, if he is pleased to call me to seal his truths with my blood. Be not ashamed of Christ, or of his gospel, though I should become a prisoner of the Lord.

Though I am bound, the word of God will not be bound: no; an open, an effectual door is opened for preaching the everlasting gospel, and men or devils shall never be able to prevail against it. Only pray, that, whether it be in life or death, Christ may be glorified in me: then I shall rejoice, yea, and will rejoice.

And now, to whom shall I address myself next?

FIFTHLY, To those, who persecute their neighbors for living godly in Christ Jesus. But, what shall I say to you? Howl and weep for the miseries that shall come upon you; for a little while the Lord permits you to ride over the heads of his people; but, by and by, death will arrest you, judgment will find you, and Jesus Christ shall put a question to you, which will strike you dumb, WHY PERSECUTED YOU ME? You may plead your laws and your canons, and pretend what you do is out of zeal for God; but God shall discover the cursed hypocrisy and serpentine enmity of your hearts, and give you over to the tormentors. It is well, if in this life God does not send some mark upon you. He pleaded the cause of Naboth, when innocently condemned for blaspheming God and the king; and our Lord sent forth his armies, and destroyed the city of those who killed the prophets, and stoned them that were sent unto them. If you have a mind therefore to fill up the measure of your iniquities, go on, persecute and despise the disciples of the Lord: but know, "that for all these things, God shall bring you to judgment." Nay, those you now persecute, shall be in part your judges, and sit on the right-hand of the Majesty on high, whilst you are dragged by infernal spirits into a lake that burneth with fire and brimstone, and the smoke of your torment shall be ascending up for ever and ever. Lay down therefore, ye rebels, your arms against the most high God, and no longer persecute those who live godly in Christ Jesus. The Lord will plead, the Lord will avenge, their cause. You may be permitted to bruise their heels, yet in the end they shall bruise your accursed heads. I speak not this, as though I were afraid of you; for I know in whom I have believed: only out of pure love I warn you, and because I know not but Jesus Christ may make some of you vessels of mercy, and snatch you, even you persecutors, as fire-brands out of the fire. Jesus Christ came into the world to save sinners, even persecutors, the worst of sinners: his righteousness is sufficient for them; his Spirit is able to purify and change their hearts.

He once converted Saul: may the same God magnify his power, in converting all those who are causing the godly in Christ Jesus, as much as in them lies, to suffer persecution! The Lord be with you all. Amen.

Sermon 56 An Exhortation

An Exhortation to the People of God not to be discouraged in their Way, by the Scoffs and Contempt of wicked Men.

Hebrews 4:9, "There remaineth therefore a rest to the people of God."

When we consider the persecutions they are exposed to, who live righteously and godly in this present world; it is amazing to consider, that the people of this generation should be so fond of a name to live, while they are in effect dead. The people of God are to expect little else but troubles and trials while they are in this world; common experience is a contradiction to my text, that there is a rest to the people of God; but the author of the Hebrews, when speaking of this rest, did not mean that they should have a rest here. No; he too well knew that the people of God, all who would seek and serve the Lord Jesus, must be despised, hated, scoffed, slandered, and evil entreated; but the time was hastening when they should have a perfect rest: there is a rest laid up for them, and this is an encouragement for you, my brethren, to hold on, and hold out your way rejoicing; after death there will be a rest for ever; at judgment, you shall be taken up to dwell with the Lord Jesus Christ; and there, you shall be for ever exempted from sin; you shall rest from all manner of sorrow, and be no more troubled with the temptations of Satan. Now, you can set about nothing for the glory of God, or for your own soul's welfare, but the devil is dissuading you from it, or distracting you in it, or discouraging you after it. Here we are scoffed and derided; as the world hated the Lord Jesus Christ, so will it hate you: but be not discouraged, though we are here the scorn and offscouring of all things; and are as a gazing stock to men and angels. Though they put us out of their synagogues, cast out our name as evil, and look on us as persons unfit for their company; yet, in that rest which is prepared for you, my brethren, we shall then be gazed at for our glory, and they shut out of the assembly of the saints, and separated from us, whether they will or no; unless the Lord Jesus Christ, by his free, rich, and sovereign grace, brings them unto himself.

The letter-learned Scribes and Pharisees of this day, look on us as madmen and enthusiasts; but though they make so much noise about the world enthusiast, it means no more than this, one in God; and what Christian can say, he is not in God, and God in him? And if this is to be an enthusiast, God grant I may be more and more so; if we being in Christ, and Christ in us, makes us enthusiasts. I would to God we were all more and more enthusiasts. They now think it strange, that we run not with them into all excess of riot, and because we will not go to the devil's diversions with them, therefore they speak evil of us. We cannot now go along the street, but every one is pointing out his finger with scorn, and cries, Here comes another of his followers; what! You are become one of his disciples too!

But there is a rest which will be a complete deliverance for you. Let none of these things move you; for, though you are thus treated here, consider, you shall in heaven have no discouraging company, nor any but what will be an assistance to you; you will have no scoffer there, all will be ready to join with heart and voice in your everlasting joy and praises. You will not be counted enthusiasts, madmen, and rabble, in that rest which remaineth for the people of God. Therefore, possess your souls in patience; account it matter of joy when you fall into tribulation; God, in his own time, will deliver us; let not their hindering us from preaching in the church, be any discouragement; do not shrink, and draw back, because of opposition; be not ashamed of your work or master; but hold fast your integrity. You must expect to go through evil report, and good report; fear not the violence of unreasonable men; let them hate you, and cast you out for the Lord's sake, behold he shall appear to your joy, and they shall be ashamed: therefore hold on, and hold out to the end. Be steadfast and patient, and bear the troubles of the world; if you are the people of God, there is a rest provided for you, which you shall certainly obtain.

I shall not speak unto you, Pharisees, this morning, nor to any, except to you who have experienced the pangs of the new-birth, or are at present under them, and who know what it is to love the Lord Jesus in sincerity and truth: do not be discouraged, or think hard of the ways of God, my dear brethren, because you are not loved by the men of this world; if you were of the world it would love you; it would then be pleased with your company; it would not thrust you from a tavern, or an alehouse; it would not dislike you for singing the songs of the drunkard, or for going to plays, balls, or other polite and fashionable entertainments, as they are called; no, these the children of the world like; but if you will sing hymns and psalms, and go to hear what God hath to say unto your souls, and spend your time in reading, praying, and frequenting religious assemblies, then it is that they dislike you, and thrust you out of their company, as unworthy thereof; but let none of these things move you, for the rest which Jesus Christ hath prepared for you, is an ample recompense for all you may meet with here.

This rest is the fruit of the blood of the Lord Jesus Christ: O how will it fill our souls with love, to think that through the streams of this blood, we have overcome the violence of the world, and the snares of the devil. My dear brethren, be not discouraged at the treatment you meet with here, but let it be a means to stir you up to advance in the love of the Lord Jesus Christ, who hath prepared a rest for you. Can you consider, what Christ has done and suffered for you, and have your hearts stupefied with vile and senseless pleasures? Can you hear of a panting, bleeding, dying Jesus, and yet be dull and unaffected? Was there any sorrow like unto his sorrow? And all this, he underwent to save you, who were vile, and polluted, and by nature, since the fall, a motley mixture of the beast and devil. Jesus Christ, by dying upon the cross, intended to take away the devil and beast from your heart, and to prepare it for himself to dwell in.

Think of the love of this your Jesus, and then, will a little reproach and scorn move you? Sure it will not. I hope better things of you, and things that accompany salvation.

O think with what pleasing astonishment you will see the Lord Jesus Christ, when he comes to take you to his rest: now his heart is open to us; but our hearts are shut against him; then, then, his heart shall be open, and ours shall be so too. O my brethren, how will your love be increased?

With what raptures will you see the Lord Jesus Christ? Therefore, undergo a few reproaches here patiently, and revile not again. Let them say what they please of me, the reproaches, scorns, and contempt of this world, will no ways hurt me, but will recoil upon their own heads; leave it to the Lord, who knows what is best for you and me: do not question his love; he will be with you; only do you, who have tasted the Lord to be gracious, follow hard after him.

And now, let me speak a word unto you, who have not yet experienced the love of Christ to your souls, but are waiting for his appearance. I shall be but very short, because I would not break in upon the duties of the day.

I shall speak unto you a word of invitation; even, to wait still on the Lord; do not forsake him, though he may not answer your petitions at once or twice seeking unto him; hold on, do not leave seeking him, and you shall have an answer of peace; remember the poor man who was lame, and had lain at the pool of Bethesda thirty-eight years for relief, yet at last he found that it was worth waiting for, he obtained his desire.

And if you are but zealous for the Lord, and seek unto Jesus, if your zeal be according to godliness, and you pray unto him for his Spirit, you shall certainly have an answer of peace; you shall find it is good to seek unto the Lord, you will be adopted into his family, and by his spirit be enabled to cry, "Abba, Father." O then do not leave, but be continually waiting at wisdom's gate, and you shall find all her ways to be ways of pleasantness, and all her paths are peace; then, you shall find that it is worth waiting on the Lord Jesus; and when you have got his Spirit within you, all the power of men or devils cannot make you forsake the ways of the Lord Jesus Christ.

If you do but once taste of his pardoning love, it will be so delightful unto you, that you will cry for more and more thereof; you will be as full as you can hold, and still not be satisfied; you will desire more and more of this love of Jesus, you will hunger and thirst, and hunger and thirst again, and never be satisfied till you come to that rest which is prepared for the people of God, where all hungering and thirsting will cease, and will be turned into songs and hallelujahs, and that for ever and ever.

As many of you as design to partake of the emblems of the body and blood of our dying Lord, examine well yourselves, lest by eating and drinking unworthily, you eat and drink damnation unto yourselves: remember the dying love of your dying Lord, and eat and drink in commemoration thereof; do not let the world keep you from partaking hereof; and when you have eaten and drank, do not go away and run into the world; let the world see that you have been with Jesus; give them no room to speak unseemly, they do that enough without occasion; but how would they rejoice if they had just reason.

Look well then unto your paths, that you do not slip; remember that all your faults are magnified, and that all your little slips are laid upon me; therefore, look well unto your ways, your words, your actions, that they may silence gainsayers; let them see that we have the presence of God with us, and that there has been good done by field preaching.

Let me exhort you once more to consider the love of the Lord Jesus Christ. O do not forget this love. Consider, I beseech you, how great it has been unto you, and do not slight this his grace, the riches, the love, the kindness of your dear Redeemer, the Lord Jesus Christ, who hath prepared this eternal rest for you; he also laid down his life for your sakes: what great love was here! that while you were enemies to the Lord of glory, he died for you, to redeem you from sin, from hell and wrath, that you might live and reign with him, world without end.

The Lamb that died, and was buried, is now risen and exalted, and sits on the right-hand of God the Father; and when he shall come to judge all the world, then, my brethren, it will be seen whether we have deserved the usage the world has given us; then it will be known who are the true followers of the Lord Jesus, and who are madmen and fools; but, may it be determined in this world, that we and our present enemies may enter into that rest which God hath prepared for those that love him.

Which God of his infinite mercy grant!

My brethren, let not these few words of exhortation be forgotten, but lay them up in your hearts, and remember they must be called over another day. I should have enlarged, but the duties of the day obliged me to forbear.

Now, to God the Father, Son, and Holy Ghost, be all power, etc.

Sermon 57 Georgia Sermon

(Preached before the Governor, and Council, and the House of Assembly, in Georgia, on January 28, 1770.)

Zech. 4:10, "For who hath despised the Day of small things?"

Men, brethren, and fathers, at sundry times and in diverse manners, God spake to the fathers by the prophets, before he spoke to us in these last days by his Son. And as God is a sovereign agent, and his sacred Spirit bloweth when and where it listeth, surely he may reveal and make known his will to his creatures, when, where, and how he pleaseth; "and who shall say unto him, what doest thou?" Indeed, this seems to be one reason, to display his sovereignty, why he chose, before the canon of scripture was settled, to make known his mind in such various methods, and to such a variety of his servants and messengers.

Hence it is, that we hear, he talked with Abraham as "a man talketh with a friend." To Moses he spoke "face to face." To others by "dreams in the night," or by "visions" impressed strongly on their imaginations. This seems to be frequently the happy lot of the favorite evangelical prophet Zechariah, I call him evangelical prophet, because his predictions, however they pointed at some approaching or immediate event, ultimately terminated in Him, who is the Alpha and Omega, the beginning and the end of all the lively oracles of God. The chapter from which our text is selected, among many other passages, is a striking proof of this: An angel, that had been more than once sent to him on former occasions, appears again to him, and by way of vision, and "waked him, (to use his own words) as a man that is wakened out of his sleep." Prophets, and the greatest servants of God, need waking sometimes out of their drowsy frames.

Methinks I see this man of God starting out of his sleep, and being all attention: the angle asked him, "what seest thou?" He answers, "I have looked, and behold, a candle-stick all of gold," an emblem of the church of

God, "with a bowl upon the top of it, and seven lamps thereon, and seven pipes to the seven lamps, which were upon the top thereof;" implying, that the church, however reduced to the lowest ebb, should be preserved, be kept supplied, and shining, through the invisible, but not less real, because invisible aids and operations of the blessed Spirit of God. The occasion of such an extraordinary vision, if we compare this passage with the second chapter of the Prophecy of the prophet Haggai, seems to be this: It was now near eighteen years since the Jewish people had been delivered from their long and grievous Babylonian captivity; and being so lone deprived of their temple and its worship, which fabric had been rased even to the ground, one would have imagined, that immediately upon their return, they should have postponed all private works, and with their united strength have first set about rebuilding that once stately and magnificent structure. But they, like too many Christians of a like luke-warm stamp, though all acknowledged that this church-work was a necessary work, yet put themselves and others off, with this godly pretense, "The time is not come, the time that the Lord's house should be built." The time is not come! What, not in eighteen years! For so long had they now been returned from their state of bondage: and pray, why was not the time come? The prophet Haggai tells them; their whole time was so taken up building for an habitation for their great and glorious Benefactor, the mighty God of Jacob.

This ingratitude must not be passed by unpunished. Omniscience observes, Omnipotence resents it! And that they might read their sin in their punishment, as they thought it best to get rich, and secure houses and lands and estates for themselves, before they set about unnecessary church-work, the prophet tells them, "You have sown much, but bring in little: ye eat, but ye have not enough: ye drink, but ye are not filled with drink: ye clothe you, but there is none warm: and he that earneth wages, earneth wages to put it into a bag with holes." Still he goes on thundering and lightening, "Ye looked for much, and lo it came to little: wand when ye brought it home, (pleasing yourselves with your fine crops) I did blow upon it: why? Saith the Lord of Hosts; because of mine house that is waste, and ye run every man unto his own house." A thundering sermon this! delivered not only to the common people, but also unto, and in the presence of "Zerubbabel, the son of Shealtiel, and Joshua, the son of Josedech the high-priest. The prophet's report is believed; and the arm of the Lord was revealed. Zerubbabel, the son of Shealtiel, and Joshua, the son of Josedech (O happy times when church and state are thus combined) with all the remnant of the people, obeyed the voice of the Lord their God, and the words of Haggai the prophets." The spirit of Zerubbabel, and of Joshua, and the spirits of all the remnant of the people were stirred up, and they immediately came, disregarding, as it were, their own private buildings, "and did work in the house of the Lord of Hosts their God." For a while, they proceeded with vigor; the foundation of the house is laid, and the superstructure raised to some considerable height: but whether this fit of hot zeal soon cooled, as is too common, or the people were discouraged by the false representations of their enemies, which perhaps met with too favorable a reception as the court of Darius; it so happened, that the hearts of the magistrates and ministers of the people waxed faint; and an awful chasm intervened, between the finishing and laying the foundation of this promising and glorious work.

Upon this, another prophet, even Zechariah, (who with Haggai had been joint sufferer in the captivity) is sent to lift up the hands that hang down, to strengthen the feeble knees, and by the foregoing instructive vision, to re-animate Joshua and the people in general, and the heart of Zerubbabel, the son of Shealtiel, in particular, maugre all discouragements, either from inveterate enemies, or from timid unstable friends, or all other obstacles whatsoever. If Haggai thunders, Zechariah's message is as lightening. "This is the word of the Lord unto Zerubbabel, saying, Not by might, not by power, (not by barely human power or policy) but by my spirit, saith the Lord of Hosts: Who art thou, O great mountain?

(thou Sanballat and thy associates, who have been so long crying out, what mean these feeble Jews? However great, formidable, and seemingly insurmountable) before Zerubbabel thou shalt (not only be lowered and rendered more accessible, but) become a plain;" thy very opposition shall, in the end, promote the work, and help to expedite that very building, which thou intendest to put a stop to, and destroy.

And lest Zerubbabel, through unbelief and outward opposition, or for want of more bodily strength, should think this would be a work of time, and that he should not live to see it completed in his days, "The word of the Lord came to Zechariah, saying, The hands of Zerubbabel have laid the foundation of this house; his hands also shall finish it, and he shall bring forth the headstone thereof with shoutings, crying, Grace, grace unto it." Grace! Grace! Unto it: a double acclamation, to show, that out of the abundance of their hearts, their mouth spake; and this with shoutings and crying from all quarters. Even their enemies should see the hand and providence of God in the beginning, continuance, and ending of this seemingly improbable and impracticable work; so that they should be constrained to cry, "Grace unto it," and wish both the work and the builders much prosperity: But as for its friends, they should be so transported with heart-felt joy in the reflection upon the signal providences which had attended them through the whole process, that they would shout and cry, "Grace, grace unto it:" or, This is nothing but the Lord's doing; God prosper and bless this work more and more, and make it a place where his free grace and glory may be abundantly displayed. Then by a beautiful and pungent sarcasm, turning to the insulting enemies, he utters the spirited interrogation in my text, "Who hath despised the day of small things?" Who are you, that vauntingly said, what can these feeble Jews do, pretending to lay the foundation of a house which they never will have money, or strength, or power to finish? Or, who are you, O timorous, short-sighted, doubting, though well-meaning people, who, through unbelief, were discouraged at the small beginnings and feebleness of the attempt to build a second temple? And, because you thought it could not come up to the magnificence of the first, therefore were discouraged from so much as beginning to build a second at all?

A close instructive question this; a question, implying, that whenever God intends to bring about any great thing, he generally begins with a day of small things.

As a proof of this, I will not lead you so far back, as to the beginning of time, when the Everlasting "I AM" spoke all things into existence, by his almighty fiat; and out of a confused chaos, "without form and void," produced a world worthy of a God to create, and of his favorite creature man, his vicegerent and representative here below, to inhabit, and enjoy in it both himself and his God. And yet, though the heavens declare his glory, and the firmament showeth his handy work, though there is o speech nor language where their voice is not heard, and their line is gone out through all the earth: and by a dumb, yet persuasive language, proves the hand that made them to be divine; yet there have been, and are now, such fools in the world, as to "say in their hearts, There is no God;" or so wise, as by their wisdom, not to know God, or own his divine image to be stamped on that book, wherein these grand things are recorded, and that in such legible characters, that he who runs may read.

Neither will I divert your attention, honored fathers, to the histories of Greece and Rome, or any of the great kingdoms and renowned monarchies, which constitute so great a part of ancient history; but whose beginnings were very small, (witness Romulus's ditch) their progress as remarkably great, and their declension and downfall, when arrived at their appointed zenith, as sudden, unexpected, and marvelous. These make the chief subjects of the learning of our schools; though they make but a mean figure in sacred history, and would not perhaps have been mentioned at all, had they not been, in some measure, connected with the history of God's people, which is the grand subject of that much despised book, emphatically called, The Scriptures. Whoever hath a mind to inform himself of the one, may read Rollin's Ancient History, and whoever would see the connection with the other, may consult the learned Prideaux's admirable and judicious connection. Books which, I hope, will be strenuously recommended, and carefully studied, when this present infant institution gathers more strength, and grows up into a seat of learning. I can hardly forbear mentioning the final beginnings of Great Britain, now so distinguished for liberty, opulence and renown; and the rise and rapid progress of the American colonies, which promises to be one of the most opulent and powerful empires in the world. But my present views, and the honors done this infant institution this day, and the words of my text, as well as the feelings of my own heart, and I trust, of the hearts of all that hear me, lead me to confine your meditations to the history of God's own peculiar people, which for the simplicity and sublimity of its language, the veracity of its author, and the importance and wonders of the facts therein recorded, if weighed in a proper balance, hath not its equal under the sun.

And yet, though God himself hath become an author among us, we will not condescend to give his book one thorough reading. Be astonished, O heavens, at this!

Who would have thought that from once, even from Abraham, and from so small a beginning, as the emigration of a single private family, called out of a land wholly given to idolatry, to be sojourners and pilgrims in a strange land; who would have thought, that from a man, who for a long season was written childless, a man whose first possession in this strange land, was by purchasing a burying place for his wife, and in whose grave one might have imagined he would have buried all future expectations; who would have thought, that from this very man and woman, according to the course of nature, both as good as dead, should descend a numerous offspring like unto the stars of heaven for multitude, and as the sand which is upon the sea shore innumerable? Nay, who would have imagined, that against all probability, and in all human appearance impossible, a kingdom should arise? Behold a poor captive stave, even Joseph, who was cruelly separated from his brethren, became second in Pharaoh's kingdom: he was sent before to work out a great deliverance, and to introduce a family which should take root, deep root downwards and bear fruit upwards, and fill the land.

How could it enter into the heart of man to conceive, that when oppressed by a king, who knew not Joseph, though they were the best, most loyal, industrious subjects this king had, when an edict was issued forth as impolitic as cruel, (since the safety and glory of all kingdoms chiefly consist in the number of its inhabitants) that an outcast, helpless infant should be taken, and bred up in all the learning of the Egyptians, and in that very court from which, and by that very tyrant from whom the edict came, and that the deliverer should be nurtured to be king in Jeshurun?

But time as well as strength would fail me, was I to give you a detail of all the important particulars respecting God's peculiar people; as their miraculous support in the wilderness, the events which took place while they were under a divine theocracy, and during their settlement in Canaan to the time of their return from Babylon, and from thence to the destruction of their second temple, etc. by the Romans. Indeed, considering to whom I am speaking, persons conversant in the sacred and profane history, I have mentioned these things only to stir up your minds by way of remembrance.

But if we descend from the Jewish, to the Christian era, we shall find, that its commencement was, in the eyes of the world, a "day of small things" indeed. Our blessed Lord compares the beginning of its progress in the world, to a grain of mustard-seed, which though the smallest of all seeds when sown, soon becomes a great tree, and so spread, that the "birds of the air," or a multitude of every nation, language and tongue, came and lodged in its branches: and its inward progress in the believers heart, Christ likens to a little leaven which a woman hid in three measures of meal. How both the Jewish and Christian dispensations have been, and even to this day are despised, by the wise disputers of this world, on this very account, is manifest to all who read the lively oracles with a becoming attention. What ridicule, obloquy, and inveterate opposition Christianity meets with, in this our day, not only from the open deist, but from formal professors, is too evident to every truly pious soul.

And what opposition the kingdom of grace meets with in the heart, is well known by all those who are experimentally acquainted with their hearts: they know, to their sorrow, what the great apostle of the Gentiles means, by "the Spirit striving against the flesh, and the flesh against the Spirit." But the sacred Oracles, and the histories of all ages acquaint us, that God brings about the greatest thing, not only by small and unlikely means, but by ways and means directly opposite to the carnal reasonings of unthinking men: he chooses things that be not, to bring to nought those which are. How did Christianity spread and flourish, by one, who was despised and rejected of men, a man of sorrows, and acquainted with grief, and who expired on a cross? He was despised and rejected, not merely by the vulgar and illiterate, but the Rabbis and Masters of Israel, the Scribes and Pharisees, who by the Jewish churchmen were held too in so high a reputation for their outward sanctity, that it became a common proverb, "if only two went to heaven, the one would be a Scribe, and the other a Pharisee." Yet there were they who endeavored to silence the voice of all his miracles and heavenly doctrine with, "Is not this the Carpenter's son?" Nay, "He is mad, why hear you him? he hath a devil, and casteth out devils by Beelzebub the prince of the devils." And their despite not only followed him to, but after death, and when in the grave. "We remember (said they) that this deceiver said, after three days I will rise again; command therefore that the sepulcher be made sure;" but, maugre all your impotent precautions, in sealing the stone, and setting a watch, he burst the bars of death asunder, and, according to his repeated predictions, proved himself to be the Son of God with power, by rising the third day from the dead. And afterwards, in pretense of great multitudes, was he received up into glory; as a proof thereof, he sent down the Holy Ghost, (on the mission of whom he pawned all his credit with his disciples) in such an instantaneous, amazing manner, as one would imagine, should have forced and compelled all who saw it to own, that this was indeed the finger of God.

And yet how was this grand transaction treated? With the utmost contempt: when instantaneously the apostles commenced orators and linguists, and with a divine profusion spoke of the wonderful things of God; "these men (said some) are full of new wine." And yet by these men, mean fishermen, illiterate men, idiots, in the opinion of the Scribes and Pharisees, and notwithstanding all the opposition of earth and hell, and that too only by the foolishness of preaching, did this grain of mustard- seed grow up, till thousands, ten thousands of thousands, a multitude which no man can number, out of every nation, language and people, came and lodged under the branches of it.

Neither shall it rest here; whatever dark parenthesis may intervene, we are assured, that being still watered by the same divine hand, it shall take deeper and deeper root downward, and bear more and more fruit upward, till the whole earth be filled with the knowledge of the Lord, as the waters cover the sea. Who shall live when God doth this? Hasten O Lord that blessed time! O let this thy kingdom come! Come, not only by the external preaching of the gospel in the world, but by its renovating, heart- renewing, soul-transforming power, to awakened sinners! For want of this, alas! alas! though we understood all mysteries, could speak with the tongues of men and angels, we should be only like sounding brass, or so many tinkling cymbals.

And yet, what a "day of small things" is the first implantation of the seed of divine life in the soul of man? Well might our Lord, who alone is the author and finisher of our faith, compare it to a little leaven, which a woman took, and hid in three measures of meal, till the whole was leavened. Low similes, mean comparisons these, in the eyes of those, who having eyes, see not; who having ears, hear not; whose heart, being waxed gross, cannot, will not understand! To such, it is despicable, mysterious, and unintelligible in its description; and, if possible, infinitely more so, when made effectual by the power of God, to the salvation of any individual soul. For the wisdom of God will always be foolishness to natural men. As it was formerly, so it is now; they who are born after the flesh, will persecute those that are born after the spirit: the disciple must be as his master: they that will live godly in him; they that live most godly in him, must, shall suffer persecution. This is so interwoven in the very nature and existence of the gospel, that our Lord makes it one part of the beatitudes, in that blessed sermon which he preached, when, to use the words of my old familiar friend the seraphic Hervey, a mount was his pulpit, and the heavens his sounding board. A part, which, like others of the same nature, I believe, will be little relished by such who are always clamoring against those few highly favored souls, who dare stand up and preach the doctrine of JUSTIFICATION BY FAITH ALONE in the imputed righteousness of Jesus Christ, and are reproached with not preaching, like their master, Morality, as they term it, in his glorious sermon on the mount; for did we more preach, and more live it, we should soon find all manner of evil would be spoken against us for Christ's sake.

But shall this hinder the progress, the growth, and consummation? And shall the Christian therefore be dismayed and discouraged? God forbid! On the contrary, the weakest believer may, and ought, to rejoice and be exceeding glad. And why? For a very good reason; because, he that hath begun the good work, hath engaged also to finish it; though Christ found him as black as hell, he shall present him, and every individual purchased with his blood, without spot or wrinkle, or any such-thing, before the Divine Presence. O glorious prospect! How will the saints triumph, and the sons of God then shout for joy? If they shouted when God said, "Let there by light, and there was light;" and if there is joy in heaven over one sinner only that repenteth, how will the heavenly arches echo and rebound with praise, when all the redeemed of the Lord shall appear together, and the Son of God shall say, "of all these that thou hast given to me, have I lost nothing." On the contrary, what weeping, wailing, and gnashing of teeth will there be, not only amongst the devil and his angels, but amongst the fearful and unbelieving, when they see that all the hellish temptations and devices, instead of destroying, were over-ruled to the furtherance of the gospel in general, and to the increase and growth of grace in every individual believer in particular. And how will despisers then behold and wonder and perish, when they shall be obliged to say, "we fools counted their lives madness, and their end to be without honor; but how are they numbered among the children of God, and how happy is their lot among the saints!" But whither am I going? Pardon me, my dear hearers, if you think this to be a digression from my main point. It is true, whilst I am musing, the fire begins to kindle: I am flying, but not so high, I trust, as to lose sight of my main subject. And yet, after meditating and talking of the rise and progress of the gospel of the kingdom, I shall find it somewhat difficult to descend so low, as to entertain you with the small beginnings of this infant colony, and of the Orphan-house, in which I am now preaching. But I should judge myself inexcusable on this occasion, if I did not detain you a little longer, in taking a transient view of the traces of divine Providence, in the rise and progress of the colony in general, and the institution of this Orphan-house in particular. Children yet unborn, I trust, will have occasion to bless God for both.

The very design of this settlement, as charity inclines us to hope all things, was, that it might be an Asylum, and a place of business, for as many as were in distress; for foreigners, as well as natives; for Jews and Gentiles.

On February 1, a day, the memory of which, I think, should still be perpetuated, the first embarkation was made with forty-five English families; men, who had once lived well in their native country, and who, with many persecuted Saltzburghers, headed by a good old soldier of Jesus lately deceased, the Rev. Mr. Boltzius, came to find a refuge here. They came, they saw, they labored, and endeavored to settle; but by an essential, though well-meant defect, in the very beginning of the settlement, too well known by some now present, and too long, and too much felt to bear repeating, prohibiting the importation and use of Negroes, etc.

Their numbers gradually diminished, and matters were brought to so low an ebb, that the whole colony became a proverb of reproach.

About this time, in the year 1737, being previously stirred up thereto by a strong impulse, which I could by no means resist, I came here, after the example of my worthy and reverend friends, Messieurs John and Charles Wesley, and Mr. Ingham, who, with the most disinterested views, had come hither to serve the colony, by endeavoring to convert the Indians. I came rejoicing to serve the colony also, and to become your willing servant for Christ's sake. My friend and father, good Bishop Bensen, encouraged me, though my brethren and kinsmen after the flesh, as well as religious friends, opposed it. I came, and I saw (you will not be offended with me to speak the truth) the nakedness of the land. Gladly did I distribute about the four hundred pounds sterling, which I had collected in England, among my poor parishioners. The necessity and propriety of erecting an Orphan- house, was mentioned and recommended before my first embarkation. But thinking it a matter of too great importance to be set about unwarily, I deferred the farther prosecution for this laudable design till my return to England in the year 1738, for to have priests orders.

Miserable was the condition of many grown persons, as well as children, whom I left behind. Their cause I endeavored to plead, immediately upon my arrival; but being denied the churches, in which I had the year before collected many hundreds for the London charity-schools, I endeavored to plead their cause in the fields. The people threw in their mites most willingly; once or twice, I think, twenty-two pounds were collected in copper; the alms were accompanied with many prayers, and which, as I told them, laid, I am persuaded, a blessed foundation to the future charitable superstructure. In a short time, though plucked as it were out of the fire, the collections and charitable contributions amounted to more than a one thousand pounds sterling.

With that I reimbarked, taking Philadelphia in my way, and upon my second arrival, found the spot fixed upon; but, alas! who can describe the low estate to which it was reduced! The whole country almost was left desolate, and the metropolis Savannah, was but like a cottage in a vineyard, or as a lodge in a garden of cucumbers. Many orphans, whose parents had been taken from them by the distresses that naturally attend new settlements, were dispersed here and there in a very forlorn helpless condition; my bowels yearned towards them, and, animated by the example of the great professor Franck, previous to bringing them here, I hired a house, furnished an infirmary, employed all that were capable of employment, and in a few weeks walked to the house of God with a large family of above sixty orphans, and others in as bad a condition.

On March 25, 1740, in full assurance of faith, I laid the foundation of this house; and in the year following, brought in my orphan family, who, with the workmen, now made up the number of one hundred and fifty: by the money which was expended on these, the remaining few were kept in the colony, and were enabled to pay the debts they owed; so that in a representation made to the House of Commons, by some, who for very good reasons wanted the constitution of the colony altered; they declared, that the very existence of the colony was in a great measure, if not totally, owing to the building and supporting of the Orphan House.

Finding the care of such a family, incompatible with the care due to a parish, upon giving previous warning to the then trustees, I gave up the living of Savannah, which without fee or reward I had voluntarily taken upon me: I then ranged through the northern colonies, and afterwards once more returned home. What calumny, what loads of reproach, I for many years was called to undergo, in thus turning beggars for a family, few here present need to be informed; a family, utterly unconnected by any ties of nature; a family, not only to be maintained with food, but clothed and educated also, and that too in the dearest part of his Majesty's dominions, on a pine barren, and in a colony where the use of Negroes was totally denied; this appeared so very improbable, that all beholders looked daily for its decline and annihilation.

But, blessed be God, the building advanced and flourished, and the wished-for period is now come, after having supported the family for thirty-two years, by a change of constitution and the smiles of government, with liberal donations from the northern, and especially the adjacent provinces, the same hands that laid the foundation, are now called to finish it, by making an addition of a seat of learning, the whole products and profits of which, are to go towards the increase of the fund, as at the beginning, for destitute orphans, or such youths as may be called of God to the sacred ministry of his Gospel. I need not call on any here, to cry, "Grace, grace, unto it." For on the utmost scrutiny of the intention of those employed, and considering the various exercises they have been called to undergo, and the opposition the building hath every where met with, we may justly say, "not by might, nor by power, but by thy Spirit, O Lord," hath this work been carried on thus far; it is his doing, let it be marvelous in our eyes. With humble gratitude, therefore, would we now set up our Ebenezer, and say, "Hitherto thou, Lord, hast helped us;" and wherefore should we doubt, but that he, who hath thus far helped, will continue to help, when the weary heads of the first founders and present helpers, are laid in the silent grave.

I am very well aware, what an invidious task it must be to a person in my circumstances, thus to speak on an affair in which he hath been so much concerned. Some may perhaps think, I am become a fool in thus glorying. But as I am now, blessed be God, in the decline of life, and as, in all probability, I shall never be present to celebrate another anniversary, I thought it best to be a little more explicit, that if I have spoken any thing but truth, I may be confronted; and if not, that future ages, and future successors, may see with what a purity of intention, and what various interpositions of Providence, the work was begun, and hath been carried on to its present height.

It was the reading of a like account, written by the late Professor Franck, that encouraged me: who knows but hereafter, the reading something of a similar nature, may encourage others to begin and carry on a like work elsewhere? I have said its present height, for I would humbly hope, that this is, comparatively speaking, only a "day of small things," only the dawn of brighter scenes. Private genius's and individuals, as well as collective bodies, have, like the human body, the nonage, puerile, juvenile estate, before they arrive at their zenith, and their lives as gradually they decline. But yet I would hope, that both the province and Bethesda, are but in their puerile or juvenile state. And long, long may they increase, and make large strides, till they arrive at a glorious zenith! I mean not merely in trade, merchandise, and opulence, (though I would be far from secluding them from the province, and would be thankful for the advances it hath already made) but a zenith of glorious gospel blessings, without which, all outward emoluments are less than nothing, or as the small dust of the balance: "For what shall it profit a man, if he shall gain the whole world and lost his own soul." Who can imagine, that the prophet Zechariah would be sent to strengthen the hands of Zerubbabel, in building and laying the foundation of the temple, if that temple was not to be frequented with worshippers that worshiped the Father in spirit and truth. The most gaudy fabrics, stately temples, new moon Sabbaths, and solemn assemblies, are only solemn mockeries God cannot away with. This God hath shown by the destruction of both the first and second temples. What is become of the seven churches of Asia? How are all their golden candlesticks overthrown? "God is a Spirit, and they who worship him must worship him in spirit and truth." And no longer do I expect that this house will flourish, than when the power of religion is encouraged and promoted, and the persons educated here, prosecute their studies, not only to be great scholars, but good saints.

Blessed be God! I can say with Professor Franck, that it is in a great measure owing to the disinterested spirit of my first fellow-helpers, as well as those who are now employed, that the building hath reached to its present height. This I am bound to speak, not only in honor to those who are now with God, but those at present before me. Nor dare I conclude, without offering to Your Excellency, our pepper corn of acknowledgment for the countenance you have always shown Bethesda's institution, and the honor you did us last year, inlaying the first brick of yonder wings: in thus doing, you have honored Bethesda's God. May he long delight to honor you here on earth! And after a life spent to his glory, and your country's good, may he honor you to all eternity, in placing you as Christ's right-hand in the kingdom above!

Next to your Excellency, my dear Mr. President, I must beg your acceptance both of thanks and congratulation on the annual return of this festival. For you was not only my dear familiar friend, and first fellow- traveler in this infant province; but you was directed by Providence to this spot, laid the second brick of this house, watched, prayed, and wrought for the family's good: A witness of innumerable trials, partner of my joys and griefs; you will have now the pleasure of seeing the Orphan- house a fruitful bough, its branches running over the wall. For this, no doubt, God hath smiled upon and blessed you, in a manner we could not expect, much less design; and may he continue to bless you with all spiritual blessings in heavenly places in Christ Jesus. Look to the rock from whence you have been hewn, and may your children never be ashamed, that their father left his native country, and married a real Christian, born again under this roof. May Bethesda's Good grant this may be the happy portion of your children, and children's children!

Gentlemen of his Majesty's council, Mr. Speaker, and you members of the General Assembly, many thanks are owing to you, for your late address to his Excellency in favor of Bethesda. etc

Your joint recommendation of it, when I was last here, which, though in some measure through the bigotry of some, for the present is rendered abortive, by their wanting to have it confined to a party, yet I trust the event will prove that every thing shall be over-ruled to the furtherance of the work. Here I repeat, what I have often declared, that as far as lies in my power before and after my decease, Bethesda shall be always on a broad bottom. All denominations have freely given; all denominations, all the continent, God being my helper, shall receive benefit from it. May Bethesda's God bless you all! In your private as well as public capacity; and as you are honored to be the representatives of a now flourishing increasing people: may you be directed in all your ways! May truth, justice, religion, and piety be established amongst you through all generations!

LASTLY, My reverend brethren, and you inhabitants of the colony, accept unfeigned thanks for the honor done me, in letting us see you at Bethesda this day. You, Sir, for the sermon preached here last year. Tell it in Germany, tell my great, good friend, Professor Franck, that Bethesda's God, is a God whose mercy endureth for ever. O let us have your earnest prayers! Encourage your people not to "despise the day of small things." What hath God wrought? From its infancy, this colony hath been blessed with many faithful gospel ministers: O that this may be a nursery to many more! This hath been the case of the New England College for almost a century, and why not the Orphan-house Academy at Georgia?

Men, brethren, fathers, as many of you, whether inhabitants or strangers, who have honored this day with your presence, give us the additional blessings of your prayers. And O that Bethesda's God may make this day, though but a day of small things, productive of great things to the souls of all amongst whom I have been now preaching the kingdom of God.

A great and good day will it be indeed, if Jesus Christ, our great Zerubbabel, should, by the power of the eternal Spirit, bless any thing that hath now been said, to cause every mountain of difficulty, that lies in the way of your conversion, to become a plain. And what art thou, O great mountain, whether the lust of the flesh, the lust of the eye, or the pride of life, sin, or self-righteousness? Before our Bethesda's God, thou shalt become a plain.

Brethren, my heart is enlarged towards you: it is written, blessed be God that it is written, "In the name of Jesus every knee shall bow, whether things in heaven, or things in earth, or things under the earth." O that we may be made a willing people in the day of his power! Look, look unto him, all ye that are placed in these ends of the earth. This house hath often been an house of God, a gate of heaven, to some of your fathers. May it be a house of God, a gate of heaven, to the children also! Come unto him, all ye that are weary and heavy laden, he will give you rest; rest from the guilt, rest from the power, rest from the punishment of sin; rest from the fear of divine judgments here, rest with himself eternally hereafter. Fear not, though the beginnings are but small, Christ will not despise the day of small things. A bruised reed will he not break, and the smoking flax will he not quench, until he bring forth judgment unto victory. His hands that laid the foundation, also shall finish it: yet a little while and the top-stone shall be brought forth with shouting, and men and angels join in crying "Grace! Grace! Unto it." That all present may be in this happy number, may God of his infinite mercy grant, through Jesus our Lord.

653

Sermon 58 The Method of Grace

Jeremiah 6:14, "They have healed also the hurt of the daughter of my people slightly, saying, Peace, peace, when there is no peace.

As God can send a nation or people no greater blessing than to give them faithful, sincere, and upright ministers, so the greatest curse that God can possibly send upon a people in this world, is to give them over to blind, unregenerate, carnal, lukewarm, and unskilled guides. And yet, in all ages, we find that there have been many wolves in sheep's clothing, many that daubed with untempered mortar, that prophesied smoother things than God did allow. As it was formerly, so it is now; there are many that corrupt the Word of God and deal deceitfully with it. It was so in a special manner in the prophet Jeremiah's time; and he, faithful to his Lord, faithful to that God who employed him, did not fail from time to time to open his mouth against them, and to bear a noble testimony to the honor of that God in whose name he from time to time spake. If you will read this prophecy, you will find that none spake more against such ministers than Jeremiah, and here especially in the chapter out of which the text is taken, he speaks very severely against them _ he charges them with several crimes; particularly, he charges them with covetousness: `For,' says he in the 13th verse, `from the least of them even to the greatest of them, every one is given to covetousness; and from the prophet even unto the priest, every one dealeth false.' And then, in the words of the text, in a more special manner, he exemplifies how they had dealt falsely, how they had behaved treacherously to poor souls: says he, `They have healed also the hurt of the daughter of my people slightly, saying, Peace, peace, when there is no peace.' The prophet, in the name of God, had been denouncing war against the people, he had been telling them that their house should be left desolate, and that the Lord would certainly visit the land with war.

`Therefore,' says he, in the 11th verse, `I am full of the fury of the Lord; I am weary with holding in; I will pour it out upon the children abroad, and upon the assembly of young men together; for even the husband with the wife shall be taken, the aged with him that is full of days. And their houses shall be turned unto others, with their fields and wives together; for I will stretch out my hand upon the inhabitants of the land, saith the Lord.' The prophet gives a thundering message, that they might be terrified and have some convictions and inclinations to repent; but it seems that the false prophets, the false priests, went about stifling people's convictions, and when they were hurt or a little terrified, they were for daubing over the wound, telling them that Jeremiah was but an enthusiastic preacher, that there could be no such thing as war among them, and saying to people, Peace, peace, be still, when the prophet told them there was no peace. The words, then, refer primarily unto outward things, but I verily believe have also a further reference to the soul, and are to be referred to those false teachers, who, when people were under conviction of sin, when people were beginning to look towards heaven, were for stifling their convictions and telling them they were good enough before.

And, indeed, people generally love to have it so; our hearts are exceedingly deceitful, and desperately wicked; none but the eternal God knows how treacherous they are. How many of us cry, Peace, peace, to our souls, when there is no peace! How many are there who are now settled upon their lees, that now think they are Christians, that now flatter themselves that they have an interest in Jesus Christ; whereas if we come to examine their experiences, we shall find that their peace is but a peace of the devil's making _ it is not a peace of God's giving _ it is not a peace that passeth human understanding. It is matter, therefore, of great importance, my dear hearers, to know whether we may speak peace to our hearts. We are all desirous of peace; peace is an unspeakable blessing; how can we live without peace? And, therefore, people from time to time must be taught how far they must go, and what must be wrought in them, before they can speak peace to their hearts. This is what I design at present, that I may deliver my soul, that I may be free from the blood of those to whom I preach _ that I may not fail to declare the whole counsel of God. I shall, from the words of the text, endeavor to show you what you must undergo, and what must be wrought in you before you can speak peace to your hearts.

But before I come directly to this, give me leave to premise a caution or two. And the first is, that I take it for granted you believe religion to be an inward thing; you believe it to be a work in the heart, a work wrought in the soul by the power of the Spirit of God. If you do not believe this, you do not believe your Bibles. If you do not believe this, though you have got your Bibles in your hand, you hate the Lord Jesus Christ in your heart; for religion is everywhere represented in Scripture as the work of God in the heart. `The kingdom of God is within us,' says our Lord; and, `He is not a Christian who is one outwardly; but he is a Christian who is one inwardly.' If any of you place religion in outward things, I shall not perhaps please you this morning;

you will understand me no more when I speak of the work of God upon a poor sinner's heart, than if I were talking in an unknown tongue. I would further premise a caution, that I would by no means confine God to one way of acting. I would by no means say, that all persons, before they come to have a settled peace in their hearts, are obliged to undergo the same degrees of conviction. No; God has various ways of bringing his children home; his sacred Spirit bloweth when, and where, and how it listeth. But, however, I will venture to affirm this, that before ever you can speak peace to your heart, whether by shorter or longer continuance of your convictions, whether in a more pungent or in a more gentle way, you must undergo what I shall hereafter lay down in the following discourse.

First, then, before you can speak peace to your hearts, you must be made to see, made to feel, made to weep over, made to bewail, your actual transgressions against the law of God. According to the covenant of works, 'The soul that sinneth it shall die;' cursed is that man, be he what he may, that continueth not in all things that are written in the book of the law to do them. We are not only to do some things, but we are to do all things, and we are to continue so to do; so that the least deviation from the moral law, according to the covenant of works, whether in thought, word, or deed, deserves eternal death at the hand of God. And if one evil thought, if one evil word, if one evil action, deserves eternal damnation, how many hells, my friends, do every one of us deserve, whose whole lives have been one continued rebellion against God! Before ever, therefore, you can speak peace to your hearts, you must be brought to see, brought to believe, what a dreadful thing it is to depart from the living God. And now, my dear friends, examine your hearts, for I hope you came hither with a design to have your souls made better. Give me leave to ask you, in the presence of God, whether you know the time, and if you do not know exactly the time, do you know there was a time, when God wrote bitter things against you, when the arrows of the Almighty were within you? Was ever the remembrance of your sins grievous to you? Was the burden of your sins intolerable to your thoughts? Did you ever see that God's wrath might justly fall upon you, on account of your actual transgressions against God?

Were you ever in all your life sorry for your sins? Could you ever say, My sins are gone over my head as a burden too heavy for me to bear? Did you ever experience any such thing as this? Did ever any such thing as this pass between God and your soul? If not, for Jesus Christ's sake, do not call yourselves Christians; you may speak peace to your hearts, but there is no peace. May the Lord awaken you, may the Lord convert you, may the Lord give you peace, if it be his will, before you go home!

But further: you may be convinced of your actual sins, so as to be made to tremble, and yet you may be strangers to Jesus Christ, you may have no true work of grace upon your hearts. Before ever, therefore, you can speak peace to your hearts, conviction must go deeper; you must not only be convinced of your actual transgressions against the law of God, but likewise of the foundation of all your transgressions. And what is that? I mean original sin, that original corruption each of us brings into the world with us, which renders us liable to God's wrath and damnation. There are many poor souls that think themselves fine reasoners, yet they pretend to say there is no such thing as original sin; they will charge God with injustice in imputing Adam's sin to us; although we have got the mark of the beast and of the devil upon us, yet they tell us we are not born in sin. Let them look abroad into the world and see the disorders in it, and think, if they can, if this is the paradise in which God did put man. No!

everything in the world is out of order. I have often thought, when I was abroad, that if there were no other argument to prove original sin, the rising of wolves and tigers against man, nay, the barking of a dog against us, is a proof of original sin. Tigers and lions durst not rise against us, if it were not for Adam's first sin; for when the creatures rise up against us, it is as much as to say, You have sinned against God, and we take up our Master's quarrel. If we look inwardly, we shall see enough of lusts, and man's temper contrary to the temper of God. There is pride, malice, and revenge, in all our hearts; and this temper cannot come from God; it comes from our first parent, Adam, who, after he fell from God, fell out of God into the devil. However, therefore, some people may deny this, yet when conviction comes, all carnal reasonings are battered down immediately and the poor soul begins to feel and see the fountain from which all the polluted streams do flow. When the sinner is first awakened, he begins to wonder _ How came I to be so wicked? The Spirit of God then strikes in, and shows that he has no good thing in him by nature; then he sees that he is altogether gone out of the way, that he is altogether become abominable, and the poor creature is made to live down at the foot of the throne of God, and to acknowledge that God would be just to damn him, just to cut him off, though he never had committed one actual sin in his life. Did you ever feel and experience this, any of you _ to justify God in your damnation _ to own that you are by nature children of wrath, and that God may justly cut you off, though you never actually had offended him in all your life?

If you were ever truly convicted, if your hearts were ever truly cut, if self were truly taken out of you, you would be made to see and feel this.

And if you have never felt the weight of original sin, do not call yourselves Christians. I am verily persuaded original sin is the greatest burden of a true convert; this ever grieves the regenerate soul, the sanctified soul. The indwelling of sin in the heart is the burden of a converted person; it is the burden of a true Christian. He continually cries out, "O! who will deliver me from this body of death,' this indwelling corruption in my heart? This is that which disturbs a poor soul most. And, therefore, if you never felt this inward corruption, if you never saw that God might justly curse you for it, indeed, my dear friends, you may speak peace to your hearts, but I fear, nay, I know, there is no true peace.

Further: before you can speak peace to your hearts, you must not only be troubled for the sins of your life, the sin of your nature, but likewise for the sins of your best duties and performances. When a poor soul is somewhat awakened by the terrors of the Lord, then the poor creature, being born under the covenant of works, flies directly to a covenant of works again. And as Adam and Eve hid themselves among the trees of the garden, and sewed fig leaves together to cover their nakedness, so the poor sinner, when awakened, flies to his duties and to his performances, to hide himself from God, and goes to patch up a righteousness of his own. Says he, I will be mighty good now _ I will reform _ I will do all I can; and then certainly Jesus Christ will have mercy on me. But before you can speak peace to your heart, you must be brought to see that God may damn you for the best prayer you ever put up; you must be brought to see that all your duties _ all your righteousness _ as the prophet elegantly expresses it _ put them all together, are so far from recommending you to God, are so far from being any motive and inducement to God to have mercy on your poor soul, that he will see them to be filthy rags, a menstruous cloth _ that God hates them, and cannot away with them, if you bring them to him in order to recommend you to his favor. My dear friends, what is there in our performances to recommend us unto God? Our persons are in an unjustified state by nature, we deserve to be damned ten thousand times over; and what must our performances be? We can do no good thing by nature: 'They that are in the flesh cannot please God.' You may do many things materially good, but you cannot do a thing formally and rightly good; because nature cannot act above itself. It is impossible that a man who is unconverted can act for the glory of God; he cannot do anything in faith, and 'whatsoever is not of faith is sin.' After we are renewed, yet we are renewed but in part, indwelling sin continues in us, there is a mixture of corruption in every one of our duties; so that after we are converted, were Jesus Christ only to accept us according to our works, our works would damn us, for we cannot pt up a prayer but it is far from that perfection which the moral law requireth. I do not know what you may think, but I can say that I cannot pray but I sin _ I cannot preach to you or any others but I sin _ I can do nothing without sin; and, as one expresseth it, my repentance wants to be repented of, and my tears to be washed in the precious blood of my dear Redeemer. Our best duties are as so many splendid sins. Before you can speak peace in your heart, you must not only be made sick of your original and actual sin, but you must be made sick of your righteousness, of all your duties and performances. There must be a deep conviction before you can be brought out of your self-righteousness; it is the last idol taken out of our heart. The pride of our heart will not let us submit to the righteousness of Jesus Christ. But if you never felt that you had o righteousness of your own, if you never felt the deficiency of your own righteousness, you cannot come to Jesus Christ. There are a great many now who may say, Well, we believe all this; but there is a great difference betwixt talking and feeling. Did you ever feel the want of a dear Redeemer?

Did you ever feel the want of Jesus Christ, upon the account of the deficiency of your own righteousness? And can you now say from your heart, Lord, thou mayst justly damn me for the best duties that ever I did perform? If you are not thus brought out of self, you may speak peace to yourselves, but yet there is no peace.

But then, before you can speak peace to your souls, there is one particular sin you must be greatly troubled for, and yet I fear there are few of you think what it is; it is the reigning, the damning sin of the Christian world, and yet the Christian world seldom or never think of it.

And pray what is that? It is what most of you think you are not guilty of _ and that is, the sin of unbelief. Before you can speak peace to your heart, you must be troubled for the unbelief of you heart. But, can it be supposed that any of you are unbelievers here in this church-yard, that are born in Scotland, in a reformed country, that go to church every Sabbath? Can any of you that receive the sacrament once a year _ O that it were administered oftener! -- can it be supposed that you who had tokens for the sacrament, that you who keep up family prayer, that any of you do not believe in the Lord Jesus Christ? I appeal to your own hearts, if you would not think me uncharitable, if I doubted whether any of you believed in Christ; and yet, I fear upon examination, we should find that most of you have not so much faith in the Lord Jesus Christ as the devil himself. I am persuaded the devil believes more of the Bible than most of us do. He believes the divinity of Jesus Christ; that is more than many who call themselves Christians do; nay, he believes and trembles, and that is more than thousands amongst us do. My friends, we mistake a historical faith for a true faith, wrought in the heart by the Spirit of God. You fancy you believe, because you believe there is such a book as we call the Bible _ because you go to church; all this you may do, and have no true faith in Christ. Merely to believe there was such a person as Christ, merely to believe there is a book called the Bible, will do you no good, more than to believe there was such a man a Caesar or Alexander the Great. The Bible is a sacred depository. What thanks have we to give to God for these lively oracles! But yet we may have these, and not believe in the Lord Jesus

Christ. My dear friends, there must be a principle wrought in the heart by the Spirit of the living God. Did I ask you how long it is since you believed in Jesus Christ, I suppose most of you would tell me, you believed in Jesus Christ as long as ever you remember _ you never did misbelieve.

Then, you could not give me a better proof that you never yet believed in Jesus Christ, unless you were sanctified early, as from the womb; for, they that otherwise believer in Christ know there was a time when they did not believe in Jesus Christ. You say you love God with all your heart, soul, and strength. If I were to ask you how long it is since you loved God, you would say, As long as you can remember; you never hated God, you know no time when there was enmity in your heart against God. Then, unless you were sanctified very early, you never loved God in your life. My dear friends, I am more particular in this, because it is a most deceitful delusion, whereby so many people are carried away, that they believe already.

Therefore, it is remarked of Mr. Marshall, giving account of his experiences, that he had been working for life, and he had ranged all his sins under the ten commandments, and then coming to a minister, asked him the reason why he could not get peace. The minister looked at his catalogue, Away, says he, I do not find one word of the sin of unbelief in all your catalogue. It is the peculiar work of the Spirit of God to convince us of our unbelief _ that we have got no faith. Says Jesus Christ, `I will send the Comforter; and when he is come, he will reprove the world' of the sin of unbelief; `of sin,' says Christ, `because they believe not on me.' Now, my dear friends, did God ever show you that you had no faith?

Were you ever made to bewail a hard heart of unbelief? Was it ever the language of your heart, Lord, give me faith; Lord, enable me to lay hold on thee; Lord, enable me to call thee MY Lord and MY God? Did Jesus Christ ever convince you in this manner? Did he ever convince you of your inability to close with Christ, and make you to cry out to God to give you faith? If not, do not speak peace to your heart. May the Lord awaken you, and give you true, solid peace before you go hence and be no more!

Once more then: before you can speak peace to your heart, you must not only be convinced of your actual and original sin, the sins of your own righteousness, the sin of unbelief, but you must be enabled to lay hold upon the perfect righteousness, the all-sufficient righteousness, of the Lord Jesus Christ; you must lay hold by faith on the righteousness of Jesus Christ, and then you shall have peace. `Come,' says Jesus, `unto me, all ye that are weary and heavy laden, and I will give you rest.' This speaks encouragement to all that are weary and heavy laden; but the promise of rest is made to them only upon their coming and believing, and taking him to be their God and their all. Before we can ever have peace with God, we must be justified by faith through our Lord Jesus Christ, we must be enabled to apply Christ to our hearts, we must have Christ brought home to our souls, so as his righteousness may be made our righteousness, so as his merits may be imputed to our souls. My dear friends, were you ever married to Jesus Christ? Did Jesus Christ ever give himself to you? Did you ever close with Christ by a lively faith, so as to feel Christ in your hearts, so as to hear him speaking peace to your souls? Did peace ever flow in upon your hearts like a river? Did you ever feel that peace that Christ spoke to his disciples? I pray God he may come and speak peace to you. These things you must experience. I am not talking of the invisible realities of another world, of inward religion, of the work of God upon a poor sinner's heart. I am not talking of a matte of great importance, my dear hearers; you are all concerned in it, your souls are concerned in it, your eternal salvation is concerned in it. You may be all at peace, but perhaps the devil has lulled you asleep into a carnal lethargy and security, and will endeavor to keep you there, till he get you to hell, and there you will be awakened; but it will be dreadful to be awakened and find yourselves so fearfully mistaken, when the great gulf is fixed, when you will be calling to all eternity for a drop of water to cool your tongue, and shall not obtain it.

Give me leave, then, to address myself to several sorts of persons; and O may God, of his infinite mercy, bless the application! There are some of you perhaps can say, Through grace we can go along with you. Blessed be God, we have been convinced of our actual sins, we have been convinced of original sin, we have been convinced of self-righteousness, we have felt the bitterness of unbelief, and through grace we have closed with Jesus Christ; we can speak peace to our hearts, because God hath spoken peace to us. Can you say so? Then I will salute you, as the angels did the women the first day of the week, All hail! Fear not ye, my dear brethren, you are happy souls; you may lie down and be at peace indeed, for God hath given you peace; you may be content under all the dispensations of providence, for nothing can happen to you now, but what shall be the effect of God's love to your soul; you need not fear what sightings may be without, seeing there is peace within. Have you closed with Christ? Is God your friend? Is Christ your friend? Then, look up with comfort; all is yours, and you are Christ's, and Christ is God's. Everything shall work together for your good; the very hairs of your head are numbered; he that toucheth you, toucheth the apple of God's eye. But then, my dear friends, beware of resting on your first conversion. You that are young believers in Christ, you should be looking out for fresh discoveries of the Lord Jesus Christ every moment; you must not build upon your past experiences, you must not build upon a work within you, but always come out of yourselves to the righteousness of Jesus Christ without you; you must be always coming as poor sinners to draw water out of the wells of salvation; you must be forgetting the things that are behind, and be continually pressing forward to the things that are before. My dear friends, you must keep u a tender, close walk with the Lord Jesus Christ. There are many of us who lose our peace by our untender walk; something or other gets in betwixt Christ and us, and we fall into darkness; something or other steals our hearts from God, and this grieves the Holy Ghost, and the Holy Ghost leaves us to ourselves. Let me, therefore, exhort you that have got peace with God, to take care that you do not lose this peace. It is true, if you are once in Christ, you cannot finally fall from God: 'There is no condemnation to them that are in Christ Jesus;' but if you cannot fall finally, you may fall foully, and may go with broken bones all your days. Take care of backslidings; for Jesus Christ's sake, do not grieve the Holy Ghost _ you may never recover your comfort while you live. O take care of going a gadding and wandering from God, after you have closed with Jesus Christ. My dear friends, I have paid dear for backsliding. Our hearts are so cursedly wicked, that if you take not care, if you do not keep up a constant watch, your wicked hearts will deceive you, and draw you aside. It will be sad to be under the scourge of a correcting Father; witness the visitation of Job, David, and other saints in Scripture. Let me, therefore, exhort you that have got peace to keep a close walk with Christ. I am grieved with the loose walk of those that are Christians, that have had discoveries of Jesus Christ; there is so little difference betwixt them and other people, that I scarce know which is the true Christian. Christians are afraid to speak of God _ they run down with the stream; if they come into worldly company, they will talk of the world as if they were in their element; this you would not do when you had the first discoveries of Christ's love; you could talk then of Christ's love for ever, when the candle of the Lord shined upon your soul. That time has been when you had something to say for your dear Lord; but now you can go into company and hear others speaking about the world bold enough, and you are afraid of being laughed at if you speak for Jesus Christ. A great many people have grown conformists now in the worst sense of the word; they will cry out against the ceremonies of the church, as they may justly do; but then you are mighty fond of ceremonies in your behavior; you will conform to the world, which is a great deal worse. Many will stay till the devil bring up new fashions. Take care, then, not to be conformed to the world. What have Christians to do with the world? Christians should be singularly good, bold for their Lord, that all who are with you may take notice that you have been with Jesus. I would exhort you to come to a settlement in Jesus Christ, so as to have a continual abiding of God in your heart. We go a-building on our faith of adherence, and lost our comfort; but we should be growing up to a faith of assurance, to know that we are God's, and so walk in the comfort of the Holy Ghost and be edified. Jesus Christ is now much wounded in the house of his friends. Excuse me in being particular; for, my friends, it grieves me more that Jesus Christ should be wounded by his friends than by his enemies. We cannot expect anything else from Deists; but for such as have felt his power, to fall away, for them not to walk agreeably to the vocation wherewith they are called _ by these means we bring our Lord's religion into contempt, to be a byword among the heathen. For Christ's sake, if you know Christ keep close by him; if God have spoken peace, O keep that peace by looking up to Jesus Christ every moment. Such as have got peace with God, if you are under trials, fear not, all things shall work for your good; if you are under temptations, fear not, if he has spoken peace to your hearts, all these things shall be for your good.

But what shall I say to you that have got o peace with God? -- and these are, perhaps, the most of this congregation: it makes me weep to think of it. Most of you, if you examine your hearts, must confess that God never yet spoke peace to you; you are children of the devil, if Christ is not in you, if God has not spoken peace to your heart. Poor soul! What a cursed condition are you in. I would not be in your case for ten thousand, thousand worlds. Why? You are just hanging over hell. What peace can you have when God is your enemy, when the wrath of God is abiding upon your poor soul? Awake, then, you that are sleeping in a false peace, awake, ye carnal professors, ye hypocrites that go to church, receive the sacrament, read your Bibles, and never felt the power of God upon your hearts; you that are formal professors, you that are baptized heathens; awake, awake, and do not rest on a false bottom. Blame me not for addressing myself to you; indeed, it is out of love to your souls. I see you are lingering in your Sodom, and wanting to stay there; but I come to you as the angel did to Lot, to take you by the hand. Come away, my dear brethren _ fly, fly, fly for your lives to Jesus Christ, fly to a bleeding God, fly to a throne of grace; and beg of God to break your hearts, beg of God to convince you of your actual sins, beg of God to convince you of your original sin, beg of God to convince you of your self-righteousness _ beg of God to give you faith, and to enable you to close with Jesus Christ. O you that are secure, I must be a son of thunder to you, and O that God may awaken you, though it be with thunder; it is out of love, indeed, that I speak to you. I know by sad experience what it is to be lulled asleep with a false peace; long was I lulled asleep, long did I think myself a Christian, when I knew nothing of the Lord Jesus Christ. I went perhaps farther than many of you do; I used to fast twice a-week, I used to pray sometimes none times a-day, I used to receive the sacrament constantly every Lord's-day; and yet I knew nothing of Jesus Christ in my heart, I knew not that I must be a new creature _ I knew nothing of inward religion in my soul. And perhaps, many of you may be deceived as I, poor creature, was; and, therefore, it is out of love to you indeed, that I speak to you. O if you do not take care, a form of religion will destroy your soul; you will rest in it, and will not come to Jesus Christ at all; whereas, these things are only the means, and not the end of religion; Christ is the end of the law for righteousness to all that believe. O, then, awake, you that are settled on your lees; awake you Church professors; awake you that have got a name to live, that are rich and think you want nothing, not considering that you are poor, and blind, and naked; I counsel you to come and buy of Jesus Christ gold, white raiment, and eye-salve. But I hope there are some that are a little wounded; I hope God does not intend to let me preach in vain;

I hope God will reach some of your precious souls, and awaken some of you out of your carnal security; I hope there are some who are willing to come to Christ, and beginning to think that they have been building upon a false foundation. Perhaps the devil may strike in, and bid you despair of mercy; but fear not, what I have been speaking to you is only out of love to you _ is only to awaken you, and let you see your danger. If any of you are willing to be reconciled to God, God the Father, Son, and Holy Ghost, is willing to be reconciled to you. O then, though you have no peace as yet, come away to Jesus Christ; he is our peace, he is our peace-maker _ he has made peace betwixt God and offending man. Would you have peace with God?

Away, then, to God through Jesus Christ, who has purchased peace; the Lord Jesus has shed his heart's blood for this. He died for this; he rose again for this; he ascended into the highest heaven, and is now interceding at the right hand of God. Perhaps you think there will be no peace for you.

Why so? Because you are sinners? Because you have crucified Christ _ you have put him to open shame _ you have trampled under foot the blood of the Son of God? What of all this? Yet there is peace for you. Pray, what did Jesus Christ say of his disciples, when he came to them the first day of the week? The first word he said was, `Peace be unto you;' he showed them his hands and his side, and said, `Peace be unto you.' It is as much as if he had said, Fear not, my disciples; see my hands and my feet how they have been pierced for your sake; therefore fear not. How did Chris speak to his disciples? `Go tell my brethren, and tell broken-hearted Peter in particular, that Christ is risen, that he is ascended unto his Father and your Father, to his God and your God.' And after Christ rose from the dead, he came preaching peace, with an olive branch of peace, like Noah's dove; `My peace I leave with you.' Who were they? They were enemies of Christ as well as we, they were deniers of Christ once as well as we. Perhaps some of you have backslidden and lost your peace, and you think you deserve no peace; and no more you do. But, then, God will heal your backslidings, he will love you freely. As for you that are wounded, if you are made willing to come to Christ, come away. Perhaps some of you want to dress yourselves in your duties, that are but rotten rags. No, you had better come naked as you are, for you must throw aside your rags, and come in your blood. Some of you may say, We would come, but we have got a hard heart. But you will never get it made soft till ye come to Christ; he will take away the heart of stone, and give you an heart of flesh; he will speak peace to your souls; though ye have betrayed him, yet he will be your peace. Shall I prevail upon any of you this morning to come to Jesus Christ? There is a great multitude of souls here; how shortly must you all die, and go to judgment! Even before night, or to-morrow's night, some of you may be laid out for this kirk-yard. And how will you do if you be not at peace with God _ if the Lord Jesus Christ has not spoken peace to your heart? If God speak not peace to you here, you will be damned for ever. I must not flatter you, my dear friends; I will deal sincerely with your souls. Some of you may think I carry things too far. But, indeed, when you come to judgment, you will find what I say is true, either to your eternal damnation or comfort.

May God influence your hearts to come to him! I am not willing to go away without persuading you. I cannot be persuaded but God may make use of me as a means of persuading some of you to come to the Lord Jesus Christ. O did you but feel the peace which they have that love the Lord Jesus Christ!

'Great peace have they,' say the psalmist, 'that love they law; nothing shall offend them.' But there is no peace to the wicked. I know what it is to live a life of sin; I was obliged to sin in order to stifle conviction.

And I am sure this is the way many of you take; If you get into company, you drive off conviction. But you had better go to the bottom at once; it must be done _ your wound must be searched, or you must be damned. If it were a matter of indifference, I would not speak one word about it. But you will be damned without Christ. He is the way, he is the truth, and the life. I cannot think you should go to hell without Christ. How can you dwell with everlasting burnings? How can you abide the thought of living with the devil for ever? Is it not better to have some soul-trouble here, than to be sent to hell by Jesus Christ hereafter? What is hell, but to be absent from Christ? If there were no other hell, that would be hell enough.

It will be hell to be tormented with the devil for ever. Get acquaintance with God, then, and be at peace. I beseech you, as a poor worthless ambassador of Jesus Christ, that you would be reconciled to God. My business this morning, the first day of the week, is to tell you that Christ is willing to be reconciled to you. Will any of you be reconciled to Jesus Christ? Then, he will forgive you all your sins, he will blot out all your transgressions. But if you will go on and rebel against Christ, and stab him daily _ if you will go on and abuse Jesus Christ, the wrath of God you must expect will fall upon you. God will not be mocked; that which a man soweth, that shall he also reap. And if you will not be at peace with God, God will not be at peace with you. Who can stand before God when he is angry? It is a dreadful thing to fall into the hands of an angry God. When the people came to apprehend Christ, they fell to the ground when Jesus said, 'I am he.' And if they could not bear the sight of Christ when clothed with the rags of mortality, how will they hear the sight of him when he is on his Father's throne? Methinks I see the poor wretches dragged out of their graves by the devil; methinks I see them trembling, crying out to the hills and rocks to cover them. But the devil will say, Come, I will take you away; and then they shall stand trembling before the judgment-seat of Christ. They shall appear before him to see him once, and hear him pronounce that irrevocable sentence, `Depart from me, ye cursed.' Methinks I hear the poor creatures saying, Lord, if we must be damned, let some angel pronounce the sentence. No, the God of love, Jesus Christ, will pronounce it. Will ye not believe this? Do not think I am talking at random, but agreeably to the Scriptures of truth. If you do not, then show yourselves men, and this morning go away with full resolution, in the strength of God, to cleave to Christ. And may you have no rest in your souls till you rest in Jesus Christ! I could still go on, for it is sweet to talk of Christ. Do you not long for the time when you shall have new bodies _ when they shall be immortal, and made like Christ's glorious body?

And then they will talk of Jesus Christ for evermore. But it is time, perhaps, for you to go and prepare for your respective worship, and I would not hinder any of you. My design is, to bring poor sinners to Jesus Christ.

O that God may bring some of you to himself! May the Lord Jesus now dismiss you with his blessing, and may the dear Redeemer convince you that are unawakened, and turn the wicked from the evil of their way! And may the love of God, that passeth all understanding, fill your hearts. Grant this, O Father, for Christ's sake; to whom, with thee and the blessed Spirit, be all honor and glory, now and for evermore. Amen.

Sermon 59 The Good Shepherd

(A Farewell Sermon - The last sermon which Whitefield preached in London, on Wednesday, August 30th, 1769, before his final departure to America.)

John 10:27-28, "My sheep hear my voice, and I know them, and they follow me. And I give unto them eternal life, and they shall never perish, neither shall any pluck them out of my hand."

It is a common, and I believe, generally speaking, my dear hearers, a true saying, that bad manners beget good laws. Whether this will hold good in every particular, in respect to the affairs of this world, I am persuaded the observation is very pertinent in respect to the things of another: I mean bad manners, bad treatment, bad words, have been overruled by the sovereign grace of God, to produce, and to be the cause of, the best sermons that were ever delivered from the mouth of the God-man, Christ Jesus.

One would have imagined, that as he came clothed with divine efficience, as he came with divine credentials, as he speak as never man spake, no one should have been able to have resisted the wisdom with which he spake; one would imagine, they should have been so struck with the demonstration of the Spirit, that with one consent they should all own that he was `that prophet that was to be raised up like unto Moses.' But you seldom find our Lord preaching a sermon, but something or other that he said was cavilled at; nay, their enmity frequently broke through all good manners. They often, therefore, interrupted him whilst he was preaching, which shows the enmity of their hearts long before God permitted it to be in their power to shed his innocent blood. If we look no further than this chapter, where he presents himself as a good shepherd, one that laid down his life for his sheep; we see the best return he had, was to be looked upon as possessed or distracted; for we are told, that there was a division therefore again among the Jews for these sayings, and many of them said, `He hath a devil, and is mad; why hear ye him?' If the master of the house was served so, pray what are the servants to expect? Others, a little more sober-minded, said, `These are not the words of him that hath a devil;' the devil never used to preach or act in this way; `Can a devil open the eyes of the blind?' So he had some friends among these rabble. This did not discourage our Lord; he goes on in his work; and we shall never, never go on with the work of God, till, like our Master, we are willing to go through good and through evil report; and let the devil see we are not so complaisant as to stop one moment for his barking at us as we go along.

We are told, that our Lord was at Jerusalem at the feast of the dedication, and it was winter; the feast of dedication held, I think, seven or eight days, for the commemoration of the restoration of the temple and altar, after its profanation by Antiochus. Now this was certainly a mere human institution, and had no divine image, had no divine superscription upon it; and yet I do not find that our blessed Lord and Master preached against it; I do not find that he spent his time about this; his heart was too big with superior things; and I believe when we, like him, are filled with the Holy Ghost, we shall not entertain our audiences with disputes about rites and ceremonies, but shall treat upon the essentials of the gospel, and then rites and ceremonies will appear with more indifference.

Our Lord does not say, that he would not go up to the feast, for, on the contrary, he did go there, not so much as to keep the feast, as to have an opportunity to spread the gospel-net; and that should be our method, not to follow disputing; and it is the glory of the Methodists, that we have been now forty years, and, I thank God, there has not been one single pamphlet written by any of our preachers, about the non-essentials of religion.

Our Lord always made the best of every opportunity; and we are told, `he walked in the temple in Solomon's porch.' One would have thought the scribes and Pharisees would have put him in one of their stalls, and have complimented him with desiring him to preach: no, they let him walk in Solomon's porch. Some think he walked by himself, no body choosing to keep company with him. Methinks I see him walking and looking at the temple, and foreseeing within himself how soon it would be destroyed; he walked pensive, to see the dreadful calamities that would come upon the land, for not knowing the day of its visitation; and it was to let the world see he was not afraid to appear in public: he walked, as much as to say, Have any of you any thing to say to me? and he put himself in their way, that if they had any things to ask him, he was ready to resolve them; and to show them, that though they had treated him so ill, yet he was ready to preach salvation to them.

In the 24th verse we are told, `Then came the Jews round about him, and said unto him, How long dost thou make us doubt?' They came round about him when they saw him walking in Solomon's porch; now, say they, we will have him, now we will attack him. And now was fulfilled that passage in the Psalms, `they compassed me about like bees,' to sting me, or rather like wasps. Now, say they, we will get him in the middle of us, and see what sort of a man he is; we will see whether we cannot conquer him; they came to him, and they say, `How long dost thou make us to doubt?' Now this seems a plausible question, `How long dost thou make us to doubt?' Pray how long, sir, do you intend to keep us in suspense? Some think the words will bear this interpretation; Pray, sir, how long do you intend thus to steal away our hearts? They would represent him to be a designing man, like Absalom, to get the people on his side, and then set up himself for the Messiah; thus carnal minds always interpret good men's actions. But the meaning seems to be this, they were doubting concerning Christ; doubting Christians may think it is God's fault that they doubt, but, God knows, it is all their own. `How long dost thou make us to doubt?' I wish you would speak a little plainer, sir, and not let us have any more of your parables. Pray let us know who you are, let us have it from your own mouth; `if thou be the Christ, tell us plainly;' and I do not doubt, but they put on a very sanctified face, and looked very demure; `if thou be the Christ, tell us plainly,' intending to catch him: if he do not say he is the Christ, we will say he is ashamed of his own cause; if he tells us plainly that he is the Christ, then we will impeach him to the governor, we will go and tell the governor that this man says he is the Messiah; now we know of no Messiah, but what is to jostle Caesar out of his throne. _ The devil always wants to make it believed that God's people, who are the most loyal people in the world, are rebels to the government under which they live; `If thou be the Christ, tell us plainly.' Our Lord does not let them wait long for an answer; honesty can soon speak: `I told you, and ye believed not; the works that I do in my Father's name, they bear witness of me.' Had our Lord said, I am the Messiah, they would have taken him up; he knew that, and therefore he joined `the wisdom of the serpent' with `the innocence of the dove;' says he, I appeal to my works and doctrine, and if you will not infer from them that I am the Messiah, I have no further argument. `But,' he adds, `ye believe not, because ye are not of my sheep.' He complains twice; for their unbelief was the greatest grief of heart to Christ: then he goes on in the words of our text, `My sheep hear my voice, and I know them, and they follow me. And I give unto them eternal life, and they shall never perish, neither shall any pluck them out of my hand.' My sheep hear my voice; you think to puzzle me, you think to chagrin me with this kind of conduct, but you are mistaken; you do not believe on me, because you are not of my sheep. The great Mr. Stoddard of New England, (and no place under heaven produces greater divines than New England), preached once from these words, `But ye believe not, because ye are not of my sheep;' a very strange text to preach upon, to convince a congregation! Yet God so blessed it, that two of three hundred souls were awakened by that sermon: God grant such success to attend the labors of all his faithful ministers.

'My sheep hear my voice, and they follow me.' It is very remarkable, there are but two sorts of people mentioned in scripture: it does not say that the Baptists and Independents, nor the Methodists and Presbyterians; no, Jesus Christ divides the whole world into but two classes, sheep and goats: the Lord give us to see this morning to which of these classes we belong.

But it is observable, believers are always compared to something that is good and profitable, and unbelievers are always described by something that is bad, and good for little or nothing.

If you ask me why Christ's people are called sheep, as God shall enable me, I will give you a short, and I hope it will be to you an answer of peace. Sheep, you know, generally love to be together; we say a flock of sheep, we do not say a herd of sheep; sheep are little creatures, and Christ's people may be called sheep, because they are little in the eyes of the world, and they are yet less in their own eyes. O, some people think, if the great men were on our side, if we had king, lords, and commons on our side, I mean if they were all true believers, O if we had all the kings upon the earth on our side! Suppose you had: alas! alas! do you think the church would go on the better? Why, if it were fashionable to be a Methodist at court, if it were fashionable to be a Methodist abroad, they would go with a Bible or a hymn-book, instead of a novel; but religion never thrives under too much sun-shine. 'Not many mighty, not many noble, are called, but God hath chosen the foolish things of the world to confound the wise, and God hath chosen the weak things of the world to confound the things which are mighty.' Dr. Watts says, Here and there I see a king, and here and there a great man, in heaven, but their number is but small.

Sheep are looked upon to be the most harmless, quiet creatures that God hath made: O may God, of his infinite mercy, give us to know that we are his sheep, by our having this blessed temper infused into our hearts by the Holy Ghost. 'Learn of me,' saith our blessed Lord; what to do? To work miracles? No; 'Learn of me, for I am meek and lowly in heart.' A very good man, now living, said once, if there be any particular temper I desire more than another, it is the grace of MEEKNESS, quietly to bear bad treatment, to forget and to forgive: and at the same time that I am sensible I am injured, not to be overcome of evil, but to have grace given me to overcome evil with good. To the honor of Moses, it is declared, that he was the meekest man upon earth. Meekness is necessary for people in power; a man that is passionate is dangerous. Every governor should have a warm temper, but a man of an unrelenting, unforgiving temper, is no more fit for government than Phaethon to drive the chariot of the sun; he only sets the world on fire.

You all know, that sheep of all creatures in the world are the most apt to stray and be lost; Christ's people may justly, in that respect, be compared to sheep; therefore, in the introduction to our morning service, we say, 'We have erred and strayed from thy ways like lost sheep.' Turn out a horse, or a dog, and they will find their way home, but a sheep wanders about; he bleats here and there, as much as to day, Dear stranger, show me my way home again; thus Christ's sheep are too apt to wander from the fold; having their eye off the great Shepherd, they go into this field and that field, over this hedge and that, and often return home with the loss of their wool.

But at the same time sheep are the most useful creatures in the world; they manure the land, and thereby prepare it for the seed; they clothe our bodies with wool, and there is not the least part of a sheep but is useful to man: O my brethren, God grant that you and I may, in this respect, answer the character of sheep. The world says, because we preach faith we deny good works; this is the usual objection against the doctrine of imputed righteousness, but it is a slander, an impudent slander. It was a maxim in the first reformers' time, that though the ARMINIANS preached up good works, you must go to the CALVINISTS FOR THEM. Christ's sheep study to be useful, and to clothe all they can; we should labor with our hands, that we may have to give to all those that need.

Believers consider Christ's property in them; he says, 'my sheep:' O blessed be God for that little, dear, great word MY. We are his eternal election: "the sheep which thou hast given me," says Christ. They were given by God the Father to Christ Jesus, in the covenant made between the Father and the Son from all eternity. They that are not led to see this, I wish them better heads; though, I believe, numbers that are against it have got better hearts: the Lord help us to bear with one another where there is an honest heart.

He calls them 'My sheep;' they are his by purchase. O sinner, sinner, you are come this morning to hear a poor creature take 'his last farewell:' but I want you to forget the creature that is preaching, I want to lead you further than the Tabernacle: Where do you want to lead us? Why, to mount Calvary, there to see at what an expense of blood Christ purchased those whom he calls his own; he redeemed them with his own blood, so that they are not only his by eternal election, but also by actual redemption in time; and they were given to him by the Father, upon condition that he should redeem them by his heart's blood. It was a hard bargain, but Christ was willing to strike the bargain, that you and I might not be damned for ever.

They are his, because they are enabled in a day of God's power voluntarily to give themselves up unto him; Christ says of these sheep, especially, 'that they hear his voice, and that they follow him.' Will you be so good as to mind that! Here is an allusion to a shepherd; now in some places in scripture, the shepherd is represented as going after his sheep; 2 Sam 7:8, Ps 78:71. That is our way in England; but in the Eastern nations, the shepherds generally went before; they held up their crook, and they had a particular call that the sheep understood. Now, says Christ, `My sheep hear my voice.' `This is my beloved Son,' saith God, `hear ye him.' And again, `The dead shall hear the voice of the Son of God, and live:' now the question is, what do we understand by hearing Christ's voice?

First, we hare Moses' voice, we hear the voice of the law; there is no going to Mount Zion but by the way of mount Sinai; that is the right straight road. I know some say, they do not know when they were converted; those are, I believe, very few: generally, nay, I may say almost always, God deals otherwise. Some are, indeed, called sooner by the Lord than others, but before they are made to see the glory of God, they must hear the voice of the law; so you must hear the voice of the law before ever you will be savingly called unto God. You never throw off your cloak in a storm, but you hug it the closer; so the law makes a man hug close his corruptions, (Rom 7:7, 8, 9) but when the gospel of the Son of God shines into your souls, then they throw off the corruptions which they have hugged so closely; they hear his voice saying, Son, daughter, be of good cheer, thy sins, which are many, are all forgiven thee. `They hear his voice;' that bespeaks the habitual temper of their minds: the wicked hear the voice of the devil, the lusts of the flesh, the lusts of the eye, and the pride of life; and Christ's sheep themselves attended to it before conversion; but when called afterwards by God, they hear the voice of a Redeemer's blood speaking peace unto them, they hear the voice of his word and of his Spirit.

The consequence of hearing his voice, and the proof that we do hear his voice, will be _ to follow him. Jesus said unto his disciples, `If any man will come after me, let him deny himself, and take up his cross and follow me.' And it is said of the saints in glory, that `they followed the Lamb whithersoever he went.' Wherever the shepherd turns his crook, and the sheep hear his voice, they follow him; they often tread upon one another, and hurt one another, they are in such haste in their way to heaven.

Following Christ means following him through life, following him in every word and gesture, following him out of one clime into another. `Bid me come to thee upon the water,' said Peter: and if we are commanded to go over the water for Christ, God, of his infinite mercy, follow us! We must first be sure that the great Shepherd points his crook for us: but this is the character of a true servant of Christ, that he endeavors to follow Christ in thought, word, and work.

Now, my brethren, before we go further, as this is the last opportunity I shall have of speaking to you for some months, if we live; some of you, I suppose, do not choose, in general, to rise so soon as you have this morning; now I hope the world did not get into your hearts before you left your beds; now you are here, do let me entreat you to inquire whether you belong to Christ's sheep, or no. Man, woman, sinner, put thy hand to thy heart, and answer me. Didst thou ever hear Christ's voice so as to follow him, to give up thyself without reserve to him? I verily do believe from my inmost soul, (and that is my comfort, now I am about to take my leave of you,) that I am preaching to a vast body, a multitude of dear, precious souls, who, if it were proper for you to speak, would say, Thanks be unto God, that we can follow Jesus in the character of sheep, though we are ashamed to think how often we wander from him, and what little fruit we bring unto him; if that is the language of your hearts, I wish you joy; welcome, welcome, dear soul, to Christ. O blessed be God for his rich grace, his distinguishing, sovereign, electing love, by which he as distinguished you and me. And if he has been pleased to let you hear his voice, though the ministration of a poor miserable sinner, a poor, but happy pilgrim, may the Lord Jesus Christ have all the glory.

If you belong to Jesus Christ, he is speaking of you; for, says he, `I know my sheep.' `I know them;' what does that mean? Why, he knows their number, he knows their names, he knows every one for whom he died; and if there were to be one missing for whom Christ died, God the Father would send him down again from heaven to fetch him. `Of all,' saith he, `that thou hast given me, have I lost none.' Christ knows his sheep; he not only knows their number, but the words speak the peculiar knowledge and notice he takes of them; he takes as much care of each of them, as if there were but that one single sheep in the world. To the hypocrite he saith, `Verily, I know you not;' but he knows his saints, he is acquainted with all their sorrows, their trials, and temptations. He bottles up all their tears, he knows their domestic trials, he knows their inward corruptions, he knows all their wanderings, and he takes care to fetch them back again. I remember, I heard good Dr. Marryat, who was a good market-language preacher, once say at Pinner's hall, (I hope that pulpit will be always filled with such preachers), `God has got a great dog to fetch his sheep back,' says he. Do not you know, that when the sheep wander, the shepherd sends his dog after them, to fetch them back again? So when Christ's sheep wander, he lets the devil go after them, and suffers him to bark at them, who, instead of driving them farther off, is made a means to bring them back again to Christ's fold.

There is a precious word I would have you take notice of, `I know them,' that may comfort you under all your trials. We sometimes think that Christ does not hear our prayers, that he does not know us; we are ready to suspect that he has forgotten to be gracious; but what a mercy it is that he does know us. We accuse one another, we turn devils to one another, are accusers of the brethren; and what will support two of God's people when judged by one another but this, Lord, thou knowest my integrity, thou knowest how matters are with me?

But, my brethren, here is something better, here is good news for you; what is that? Say you: why, `I give unto them eternal life, and they shall never perish, neither shall any pluck them out of my hand.' O that the words may come to your hearts with as much warmth and power as they did to mine thirty-five years ago. I never prayed against any corruption I had in my life, so much as I did against going into holy orders so soon as my friends were for having me go: and bishop Benson was pleased to honor me with peculiar friendship, so as to offer me preferment, or do any thing for me. My friends wanted me to mount the church betimes, they wanted me to knock my head against the pulpit too young; but how some young men stand up here and there and preach, I do not know how it may be to them; but God knows how deep a concern entering into the ministry and preaching, was to me; I have prayed a thousand times, till the sweat has dropped from my face like rain, that God, of his infinite mercy, would not let me enter the church before he called me to, and thrust me forth in, his work. I remember once in Gloucester (I know the room, I look up at the window when I am there and walk along the street; I know the window, the bedside, and the floor, upon which I have lain prostrate) I said, Lord, I cannot go, I shall be puffed up with pride, and fall into the condemnation of the devil; Lord, do not let me go yet; I pleaded to be at Oxford two or three years more; I intended to make an hundred and fifty sermons, and thought I would set up with a good stock in trade but I remember praying, wrestling, and striving with God; I said, I am undone, I am unfit to preach in thy great name, send me not, pray, Lord, send me not yet. I wrote to all my friends in town and country, to pray against the bishop's solicitations, but they insisted I should go into orders before I was twenty-two. After all the solicitations, these words came into my mind, `My sheep hear my voice, and none shall pluck them out of my hand.' O may the words be blessed to you, my dear friends, that I am parting with, as they were to me when they came warm upon my heart; then, and not till then, I said, Lord, I will go, send me when thou wilt. I remember when I was in a place called Dover-Island, near Georgia, we put in with bad winds; I had an hundred and fifty in family to maintain, and not a single farthing to do it with, in the dearest part of the king's dominions; I remember, I told a minister of Christ, now in heaven, `I had these words once, sir, "Nothing shall pluck you out of my hand." `O', says he, `take comfort from them, you may be sure God will be as good as his word, if he never tells you so again.' And our Lord knew his poor sheep would be always doubting they should never reach heaven, therefore says he, `I give to them eternal life, and they shall never perish.' Here are in our text three blessed declarations, or promises: First. I KNOW THEM.

Second. THEY SHALL NEVER PERISH; though they often think they shall perish by the hand of their lusts and corruptions; they think they shall perish by the deceitfulness of their hearts; but Christ says, 'They shall never perish.' I have brought them out of the world to myself, and do you think I will let them go to hell after that? 'I give to them eternal life;' pray mind that; not, I will, but I do. Some talk of being justified at the day of judgment; that is nonsense; if we are not justified here, we shall not be justified there. He gives them eternal life, that is, the earnest, the pledge, and assurance of it. The indwelling of the Spirit of God here, is the earnest of glory hereafter.

Third. NEITHER SHALL ANY PLUCK THEM OUT OF MY HAND. He holds them in his hand, that is, he holds them by his power; none shall pluck them thence. There is always something plucking at Christ's sheep; the devil, the lust of the flesh, the lust of the eye, and the pride of life, all try to pluck them out of Christ's hand. O my brethren, they need not pluck us, yet we help all three to pluck ourselves out of the hand of Jesus; but 'none shall pluck them out of my hand,' says Christ. 'I give to them eternal life. I am going to heaven to prepare a place for them, and there they shall be.' O my brethren, if it were not for keeping you too long, and too much exhausting my own spirits, I could call upon you to leap for you; there is not a more blessed text to support the final perseverance of the saints; and I am astonished any poor souls, and good people I hope too, can fight against the doctrine of the perseverance of the saints: What if a person say they should persevere in wickedness? Ah! That is an abuse of the doctrine; what, because some people spoil good food, are we never to eat it? But, my brethren, upon this text I can leave my cares, and all my friends, and all Christ's sheep, to the protection of Christ Jesus' never- failing love.

I thought this morning, when I came here, riding from the other end of the town, it was to me like coming to be executed publicly; and when the carriage turned just at the end of the walk, and I saw you running here, O, thinks I, it is like a person now coming just to the place where he is to be executed. When I went up to put on my gown, I thought it was just like dressing myself to be made a public spectacle to shed my blood for Christ.

I take all heaven and earth to witness, and God and the holy angels to witness, that though I had preferment enough offered me, that though the bishop took me in his arms, and offered me two parishes before I was two-and-twenty, and always took me to his table; though I had preferment enough offered me when I was ordained, thou, O God, knowest, that when the bishop put his hand upon my head, I looked for no other preferment than publicly to suffer for the Lamb of God: in this spirit I came out, in this spirit I came up to this metropolis. I was thinking, when I read of Jacob's going over the brook with a staff, that I could not say I had so much as a staff, but I came up without a friend, I went to Oxford without a friend, I had not a servant, I had not a single person to introduce me; but God, by his Holy Spirit, was pleased to raise me up to preach for his great name's sake: through his divine Spirit I continue to this day, and feel my affections are as string as ever towards the work and the people of the living God. The congregations at both ends of the town are dear to me: God has honored me to build this and the other place; and, blessed be his name, when he called me to Georgia at first, and I left all London affairs to God's care, when I had most of the churches in London open to me, and had twelve or fourteen constables to keep the doors, that people might not crowd too much; I had offers of hundreds then to settle in London, yet I gave it all up to turn pilgrim for God, to go into a foreign clime; and I hope with that same single intention I am going now _ Now I must come to the hardest part I have to act; I was afraid when I came out from home, that I could not bear the shock, but I hope the Lord Jesus Christ will help me to bear it, and help you to give me up to the blessed God, let him do with me what he will. This is the thirteenth time of my crossing the mighty waters; it is a little difficult at this time of life; and though my spirits are improved in some degree, yet weakness is the best of my strength: but I am clear as light in my call and God fills me with a peace that is unutterable, which a stranger intermeddles not with: into his hands I commend my spirit; and I beg that this may be the language of your hearts: Lord, keep him, let nothing pluck him out of thy hands. I expect many a trial while I am on board, Satan always meets me there; but that God who has kept me, I believe will keep me. I thank God, I have the honor of leaving every thing quite well and easy at both ends of the town; and, my dear hearers, my prayers to God shall be, that nothing may pluck you out of Christ's hands. Witness against me, if I ever set up a party for myself. Did ever any minister, or could any minister in the world say, that I ever spoke against any one going to any dear minister? I thank God, that he has enabled me to be always strengthening the hands of all, though some have afterwards been ashamed to own me. I declare to you, that I believe God will be with me, and will strengthen me; and I believe it is in answer to your prayers that God is pleased to revive my spirits: may the Lord help you to pray on. If I am drowned in the waves, I will say, while I am drowning, Lord, take care of my London, take care of my English friends, let nothing pluck them out of thy hands.

And as Christ has given us eternal life, O my brethren, some of you, I doubt not, will be gone to him before my return; but, my dear brethren, my dear hearers, never mind that; we shall part, but it will be to meet again for ever. I dare not meet you now, I cannot bear your coming to me, to part from me; it cuts me to the heart, and quite overcomes me, but by and by all parting will be over, and all tears shall be wiped away from our eyes. God grant that none that weep now at my parting, may weep at our meeting at the day of judgment; and if you never were among Christ's sheep before, may Christ

Jesus bring you now. O come, come, see what it is to have eternal life; do not refuse it; haste, sinner, haste away: may the great, the good Shepherd, draw your souls. Oh! If you never heard his voice before, God grant you may hear it now; that I may have this comfort when I am gone, that I had the last time of my leaving you, that some souls are awakened at the parting sermon. O that it may be a farewell sermon to you; that it may be a means of your taking a farewell of the world, the lust of the flesh, the lust of the eye, and the pride of life. O come! Come! Come! To the Lord Jesus Christ; to him I leave you.

And you, dear sheep, that are already in his hands, O may God keep you from wandering; God keep you near Christ's feet; I do not care what shepherds keep you, so as you are kept near the great Shepherd and Bishop of souls. The Lord God keep you, lift up the light of his countenance upon you, and give you peace. Amen.

Also from Benediction Books ...

Wandering Between Two Worlds: Essays on Faith and Art
Anita Mathias
Benediction Books, 2007
152 pages
ISBN: 0955373700

Available from www.amazon.com, www.amazon.co.uk
www.wanderingbetweentwoworlds.com

In these wide-ranging lyrical essays, Anita Mathias writes, in lush, lovely prose, of her naughty Catholic childhood in Jamshedpur, India; her large, eccentric family in Mangalore, a sea-coast town converted by the Portuguese in the sixteenth century; her rebellion and atheism as a teenager in her Himalayan boarding school, run by German missionary nuns, St. Mary's Convent, Nainital; and her abrupt religious conversion after which she entered Mother Teresa's convent in Calcutta as a novice. Later rich, elegant essays explore the dualities of her life as a writer, mother, and Christian in the United States-- Domesticity and Art, Writing and Prayer, and the experience of being "an alien and stranger" as an immigrant in America, sensing the need for roots.

About the Author

Anita Mathias was born in India, has a B.A. and M.A. in English from Somerville College, Oxford University and an M.A. in Creative Writing from the Ohio State University. Her essays have been published in The Washington Post, The London Magazine, The Virginia Quarterly Review, Commonweal, Notre Dame Magazine, America, The Christian Century, Religion Online, The Southwest Review, Contemporary Literary Criticism, New Letters, The Journal, and two of HarperSanFrancisco's The Best Spiritual Writing anthologies. Her non-fiction has won fellowships from The National Endowment for the Arts; The Minnesota State Arts Board; The Jerome Foundation, The Vermont Studio Center; The Virginia Centre for the Creative Arts, and the First Prize for the Best General Interest Article from the Catholic Press Association of the United States and Canada. Anita has taught Creative Writing at the College of William and Mary, and now lives and writes in Oxford, England.